In the Beginning was the Name

Selected Essays by Professor W. F. H. Nicolaisen

Published by the Scottish Place-Name Society
2011

In the Beginning was the Name
Selected Essays by Professor W. F. H. Nicolaisen

ISBN 978-0-9565172-2-7

Published by the Scottish Place-Name Society, 2011.

Printed by
Shetland Litho,
Gremista, Lerwick,
Shetland ZE1 0PX

In the Beginning was the Name

Bill Nicolaisen with School of Scottish Studies colleagues Donald Archie MacDonald and Hamish Henderson in Athens in 1964.
Photograph from the Kätzel Henderson Collection.

Thanks to Kätzel Henderson for permission to publish.

CONTENTS

Professor W. F. H. Nicolaisen

THIS collection of papers is the result of a lifetime's study and research by one of the most prominent and productive onomasticians of the twentieth century.

Few scholars have truly mastered the craft of assembling the disparate themes of human knowledge which the subject fairly merits. The various strands of linguistic, historical, geographical and sociological information are seldom fully exploited by those whose business is the science of names and naming. Bill Nicolaisen, as he is generally known, is recognised as a master of this craft, having established himself as being proficient in the many aspects of onomastic research which satisfy the most demanding academic criteria.

Born in Halle, Germany, in 1927, he studied Comparative Linguistics, English, German and Folklore at the Universities of Kiel, Tübingen and King's College, Newcastle-upon-Tyne, before graduating with a D.Phil, *magna cum laude*, at Tübingen in 1955. In the years before this, he had worked as 'lektor' in the German departments both at Glasgow University and University College Dublin. In 1956 he graduated from the University of Glasgow with a B.Litt. on his thesis 'Studies on Scottish Hydronymy'.

Bill Nicolaisen's first major academic post was in the School of Scottish Studies of Edinburgh University, from 1956 to 1969, where he was in charge of the Scottish Place-Name Survey. Here he was to develop the study of Scottish place-names in a scientific and systematic manner, exploiting all the sources available for the elucidation of names. The usual documentary and early map evidence was pursued, but as the School's main activities involved the recording of oral tradition from informants in the field, Nicolaisen established a system of collecting place-name evidence from tradition-bearers in many parts of Scotland. He recognised the necessity of recording on tape those informants who lived in the areas of Scotland where Gaelic was on the point of extinction, so his early recordings were conducted in Perthshire, Arran and the Great Glen, where reliable Gaelic speakers were becoming increasingly scarce.

With such a range of expertise in Celtic and Germanic languages, Bill Nicolaisen found an increasing interest in folk studies. This was, for an onomastician, an opportunity to expand academic interests in a truly international manner. As Organising Secretary of the Third International Congress of Celtic Studies in Edinburgh in 1967, he was instrumental in bringing together scholars from all over the world, and in the process, building up important academic contacts in Europe and North America. He had already acted as Secretary of the Council for Name Studies in Britain and Ireland, which was forging important links between onomasticians from Scotland, England, Wales and Ireland, and encouraging scholars from Scandinavia to develop and exploit studies in place-names which were to prove beneficial to both areas of interest. He personally reinforced this process as Secretary to the University of Edinburgh's Northern Scholars Committee and by regular participation in the conferences and congresses of NORNA (Nordic Cooperative Committee for Onomastic Research) and by a lecture tour of academic centres of name studies in the northern countries.

The Scottish situation, of course, was fruitful ground for onomasticians, since Gaelic, Cumbric, Pictish, Old English and Old Norse place-names formed the onomasticon. Nicolaisen produced the standard text for Scottish place-name studies in his *Scottish Place-Names: Their Study and Significance* in 1976. This, and its new edition (2001), reprinted (2011), is regarded as the authoritative work on the subject, since virtually all studies on Scottish place-names have quoted it, or some part of it, while all bibliographies of any significance include reference to it.

The U.K.-wide aspect of place-name studies was not neglected, as Bill Nicolaisen, with Dr. Margaret Gelling and Professor Melville Richards produced *The Names of Towns and Cities in Britain* in 1970. This popular volume was an attempt to introduce serious place-name research to a wider public. The 1970s saw an expansion of local history societies, and Bill Nicolaisen was keen to preach the gospel of place-name studies to a wider audience. Besides contributing a series of important articles in the School of Scottish Studies journal *Scottish Studies*, he contributed a regular column in the *Scots Magazine*, 'The Story Behind the Name', for many years. This, as much as any other publication, made his name well known to that section of readership who enjoyed the various strands of Scottish life which the magazine features.

In 1966, Nicolaisen was invited to become Visiting Professor in the Department of English of Ohio State University, and while acting Head of

Department in the School of Scottish Studies in 1968, he was awarded the Norse Prize from the University of Glasgow. In 1969, however, he accepted the post of Associate Professor of English in the State University of New York, at Binghamton, where he enjoyed a successful and fruitful scholarly career. Over the next two decades, he became heavily involved in place-name studies in the U.S., as well as in folklore, ethnology and literature. In 1969 he became Chairman of the Place-Name Survey of New York State, as well as chairing a Committee for an American Folklore Atlas for the American Folklore Society. Awarded a full professorship at Binghamton in 1973 (English and Folklore) and appointed Distinguished Professor in 1985, he rose to President of the American Name Society in 1977, and President of the American Folklore Society in 1983. His volume on *Scottish Place-Names* won joint first prize in the Chicago Folklore Competition in 1977. He was President of the Fourteenth International Congress of Onomastic Sciences in 1981, in Ann Arbor.

These positions, as well as membership of many other similar organisations in the U.S. and Canada served to establish Bill Nicolaisen's reputation as an outstanding scholar, with a versatility that few of his American contemporaries could boast. In addition, his consummate skill as a chairperson of many learned societies is recognised both in the U.S. and in Scotland.

On his return to Scotland in 1992, Bill immersed himself in the task of compiling the *Dictionary of Scottish Place-Names* on which he had long laboured. This immense task was interwoven with writing and research on many onomastic and folkloristic topics, as well as teaching onomastics and folklore in the Centre for Continuing Education at Aberdeen University, where he was warmly welcomed, first as an Honorary Research Fellow (1992-1997) and then as an Honorary Professor of English (1998-), as well as an Honorary Fellow of the Elphinstone Institute (1999-). In 1996, he organised the XIXth International Congress of Onomastic Sciences in Aberdeen, the Proceedings of which he edited in 1998. In 2006, the University of Aberdeen awarded him a doctorate *honoris causa*. He continued to contribute articles to a wide range of scholarly journals, in Europe, the U.S.A. and Canada, and having been an enthusiastic attendee at academic conferences for much of his life, was often called on to deliver keynote papers. His output of articles and reviews has been nothing short of staggering – nearly 700 for his entire career. Quite apart from academic papers, he has the rare ability to write for the popular press, including *The Leopard*, Aberdeen's successful regional magazine. Work on his *magnum opus* dictionary continues, with assistance from an editor at Scottish Language Dictionaries, and his harvest of publications also continues unabated.

In addition to his involvement in learned societies in the U.S., Bill was elected President of the Society for Name Studies in Britain and Ireland (1993-96), President of the International Council of Onomastic Sciences (1993-96), President of the Scottish Medievalists (1994-97), President of the Folklore Society (1999-2002), Honorary Praeses of the Scottish Place-Name Society (1996-), President of the Scottish Society for Northern Studies (2000-2003) and Honorary Vice-President of the English Place-Name Society (2008-) to name but a few of the more prestigious. But the most significant of his talents must be the winning of the American Folklore Society 'Lifetime Scholarly Achievement Award' in 2002. He was first recipient of this prize, and it recognises the substantial contribution he has made to folklore studies in the U.S.

This selection of Bill Nicolaisen's papers has been a difficult, although pleasant, task for the editors. We have attempted to include a wide range of articles which reflect the purely onomastic side of his production. Yet these, while primarily of relevance to onomasticians, frequently include aspects of the man's broader interests. So they are often redolent with references to historical incidents, dialectal nuances, recondite documentary notes, examples of material from oral tradition and folk-literature, as well as detail from narrative traditions of Europe and North America.

All of Bill Nicolaisen's students would agree that he is a clear lecturer, with a marvellous command of English, and a delight in the craft of wordplay, which he employs on a frequent basis. He has an inherent love of puns and spoonerisms, and the many twists of verbal complexity that he is able to dredge from his vast knowledge of literature. No student of onomastics has remained immune to his influence, while it is no exaggeration to say that he has inspired several generations of scholars, not merely in the field of name studies, but in a whole range of studies in language, history, ethnology and literature. These papers therefore reflect his command of a range of disciplines, and are a real insight into the career of a very distinguished, and distinctive, scholar.

I. A. F.

PREFACE

THE primary purpose of this collection of essays is to provide a sequel to my book *Scottish Place-Names: Their Study and Significance*, published in 1976, followed by two reprints in 1979 and 1986 and a new edition in 2001, reprinted in 2011. It does, however, differ from its predecessors in a number of important ways, the most noteworthy being that, whereas in the earlier versions the various separate articles which had been incorporated in them were moulded into a cohesive narrative, structured by chapters devoted to the place-name evidence for the several discernible strata in Scotland's linguistic settlement history, this new volume presents the included collected papers in their original, independent form, in order of their dates of publication. In principle, therefore, this compendium is intended to inform its readers conveniently of the scope and contents of the author's work from 1976 to the present day, thus responding to the express need to bring together articles which have appeared over the years in a wide variety of journals, magazines, conference proceedings, festschriften, thematic collections, etc., and this aim has been a strong motivating factor in their selection from sources often frustratingly difficult of access.

In acceptance of the chronological restrictions imposed by this concept, the essays chosen consequently either appeared or were written after the publication of the first edition of *Scottish Place-Names* in 1976. Exceptions are "The Semantic Structure of Scottish Hydronymy" (1957), a chapter in my Glasgow BLitt-thesis of 1956; "The Prodigious Jump" (1968) but not thematically suitable for *Scottish Place-Names*; "Falkirk" (1969) but not included in *Scottish Place-Names* in its entirety; and "Post-Norse Place-Names of Shetland", written in 1969 but not published until 1983.

In keeping with the nature of the previous volumes and in answer to the Scottish Place-Name Society, the chief supporter of this undertaking, the collection predictably contains a high proportion of toponymic studies, many of them devoted to the Scottish scene. It does, however, also reflect at least tangentially, without blurring this special focus, through some adjacent links the author's extensive research interests and more rounded academic preoccupations.

In the absence of a connecting commentary, it may be helpful to highlight the major topics touched upon and to supply a guide to their relevant illustrations, without attempting a complete overview. Articles continuing or elaborating on themes and discussions associated with the 1976/2001 volumes are "Thirty Years Later: Thoughts on a Viable Concept of Old European Hydronymy" (1982), "Gaelic Place-Names in Scots" (1986), "Imitation and Innovation in the Scandinavian Place Names of the Northern Isles of Scotland" (1987), "Aberdeen: A Toponymic Key to the Region" (1990), "Names in the Landscape of the Moray Firth" (1983), "English and Gaelic Place-Names in Mediaeval North-East Scotland" (2003), "Perspectives on the pre-Norse Language(s) of Orkney" (2003), and "Scottish Loch Names" (2005). Also concerned with place-names but in a wider context or dealing with more general toponymic issues are "Onomastic Dialects" (1980), "Maps of Space – Maps of time" (1984), "Burnside of Duntrune: An Essay in Praise of Ordinariness" (1985), "Semantic Causes of Structural Changes in Place-Names" (1987), "Place-Name Maps: How Reliable Are They?" (1989), "Scottish Place-Names as Evidence for Language Change" (1993), and "Is There a Northwest Germanic Toponymy?" (1995). One article builds bridges between place-names and personal names: "Pictish Place-Names as Scottish Surnames" (1991-2), and two papers deal with facets of personal names; one, "Tension and Extension: Thoughts on Scottish Surnames and Medieval Culture" (1980), concentrates on social issues; the other, "An Onomastic Autobiography, or In the Beginning was the Name" (1999), as the title indicates, with concerns of selfness in the light of onomastic criteria. The author's increasing interest in literary onomastics is reflected in "Names as Verbal Icons" (1974), "Landscape as Plot: Place-Names in R.L. Stevenson's Fiction" (2000-2991), and "A Change of Place is a Change of Fortune" (2001). A variety of problems involving the study of names and adjacent disciplines, persuasively showing that it is profitable to look beyond the narrow boundaries of name studies, are at the heart of such articles as "Socio-onomastics" (1985), "Names and Politics" (1994),"Name and Appellative" (1995), "One Name but Many Systems" (1996), "Teaching Names: A Personal Account" (2004), and, as instances of the writer's long-standing fascination with folklore, especially folk-narrative, "The Prodigious Jump" (1968) and "The Past as Place: Names, Stories and the Remembered Self" (1991).

As these titles and the fuller list of publications at the end of the volume demonstrate, the widening of the author's horizons and therefore also the expansion of the range of the resulting publications are closely connected with changes in his personal circumstances. While the 1976 book was based on and derived its mainly Scottish impetus and direction from his position as Head of the Scottish Place-Name Survey of the School of Scottish Studies in the University of Edinburgh (1956-1969) and valuable benefits from contacts with the Society for Name-Studies in Britain and Ireland, as well as NORNA, the Nordisk Samarbejdskomite for Navneforskning, later research and its concomitant publications became possible, perhaps even inevitable, after his 1969 move to the State University of New York in Binghamton in the United States and his subsequent close involvement in the activities of the American Name Society and the International Council of Onomastic Sciences and, after his return to Scotland, similar participation in the Scottish Society for Northern Studies and, at a later stage, in the newly-founded Scottish Place-Name Society. Biography and Bibliography are thus found to be inseparable.

The fuller bibliography also gives a hint as to the difficulties encountered in the selection and arrangement of articles for this volume. Fortunately a very competent and willing sub-group of the Scottish Place-Name Society chaired by Doreen Waugh, took on these tasks, in close co-operation with the author who thanks them deeply for their commitment. A special debt of gratitude is due to Nancy Robertson who generously and efficiently put her considerable expertise to use in transforming the greatly varying originals into a uniform format for the benefit of the proofreaders.

May the readers of this book derive as much pleasure and profit from the finished product and its making as the team has.

W. F. H. N.

ACKNOWLEDGEMENTS

THE essays which appear in *In the Beginning was the Name: Selected Essays by W.F.H. Nicolaisen* were chosen from his extensive bibliography of published articles by a sub-group of the Scottish Place-Name Society (SPNS) committee. This was done in close consultation with Bill Nicolaisen and with the support and encouragement of all other SPNS committee members.

Various societies and organisations have contributed financially towards publication and promotion of this book. They are:

Scottish Place-Name Society (SPNS)
Ortnamnssällskapet i Uppsala/ The Place-Name Society of Uppsala
International Council of Onomastic Sciences (ICOS)
Society for Name Studies in Britain and Ireland (SNSBI)
Shetland Place-Name Project
School of Scottish Studies Archives
Dorothea Coke Memorial Fund
Scottish Society for Northern Studies (SSNS)

It is a condition of the Dorothea Coke Memorial Fund that, when printed, the book should carry the following notice:

The printing of this book is made possible by a gift to the University of Cambridge in memory of Dorothea Coke, Skjaeret, 1951.

The same can be said of all the donors listed above. The printing of this book would certainly not have been possible without their kindness.

Members of the sub-group of SPNS were Ian Fraser, Alison Grant, Arne Kruse, Bill Patterson and Doreen Waugh, all of whom gave very generously of their time, whether at the selection stage or at the later stage of proofreading and preparing the articles for re-printing. They were ably assisted in their proofreading by Pauline Cairns-Speitel and John Waugh. Ian Fraser, who was a colleague of Bill Nicolaisen in the Scottish Place-Name Survey, prepared the introductory tribute and Bill Patterson, helped by Bill Nicolaisen, undertook the task of writing to previous editors to request permission to re-publish the chosen articles. Their enthusiasm for our proposed volume has been most encouraging and we thank them for making this book possible by giving their permission to use the selected articles again. Further assistance was given by Margaret Mackay and various members of staff in the School of Scottish Studies Archives, Celtic and Scottish Studies, University of Edinburgh, who helped in the locating and selecting of photographs for the book. It proved a fascinating exercise.

All of the people mentioned above gave of their time and expertise most willingly because they wished to mark their appreciation of a lifetime's work by Bill Nicolaisen, whose lengthy association with Scotland is a matter of great pride. Bill has taken a very personal interest in our work throughout and kindly agreed to contribute the explanatory Foreword which follows.

D. W.

Names 47, 3 (Sept. 1999) 179-190

An Onomastic Autobiography, or, In the Beginning was the Name

ON Monday, June 13, 1927, at a quarter to two in the afternoon, Frau Paula Elisabeth Nicolaisen, herself twenty-three years old and only in the seventh month of her first pregnancy, gave birth to a son, weighing just over five pounds, to whom she and her husband, Andreas Wilhelm Albert Nicolaisen, gave the three names *Wilhelm Fritz Hermann*. These three names, confirmed in baptism on August 28, 1927, have, for over 70 years, been the official forenames of your honoree individualising him, in conjunction with his surname, in society and distinguishing him from all other Nicolaisens in a fairly large family. One might say that such a triple designation sanctioned by state and church should have been sufficient identification for the little male baby as well as the retired professor, and in a very limited sense this has been the case, of course, but the mere fact that I am often introduced or referred to as *Bill Nicolaisen* and the realisation that the *Wilhelm Fritz Hermann Nicolaisen* has probably been my least used appellation over seven decades (so rarely, in fact, that to many people who have known me for a long time, this is news), are clear indications that the official birth certificates, even

Mother and son, October 1927, Halle/Saale.

1 ———

when supported by the ecclesiastical powers that be, are severely restricted in their application and documentary value. It is probably true to say that I have been officially *Wilhelm Fritz Hermann Nicolaisen* only to issuers, perusers and processors of such and similar documents (like passports, marriage licences, visas, and so on), and not to anybody else, and that consequently the actualisation of my identity has almost exclusively been expressed in other, unofficial, onomastic terms. It is this variety of names that I have been called over the years by different people, in different situations, in different languages, in different registers, and that have shaped me as a person during that time, have made me and labelled me, that I want to parade and discuss in this "onomastic autobiography", in an account of "My Names and I", if you like.

Father in the 1950s, Hanover.

Before I do so, however, allow me briefly to return to the *Wilhelm Fritz Hermann* of my birth certificate because, unrelated to the practical demands of daily living as this triad of names may be, they anchor me firmly in my family and even in a little bit of German history. In particular, they make me the onomastic descendents of my closest male ancestors, my father and my two grandfathers. My father bestowed on me the name *Wilhelm*, the middle one of his three forenames, the other two of which were never used. I am therefore undoubtedly my father's son; the complications which such identical naming can produce I will refer to later. I am, however, also my two grandfathers' grandson, not just genetically but also onomastically, for *Fritz Nicolaisen* was my father's

Grandfathers Fritz Nicolaisen and Hermann Kähler, 1960s, Flensburg.

father and *Hermann Kähler* my mother's father. According to the prevailing naming practices at the time, I could therefore not be mistaken for anything else but what I was: The eldest son of my father's and the eldest grandson of my grandfathers'; my names said and still say so quite clearly, and there is no escaping from this status. Fortunately, the chains which this onomastic triplet has placed on me have been very light, even comfortable, sartorial items, and I have never thought of them as a burden or felt the need to divest myself of them in any mood of protest or resentment or because of a feeling of inappropriate identity. Of these three names, *Wilhelm* has further implications because my father was named after one of his uncles, and his uncle bore the name of the first German Kaiser, demonstrating my ultimate onomastic involvement in the German monarchy, with a chronological depth of about 125 years. One does not have to be a name scholar to recognise that a tripartite combination like *Wilhelm Fritz Hermann* was a little old-fashioned even in 1927, the year of my birth, and could easily have been given a generation or two earlier. In this connection, it is worth mentioning that all three names cannot, and in 1927 would not, deny their patently Germanic origins or flavour although their lexical etymologies never entered into my naming: I am not, never have been, and my parents never thought of me as a "helmet of resolution"; nor am I someone "mighty in

3

peace" or an "army-man". My onomastic persona was created under the fairly conservative, social pressures of the time which assigned it a clearly appointed place in my family genealogy. "Eldest son and grandson" are the onomastic contents of my forenames, and that is good so. (In parentheses, I should add that my Jutland surname, *Nicolaisen*, of course, also no longer corresponds to its lexical meaning "son of Nicolai or Nicholas"; if patronymic surnames had not yet become hereditary in Danish at the time of my birth, I would naturally have been *Wilhelmsen* or perhaps *Andresen*.) Lexically, therefore, I am a fraud, but onomastically my individual niche could not have been more definitely and appropriately selected.

Once the birth certificate had been filed and the drops of water that had been sprinkled on my forehead at the baptismal font had dried, however, good old (or young) *Wilhelm Fritz Hermann* had seemingly been filed and dried with them, for even a photograph which shows me as a three-month-old in my mother's arms is signed by her on my as yet preliterate behalf as *Klein-Willi*

"little Willi", distinguishing me not just in size and age but also in name from my father who was always known in the family as *Willi*. I see the addition of *Klein-* to my name not as a belittling act but rather as a small but significant gesture of providing me with an identity different from my father's, an early step in the direction of becoming myself.

Exactly how long this designation lasted is difficult to tell in retrospect, but undoubtedly a further emancipatory move on the onomastic front had taken place before I was two years old because the next photograph that can be dated is signed, in my mother's handwriting, by somebody called *Putzi*. How the transformation from *Klein-Willi* to *Putzi* came about, I cannot now say since there is no phonological law in the Indo-European languages from Verner's to Grimm's, no Lautverschiebung known

Putzi, May/June 1929, Halle/Saale.

to learned linguists, which would explain even with a high degree of speculation and uncertainty this curious metamorphosis. I have a suspicion that it is the combined effect of early babbling by its bearer (perhaps ineptly echoing the German adjective *putzig* "cute") and the desire in that strange age of emerging identities to name oneself. For whatever reason, *Putzi* was the name I gave myself, clumsily perhaps but also effectively because nobody could confuse *Putzi* with *Willi*, my father (a former colleague of mine, when he heard about this project suggested that I should call it "Putzi's Progress").

Thus, for better or worse, *Putzi* became my pre-school-age name, and I connect it with a carefree, sheltered life on Halle University's research farm, frequent visits from grandparents and doting aunts, very occasional trips to my mother's beloved Schleswig-Holstein, years full of play including playful chores like feeding the hens, a near-fatal encounter with a Model T Ford which crushed my tricycle but not me, with sun in the summer and snow in the winter, just as things should be when you are a child, later in the company of *Didi* and *Spatzi*, my two brothers who also quickly outgrew their childhood names.

Putzi, 1928, Halle/Saale.

Putzi, Didi (Dieter), Spatzi (Heiner), July 1932, Halle/ Saale.

5

Willi's first day at school, April 1933, Halle/Saale.

The final onomastic demise of *Putzi* came just after Easter 1933 when, not yet six, I was required to attend to the daily task, Monday through Saturday, of going to school. The first day was made very much easier by a tradition, still observed today, of the Zuckertüte, a cone-shaped receptacle coming in all sorts of sizes, of which mine was not the smallest, filled with a variety of sweets. This would be handed to brand-new first-graders by their mothers, anxiously awaiting their offsprings' re-emergence from the school portals that had swallowed them up earlier for the incredible ordeal of one or two initial hours in a classroom with thirty or so other children, in my case, because of the system prevailing at the time, all of them boys. A photograph shows me on the way home, none the worse for that daunting experience, proudly clutching my Zuckertüte in keen anticipation of the demolition of its content. This may well be the first picture of the post-*Putzi* Willi, for I am told that, on the eve of my first schoolday, I declared in full appreciation of the rite of passage: "Now *Putzi* is no longer *Putzi;* from now on *Putzi* will be *Willi;*" and *Willi* I have been in my family ever since, for nobody dared oppose such a determined and, I think, reasonable edict. Cloaking one's new identity – in this case, that of a schoolboy – in a different name is obviously not a recent discovery by name scholars but an instinctive response by the naively and innocently young (or do I detect in *Putzi's* determined decree an early act of the future onomastician?).

Well, determined and timely the act may have been for it placed the newly renamed *Willi* as an individual in a whole class of little boys whose teacher, now in her nineties, with whom I am still in touch. To her I am still *Willi Nicolaisen* today but in deference to my academic status she refuses to use the familiar "Du" as a form of address, preferring the more formal "Sie". While *Willi* served

First year at Freiimfelder Volksschule, Halle/Saale.

well my new public image, it created a fresh ambiguity on the domestic front for now there were again two *Willis* in the house, my father and myself. This potentially confusing situation was resolved in two ways: When neither of us was present we were referred to in family circles as *der grosse Willi* and *der kleine Willi* which at the time apparently distinguished us sufficiently by age, status and generation. As the years went by, however, the two epithets which were employed to distinguish us became less and less applicable if taken literally but I remained *der kleine Willi* even after my father's death in 1973, and my only surviving aunt still uses that designation although *der grosse Willi* has unfortunately not been with us anymore for over twenty-five years. The second solution evolved within the closest family circle in which my father, whether present or not, was referred to as *Vati*, and I thus became the only *Willi*, neither *gross* nor *klein*. A little later – and I remember being distinctly aware of this and somewhat disturbed by it as a boy – my parents stopped calling each other *Willi* and *Paula*, at least in public, addressing each other instead as *Vati* and *Mutti*, switching onomastically from a fundamentally conjugal role to an essentially parental mode of existence and of self-perception. This practice continued until grandchildren came along when *Opa* and *Oma* replaced *Vati* and *Mutti* in their presence. Otherwise, the latter pair continued right until death separated them.

Always a reader, c. 1937-8, Kiel.

Willi remained my chief name even after our move to my mother's birthplace, Kiel, in the German north, where my father had been given a professorial appointment at the university in 1935. Indeed, *Willi* is still my name within my nuclear family, except for the next generation which, acknowledging my avuncular status, calls me *Onkel Willi*. This is, however, by no means the end of my onomastic story for as soon as I started going to high school, and without any prompting, I was given the same nickname which my father had had in his own high school and student days: *Nico*. In fact, I shared this fate with my

Birthday party, June 1937, Kiel.

two brothers. Among the few of my classmates who survived World War II, there are still some who, on the rare occasions on which we meet, will call me *Nico* and who may not even remember my real first name. Only our Physical Education teacher, for some reason, insisted on calling us *Nike*, especially in the memorable, though highly critical, phrase, which has entered the Nicolaisen family oral tradition: "The whole *Nike* family cannot swim!"

It was in the early post-war years that various people outside my family started to call me *Wilhelm*, beginning on the farm on which I worked for a year and a half after my release as a P.O.W. Even during those 18 months there were variations, however: as we almost exclusively spoke Low German (Plattdeutsch) I tended to be called *Willem* by the farmer, his family and neighbours in the village, with the exception of the farmer's wife who, presumably because I had been cajoled into teaching them English one evening a week (without much success, I must admit), honoured me with the classical designation *Wilhelmus* and continued to call me that until her death a few years ago. Otherwise, however, I had become *Wilhelm* to my friends and acquaintances from the time I resumed my schooldays which at the end of the war had been severely interrupted, to the time when I was working on my dissertation at the University of Tübingen, and beyond.

Two other names, however, enriched and confused, whatever way you want to look at it, my onomastic existence as a student. In early 1950, while I was still at the University of Kiel, I got

School-leaver, May 1948, Herford.

At work on Ph.D. dissertation, 1954, Tübingen.

involved in the English Dramatic Club and, apart from being a hare in first grade in a dramatisation of the fable of "The Hare and the Hedgehog" at the age of six, made my acting debut in the part of *Nicola* in Shaw's "Arms and the Man". As frequently happens among amateur thespians, we started to call each other by our stage names, and I am still in touch with one of the actresses who, in her occasional correspondence, is very uncomfortable calling me anything other than *Nicola*, while she to me remained *Raina* and has not become *Ursel*.

The other additional name had more serious repercussions because it involved not just a switch in the linguistic register but a change from one language to another, in this case from German to English. When, in April 1950, I first stepped onto English soil as an exchange student at King's College Newcastle, now the University of Newcastle, I was immediately and without being consulted in the matter called *Billy* – by professors, fellow students, my landlady, and others. I am glad to say that this name did not survive my stay in Newcastle and the summer which followed (including a short spell on a farm near Bridgwater in Somerset), for I never took to it; it somehow was not me, at least not from my own

As Nicola in Shaw's Arms and the Man, *January 1950, Plön, nr. Kiel.*

Billy at Capernwray Hall, Lancs., September 1951.

11

point of view, although others who had known me for only a short time appeared to have no difficulty in equating it with me. I might have been happier with it as a younger boy but at the time I was in my twenties *Billy* seemed so immature, so juvenile, so insubstantial, almost trivial.

One year later, however, I graduated to my real name, and this happened in connection with my first full-time academic appointment at the University

Head of Scottish Place-Name Survey, School of Scottish Studies (1956-69), Edinburgh.

of Glasgow which was also, although it could not have been foreseen at the time, the beginning of an academic career in English-speaking countries, a career which has lasted for more than 47 years. I do not know who first called me *Bill*, nor do I remember whether I actively discouraged people from calling me *Billy* again, but certainly *Bill* I became and have stayed ever since. It is as if all the other names had just been preparations or rehearsals for this one and as if *Bill* then perfectly expressed who I was meant to be. Undoubtedly, more people know me as *Bill* or *Bill Nicolaisen* now than by any other name. Naturally, such people are chiefly speakers of English but even to German speakers who have met me since 1951 I am now usually *Bill*. In that respect, I was particularly touched when my mother started referring to me as *Bill* when my wife was around. Anyhow, the person who first called me *Bill* deserves a medal.

What else was there in store for me? Marriage in Scotland in 1958 and fatherhood in 1959 earned me the name of *Dad* or *Daddy*, finally in quadruplicate, to which was added in due course the title of *Opa* (Grandpa). Professionally, *Dr. Nicolaisen* made his appearance in the University of Edinburgh in 1956 (although I was and

Daddy and daughter Fiona, October 1959, Edinburgh

With wife May and daughters Fiona, Kirsten, Moira and Birgit on my 60th birthday, June 1987, Edinburgh.

13

Visiting Professor at Ohio State University (1966-7), Columbus, Ohio.

still am *Willie Nick* to some of my former colleagues there), and the first time anybody ever addressed me as *Professor Nicolaisen* or just plain *Professor* was during my visiting professorship at Ohio State University in 1966-1967. This appellation is still with me now although one generation of graduate students a few years ago chose to call me, among themselves, "Nickey". As a publishing scholar – in contradistinction to my father who was also a well-published academic – I started out as *Wilhelm F.H. Nicolaisen* but soon decided on the initials *W.F.H.*, the old *Wilhelm Fritz Hermann* reduced to an acronym; curiously, though, and for no reason I can discern, the order of

PLANSUS Meeting, c. 1991, Washington D.C.

these initials is frequently changed by all kinds of people on both sides of the Atlantic, especially by editors, and I am as often as not referred to as *W.H.F.* which I am *not* and which sounds more like the call sign of a radio station. Similarly, the first initial is sometimes expanded to *William*, or much to my chagrin, to *Will*, which I am *not* either. What's good enough for Shakespeare is not necessarily good enough for Nicolaisen. I regard these aberrant variants not as true names of mine, not even as acceptable variants, but as mistakes that have more to say about the people who use them than about me.

This also applies to various erroneous pronunciations of my surname – like [niko'le:sən] or [niko'la-i-sən] – which seem to have become inevitable though not less annoying whereas [niko'laɪsən], with a voiceless fricative, instead of the German [niko'laɪzən], with its voiced counterpart, has become the norm and more than just acceptable, especially since my father also used that pronunciation, having been brought up close to the Danish border where Danish has influenced the language of his birthplace, Flensburg. I am pleased to be *Bill Nicolaisen* and undoubtedly will remain so. Perhaps an anecdote illustrating the dangers involved in insisting on retaining one's surname more or less intact in a different linguistic and cultural environment, rather than changing it to *Nicolson* or *MacNicol*, may be illuminating at this point: When we still lived in Edinburgh, from time to time I had to take shoes to the cobbler's or a suit to the cleaner's, and almost invariably after giving my name as *Nicolaisen*, I was asked "How do you spell that?". I thought I might be able to avoid this question and therefore on one occasion gave my name as *Nicolson* whereupon I was asked "With or without

Distinguished Professor of English and Folklore, State Unversity of New York at Binghamton (1969-92).

an -h-?". When I explained that it did not matter because it was not *Nicolson* anyhow, the shop attendant almost refused to take my suit! What can one say?

Allow me to add a few more *allonyms* which are infrequent in their application: Some old-fashioned academics on both sides of the Atlantic refer to me simply by my surname – *Nicolaisen*. A few of my Scottish friends who are native speakers of Gaelic sometimes Gaelicise my name into *Uilleam MacNeacail(l); the* Anglicised form of the latter is, of course, *MacNicol(l).* A couple of nephews and nieces and a few young children of family friends call me *Uncle Bill,* and one German niece whose legal guardian I was when she was staying in upstate New York while attending Vestal High School for a semester, still addresses me as *Guardian.* I should perhaps also point out that *Putzi* has not been the only self-imposed name. On a family tour of Germany, the eleven-year old *Willi* decided to call himself *Alter Mann* (Old Man), and almost fifty years later I told the students in our London Program that I was *Big Bad Bill* (in both these instances I used to speak of myself in the third person). Both of these names did not outlast their specific short-term usage but I find the use of the third person that went with it, as it had done with *Putzi,* a fascinating way of looking at oneself from the outside and of relinquishing one's first-person egocentricity.

So, what is my onomastic identity now after 70 years of meandering shaping and reshaping? Well, it is obviously centrally enshrined in *Bill* or *Bill Nicolaisen* but the issue is not that simple, and I have often wondered if I have any identity at all since I am so many names to so many people. Let me try to list these allonyms: *Bill, Bill Nicolaisen, Uncle Bill, Willi, der kleine Willi, Onkel Willi, Willi Nicolaisen, Wilhelm, Wilhelm Nicolaisen, W.F.H. Nicolaisen, Nicolaisen, Nico, Nicola, Guardian, Dr. Nicolaisen, Willie Nick, Professor Nicolaisen, Professor, Dad, Daddy, Opa,* and, of course, good old birth-certificate *Wilhelm Fritz Hermann Nicolaisen.* What a bewildering array! And how important the socio-onomastic aspects are of this list, like register and usage! I respond to all these names in their appropriate situations, and each one of them presents or reflects a different side of me to the world, and to myself, I presume.

To round off this onomastic autobiography of mine, here is a final image based on a photograph taken by my good friend Professor Eichler: In March 1980, I had an opportunity to revisit my birthplace Halle for the first time in almost forty years and, in the process, got very close to where *Putzi* had grown up but not close enough, for the authorities of what was then still East Germany, the DDR, had put a wire fence round the whole property and a very securely locked gate across the path along which the newly transformed Willi had proudly marched home with his Zuckertüte in 1933. The house itself, or what one could see of it in the middle distance in the sulphurous smog, looked neglected and in considerable need of repair. It also looked smaller. When I studied this photograph again of *Professor W.F.H. Nicolaisen* or *Bill* standing outside the gate and barred from *Putzi's* home, it occurred to me that this is probably as close as we will ever get to our childhood again, to our past as place, and that even documents, a set of pictures, and a series of names will not help us to do more than reminisce about the children we imagine ourselves to have once been. Even an onomastic autobiography can do no more than create true chunks of a past that never was. Presumably it is at this point that "story" and "history" regain their original etymological unity. Nevertheless, *Bill Nicolaisen's* account of *Putzi's Progress* is bound to remain just that – *Bill Nicolaisen's* account of *Putzi's Progress*, and not *Putzi's* or *Willi's* or *Nico's* own unfiltered, unrefracted stories.

Outside boyhood home, Halle/Saale, March 1980.

Scottish Studies 1 (1957) 211-240

The Semantic Structure of Scottish Hydronymy

Introduction

SCOTTISH place-names have never suffered from lack of interest. On the contrary, there have always been people, from all walks of life, who have dedicated a considerable amount of their time to the study of Scottish toponymy. Very often the reason for this has been an academic one: an antiquarian's interest in local history, an archæologist's desire to find confirmation of his own research in the place-nomenclature of the region, a geographer's attempt at solving the problems of human settlement or a philologist's quest for data relating to the linguistic past of a district. The most important factors taken into account by these students of place-names are usually the distribution of certain elements, the morphological formation of names, the sound changes they imply and the definition of the language and linguistic stratum to which they belong.

But besides this academic approach there has always been a genuine interest in place-names on the side of the general public, although with a completely different emphasis and attitude. To the archæologist, the geographer, the historian – and even to the philologist, semantic considerations may only be of secondary importance. To them it does not really matter what a name "means". Not so with the ordinary enquirer and place-name enthusiast. His first, and normally his only, question is "What does this name mean?" And if the name is not easily explained and understood, he resorts to what is usually called "folk-etymology" until its obscurity is made intelligible. Just as a thing, an idea, an event cannot be "mastered" by the human mind until it can be put into words, so one's geographical surroundings cannot be "mastered" till one has given them intelligible names or till one understands the names they already possess. So, this popular approach to a place-name – in contrast to the scholarly one – reflects in its special interest in the "meaning" of the name the tendency of the human being to "master" his world – and that includes his geographical surroundings – linguistically.

The Scot – and the Scottish Highlander in particular – seems to have developed an even stronger inclination towards this merely semantic interpretation of toponymic evidence, than members of other nations, as any visitor, especially to the Gaelic-speaking areas, who has ever made any enquiries about a place-nomenclature will testify. The crofter, the shepherd, the local schoolmaster – not only will they supply him with the "correct" form of the name and its meaning, but most probably also with a story that explains and underlines this particular meaning. Etymological speculation and imaginative interpretation are applied to the name in question and both have undoubtedly been very strong formative powers in the creation of new names, or the adaptation of old and obscure ones, throughout all phases of Scottish toponymy.

It is typical of this popular approach to the understanding of a place-name – and, indeed, of many a pseudo-scholarly attempt at such an understanding as well – that a linguistic explanation is looked for only in the modern language spoken in that particular area at the time of the enquiry. This is where the peculiar nature of place-names is completely misunderstood, a nature which makes them important source-material of the linguistic history of any country. Personal names wander and migrate with the people that bear them and only in exceptional cases throw much light on the nature of the language or languages spoken in a certain area in the past. But place-names are more stationary, as is to be expected because of their close connection with the land.[1] They also possess a remarkable power of survival. When, in the course of extensive migrations and re-settlement people of different linguistic stock arrive in a certain region, settle there and, finally, dominate the earlier inhabitants, politically and linguistically, not every geographical feature is named afresh. Old names are translated, either in part or in whole, or are just adapted in accordance with the phonetic possibilities of the new language; sometimes elements belonging to the old language are used in conjunction with elements that are part of the new one, resulting in a not inconsiderable number of toponymical hybrids. The main fact emerging from these observations is, that when new place-names are coined in a different linguistic medium, not all the old names are replaced and disappear, but a certain number of them remains, although often disguised and hardly recognisable.

The result is a stratification of various layers of linguistic sediments, the lowest of which leads us much further back into history and prehistory than any other linguistic evidence. It is the task of the place-name scholar to remove layer after layer, examining the morphological and semantic structure of the names each contains and utilising them in the interpretation of the early stages of those languages to which they can be assigned. When the "lowest" stratum is reached that can still be interpreted with the linguistic knowledge now at our disposal, there will still be a number of names left that have defied all attempts at an explanation, but it would be dangerous to treat obscurity as a sign of the great age of a name. Oral tradition of a name is subject to so many influences, especially when more than one language is involved in its execution, that it would be surprising if every single name could be satisfactorily analysed in the course of our investigations.

Generally, place-names ante-dating names of human settlements are those denoting water-courses or mountains and hills, and especially names of burns and rivers. These may throw much light on the problems of linguistic prehistory and so of prehistory in general. The oldest of them are like fossils preserved in later surrounding linguistic media, and it is not too bold to say that the oldest Scottish river-names give us information about the language or languages spoken on the banks of the water-courses they denote, more than 1000 years B.C.

This is not the place for us to outline the course of our investigations in that particular field of research. It will suffice for our immediate purposes to state the results of that enquiry: there are at least five layers of Scottish hydronymy, the English, the Norse, the Gaelic, the "p"-Celtic and the pre-Celtic Indo-European. A closer examination, however, shows that there are really two English strata, one linked up with northern English stream-nomenclature and one moulded upon underlying Gaelic patterns when English began to invade the Highlands. Furthermore, the Norse layer may be divided into three sub-sections, one supplying the generic terms Old Norse á, gröf and – possibly – lón, the second introducing the beck-names near the English border, the third providing the Scots dialect with the term grain. Only two strata cover the whole of Scotland: the latest, the English, and the earliest, the pre-Celtic one. All others are confined to a certain part of the country and usually to a certain period of name productivity.

Morphologically, the top strata of Scottish hydronymy – as those of the other parts of the British Isles and of other European countries – consist of compound names, regardless of the language to which they belong. But underneath these a different class of names is to be found characterised by the formation: stem + suffix. This group only amounts to 8 per cent of all Scottish river-names marked on the one inch Ordnance Survey maps, with the following subdivision: Gaelic names 5.3 per cent, p-Celtic names 1.8 per cent, pre-Celtic names 0.8 per cent. With two possible exceptions, Germanic names do not appear in this category, and the formation of river-names by suffixing seems to have ended in their respective, languages before the Norsemen and Anglo-Saxons reached Scotland. A number of simple stems occurs in the early hydronymic strata. Even if these early names are few in comparison with the overwhelming majority of modern names, they prove how futile it would be to try to explain every single name of a Scottish water-course from the vocabulary of Modern Anglo-Scottish or Modern Scottish Gaelic.

It is against this morphological and historical background that we wish to outline the semantic structure of Scottish river-nomenclature, i.e. we want to apply scholarly and linguistic methods to that aspect of a section of Scottish toponymy that is normally the prerogative of popular and imaginative speculation. The form in which this will be done will be a systematic classification of names of Scottish water-courses that covers all the categories of meaning which appear in this nomenclature. Significant examples will be chosen from all hydronymic layers, from all dialect areas and from all morphological classes. We shall examine whether and how the predominance of certain aspects of meaning changed in the course of time, and how much each stratum of Scottish hydronymy has to contribute towards each semantic group. We shall also attempt to illustrate, by these examples and by the changes they imply, the change of attitude in the minds of the people who created this Scottish river-nomenclature in its various phases.

The system of classification used will be, in principle, the one worked out by Bach (1953) for the names of German water-courses. It will be adapted to the special Scottish situation and enlarged to be applicable to the whole of our hydronymy. Comparative notes will be supplied wherever the river-nomenclature of other parts of the British Isles or of other countries in which an Indo-European language is, or used to be, spoken seems to throw light on our particular Scottish problem. Scottish hydronymy is not an isolated entity – either in its semantic or its morphological aspect – and cannot be treated without comparative reference to the terminology applied to rivers and streams in those countries from which the languages, traceable in Scotland's linguistic history, originally emigrated. Scandinavia, Ireland, England, Wales, the European continent proper all have much to contribute to toponymic research in Scotland. Scottish hydronymy, and Scottish toponymy in general, may have many peculiarly "Scottish" features, but nothing could more dangerously impair a satisfactory progress in their investigation than a parochial or national outlook that, apart from ignoring the toponymic situation and research south of the Tweed, refused to look for elucidation from beyond the North Sea, the Irish Sea and the English Channel. The study of place-names in any country must be based on the methods and results of *comparative* linguistics.

The basic material for the following survey has been excerpted from Ordnance Survey maps, scale 1 inch: 1 mile, and supplemented by derivations and explanations of Scottish rivers and burns, given in various place-name studies of which there are not very many that can be accepted and approved without some considerable hesitation. The acceptance of this kind of material as a basis for a genuinely linguistic investigation entails certain handicaps, limitations and inaccuracies, due to the nature of geographical names printed on Ordnance Survey maps covering Scotland, especially in respect of Gaelic names. But it seems that these inexactitudes, slight or grave as they may be, do not seriously impair the validity of the conclusions reached at this stage of Scottish hydronymic research especially in a study of this nature, in which neither comprehensiveness nor finality can be attempted. The advantage of the Ordnance Survey maps is that they cover the *whole* of Scotland, and the 1 inch: 1 mile edition provides a suitable number of names of rivers and burns.

The spellings given will be normally those to be found on these maps, and the county abbreviations, used to indicate the geographical situation of the water-courses concerned, will be those adopted by the place-name department of the School of Scottish Studies. A complete list of these abbreviations will be provided at the end. Names in the Western Isles will be followed by the name of the island in which they occur, not by the county name. Older forms will generally not be mentioned, as that would only extend the already lengthy lists of names without contributing much to our particular attempt at *a classification of Scottish river-names according to their meaning*. Normally only one instance of a name will be mentioned, even if it occurs several times, as is often the case with the names of smaller water-courses.

Classification[2]

A. Streams named after Characteristics of the Water
(a) *The* colour *of the water*

O.S.M. 1 inch (Scotland)[3] have 412 stream-names derived from the colour of the water. This naming of a water-course after the special characteristics impressed upon the people living near it, through the medium of the eye, is by far the most common, compared with the other groups of names that express a special quality of the water of a stream or river. The figures for these groups are: the *taste and smell* of the water 8; *temperature* of the water 6; *noise* of the flowing water 53; *effect* of the water 12.

Almost the whole colour-scheme is represented in this category, some colours more frequently than others. Yet although, in the majority of cases, the actual colour of the water of a stream may have prompted the name it bears, we must take into consideration the possibility of fashionable name patterns and semantic models. Moreover, in quite a number of instances *black* and *white* do not so much serve to describe the colour of the water as to distinguish between two water-courses that flow into each other, are parallel tributaries of the same river or bear the same name and could be confused because of their geographical proximity.

Here are some examples for the various colours:

Black: *Abhainn Dubh* ROS, *Alltan Dubh* SUT, *Allt Dubh* SUT, *Alt Dubhagan* PER, *An Dubh-Alltan* SUT, *Black Burn* MOR, *Black Sike* SLK, *Black Water* ROX, *Caochan Dubh* INV, *Douglas Water* ARG, *Duack Burn* INV, *Dubh Uisge* INV *Dupple Burn* DMF, *Dye Water* BWK, *Féith Dubh* SUT, *Lón Dubh* SKYE, *River Divie* MOR, *Uisge Dubh* INV.

Blue: *Allt Ghormaig* INV, *Allt Gorm* INV, *Gormack Burn* ABD, *Feadan Gorm* LEWIS.

Bright: *Light Water* KCD, *Lochar Water* DMF, *Luggie Water* DNB/LAN-DNB, *Peffer Burn* ELO, *River Loyne* INV, *The Lussa* ARG.

Brindled: *Alltan Riabhach* SUT, *Allt Riabhach* ROS, *Caochan Riabhach* INV, *Féith Riabhach* SUT.

Brown: *Caochan Donn* INV, * *Duinnid* (in Inver*inate*) ROS.

Dark: *Alltan Dorch* ROS, *Leuchar Burn* ABD, *River Lochy* INV.

Dun: *Alltan Odhar* ROS, *Allt Odhar* INV, *Féith Odhar* PER.

Filthy: *Mossat Burn* ABD, *Salachie Burn* ROS.

Green: *Abhainn Glas* PER, *Abhainn Uaine* LEWIS, *Allt Glas* PER, *Allt Uaine* INV, *Glas Allt* ABD, *Glas Burn* ANG, *Glas Féith* PER, *Greenburn* BNF, *Lón Glas* SKYE, *River Glass* ROS.

Grey: *Allt Liath* SCALPAY.

Pie-bald: *Allt Drimmeach* INV.

Red: *Abhainn Dearg* ROS, *Alltan Dearg* SUT, *Alltan Roy* ABD, *Allt Dearg* ROS, *Allt Ruadh* INV, *Dearg Abhainn* ARG, *Dearg Allt* INV, *Red Burn* MOR, *River Roy* INV.

Silver: *Silver Burn* ABD.

Speckled: *Allt Ballach* INV, *Alltan Breac* ARG, *Allt Breac* ROS, *Caochan Breac* INV.

White: *Allt a' Gheallaidh* MOR, *Allt Bàn* INV, *Allt Geal* SUT, *Burn of Canny* ABD, *Cander Water* LAN, *Dìg Bhàn* ARG, *Féith Bhan* ARG, *Fender Burn* PER, *Finglas Water* PER, *Fionn-abhainn* ROS, *Fionn Allt* LEWIS, *Geldie Burn* ABD, *Gelder Burn* ABD, *Lón Bàn* SKYE, *River Finnan* INV, *Sruthan Bàn* S. UIST, *Sruth Geal* PER, *White Burn* ANG, *White Grain* SLK, *White*

Sike SLK, *White Water* ANG.

Yellow: *Allt Buidhe* ARG, *Féith Buidhe* SUT, *Pollan Buidhe* ROS.

Colour adjectives are often used to distinguish between two related water-courses, as for example:

Allt Bàn – Lower part *Allt Dubh* SKYE.

Dubh Lighe – Fionn Lighe (parallel streams) INV.

White Burn joins *Black Burn* ANG.

Black Cart Water RNF joins *White Cart Water* LAN/RNF-RNF.

Black Laggan Burn→ *White Laggan Burn* KCD.

Blackadder Water→ *Whiteadder Water* BWK.

River Findhorn (**Fionn* Earn) – *River Deveron* (**Dubh* Earn) – identical primary river-names in the same district.

That this practice is not confined to Scotland is shown by Welsh doublets like *Braenan Ddu* and *Wen*, *Claerddu* and *Claerwen*, *Cleddy Ddu* and *Wen*, as well as by the German river-names *Schwarze* and *Weisse Elster*.

In a few instances colour adjectives seem to have become generic terms for "water, river". The Gaelic and Welsh term *glais*, "a stream" is based on Welsh *glas* "blue, grey, pale", Gaelic *glas* "grey, green", Breton *glaz* "green", etc. According to Wilhelm Schulze (1934) a similar derivation is to be considered for Gaelic *dobhar* and Welsh *dw(f)r*, "water", which are connected with Gaelic *dubh*, Welsh *du*, etc. "black"; so the original meaning of these two hydronymic terms seems to have been "the green one" and "the black one", respectively.

(b) *The* taste *and* smell *of the water*

This group of names is small compared with the preceding one, no doubt due to the fact that the senses of taste and smell are easily overruled by the eye and the ear in the determination of the main characteristics of a water-course, nevertheless we can list *Allt Bhrachain* PER ("putrefaction"), *Allt Breinag* INV ("putrid"), *Allt Shallainn* PER ("salt"), *Almeel Burn* STL ("sweet"), *Foul Burn* BWK, *Garroch Burn* KCD ("having a bad odour"), *Grotaig Burn* INV ("putrid"), *Sweet Burn* ARG.

(c) *The* temperature *of the water*

This group of names forms an even smaller category, numerically, in Scottish hydronymy. The hotness or coldness of water have to be extremely intensive before they form the main quality of a stream. Instances are *Burn of Brown* INV/BNF (**Brutonā*), *Cald Burn* ANG, *Cauld Burn* ELO, *Coldstream Burn* KCD, *Uisge Fuar* ISLAY, *Warm Burn* KNR.

(*d*) *The* noise *of the flowing water*

This group contains about one-eighth of the number of names in the category referring to the colour of the water, but it is considerably stronger than *b*, *c* and *e*. Its outstanding feature is the great variety of defining elements which are used to describe the kind of noise peculiar to a certain stream. One has to listen very long and carefully before one is justified in applying any of these 53 names. *Labhar*, "talkative" seems to be one of the most favoured defining elements, and there are indications that its *p*-Celtic equivalent was used just as readily. In any case, the number of early names in this group is remarkable. – These are some of the names: *Allt Darrarie* ABD ("rattling"), *Allt Eigheach* PER ("noise"), *Allt Gleadhrach* ROS ("shrill"), *Blye Water* BNF ("noise"), *Calair Burn* PER ("loud"), *Clattering Burn* LAN, *Kale Water* ROX (**Calonā*), *Lavery Burn* AYR (**Labharag*), *Levern Water* RNF (**Labaronā*), *Liddel Water* ROX ("loud"), *River Balvag* PER ("silent"), *River Braan* PER ("bleating"), *River Garnock* AYR ("noisy"), *River Ythan* ABD ("talkative"), *Rumbling Burn* AYR, *The Shevock* ABD ("quiet"), *Uisge Labhair* INV ("loud"), *Water of Gairney* ABD ("loud").

(*e*) *The* effect *of the water*

Names in this section refer to the health-giving quality of the water, to its blessedness, and to other virtues. They do not necessarily prove any kind of river-worship, but only point to a certain amount of superstition in the medical ideas or practice of the people living on the banks of these streams and possibly to some genuine health-promoting faculty of the "waters", when drunk by the patient. In this connection the usage of Gaelic *fion*, "wine" is interesting (Watson 1926, pp. 436-7). Examples from O.S.M. 1" are *Abhainn Eilg* INV ("virtue"), *Abhainn Bhuachaig* ROS ("virtue"), *Alltan Buadh* CAI ("virtue"), *Allt an Fhiona* INV ("wine"), *Allt Mathaig* PER ("good"), *Allt na Slànaich* IN\' ("having a healing virtue"), *Allt Sealbhach* SUT ("lucky"), *Allt Slanaidh* PER ("healthy"), *Hallow Burn* PEB, *Polmath Burn* AYR ("good"), *Sound Burn* LAN, *Water of Buchat* ABD ("abounding in virtue").

B. Streams named after Characteristics of the Water-Course

(*a*) *The* size *and* length *of the stream*

In 211 cases Scottish stream-names marked on O.S.M. 1 inch seem to refer to either the size or the length of the stream, and amongst these, names referring to the size are in a great majority. The most popular Gaelic name of this category is *Allt Mór*, of which there are at least 61 instances. *Mór* is in these cases seldom used in a relative sense, being meant to denote the absolute size of the stream, although one cannot escape the impression that it is very often just the imitation of a semantic name pattern not referring to the actual size of the water-course. But in some instances an *Allt Beag* runs parallel to an *Allt Mór* and quite frequently *Mór* and *Beag*, *Big* and *Little* are attached to the names of parallel streams to distinguish them from each other. *Beag* and *Little* are also used to denote a tributary that bears the same name as the river into which it flows.

Examples: *Abhainn Bheag* JURA, *Abhainn Mhór* ARG, *Allt Beag* INV, *Allt Fada* LEWIS ("long"), *Allt Mór* ARG, *Allt Yairack* INV ("short"), *Beg Burn* ROS ("small"), *Big Burn* INV, *Caochan Mór* ABD, *Faeshealloch Burn* INV ("short"), *Feadan Mór* LEWIS, *Féith Mór* INV, *Gearr Abhainn* ARG, *Little Burn* SLK, *Little River* CAI, *Little Water* ABD, *Long Burn* ROX, *Long Grain* SLK, *Long Latch* BWK, *Lón Mór* SKYE, *Meikle Burn* LAN, *Muckle Burn* ANG, *Pillmour Burn* ELO, *River Morar* ROS, *Wee Burn* AYR.

Instances of two *parallel water-courses* distinguished by *mór* and *beag* are *Allt Beithe Mór* and *Beag* PER, INV; *Allt Chaorach Mór* and *Beag* INV, *Allt Dearg Mór* and *Beag* SKYE, *Allt Dhaidh Mór* and *Beag* ABD, *Allt Mór* and *Beag* ARG, ROS, *Allt Ruadh Mór*, and *Beag* INV, *Féith Odhar Mhór* and *Bheag* PER, *Feochan Mhór* and *Bheag* ARG, *Fionn Allt Mór* and *Beag* LEWIS, *Scaladale More River* and *Scaladale Beg River* LEWIS. Here also belong *Allt Mhuic Bheag* INV, flowing parallel to *Allt Mhuic* and *Little Gruinard River* ROS, flowing parallel to *Gruinard River*.

Examples of *Little* and *Beag* being used to denote a *tributary* that bears the same name as the river into which it flows are *Allt Borgidh Beag* SUT→*River Borgie*, *Beanaidh Bheag* INV →*Am Beanaidh*, *Duibhe Bheag* PER→*Abhainn Duibhe*, *Garbh Uisge Beag* BNF→*Garbh Uisge*, *Kish Beg River* LEWIS→*Kish River*, *Little Allt Bheitheachan* BNF→*Allt Bheitheachan*, *Little Calder* LAN→*Calder Water*, *Little Eachaig River* ARG→*River Eachaig*, *Little Tarras Water* DMF→*Tarras Water*, *Luibeg Burn* ABD→*Lui Water*. – Sometimes the main river shows an additional *mór*: *Allt Cristie Beag* ABD→*Allt Cristie Mór*, *Féith Gaineimh Bheag* CAI→*Féith Gaineimh Mhór*, *Glas Féith Bheag* PER→*Glas Féith Mhór*.

Two water-courses that *join*, belonging to this category, are *Little* and *Big Water of Fleet* KGD which flow together to form the *Water of Fleet*.

Just as in the case of the juxtaposition of Gaelic *dubh* and *bàn* (or *fionn*), English *black* and *white* in the description of parallel or joining streams of identical names, the usage of Gaelic *mór* and *beag* can be paralleled outside Scotland. In Wales we find, amongst others, *Anghidi Fawr* and *Fechan*, *Dwyfawr* and *Dwyfach*, *Llynfi Fawr* and *Fechan*, etc.

Edward Schröder (1944) in his *Deutsche Namenkunde* points out that tributaries can be named by forming diminutives from the names of the rivers into which they flow; he mentions as examples the continental river-names *Selke* (<*Selica*) →*Sala* and *Mürz* (<*Muoriza*) →*Muor*. Schwarz (1950) is of the opinion that this type of name is especially common in the Slavonic languages and that there even the upper reach of a water-course may be called *Little River*. A possible Scottish example of this type is *Spean* INV, if it may be taken to be a diminutive of *Spey* (Watson 1926, p. 474), although it does not, of course, flow into that river. In England and Wales this category is well represented, cf. *Erthig* (Cardigansh.) →*Arth*, *Sochan* (Caernarvonsh.) →*Soch*, *Sturkel* (Dorsetsh.) →*Stour*, OE. *Temedel* (Worcestersh.) →*Teme*, etc.

(*b*) *The* form of the bed *of the stream*

In the 184 examples of stream-names referring to the form of the water-course various comparisons with human instruments and tools are made in order to describe the shape most appropriately. We meet the *fork*, the *vat*, the *bag*, the *bowl*, the *ampulla*, the *needle* and the *trough*. This is a type especially common in Wales (cf. Thomas 1938 p. 128) where the names of many tools and instruments have become names of water-courses. In this hydronymic usage names of containers are to be found throughout Britain, the most frequent of them being *cup* or *bowl*, cf. besides the *Quoichs*, *Quaichs* and *Cuachs* of Scotland, *Bune* (Oxfordsh.), *Cogan Pill* (Glamorgansh.), *Sence* (Leicestersh.). Obviously, adjectives like *crooked, narrow, round, pointed* were not sufficiently expressive in the opinion of the name-givers, but they saw the river as being *crooked like tongs, pointed like a needle, round like a cup*, etc., and so the water-course became itself *tongs, needle, cup*, etc. The same applies to those stream-names that are identical with names of animals or trees.

Besides these metaphorical terms mostly adjectives are used, among which *crom* and *cam* are the most frequent not only in Gaelic hydronymy but also in earlier Celtic river-names. In *Leth Allt* – in the following list the Ross-shire name serves as one example for many instances of this name throughout the Gaelic area – the intermediate meaning of *allt* as "a burn with steep banks" is preserved, for *leth allt* "half burn" denotes a burn with only one steep bank. References to the form of a water-course in Scotland are much more common in Celtic than in Germanic river-names.

Some typical examples are: *Abhainn Shlatach* INV ("branchy"); *Allt an t-Sniomh* LEWIS ("twist"), *Allt Briste* SUT ("broken"), *Allt Cam* INV ("crooked"), *Allt Caol* CAI ("narrow"), *Allt Chernie* SUT ("angular"), *Allt Domhain* ROS ("deep"), *Allt Gobhlach* SUT ("forked"), *Allt Leathan* PER ("broad"), *Allt nan Criopag* SKYE ("wrinkles"), *Allt Nealagro* LEWIS ("needle"), *Allt Utha* INV ("udder"), *An Cam-allt* INV, *Braid Burn* MLO ("broad"), *Broad Burn* MOR, *Builg Burn* ABD ("bag"), *Burn of Ample* PER ("ampulla"), *Burn of Breitoe* SH ("steep"), *Cam Alltan* ROS, *Cammock Burn* AYR, *Campel Water* DMF, *Caochan Cam* INV, *Caochan Crom* SUT ("crooked"), *Caochan Uchdach* INV ("steep"), *Caolie Water* INV, *Crom Allt* ROS, *Crombie Burn* BNF, *Crook Burn* BWK, *Deep Sike* ROX, *Fiar Allt* LEWIS ("winding"), *Gable Burn* SUT, *Gowl Burn* ELO, *Leth Allt* ROS ("half-burn"), *Loop Burn* CAI, *Meoir Veannaich* ABD ("forked"), *Old Hangy Burn* KNR ("slender"), *Poldivan Lake* DMF ("deep"), *Quoich Water* ABD ("bowl"), *Rigging Sike* ROX ("meandering"), *River Bogie* ABD ("bag"), *Smail Burn* SLK ("narrow"), *Snaid Burn* STL ("needle"), *Trough Burn* AYR, *Vat Burn* SUT, *Woo Burn* SLK ("crooked").

(c) *The* speed *and* movement *of the flowing water*
 A smallish category in Scottish hydronymy, this group comprises about 70 names extracted from O.S.M. 1 inch (Scotland). Very often terms normally applied to human moods and states of mind are used to denote the velocity of the flowing water. A rushing stream is *angry* or *quarrelsome* or *boisterous* or *wild*; references to the *fierceness, gaiety* or *madness* of a river also occur. Slow burns suggest *sadness, tranquillity, laziness* or the *stately* movement of a procession. A stagnant brook is *dead*.
 The following names may be noted as significant examples: *Abhainn Sithidh* ROS ("stately"), *Allt Bheargais* ROS ("anger"), *Allt Bhuailteach* CAI ("quarrelsome"), *Allt Chriosdain* BNF ("quick"), *Allt Sgualach* INV ("moving with a sweep"), *Allt Sniomhach* INV ("sad"), *Allt Socrach* ROS ("slow"), *Bruar Water* PER ("boiling"), *Burn of Sheeoch* KCD ("tranquil"), *Dead Water* ANG ("stagnant"), *Luther Water* KCD ("swift"), *Mad Burn* WLO, *Maldie Burn* SUT ("slow"), *Powgavie Burn* PER ("boisterous"), *River Farg* PER ("anger"), *River Kingie* INV ("striding"), *Standing Burn* LAN, *Still Burn* MLO.

(d) *The* geological nature of the bed *of the stream*
 Whereas the form of the bed and the movement of the flowing water are described by unusual and imaginative defining elements, the geological nature of the bed is denoted by ever recurring matter-of-fact terms, especially referring to the roughness of the bottom of the stream. So Gaelic *Garbh Allt* with its variants occurs at least 50 times; Calder-names are widespread and at an earlier period *Carron* is extremely common, almost suggesting appellative usage of that term, at one stage.

This is a short list of examples: *Allt Carnach* PER ("stony"), *Allt Creagach* INV ("rocky"), *Allt Lathach* INV ("clay"), *Allt Leacach* ARG ("stony"), *Allt Tollaidh* ROS ("full of holes"), *Burn of Turret* ANG ("dry"), *Calder Water* LAN ("hard"), *Carron Water* DMF ("hard"), *Dry Burn* AYR, *Gana Burn* LAN ("sandy"), *Garbh Allt* ARG ("rough"), *Garbh Uisge* BNF, *Garple Burn* KCB, *Grudie Burn* SUT ("gravelly"), *Keltie Burn* PER ("hard"), *Megen Burn* ABD ("boggy"), *Meggat Water* DMF, *Moo Burn* SH ("sandy"), *River Clachaig* ARG ("stony"), *River Elchaig* ROS ("rocky"), *River Greeta* LEWIS ("gravel"), *River Lonan* ARG ("boggy"), *River Pattack* INV ("full of potholes"), *River Polloch* ARG ("full of holes"), *River Sligeachan* SKYE ("shelly"), *Rough Burn* AYR, *Sandy Burn* LAN, *Sleach Water* CAI ("slimy"), *Stone Grain* PEB, *Yarrow Water* SLK ("rough").

C. Streams named after the Surroundings of the Water-Course

(*a*) *The* terrain *through which the stream flows*

It is impossible to give an adequate representation of the more than 1800 Scottish stream-names which qualify for this category. It is the largest semantic group, containing about one-quarter of all names of water-courses marked on the 92 Scottish O.S.M. 1 inch. Reference to the natural features of the terrain through which a stream flows has provided ample possibilities for the naming and re-naming of burns; the corrie, the pass, the hill, the fir-grove, the bog, the water-fall, the valley, the hollow, the point, the field, the slope, the haugh, the meadow, the rock, the marsh – they, and many other natural features of the countryside, all enter Scottish hydronymy as defining elements, as a rule in the names of smaller water-courses. Many of these descriptive names contain quite a number of words as, for instance, *Allt Cnoc Airidh an t-Seolich Bhig* SUT or *Uisge Dubh Poll a' Choin* INV, and one is entitled to ask how far these accurate *descriptions* are really *names*. Quite a number of them bear much more resemblance to the directions given by a farmer to his shepherd or by a laird to his foresters than to a short, practicable and current proper name. It may very well be the map that will finally turn these descriptions into names and will preserve them as such. Here are a few out of this host of names: *Abhainn Droma* ROS, ("ridge"), *Abhainn na Coinnich* ARG ("moss"), *Akran Burn* SUT ("field"), *Allt an Doire-giubhais* ROS ("fir-grove"), *Allt an t-Sneachda* ABD ("snow"), *Allt Bad nan Clach* SUT ("clump"), *Allt Bealach Easain* INV ("pass"), *Allt Choire Phiobaire* INV ("corrie"), *Allt Creag a' Chait* NAI ("craig"), *Allt Eas na Maoile* SUT ("water-fall"), *Allt Lón Ghlas Bheinn* INV ("morass"), *Allt na h-Innse Buidhe* ARG ("haugh"), *Allt Ruigh na Cuileige* ABD ("slope"), *Allt Uamha na Muice* ARG ("cave"), *Caochan Glac na Crìche* INV ("hollow"), *Cleuch Burn*

LAN ("ravine"), *Coillechat Burn* PER ("wood"), *Dale Water* SH, *Hamra River* SKYE ("rock"), *Howe Burn* BWK ("hollow"), *Kames River* ARG ("bay"), *Knock Burn* KCB ("hill"), *Laggan Burn* BTE ("hollow"), *Linnshaw Burn* AYR ("copse"), *Loch Strand* WIG, *Longhill Burn* MLO, *Lón Horro* SKYE ("moor"), *Mire Burn*, ROX, *Perter Burn* DMF ("copse"), *Strath Burn* CAI ("valley"), *Strone Burn* PER ("point").

(b) Tree vegetation *associated with the water-course*
    This group and the following one are not only of interest to the linguist but also the botanist, for if the modern names of this type reflect the distribution of trees and plants as we find it in our own time, older names can contribute towards the knowledge of the distribution of these in earlier periods. At least 16 different tree-names enter into Scottish hydronymy; the birch, the fir, the rowan, the alder, the willow, and the hazel are especially well represented in younger names, whereas the elm only comes into names of the *p*-Celtic period. Remarkable absentees are the beech and the ash. Apparently, conspicuous single trees, as well as clusters of trees or little groves and larger forests, can contribute towards the making of a name for the stream that flows past them. O.S.M. 1 inch has 169 names of this type altogether; in the following list we shall give one or two examples under each tree-name:
    Alder: *Alltan Feàrna* SUT, *Alder Burn* LAN.
    Birch: *Allt Beithe* ROS, *Birken Burn* STL.
    Bird-cherry: *River Fiag* SUT.
    Blackthorn: *Allt Dregnie* BNF.
    Elder: *River Tromie* INV.
    Elm: *River Leven* INV/ARG, *Glen Almagro* LEWIS.
    Fir: *Allt Giubhais* ROS.
    Hawthorn: *River Skiack* ROS.
    Hazel: *Cowie Water* KCD, *Hazel Burn* ANG.
    Holly: *Allt a' Chuilinn* SUT.
    Juniper: *Allt Staoine* CAI.
    Oak: *Derry Burn* ABD, *Oak Burn* SLK.
    Rowan: *Allt a' Chaoruinn* ROS, *Rowantree Grains* LAN.
    Sloe: *Allt a' Droighinn* ROS.
    Willow: *Allt nan Seileach* BNF, *Willow Burn* DMF.
    Yew: *River Ure* ARG, *Glen Ioagro* LEWIS.
    Not all names mentioned in this list are necessarily derived from trees growing, singly or in clusters, near or on the banks of the water-course they denote. In a number of cases the streams can be rather thought of as being

identified with these trees, just as in group B.*b.* above we find river-names identified with names of tools, instruments and containers. The link between tree-name and river-name may be the shape of the water-course or some other quality that seemed to be common to both the tree and the river in question. But it is quite possible that this identification was due to some other imaginative process in the mind of the name-giver(s) which we are now unable to follow. Of course, the possibility of imitation must be taken into consideration; one river-name derived from a tree-name created another, and so forth.

In the above list, *River Fiag* SUT (= Gael. *fiodhag* "bird-cherry"), *River Tromie* INV (= *tromm-de* "of elders"), *River Skiack* ROS (= Gael. *sgitheach* "hawthorn", or < *Allt na sgitheach*), *Cowie Water* KCD (= O.Ir. *collde* "colurnus") and *Derry Burn* ABD (= O.Ir. *dairde* "oaken") seem to belong to this category, although the meaning "abounding in elders, hazel, oaks" is not ruled out for the names in *-ie, -y.* For this type of name in Russian and Polish hydronymy refer to Paul Trost, *Der blosse Baumname als Gewässerbezeichnung,* Zeitschrift für Namenforschung XIV (1938), p. 170. Nearer home Wales provides quite a number of examples, cf. *Castan* (Glamorgansh.), *Cerd(d)in* (several), *Coll* (Cardigansh.), *Helygen* (Cardigansh.), etc.

(c) Plants, other than trees, *associated with the water-course*

Various other plants, besides trees, enter into Scottish river-names. Most of them are referred to just once, and there are hardly any doublets, except for names indicating an abundant growth of fern or berries in the neighbourhood of the stream. This section is small and contains only 63 names, perhaps because plants are not conspicuous enough to be the most impressive factor in the natural surroundings of a water-course. Examples of this group are *Allt a'Chreimh* SUT ("wild garlic"), *Allt Dogha* INV ("burdock"), *Allt Luachair* INV ("rushes"), *Allt na Cuilce* INV ("reed"), *Allt nan Eithreag* SUT ("mountain-strawberry"), *Allt Raineach* ARG ("fern"), *Berry Grain* DMF, *Blaeberry Burn* LAN, *Féith Shiol* INV ("oats, corn"), *Feuchaw Burn* DMF ("heather"), *Hay Sike* SLK, *Lusragan Burn* ARG ("herb"), *Nettly Burn* FIF, *River Cannich* ROS-INV ("bog-myrtle"), *River Nant* ARG ("nettle"), *Starragro* LEWIS ("rough grass").

(d) Animals, birds, fishes, *etc, associated with the stream*

A great variety of names of animals, birds, and fishes must have seemed to be apt characterising elements to those responsible for the creation of Scottish hydronymy. Foxes that had their dens near the stream, horses that came to drink out of it, heifers that grazed in the neighbourhood, birds that built their nests somewhere on its banks, trout and salmon that filled its pools – they all attracted the attention of the name-givers, and apparently most of our stream-names which contain names of animals, etc. refer to the living fauna near the water-course.

But there seems to be another kind of relationship between animal or bird or fish on the one hand, and the stream on the other. Rivers were called after animals whose special characteristics seemed to express the peculiar qualities of the water-course, and so were more or less identified with these animals. This is suggested by names like *River Bran* ROS ("raven"), *River Tarff* INV ("bull"), *River Einig* ROS ("little bird"), *River Enrick* INV ("snipe"), etc., where we need not suppose any genitival relationship as in the usual name pattern *Allt nan Each* ("Burn of the horses") or *Caochan na Feòraige* ("Streamlet of the squirrel"). A similar identification can be assumed for names which are derived by suffixing *-aidh* (*-ie*, *-y*) to the name of the animal, for instance: *Burn of Buckie* BNF ("buck"), *Kirkney Water* ABD ("hen"), *Brocky Burn* KCD ("badger"), *Markie Burn* INV ("horse"), *Tarvie Burn* PER ("bull"). There are also diminutives like *Abhainn Chonaig* ROS ("little wolf"), *River Eachaig* ARG ("little horse"), *Allt Laoghainn* PER ("little calf").

Again, many names of this latter kind are to be found in Welsh river-nomenclature (Thomas 1938, p. 52; *Bulletin of the Board of Celtic Studies* 1935, p. 128). There not only the names of almost all domestic animals, but also those of wild beasts, birds and insects, have been employed in the naming of water-courses. An instructive example is *banw* "young pig". This term (*Archiv für Celtische Lexicographie* 1907, p. 43) is applied to water-courses "forming deep channels or holes in which they sink into the earth and are lost for a distance". It is only a short step to calling a tributary of this stream *twrch* "boar". As in the case of river-names, identical with names of trees, we have to consider the influence of analogy, but a river like *Bran* ROS may have received its name because of its dark colour and *Tarff* INV may be due to the wild speed of its flow (Trost 1936, 1938; Schröder 1937, Pokorny 1954, Krahe 1951-52).

But it is the former category that interests us here. For it, the following names may serve as illustrations: *Allt a'Ghamhna* SUT ("stirk"), *Allt a'Ghobhair* SUT ("goat"), *Allt an Daimh* ROS ("ox, stag"), *Allt an t-Seangain* PER ("ant"), *Allt na Feadaige* INV ("plover"), *Allt na Muic* SUT ("pig"), *Allt na Seabhaig* ARG ("hawk"), *Allt Nathrach* INV ("snake"), *Bo Burn* KCD ("cow"), *Caplaich Burn* CAI ("horse"), *Cock Burn* ABD, *Conglass Water* BNF ("wolf"), *Crow Burn* SLK, *Ishag Burn* PER ("lark"), *Lamb Burn* ELO, *Lón nan Earb* SKYE ("roe"), *River Laxay* LEWIS ("salmon"), *Stag Burn* KCD.

(*e*) *The* situation *of the water-course*

This is, with more than 300 names, an astonishingly large group. The names it contains not only express the absolute position of the water-course but also the position in relation to other streams or to other geographical features. In this latter sense, the names of the four chief points of the compass are frequently used; other favourite terms are words meaning "back", "fore" or "across, transverse". Very often water-courses form the boundary of some piece of land, be it a field or an estate or a county, and in many instances this stream is just called the *boundary river*.[4] There are plenty of examples of this, in this category. Most of the names occur over and over again; so a few examples may suffice: *Allt Deas* ABD ("south"), *Allt na Criche* INV ("boundary"), *Allt Shios Bhreacachaidh* ARG ("below"), *Allt Tarsuinn* ROS ("cross"), *Back Burn* MOR, *Burn betwixt the Laws* BWK, *Cross Burn* BWK, *Easter Burn* ANG, *Fore Burn* BNF, *March Burn* INV, *Meur Tuath* NAI ("north"), *Mid Grain* DMF, *North Burn* SUT, *Powmeadow Burn* LAN ("middle"), *Thorter Burn* PER ("transverse"), *Twart Burn* SH, *West Water* ANG.

Besides colour-adjectives and words denoting the size of the stream, terms referring to the relative situation of the water-course are used to distinguish between two burns bearing the same name and flowing parallel to each other or joining each other. For *parallel* streams we may list: *Auchlyne East* and *West Burn* PER, *East* and *West Burn* AYR, *Easter* and *Wester Burn* ROX, *Eastplace* and *Westplace Burn* PER, *High* and *Low Mill Burn* KCB, *North* and *South Black Burn* AYR, *North* and *South Burn* AYR, *North* and *South Burn of Grimista* SH.

Examples of *joining* water-courses are: *Allt Shios* and *Shuas Chulaibh* PER, *Back* and *Fore Burn* BNF, *East* and *West Burn of Builg* KCD, *East* and *West Burn of Glenmoye* ANG, *East* and *West Grain* ANG, *Easter* and *Wester Burn* BWK, *Easter* and *Wester Glen Quoich Burn* INV, *Eastrig* and *Westrig Burn* PER, *North* and *South Garvan River* ARG, *River North Esk* and *River South Esk* MLO, *Warroch East* and *West Burn* KNR.

D. Water-courses named after Human Institutions and Human Beings
(a) Water-courses associated with human institutions
This category is represented by 366 names; it does not include stream-names derived from place-names proper, which will be listed separately under E.*a*. We cannot even attempt to give a representative cross section of this name group because the range of defining elements referring to human life and institutions on the banks of the respective water-courses is far too wide. It comprises mill and fort, creel and deer-trap, bridge and booth, church and mill-dam, hospital and sheep-pen, gallows and kiln, mine and penny-land, orchard and byre and many another imprint of human culture and civilisation upon the neighbourhood of our Scottish streams. We select at random, and mention *Abbey Burn* KCB, *Abhainn Rath* INV ("fort"), *Allt a' Mhuilinn* JURA ("mill"), *Allt na Craidhleig*

INV ("creel"), *Allt na h-Eaglaise* SUT ("church"), *Allt nah-Eilrig* INV ("deer-trap"), *Allt na Làrach* INV ("ruin"), *Allt nan Ramh* SUT ("oars"), *Bught Sike* ROX ("sheep-fold"), *Castle Burn* STL, *Kiln Burn* DMF, *Kirk Burn* DMF, *Lead Mine Burn* AYR, *Mill Burn* LAN, *Puball Burn* ARG ("tent"), *Pulharrow Burn* KCB ("wall"), *River Borgie* SUT ("fort"), *River Brora* ROS ("bridge"), *River Ericht* PER ("assembly"), *River Housay* HARRIS ("house"), *Smithy Burn* ANG, *Spittal Burn* PEB, *Tower Burn* DMF, *Whitehouse Burn* ARG.

(b) Water-courses connected with human beings

Not only have human activities and institutions been recorded in Scottish river nomenclature, but also names of gods[5] and saints, personal names, or names referring to personal callings or titles, are frequently to be found. This group comprise almost 200 names, *all* of the modern compound type.

Personal names, names of saints, gods and goddesses: *Abhainn Catriona* HARRIS, *Allt Eoghainn* MOR, *Allt Màiri* INV, *Allt Mhàrtuin* ROS, *Allt Rostan* DNB (saint's name), *Allt Uilleim* INV, *Bennet's Burn* ELO, *Caochan Roibidh* INV, *Duncan Gray's Burn* ABD, *Murray's Burn* KCB, *Patrick Burn* AYR (saint's name), *River Tora* SKYE (god's name).

Human occupations, titles, etc.: *Allt a' Bhodaich* INV ("old man"), *Allt an Airich* ARG ("shepherd"), *Allt na Caillich* SUT ("old woman"), *Altgillie Burn* ANG ("lad"), *Caochan Greusaiche* PER ("shoemaker"), *Fiddler Burn* LAN, *King's Beck* LAN, *Laird's Burn* ABD, *Lón a' Chleirich* SKYE ("clergyman"), *Pollgowan Burn* AYR ("smith"), *Priest's Water* ABD, *Salter Grain* DMF ("salt-dealer"), *Scots Burn* LAN, *Thief Sike* ROX.

E. Water-courses containing the Name of Named Objects

(a) Water-courses named from the names of human settlements

In this category of "names from names", there are more than 1000 place-names proper used as defining elements, the second largest sub-section in Scottish hydronymy. In these cases, as well as in the following groups, we would describe the river-name as being *secondary*, i.e. based on the name of some other geographical feature or on a primary river-name. Of course, we cannot expect any discrimination as to the origin, age or linguistic make-up of the place-names which occur as hydronymic elements, and so we find names of all strata of languages in this group. It will suffice to mention a few of them, as they all follow an ever recurring morphological pattern. *Allt Baile nan Carn* INV (Gael. Pl. N.), *Allt Gharbh Ghaig* INV (<pass-name), *Balnakailly Burn* BTE (<Gael. farm-name), *Burn of Auchentumb* ABD (<Gael. field-name), *Forrestburn Water* LAN-WLO (<Engl. river-name), *Golspie Burn* SUT (<ON.

Pl. N.), *Gruinard River* ROS (<ON. bay-name), *Inveruglas Water* DNB (Pl. N., containing Celt. river-name), *Keith Water* MLO-ELO (<*p*-Celt. wood-name), *Kilfinnan Burn* INV (<Gael. church-name), *Lealt River* SKYE (Pl. N. <Gael. river-name), *Monynut Water* ELO (<Celt. hill-name), *Nethertown Burn* MLO (Engl. Pl. N.), *Pitcarmick Burn* PER (Pict. farm-name), *River Alness* ROS (Pl. N., containing pre-Celtic river-name), *Wauchope Burn* ROX (<valley-name).

(*b*) *Water-courses named from the* names of hills

In section C.*a.* we came across river-names referring to hills, rocks and knolls past which the stream flows. But the defining elements used in those cases were purely appellative and descriptive, or at least appeared to be so from map evidence. The names of this present group, on the other hand, contain the proper name of the hill or height after which they are called, and so, in our terminology, would have to be classified as "secondary" stream-names. The generic terms used in this category are almost exclusively *burn* and *allt*; we find *burn* qualified by Gaelic hill-names but have no example of *allt* alongside a hill-name of Anglo-Saxon derivation. Here is a short list of examples:[6] *Allt a' Chnoic* DNB (1614), *Allt a' Mhàim* SKYE (1335), *Allt an Tuirc* INV (2422), *Allt Bhuidheannach* PER (3064), *Allt Càrn na Fiacail* INV (1913), *Allt Creag an Lèth-choin* INV (3448), *Allt na Glas Bheinne* INV (2127), *Benbrack Burn* KCB (1900), *Ben Glas Burn* PER/DNB (2037), *Carewoodrig Burn* DMF (1117), *Cruach Neuran Burn* ARG (1988), *Cuff Burn* LAN (1111), *Kingsseat Burn* ROX (1747), *Risingclaw Burn* LAN (1591), *Shalloch Burn* AYR (1777), *Toardy Burn* ANG (1935), *Tushielaw Burn* SLK (1431), *River Horneval* SKYE (218).

(*c*) *Water-courses named from the* names of valleys

Naturally, a river and the valley through which it flows are very closely associated in the minds of the people living near them, and so it is not surprising that large numbers of streams are named after the glen, dale or dean that houses them. The O.S.M. 1 inch (Scotland) has at least 469 of them, not counting valley-names now only used as names of human settlements. These are some of them: *Allt Gleann Gniomhaidh* INV, *Allt Scamodale* ARG, *Burn of Glendui* ABD, *Finland Burn* DNB, *Glendow Sike* DMF, *Glensherup Burn* PER, *Greenhope Burn* BWK, *Lón a' Ghlinne Bhig* SKYE, *Ravendean Burn* PEB, *Rimsdale Burn* SUT, *River Erradale* ROS, *Strathmore Water* CAI.

(*d*) *Water-courses named from the* names of lakes

The "normal" practice in Scottish hydronymy, especially as far as the larger water-courses are concerned, seems to have been to derive the lake-name from the name of the river which flows out of, through or into the loch. We need only think of *Loch Tay, Loch Earn, Loch Awe, Loch Shin, Loch Carron, Loch Ness* to realise this pattern. But there are almost a hundred, usually smaller, streams mentioned on the Scottish O.S.M. 1 inch that show the opposite semantic development: they are named after the loch out of which they issue.[7] Here belong amongst others: *Abhainn an Loch Bhig* SUT (→Loch Beag), *Abhainn Caslavat* LEWIS, *Allt an Lochain Duibh* INV, *Allt Loch a'Ghael* ARG, *Burn of Pettawater* SH, *Gossawater Burn* SH, *Lochbroom Burn* PER, *Loch Gower Burn* WIG, *Loch of the Lowes Strand* KCB, *Lón Loch Mhóir* SKYE.

(*e*) *Water-courses connected with* primary river-names

Pleonastic usage of generic terms denoting "water, river" seems to have been common in all periods of Scottish hydronymy. It is normally an expression of a change from one language to another, probably starting with an explanatory quality in a time of bilingual transition, but becoming petrified and losing its interpretative character when the older language dies out and is no longer understood. The oldest instance in Scottish hydronymy is apparently *Allander Water* DNB, where Celt. *dubron* was added to a pre-Celtic *Alaunā*. Celt. *dubron*, in its Gaelic and Brythonic variants, is, on the other hand, furnished with a pleonastic *burn* or *allt*, as in *Gelder Burn* ABD, *Allt Calder* INV, *Deer Burn* DMF. Three linguistic strata are represented not only in *Allander Water* but also in *Feardar Burn* ABD: Brit. **dubro-* or Early Gael. *dobur*, Gael. *féith* and Engl. *burn*. To names in *-glais* usually an explanatory water is added as in *Finglas Water* PER and *Douglas Water* DNB, whereas river-names containing *poll*, *pwll* are, as a rule, followed by an additional *burn*, cf. *Polmood Burn* PEB, *Dipple Burn* LAN, *Pillmour Burn* ELO. ON. *ā* enters into quite a number of hydronymic compounds, but always – with the possible exception of *The Lussa* ARG (but cf. also *Lussa River* JURA) – demands a more "modern" pleonastic term; as we see it in *Allt Torray* LEWIS, *Laxo Burn* SH, *Iorsa Water* ARRAN. A few river-names with other pleonastic hydronymic elements suggest that the south-western counties at one time knew *allt* as a river-name element, but it cannot have been very prolific. There are *Garwald Water* and *Garrell Water* in DMF and *Garvald Burn* on the LAN-PEB border, all of which probably stand for Gael. *garbh allt* "rough burn"; *Altigabert Burn* in AYR, *Burn of Altibrair* and *Allivolie Burn* in WIG and possibly *Old Water* in KCB. The maps show 24 names of water-courses altogether in which the primary *allt*-name has been supplemented by a Germanic hydronymic term.

Difficult, in this connection, is the interpretation of the usage of Engl. *river* (and in many cases also *water*). It does occur as a genuine generic element, but where it is attached to a "primary" river-name it is doubtful if it is an integral part of the resulting secondary name, at all. Is it just map-usage or is it an early stage of pleonastic interpretation and addition? We suspect the former although the latter is just possible.

F. "Water-Words"

By this term we mean names which simply mean "river" or "stream" or "flowing water", without any reference to any particular characteristics of the water-course itself or the countryside through which it flows. Names of this kind are to be found in most strata of Scottish hydronymy although they are not very common in modern river-nomenclature. They are well represented amongst the names that have come to us from early linguistic periods, and all names to be ascribed to the pre-Celtic stratum are, without exception, to be classed here. There are 95 of them altogether, 75 of which belong either to the *p*-Celtic or the pre-Celtic layer, and so it is not surprising that we find here most of the names of the larger Scottish water-courses. Examples are: *Allan* (Water) PER-STL, *Armet* (Water) MLO, *Avon* (Water) LAN, (River) *Awe* ARG, (River) *Ayr* AYR, (River) *Clyde* LAN, (River) *Doon* AYR, (River) *Eden* KNR/FIF, (River) *Esk* DMF, *Leithen* (Water) PEB, *Lyne* (Burn) FIF, (River) *Lyon* PER, (River) *Naver* SUT, *Pow* (Water) PER, *Rye* (Water) AYR, (River) *Sheil* ROS, (River) *Tay* PER, (River) *Tyne* ELO.

Statistical Summary and Conclusion

In this study examples of the various semantic groups have been chosen from all temporal and morphological strata of Scottish hydronymy. It remains now to find out how the semantic categories are distributed over these strata, whether certain morphological types of names are connected with certain semantic aspects and whether certain periods preferred reference to certain characteristics of the water, the water-course, the surroundings, etc.

The table overleaf shows the semantic structure of all Scottish river-names to be found on O.S.M. 1 inch. Its figures are by no means final and may be subject to slight alterations, but the over-all picture is undoubtedly correct.

Morphological Group	Linguistic Stratum	Element	A: a. colour	A: d. noise	B: a. size	B: b form	B: c. speed	B: d. bed	C: a. terrain	C: b. trees	C: c. plants	C: d. animals, etc.	C: e. situation	D: a. human institutions	D: b. persons	E: a. place-names	E: b. hill-names	E: c. valley-names	E: d. lake-names	E: e. river-names	F: water words	Miscellaneous	Obscure
Compounds	Anglo-Scottish	burn	79	10	17	30	15	25	426	24	12	36	111	155	59	634	129	247	14	212	2	21	131
		burn of	1	...	1	1	...	...	54	1	2	3	2	3	...	97	17	14	7	30	...	...	16
		water	16	2	1	1	1	5	38	...	2	7	9	10	2	59	1	25	...	104	...	1	34
		water of	...	1	...	...	...	...	1	1	...	3	...	...	...	4	...	2	...	26	...	...	8
		river	2	...	1	2	...	...	36	2	3	5	4	7	2	110	6	57	2	173	...	5	15
	Old Norse	á	7	...	...	1	1	5	8	...	...	8	...	5	4	...	...	...	...	...	...	1	...
	Gaelic	allt	101	11	62	88	22	90	1075	87	27	131	70	139	75	61	51	71	61	43	1	40	55
		abhainn	17	1	12	5	4	3	84	2	1	6	5	11	4	18	4	41	9	13	1	2	6
		uisge	11	...	...	...	...	3	3	...	...	...	1	...	...	...	...	1	...	1	...	2	2
	Early Celtic	glais	7	...	...	...	...	...	...	...	...	4	...	...	...	...	...	...	...	...	...	3	...
		pow, poll	7	1	1	5	1	6	14	7	4	22	4	10	9	1	...	...	...	...	...	11	10
		dubro-	4	...	1	1	...	20	...	...	2	...	...	...	...	...	...	...	...	1	...	6	...
Suffixes and Simple Stems	Gaelic	-ach	15	3	1	12	7	41	6	8	6	6	3	...	...	...	...	...	...	...	3	8	5
		-ag	5	6	2	5	3	9	...	...	...	7	...	...	...	...	...	...	...	1	2	6	2
		-an	6	1	...	3	4	9	3	5	3	4	...	...	...	...	...	...	...	2	3	1	...
		-agan	2	...	...	...	...	1	...	1	1	2	...	...	1	...	...	...	...	...	1	...	...
	Early Celtic	-aidh	23	5	...	17	9	26	7	5	4	26	3	...	...	...	...	...	...	1	7	...	...
		p-Celtic	27	14	...	...	5	22	1	3	...	...	1	...	...	...	...	...	...	...	32	12	8
	pre-Celtic		...	...	...	...	...	...	...	...	...	...	...	...	...	...	...	...	...	...	43	...	3

In examining the most modern names first, we leave aside all smaller groups like names in *sike*, *lane* or *grain*, as well as those in *féith, lón, dìg*, etc., and concentrate on the two most prolific river-name elements: Engl. *burn* and Gael. *allt*. Names containing these generic terms refer, in the majority of cases, to the surroundings of the water-course, be it natural or man-made. But the difference between the percentage figures is significant. Whereas 64.9 per cent of all *allt*-names refer to the *natural* surroundings of the water-course and only 11.3 per cent to the *human imprint* on them, the respective figures for the *burn*-names drop to 42.1 per cent referring to the *natural* surroundings and rise to 35 per cent for names incorporating names of *human* settlements, institutions, occupations and personal names. The difference is especially striking as far as the derivation of river-names from place-names is concerned; names of that category amount to a mere 2.5 per cent in *allt*-names but include more than a quarter (26.2 per cent) of all *burn*-names, *expressing the high degree of influence human civilisation and culture has had on the naming of our younger and smaller Anglo-Scottish stream-names*. Not even half of all names containing *burn* as a generic term are primary river-names, for 53.4 per cent are "names from names" (place-names, hill-names, valley-names, lake-names, personal names, primary river-names), including 8.7 per cent in which *burn* is used pleonastically. The respective figures for Scottish *allt*-names are 14.9 per cent and 1.7 per cent. Only 15.4 per cent of all *allt*-names and 7.3 per cent of all *burn*-names refer to characteristics of the water and the water-course themselves.

The share of secondary names is even greater in the special type "*burn of-*". Here 63.2 per cent are "names from names", including 37.2 per cent place-names and 11.5 per cent primary river-names. Whereas 76.6 per cent of all names of this group point to the surroundings, natural or artificial, of the stream, only 1.1 per cent (3 names) refer to characteristics of the water and the water-course. With the pattern "*burn of-*" we may link the type "*water of-*"; "names from names" are represented by an almost identical percentage, i.e. 62.7 per cent, but the distribution is very different, for this figure is made up of 51 per cent primary stream-names, 7.8 per cent place-names and 2.9 per cent other names, stressing the strong accent on pleonastic usage which this type has in modern Scottish hydronymy. 13.7 per cent of all names speak of the natural surroundings of the river and 1.9 per cent (1 name!) of the water itself. *Water* in the more "normal" morphological pattern, i.e. *following* the defining element, again is qualified by terms pointing to the surroundings of the water-course or by primary geographical names: 25.3 per cent refer to the natural surroundings of the stream, 21.9 per cent to traces of human civilisation in the neighbourhood, 32.1 per cent show pleonastic usage; the share of "names from names" is just over

50 per cent. We arrive at similar figures for the usage of Engl. *river* in Scottish hydronymy: natural surroundings 26.4 per cent, human influence 27.3 per cent, pleonastic usage 39.7 per cent; but the category of "names from names" goes up to 78.9 per cent, a confirmation of the view expressed earlier that *river* has no real creative value, in the "primary" sense, in Scottish river-nomenclature.

The Gaelic generic elements corresponding to Engl. *water* and *river* – *uisge* and *abhainn* – preserve more of the primary hydronymic character than their English equivalents. Exactly half of all *uisge*-names refer to the water or the water-course and another 18.4 per cent to the natural surroundings; only 2 names (6.8 per cent) are "names from names", one of them with pleonastic *uisge*. *Abhainn* approaches more closely to the usage of Engl. *river* than *uisge* to that of Engl. *water*, but *the highest percentage – 60.1 – goes to streams named after the natural surroundings of the water-course and only 13 per cent to those referring to human settlements, institutions and personal names*. Characteristics of the water or water-course are denoted by 17 per cent of the defining elements used. The share of "names from names" is 35.2 per cent. So the main usage of *abhainn* corresponds to that of Gael. *allt:* neighbouring geographical features supply the defining term. In this respect, *abhainn* and *allt* are joined by Gael. *poll*, W. *pwll*, Scot. *pow*, for 45.3 per cent of the names of that class refer to the surrounding countryside and only 11.1 per cent to human civilisation.

It is interesting to compare, at this point, the semantic aspects of the defining elements qualifying ON. *á* in Scottish hydronymy, for we find that *á* does not go together with the other Germanic terms mentioned – *burn*, *water*, *river* – but can be classed with their Gaelic equivalents in so far as the natural surroundings of the water-course are referred to in 40 per cent of all cases, whereas only about half that number has any connection with human life in the neighbourhood. But in one respect the usage of *á* points away even from *allt*, *abhainn* and *uisge:* 35 per cent of all *á*-names indicate special qualities of the stream itself.

Here *á* (itself belonging to a fairly early Germanic stratum) links up with those two Celtic terms which must be thought of as part of an older layer of Scottish hydronymy than the one *allt*, *abhainn* and *uisge* belong to: *glais* and *dobhar* (*dw(f)r*). Not a single one of the names which contain them as generic terms implies a reference to human activity in the neighbourhood of the stream referred to, though the natural surroundings are mentioned in 28.6 per cent of all *glais*- and in 5.9 per cent of all *dobhar*-names. The decisive difference, however, is expressed by the fact that 50 per cent of the names containing *glais* and 76.5 per cent of those containing *dobhar* (or *dwr*) speak of special characteristics of the water or the water-course. This semantic evidence underlines and confirms the view, based on morphological grounds, that names containing Celt. *dubron* belong to the earliest stratum of hydronymic compounds in Scotland, for it closely corresponds to the distribution of semantic aspects in names formed by adding a suffix to a word or word-stem, a group that, on the whole, undoubtedly belongs to an earlier period than compound names.

If we first look at the names ending in *Gaelic* suffixes, we find that the basis of 80.9 per cent of all these names is a word or stem referring to the water or water-course, whereas only 17 per cent point to the natural surroundings of the stream (including names in *-ach*, derived from names of animals, etc.). Names of human settlements, human activities and institutions and personal names are not incorporated, four names are examples of pleonastic usage (1.1 per cent) and the rest come under the headings "miscellaneous" and "unexplained". For *p-Celtic* names almost the same remarks apply, for, as to their name-bases, 80 per cent mean special characteristics of the flowing water or its course, in contrast to 3.2 per cent (4 names) that point to the countryside near it and 16.8 per cent miscellaneous and unexplained names. Again human civilisation does not come into the nomenclature of this morphological stratum, at all. If we step even further back to examine the Scottish river-names which we believe to have come down to us from a *pre-Celtic* period, we find that even references to the natural surroundings are not implied by the stems used, but that all explainable names (93.5 per cent) refer to the water or water-course, most of them simply meaning "water" or "river" or "something flowing", probably with various and sensitive shades of meaning which we can no longer detect.

A comparison with figures given by Hans Krahe (1949) for the semantic structure of the river-names in the catchment area of the River Main in Germany may be very instructive at this point. There the youngest, German, layer – compound names containing the element *-bach* – consists of 41 per cent of names referring to human beings and human civilisation, 46 per cent pointing to the natural surroundings and 13 per cent to the water itself and its characteristics. This corresponds roughly to our *burn*-names, where the equivalent figures are 35, 42 and 7 per cent. In the Main area the main basic element in the older, Germanic, stratum of compound names is *-aha*, cognate with OE. *ēa* and ON. *á*. Names belonging to this group show a different distribution of the semantic categories: only 6 per cent are derived from human activities and institutions, 54 per cent are connected with the natural surroundings and 40 per cent describe characteristics of the flowing water itself. With these formations in *-aha* we may compare our Gaelic river-names containing *allt* or *abhainn* as generic elements, but it must be noted here that *allt-* and *abhainn*-names show a more "modern" trend in so far as they include a higher percentage of names derived from the human imprint on the surrounding countryside and, at the same time, do not refer as often to the water or the water-course themselves. No name-group comparable with our category ending in Gaelic suffixes is mentioned in Krahe's short survey, based on a dissertation by M. Belschner (1943); but our *p*-Celtic simple stems have an equivalent in Early Germanic names of the same morphological structure, and what Krahe says about the latter is just as applicable to the former (Krahe 1949, p. 24):

> And here man is not mentioned anymore, here everything is only nature, or – more precisely – only the water itself. At this early stage the mere description as "river" is predominant, and only here and there a special quality of its course or its character is referred to more explicitly.

As the oldest accessible hydronymic stratum seems to have been the same in the part of Britain examined by us and in the catchment basin surveyed by Krahe – a pre-dialectal Indo-European group of simple stems – it is not surprising that they are identical semantically in both areas, i.e. they consist exclusively of a great variety of "water-words" describing only the water itself.

If we interpret the above lists and the subsequent summary and examine the development and changes in the semantic aspects expressed in the various strata of Scottish river-nomenclature, we find that the oldest names just refer to the water itself and its flowing. It suffices at this early stage to call the river "the flowing one"; and even the colour and noise of the flowing water do not play any part yet, but only become significant attributes, together with the nature of the bed in which the stream flows, in the slightly later Early Celtic hydronymy. In the next layer the importance of that aspect is still obvious but references to the natural surroundings occur, first of all to the flora and fauna on the banks of the water-courses, then also to hills, woods and glens. Names including the surrounding terrain, plants, trees, animals, become more common during the following period and form, in our most "modern" river-nomenclature, the strongest semantic subsection, although greatly challenged for pride of place by the numerous names to be connected with human life near the water-course. The growing number of references to human activities in the widest sense becomes especially apparent in the group of names containing Engl. *burn* as a generic term; here man and his civilisation are, as we have seen above, referred to in at least 35 per cent of all examples found on the Scottish O.S.M. 1 inch.

In this youngest semantic stratum – in which reference is made to the natural and artificial surroundings of the water-course – the number of compound names is extremely great. It is possible to say that the inclusion of the surrounding countryside as a source for river-nomenclature is the semantic equivalent of the morphological development from simple stems and suffixed formations to compound names. The form and meaning of a name prove to be almost interdependable. A change in the morphological structure, i.e. the creation of new morphological types, seems to have made possible, or even necessary, a new semantic aspect, and, on the other hand, an altered semantic attitude has necessitated new modes of morphological expression.

As references to foreign hydronymies have shown, this semantic structure and development is not confined to Scotland or to the British Isles. It represents a change in the connection between name and meaning and in the creative process of naming in general, at least in those parts of the world in which Western European languages have formed the structural basis for the linguistic expression of thought.

County Abbreviations

ABD	Aberdeenshire	LAN	Lanarkshire
ANG	Angus	MLO	Midlothian
ARG	Argyllshire	MOR	Morayshire
AYR	Ayrshire	NAI	Nairnshire
BNF	Banffshire	ORK	Orkney
BTE	Buteshire	PEB	Peeblesshire
BWK	Berwickshire	PER	Perthshire
CAI	Caithness	RNF	Renfrewshire
CLA	Clackmannanshire	ROS	Ross-shire
DMF	Dumfriesshire	ROX	Roxburghshire
DNB	Dunbartonshire	SH	Shetland
ELO	East Lothian	SLK	Selkirkshire
FIF	Fife	STL	Stirlingshire
INV	Inverness-shire	SUT	Sutherland
KCB	Kirkcudbrightshire	WIG	Wigtownshire
KCD	Kincardineshire	WLO	West Lothian
KNR	Kinross-shire		

References

Archiv für Celtische Lexicographie, 1907. *Archiv für Celtische Lexicographie* iii, 43. Halle.

Bach, A., 1953, *Deutsche Namenkunde* ii, 278-84. Heidelberg.

Belschner, M., 1943, Das Stromgebiet des Mains. Eine flussnamenkundliche Untersuchung. Würzburg. Typescript only.

Bulletin of the Board of Celtic Studies, 1935, *Bulletin of the Board of Celtic Studies* vii, 128.

Krahe, H., 1951-52, *Beiträge zur Namenforschung* iii, 14. Baltic river names of this kind containing *nt*-suffix are here listed.

Krahe, H., 1949, *Ortsnamen als Geschichtsquelle*. Heidelberg, 21-25.

Pokorny, J., 1954, *Beiträge zur Namenforschung*, 92.

Schröder, E., 1944, *Deutsche Namenkunde*. Göttingen, 371. (2nd Ed.).

Schröder, E., 1937, Zum Thema: Tiernamen als Flussnamen. *Zeitschrift für Ortsnamenforschung* xiii, 63.

Schulze, W., 1934, *Kleine Schriften*. Göttingen. p. 120 with note 2.

Schwarz, E., 1950, *Deutsche Namenforschung II (Orts- und Flurnamen)*. Göttingen, 94.

Thomas, R.J., 1938, *Enwau Afonydd a Nentydd Cymru*. Caerdydd. Under Gwachell, 99-100. Under Cathan, 52.

Thomas, R.J., 1935, *Bulletin of the Board of Celtic Studies* vii, 128.

Trost, P., 1936, Der blosse Tiername als Gewässerbezeichnung. *Zeitschrift für Ortsnamenforschung* xii, 89. Gives this type of name in general.

Trost, P., 1938, *Zeitschrift für Namenforschung* xiv, 172, note 5.

Watson, W.J., 1926, *The History of the Celtic Place-Names of Scotland*. Edinburgh and London.

Notes

1   This does not, of course, mean that they cannot be transplanted; names of European settlements in the "New World" prove the contrary; but, in these cases, the original name usually stays behind and remains a stationary feature of the emigrants' home-land.

2   The following name-lists were first compiled for the third chapter of my thesis *Studies in Scottish Hydronymy*, submitted for the degree of B. Litt. Glasgow University in 1956.

3   O.S.M 1 inch will be used in this article as the abbreviation for Ordnance Survey map, scale 1 inch: 1 mile, 4th edition.

4   Continental river-names derived from the fact that the water-courses they denote form boundaries, are dealt with by Hans Krahe in *Beiträge zur Namenforschung* VI (1955), 1-13.

5   Difficult to assess are mythological names like the two *Dees* (< *Dēuā) in ABD and KCB and the *Don* (*Deuonā) in ABD. In these cases the river-name seems to mean simply "goddess", implying in all probability, river-worship on the part of the Celtic name-givers.

6   The numerals in brackets denote the height of the hill in feet, as given on O.S.M. 1 inch.

7   There are one or two exceptions, where the defining element is supplied by the name of the lake into which or through which the stream flows.

Volksüberlieferung: Festschrift für Kurt Ranke
Fritz Harkort et al. (eds.) (1968) 531-542

The Prodigious Jump

A contribution to the study of the relationship between folklore and place-names.

ALTHOUGH there is a school of thought amongst folklorists which would claim the collection and study of place-names as a legitimate pursuit of those interested in folklore, name studies are usually taken to be the task of the linguist. Toponymic research is consequently often conducted side by side with the investigation of dialects or regional variations of language, or figures as a kind of appendix to – less often as an integral part of – lexicographical enterprises and dictionary work. When this happens the primary qualities of names as *words* are duly recognised and usually taken care of in a satisfactory manner. However, the extralinguistic characteristics which go beyond the question of etymology and meaning tend to be ignored or at least to be obscured by this approach, and names are hardly ever treated as *names*.

Those who would insist on an onomastic rather than a purely linguistic or etymological examination of names, on the other hand, would want to consider a great many facets of a name which are of little or no use to the linguistic investigator. One of these aspects would be the folk-etymological re-interpretation of local names which have become meaningless as words because the language which coined them is no longer spoken in the area or because the elements which created them have become obsolete or phonologically disguised. More often than not these re-interpretations are told in the form of explanatory stories, and *Sagenbücher* or miscellaneous collections of local folklore are full of them. As one example I quote a book which happens to be on my desk at the moment, (Richard Kühnau's *Sagen*[1]) in which literally dozens of the 589 individual items are of the type "Wie die Ortschaften Schweinebraten, Großburg, Michelwitz und Haltauf zu ihrem Namen kamen" (No. 63), "Woher der Name des Dorfes Wilkawe" (No. 116), "Woher der Spittelberg bei Olbersdorf seinen Namen hat" (No. 252), etc., etc. One of my favourites in this genre of the explanatory legend is one which originally appeared in the *Journal of American Folklore,*[2] but was recently republished in Coffin's and Cohen's collection of *Folklore in* America.[3] This explains how a certain Iowa town was named *Elkader*. It first of all rejects the story that "Abt El Kader, after deeds of heroism in remote Africa, lent his name to this Iowa village that it might be a place of courage" on the grounds that this is "a story like all the answers grownups give when they don't understand the question", and then proceeds to relate "what really happened". The 'real' explanation is said to be that a little Indian princess who loved the hills but had been forbidden to "go up in them alone," one day in her childish enthusiasm disobeyed this injunction, and "high in the hills, *an elk ate her*". What is so intriguing about this Iowa story is the way in which it operates on two levels, first of all making use of the privilege normally only accorded to the 'academic', and foreign to folk-tradition, of demolishing an obviously 'impossible' theory, and then replacing it by the allegedly 'real' but in reality just as unscientific notion of the carnivorous elk.

Local legends of this kind are numerous and certainly worth studying as they afford a convenient entry into the 'folk-mind'. To the best of this writer's knowledge they have, however, never been investigated systematically, and even comprehensive collections within any one language area are still lacking although at least one has been started and should at least allow a fairly satisfactory, albeit limited, analysis in the not too distant future. This is where the place-name scholar can safely leave his linguistic training behind and put on his folklorist's cap, and whereas it is highly doubtful that those interested in the proper origin and meaning of a name will derive anything of benefit from an examination of stories of this type, the onomastician will probably find that it makes for a more rounded knowledge of toponymic matters. When this or similar material are handled by the folklorist, on the other hand, as a kind of ancillary to folk-narrative research, the warning is in order that it takes a fair amount of linguistic training coupled with local historical and topographical knowledge to determine what is the scientific and what the folk interpretation, or whether the two are identical. Otherwise he too will move in a world full of carnivorous elks.

This, then, is one – quite well known – area which serves as a common hunting ground for the linguist, the onomastician and the folklorist. What is important here is the sequence of events: the name existed first as a meaningful entity, then, for some reason or other, became meaningless as far as its word content was concerned, and subsequently was given a new meaning, or several new meanings, in the explanatory legend. Folklore comes to the rescue when linguistic ability has failed. There is, however, another process in which folklore reveals a special relationship to place-names. In a way, it may be regarded as the opposite to the folk-etymological explanation of a given name because, in this second situation, folklore *creates* the name; the meaning of the name is therefore to be found in folklore, particularly folk-belief, and a purely linguistic interpretation will for this reason be superficial and insufficient. Because of their preoccupation with linguistic derivation, place-name students appear to have paid very little attention to this type of name in the past although folklorists are aware of its existence.[4] They have, however, sometimes tended to confuse the two processes described. Regarding as secondary and explanatory a story which is, in fact, the very basis of the name, and therefore prior to it. Names like *Devil's Elbow*, *Devil's Beeftub*, *Devil's Dyke* (all in Scotland) would belong here, or *Saothair an Daoi* 'the devil's work' (in the Scottish island of Colonsay). Not always does one find stories attached to these particular geographical features. In the case of the first three it is simply their shape and especially their size which links them with the supernatural (I have not seen the fourth), and it is at least questionable whether anybody ever believed any association with the devil; in numerous other names that belief is of course very real.

In the name-type central to our discussion, however, the legend is a definite prerequisite, even if it is not always possible for us to recover it, so that nothing but the name remains. The legend may also exist, and does exist, in certain localities without ever producing a place-name; this also applies when the spot to which it has become attached is well enough known. Thirdly, the legend may be in living tradition without any particular localisation, which again proves that it does not simply thrive on existing names but precedes the creation of a derivative name. The legend is the source of the name, not the name the source of the legend. There are several legends which would be relevant here but the one chosen for discussion is one which in Stith Thompson's *Motif Index*[5] has received the classificatory label F 1071 "Prodigious Jump", although motifs like A 972.5.2. "Chasms between rocks mark leaps of giants, heroes, etc.", F 684 "Marvellous Jumper", F 989.1.1 "Horse's tremendous leap", F 1071.2.1 "Man clears river of enormous width in one leap", H 1149.10 "Task: jumping across river in one bound", and H 1562.4 "Test of strength: prodigious jump", would also appear to belong here. At least one form of it has entered AT 530 "Princess on the Glass Mountain", and its existence in traditional folk-narrative, as an element of a more complex tale or more usually alone, is therefore presumably indisputable. The present writer first became aware of this legend as a name-forming factor in Scotland when confronted with the Perthshire name *The*

_____

Soldier's Leap which is attached to two rocks on opposite sides of the river Garry in the Pass of Killiecrankie. The events behind this name are described as follows in a book on the local history of the area:[6]

> "A lowland sentry, who had been stationed at the head of the Pass of Killiecrankie, first knew the result of the battle [of Killiecrankie on July 27th, 1689] by seeing a party of Highlanders rushing down upon him. He ran before them and when they were overtaking him, and had actually wounded him in the shoulder, he leapt across the River Garry where the gorge is narrowest and so escaped, for they dared not leap after him. The place is called the "Soldier's Leap," and every visitor to the pass has a look at it. The soldier lived many years afterwards and was employed by General Wade who began to make roads in the Highlands thirty-five years later. The soldier often told his story and showed the wound he received in the moment of the leap."

Apparently initially told as a *memorate*, to use von Sydow's terminology, the story has actually become part of Perthshire local history, and practically of Scottish history in general, because it crystallises and personalises the battle in question which was fought between the troops of the exiled King James II (and VII) under Claverhouse and the forces of William and Mary under General Mackay. There is no doubt about the date and the place; the soldier, although we do not know his name[6a], is shown as a live human being who later worked for General Wade, had his wounds to show for his exploits and, thanks to his prowess at the right moment, lived for many years after the battle. There is not the slightest doubt about the authenticity of the account, and the visitors mentioned stand at the place in question, viewing it from a vantage point, discussing amongst each other whether they would be able to perform the same feat, and usually agreeing that this would be a remarkable but probably impossible thing to accomplish, unless under the same or similar pressure as the soldier in 1689 when a successful jump meant life, failure certain death.

The historicity of the events as told becomes somewhat doubtful when one discovers that

> "Midway down this stretch of the River Findhorn to Sluie is *Randolph's Leap* where in olden days the chasm about eight feet wide, was crossed by a chained plank bridge ... Some time before the final stages of the battle of the 'Lost Standard' were fought here. Cut off and surrounded on all sides, Alastair Cumyn of Dunphail and four companions leapt over and fought their way to safety. Randolph's forces were in pursuit and no doubt crossed as well" (*Scots Magazine*, Nov. 1958).

This place may be less well known generally than the *Soldier's Leap* but the story has the same localisation in time and space, with a personal and identifiable hero. It differs in so far as the pursuer manages to leap the chasm as well, and as the spot is named after him and not the pursued. One is left wondering whether there has been some kind of confusion in the oral transmission of the narrative, or whether the political viewpoint has changed.

Very close to the story behind the *Soldier's Leap* are also the circumstances which are said to have led up to *Donnacha Reamhar's Leap*[7]:

"There is a battlefield on the side of the river Errochd, about two miles above the point where it falls into Loch Rannoch. The battle was part of. the War of Independence, and was fought between Donnacha Reamhar, ancestor of the Robertsons of Strowan, and Alexander MacDougall, chief of Lorn. Donnacha was a Bruceite. MacDougall was son-in-law of the Red Comyn, whom Bruce slew in the Dominican church at Dumfries. This made him and his family mortal enemies of Bruce, and zealous partisans of the English faction. With the view of joining a band of the English who had found their way to Rannoch, the MacDougalls came as far into the district as Errochd. Donnacha Reamhar collected his followers, and lay concealed by the side of the river, to oppose the invaders, and to drive them back. Anxious to learn their number and strength, he disguised himself as a beggar, and ventured into their camp. Having gained his object he left; but by that time the Lorn men suspected their visitor to be a spy, if not Donnacha himself, and pursued him. He distanced all of them but one, on whom he turned and despatched him. Resuming his run, he came to the Errochd at a place where the rocks confined it to a breadth of sixteen feet. He cleared the chasm with a bound, at a point which is known to this day as Donnacha Reamhar''s Leap. After this he recrossed the river with his followers; came upon the Lorn men almost unawares; vanquished them in a fierce and bloody battle; and took their chief a captive."

Only a little more casting around produces more leaps (or *loups*) from the Scottish scene. On Loch Ness side we have *Leum Ailein Mhic Raonuill* "Allan MacRanald's Leap" where Allan MacRanald of Lundie when pursued after the massacre of the Mackenzies at Killchrist near Beauly, escaped by two desperate leaps, one across a deep chasm in a stream and another into the loch itself from which he was ultimately rescued – an event said to have taken place at the beginning of the 17th century. On Crichope Linn there is *Burleigh's Leap* where a Covenanter, Balfour of Burleigh, escaped from the dragoons by leaping over the Linn. "Such are the feats of desperation", is the comment made by a recent writer (*Scots Magazine*, March 1960). Another similar, although slightly more humorous, story is told about the *Tinker's Loup*, a gorge in the River Deuch in the parish of Carsphairn (Kirkcudbrightshire):[8]

"A tinker who passing along the road entered a house in which 'bleedy puddins' [blood puddings] were being cooked for supper. No one was in the house. He seized the puddings and made his escape from the house. He was seen and pursued. He was on the point of being caught. To save himself he leapt over the river at the spot that bears his name, and then sat down on the opposite side to rest and enjoy his feast of 'bleedy puddins'."

There is also *McGregor's Leap* in the parish of Weem (Perthshire), the Gaelic name for which is usually *Leum a' Chleasaiche* "The Trickster's Leap" because an acrobat or juggler had come to the glen and tried to leap across a gully to show his skill but was killed on the rocks. On Euchan Water, near Sanquhar in Dumfriesshire, we have *McCririck's Loup*, a name referring to an incident in the rising of 1745; and in Ardalanish there is *Leum a' Mhinister* "The Minister's Leap," although no story has come to us to explain this name. As it is on the coast, it is probably only remotely related to our theme.

And so one could go on, for Scotland also provides *Rob Roy's Leap* in the Macgregor country, *Maggie's Loup* in East Lothian, *Leum Ruaraidh* "Rorie's Leap" in Ross-shire, *Leum na Feinne* "The Fenian's Men's Leap" in Badenoch, *Leum Odair* "Odin's Leap" in North Uist, *Barry's*, *Scabby's*, and *Matty's Loups* in the Rinns of Galloway, and several others; and although the history of these names is by no means always known, they obviously stand in the same tradition as those for which we do have explanations. The claim for the historic authenticity of the *Soldier's Leap* at Killiecrankie has lost a great deal of conviction in the light of all this evidence, and the character of the story as *Sage* rather than actual event is clearly shaping. For those who are not yet convinced, evidence from outside Scotland may be adduced as further proof, for "near Rimington in Lancashire is *Pudsay's Leap*. This is the spot where a man called William Pudsay, by the help of a magical bit which had been given him by the fairies, leaped his horse right across the Ribble, and so escaped from his foes."[9] The circumstances surrounding *Bayard's Leap* near Sleaford are somewhat different.[10]

Ireland has such an abundance of names in this category that it would be impossible to list them all in this context or quote the stories behind them. It simply must suffice for the time being to state that my friends Seán ó Súilleabháin of the Irish Folklore Commission and Éamonn de hóir of the Irish Placename Commission have provided me with at least eighty Irish place-names containing the element *léim* (Anglicised *Leam-* or *Lem-*) "leap", or the word *leap* itself. About one of them, *Maggie's Leap* near Newcastle, Co. Down, the following story is told: "… there is a remarkable crevice or fissure in a rock, open to the foaming waves below. It is of considerable width and is known as "Maggie's Leap". The story goes that a very agile young woman, Maggie, when pursued by some ruffians, escaped by leaping across the great chasm, and her pursuers were afraid to follow."[11] *Léim an Eich* or *Horseleap* in Co. Westmeath preserves the story of Sir Hugh de Lacy's great leap on a horse "over the drawbridge in this place", and *Léim na Mná* "The Woman's Leap" in Co. Cork is so called from a leap made by a girl fleeing from the "Redcoats": marks of her feet are still visible where she landed. In Jeremiah Curtin's *Tales of the Fairies*, the story of *Trant's Leap* (Irish *Léim an Treanntaigh*) in Co. Kerry is told as part of the tale of "The Knights of Kerry",[12] and a manuscript version in Irish in the IFC shows it to be still in oral tradition in our time.

In Norway the best known name and story of the prodigious jump appears to be that of the *Riddersprange* "the rich farmer's leap"[13] but from its manuscript collections the Norsk Folkeminnesamling in the University of Oslo was able to supply another half dozen examples. In spite of intensive enquiries, the other Scandinavian countries have so far not yielded any example although one would have expected them to have produced at least a few in certain parts of Sweden, for topographical reasons.

The German-speaking area, on the other hand, has many localisations of our legend and consequently numerous place-names of the type under discussion. The best known is probably the Harz legend of the *Rosstrappe* of which the brothers Grimm print five different versions.[14] In one, a giant princess makes a bet that she will be able to jump her horse over the chasm called *Kreetpfuhl*. Twice she succeeds but the third time topples over backwards on her horse and falls into the gorge where she is still doing mischief. In the second version, a prince persuades the devil to give him a horse from hell. On this he elopes with a princess, leaping the chasm in the process, with the horse leaving an imprint of this shoe in the rock (which explains the name). The third version gives an account of a princess who, against her father's will, has a secret love affair. In order to save herself from his wrath she jumps the chasm on her horse, again leaving an imprint of one hoof in the rock. In the fourth variant, Bodo the giant is said to have ruled over everybody except Emma, a princess from the "Riesengebirge". On what he deems a suitable occasion he pursues her on horseback but whereas she and her horse escape by jumping the chasm, Bodo and his mount perish in the attempt and fall to their death below. In this version, both the name of the *Rosstrapp(e)* and of the river *Bode* are aetiologically explained in the same *Sage*. The fifth variant closely follows the fourth, only in this case the princess and her lover escape from the giant on the giant's own outsize horse whereas he has to ride after them on a normal horse and falls into the chasm because he is too heavy a burden.

Perhaps it is necessary at this point to emphasise that the writer is aware of the fact that the leap is only incidental to this particular legend which is primarily designed to explain what looks like the imprint of a horseshoe in one of the rocks. The resulting name therefore refers to this imprint and not to the leap itself. Another example .of our *Sage* is printed by the Brothers Grimm as their No. 141,[15] the legend of the mountain called *Jungfrausprung* near Grätz in Steier, which takes its name from an event in which a peasant girl when trying to escape the lustful designs of an unwanted lover, leaps the river Mur from the mountain in question to one on the other side. Similarly, St Mang jumped from one rock to another across the river Lech near Füssen, a legend which produced the name *St. Mangsprung* for the chasm.[16] According to some, the saint was pursued by a dragon at the time,[17] although others credit Julius Caesar with the leap (*Jusulte* = saltus Julii, as an alternative name for the *Mangsprung* or *Mangtritt*) and the imprint of the horseshoe in the stone surface. In the Black Forest the story is told of a maiden who, when followed by her pursuers, asked God to carry her across the Lierbachtal; in answer to her prayer angels carry her without harm to the other side, and the spot from where she jumped has since been known as the *Engelskanzel* "Angels' pulpit".[18] The question arises, however, whether our legend is not perhaps secondary to this spot, having become localised here when the original legend which had produced the name, had for some reason or other been lost in living tradition, for it is much more likely that the original story was something like the one told for the *Engelskanzel* near Baden-Baden where it is opposed to a *Teufelskanzel* from where the old enemy used to preach; but from the *Engelskanzel* on the other side a good angel talked to the tempted and led them back to the path of salvation. In Siebenbürgen, the Hungarian name of the village of Gait, *Ugra*, is linked in a legend with the verb *ugrani* "to jump" and with the explanation that once a maiden, followed by her enemies, leapt over the river Alt at this point to save herself, most probably a case of secondary aetiology rather than name giving.[19] The Rhineland furnishes the story of the three beautiful and pietous sisters Irmina, Adela and Klothildis who lived in the nunnery of Mons at the time of King Dagobert I. The king wanted to win them by fair means and foul but they escaped with the help of a Franconian officer. Although the king managed to catch up with them in his pursuit and killed all their helpers, the three maidens, after having prayed to God for His assistance, mounted their donkey and on it miraculously leapt the valley of the river Kyll near Auw. The rock face on the other side on which they safely landed is still called *das Eselchen* "the little donkey."[20] In the Swiss canton of Uri, the name *Pfaffensprung* "priest's leap" is explained by the fact that two men of the cloth had attempted to jump across the river Reuss at this point, one succeeding, the other perishing.[21] In Czechoslovakia, a relevant legend is linked with the *Reitstein* (near Reichenberg), a formation consisting of two rocks standing some distance part. Here an earl escaped from his pursuer by jumping on his horse from one rock to the other, whereas his enemy while attempting to do the same fell into the chasm and perished "with his horse".[22] Again, one must at least ask whether this is not rather a *Namensage* than a *Sagenname*, as the name by no means implies a leap.

This list in no way exhausts the number of variants of our legend from the German language area. There are many other places with similar names and origins, and there are also many versions which are told without any definite localisation. However, in this context the summaries given will at least give an impression of the kind of shape the *Sage* has in Germany, Austria and Switzerland, and in some German minority settlements in neighbouring countries.

That it is also known in France appears evident from a remark by Paul Sébillot[23]: "Le nom de quelques rochers suppose que des personnages y ont pris leur élan pour accomplir un saut prodigieux; ordinairement, ils y laissent leur empreinte; et c'est a ce chapitre que je raconterai leur legende; parfois le nom seul rappelle le souvenir de cet acte." The present writer does, at the moment, not have any concrete examples of such names in France, nor can he say how much further the legend is known in Continental Europe and where it has produced place-names. He is, however, aware of at least one instance in the New World which belongs here and which may conveniently finish this short and tentative survey. It concerns Captain Samuel Brady's leap across the Cuyahoga River in Ohio and, as will be noticed, bears all the hallmarks of our legend although it is treated by many as a historical incident. E.O. Randall, for instance, writes; "That a famous leap by Brady was made, at the place generally designated as the site, there is little or no doubt".[24] Others as early as 1856 bemoaned the fact that "the numerous traditions respecting Brady's Leap across the Cuyahoga River, and many other hair breadth escapes and adventures of that old frontiersman grow more and more vague and conflicting with the lapse of time".[25] According to Randall, our knowledge of *Brady's Leap* is based mainly on a letter written by Frederick Wadsworth in Akron, Ohio, in 1856, in which he relates Brady's adventures as heard from "a man by the name of John Sumerall" whom he met in Pittsburgh in 1802 and who had been an "intimate friend of Brady". Here is the story with comments as printed by Randall:[26]

> "According to Sumerall's account Samuel Brady 'a powerful strong man, kind hearted, but an uncompromising and deadly enemy to the Indians,' lived in his youth in Pennsylvania. During an Indian raid the people of Brady's settlement were killed and Brady escaping 'swore eternal enmity to the whole Indian race.' Sumerall relates to Wadsworth many of the encounters Brady had with the red men and among escapades the one involving the famous leap. Sumerall gave Wadsworth the date of this feat but the latter failed to remember it. This lapse of memory by Wadsworth is unfortunate as that is the main point in dispute by different relators of the incident.

Wadsworth recites the story at some length as he had it from Sumerall who had it from Brady. Briefly the account is that Brady – at the time in question, date not given – left Pittsburgh with three or four companions, 'on a scout toward the Sandusky villages', and arrived there only to be captured by a party of twelve Indians. His companions were killed in the encounter. The Indian captors hastened their prize prisoner to their village amid great rejoicings of the tribesmen. His execution at the stake was decreed. The tribesmen assembled to witness the burning. There seemed to be no hope for Brady when he espied the renegade Simon Girty in the Indian crowd. They had been boys together and had been companions in frontier adventures. Brady plead with Girty to rescue him from his fate but to no avail as Girty, at first pretending not to recognize his old friend, finally refused to aid him. He now 'begged Girty to furnish him with the means to take his own (Brady's) life' and thus escape the horrible tortures awaiting him. But without effect. Girty was implacable. The victim was tied to the stake; the fagots heaped about him; 'the fires were lighted and the excitement among the Indians intense.' The Indian circle around him drew closer and he began to feel the flames. He watched his opportunity, when in the confusion of the scene, a fine looking squaw, belonging to one of the chiefs, ventured too near him for her own safety. With a mighty effort, Brady broke the withes that bound him, leaped over the burning fagots, caught the squaw by the head and shoulders and threw her into the burning pile and amid the consternation and panic following, sprung forth and fled for the forest. Brady was a swift runner and easily outdistanced his pursuers. The Indians were of course soon in hot pursuit and a long chase, lasting a day or more, ensued. It continued for a hundred miles until he reached the Cuyahoga river in Franklin Township, Portage County, at what is now the town of Kent. The Indians were close upon him, and a number of times came near overtaking him. He had intended crossing the Cuyahoga at a place called 'Standing Stone' on the Indian trail from Sandusky to the Salt Springs, a few miles south of Warren, Trumbull County. He was obliged to change his course and followed down the river until he found himself at the Narrows, the narrowest place in the river channel, 'the Indians close on his track behind him; he had not a moment to spare and as it was life or death with him he made the famous Brady's leap across the Cuyahoga River.'

Some years before writing the letter, giving this account, Wadsworth visited the site of this leap, accompanied by a Mr. Haymaker who had personally known Brady: 'We measured the river where we supposed the leap was made and found it between twenty-four and twenty-six feet. Brady jumped from the west to the east side; the banks on each side of the stream were nearly of the same height, the flat rock on the west side descending a very little from the west to the east. Brady 'caught the bushes on the bank as he landed and fell some three or four or five feet before he recovered and got out.' By this time the Indians were within a few rods of the river and when they saw him on the opposite bank of the river they set up a terrible yell; 'but none attempted to follow in jumping the river.' Three or four Indians fired at him, and wounded him slightly in the leg."

Nevertheless Brady managed to conceal himself in *Brady's Pond*, about a mile east of the Cuyahoga River, and the Indians gave up the chase. It is Randall's conclusion that the events described occurred in 1780.

The circle is complete. The circumstances surrounding the Scottish *Soldier's Leap* and *Brady's Leap* in America are so similar that there can be little doubt that we are dealing with the same story. Even the slight wounding is there; the Scotsman was wounded in the shoulder, the American in the leg – wounds which make the feat even more remarkable. In addition one may say that the account of *Brady's Leap* contains many other stock features of the American frontier hero: He was "a powerful strong man, kind hearted, but an uncompromising and deadly enemy to the Indians," he made a last minute escape when already tied to the stake, shows himself to be a swift runner, and, after his leap, "secreted himself under water; …he found a hollow weed which he could breathe through with his head under water".[27] If there are no *Daniel Boon's* or *Jessie James' Leaps* in America yet, they should be there and probably will be one day.

Two main features stand out in the analysis of our legend. Whenever it appears in local history publications, as in Scotland and America, any suggestion of intervention by the supernatural and any other miraculous trimmings are missing. When, on the other hand, the legend even to those who tell it, is merely and clearly a legend we find an accretion of other motifs from the realm of folk-belief, like the imprint of the horse's hoof, the horse from hell, the magic bit, the princess' crown which falls off her head in the jump and can still be seen in the chasm or river on certain days, angels as God's agents to carry the pursued maiden across, the 'good' person accomplishes the jump, the 'evil' enemy perishes in the attempt, etc. From this point of view, *memorate* and *fabulate* definitely differ in presentation and contents, the second being much closer to the *Märchen* – and are yet the same story.

It needs not be stressed that wherever the topographic circumstances are right, this particular legend might become localised. Two rocks seem to be the main requisite, preferably on either side of a chasm with a river flowing underneath it or in between. The historical conditions, for the *memorate* anyhow, needed to produce a suitable localisation are also more or less predictable: a clash of two opposing forces, whether in a warlike situation over many years (as on the American frontier), or in a single battle (as at Killiecrankie). One side of this dispute usually becomes personalised, sometimes both, as in *Randolph's Leap*, and it is interesting to note that this personalisation usually reveals the sympathies of the teller of the legend. Neutrality is not allowed, and it is therefore of the greatest significance to see who is pursuing whom: the dragoons the Covenanter, the English 'redcoats' the Irishman, one clansman another, the

Indians the European frontiersman, etc. Each historical situation produces its own loyalties, and even in the Central European medieval background of kings, princesses, knights, giants, giants' daughters, lustful hunters, pietous virgins, angels, devils, saints and dragons, the division into good and bad is always clear.

As the material presented shows, the distribution of place-names arising from our legend is obviously over a wide area, including the British Isles, northern and central Europe, and North America (and it is suspected that a more thorough search will probably enlarge this area still further). In view of the internationality of our legend, would it be right to regard it as migratory, in Christiansen's sense? If "only the *fabulates* are truly migratory and will pass from one country to another",[28] is our legend a *fabulate*? It is interesting that Christiansen does not include the *Riddersprange* legend in his classification. Is this because the Norwegian variants still have too much of the *memorate* about them, and not enough of the *fabulate*? Where indeed is the line between *memorate* and *fabulate*? If *memorates* are "accounts of actual experience at either first or second hand and almost always connected with some landmark, locality or person" and if *fabulates* "may also be so localised but the story no longer has the direct personal touch and instead follows a definite pattern",[29] then the legend under discussion seems to lead a kind of schizophrenic existence, at least as far as Scotland is concerned. Also, the story of *Brady's Leap*, although clearly a *memorate* within the definition, appears to have most of the traits of another *memorate*, the *Soldier's Leap*, on the other side of the Atlantic. Here it may be helpful to note that Archer Taylor regards the story of the *Lover's Leap* in American tradition as a migratory legend. "It tells of a maiden who jumps from a cliff to her death in order to avoid an unwelcome suitor or some other embarrassment. It is localized in many places and passes for a historical event of a sort but was no doubt disseminated orally and, in some instances, deliberately transferred from one scene to another".[30] Well, this article is not intended to solve the intricate problems of terminology and classification with regard to the *Sage* but the material in hand certainly does show up some difficulties, in so far as some variants are supposedly autobiographical, or biographical, but nevertheless seem to have travelled long distances.

Another factor must be taken into account; this is implied in Dixon's version of the *Soldier's Leap* (see Tafel XIV) when he says that "every visitor to the pass has a look at it". This indeed seems to me to be the very point at which the legend (and the place-name) have their origin: the desire of the visitor to gorges, chasms and rock formations so named, to be able to jump across a gap which, objectively, could perhaps be leapt by an Olympic champion under

Tafel XIV – The rocks at the Soldier's Leap, Pass of Killiecrankie.
Property of the National Trust for Scotland.

ideal conditions but would normally be just a little too wide even for him. This psychological impulse is compensated for by the creation of a 'superman' who, at one time or another, was indeed able to perform this impossible leap when his life was at stake; once the story exists we wonder if we could perhaps do the same under the same perilous circumstances.

Closely allied to the prodigious jump as expressed in legend and place-name is the leap from a height, rock or castle into the deep, usually a river or some kind of valley. This, too, has produced many place-names which occur side by side with those of "prodigious jump" origin, although they seem to be more numerous in Central Europe than in the British Isles. The 'leap down' normally requires supernatural help, of course, if it is to be executed successfully. It is seldom simply a feat of prowess like the 'leap across', although there are one or two exceptions to the rule, notably *McCulloch's Leap* near Wheeling in West Virginia where the feat is definitely attributed to Major Samuel McCulloch's horsemanship. The height of the precipice is variously given as 150, 200, and 300 feet, the adversaries again being Indians. The date is supposed to have been 1777.[31] Sometimes a cushioning effect is mentioned and explained both supernaturally (angels) or naturally (a girl's petticoat), but always with special emphasis on the miraculous; in other instances no explanation is given. The impression made by the horse at the jump-off in the 'leap across' stories is frequently parallelled by the imprint of the maiden's feet or the horse's hoofs when landing on the ground, and if such a footprint is produced by a saint, the water that collects in it after a heavy rainfall has special healing qualities. Sometimes even a medicinal spring originates in this way. This 'leap down' legend, too, seems to have its beginnings in the psychological urge many people feel when standing on high towers or on precipitous cliffs: They want to jump down. The present writer, for one, must confess to such an urge which is accompanied by the conviction that the fall will just be a floating through the air and the landing a soft one. It is at least partly this personal experience which has created the special personal interest in this particular legend and has, maybe, added to the belief that the desire to achieve successfully either or both leaps is deep-rooted in many people and might therefore be responsible for the spontaneous creation of similar accounts in different places so that not all variants in our survey may be regarded as migratory variations of the same theme and localisations of the identical legend.

Be that as it may, whatever the ultimate explanation may be, whether memorate or fabulate, whether polygenesis or migration, or memorate *and* fabulate *and* polygenesis *and* migration, the legend of the prodigious jump is undoubtedly a fine example of folklore as a source of place-names, and a strong reminder that onomasticians who ignore the folkloristic element in whatever regional toponymy they study, will be all the poorer for that omission.

Notes

1   Richard Kühnau, Mittelschlesische Sagen geschichtlicher Art, Breslau 1929.

2   *Journal of American Folklore*, vol. 62 (Philadelphia 1949), p. 318.

3   Tristam P. Coffin and Henning Cohen, *Folklore in America*, New York 1966, p. 41 f.

4   See, for instance, Mary Williams, Folklore and Placenames; in *Folklore*, vol. 74 (London 1963), pp.361-376.

5   Stith Thompson, *The Motif-Index of Folk-Literature*, rev. and enl. ed., six vols., Copenhagen 1955/58.

6   John H. Dixon, *Pitlochry Past and Present*, Pitlochry 1925, p. 110 f.

6a   In the official guide to "Places in Perthshire" by the National Trust for Scotland which administers "The Soldier's Leap", George Scott-Moncrieff-seemingly not doubting the historicity of the event-thinks that "the hero of the Leap was probably the Highlander, Donald MacBean, who was one of Mackay's army and published a memoir of his life, printed in Glasgow in 1728". Scott-Moncrieff prints the relevant passage from this autobiography (p. 10), and it is significant that MacBean only claims to have lost a shoe in the jump.

7   William Marshall, *Historic Scenes in Perthshire*, Edinburgh 1881, p. 435.

8   British Association Report, London 1897, p. 493 f.

9   Henry Bett, *English Legends* London 1950, p. 89.

10   *Ibid.*, p. 88 f.

11   Ireland's Own (October 25, 1947), p. 9.

12   Jeremiah Curtin, Tales of the Fairies and of the Ghost World, collected from Oral Tradition in South-West Munster, London 1895, p. 34.

13   Ivar I. Kleiven, *Segner fraa Vaagaaa*, Kristiania 1894, pp. 51-59; also J. J. Alnees, *Norske Sagn*, Oslo 1947, pp. 120-121.

14   Brüder Grimm, Deutsche Sagen, 4. Aufl., Hrg. von Reinhold Steig, Berlin 1905, pp.226-229. The first edition appeared in 1818.-See also Gust. Ad. Leibrock, Sagen des Harzes, 4. Aufl., Quedlinburg [1888], pp. 1-11, and C. Förstner, Sagen- und Märchenwelt des Harzes, Quedlinburg [1888], pp. 61-65 (for the Mägdesprung).

15   *Ibid.*, pp. 118-119 (after Abraham a Santa Clara).

16   Friedrich Panzer, Bayerische Sagen und Bräuche, hrg. von Will-Erich Peuckert, Göttingen 1954, p. 53.

17   Ignaz V. Zingerle, Sagen aus Tirol, 2. Aufl., Innsbruck 1891, p. 491.

18   Johannes Künzig, Schwarzwald Sagen, Jena 1930, pp. 192-193.

19   Friedrich Müller, Siebenbürgische Sagen, Wien 1885, p. 17.

20   Paul Zaunert, Rheinland Sagen. Bd. 1, Jena 1924, pp. 285-286.

21   Josef Müller, Sagen aus Dri. Bd. 3. Hrg. von Robert Wildhaber, Basel 1945, Nr. 223.

22   Gustav Jungbauer, Deutsche Sagen aus der Čechoslovakischen Republik, 1. Teil, Prag 1934, 92 Nr. 152.

23   Paul Sébillot, Le Folk-Lore de France. Tome Premier: Le Ciel et la Terre, Paris 1904, p. 321.

24   E.O. Randall, Brady's Leap; in: Ohio Archaeological and Historical Society Publications, vol. 20, (Ohio 1911), p. 457.

25   Mr. L.V. Bierce, quoted by Randall, loco cit.

26   *Ibid.*, pp. 457-459

27   *Ibid.*, p. 459.

28   Reidar Th. Christiansen, The Migratory Legends, Helsinki 1958, No. 5 (FF Communications, No. 175).

29   *Ibid.*

30   Western Folklore, vol. 21, Los Angeles 1962, p. 131. – The jump over some extremely high obstacle like a wall or a gate to a castle is, of course, another closely related legend in our group.

31   Phil Conley, Beacon Lights of West Virginia History, vol. 1 (Charleston, W. Va., 1939), p. 177; and West Virginia, a Guide to the Mountain State, New York 1941, sec. print. 1943, pp. 293, 296, 488 and 519.

Scottish Studies 13 (1969) 47-57

Falkirk

T HE situation with regard to the study of individual Scottish place-names is such that, unless there exists a competent regional account of the place-nomenclature of a certain area – and there are very few such accounts –, even names of larger inhabited places, such as towns and cities, lack the kind of near-comprehensive documentation which allows a detailed analysis. Glasgow, Dundee, Paisley, Kilmarnock, Lanark, Peebles, Kirkcaldy, Banff, Nairn and many others all fall within this category. This does not mean that the etymology of these names is not known; in fact, we can fairly confidently etymologise all the names just listed. However, the gradual development of the name, both in form and application, and the ultimate emergence of the modern spelling cannot normally be followed from any printed discussion of these names. In each case it is necessary to amass one's own list of spellings by laboriously searching through the relevant records. This task should become considerably easier once the archives of the Scottish Place-Name Survey have been arranged in such a way that the hundreds of thousands of early spellings they contain are accessible in conjunction with each name, but such an arrangement cannot be expected to be available for quite a number of years to come.

It appears necessary therefore that, from time to time, the present series of place-name articles should, in addition to the discussion of broader issues such as historical stratification and geographical distribution, devote some space to the examination of individual names such as the ones listed above; this particular note is therefore concerned with the name *Falkirk* which might with justification have been added to the group of names in question. Falkirk is a fascinating name in many respects but in this context and on the basis of our present knowledge it will not be possible to touch on all of these. We are also more fortunate than with most individual names in so far as there does exist at least one quite detailed attempt at an account of the derivation and meaning of the name. This account was published almost eighty years ago (Miller 1893) and elucidates much of what we have to know about the historical background of the place called Falkirk, beyond the purely linguistic data necessary to establish a reliable etymology. Unfortunately the author of that treatise does not show the same competence when it comes to the discussion of the meaning of the name and squanders his hard-earned documentary knowledge on an unacceptable etymology which we shall allude to below (note 12).

First of all, it is necessary to present a list of the various forms as they occur from the eleventh century onwards (or at least from the twelfth). This list cannot be comprehensive, especially from the sixteenth century onwards, but all the relevant spellings will be shown:

(a)	*egglesbreth*	*c* 1120 (1165-70) Symeon of Durham
		c 1150 Historia post Bedam
	Eglesbreth	? 12th cent. (16th cent.) Leland I, 384
	eaglesuret	1185-98 Chron. Melrose[1]
	Eglesbryth	1268 Holy. Lib.
(b)	*Egelilbrich*	1164 Holy. Lib.
	Eiglesbrec	1166 Holy. Lib.; *Egglesbrec* Stevenson, *Illustrations*
	Egelbrech	1190-1200 Roger de Hoveden
	Eglesbrich	1247 Holy. Lib.
	An Eaglais Bhreac	Mod. Gaelic
(c)	*Varia Capella*	1166, 1240, 1247, 1319 Holy Lib.;
		1242 Pontifical of St Andrews
	Varie Capelle	(gen.) 1319 Holy. Lib.; 1531 (1534), 1537 RMS
(d)	*la Veire Chapelle*	1301 CDS
	la Vaire Chapele	1303-4 CDS
	la Veyre Chapele	1304 CDS
	la Veire Chapele	1305 CDS
(e)	*la Faukirk*	1298 CDS
	Faukirk	s.a. 1298 Chron. Lanercost; 1391, 1468 ER;
		c 1460 Harding Map of Scotland; 1511 RMS;
		c 1564 Nowell Map of Scotland
	Fawkirk	1391, 1392 Holy. Lib., 1537, 1632, 1634 RMS
	Fawkirc	1391, 1392 RMS
	Fawkyrk	1531 (1534) RMS (twice)
	Fauskyrk	1564 Mercator Map of British Isles
	Fauskirk	1570 Ortelius Map of British Isles
(f)	*Falkirk*	1458, 1557 (1580), 1580, 1581, 1587, etc. RMS;
		1546 Holy. Lib., 1551, 1591-2 ER; 1594 Brech. Reg.,
		1595 Mercator Map of Scotland

A discussion of this unusually great variety of forms and spellings must of necessity be preceded by some comment on the identification of the forms listed under *(a)*, with Falkirk, and of their relationship to each other. The first four, as well as Hoveden's *Egelbrech* under *(b)*, all occur as part of an annal for 1080 which in more or less identical terms states that 'Quo anno idem rex Willelmus autumnali tempore Rodbertum filium suum Scotiam contra Malcholmum misit. Sed cum pervenisset ad Egglesbreth, nullo confecto negotio reversus, Castellum Novum super flumen Tyne condidit'.[2] From this entry it is, of course, by no means clear where in Scotland *Egglesbreth* lies, and it is only natural that at first it should have been looked for in the most southern parts of the country. Sir David Dalrymple, for instance, equated it with Bridekirk near Annan, regarding *Eggles-* as standing for *Ecclesia* and the whole name for Latin *Ecclesia Bridgidae* (Dalrymple 1776: 19 *n*); and in his index to the works of Symeon of Durham, Arnold thinks of a possible identification with Eccles in Berwickshire (Arnold 1885: II, 416).Whereas Egglesbreth led Sir David Dalrymple to Bridekirk, the reading Egglesbrech suggested '*Eglesbrec*, the old name of *Falkirk*' to Chalmers who further argues (1807: I, 419 note *h*) that 'if Robert had penetrated to *Annan*, he must have entered Scotland, from Cumberland, on the west: but, as his irruption was bounded by Falkirk, he must have come down to this well-known town, the scene of so many conflicts, through Northumberland, whether he certainly returned', to found Newcastle. Chalmers' view has become the generally accepted one, but although we are in agreement with it too, it was necessary to point out the, at least partly, extra-linguistic nature of the argument.

Although a detailed account of the history of the chronicles involved cannot be part of this discussion, it is however essential to give a brief survey of the relationship of the spellings to each other in order to assess their value and standing as the earliest, and therefore extremely important, forms of our name. The main question which arises in this respect is whether these spellings have come down to us independent of each other or have some kind of connection. The fact that they all occur in practically identical annals referring to the same year (1080) rules out the first alternative or at least makes it very unlikely; what we must determine therefore is the nature of the connection which exists between these five spellings. This in turn depends on the nature of the relationship of the sources. As far as Hoveden is concerned, both the *Historia Regum* ascribed to Symeon of Durham and the so-called *Historia post Bedam* (Stubbs 1868: I, xxvi and xxxi-xxxiii) are considered to be among his sources, a supposition supported by the presence of the phrase *autumnali tempore* which only occurs in these three versions (see note 2 below). For the Chronicle of Melrose, the

when trying to distinguish between *c* and *t*, or other letters for that matter, since the *eaglesuret* of the Melrose Chronicle, if found in isolation, would hardly have allowed even the most daring scholar to amend it to **egglesbret(h)*. With this background in mind, we have to take our starting-point as being a spelling ending in *bret(h)*. Seeming confirmation of such a form comes from a much later and completely independent source, a charter in 1268 by Gamline, Bishop of St Andrews to the Church of Holyrood, listing amongst other possessions 'Ecclesiam de Eglesbryth que hodie varia capella nuncupatur' (Innes 1840: 66). This is in confirmation of an earlier charter of 1240 in which unfortunately our name becomes illegible after *Egl-* (Innes 1840: 64). We are therefore not in a position to judge whether the *-th* is a misreading for *-ch* or an accurate copy. One is inclined, under the circumstances, to decide in favour of the former,[6] as a singular *-th* appears to be somewhat out of place in a series of charters and bulls which otherwise only show *-ch*, but certainly its existence must be taken into account in any evaluation of the *-th* spellings for the annal of 1080.

With or without support from the Holyrood charter, however, these spellings and their hypothetic source are there for us to interpret and should not be pushed aside lightly by emendation, as everybody before Watson used to do, who threw out the suggestion that Symeon's *Egglesbreth* might be a British form (1926: 349), a proposal which prompted Johnston to add to his earlier derivation as Gaelic *eaglais breac*, the alternative 'or W[elsh] *eglwys brith*', 'speckled church', in the third edition of his dictionary (1934: 176). How serious and acceptable is the notion that a spelling occurring in a late eleventh- or early twelfth-century Northumbrian (monastic) annal might represent a genuine British (=Cumbric) place-name in Central Scotland? First of all, it must be stated that, as *eglwys*<Latin *ec(c)lesia* is feminine in Welsh, the adjective would be *braith*<*breith* and not *brith* and also should show soft mutation after a feminine noun, *i.e. fraith*. Presumably a late eleventh-century form would have been something like **egluis breith* (Jackson 1953: 330; 1954: 71-3). However, as the corresponding mutation is never shown in the Gaelic form of the name (where one would have expected at least the occasional Anglicised **vrech*, or the like), it is perhaps not necessary to take the apparent non-lenition of the initial consonant too seriously in this context. Perhaps more difficult to accept is the representation of *-ei-* by *-e-* in *breth* for *breith* although this would seem to have a parallel in *Eden-*<*Eidyn* in the twelfth-century forms of the name Edinburgh (Jackson 1959: 42), nor is it easy to understand why the alleged Cumbric name should have contained an adjective etymologically less closely related (*brith*<**brikt-*) to Gaelic *breac* rather than the cognate *brych* (feminine *brech*)<**brikk-*. In addition to these two arguments, even bearing in mind the great power of survival inherent in place-names, it is not at all plausible that, unless a Strathclyde source with a Strathclyde version of the name was involved, a Northumbrian chronicler of the late eleventh century should retain a pre-Gaelic Cumbric form of the name at a time when Gaelic must have been spoken in the Falkirk area for at least 300 years, at the most conservative estimate. In the present writer's opinion, the Northumbrian source which provided the Chronicle of Melrose, Symeon of Durham, *the Historia post Bedam*, and the Lindisfarne chronicle quoted by Leland with the spelling **eg(g)lesbreth* was probably a fair copy of either a whole chronicle or, which is more likely, a number of draft annals, including the one for 1080, in which a copyist unfamiliar with the place-name misread a -c- in the draft version for -t-. We would therefore put a draft annal, perhaps not written much after the year 1080, before the fair annal in the Northumbrian source which all three (or four) chroniclers used, and assume that **eg(g)lesbreth* was a misreading for **eg(g)lesbrech*. This would, of course, not turn it into a Gaelic name on phonological grounds but would at least allow us not to attach too much importance to the Northumbrian spelling as an indication of the survival, and therefore previous existence, of a Cumbric name for Falkirk.[7] The isolated *Eglesbryth* in the Holyrood Charters would be explained in a similar fashion (see above).

We must now consider what are, in the light of the modern Scottish Gaelic name for Falkirk and for historical reasons, apparently Gaelic forms of the name. Of these, the spelling in the confirmation charter of 1166, by Bishop Richard of St Andrews to the Canons at Holyrood, is the most straightforward for it presents us with an unequivocal *-brec* as the second element. The fact that the editor of the Holyrood charters read *Eigles-* whereas Stevenson has *Eggles-*, has no influence on the etymology and only illustrates the difficulties even nineteenth-century and earlier experts encountered when transcribing these charters.[8] Undoubtedly *Eiglesbrec* (*Egglesbrec*) stands for something like **Eaglais B(h)rec* which must have been the twelfth-century Gaelic form of our name. The charter spelling is vital when it comes to the interpretation of the respective references to Falkirk in the Bulls of Pope Alexander III in 1164 (*Egelilbrich*) and Pope Innocent IV in 1247 (*Eglesbrich*) as both of these, on the surface, show Brythonic rather than Gaelic forms of the adjective 'speckled'. The final *ch* does not seem to have presented a problem to any other scholar discussing this name[9] but is in need of some explanation. Everything hinges, of course, on the question as to whether it represents an unvoiced spirant [χ] or the homorganic stop [k] in pronunciation. Unfortunately there is nothing in these two Bulls to indicate what *ch* normally stands for but as the names were presumably not taken down from oral dictation but copied from documents which had reached Rome from Scotland previously,[10] it is perhaps not the orthographic habits of the scribes at the Holy See which matter here, but rather the significance of these spellings within a Scottish context. It should, however, be noted that Heriot appears in both Bulls as *Herth* which undoubtedly means a voiceless dental stop (perhaps with strong post-aspiration), and that Bathgate is given as *bathcat* and *Bathketh*, respectively, where both spellings must have the same phonetic value. It is reasonable to assume that like -*th* and -*t*-, Anglo-Norman -*ch* and -*c*- might also be interchangeable in final position, or at least that -*ch* does not indicate a spirant. Then there are, if our previous arguments are acceptable, those other two spellings in -*ch* in addition to those occurring in the Bulls, *i.e.* the *egglesbrech of the Northumbrian annal and the emended *Eglesbrych of the charter of 1268 (and its predecessor of 1240). As far as the latter is concerned, the same situation appears to have existed as in the Bulls, *i.e.* both charters have *Herth* and *Bathketh* for Heriot and Bathgate, respectively. The *Eglesbryth* for *Eglesbrych* (=*Eglesbryc*) sequence gains support from the spellings which are found in the same chartulary for the name Kirkcudbright which, after being mentioned properly as *Kyrkecuthbert* in the twelfth century, is shown as *Kyrcudbryth* and *Kircudbrich* in the fourteenth and finally as *Kyrkcuthbryt* in the sixteenth. For Symeon's version *egglesbreth* = *egglesbrech*, it is significant that in the same annal he has *Malcholmum* which is rendered by Hoveden and the Melrose Chronicle as *Malcolmum*, and that elsewhere he has *Uchthredum* against Hoveden's *Uchtredum*. It is therefore not unlikely that his source had -*brec* and not -*brech* and that the ending -*et* in the *eaglesuret* of the Melrose Chronicle is a copy of an earlier -*ec*.[11] In this writer's opinion, there seems consequently little doubt that we are here dealing with various versions and developments of an original final -*c*, or rather a velar voiceless stop [k], which points to a Gaelic -*brec* as the second element in our name.

This leaves us with the presence of the vowel -*i*- (or -*y*-) in the spellings found in the two Bulls and in the charter of 1268, and presumably also that of 1240. It is difficult to think of this as a mere spelling variation as the full stress would be on this syllable, and one can only assume that this might be a reflection of a dative used as a locative, although Modem Gaelic appears to have standardised the nominative in this particular name.

Having dealt with the recorded Gaelic forms of the name, we must now look at the Latin versions which invariably are *Varia Capella* in the nominative and *Varie Capelle* in the genitive. They all occur in Latin texts, but Miller alleges (1893: 60) that 'there are no historical documents showing the exact significance of the words *Varia Capella*, usually translated as meaning "the Spotted or Speckled Church"'. His own conclusion is that 'the term "Varia Capella" is...a figurative form of expression in which the unsatisfactory relations subsisting between the parties interested are ascribed to the church itself' and he feels that the term 'the broken church' quoted in the First Statistical Account (vol. 19, p. 72) 'exactly expresses what took place when its status was reduced to that of a chapel in 1166' (*ibid.* 61).[12] In contrast to Miller, it is our own contention that the existing documentary evidence provides us with a very good insight into the exact usage and meaning of *Varia Capella* which cannot be construed simply to mirror unsatisfactory ecclesiastical arrangements and developments. The first important pointer in this respect is the observation that, from the very first, *Varia Capella* almost exclusively occurs in the phrase *Eiglesbrec que Varia Capella dicitur* (1166). Sometimes the word *nuncupatur* is used instead of *dicitur* and the charters of 1240 and 1268 even add the word *hodie* 'to-day' before the Latin name. Only in the charter of 1319, the Pontifical of St Andrews (1242) quoted by Anderson (1922: II, 522) and the reference in the Register of the Great Seal of 1531 does the term appear alone; and only in one instance, the last, is it linked with *Fawkirk* (RMS 1537: apud ecclesiam Varie Capelle *alias* Fawkirk).

Obviously the phrase '*Eiglesbrec* which is (now) called *Varia Capella*' implies that a change of name has taken place. It does not simply mean that 'Mediaeval records use the Latin synonym' (Stirlingshire Inventory 1963: 150, note 7). As *Varia Capella* in this phrase fills the exact slot normally allotted to the vernacular term in Latin documents of this kind, the conclusion is not that the Gaelic name has been translated into Latin but that here we have the Latin version of the new English translation of the Gaelic name, *Faw Kirk*. It is therefore evidence of the fact that by 1166 English was already so widely spoken in the area that, in a bilingual situation, the Gaelic place-name could be translated into the incoming language, whereas there was probably very little, if any English influence in the Falkirk region in 1080.[13] After 1268, nobody seems to have used the Gaelic name anymore, and by 1319 *Varia Capella* is probably accepted scribal and ecclesiastic usage for *Faw Kirk*. That this is likely to have been the case is supported by the Norman French form *la Veire Chapelle* which, with variations, appears in Norman writs of the first decade of the fourteenth century.[14] The Latin term bows out in 1537 when *Fawkirk* is acknowledged to be the (vernacular) alternative.

Without the Latinised evidence we would not have known of the existence of the English name until 1298 when significantly it first appeared with the (French) definite article; and another century goes by before it is quite frequently found in official documents. The first element in *Faukirk, Fawkirk* is Middle English *fawe, fahe* 'variegated, of various colours' (*Dictionary of the Older Scottish Tongue* 2, 426) which is not unknown in Scottish place-nomenclature, one of the chief examples being a compound with *side*, as in Fallside in Lanarkshire, Falside in East Lothian, Fife (2), Roxburghshire, and West Lothian, Fawside (Berwickshire) and Fawsyde (Kincardineshire). Various forms of the English name are used right into the seventeenth century, including the curious *Fauskyrk*, *Fauskirk* which only occurs on maps[15] and clearly shows that the adjective *faw(e)* is no longer understood so that on the analogy of other names, it seems to have been taken to be a personal, perhaps a saint's, name.

The last important phase of the history of our name starts in 1458 when we have the first isolated instance of the spelling *Falkirk* which from the second half of the sixteenth century onwards dominates the scene although as late as 1634 it shares the references to the place with *Fawkirk* in one and the same charter. This new spelling must be understood as a result of false analogy, because the first element of our name was obviously considered to be in the same category as Scots *ba'* <*ball*, *wa'*<*wall*, *fa'*<*fall*, etc. An unhistorical -*l*- was therefore introduced into the 'standard', non-dialect spelling and has remained there ever since. In its turn it has produced the modem pronunciation-spelling ['fɔlkɛrk] which is now used by everybody except the inhabitants of the town itself who still call it Fawkirk ['fɔ:kɛrk]. How long they will be immune to the influence of the spelling is another question.

Our name can therefore demonstrably be shown to have started out as a Gaelic *Eaglais B(h)rec* before 1080 (with a reasonable possibility of an earlier Cumbric name) and to have been translated into English by 1166 although there is initially only indirect evidence for this in the Latin *Varia Capella* and the Norman French *la Veire Chapelle*. This new English name is *Faw Kirk* which like the Gaelic and the Latin names means '(the) speckled church', a meaning which must have been derived from the peculiar (sand-stone?) aspect of the church,[16] unless a painted wooden church or one built in wood and stone can be envisaged. By false analogy, a new spelling *Falkirk* is produced from the middle of the fifteenth century onwards which in turn has given rise to a new pronunciation ['fɔlkɛrk] although this is hardly used in Falkirk itself, The Gaelic name has survived as *An Eaglais Bhreac* but because of the modern English spelling and pronunciation, the connection between *Breac* and *Fal*- is now obscured and no longer immediately discernible.

The documentary evidence reflecting this development can, in conclusion, be summarised as shown in the table opposite.

Century	Gaelic	Latin	Norman French	English Faw-. Fau-	Fal-
11	*egglesbreth (= egglesbrec) (1080)				
12	egglesbreth (?) Eglesbreth Egglesbrec Egelibrich Eglesbrich eaglesuret	Varia Capella (1166)			
13	Eglesbryth (1268)	Varia Capella		(la) Faukirk (1298)	
14		Varia Capella Varie Capelle	La Veire Chapelle etc. (1301–1305)	Faukirk Fawkirk (1391) Fawkirc	
15				Faukirk	Falkirk (1458)
16		Varie Capelle (1531,1537)		Faukirk Fawkirk Fawkyrk Fauskirk Fauskyrk	Falkirk (1546, etc.)
17				Fawkirk (1622,1634)	Falkirk
18					Falkirk

Notes

1   Wherever possible the source abbreviations are those recommended in the 'List of Abbreviated Titles of the Printed Sources of Scottish History to 1560' which was originally published as an Appendix to *The Scottish Historical Review* 42 (1963) but is also available as a separate reprint.

2   This is the Symeon of Durham version (Arnold 1885: II. 211); in the greatly abbreviated version of the *Historia Regum* in the Bibliotheque Nationale in Paris (ms. nouv. acq. lat. 692) our passage reads (f. 35-35v): 'quo anno idem rex Willelmus autumnali tempore Rodbertum filium suum scotiam contra Malcolmum (f. 35v) misit. Sed cum pervenisset ad egglesbreth nullo confecto negotio reversus castellum novum super flumen Tine condidit' (Communication from M. Pierre Gasnault, Conservateur, in a letter of 24 February 1969).

    The phrase 'autumnali tempore' is found here, in the *Historia post Bedam* and in Hoveden but is missing in the Melrose Chronicle and Leland's excerpt. Its presence in the *Historia post Bedam* was kindly confirmed by Mr H.M. Colvin and Miss P.M. Higgins (see note 5).

3   Earlier, however, he had stated (Anderson 1922: I, 46 note 2) that the paragraph containing our name 'is derived from S.D., II, 211' but even then pointed out the fact that 'S.D. says that the invasion took place in the autumn time'. Stubbs was of the opinion that Hoveden's immediate predecessor was the compiler of the *Historia post Bedam* (1868: xxx-xxxi) which 'in its turn resolves itself into two elements, the compilation known as the "History of Simeon of Durham", and the "History of Henry of Huntingdon" (*op. cit.:* xxvii).' Blair, although accepting and ably summarising most of Hoveden's arguments (1939: 91-2), however, states quite firmly that the two versions of the joint sources as surviving in Symeon and the *Historia post Bedam* 'are not derived directly one from the other, but are laterally related', the latter in fact being a reduction of the two conjoined chronicles it incorporates rather than a faithful copy.

4   See Blair 1963: 112 and 117. For the non-Northern and non-Scottish parts this is almost completely derived from Florence of Worcester, but our part of the annal for 1080 is not from that source. As a whole, the manuscript of the so-called *Historia Regum* was evidently 'written at Sawley in the West Riding of Yorkshire during the second half of the twelfth century, probably *c.* 1165-70' (*op. cit.:* 116).

5   Dr R.L. Page, Librarian of Corpus Christi College, Cambridge, has kindly checked this spelling, at my request, in the only full MS extant of Symeon. He comments (letter of 21 January 1969): 'I have checked MS 139 new foliation 112v; the name form is *egglesbreth* as in the Rolls Series edition. There is similarity between *t* and *c* letter forms in this hand, but I think no doubt that the name form you want ends in -*th*'. The spelling is confirmed as *egglesbreth* in the abbreviated MS of the *Historia Regum* in the Bibliotheque Nationale in Paris by M. Pierre Gasnault, Conservateur (see note 2). Similarly, Mr H.M. Colvin, Librarian of St John's College, Oxford, has kindly looked at f. 54v of their MS 97, the so-called *Historia post Bedam*, and informs me (letter of 22 February 1969) that 'the place-name is written "egglesbreth". The "t" could be read as "c", but comparison with other *t*s and *c*s makes it clear that it must be regarded as the former letter.'

    In the other MS of the *Historia post Bedam* (Royal MS 13.A.6, f 72) the name is also written as *Egglesbreth*, according to Miss P.M. Higgins, Assistant Keeper of Manuscripts in the British Museum.

    Apart from confirming this spelling, Miss Higgins has also taken the trouble to look at the name-forms in the various Hoveden MSS in the British Museum. Her comments (letter of February 26, 1969) are as follows: 'The name is spelt "Egelbreth" in Royal MS 14.C.2, f. 62b and in Arundel MS 150, f. 30. However, the folio in the latter is a post medieval insertion by William Howard. "t" and "c" are frequently written in precisely the same way in the hand employed for Arundel MSS 69 f. 47b, moreover the word in question is smudged, but it is probably "Egelbrech" rather than "Egelbreth".'

    Evidently the spelling printed by Stubbs in the Rolls Series was taken from the last MS but as it appears to be the odd one out at best, we can probably assume Egelbreth for Hoveden, too. In that case Leland's *Egelbereth* ttom Hoveden would not be so curious, as he may have seen another MS. It is interesting, however, that the, perhaps unjustified and certainly unqualified, -*ch* ending led to the identification of the name mentioned in the 1080 annal, with Falkirk.

6   Miller (1893: 60) does not seem to see any problem here and without hesitation extends *Egl-* to *Egl[isbrich]* in the 1240 charter.

7   Skene (1887: 36 note 75) considers our name in conjunction with the personal name *Brychan* and makes the church of Falkirk 'the chief church' in *Manau Guotodin*, although he quotes the name in the form *Ecglis Breacc*. There is no indication in any of the primary sources known to the present writer to substantiate that claim or, indeed, to show that the church at Falkirk existed in the time of the Gododdin.

8   It looks as if Stevenson transcribed the original Harleian charter, III. b. 14 (Stevenson 1834: 13), whereas the version printed in the *Liber Cartarum Sancte Crucis* is from a copy in the then Advocates' Library (Innes 1840: lxxx).

9   It is possible that they simply regarded it as an indication of a pre-aspirated consonant, but did pre-aspiration exist as early as the twelfth century and, if so, was it a feature of this particular dialect?

10   The obvious copyist's error *Egelil-* for *Egles-*, or the like, is probably to be attributed to the later notary's transumpt which is published in the *Holyrood Charters*.

11   In their introduction to the facsimile edition of the Chronicle, the editors particularly draw attention to the presence of 'occasional confusion between *c* and *t; e.g. Stoctorum* stands for *Scottorum* ...(Anderson 1936 : lxxix).

12   In the rest of his paper which otherwise is an excellent collection of source material, Miller goes on to argue that both *Eglesbrich* and *Fawkirk* mean 'the church at, or on the wall', a view which for many reasons is wholly unacceptable.

13   To say that 'on this showing Gaelic was still spoken in the district in 1080' as the Stirlingshire Inventory does (1963; 150 note 7) would be applying the wrong kind of emphasis. It would be more correct to state that, on the evidence of the 1080 anual, the district of Falkirk was still largely monoglot Gaelic in that year or a little later. The peculiar function of the phrase *que* (*hodie*) *Varia Capella dicitur* also evidently rules out the theoretical possibility that *Fawkirk*, although not recorded until the medieval period, is really some centuries older and goes back to the time when the Falkirk region was part of English-speaking Northumbria, before the Scots crossed the Forth to the South.

14   Unfortunately I have not been able to trace Johnston's reference '*a.* 1300 MS *Digby* Locus qui Anglice vocatur ye fowe chapel' (1934: 174) which shows a similar use of the definite article and points to the Norman term as being a translation of the English.

15   The map evidence was kindly supplied by Dr A.B. Taylor. Only spellings not genealogically derived from each other have been quoted in our list.

16   The *Stirlingshire Inventory* (1963: 150) feels that the form in the anual for 1080 'suggests that the building was parti-coloured, perhaps through the use of two

kinds of stone occurring in the same quarry'. In addition, we are informed that 'in 1810-11 the whole structure was demolished, apart from some portions of the tower' and that a new church was 'added to the existing steeple'.

Acknowledgement

I gladly acknowledge the help given to me by Professor K.H. Jackson and my colleague, Mr John MacInnes, who both very kindly read a draft version of this note. Without their critically constructive comments, my arguments would very often have gone astray and would certainly have been less convincing.

References

Anderson, A.O., 1922. *Early Sources of Scottish History 500 to 1286*. 2 vols. Edinburgh.

Anderson, A.O., *et al*. (eds.), 1936. *The Chronicle of Melrose* (Facsimile Edition). London.

Arnold, Thomas (ed.), 1885. *Symeonis Monachi Opera Omnia*, Vol. II. Rolls Series 75. London.

Blair, Peter Hunter, 1939. 'Symeon's History of the Kings'. *Archaeologia Aeliana*, Fourth Series, 16: 87-100.

Blair, Peter Hunter, 1963. 'Some Observations on the *Historia Regum* attributed to Symeon of Durham'. In: *Celt and Saxon*. Ed. N.K. Chadwick. Cambridge, 63-118.

Chalmers, George, 1807. *Caledonia*, Vol. 1. London.

Dalrymple, Sir David. 1776. *Annals of Scotland from the Accession of Malcolm III surnamed Canmore, to the Accession of Robert I*. Edinburgh.

Innes. Cosmo (ed.), 1840. *Liber Cartarum Sancte Crucis*. Bannatyne Club, Edinburgh.

Jackson, K.H., 1953. *Language and History in Early Britain*. Edinburgh.

Jackson, K.H., 1954. 'The British Language during the Period of the English Settlements'. In: *Studies in Early British History*. Ed. N.K. Chadwick. Cambridge, 61-82.

Jackson, K.H., 1959. 'Edinburgh and the Anglian Occupation of Lothian'. In: *The Anglo-Saxons*. Studies …presented to Bruce Dickins. London, 35-42.

Johnston, James B., 1934. *Place-Names of Scotland*. Third edition. London.

Leland, John, 1770. *Joannis Lelandi Antiquarii de rebus Britannicis Collectanea*. Editio Altera. London.

Miller, P., 1893. 'Notes on the Derivation and Meaning of the Place-Name of Falkirk, as ascertained from charters and other historical documents'. *Proceedings of the Society of Antiquaries of Scotland* 27 (1892-3): 58-65.

Skene, William F., 1887. *Celtic Scotland*, vol.II. Second Edition. Edinburgh.

Stevenson, Joseph, 1834. *Illustrations of Scottish History, from the twelfth to the sixteenth century*. Maitland Club, Glasgow.

Stirlingshire Inventory 1963. *Stirlingshire – An Inventory of the Ancient Monuments*, vol. I. H.M.S.O.

Stubbs, William (ed.), 1868. *Chronica Magistri Rogeri di Howedene*, vol. I. Rolls Series 51. London.

Watson, William J., 1926. *The History of the Celtic Place-Names of Scotland*. Edinburgh.

Names 22, 3 (Sept. 1974) 104-110

Names as Verbal Icons[1]

> "And in the end, their names were only names and names – and nothing more.
> Or, if their names were something more than names ... "
>
> Thomas Wolfe, *Of Time and the River*.

IN a detailed discussion of the process of semantic change involved when words become names, I have suggested elsewhere[2] that names reflect at least three levels of meaning:

(a) the *lexical* level, i.e. the dictionary meaning of the word or words comprising the name;

(b the *associative* level, i.e. the reason or reasons why the particular lexical (or onomastic) items were used in the naming process – this, incidentally, is also the level on which connotative names operate;

(c) the *onomastic* level, i. e. the meaning of a denotative name as a name, or its application based on lexical and associative semantic elements, but usually no longer dependent on them.

If this assumption of a threefold semantic tier is correct, *naming* might be paraphrased as "the process by which words become names by association". It is also worth reiterating that as part of the final stages of this process the end-product, the name,[3] frequently loses its lexical meaning and, divested of the associations which initially caused the transition from word to name, more often than not operates, from a semantic point of view, on the onomastic level alone. Consequently, while for the correct usage of a name it is necessary, indeed essential, that the user know it, it *is* not expected of him that he also understand it, since that would demand a survival or at least a recovery of the lexical meaning. Such a reduction to the lexical level is, however, normally uncalled for, in view of the fact that even when the word meaning of a name is accessible without any special effort or knowledge, it is ordinarily ignored by the name user, to the point of total unawareness; therefore the fact that Mr. Baker is a butcher does not bother anyone.

While the linguistically oriented onomastician – and practically all name scholars have so far almost by definition, but certainly by training, been linguists, and especially linguistic historians – shows a primary concern in the task of making a name lexically meaningful again, the creative writer, and particularly the poet, has gladly accepted the lexically meaningless name as a literary device of no mean possibilities. This is not to say that all writers and poets have in fact seen the creative possibilities of names in this way; indeed, many have approached and employed them rather like the linguistic historian – it did matter to them what the real or perceived lexical meanings of the names of their characters or localities were, and it is therefore quite a legitimate pursuit on the part of literary onomastics to ferret out the author's etymological intentions, as an important aspect of the literary function of names.

However, what this paper is attempting to do goes beyond such direct relationship between name etymology and quality of character or place; its concern is to be rather the deliberate poetic usage of the lexically meaningless name as a foregrounding device by the creative artist who seizes upon the onomastic item as a welcome means of enriching and condensing the texture of his work. This is true of both oral tradition and written composition, and it is therefore just as helpful to illustrate our line of argument by examples from, let us say, popular balladry[4] as from conscious art poetry, whether imitative of the ballad or not.

At its simplest, in such usage, the name – and I am obviously thinking particularly of place-names in this context – becomes a convenient localising device, pinpointing the external or internal event of the poem:

> "The king sits in Dunfermling town / Drinking the blude-reid wine"
>   (Sir Patrick Spens)
> "There lived a wife at Usher's Well, / and a wealthy wife was she"
>   (The Wife of Usher's Well)
> "I have a bower at Bucklesfordberry, / full daintily it is dight"
>   (Little Musgrave)
> "There dwelt a man in fair Westmoreland, / Johnie Armstrong.men did him call"
>   (Johnie Armstrong)
> "There lives a lad in Rhynie's lands, an' anither in Auchindore"
>   (Lang Johnny More)

These randomly chosen lines from Sir Francis James Child's canon of traditional ballads,[5] can easily be matched by instances from art poetry:

"In Xanadu did Kubla Khan a pleasure dome decree"
  (Samuel Taylor Coleridge, *Kubla Khan*)
"All in the Downs the fleet was moored, / The streamers waving in the wind"
  (John Gay, *Sweet William's Farewell to Black-eyed Susan*)
"Let Observation, with extensive view, / Survey mankind, from China to Peru"
  (Samuel Johnson, *The Vanity of Human Wishes*)
"Sweet Auburn! loveliest village of the plain"
  (Oliver Goldsmith, *The Deserted Village*)
"Ye flowery banks of bonnie Doon, / How can ye blume sae fair"
  (Robert Burns, *Bonnie Doon*)

In calling such usage "simple", one may with justification be accused of trivialising the poet's or singer's intent and of neglecting important facets of poetic strategy. In order to answer such criticism, the quotations just listed were therefore chosen deliberately to represent various degrees of simplicity or complexity. Dunfermline, Westmoreland, Rhynie, Auchindore, and the Downs are very real and identifiable geographical locations, some of them more widely known than others, which serve the purpose of localisation and that alone. China and Peru are just as real and identifiable, but in the context of the Johnson poem are clearly not meant as actual locations but rather as limiting geographical references. Usher's Well and Bucklesfordberry sound real, and certainly are real as locations anchoring the respective ballad narratives "to the ground", so to speak, within the ballad "world", but to the best of this writer's knowledge have never been identified and might consequently just as well be termed imaginary in the same sense in which, in spite of its basis in historical reality, Xanadu might be called imaginary. Sweet Auburn and Bonnie Doon are by no means localities invented by Oliver Goldsmith and Robert Burns but the epithets added, as well as the evocative address, intimate that our two poets had obviously more in mind than a toponymic shorthand for a geographical setting, a more limited kind of poetic technique which is akin to the place-name rhyme of oral tradition.[6]

As regards lexical meaning, English-speaking readers – and these ballads and poems are, after all, in English – may recognise certain elements in such names as Usher's Well, Bucklesfordberry, Westmoreland, Auburn, and the Downs, and are likely to be aware of at least partial meanings. There is, however, no poetic significance in such partial transparence, and these names might on the whole be as semantically opaque as the others – Dunfermline, Rhynie, Auchindore, Doon, and Xanadu, China and Peru, although the opacity of the first four of these is, of course, less formidable to speakers of Celtic languages. The main point to remember is that etymologies, or attempts at etymologisation, simply do not enter into the picture.

The hints contained in Goldsmith's "Sweet Auburn" and Burns' "Bonie Doon" are sufficient to make us realise that a name may function in a poem in more than one way, quite regardless of its etymology, real or perceived. In addition to is localising effect, it may have other qualities, notions, feelings, impressions to convey which may or may not have a direct connection with its location. Instances in the first category, i.e. in the group for which it does matter where the names are located, would be, it seems, Westmoreland, the Downs, Dunfermline, Rhynie, Auchindore, Xanadu, China and Peru which, in their own different fashions, provide the reader or listener with some of the flavour of the places so named, whether it be the peculiar scenic beauty of the English Lake District, the historical associations of the royal residence on the River Forth, the cultural landscape of the farming communities of the Scottish northeast, or the exotic appeal and otherness of places and countries far from home. Much will depend in each case on the knowledge which the reader or listener has of the places concerned. It is more than likely, for instance, that names like Dunfermline, Rhynie, and Auchindore convey very little topographic or cultural detail to most people outside Scotland or Britain, whereas their isolating onomastic burden is far greater for a Scot, especially for Dunfermline, less so for Rhynie, and least for Auchindore, although the general picture of the landscape of the north-east of Scotland still remains.

To the second category, i.e. to those names which have a secondary function not directly related to their location, would belong such names as Usher's Well, Bucklesfordberry, Auburn and Doon. For the first two examples, no location is known anyhow, and any secondary role, apart from the apparent authenticity conferred on a ballad narrative by the mention of a place-name, however unidentifiable or fictitious, will for that reason have to be deduced from internal evidence. For the name Usher's Well there is next to no information of this kind, and we must come to the conclusion that it only has a localising function, albeit a fictitious one, in the ballad.[7] For Bucklesfordberry, on the other hand, the night of love and morning of disaster for Little Musgrave and Lady Barnard (they spend the night together at Bucklesfordberry and are both killed by the irate and jealous Lord Barnard on his unexpected return in the early morning) creates a new literary meaning which one can no longer ignore or dismiss from one's mind whenever the name is mentioned. Auburn and Doon, too, although primarily this English village in Yorkshire and that Scottish river in Ayrshire, take on a new literary role as a result of the poems in which they occur so that Auburn, as "Sweet Auburn, loveliest village of the plain", becomes the poetic prototype of a Deserted Village, and Doon, as "Bonnie Doon", can no longer be disassociated from false love and deceit which makes mockery of appearances.

Bucklesfordberry, Auburn, and Doon carry out this their secondary function successfully, whether their location is known and appreciated or not. For those who do know the Yorkshire Auburn and/or the Ayrshire Doon, their empirical personal knowledge will allow them to appreciate the poetic works in question on an additional level which generates visual association with topographic detail. The point at issue, however, is that such knowledge is not essential for a full understanding of these poems.

There would undoubtedly be considerable justification in detecting in this latter group traces of metonymic transference of meaning, although the contrast literal versus figurative is so much more easily handled with regard to non-onomastic lexical items. When somebody says "The whole village rejoiced,"[8] it does not need much experience in the language of literature to understand the noun phrase "the whole village" as standing for "all the people in the village". When a newscaster tells us that "Washington has reacted cautiously to the latest peace proposals", most of us also realise that the place-name Washington here represents "the people in Washington who run the American government", but since Washington has no, or at best partial, lexical meaning, the literal use to which the figurative one is here contrasted must of necessity be a purely onomastic one, i.e. Washington, capital of the United States, situated at such and such a latitude and longitude, of the following size and extent, administrative status, etc., whereas the derivation of the name from that of the first President of the United States, the conversion of a personal name into a place-name, does not come into play at all. For most names there is no "literal" usage-cum-meaning in the ordinary sense. Because of the shift in the level of meaning outlined at the beginning, most names, even when accessible on the lexical level, are basically figurative in so far as their application tends to vary from orthodox language usage and introduces a measure of noticeable linguistic abnormality or even downright audacity, as when a place is given the name of "Wounded Knee".

It is against this background of onomastic "figurativeness" that we have to contrast the figurative usage of names in a literary sense, a poetic deployment which permits the writer to build a name into his general metonymic and symbolic strategies, even to the extent of metaphorical application, stimulating and encouraging the thinking in names, in onomastic images, rather than in words. The onomastic metaphor "Wounded Knee", for example, turns into a literary metaphor in the last line of Stephen Vincent Benéts toponymically oriented poem "American Names", in the injunction "Bury my heart at Wounded Knee" (which, recently, moved further along the figurative route as the title of a book). In the context of Benét's poem, "Wounded Knee" becomes the culminating, ultimate, non-reducible distillation of a cultural essence. Together with "the plumed war-bonnet of Medicine Hat, Tucson and Deadwood and Lost Mule Flat" and such others as Harrisburg, Spartanburg and Painted Post, it is moulded by the poet into a set of verbal icons, of pseudo-sacred images, in both sound and sense, not only foregrounding his self-confessed love for American names but also removing them irrevocably from the realm of lexicographical definition and from the normal linguistic processes of encoding and decoding.

Similarly, the opening two lines of Carl Sandburg's poem *Localities* – "Wagon Wheel Gap is a place I never saw / And Red Horse Gulch and the chutes of Cripple Creek" – in their insistence on the enumeration of quaint onomastic reminders of the romanticised life of the American frontiersman and the great move west, are an attempt at creating a particular atmosphere through metaphors that turn what are to all intents and purposes recognisable, meaningful lexical compounds into semantically denuded poetic sound symbols of American geography and popular culture.

Perhaps the strongest and most densely textured examples of what might be called the poetic prose of name worship, i.e. an iconically perceived accumulation of figurative geographical names turned metaphors, occur in Thomas Wolfe's epic *Of Time and the River*. Having in an earlier passage put into words his conviction as to the identity of name and place, at least in a French setting (" … what name could more perfectly express Arles than the name it has – it gives you the whole place, its life, its people, its peculiar fragrance … "),[9] the author extols in several ecstatic paragraphs "the thunder of imperial names, the names of men and battles, the names of places and great rivers, the mighty names of the States."[10] Battles, states, Indian nations, railroads, engineers, engines, sleeping-cars, tramps are pressed into service, savoured, proudly offered to tongue and ear and mind as thundering hymns of worship and intoxicating songs of patriotism in onomastic garb; and all are just a preparation, a prologue for the concluding hydronymic extravaganza, echoing the main theme of the book:[11]

> Finally, the names of the great rivers that are flowing in the darkness (Sweet Thames, flow gently till I end my song). By the waters of life, by time, by time: the names of the great mouths, the mighty maws, the vast, wet, coiling, never-glutted and unending snakes that drink the continent. Where, sons of men, and in what other land will you find others like them, and where can you match the mighty music of their names. – The Monongahela, the Colorado, the Rio Grande, the Columbia, the Tennessee, the Hudson (Sweet Thames!); the Kennebec, the Rappahannock, the Delaware, the Penobscot, the Wabash, the Chesapeake, the Swannanoa, the Indian River, the Niagara (Sweet Afton!); the Saint Lawrence, the Susquehanna, the Tombigbee, the Nantahala, the French Broad, the Chattahoochee, the Arizona, and the Potomac (Father Tiber!) – these are a few of their princely names, these are a

few of their great, proud, glittering names, fit for the immense and lonely land that they inhabit.

No historical dilutions or delusions here, no search for origins, just locations and sounds, sounds, sounds – to use the author's epithets "princely, great, proud, glittering" sounds, a "mighty music … fit for the immense and lonely land." A poetic illusion, perhaps; a linguistic distortion, possibly; a perpetuation of a myth, probably; an aesthetic pleasure, certainly – but also a feast (or is it a surfeit?) of names as metaphors, and a delight for the onomastic iconographers – us.

Notes

1   This is a considerably revised version of a paper read at the Annual Meeting of the American Name Society in Chicago on December 30, 1973. It is affectionately dedicated to Margaret Bryant, not only because she did not hear the first version.

2   "Linguistics in Place-Name Studies," in *Current Trends in Onomastics in the United States* (in preparation).

3   Or, in Algeo's terms, "a word people use to call someone or something by." See John Algeo, *On Defining the Proper Name*, University of Florida Humanities Monographs, no. 1 (Gainesville, Florida), p. 87.

4   "Place-Names in Traditional Ballads," *Folklore* 84 (1973), pp. 299-312.

5   Francis James Child, *The English and Scottish Popular Ballads* (New York: Houghton, Mifflin and Company, 1882-1898).

6   See, for example, W.F.H. Nicolaisen, "Some Gaelic Place-Rhymes", *Scottish Studies* 7 (1963), pp. 100-102.

7   In his adaptation of this traditional ballad under the title of "The Sea-Wife", Rudyard Kipling, for instance, substitutes the equally unidentifiable *Northern Gate* for *Usher's Well*.

8   This example and the next are used by Geoffrey N. Leech, *A Linguistic Guide to English Poetry* (London: Longmans, 1969), pp. 148-149.

9   Thomas Wolfe, *Of Time and the River* (New York: Charles Scribner's Sons, 1935), p. 608.

10   *Ibid.*, p. 866.

11   *Ibid.*, p. 867.

Journal of Popular Culture 14, 1 (1980) 119-130

Surnames and Medieval Popular Culture. Tension and Extension: Thoughts on Scottish Surnames and Medieval Popular Culture

> Our names preserve a record of the
> government, industries. habits. beliefs.
> and fancies of our ancestors.
> Donald Mackinnon (1887).[1]

NAMES are initially, one might even say primarily, linguistic items. When first given they usually mean in the way in which words mean, and when used they are embedded in linguistic contexts – phonologically, morphologically, syntactically. It is therefore fair to expect them to yield, when studied, chiefly linguistic information. As markers of different strata in linguistic history, for example, and of the relative chronology of that stratified history, they have provided invaluable evidence, especially in countries with a long and diversified sequence of immigrant languages as, let us say, Scotland.[2] Place-names have proved to be particularly instructive material in this respect, supplying, most as names of major water courses, information about early, prehistoric strata for which no written record of any other kind is available. In such forays into linguistic prehistory they have become equivalent in significance and expressive force to the surviving items of material culture which are the archaeologist's sources of information and objects of research.

Although perhaps less dramatically, place-names have also served well the student of medieval matters linguistic in Scotland, helping effectively to determine the extent of Scandinavian linguistic (and political) domination of the Scottish north and west, to chart the gradual progress of Gaelic in the kingdom of Strathclyde, and to reconstruct some of the aspects of the ousting of Pictish, to cite but three important examples.[3] In all three instances, the history of the languages involved and the settlement of the speakers of these languages are so intertwined that it is practically impossible, and probably also undesirable, to separate them. A large variety of extra-linguistic information is, it appears, readily available in toponymic evidence, as long as one knows how to extract it and, equally important, as long as the limitations of that evidence, as well as its scope, are recognised.

Our knowledge of medieval popular culture is not only likely to benefit from such evidence, but it can be expected to be one of the chief beneficiaries, for the act of naming and the use of names are, after all, first and foremost aspects of culture-bound behaviour on a "popular" level, in the broadest sense of that term. Whether we give names to places or persons, or call them by their names, this will only in a small number of instances involve official decrees or sanctions: naming and using names is an essential privilege of the people. With the help of place-names people turn a threatening wilderness into a habitable landscape; with the aid of personal names people transform the perplexing human environment into a structured society. The investigation of naming strategies and of the employment of names consequently will of necessity throw light on several aspects of popular culture, the medieval period being eminently suited for the task.

II

Through a systematic scrutiny of the appropriate specifics, or defining elements, in compound place-names, for instance, it is possible to reconstruct a fairly accurate, though because of the survival factor and the "accidental" nature of names, by no means comprehensive picture of animal husbandry or other noteworthy agricultural and pastoral practices. The island of Lewis, northernmost part of the Outer Hebrides, like the rest of the Western and Northern Isles of Scotland, and the adjacent mainland, under Scandinavian domination from the 9th to the 13th century, abounds in Scandinavian place-names of both man-made and natural geographical features. A careful perusal of these names provides some intriguing and instructive facts[4]: Names like *Quier* 'cattle-folds', *Croigary* 'pasture of the cattle-fold', and *Garrabost* 'enclosed farm' indicate the keeping of cattle and the consequent necessity for enclosed pasture and fields. *Rossal* 'horse-field', *Hestaval* 'horse-hill', *Hestam* 'horse-islet', and *Roisnish* 'horse-headland' inform us that horses were also kept and that there must have been special grazing grounds for them. Some of them seem to have been pastured on islands for at least part of the year, and there appear to have been other islands which were primarily used for the pasturing of sheep

(*Soay*), lambs (*Lampay, Lamalum*) he-goats (*Haversay*), and calves (*Calva*), although the latter name is also applied metaphorically to small islands situated close to a larger one. Besides *Hestaval*, there are *Soval* 'sheep-hill' and *Neidal* 'rough hill ground for cattle', supplying further evidence for the practice of transhumance in Scandinavian Lewis, and in the Hebrides in general. Certain farms seem to have specialised in the keeping and breeding of certain animals, like *Geshader* 'goat-farm' and *Galson* and *Griosamul*, both referring to a pre-occupation with pigs. Other farms concentrated the growing of corn (*Cornabus*) or flax (*Linshader*); there is also the name Lionel 'flax-field'. The economic and culinary importance of fishing in both river and sea is reflected in such names as *Laxay* 'salmon-river' and *Shilten* 'herring-promontory'. Other names comment on the presence of fortifications (*Borue, Boreray*), of a bridge (*Brue*) and of ecclesiastical buildings (*Kirkebost, Kirkipul*); others again convey a notion of personal ownership of permanent farms, as *Swanibost* 'Sveini's farm', *Tolsta* 'Tholf's farm', *Grimshader* 'Grim's farm', and others. *Eoropie* 'Jorunn's farm' speaks of female ownership. Considering the paucity of our documentary evidence for Lewis and other Hebridean islands during the early Middle Ages, this toponymic information is a welcome and quite detailed addition. Naturally, it is possible to reconstruct similar pictures for other parts of the country.

The gap between place-names and personal names is bridged by surnames derived from the names of locations, including fully-fledged place-names. Hereditary surnames (about which more below) came into being in lowland Scotland mostly in the 13th and 14th centuries, while the Highlands followed suit much later.[5] When counted individually as names, this group of local surnames is much larger than any of the other three surname categories,[6] but undoubtedly the proportions would change if the individual bearers of all types of surnames were to be counted instead. It is significant in this respect that in both a list of tenants of the lordship of Fermartyne of 1382 and a list of members of the Guild of Ayr, *circa* 1431, surnames of relationship (the so-called "patronymics") are the most numerous.[7] This change in emphasis does not, however, detract from the fact that in the Middle Ages many people were identified by an indication of their place of origin, like *Abercorn, Aberdour, Amisfield, Belhelvie, Colston, Eshiels, Fenwick, Glendochart, Hangingshaw, Kilconquhar, Middleton*, etc. Almost invariably, and certainly not surprisingly, persons bearing such names are mostly on record in places other than the ones from which they originated, according to their surnames, whether they were actually born there or had only lived there for a while.[8] For this reason, local surnames can be exploited as raw material for research on two topics about which otherwise there is very little known, i.e., the medieval hinterlands of some of the big cities and the degree and range of mobility exhibited by medieval people. Obviously, also, persons bearing surnames belonging to one of the other three classes – patronymics, occupational surnames and nicknames – did not necessarily remain stationary but, for one reason or another, changed their places of residence; the picture is therefore incomplete because their movements are not as directly traceable. It is, on the other hand, unlikely that their patterns and degree of mobility were very different from those of the sample group that carries their status as strangers or newcomers in their communities on their anthroponymic sleeves, so to speak. It is by implication the volume of movement, rather than the range, which eludes the name scholar, as long as the assumption is correct that persons bearing local surnames in the 13th, or perhaps even 14th or 15th centuries, had either themselves comes from the places indicated or had recent forebears who had left those localities, more often than not small places, both in size and importance.

A preliminary investigation of the hinterlands of the cities of Edinburgh and Aberdeen, as demonstrated by the presence of medieval bearers of local surnames, has shown that these are not terribly extensive and easily restricted by sizeable natural barriers such as river estuaries or hill ranges.[9] Cities or big towns, according to this evidence, were clearly more attractive to those living in their vicinities, and their reputation as desirable places of work and residence for those with certain skills and inclinations did not usually outweigh the reluctance to travel long distances and leave one's familiar social environment behind. It should be possible to corroborate this conclusion by tests examining the occurrence of local surnames in terms of distance from their locations of origin,[10] but this is not an easy task to accomplish because of the skimpiness of the Scottish evidence.

The record is flawed in quite a number of ways, and consequently the demonstrable occurrence of surnames which can reliably be ascribed to definite localities of origin is sporadic with regard to the general populace before 1500. A major obfuscating factor is the recorded presence of many persons having surnames derived from the lands they own or the titles they bear. Since members of this "upper", frequently aristocratic, layer of society tend to hold military, political or ecclesiastical office, they are also found to be travelling or employed much farther afield, but without losing their direct links with the eponymous piece of land they own or which gave them their titles. Their presence at the royal court or at an important religious house hundreds of miles away from home does therefore not throw any light on the question of popular mobility. The record becomes much fuller after 1500, but whether this is to be attributed to the much larger number of documents available or a genuine scarcity of non-aristocratic surnames of local origin before the end of the 15th century is, at present, difficult to say. Only a systematic and comprehensive survey of the surnames of Scotland will tell.[11] Until the results of such a vast undertaking are available, one has to be content with meagre and spotty medieval evidence and with the projection of such observations, as the distinct regionality of certain modem surnames with toponymic affiliations, to the Middle Ages. After all, the distribution of such surnames is not likely to have been less restricted then that now, but rather more so.

We are on much less controversial ground in the assessment of surnames derived from a particular trade, occupation or office; name scholars and medieval historians alike have seized upon this extensive category as a potential source for the study of certain facets of medieval society.[12] Two issues in particular have attracted scholarly attention: the survival, in the form of surnames, of numerous medieval occupations which have ceased to exist as the result of industrialisation and changing commercial practices, on the one hand; and "the surprising variety and specialised nature of medieval occupations",[13] on the other.

In the former category, the name *Barker* (Patrick Barcar 1200)[14] recalls the now obsolete occupation of bark-stripper who produced and prepared an important ingredient for the process of tanning. *Bellman* (Gilbert Belman 1398) makes reference to the office of town-crier whose significance in the system of communications of a medieval town was considerable, putting official announcements against rumour rampant. Somebody would be called *Blindseil* (William Blindcele 1398), if he had the special job of sealing, or covering, the eyes of falcons used in hawking. A *Boyter* (Andrew Boytour 1510) would make 'boxes', a *Buckler* (Robert Buklar 1402) 'buckles', a *Challoner* (Robert Chaloner 1472) 'chalons', i.e., coverlets for beds, a *Cordiner* or *Cordwayner* (Thomas Cordonar 1442) 'shoes of goat-skin leather', a *Cutler* (Matthew de Coteleir 1296) 'knives', a *Horner* (Nicholas Horner late 15th cent.) 'horn-spoons', a *Lorimer* (Matthew Lorimer 1463) 'bits, spurs, stirrup-irons, etc.', a *Naesmith* (Adam Nasmith 1420) 'knives', a *Patternmaker* (Henry Patynmakar 1427) 'patterns', i.e., 'clogs', etc., etc. A *Brander* had the task of 'branding' (fish) barrels. Hay was put up in 'cocks' by a *Cocker* (Alexander Cokker 1363), and charcoal burned by a *Collier* (John Colzear 1582). The list of such obsolete or obsolescent occupations, as represented by modem surnames, is obviously much longer, but even from this brief example it becomes clear that it is of no consequence in this context whether a name is still semantically transparent (*Barker, Bellman, Buckler, Cutler, Brander*), merely suggestive as to its original meaning (*Naesmith, Cocker, Collier*), or totally opaque (*Boyter, Challoner, Cordinar, Lorimer*). As a record of medieval life they all carry equal weight, just as hereditary surnames, they are now all equally detached from their primary lexical meaning, despite a high instance of transparency or suggestiveness in quite a few examples.

In certain respects the list of names just paraded has already been illustrative of the second extraordinary phenomenon which has given scholars something to write about – the remarkable degree of specialisation in medieval occupations, resulting in a wide terminological spectrum with fine distinctions and nuances and, subsequently, in a large variety of surnames originating from that finely shaded terminology. The brief catalogue of names derived from nouns depicting objects of manufacture (*Buckler*, *Challoner*, *Cordiner*, etc.) is a case in point; a full inventory of such names would naturally be even more persuasive. A similarly diversified background in the "making" of things has given us the many different kinds of names ending in -*smith* 'a worker mostly in metal' and -*wright* 'a worker mostly in wood'. In addition to the simple names *Smith* (Robert the smith c. 1199) and *Wright* (Rauf le Wrighte 1296), we have compounds such as *Goldsmith* (Walter the goldsmith 1296), *Locksmith* (Robert Lokessmyth 1214) 'maker of locks', *Naesmith* (Adam Naesmith 1420) 'knife-maker', *Shearsmith* (Andrew Schiersmythe 1479) 'maker of shears', *Whitesmith* 'worker in white metals', and *Wildsmith* (John Wyldesmyth 1259) 'wheel-smith,' as well as *Glasenwright* (Johannes Glasinwricht 1406) 'glazier', *Plewright* (William Plewryght 1649) 'plough-maker', *Sawright* (John Sawright 1570) 'saw-maker', *Sievewright* (William Suffwricht 1512) 'sieve-maker', and *Slavwrock* (Metylda Slaywrock 1348) 'slay-maker' (Slaywright?), and *Wheelwright* (Johannes Quwelwrycht 1361-65) 'maker of wheels and wheel-carriages'.[15] In addition, a detailed analysis of the medieval surnames of neighbouring England has produced 99 compounds of -*maker*. The same studies have collected 40 names ending in -*monger*, reflecting an almost corresponding specialisation in the handling of saleable commodities; often, of course, the maker, seller and mender of particular items was the same person.

When considering individual trades or industries, the degree of differentiation which emerges from an examination of documented surnames is even more astonishing. In England, as many as 165 medieval surnames refer to the cloth industry, names connected with weaving and dyeing being especially numerous; according to Reaney, "there are 18 different surnames denoting makers or sellers of hats, caps, hoods, etc."[16] It is worth noting in this connection that the output of cloth for export was highest at the end of the late 15th and the beginning of the 16th centuries,[17] so that a large and varied labour force was required in that particular industry. Other occupations and services well represented by surnames are the metal trades (108) and the provision dealers (107).[18]

Specialisation was, however, not merely an urban trait in medieval society, as the various 'herdsmen' in the personal nomenclature indicate: *Bulman* (Stephen Bulman 1662) 'bull herd (?)', *Calvert* (Johannes Calfhyrd c. 1350) 'calf-herd', *Coltart* 'colt-herd', *Femister* (Alexander Feemaister 1458) 'flock-master', *Gosman* 'tender of geese', *Hird* (*W. dictus* Hyrd 1328) 'herdsman, shepherd', *Hoggart* (Henry Hoggart 1525) 'one in charge of hogs, i.e., young sheep', *Pastor* (William and Walter Pastor 1262) 'shepherd, also clergyman', *Shepherd* (Henricuv Scyphard 1363), *Stoddard* (David Stodhirde 1376) 'stot-herd', i.e., herder of bullocks', *Storrar* (William Sturor 1534) 'in charge of flocks or herds', and *Wetherherd* (Thomas dictus Wethyrhyrde c. 1200) 'wether-herd'. Apparently bulls, calves, colts, geese, hogs, sheep, bullocks and wethers required their own herdsmen with special expertise concerning the animals in their keeping and, of course, separate pastures.[19] At the other end, some of the major products of these herding activities, meat and hides, were handled by correspondingly specialised slaughterers and a large number of occupations associated with tanning and the manufacture of leather goods. The processing of wool obviously became part of the cloth industry (see above).

An intriguing sidelight is thrown on occupations likely to have been carried out by women, by a small morphological group of names ending in -*ster*: *Baxter* (Reginald Baxter 1200-1240) 'female baker', *Brewster* (Thomas le Breuester 1296) 'female brewer', *Dempster* (Andrew Dempster 1360) 'judex', *Litster* (Pieres le litstere 1296) 'female dyer', *Sangster* (James Sankster 1452) '(female) chorister', *Walkster* (William Walkster 1739) 'female fuller', *Webster* (Malcolm Wobstare 1436) 'female cloth-weaver'. The medieval evidence, and certainly that afforded by our surnames, is by no means unambiguous insofar as even Old English -*estre* was sometimes used to designate male persons. The suffix was, however, the most productive of the very few derivative endings available to distinguish women, and it has been shown that there are at least thirty-eight Old English examples in which -*estre* is exclusively a feminine suffix,[20] like *keppestre* 'saleswoman' *webbestre* 'female weaver', *hoppystre* 'female dancer', and *hearpestre* 'female harper'. Since many occupations could be carried out by both men and women, the suffix became neutral with regard to the indication of sex, in the early Middle Ages, and certainly names like *Dempster* and *Sangster* cannot be said to refer to women in our context. The other names, however, significantly denote tasks performed around the home – baking, brewing, dyeing, fulling, weaving – as part of the production of food and clothing,[21] an extremely limited and limiting circle of activities. In this respect, it is also worth recalling that -*estre* appears to have been created, in most cases, as the feminine equivalent of masculine agent nouns in -*ere* (Modern English -*er*), so that we have *Baxter* besides *Baker*, *Brewster* and *Brewer*, *Walkster* and *Walker*, *Webster* and *Webber*, but also the English *Dyster* and *Dexter* besides *Dyer*.[22] An enlightening glance at the world of medieval woman through the telescope of surnames!

III

Whether one seeks information about agricultural and pastoral activities in a Hebridean island under Norse rule, the hinterland of medieval Scottish cities, the mobility of Scottish persons in the Middle Ages, the occupational composition of medieval Scottish society, or the tasks performed by women in that society, names provide important clues, if sensitively and sensibly utilised. There are also numerous other aspects of popular culture in medieval Scotland for the elucidation of which names might be similarly and appropriately employed. Indeed, in all these pursuits, onomastics [the study of names] plays a handmaiden role, supportive of other disciplines, especially medieval social history, but also linguistics, archaeology, geography, ecclesiastical history and others. Because of the effectiveness of secondary extra-onomastic results achieved through the study of names, it is easily forgotten that, above all, names should be studied as *names* and should therefore be expected to have something to say about the act of naming and of name usage, both of which are, as we have already seen, processes involving most directly and essentially the 'people' themselves.

Any essay trying to put into words some so-called "thoughts" concerning the significance of surnames in the popular culture of medieval Scotland would consequently have to be considered severely deficient if it neglected to pay any attention to these peculiarly onomastic properties and functions of names. In fact, everything said so far (especially since it cannot be claimed to be truly "new", except as a personal synthesis) can only act as a focusing device that will give selective substance and direction to the ideas and notions which are expressed in the following. Otherwise these reflections are bound to lose their most telling dimension.

As must have become apparent in the previous discussion, the various extra-onomastic conclusions, arrived at on the basis of onomastic evidence, without exception rely on, indeed require, the prior competent etymologisation of the names in question, i.e., the successful reduction of these names to the words they once were and the disclosure of their embeddedness in the lexicon. Without this rediscovery of lexical meaning and the corresponding re-allocation of a slot in a live and meaningful vocabulary, the semantic opacity of a fair proportion of the evidence would prevent a convincing presentation and acceptance of such conclusions. If one extends Reaney's dictum that 'occupational surnames originally denoted the actual occupation followed by the individual',[23] to the other three categories of surnames, by stating that "surnames of relationship originally denoted the actual (paternal) parent whose child the individual was", that "local surnames denoted the actual place from which an individual had come", and that "nicknames referred to an actual characteristic of the individual so named", then this retrospective identification of name and word is, of course, justified. It is, however, necessary to stress in this context that these actual circumstances which gave rise to recorded surnames, regardless of whether they have survived or not, obtained only at that time when these very surnames were first created, i.e., when they became hereditary. At that time, as it had been for generations before, a person called *Crocker* was a *crocker* (or potter), a person called *Aberdour* had come from *Aberdour* in Fife or in Aberdeenshire, a person called *Thomson* had a father called *Thom(as)*, and a person called *Thin* was indeed of slender build.

Such lexically meaningful *by*-names or *to*-names were added to a comparatively small number of *font*-names, i.e., names given in baptism, that were, with few exceptions, no longer transparent semantically, having frequently entered English naming traditions from other languages, in quite a few instances through Biblical influence. In a manner of speaking, they were all nicknames (*eke*-names 'additional names') needed to identify individuals in a society which had largely lost the knack of creative first-naming. Naming as the deictic act of identification was, however, not an isolating process, but one which placed the name bearer in a complexly structured societal setting. This was, of course, only possible if an identifying name was not only knowable but understandable. This excluded not only opacity but also privacy and secretiveness, and the facts from which recognisable characteristics were selected had to be publicly discernible.

This need probably also accounts for the comparative lack of offensive nicknames in the surname network. Most of these would be used behind the individuals' backs or in their absence and would not be known to them; this would give them a semi-privacy which practically excluded them from ubiquitous, public knowability. Otherwise the four major categories of potential surnames are excellently suited for this purpose, and it is not surprising that one eminent modern name scholar calls the division into these 'four broad classes ... the only sure ground' of surname lexicography.[24] One's genealogical links, one's place of birth or origin, one's occupation or office, and one's physical, sartorial and behavioural qualities are, in a sense, 'outward' attributes which allow others to name and identify, and through the use of such names to re-identify, an individual. While the first three categories, if applied competently and correctly, contain factual information which permits no choice on the part of the outside names giver and names user, the fourth class – the so-called nicknames proper –

admits of a certain degree of spontaneity and chance. After all, somebody may be *Brown, Thin, Little, Swift, Wise*, and a *Makepiece* at the same time, and other things besides. It is by no means predictable what will strike his neighbours as his most noticeable peculiarity. Not unexpectedly, however, the number of nicknames in the Scottish surname repertoire is much smaller than that of any of the other three categories which are based on indisputable fact and not on imaginative interpretation of, or emotional response to, someone's visible nature.[25]

The act of lexically meaningful naming, then, puts the identified and identifiable individual into a social context. A person called *Aberdour* may thus be labelled as an incomer and be accorded stranger value and suspicion in Kirkcaldy and Aberdeen; an individual onomastically depicted as *Thomas(s)-son* is primarily seen as his father's offspring and made conscious of his family ties with the past; a man named *Goldsmith* may be associated with the excellence of the craft and the reputation of the guild. Thus names do not exist in a vacuum, have no real significance on their own, but function in contrast to other names, just as their bearers live in competition with and contrast to other persons. As a socio-cultural item, the meaningful by-name (the proto-surname), has its existence in the tensions of the lexical field in which the word from which it derives has its structural slot. A name locates an individual in society, not just in a geographical sense, as in the case of surnames derived from actual place-names or from vague topographical ascriptions like *Hill, Wood, Milne*, or *Shaw*. Location through genealogical or occupational associations is just as common and just as valid. Quite apart from one's identification as a social individual, society itself is given, on this level and in this respect, a structure and cohesion, not easily reflected in any other linguistic manner. In this setting, naming reinforces identity in the context of socio-cultural relationships.

The changes triggered in the anthroponymic system – the havoc wrought is perhaps a more appropriate phrase – by the introduction of hereditary surnames can hardly be overestimated. This is not the place to present the apparent reasons for their introduction, except to say that they seem to have been Anglo-Norman rather than Germanic in origin, and that they were brought into being by the needs of administrators and officialdom rather than by a change of attitude among the people themselves. Although their development was gradual, beginning with the land-owning classes in the 12th century, the repercussions were nothing short of revolutionary and are most poignantly epitomised by an entry in the Royal Burgh Records of Stirling of 1525 in which *Agnes Beltmakar* is described as a *kaikbakstar!*[26] Two or three hundred years earlier she would clearly have been a 'maker of belts and girdles,' not a 'baker of cakes'.

As this example shows, the hereditary principle had some major consequences: the surname became detached from its lexical etymon and, even if word meaning was accessible as in the case of *Beltmakar*, ceased to function within the tensions of a current semantic field. In addition to many meaningless font-names, people were also more and more beginning to bear meaningless surnames. This increasing semantic opacity or irrelevance eliminated the surname as a viable locating device placing identified individuals in their rightful slots in contemporary society. Seeming contradictions like the one mentioned above no longer disrupt when the surname is no longer expected to mean as a word. Somebody called *Aberdour* may now have been born in Kirkcaldy, somebody named *Thomson* may have Peter as a father, and somebody bearing the name of *Little* may be of considerable physical stature. When the very occupations denoted by surnames have perished or decayed (*Barker*, *Gosman*, *Cordiner*, etc.), then the surname becomes nothing but a linguistic fossil useful perhaps in the reconstruction of medieval popular culture but without much direct relevance to the contemporary scene.

Instead of the semantic tension of fields of lexically meaningful surnames, we now find an extension of the genealogical principle of the *Thomson* and *Macdonald* variety, by which an individual is not so much identified in the present as in the past. All surnames have become surnames of relationship, and are, metaphorically speaking, 'patronymics'. In the chapter on "Scotland before the Reformation" in her book *Life in Scotland*, Rosalind Mitchison makes the following observation: "A kinship society ... will be a status-dominated society with the key to that status, family, lying in the past. Not for nothing did most highland clans use as surname some filial derivative. A man's lineage was what mattered most to him".[27] Without wishing to stretch this point too far, one might argue that the introduction of hereditary surnames effectively turned medieval popular society into a kinship-oriented one.[28]

In such a situation, surnames function on an onomastic, albeit intra-cultural, level only; etymological strategies are no longer capable of revealing their meaning; and their knowability is not dependent upon their understandability. Their contents instead depends chiefly on what other individuals know about the bearer. Consequently, competence in name usage has much to do with the scope and intimacy of that name knowledge. Identification of individuals through surnames, hinging greatly on filial and uxorial links, is achieved almost exclusively through extra-linguistic processes. Administrative necessity has destroyed, or at least considerably affected and distorted, the denotation of individuality through multifaceted locatory devices. The knowledge that John is the son of Thom, comes from Aberdour, works as a beltmaker, and is small in size, is not conveyed by his hereditary surname *Smith*, or even by a less ubiquitous name like *Latimer*. To 'know' the person John Smith or Latimer, such information has to be obtained independent of the lexically opaque onomastic evidence. In the later Middle Ages, therefore, onomastic fields no longer function in conjunction with the corresponding lexical fields, but only as a reflection of the socio-cultural constellation of their bearers, in relationship to each other. The onomastic revolution, caused by the introduction of hereditary surnames, has produced a new concept of self by abandoning the old language-bound devices of social location. It has also shifted the locus of identity and knowability from the name of a kinship-dominated system of linguistically opaque signs and ultimately to the labelled individuals themselves. The function of surnames as sanctuaries and reservoirs of identity has become quite circumscribed. A new era has begun.

Notes

1 (Donald) Mackinnon. "Place-names and Personal Names in Argyll. V. Archaic Words and Forms." *The Scotsman*, Nov. 29, 1887, p. 7.

2 For details see W.F.H. Nicolaisen, *Scottish Place-Names* (London: B.T. Batsford, 1976).

3 See the appropriate maps and text in *An Historical Atlas of Scotland c. 4000-c. 1600*. Eds. Peter McNeill and Ranald Nicholson (St. Andrews, Trustees of the Conference of Scottish Medievalists, 1975); also Nicolaisen, *loc. cit.*

4 See Nicolaisen, 'Life in Scandinavian Lewis', *The Scots Magazine* 78, No. 4 (Jan. 1963), p. 329; also *Scottish Place-Names*, pp. 97-98.

5 "Surnames were rare in the Highlands till the sixteenth and seventeenth centuries when the younger and minor clans escaped the tutelage of the Island lords and the 'lieutenancies' of Huntly and Argyll. Individuals were designated by a string of ancestors, ending usually with the name of the croft or farm occupied, such as: John MacHamish vic Aonas vic Allister Reoch *in* Ballachroan (1679). After the '45 matters rapidly changed; movements and expeditions to the Lowlands necessitated surnames; and these were adopted either from the clan to which the individual really belonged or to which he attached himself, or from the name of the district or place of origin. It has been a common thing for the smaller septs to sink their real surname in the bigger tribal or clan name." Alexander Macbain, "The Study of Highland Personal Names", *Celtic Review* 2 (1905-06), p. 63.

6 According to P.H. Reaney, *A Dictionary of British Surnames* (London: Routledge & Kegan Paul, 1958), p. xv. See also Basil Cottle, *The Penguin Dictionary of Surnames*. Second Edition (London: Allen Land, 1978), p. 18.

7 The exact figures are given by George F. Black, *The Surnames of Scotland: Their Origin, Meaning, and History* (New York: The New York Public Library, 1946), pp. xxiii-xxiv.

8   See Cottle, p. 19: also P.H. Reaney, *The Origin of English Surnames* (London: Routledge & Kegan Paul, 1967), p. 36.

9   The studies are still in progress and therefore not yet available in published form. As models might serve Rolf Bergmann, "Ein Kölner Namenverzeichnis aus der Zeit Erzbischof Hermanns I." *Rheinische Vierteljahrsbläter* 29 (1964), pp. 168-74; Rudolf Schützeichel, "Köln und das Niederland" (Groningen: J.B. Wolters, 1963); 'Die Kölner Namenliste des Londoner Ms. Harley 2805.' *Namenforschung– Festschrift für Adolf Bach* (Heidelberg: Carl Winter, 1965), pp. 97-126.

10   Some interesting facts and observations on this topic are contained in Gillis Kristensson, *Studies on the Early 14th-century Population of Lindsey (Lincolnshire). Scripta Minora Regiae Societatis Humaniorum Litterarum Lundensis* 1976-1977: 2 (Lund: W.K. Gleerup, 1977). See especially pp. 6-12.

11   There is at present no surname equivalent to the Scottish Place-Name Survey of the School of Scottish Studies in the University of Edinburgh, and George Black's *Dictionary* (see note 7) remains the only extensive collection of Scottish surnames and their early recorded forms. David Dorward, *Scottish Surnames* (Edinburgh: William Blackwood, 1978) is a popular presentation of familiar names and their background.

12   G. Fransson, *Medieval English Surnames of Occupation, 1100-1350* (Lund: C.W.K. Gleerup 1950); B. Sundby, 'Some Middle English Occupational Terms.' *English Studies* 33 (1952), pp. 18-20; M.M. Postan, *The Medieval Economy and Society: An Economic History of Britain in the Middle Ages* (Harmondsworth: Penguin Books, 1975), pp. 226-227.

13   Reaney, *Dictionary*, p. xxxviii.

14   Early documentation, when given, is from Black, s.v.

15   These lists can be considerably expanded by the inclusion of complementary evidence from England, for which see, for example, Reaney, *Origin*, pp. 204-08. See also Elsdon, C. Smith, *The Book of Smith* (New York: Nellen, 1978).

16   Fransson, p. 30, and Reaney, *Origin*, pp. xxxviii and 181.

17   Postan, p. 227.

18   Reaney, *Origin*, p. xxxviii (after Fransson).

19   From England we might add *Coward, Eweart, Gathard, Geldart, Lambert, Nothard, Oxnard*, and *Swinard* (Reaney, *ibid.*, p. 177).

20   Bogislav von Lindheim, 'Die weiblichen Genussuffixe im Altenglischen.' *Anglia* 76 (1958), p.500.

21   *Spinster* besides *spinner* would also belong here but does not seem to have resulted in a surname. The Modern English word has, of course, undergone a semantic shift.

22   Reaney, *Origin*, p. 356.

23   Reaney, *Dictionary*, p. xxxviii.

24   Cottle, p. 9.

25   Most nicknames appear to be based on eye-judgments, but some moral and mental characteristics are also singled out.

26   Black, p. 68.

27   Rosalind Mitchison, *Life in Scotland* (London: B.T. Batsford, 1978), p. 15. See also note 5 above.

28   One curious side-effect has been that modern surname lexicographers have been forced to emphasise expressly that "the purpose of a Dictionary of Surnames is to explain the meaning of names, not to treat Genealogy and family history" (Reaney, *Dictionary*, p. x), or that 'names, not their bearers, are the characters' in such a compendium (Cottle, p. 10).

American Speech **58, 1 (Spring 1980) 36-45**

Onomastic Dialects

D ESPITE its assertive title, this essay is not intended to be conclusively descriptive but is rather a quest for something that is linguistic in nature – dialect – but that is also onomastic. It is a quest that has to define its goal as it progresses, for, to the best of my knowledge, the term Onomastic Dialect has hitherto only once appeared in print and has no precise definition yet.[1] It is therefore necessary to interpret the term as well as to give it theoretical underpinning.

Linguistic and onomastic items are sometimes appropriately treated alike, particularly in dialect study or linguistic geography. It would be unwise to introduce the term 'regional' at this point, not only because the plea has recently been made that the neighbouring discipline of folklore should employ the term 'region' more precisely (Nicolaisen 1976b), but also because the term may suggest ready-made areas defined largely on the basis of extralinguistic and extraonomastic factors.[2] To be sure, some linguistic and onomastic regions coincide with other kinds of cultural regions because they have arisen from similar sociocultural responses to the natural habitat.[3] Yet, despite the recognition of various dialect areas in the recent linguistic-geographic research of the Linguistic Atlas of the United States and Canada and the Dictionary of American Regional English, we are still far from the designation of regions, whether "functional" or "formal" (Minshull 1967, pp. 18, 25), with a complex interdependence of several phenomena. Nevertheless, it is possible to examine the geographical distribution of words and names and their potential interrelationship.

Linguistic geography and toponymic research have so much in common that it is reasonable for a leading dialectologist (McDavid 1958) to call for the joint study of the "underlying cultural forces" that cause, for example, some of the major differences in place-name syntax, and to request more cooperation that would "utilize the answers obtained in one field as an aid toward solving the problems of the other".[4] Certainly the study of language and the study of names are highly compatible pursuits, as the overlapping membership rosters of the American Dialect Society and the American Name Society show. The most obvious onomastic parallel to dialect geography is the study of the geographical distribution of place-names. Endeavours so far have concentrated on determining the spatial scatter of 'generics' (common nouns like *creek* and *brook* used as part of proper names). Of these there are, as Meredith Burrill (1956, p. 226) has determined, "something over 750", of greatly varying frequency, distribution, and linguistic origin. Wilbur Zelinsky (1955, p. 346), who has done research on generics in the northeastern United States, concludes that "no two of the terms studied have identical or even near identical patterns of distribution".

The generics *creek* and *brook* are complementary in their distribution. *Creek* "occurs in considerable numbers almost everywhere west and south of the Adirondacks and Hudson River in association with medium-sized streams", whereas the distribution of *brook* is "in most respects the converse of that of *creek*, for it is well represented in New England, New York, New Jersey, and northern Pennsylvania but is relatively uncommon elsewhere" (Zelinsky 1955, pp. 324-25).[5] These two contrasting distribution patterns reflect dialect differences in the use of *creek* and *brook* as appellatives in nontoponymic contexts, although it appears that the distribution of toponymic generics is, in this case, slightly more limited (Kurath 1949, p. 61, fig. 93).[6]

Although linguistic, geographic and toponymic research are bound to reinforce each other, the sources of relevant information will of necessity differ considerably.[7] Lexical items to be studied will come from selected native speakers of the geographical varieties of American English, whereas onomastic items will be mostly culled from printed maps, some perhaps from oral tradition, but in all cases from sources anchored to the ground and therefore much less mobile than individual informants. This is not to say that place-names never migrate – they do, especially in this country – but toponymically applied generics are less easily up-rooted than their non-onomastic counterparts in the general lexicon. Words are as footloose as the people who use them, while place-names tend to be stationary.

In comparison with *creek* and *brook*, both used widely and densely in the names of medium-sized and smaller watercourses, the generic hydronym *lick* has quite a different distribution. On the basis of his map evidence for the American northeast, Zelinsky (1955, p. 329) adjudges it to be a "Southernism, probably of late origin along the frontier", but despite its much more limited distribution, *lick*, like *creek* and *brook*, has a toponymic scatter similar to that of its lexical use.[8] All three terms are semantically accessible and productive in the speech of the areas where they occur. *Creek*, *brook*, and *lick* indicate by their spatial scatters different lexical choices for the naming of streams in American English. These three hydronyms suggest one criterion for toponymic dialects: onomastic variation influenced by dialectal variations in the lexicon. In this category – and there are many thousands of such names on the American map – the relationship between lexicon and onomasticon is very close, and it is therefore not always easy to make a persuasive distinction between linguistic and onomastic dialects; nevertheless they are not identical.

The distribution of the generic *kill*, as in *Fishkill*, *Catskill*, and *Cobleskill*, also studied and mapped by Zelinsky (1955, p. 330), has different implications, stemming mainly from two facts. On the one hand, *kill* is not of English origin; and, on the other, it is absent from nontoponymic use in the English dialects of the area in which it occurs as a part of place-names. It is derived from Dutch *kil* 'stream' and is limited "to the Hudson Valley, Catskills, and upper Delaware Valley" (Zelinsky 1955, p. 329), the area settled by the Dutch. Despite its lack of integration into the English dialects of the area as an appellative, it is a significant feature in the determination of onomastic dialects.[9] For present-day English speakers in the Hudson valley, the Catskills, and the Delaware valley, the hydronymic element *-kill* and names formed from it are semantically opaque, whereas *creek* and *brook* are transparent. It is the opacity of *-kill* that permits its use in the name of an extensive mountain range, the Catskills, which would otherwise have been semantically confusing. Names containing *-kill* are only slightly more accessible in ordinary lexical meaning than pre-European native American names like Delaware, Susquehanna, and Chenango. It is present in the onomasticon of the area but not in its lexicon.

In another part of the country, the distribution of the generic *bayou* in stream names is "a partial index to the areal spread of the cultural influence of a given ethnic group during the 18th century" (West 1954, p. 73), in this case of the Louisiana French. Radiating from Louisiana, *bayou* is found along much of the Gulf Coast and northwards up the Mississippi and sporadically along the lower Ohio and Wabash rivers. Some names formed with this generic occur outside its focal area.[10] Unlike *kill*, *bayou* (French *bayouc* or *bayouque* from Choctaw *bayuk* 'sluggish water course') has passed into English as an appellative and has developed a wider range of connotations. West has argued (and I understand that his conclusions have support in the evidence collected for the Dictionary of American Regional English) that the present-day lexical use is both more extensive and later than the employment of *bayou* as a toponymic generic, though some names containing the element may have disappeared from our maps. Whatever the status of *bayou* as a borrowed lexical item in English, it is

97

certain that most names containing *bayou* – *Bayou Beaucoup*, *Bayou Gauche*, *Bayou Jaune*, *Bayou L'Ours* – were created by speakers of American French, not American English (Leeper 1976, pp. 25-29).

Apart from the New York Dutch *kill*, then, all the hydronymic generics discussed so far have parallels in the current English dialects of the areas in which they occur. Since their lexical meaning is accessible to the user, connotations might interfere in the denotative onomastic function. Although the distribution of lexically meaningful toponymic elements, such as these, can be useful in defining dialect areas, its value for establishing onomastic or, more precisely, toponymic dialects is less obvious. What is needed is research into the geographical distribution of particular types of 'whole' names, especially those that are meaningless on the lexical level, not compounded with the same generic, and unanalysable morphologically. This is not to say, however, that the absence of lexical meaning somehow turns an onomastic item into a better, or more complete, name; to function denotatively, or to perform satisfactorily what Searle (1969, p. 174) has called the "speech act of identifying reference", a name does not have to be meaningless lexically, although it frequently is.

Similar to *kill* in their opacity to Americans, are the geographic names of Spanish linguistic origin utilised by H.F. Raup and W.B. Pounds (1953) to determine the sphere of Spanish-Mexican influence in California. Words such as *Fresno*, *Madera*, and *Manteca*, although descriptive in Spanish, have lost their connotative potential since passing into English names, and place-names derived from family names like *Vallejo*, *Vaca*, and *Amador* have shared that fate. It is open to question whether Spanish place-names commemorating saints, such as *San Diego* or *Santa Barbara*, are lexically meaningless in English. The very forms of the words for 'saint' – *san* or *santa* – stamp them as exotically unEnglish. These names are on the map today as the result of what can be termed onomastic dialect variation; though ultimately of Spanish origin, the names are now regarded as typically Californian and Southwestern.

There are some American place-names that have never had any connotative function on this side of the Atlantic; nor did they have lexical meaning when first given. They are the so-called classical town names (Zelinsky 1967), the heartland of which is central New York State with its Homer, Marathon, Ithaca, Syracuse, Troy, Rome, Attica, Cincinnatus, and Vestal. Unlike other cultural transfers, such as Plymouth, Andover, Hamburg, and Warsaw, the classical names were not transported from Europe because of any direct contact with their native locale but were rather created as an onomastic expression of the Classical Revival, based on "the notion ... that the United States is the latter-day embodiment of the virtues and ideals of ancient Greece and Rome" (Zelinsky

1967, p. 463). Starting in west-central New York in the last two decades of the eighteenth century, this toponymic innovation continued to spread across the country from east to west until the present century (Zelinsky 1967, figures 3-14), providing fascinating data for "the historical geography of an American idea" (as Zelinsky subtitled his 1967 article).[11] Whether or not one accepts completely Stewart's (1945, p. 185) imaginative reconstruction of a committee deliberating and conceiving this nomenclature, there are almost 3000 names representing an onomastic dialect unknown in this country as recently as two centuries ago. There are noticeable centres of gravity for this feature, as in the states of New York, Ohio, Iowa, Missouri, Illinois, Kansas, and Pennsylvania, each of which has over a hundred occurrences of classical town names; but none of the first forty-eight states is without examples (Zelinsky 1967, figure 1). It is a dialect feature current everywhere, but it cannot be linked directly to anything a linguistic atlas will ever show, being closer to transferred nonlinguistic cultural traits, like the imitation Greek column (Zelinsky 1967, p. 486), than to the lexicon of American English.

The subcategory that shifts classical personal names to place-names, including *Homer, Cincinnatus, Hector,* and *Virgil,* is tied to another American specialty in place nomenclature, the use of surnames like *Washington, Worthington, Endicott, Jefferson,* and *Dewey* as names of places, without the addition of a generic – although the latter formation also exists, as in *Johnson City* or *Broome County.* It would be equally fruitless to look for lexical etymologies in this toponymic category, although the easy shift from one name class to another awaits satisfactory explanation,[12] as does the geographical distribution and diffusion of this name type. There are many more than 3000 such names to investigate, not only for their chronological and geographical distribution, but also for their role in the human endeavor to continue life beyond its natural limit. The classical town names and the surnames turned place-names have a sociocultural dimension that goes beyond the traditional concept of dialect.

When a name does contain a lexically meaningful generic, that term must be mapped in relationship to other generics for similar features. For example, *river* and *creek* contrast in the size of their referents, but a different contrast is involved when there are three terms – *river, creek,* and *branch.* or *river, creek,* and *run* – rather than two only (McDavid 1958, p. 71; Zelinsky 1955, p. 322). All terms in such a set should be mapped together, with an identification of the relative sizes of the watercourses and a complementary mapping of any homonymous terms, such as *creek* 'inlet from the sea'. All semantic features distinguishing the members of a set need to be identified. Celia Millward (1972), in her study of the place-name generics of colonial Rhode Island, pointed out nine oppositions that structure the toponymic vocabulary, for example, water versus land, contiguity versus noncontiguity to water, natural versus artificial, vegetation versus lack of vegetation, isolation versus continuity, and the one just mentioned – relative size: "For example, a *brook* in Rhode Island is distinguished from a *river* by relative size, from a *pond* by its lack of isolation, from a *creek* by its fresh water, and from a *neck* by its liquidity" (p. 51). Such binary contrasts structure the "lexical field" of topographic terms and the names formed with generics chosen from that "field". Whether the notion of "lexical field" can be extended as an "onomastic field" for names lacking generics or other lexically meaningful parts is a question that needs separate treatment (Nicolaisen, 1982).

Neither the mapping of lexical items culled from the toponymic sector of the vocabulary nor the patterning of lexically meaningless whole names can by itself lead to a full understanding of onomastic dialects. Although onomastic dialects will always have connections with linguistic dialects and an onomasticon will always have parallels with the relevant lexicon, it is necessary to emphasise the nonlinguistic onomastic criteria (see, however, note 7). What counts is not whether a name is lexically meaningful but that it functions differently from lexical items. The denotative isolation of a person or place (or boat or horse or hurricane) is a mental process very different from the connotative, inclusive embracing of a set of similar items. It is the difference between *Callas* and *opera singer*, *Chicago* and *city* (or even *metropolis*), *Secretariat* and *racehorse*. The recognition of such isolating names demands a kind of knowledge not required of words (Nicolaisen 1978) but makes understanding in the true sense unnecessary. So much is usually made of the naming process, the creation of names, that it is easy to forget that in the vast majority of instances we are called upon not to name but to know names; some of us may never be asked to name at all.

In the sense in which it is presented here, the notion of an onomasticon, as separate from though related to a lexicon, first suggested itself to me during a detailed examination of the naming needs and naming practices of settlers in a new country. Ninth-century Norse settlers in the Scottish north and west had to convert a virtually nameless natural landscape into a cultural one through naming (Nicolaisen 1979-80), an existential act that relied partly on name models and actual names with which the settlers were familiar in their home countries. Likewise in that other big area of onomastic endeavour, the naming of children, parents depend on a conventionally accepted onomasticon of personal names, from which only the very rich, the very stupid, or the very enterprising dare to depart.

We all acquire an onomasticon as well as a lexicon, and use it appropriately in recognition, in thinking, and in talking. The result is a large number of onomastic idiolects, individual name repertoires, with the range and degree of competence varying from person to person. Naturally, each such onomastic idiolect is strongly influenced by its community of name users and name givers, who make up an onomastic dialect area that is also culturally and socially stratified. A toponymic dialect would be shaped by toponymic items from the lexicon and their geographical distribution (like *creek*, *brook*, and *lick*), but also by other important factors: by the impact of linguistic and onomastic substrata (French *bayou* and Dutch *kill*), by the toponymies created by earlier settlers (*Fresno* and *San Diego* from the Spanish, but also *Susquehanna* and *Chenango* from the American Indians), by the creation of new name types through cultural transfer (*Homer*, *Syracuse*, *Marathon* from a Mediterranean civilisation) or shift from personal name to place-name (*Washington*, *Endicott*, *Jefferson*), by the structuring of onomastic fields (*Homer*, *Syracuse*, and *Marathon* as interdependent in meaning), by the sequence of naming, by the selection of features named (Stewart 1943), and above all by the configuration of the topography.

It is worth reiterating that, if there is one major difference between a structured lexicon and a structured onomasticon, it is that the latter has no contents, cannot function as an onomastic web, without a direct link between each name and the discrete, single, frequently unique feature – whether man-made or natural, whether fictitious or real – that has been chosen to bear it. Just as names identify individual features, so the nameability of such features is predetermined by a culture's structured view of the world "out there".[13] We cannot name what we do not perceive, but we do not properly perceive a thing until we have named it. As a result of this paradox, a direct, close, and knowable relationship develops between the name and the feature (or person) named.

The isonyms that determine onomastic dialects are not always related to the lexical isoglosses of linguistic dialects; and, even when they are, only partial identity can be expected. Realising that there is such a communicative phenomenon as an onomasticon, with dialectal and idiolectal varieties, is one thing; it is quite another to study it in detail – to discover its structure; to delineate its boundaries and its areas of overlap with related linguistic dialects; to identify the geographic, sociocultural, and personal features that shape it; to find its relationship to topography and social conditions; to gauge its relative density; to monitor its gradual acquisition; to measure competence and even felicity in the use of names; to investigate active and passive name knowledge; to do the hundred and one different things that have already been done in the study of the lexicon. These important tasks should be undertaken, for the innovative concepts of an onomasticon and of onomastic dialects promise to be valuable in the study of names and especially in the development of methods that are as appropriate, sophisticated, and adequate as that study requires.

Notes

1   I have used the term in my own teaching, in a number of public lectures, and in a preliminary fashion in print in 1978.

2   Forty definitions of the geographical concept 'region' are given by Odum and Moore (1938, p. 2).

3   As early as 1911, R.H. Whitbeck claimed that "the place-names of the region will reflect the social and economic conditions of the people who bestowed the names" and that "the peculiarities of the people of different regions record themselves, not only in customs, laws, and institutions, but also in the names of places" (p. 281).

4   McDavid and O'Cain (1976, p. 28) also attempt "to indicate some of the possible ways in which data from the Linguistic Atlas may be of interest to the name researcher". Some topographical terms are part of that data.

5   Edward Hale (1930, p. 158) states that "one will generally find the word creek up and down the Hudson and the Mohawk and on each side back in the country. Further one will generally find the small streams called creeks in parts of the country settled by people who came from this district, as westward through the Mohawk gap, or to the southwest down Otsego Lake and the Susquehanna." Both Hale and Burrill (1956, p. 233) associate brook primarily with New England. Burrill says, "In its widely scattered occurrences [it] sticks fairly close to the New England concept of a small, short, perennial, fairly high gradient, clear stream in hilly or mountainous terrain, though some have trouble with the clearness qualification." Burrill also points out that brook, "thanks to the power of literature, has that 'nice' or 'pleasant' connotation".

6   Zelinsky (1955, p. 320, n. 6) calls the "problem of the relationships between vernacular 'topographic' language...and the generic terms employed in place-names" a "vexing" one and deplores the fact that in 1955 it had "apparently been left wholly unexplored". This situation has since improved, but the correlation still requires much research. Two fine studies are those by Eugene Green and Rosemary M. Green (1971) and by Robert W. Bastian (1977).

7   In the past, onomastic dialects have usually been subsumed under linguistic (or lexical) dialects, a procedure that obscures the need for recognising discrete dialects in the onomasticon apart from the lexicon. Even Burrill's (1956, p. 240) "nomenclature regions", which probably come closest to my notion of "onomastic dialects", are expressly based on "a reasonably homogeneous complex of generic terms and applications", almost equal to "the distribution of individual terms or groups of terms". An innovative concept of linguistics that (without becoming amorphous) is wide enough to embrace onomastics, despite the semantic and functional differences between words and names, would require certain modifications in the present discussion but not make it unnecessary (Nicolaisen 1974, 1976a). One of the terminological desiderata, in that respect, would be an

"umbrella" term for both words and names. If it could be prized away from the traditional grammatical usage, appellative might be a good candidate for that slot, as it would lucidly state one of the major functions of both lexical and onomastic items. In this paper, however, the long accepted, though not very satisfactory, classical use of the term *appellativum* in contrast to the nomen proprium has been retained, in order to avoid further confusion.

8 The primary meaning of lick "spot to which animals resort to lick the salt or salt earth" is of only marginal concern here. Its toponymic use has not been mapped, but according to Zelinsky (1955, p. 331), "the use of lick as a full generic term for stream occurs in scattered localities in West Virginia and in the adjoining portions of Virginia, Kentucky, Ohio, and western Maryland – as well as in north-central Pennsylvania".

9 Kurath (1949) stresses several times that "the Dutch word kill for a small watercourse survives only in the names of certain creeks or rivers in the Dutch settlement area" (p. 61) and "is no longer used as a common noun" (p. 24, also p. 13). In his figure 93 he maps only place-name use. Stewart (1945, p. 110) asserts that kill is one of the Dutch words which "the English never accepted".

10 Burrill (1956, pp. 227-28) points out that there are "outlying occurrences in New Jersey, Michigan, Nebraska, Montana, California" which West's method did not catch, but such outliers are only to be expected and do not compromise the validity of West's description of the main distribution.

11 According to Zelinsky (1967, p. 466), the names were spread in three ways: (1) by diffusion between neighbouring communities and persons, (2) by transportation over considerable distances as part of the mental baggage of pioneer settlers, and (3) by nearly instantaneous, but scattered, adoption over a wide territory by the social elite.

12 Kolin (1977) offers some good insights into the process.

13 Some of the best things on this subject have been said by geographers who are usually more aware than linguists of the importance of names in the cultural landscape (Burrill 1968, Orth 1972).

References

Bastian, Robert W. 1977. "Generic Place-Names and the Northern-Midland Dialect Boundary in the Midwest." Names 25: 228-36.

Burrill, Meredith F. 1956. "Toponymic Generics." Names 4: 129-37, 226-40.

——— 1968. "The Language of Geography." Annals of the Association of American Geographers 58: 1-11.

Green, Eugene, and Green, Rosemary M. 1971. "Place-Names and Dialects in Massachusetts: Some Complementary Patterns." Names 19: 240-51.

Hale, Edward E. 1930. "Dialectal Evidence in the Place-Names of Eastern New York." American Speech 5: 154-67.

Kolin, Philip C. 1977. "Jefferson Davis: From President to Place-Name." Names 25: 158-73.

Kurath, Hans. 1949. A Word Geography of the Eastern United States. Ann Arbor: Univ. of Michigan Press.

Leeper, Clare D'Artois. 1976. Louisiana Places. Baton Rouge: Legacy Pub. Co.

McDavid, Raven I., Jr. 1958. "Linguistic Geography and Toponymic Research." Names 6: 65-73.

McDavid, Raven I., Jr., and O'Cain, Raymond K. 1976. "The Name Researcher and the Linguistic Atlas." Names in South Carolina 23: 23-28.

Millward, Celia M. 1972. "Universals in Place-Name Generics." Indiana Names 3, no. 2: 48-53.

Minshull, Roger. 1967. Regional Geography. London: Hutchinson.

Nicolaisen, W.F.H. 1974. "Onomastics – An Independent Discipline?" Indiana Names 3, no. 2: 33-47.

—— 1976a. "Words as Names." Onoma 20: 142-63.

—— 1976b. "The Folk and the Region." New York Folklore 2, nos. 3-4: 143-49.

—— 1978. "Are There Connotative Names?" Names 26: 40-47.

—— 1979. "Early Scandinavian Naming in the Western and Northern Isles." Northern Scotland 3, 2: (1979-1980) 105-121.

—— 1982. "Lexical and Onomastic Fields." In Proceedings of the Thirteenth International Congress of Onomastic Sciences, Cracow 1978.

Odum, Howard W., and Moore, Harry Estill. 1938. American Regionalism. New York: Holt.

Orth, Donald J. 1972. "Words, Thought, and Landscape." Surveying and Mapping 32: 363-67.

Raup, H.F., and Pounds, William B., Jr. 1953. "Northernmost Spanish Frontier in California As Shown by the Distribution of Geographic Names." California Historical Society Quarterly 32: 43-48.

Searle, John R. 1969. Speech Acts: An Essay in the Philosophy of Language. Cambridge: Cambridge Univ. Press.

Stewart, George R. 1943. "What Is Named? – Towns, Islands, Mountains, Rivers, Capes." University of California Publications in English, no. 14: 223-32.

—— 1945. Names on the Land. New York: Random House.

West, Robert C. 1954. "The Term 'Bayou' in the United States: A Study in the Geography of Place-names." Annals of the Association of American Geographers 44: 63-74.

Whitbeck, R.H. 1911. "Regional Peculiarities in Place-names." Bulletin of the American Geographical Society 43: 273-81.

Zelinsky, Wilbur. 1955. "Some Problems in the Distribution of Generic Terms in the Place-Names of the Northeastern United States." Annals of the Association of American Geographers 45: 319-49.

—— 1967. "Classical Town Names in the United States: The Historical Geography of an American Idea." Geographical Review 57: 463-95.

Festschrift für Johannes Hubschmid zum 65.
Geburtstag. Beiträge zur allgemeinen, indogermanischen
und romanischen Sprachwissenschaft.
Otto Winkelmann & Maria Braisch (eds.) (1982) 551-563

Thirty Years Later:
Thoughts on a Viable Concept of an Old European
Hydronymy

W HEN, more than a generation of name scholars ago, the late Hans Krahe
developed and formulated his revolutionary theory of an "Old European"
stratum in the prehistory of western Indo-European languages in Europe,[1] one
of its main thrusts was the establishment of an early pre-dialectal, apparently
highly unified linguistic phase, in direct contrast to previous claims by other
scholars in support of the widespread domination of individual languages, like
Illyrian,[2] at one time or another, in many parts of central, northern and western
Europe. As is, of course, well known, Krahe partially based his controversial
concept on the perceived occurrence, in many parts of Europe north of the
Alps, of a large number of river names which, for phonological, morphological,
semantic, or distributional reasons – and sometimes a combination of several of
these – could only with difficulty, or not at all, be ascribed to individual Indo-
European languages known to have been spoken in the areas in which the names
in question occurred, but were nevertheless clearly Indo-European in character.
In a series of closely argued articles and monographs, Krahe not only attempted
to present the hydronymic materials which gave his theory substance but also
to hone that theory itself in terms of precision and persuasiveness. What had
emerged, at the time of Krahe's untimely death in 1965, was the clearly defined
notion of a system of river names which preserved for us, as no other relevant
evidence could, an echo of extraordinary linguistic unity and cohesiveness,

within the framework of the Indo-European family of languages, in what might be archaeologically termed Bronze Age Europe.

Like all new theories, the idea of a linguistic Old Europe embodying the potential of language individuation but not yet realising it had its supporters and its antagonists. One of the main arguments put forward by the latter was directed against the assumption of a "system" of river names, especially since this was perceived by them in much more rigid structural terms than Krahe had ever intended who, on the whole, preferred to speak of a much more loosely articulated hydronymic "network", a metaphor which would allow much greater openness and flexibility in determining the ways in which the various names related to each other. One of the drawbacks of the scholarly exchange which ensued was the fact that the names in question were, by and large, looked upon as lexical items with certain peculiar properties, an opinion which led to various misconceptions regarding the nature of names and their meaning and function, therefore distorting their role as evidence suitable for the investigation of linguistic archaeology. Another shortcoming of the debate was the underlying, though hardly ever clearly voiced, supposition of a more or less static linguistic stratum in which change seemed to be almost ruled out and which made it difficult to understand how the several individual languages could later emerge from it as discrete entities. It is the argument put forward in this paper that Krahe's concept of a linguistic Old Europe would have gained a greater degree of acceptance among both name scholars and linguists, but especially among the latter, if the river names concerned had been seen primarily as part of an onomasticon, or more precisely a hydronymicon, than a lexicon, and if the Old European stratum had been viewed as dynamic, not static, and as being capable of both diachronic change and synchronic variation.

The initial stimulus which had led to this judgment, was the observation that, in the river nomenclature of the British Isles, many of those names which appear to show some close affiliation with the "Old European" hydronymy of the continent,[3] sometimes as demonstrably identical equivalents of individual continental names, neither covers the whole potential hydronymic spectrum nor displays totally haphazard geographical distribution. The British Isles, especially the British mainland, are so important in this respect because in contrast to many areas of continental Europe, both the river names of the Old European stratum and the geographical names of later individual Indo-European languages, particularly of the Celtic and Germanic varieties, must have been introduced into Britain from the continent at different times. Britain is therefore obviously an area of expansion and migration for Old European which is therefore not the earliest reachable linguistic layer beyond which there is only uncertainty, if anything. Similarly, the main representatives of Celtic – Cornish, Welsh, Cumbric, Pictish, Gaelic – and of Germanic – English, Scandinavian – spoken at one time or another in the British Isles or still spoken there today, are not the local descendants of the earlier insular Old European stratum but rather emigrant offshoots of the continental descendants of continental Old European. No modern language spoken in Britain is therefore directly, genetically traceable through its earlier phases, to insular Old European. This undoubted lack of continuity in linguistic evolution, despite the cognate character of the languages involved, has, however, the advantage of permitting us to make certain pronouncements which are not possible in areas of unbroken linguistic evolution. In particular, it gives us the opportunity to de-emphasise the static aspects of the Old European stratum and to parade its obvious dynamism as inherent in geographical expansion, and to explore particular kinds of names which can be shown to have crossed the Channel, always bearing in mind the vagaries of survival, especially of detectable and detected survival, from a period about 3500 years ago.

Given these encouraging opportunities, it is incumbent upon us to go beyond the statement that certain river names demonstrate the presence of speakers of Indo-European in Britain before any Celt ever set foot on British soil. The isolation of such names in the extensive river-nomenclature of the British Isles is only a first step in this respect, albeit an essential one, and even the exciting discovery that, let us say, the Scottish river names *Adder* and *Ayr* have identical equivalents in the German river names *Oder* and *Ahr,* or that the name *Yealm* in Devonshire has a twin in *Alma* (Esturia), or that the several British river names *Hail, Hayle, Haill,* etc. are identical with French *Seille,* Spanish *Sella* (<*Salia) and that Scottish *Shiel* probably also belongs to this group, in only a broad hint of the complex relationships which may be laid bare if painstakingly investigated.[4] Naturally such proven identity is stronger evidence than mere derivation from the same root or use of the same morphological elements but, in the long run, does not have greater plausibility than these if it continues to be interpreted as either accidental or as a purely lexical response to the nature of the watercourses in question. Anyone who has seen the *Blackadder* and *Whiteadder* in Berwickshire, as well as the *Oder,* or the *Ayr* as well as the *Ahr,* will have great difficulty in defining what the common environmental conditions might have been which provoked the same semantic response. A more satisfying, and potentially more successful, question might well be what onomastic items were transferred from the continent to Britain rather than what lexical material appropriate for the naming of streams made it across the Channel, or, put somewhat differently, what significant features of the Old European hydronymicon, i.e. onomasticon, were transferred rather than what selective parts of the Old European lexicon.

It is, after all, unlikely that the speech acts of naming and of using names were notably different in the second millennium B.C. from two or three thousand years later, and careful adaptation of recent research into the early names given by the Anglo-Saxons after their arrival in England,[5] or of the naming habits of the earliest Scandinavian settlers of Scotland,[6] or the naming strategies of Europeans as part of their settlement of the American Eastern Shore[7] can be expected to throw light on a similar situation in linguistic prehistory (or is it *onomastic* prehistory?). As a result of such investigations it has become very clear that the traditional quest for the earliest toponymic element or place-name type employed in a particular linguistic invasion is bound to produce misleading results because it asks a practically unanswerable question. The nature of sources relevant to toponymic research is such that they will hardly ever provide clear cut evidence about the beginnings of a naming process but will with much greater ease and persuasiveness supply pointers indicative of the end of such a process. The question as to which name type or element was first used is much less answerable than the question as to which name type or element first ceased to be used. Indeed, it is altogether erroneous to assume that the early naming process consisted solely of the consecutive employment of certain elements or formations when commonsense and contemporary, as well as historically documented, experience tell us that settlers will employ different elements, types, and formations simultaneously from the very beginning.

This is where the notion of an onomasticon, distinct from, although linked to, a lexicon is so helpful. Like their later successors, the Anglo-Saxons in England, the Scandinavians in England and Scotland, or the English on the Eastern Shore, the "Old Europeans" arriving in Britain must have been familiar with the characteristics of both names and naming in those parts of the European continent from which they had come and they must have continued that onomastic usage similarly to the way in which they would continue familiar lexical usage in day-to-day communication. This would include the coining of names from suitable word stock, the transfer of particular names from their "homeland", and the giving of, probably unanalysed, name types. As far as the Old European hydronymy of Britain is concerned, we must therefore expect to find all three categories, including the *ad hoc* combination of well known bases and affixes. This might produce a name identical with one already existing on the continent or it might, through an untried permutation of elements, create a name which in that particular form had no antecedents anywhere. With regard to other identical equivalents, these might arise either from the direct transfer of a particular name or from the recreation of a special name type under appropriate circumstances, without deliberate reference to any identifiable continental name.

Those settlers naming the rivers *Adder* in Scotland may ultimately have come from the banks of the *Oder* or, which seems more likely, may have applied the name type *Oder* without necessarily analysing it lexically or etymologically. *Oder* was the kind of name one gave to rivers in Old European times. Such onomastic appropriateness would be even more applicable in the cases of names which occur several times over both on the continent and in Britain; the series *Hail, Haill, Hayle, Shiel, Seille, Salia* (< *Salia*) might be a good illustration of this principle. One might indeed extend to the Old European period the notion that migrating people carry with them in their mental baggage, not only their linguistic, especially lexical, dialects but also their onomastic dialects[8] and use these whenever naming becomes a necessary part of settling in a new and, for the incomer, virtually nameless environment.

Such a procedure essentially presupposes that, in the case of the Old Europeans, their "network" or "system" of river names was not undifferentiated either geographically or chronologically and that, consequently, through appropriate methods, it might be possible to detect some indication as to where in that vast area of Europe in which river names belonging to this stratum have been found the settlers reaching Britain may have come from, and at what time within the Old European period they may have crossed the Channel. Neither conclusion will be easily reached but there may be clues which we have been overlooking simply because unity rather than diversity has been the overriding image of that prehistoric stratum. Naturally, such correlations would be most convincingly established if it could be shown that certain areas on the continent favoured certain river names and that there were corresponding areas in Britain.

It is, on the other hand, of course, also possible, indeed probable, that the character of Old European as brought into Britain did not remain unchanged but continued to develop, a process which included the creation of new types or putting special emphasis on certain existing name types either in the whole of Britain or in more limited regions. If the five rivers *Carron* in Scotland, for example, are definitely Old European, and not Early Celtic, they may well be instances of regional innovation in Britain, as the *-no-/-nâ-* formation from the root *kar-* "hard" is only found in an insular context whereas *-nt-* formations abound on both the continent and in Britain. The formation *Karīsâ,* on the other hand, seems to be limited to south-west Britain (Carey, Cary, Ceri [2]). Both *Kar(r)ona* and *Karisa* may, by implication, also be late Old European, at least within a context of its "insular" variety, for it is surely legitimate to ascribe names to this pre-Celtic Indo-European stratum in Britain, even if they have no exact counterparts in the continent. By extending this methodological principle a little further, it may also be claimed with reasonableness that the onomastic dialect of Old European, as introduced into and further developed in the British Isles, may well have created new hydronymic preferences in its insular environment. By definition, it is much more difficult to prove conclusively the embeddedness of such favourite names in the Old European hydronymic "network" but if they turn up in large numbers – as a consequence of their favourite status! – and are only uncomfortably associated with the Celtic stratum, lacking plausible lexical links, for example, there is every reason to think of them in Old European terms, especially if etymologically and morphologically their Indo-European-ness is not to be doubted. In Britain, these criteria would apply to that extensive group of river names derived from the Indo-European root *tâ-/*tə- 'to flow', particularly its *m-*, *n-*, and *_l-* formations (*Team, Tame, Teviot, Thames; Tone, Tain, Tean; Taw, Tay;* and others, respectively). For this group of names the number of continental equivalents is small; for many individual names there is none. It seems compelling, therefore, to regard them under the rubric "insular Old European" and to see them as proof not only of the existence of an Old European linguistic stratum in Britain but also of its dynamic nature.

While it is always easier to associate, indeed pinpoint, the variability of linguistic and onomastic features in conjunction with new settlement areas – the English and Scandinavians in Britain, the Europeans in North America – it would be unnatural to expect a nomenclature, whether of watercourses or of other geographical features, to have remained static in areas in which population movement is not easily demonstrated or did not occur. Linguistic and onomastic changes do not only take place in "colonial" territory; they are just as likely to happen in the "homeland". In addition to searching, through careful, detailed and critical scrutiny of all the salient evidence, for discernible patterns in the geographical scatter of Old European river names on the continent, it is therefore also necessary to lay bare, if possible, chronological strata within the stratum. Not only would this approach reveal Old European as a viable entity in the linguistic prehistory of Europe, it would also provide guidance for the recognition and ultimate description of individuation, the process by which the later individual Indo-European languages said to be descendants of Old European (Germanic, Celtic, Illyrian, Venetic, Italic, and Baltic), gradually developed as discrete entities.[9] Until at least a serious attempt has been made at throwing some light on these important matters, the concept of Old European is unlikely to convince the sceptics and have the full impact which it deserves on the thinking of those engaged in unravelling the various strands of European linguistic prehistory. Both the recognition of distinct onomastic dialects and the display of chronological stratification within the stratum are essential strategies in this scholarly activity, and the insular evidence, in this respect, may well help us to understand the situation on the continent.[10] Retention and innovation, as basically opposing, but complementary forces of onomastic history, will both serve to substantiate that understanding. We cannot afford to neglect that task any longer, an undertaking which would also be quite responsive to Krahe's own intentions.[11]

References

1   Beiträge zur Namenforschung 1 (1949-50) – 6 (1955); Sprache und Vorzeit (Heidelberg 1954); Unsere ältesten Fluânamen (Wiesbaden 1964; and elsewhere).

2   For example, Julius Pokorny, Zur Urgeschichte der Kelten und Illyrer (Halle 1938).

3   See W.F.H. Nicolaisen, "Die alteuropäischen Gewässernamen der britischen Hauptinsel", Beiträge zur Namenforschung 8 (1957) 209-268; "Great Britain and Old Europe", Namn och Bygd 59 (1971) 85-105; also Scottish Studies 2 (1958) 189-196; 10 (1966) 78-87, and Chapter 9, "Pre-Celtic Names" in Scottish Place-Names: Their Study and Significance (London 1976) 173-191.

4   It is not the purpose of this paper to present new material but a new perspective. The examples mentioned have therefore been culled from the publications cited in note 3.

5   See, for instance, Margaret Gelling, Signposts to the Past: Place-Names and the History of England (London 1978) and its bibliography.

6   W.F.H. Nicolaisen, "Are There Connotative Names?", Names 26 (1978) 40-47; "Early Scandinavian Naming in the Western and Northern Isles", Northern Scotland 3, no. 2 (1979-80) 105-121.

7   Janet H. Gritzner, "Seventeenth Century Generic Place-Names: Culture and Process on the Eastern Shore", Names 20, no. 4 (1972) 231-239.

8   On this notion see W.F.H. Nicolaisen, "Onomastic Dialects", American Speech 55 (1980) 36-45.

9   An important initial attempt in this direction is Wolfgang Meid's study "Indo-European and Celtic", Proceedings of the Third International Congress of Celtic Studies (Edinburgh 1968) 45-56.

10   Evidence from the Iberian and Apennine Peninsulas may, of course, serve a similar purpose.

11   See, particularly, Unsere ältesten Fluânamen, 84-86, where he argues for the highly "dialectal" character of Old European and invited further research.

Språk och Tradition: Festskrift till Sven Benson
Svenska Landsmål och Svenskt Folkliv 106 (1983) 144-152

Scandinavian Shore Names in Shetland:
The Onomastic Sub-Dialect of a Coastscape

STUDENTS of names, as well as historians, cultural geographers, linguists, and others who explore place-names as potential raw material for their scholarly pursuits, have for a long time been aware of the value of discernible distribution patterns of names, name types, name elements, name formations, and the like, and have interpreted these both synchronically and diachronically. The most popular of such approaches has probably been the attempt to link the geographical scatter of toponymic evidence with the historical stratification of languages, or phases of languages, in a given area. More recently, paralleling the dialect geographers' treatment of regional variation in the, mostly, phonological and lexical aspects of language, it has been suggested that variations in the onomasticon, and particularly in the toponymicon, similar to those in the lexicon, fully justify the assumption of onomastic as well as linguistic dialects (Nicolaisen 1980a). Naturally, the two are frequently quite closely connected although such connection is not a prerequisite. Thus, at one end of the taxonomic spectrum of an onomastic dialect would be those lexical items in the topographic sector of the vocabulary from which names, especially name generics, are commonly formed, whereas at the other end would be fully-fledged names which, because of their linguistic provenance, have no lexical counterparts in the contemporary regional variety of the current language. Inherited name models would be somewhere in the middle, although perhaps tending towards the latter rather than the former, despite their semantic accessibility.

If the existence of onomastic dialects is an acceptable notion, then it follows that, just like their linguistic (lexical) counterparts, such dialects are capable of migrating with those whose part of their cultural profile and heritage they are.

Both groups and individuals can carry their onomastic dialects to other parts of the same country or even to other countries, as ingredients of their mental baggage and, if called upon to name, may utilise these dialects in new territory. I have previously on several occasions (Nicolaisen 1969, 1976a, 1976b, 1979-80, 1980b, 1982a) drawn attention to the ways in which Scandinavian settlers from certain parts of Norway applied their onomastic dialects to the landscape of Scotia Scandinavica from the ninth century onwards, and within that general framework it has been my special concern to point out the frequently overlooked role which the realisation and actualisation of name models played in situations in which people unskilled and inexperienced as namers were called upon to name many geographical features in a hurry (Nicolaisen 1978).

It is, of course, profitless to discuss the existence and characteristics of onomastic dialects in the abstract, even in terms of the more limited use of ninth- to thirteenth-century Norse dialects in Scotland. Particularly toponymic dialects, in their earth-bound qualities, only make sense, only have substance, in their selective, structured application to the topography of an island, let us say, or of a valley or perhaps of an area within some administrative boundary (Nicolaisen 1982b), as long as the old paradox is remembered which, on the one hand, claims that no feature of the landscape exists until it has been named, while names are, on the other hand, only given to perceived features of the landscape. Instead of regarding this as a confusing chronological conundrum, it is probably better to acknowledge that perception and naming go hand in hand, are, indeed, inextricably linked.

In this brief essay, I intend to regard the names of natural features in Shetland as part of such an onomastic dialect imported from Norway but adapted and further developed in "colonial" territory. In order to prevent the discussion from becoming either too shallow or too unmanageable I wish, within this dialect, to examine in some detail the sub-dialect of names found on or near the coast, while paying only brief attention to names associated with inland or maritime features. Particular thought will be given to the kinds of features named, as well as to the semantic status of the elements employed. As basic evidence will serve chiefly the alphabetic list of Norse appellatives found in Shetland place-names, as compiled and presented by Jakob Jakobsen in his pioneering study of *The Place-Names of Shetland* (Jakobsen 1936: 18-125; Jakobsen's name spellings are here retained). It goes without saying that such a list, first put together almost a century ago from a well informed, but somewhat idiosyncratic point of view, cannot be used uncritically in its entirety. I have, for example, for reasons stated extensively elsewhere (Nicolaisen 1959, 1960, 1965, 1976a: 57-64), not taken into account names of the type *de Bārd o' Bressay* (Ordnance Survey: Bard), *de*

Grøt o' Stavaness (O.S.: The Groot), *de Holm o' West Sandwick* (O.S.: Holm of West Sandwick), *de Hevdin o' Wadderste* (O.S.: Hevden Ness, Wetherstaness), etc. Although there cannot be any doubt that they ultimately contain Old Norse (ON) *barð, grjót, hólmr* and *hǫfði,* respectively, they must be regarded as Scottish-English formations, as attested by the definite article, the use of the preposition *o(f)* and, in some instances, the English plural *–s.* That they include Old Norse words in their Shetland Norn disguises is an indication that these terms continued to be used and understood in post-Norn times. Where the Old Norse definite article is preserved, as in *de Hevdin,* its duplication by the English definite article *de* is not tautological redundance or translation from the Old Norse but rather a sign that the Old Norse definite article was now regarded as part of the name which was no longer morphologically analysed as complex. In other words, it is highly doubtful whether there is, typologically, an Old Norse **klettar* behind every *de Kletts,* like *de Kletts o' Sjina hwita,* or **klettarnir* behind *de Klettins.* Sometimes such "morphological translations" may have taken place but as evidence from other parts of Scotland shows – in Gaelic-English bilingual contact, for example – translations of place-names are not as common as is often assumed (Nicolaisen 1975, 1976a: 53-56). Difficult to prove, it should never be taken for granted. Jakobsen himself puts forward the theory that "such words … are vividly present to the mind of the people, and are partly understood as common nouns", in Shetland English usage (Jakobsen 1976: 9).

I have also, for different reasons, separated out from my primary source material all Old Norse appellatives which occur only as specifics in compound names but never as generics. Admittedly, this may be, in some instances, due to the quirks of chance survival but since the semantic range of specifics is so much wider than that of suitable generics and reaches beyond mere topographic items, it is not surprising that specifics are more numerous, or at least less restricted, than generics which are, quite appropriately, at the heart of any onomastic dialect.

Thirdly, I have treated with caution Jakobsen's tacit assumption that all etymologically retrievable elements were semantically transparent appellatives at the time the names in question were given. I do not, for instance, share his conviction that the presence, in Shetland, of names (not on the coast, of course) containing ON *vin* "pasture" implies Scandinavian settlement earlier than 800 A.D. since *vin* was obsolete by that time in the Norwegian homeland (See also Fellows-Jensen, 1984, 154). All sorts of names, whether semantically and morphologically accessible or not, formed part of the onomastic dialect which Scandinavians transferred across the North Sea to Shetland. Every name or name type which existed in Norway at the time qualified, and it is not necessary to assume that its components were toponymically productive and lexically meaningful. Many of them, perhaps most of them, were, but this was not a precondition for their usefulness in the naming of a virtually nameless landscape.

Despite these eliminations, the remaining corpus of elements is still impressively large and quite suitable for our purposes. If one oversimplifies a little what is really a more complex picture and equates the known meaning of the underlying appellatives with the conjectured original meaning of the name generics, certain broad generalisations can be made and some informative conclusions reached.

In a conglomeration of islands, like Shetland, the network of toponyms, and especially of toponymic generics, employed to produce a structured landscape by isolating perceived topographic features and relating them to each other through naming, is generally divisible into names (and name generics) which apply to coastal features and those which are largely used in inland settings. That there are some onomastic items which may be found in both is understandable, as, for example, ON *bak(r)* 'back', *bakki* 'steep bank', *botn* 'bottom', *hamarr* 'steep rock', etc. It simply means that the appellatives incorporated in these names had a sufficiently broad semantic range, so as not to be associated with either one or the other of the two major sub-divisions. Naturally, in toponymic usage their specific 'meaning' may differ somewhat depending on whether they apply to coastal or inland features: ON *bakki* (Shetland *bakka, bakk*) refers either to a 'steep coast' (*Dunabakka* < **dunubakki*, *Sundebakk* < **sundbakki*) or to a 'bank' or 'slope' (*Swartabakk*); ON *bak(r)* is represented by the sea rocks called (*de*) *Hwālbak* 'whale back' and by the inland name *Kaldbak* 'cold ridge of hills'; ON *botn* can either be the 'head of a bay' (*Vōboiten* < **vágs-botn*) or the 'head of a little round valley' (*Gardabotten* < **garða-botn; de Hwibodden* < **kví-botn*); ON *hamarr* might be a 'ledge of rock in the hillside' (*Bratthāmar* < **bratthamarr*) or 'a flat rock by the seashore' (*Lāhamar, Lēhamar, Lāmar* < **hlað-hamarr*), etc.

The number of generic elements which have gone into the Shetland coastal nomenclature is large and their application varied as well as telling, insofar as we are given through them a glimpse of what the Norse settlers' notion of "coast" appears to have been, perceiving its dual and contradictory nature as separating land from sea while linking them at the same time. "Coast" does therefore not necessarily end where the water begins but rather, on the one hand, includes natural features which might be understood as encroachments of the sea upon the land while, on the other hand, also comprising features that are like extensions – however unconnected – of the land into the sea. Coastscapes also reveal their januslike duality insofar as they present different aspects to those who view them mostly from the land and to those who see them primarily from the sea (Eunson 1961). Sometimes the same feature may therefore well have two different names, representing two different visions, although an investigation of that kind of onomastic doubling is not part of this essay.

In view of this mediating function of the idea of "coast" or "shore", the number of generics (and their corresponding topographic features) emphasising the notion of "edge" or "separation" is quite small; examples would be *bakki* 'steep coast' in *Dunabakka* < ON **dunubakki* and *Sundebakk* < ON **sundbakki* (note, however, that in both instances the specifics refer to the sea and not to the land!); *berg* 'rock' in *Brattaberg* < ON **brattaberg* 'steep rocky coast' and *Dunaberg* < ON **dunuberg* 'roar (of the surf) rock'; *bust* 'bristle' > 'steep part of coast, tapering into point or ridge' in *Sinnabust* < ON **sinu-bust* 'grass ridge'; *eið* 'isthmus, neck of land' in *Brē* < ON **breið-eið* 'broad neck of land' and the neighbouring *Mēves* (*grind*) < **Mēved* < ON **mæf-eið* 'narrow neck of land'; *klif* 'cliff, bank' in *de Hedliklif* < ON **hellu-klif* 'rocky cliff'; and *pallr* 'step, shelf' > 'high plateau' in *de Fjardepall* < ON **fjarðar-pallr* 'firth plateau' (note again the reference to the sea in the specific).

As far as names are concerned that single out land features jutting out into the sea, there are two basic categories – those actually connected with the land above water level and those separated from it by water. To the first category would belong such elements as *blað* 'blade, leaf' in *Ørablā* < ON **<øyrar-blað* '(leaf-shaped) tongue of land near a sandbank'; *gajl* 'gable' in *Orknagabel*, referring to a steep, projecting part of the coast originally called *Orka; hǫfði* 'promontory' in *Hohevd(a)* < ON **há-hǫfði* 'high promontory', *Lambahefda* < ON **lamba- hǫfði* 'lamb promontory', *Stūrhevda* < ON **stór- hǫfði* 'big promontory'; *koddi* 'pillow' > 'something baggy' in *Lambakodda* < ON **lamba-koddi* 'rounded point of land of the lambs', *Runkakoddi* 'point of land with the bulky rocks' (ON *hrúnki* 'a big person'), and *Tøfakoddi, Tēfakodda, Tøvakoddi*, and the like, < ON **þæfakoddi* 'fulling point' (Jakobsen 1936: 68 explains this compound as 'rounded rock, point, or small basin at the shore, where wadmal formerly was stretched out to be fulled by the alternating tides'). Like, for instance, *Hundikoddi* 'place where puppies were usually drowned', the term may therefore refer to either (or both) the point and the adjacent water feature; the latter is described by the names *Flukodda* < ON **flóð-koddi* 'floodbay' ('a small semicircular bay, surrounded by rocks which are partly submerged at flood-tide'); *lúðr* 'stick, rod' in *Longaluder* < ON **langi lúðr* 'long tongue of land'; *múli* 'muzzle' > 'rounded promontory' in *Blōmul, Blūmul* < ON **blá-múli* 'blue promontory'; *nes* 'promontory' in *Brimnes* < ON **brim-nes* 'surf promontory',

Hwidanes < ON **hvita nes* 'white promontory', *Mjōnes* < ON **mjáfa nes* 'slender promontory', and many others; *(h)núfr* 'promontory' in *de Bānuf* < ON **boða-núfr* 'breakers-promontory', *Blōnuf* < ON **blánúfr* 'blue promontory', *Hulmsnof* < ON **hólms-núfr* 'islet promontory'; *nos* 'nose' > 'point of rock' in *de Skarfsnos* < ON **skarfs-nos* 'barren point of rock' or 'cormorant point'; *pallr* 'step, bench' > 'angling rock' in *de Sōpall* < ON **sá-pallr* 'bait rock'; *pynt* 'something jutting out' in *Stūrapont* 'big point'; *sporðr* '(fish) tail' in *de Hellaspor* < ON **hellu-sporðr* 'flat, rocky point'; *tangi* 'tongue of land' in *Fiska-teng*, etc. < ON **fiska-tangi* 'fishing rock', *Gronateng, Grønitong* < ON **grænitangi* 'green point', *Nestonga* < ON **nes-tangi* 'promontory point', and several others; and *øyrr (eyrr)* 'a flat sand- or gravel-bank, jutting out into the sea' in *Littlør* < ON **litla øyrr* 'little sandbank', *Muklør* < ON **mikla øyrr* 'large sandbank', *Vadlør* < ON **vaðil-øyrr* 'shallows point', and others.

In the naming of coastal features completely surrounded by water, sometimes submerged or partially submerged in it, the following generics are involved: *boði* 'breakers, sunken rock' in *Gamlebā* < ON **gamli boði* 'old rock' or *Litlabā* < ON **litli boði* 'little rock'; *fles* 'a flat skerry in the sea' in *de Maraflesjins* < ON **mara flesjarnar* 'horse skerries'; *hólmr* 'islet' in *Brattholm* < ON **bratthólmr* 'steep islet', *Fladholm* < ON **flathólmr* 'flat islet', *Nøstholm* < ON **nausthólmr* 'boat-berth islet', etc.; *klettr* 'rock' in *Stūraklett* 'big rock (in the sea)'; *látr* 'litter, resting place (for seals)' in *de Fiskalōders* < ON **fiska-látr* 'fish skerry'; *lúðr* 'stick, rod' in *Ongerste luder*, a rock in the sea; *rif* 'reef in the sea' in *de Hevdariv* < ON **hofða-rif* 'promontory reef' (or 'the reef of *Hevda*'); *sker* 'skerry' in *de Utskerris* < ON **útsker* 'outer skerry', *Brōrien Skerri* < ON **bræðranna sker* 'the brothers' skerry'; *stakkr* 'stack, pile' in *Blōstakk* < ON **blá-stakkr* 'blue high rock (in the sea)', *Grōstakk* < ON **grá-stakkr* 'gray high rock (in the sea)', *Gronastakk, Gronistakk* < ON **græni stakkr* 'green high rock' (with grass growing on top), etc.; *steinn* '(sea) rock' in *Lōrasten* (= *stenlōra*) < ON **ljóra-steinn* 'high rock in the sea with an opening through the centre of it'; and *øy* 'island' in *Balta* < ON **Balt(a)-øy* 'Balti's Island', *Bressa(y)* < ON **Brús(a)-øy* 'Brúsi's island', *Burra* < ON **borga(r)-øy* 'fortification island', and many others. These names in -*øy* pose a dilemma because many of them, especially those associated with sizable islands, can be seen as separate entities forming their own circumscribed, insular onomastic fields.

Names primarily associated with the sea often apply to features shaped by the land and therefore contiguous to it; in some instances, however, the features named are found on the land as the result of inroads made by the force of the water. All the features involved represent the notion of "water vs. land", one of the most basic distinctions (Millward 1972: 50). Toponymic generics employed in this category are: *bogi* 'bend' > 'cove' in *de Ørabog* < ON **øyrar-bogi* 'sandbank cove'; *botn* 'end' in Vōboiten < ON **vágsbotn* 'bay-head'; *fjǫrðr* 'firth, bay', usually now superseded by English *firth* as in *Burrafirth, Catfirth, Collafirth*, etc. (names of fishing grounds are not included in this paper); *gjá* 'ravine' in *Blōgjo* < ON **blá-gjá* 'blue ravine', *Brēgjo* < ON **breið-gjá* 'broad ravine', *Gulgjo* < ON **gul-gjá* 'gold ravine', and several others; *hellir* 'cave' in *Dūnheljar* < ON **dyn-hellir* 'cave of the roar (of the sea)', Hondsheljar < ON **hunds-hellir* 'dog cave' (a place where pups were drowned); *ker* 'tub, vessel' > 'cave' in *de Selkēr* < ON ** sel-ker* 'seal cave'; *mynni* (*minni*) 'mouth, opening' > 'inlet' in *Kleverminn* < ON **kleberg-mynni* 'soapstone inlet' or *'Kleberg* inlet', *Vog Minn* < ON **vág-mynni* 'the inlet to Gunnister Voe'; *sund* 'sound' in *Hul(m)sund* < ON **hólmsund* 'islet sound'; *vágr* 'creek, bay' in *Hamnavoe* < ON **hafnar-vágr* 'harbour bay'.

It goes without saying that the coastscape portrayed by the generics cited, and by the names in which they occur, is a highly visual one, regardless of whether the names in question isolate features seen as part of the landscape or the seascape or as belonging to both. For this reason, the major characteristics of generics differentiating otherwise similar features are size and shape – *hólmr* vs. *øy*, *vík* vs. *vágr*, *steinn* vs. *stakkr* or *klettr*, and the whole array of *blað*, *hǫfði*, *koddi*, *lúðr*, *múli*, *nes*, *(h)núfr*, *nǫs*, *pynt*, *tangi* for differently sized and shaped promontories, emphasising the continuous interaction between land and sea. Many specifics reinforce these primary qualities but also add other visual characteristics, especially colour, as part of a quest for greater discrimination and precision achievable through the use of compound names. Another important facet of several toponymic compounds is the employment of other lexical items or of names referring to nearby geographical features, as specifics, thus confirming our contention that both *nomina* and *nominata*, i.e. names and features named, are perceived to exist through interaction with other *nomina* and *nominata*. In this respect, coastal names do not differ significantly from inland or seaward names, although generics in inland names add, among others, the predominant notion of "height", even in an island archipelago not noted for its high elevations. Inland names also make even greater use of "metaphorical generics", as exemplified in coastal names by *blað*, *bu(r)st*, *gafl*, *ker*, *koddi*, *lúðr*, *múli*, *mynni*, *nebb(nef)*, *nǫs*, *sporðr* and *tangi*, adding, for example, *bak(r)*, *bringa*, *brjóst*, *hals*, *hamarr*, *kambr*, *kjalki*, *(h)rygr*, as well as *belti* and *teinn*. What is particularly striking in most of these generics is the analogical use of parts of the "bodyscape" of human beings in the designation of topographic features – namers through naming mirroring and enlarging themselves in the named world out there.

Although "Shetland English" formations such as *de Bārd, de Berri, de Bōd, de Bogi, de Botten, de Bost, de Fjord, de Fles, de Grūd*, etc. have been expressly excluded from this study, for linguistic as well as chronological reasons, the fact that, with few exceptions, every generic examined has a counterpart in simple names of this kind cannot, of course, be overlooked. Not only are the lexical items in question of Norse (= Shetland Norn) origin, they also testify to their continued use as appellatives hovering themselves in their toponymic application on the boundary between words and names. There cannot be any doubt therefore that the onomastic subfield under discussion has from the very beginning of its gradual creation been closely linked with the corresponding lexical subfield. Toponymic generics and lexical appellatives are quite frequently indistinguishable in this particular setting, and it is only their denotative or connotative functions which set them apart.

The onomastic sub-dialect of the Shetland coastscape is consequently not only a "colonial" extension of the onomastic sub-dialect of the coastscape of the Norwegian homeland but also still has, hundreds of years later, viable and invigorating ties with the contemporary lexicon, thus structuring the phenomenon of "shore" not only in onomastic perceptions. Onomasticon and lexicon continue to be reinforcingly interactive for speakers of Shetland English while lacking that, or any, connection for those who are not familiar with that dialect because they themselves are recent incomers speaking Scots or some British or American regional variety. However, even when the ties between onomasticon and lexicon are close, the structured place-nomenclature and the structured topographic vocabulary of the coastscape are not identical, and it takes more than a linguist to unravel the intricate internal inter-relationships of the former, since the concept of "coast" is, after all, more than a linguistic phenomenon. Through naming that concept is made both systemic and actual, and where land and sea meet, define each other and encroach upon one another, becomes a thinkable reality.

References

Eunson, Jerry, 1961: The Fair Isle Fishing Marks. (Scottish Studies 5, pp. 181-198.)

Fellows-Jensen, Gillian, 1984: Viking Settlement in the Northern and Western Isles – the Place-Name Evidence as seen from Denmark and the Danelaw (The Northern and Western Isles in the Viking World. Eds. A. Fenton and H. Pálsson. Edinburgh, pp. 148-168).

Jakobsen, Jakob, 1936: The Place-Names of Shetland (Shetlandsøernes Stednavne). London – Copenhagen.

Millward, Celia, 1972: Universals in Place-Name Generics. (Indiana Names 3, 2, pp. 48-53.)

Nicolaisen, W. F. H., 1959: The Type 'Burn of –' in Scottish Hydronymy. (Scottish Studies 3, pp. 92-102.)

—— 1960: Names Containing the Preposition *of.* (Scottish Studies 4, pp. 190-205.)

—— 1965: Scottish Place-Names: 'Hill of –' and 'Loch of –' (Scottish Studies 9, pp. 175-182.)

—— 1969: Norse Settlement in the Northern and Western Isles. (Scottish Historical Review 48, pp. 6-17.)

—— 1975: Place-Names in Bilingual Communities. (Names 23, pp. 167-174.)

—— 1976a: Scottish Place-Names. London.

—— 1976b: Scandinavian Place-names in Scotland as a Source of Knowledge. (Northern Studies 7/8, pp. 14-24.)

—— 1978: Are There Connotative Names? (Names 26, pp. 40-47.)

—— 1979-80: Early Scandinavian Naming in the Northern and Western Isles. (Northern Scotland 3, 2, pp. 105-121.)

—— 1980a: Onomastic Dialects. (American Speech 55, pp. 36-45.)

—— 1980b: Place-names as Evidence for Linguistic Stratification in Scotland. (*NORNA-rapporter* 18, pp. 211-231.)

—— 1982a: The Viking Settlement of Scotland: Evidence of Place-Names. (The Vikings. Ed. R.T. Farrell. Chichester, pp. 95-115.)

—— 1982b: Lexical and Onomastic Fields. (Proceedings of the Thirteenth International Congress of Onomastic Sciences, Cracow, 2, pp. 209-216.)

Shetland and the Outside World 1469-1969
Donald J. Withrington (ed.) (1983) 69-85

The Post-Norse Place-Names of Shetland

IN my view, it can be demonstrated quite clearly that when the Norsemen arrived in Shetland almost 1200 years ago they not only carried with them in the vocabulary of their language a large number of words suitable for the naming of geographical features of all kinds, whether natural or man-made, but also a stock of actual names which could be drawn upon whenever applicable. The giving of Norse names to places in Shetland – and this statement has, of course, more general implications and could be said to be true of all areas into which speakers of a new language move in large numbers – was therefore not entirely a process of creating appropriate distinguishing labels from suitable lexical items. Although this spontaneous creation did take place naturally, there must have been also many occasions when a ready-made name from the homeland was pulled out of the onomastic bag, simply because such and such a feature always had such and such a name at home. In some cases, there may have been an element of nostalgia involved as well but, on the whole, I feel that the use of this kind of commemorative naming is usually overstressed, perhaps because of the important part it has played in the naming of settlements in the New World across the Atlantic in more recent times. Naturally, it is not always easy to decide which aspect is involved in the act of naming, but I suspect that in cases like Lerwick, Dale, Tingwall, Linga, Breiwick, Twatt, Voe, Melby, Houlland, which all have not only close but identical parallels in Norway and sometimes several of these, we may with some confidence consider the possibility of onomastic rather than linguistic naming: by which I mean that a ready-made name was re-applied rather than freshly created.

This is the subject I first thought of exploring in this lecture, but it is more appropriate that I should turn rather to a discussion of the place-names of

Shetland after 1469 rather than before that date. I do so with some hesitation, even trepidation.

First of all, there is the regrettable fact that this is my first visit to Shetland, which makes clear my presumption in attempting an account of Shetland place-names under Scottish and British rule. Secondly, Shetland has been extremely fortunate in having experienced – mainly in the last decade of the nineteenth century but also in the ten or fifteen years which followed – the stimulating influence of that great scholar, Jakob Jakobsen, still fondly remembered by so many.[1] The existence of his book on the place-names of Shetland, now unfortunately only obtainable at a premium, has so far persuaded us in the Scottish Place-Name Survey not to conduct any systematic collecting and recording of place-names in these islands, since the more urgent task seemed to be the carrying out of field-work in areas in which Scottish Gaelic is disappearing fast. I do not know whether the expression 'carrying coals to Newcastle' is still apposite in our day and age, but if it is, then 'talking about place-names in Lerwick' carries just about the same indication of superfluity. Thirdly, and this point is linked with the last, I am only too well aware that I am addressing an audience in which at least every Shetlander present is an expert in, or at least has some knowledge of, local place-names, and among whom one in particular – a Whalsay man, a schoolmaster in Aberdeen[2] – knows a great deal more about the place-names of this group of islands and has done more research into them than I could ever know or do. Lastly, the post-Norse place-names of Shetland do not have anything like the glamour of their Norse predecessors.

Yet there are good grounds for addressing ourselves to this topic. Firstly, the place-names of the post-Norse era in Shetland have never been looked at systematically but have only had a few pages or paragraphs in even the best accounts of Shetland names published so far; their detailed investigation is more than overdue. And, secondly, it appears reasonable that an elucidation of problems and questions rather than solutions and answers may be useful to any future scholar or scholars who may want to devote time and energy to a more comprehensive study of the subject under discussion. I have therefore come from Edinburgh to bemoan the fact so little has been done in this field, to suggest what might be done and to put in a plea for work to be carried out locally, not only with regard to the place-names of Shetland coined or adapted after 1469 but also for those of earlier periods. There is, after all, no reasonably complete and systematic published account of the place-names of these islands.

Not being a Shetlander nor a Scot, I can perhaps walk where angels would fear to tread and state categorically at the outset that the question of whether Scottish and English or Scotticised and Anglicised place-names in Shetland are desirable or not is not going to enter into or colour my arguments. I am neither celebrating their existence nor holding a wake for them: but I shall be looking at them in the way in which I would look at the place-nomenclature of any region in which one language has been superseded by another. I shall look for survivals, for adaptations, for new coinings, and for all the other phenomena associated with the place-names of what must have been for centuries a bilingual community. It is perhaps also well worth remembering in this respect that almost as much time has passed since 1469 as elapsed during the period between the arrival of the Norsemen about 800 A.D. and the year of the fateful pledging. Indeed, if we take into account a certain amount of Scottish infiltration into Shetland before that date, the Norse and the post-Norse periods are practically of equal length.

It does not need a place-name expert to tell you that the earlier of these two periods has had a much profounder influence on Shetland place-names than the second, certainly with regard to individual names. The evidence is all around us and exemplified by the many names, mainly of human settlements but also of natural features, which Shetlanders without any special instruction no longer easily understand – neither through their own dialect of Scottish nor via Standard English – but which, I believe, still give Norwegian and other Scandinavian visitors the feeling that they are not far from home. This is no idle statement, for comprehensibility plays an important part in people's attitudes to names. As soon as a name is no longer understood it is removed even further from the realm of ordinary words than a name of which the meaning is still clear. Then only its onomastic qualities survive since it is no longer of any practical use as a lexical item. Such a shift, from the immediately or relatively meaningful to the partly or totally meaningless, takes on immense proportions when we go beyond the obsolescence of individual name-elements within the medium of the same language[3] to the replacement of one whole language by another. Depending on the kind of replacement and its speed, we have a gradual or sudden drifting into meaninglessness of hundreds or even thousands of names. This is the sort of process which must have taken place in Shetland some time between the middle of the fifteenth and the middle of the eighteenth century, and it is not surprising therefore that linguistic and local historical scholarship has since then, but mainly during the last hundred years or so, been concerned with the retrieval of these lost meanings. The driving force behind this has been largely the community's interest in its linguistic past or its roots in general. There has also, however, one suspects, been the age-long curiosity and imagination which imbues the meaningless shape with romantic ideas and notions, identifies the lost meanings of names with the loss of an age in which everything was good and lovely, and so there seems to be some hope that the recovery of the meaning of names may also bring back (or strengthen the demand for the return of) at least some aspects of that golden time. Would the same amount of scholarship, energy and interest have been spent on such a quest if Lerwick had been known as Mud-Bay, Linga as Heather-Island, and Houlland as High-Land? I personally doubt this very much, for I never receive requests for help with the investigation of names like Bankhead, Middleton and Stonehouse although such names are by no means as clear as they look. It is a fallacy anyhow to suppose that we can handle place-names better if we know what they mean.

This is not as much of a digression as it may seem, for it explains why the Norse ingredient in Shetland place-nomenclature has had so much attention whereas the English and Scottish names have not. Our starting-point nevertheless must be this Norse nomenclature which, in the context of this paper, is simply regarded as existing at the time when the islands were pledged to the Scottish crown. That these names must have been dense and numerous on the ground there is no doubt. If it is correct that the population figure soared to the region of 20,000 at one stage of the Scandinavian period, many individual dwellings and clusters of dwellings must have been needed, and each required a name; and even if, as I suspect, the population figure was a little lower, a large number of settlement-names was still needed and doubtlessly existed. Obviously these names were not all created at the same time nor even within a few years of each other. As settlement became denser, as families grew, as new settlers arrived, the need for new names increased and must have been met. It is therefore possible to detect strata within the Scandinavian stratum, and I have recently published an attempt to disentangle these layers and to establish a sequence of names or at least of name-elements, not only for Shetland but for the whole sphere of Norse influence in the Northern and Western Isles and on the adjacent Scottish mainland.[4] This sequence does not concern us here, for all that matters to us is the fact that in 1469 there was a dense network of Norse settlement names in Shetland so that the Scottish incomers came across the *staðrs*, and the *bólstaðrs*, and the *boers*, and *kvís*, and *setrs*, and names compounded with similar elements referring to man-made settlements.[5] In addition, there were almost uncountable numbers of Norse names of natural features and of settlements which had derived their names from natural features: *víks* and *vágrs* and *ás* and *nes's* and *fjalls* and *vatns*, and dozens more. Personally, I would not entirely support the claim that every feature had a name in 1469, and certainly not that every feature had a Norse name. Quite clearly, some pre-Norse names have survived even if we can't yet ascribe all of them to any particular language.

What, then, happened to these Scandinavian names? As far as I can see, there are three main possibilities in this kind of bilingual situation when one language is increasingly ousting another.[6] Names are adapted in some way, they are replaced, or they drop out altogether.[7] And this process goes on while new names are being coined in the new language for new settlements which may spring up or for natural features which apparently had no name in the earlier language. Let us look at these various possibilities in turn.

First of all, there are the adaptations, using that word in its widest sense. Here we have a number of possibilities. Names may be fully translated, a process which requires practically full bilingualism and would therefore not be associated either with the earliest phases of Scottish influx nor with the later stages when Scots had become so dominant that there was very little left of Shetland Norn. One might be inclined to think of the sixteenth and seventeenth centuries as suitable periods when conditions were right. Or again, only one part of the name may be translated whereas the other part is left intact. This usually happens to generic elements but sometimes also affects the explanatory part of a word. Theoretically it could probably take place at any stage during a bilingual period. A third form of adaptation takes place when words of the new language are added tautologically – that is, they mean the same thing and describe the same feature as the whole name (if it is an uncompounded name) or as one element of it (if it is a compound one). This is not the same as translation because tautologies normally arise when the meaning of the original name or name-part is no longer known. They are therefore mainly late phenomena. Fourthly, there is the possibility of extensions or incorporations. What I mean by this is that a word or words belonging to the new language are added to an existing name to describe a feature nearby, i.e. the old name is incorporated in the new one. Occasionally this also happens in the case of the same name but the extension is then not tautological. Lastly, the name may be phonologically adapted; that is, it is left untranslated but its sound-shape is changed according to the sounds available in the new language. Sometimes this produces the possibility of a folk-etymology on the basis of the receiving language. Phonological adaptation may, and usually does of course, also happen as an integral part of part-translations, tautologies and extensions, and we can say straightaway that it is always the most common treatment given to existing names by the incoming speakers of a new language.

So far as Shetland is concerned all these five varieties of adaptation of older names did happen in the Norse>Scottish change-over. The first of these, full translation, is the most difficult to prove and indeed frequently unprovable unless there is conclusive documentary evidence. Jakobsen[8] cites at least two instances. These are Black Loch (in Unst) and Black Water (Nesting) which, in his terminology, 'correspond' to a name such as *Swartasjøn* from the Old Norse **svarta tjǫrn* (black tarn): according to him we have a plural in West Sandwick in Yell, but on the Ordnance Survey one-inch map this is spelled in the singular form *Swarta Shun*. Jakobsen may be right or he may be wrong; the documentary evidence being what it is, we have no means of proving the case either way. I do not know of a single instance in which the written record demonstrates or suggests full translation of an existing Norse name by the incoming Scots. We are nevertheless entitled, I think, to assume that this variety of adaptation did take place to a limited extent although it is not one of the most common phenomena in other bilingual regions, even in the Gaelic-speaking parts of Scotland where we can check the various processes in present-day conditions because they are happening under our very noses.

We are in a much stronger position with regard to part-translations, of which there are several good examples in Shetland.[9] Woodwick in Unst, for instance, probably goes back to an Old Norse **við-vík*, in the same way as Woodwick (Orkney) which has an earlier spelling Weidwick. Dyke-end may be a rendering of an earlier Old Norse **garðs-endi*, with the same meaning.[10] In fact, this may almost be called a full translation since *-end* may well be the Lowland Scots cognate of Old Norse *endi*. Transition from Norse to Scots was often facilitated by such cognate words, and one suspects that loch-names ending in -water, like Fugla Water (Yell), Papil Water (Fetlar), Gorda Water (Papa Stour) and Gossa Water (Sandsting), originally ended in Old Norse *vatn*. Similarly in Cat Firth, Lay Firth, Colla Firth, Whale Firth and the like, firth is surely the replacement of Old Norse *fjǫrðr* by its Scots cognate. The element *land*, too, was easily 'translated', as very little sound substitution was necessary; and the same is true of *dalr* and dale, *bakki* and bank, *borg* and brough, *hólmr* and holm, *hús* and house, *gata* and gate, *hǫfði* and head, *sund* and sound, and many others. (I am quoting the Old Norse forms, although the Shetland Norn versions are sometimes even closer to Scots). In the case of non-generic first elements, certain adjectives lend themselves to the kind of treatment just described, particularly Old Norse **djúpi* which easily becomes 'deep' as in Deepdale (Sandwick and Sandness); *hvíta* which is without difficulty turned into 'white' as in Whiteness (Tingwall); *grœn* for 'green', which must have been substituted at an early date in such names as Greenmow (Dunrossness) and Greena (Tingwall). Adjectives of position like (*ǫfri* and *neðri*; must also have invited quick replacement by 'over' and 'nether', and a similar correspondence existed between terms for the directions of the compass. In some instances, both the first *and* the second element have found easy substitution in this way. We have already mentioned Deepdale, in which both elements are cognates of the kind just described; Greenland in Walls would also belong here, and all these examples (but the last two in particular) are reminders that the Shetland variety of Norse and the Scots variety of English were closely related languages when the linguistic confrontation took place: they did not, therefore, create the same problems which exist, for example, in an English-Gaelic or English-Welsh bilingual community. People must have understood each other fairly quickly and easily, especially since Scots in general was very strongly influenced by Norse. The modern Shetland dialect seems to demonstrate very clearly this kind of easy amalgamation.

This brings us to the so-called tautologies, which can be quite misleading in so far as they appear to contain an element of translation and are therefore often regarded as such. In my own view this element, although natural in one way, is purely accidental in another. And it is certainly unpredictable which word in the new language is going to be used when it is applicable. In their very nature, these names presuppose that the earlier of the two (or sometimes three) tautological elements had become meaningless; consequently, they must be reckoned mostly to have arisen at the tail-end of a bilingual situation. This type of name is practically unknown in Shetland, for one suspects that, in Yell coastal names like Bay of Whinnifirt and Point of Ness, Whinnifirt and Ness are not really regarded as names of the same feature, and Head of Hevdagarth, in the same island, with its doubling of *hevda* (Old Norse *hǫfði*) by 'head' would also not be an instance of straightforward tautology. The almost total absence of this kind of adaptation of earlier names can only be explained by the assumption that most generic elements referring to geographical features never really lost their meaning; but were retained in the emerging Shetland variety of Scots so that there was no need for re-describing the voes, wicks, geos, and nesses by words of English origin. Indeed, most of these are still alive in Shetland today and have been used in the formation of new English names, as we shall see.

Whereas tautologies were uncalled for, the extension or incorporation of earlier Norse names in their Scotticised forms is a normal feature of post-Norse naming in Shetland. In a number of cases this extension may have taken place in Norse times and was obscured later by a kind of part-translation, but such instances are difficult to establish. That that extension is also a pre-1469 phenomenon is, I think, shown by such names as Lunda Wick (Unst) incorporating the early name Lund, Laxabigging (Melby) and the many sound-names like Uyea Sound, Hascosay Sound, Yell Sound, Bressay Sound which contain the names of adjacent islands and undoubtedly go back to names originally ending in Old Norse *sund*. Post-Norse examples would be Sumburgh Head, New Grunasound (East Burra), Wormadale Hill (Tingwall), Lerwick Harbour, and Pettadale Water (North Roe); but probably also Kirkabister Ness (Bressay) and Papa Skerry in spite of the Norse origin of *nes* and *skerry*. In these names and some others they were probably used as Norse loan-words in a Scots dialect rather than as genuine Scandinavian elements in Norse times. Such a statement as this is not easily proved, and only clearly-dated documentary evidence will help in time to solve this problem.

The most common type of post-Norse Shetland name which incorporates an earlier Norse one relating to a neighbouring geographical feature is that exemplified by the construction, 'A of B': Hill of Dale, let us say, or Noup of Noss. These names occur in abundance on the Shetland map, and have such an interesting history that we should look at them in a little more detail.[11] It must be stated at the outset that I feel that, in the interpretation of this name-type, Jakobsen was incorrect in assuming a Norse origin for this construction.[12] I have very carefully examined the various Scandinavian place-name archives and have also consulted colleagues in Norway, Denmark and Sweden; and there appears to be no trace of any similar name-type in those countries. We must therefore look elsewhere for its origins, and it is significant here that Shetland and Orkney are by no means the only regions of present-day Scotland in which this type of name is to be found. If we look, for instance, at a map showing the distribution of 'Burn of-' names (95 out of a total of 135 stream-names in Shetland marked on the one-inch Ordnance Survey maps bear such a name), we discover that the Scottish north-east also shows a remarkable density of these names. Such Shetland names as Burn of Russdale, Burn of Geosetter, Burn of Aith, Burn of Hamnavoe, are paralleled in the north-east by Burn of Birse (Aberdeenshire), Burn of Longshank (Angus), Burn of Boyne (Banffshire), Burn of Melmannoch (Kincardine), Burn of Clashgour (Moray) and many others. In my opinion, it is here that we can expect to find the roots of our Shetland name-type, for it is remarkable how often the element B in this 'A of B' construction is a name of Gaelic origin. In our selection we have Birse, Boyne, Melmannoch, and Clashgour. It is therefore tempting to derive the 'A of B' pattern from a Gaelic source and, without wanting to make this too much of a mystery, I suggest that the stages in which this development took place may have been as follows:[13]

1st stage   Gaelic *Allt an t-Sluic Leith*, i.e. burn of the grey hollow;

2nd stage most commonly (a) Burn of Sloch Lee, with 'Burn of' translating the Gaelic *Allt (an)*, anglicisation of the Gaelic element 'B' as in Sloch Lee, and with substitution of the nominative for the genitive: or sometimes (b) where the whole name is translated; thus the Angus names Burn of Blackpots and Burn of Oldtown are strongly suggestive of being full translations of Gaelic **Allt na(n) Linneacha(n) Dubh(a)* and **Allt (an t-Sean(a)-bhaile* respectively;

3rd stage: 'Burn of', followed by any (usually anglicised) Gaelic element, whether or not it has been part of an original stream-name in *allt*, e.g. Burn of Knock (Kincardine), Burn of Corrhatrich (Moray), Burn of Badenhilt (Aberdeenshire) ;

4th stage: 'Burn of', followed by any defining element regardless of its linguistic origin, cf. Burn of Berryhill (Angus), Burn of Cauldcots (Kincardine), Burn of Davidston (Aberdeenshire). (The two names mentioned in the 2nd stage (b), Burn of Blackpots and Burn of Oldtown, may also belong here.)

The third and fourth stages of this development bring the complete emancipation of this new name pattern and its independence from the original stimulus. Nevertheless it must have come about in a Gaelic-Lowland Scots bilingual situation particular to the Scottish north-east, and could not and cannot emerge in the south-east where there was no Gaelic stimulus or in the present-day Highlands and Islands where Gaelic is being replaced by a variety of Standard English, and not Scots, under completely different economic and educational circumstances.

That the distribution of the 'Burn of-' type is no matter of mere chance is shown by the geographical scatter of such name patterns as 'Water of-', 'Mains of-' 'Mill of-', 'Hill of-' and others. In this respect, it is interesting to note that Shetland does not share the types 'Water of-', 'Mains of-' and 'Mill of-' with the north-east. 'Water of-' could not be used here for the naming of water-courses because its Norse cognate *vatn* had already been assigned to denote 'loch'. 'Mains of-' and 'Mill of-' were probably unsuitable because of the differences in agricultural organisation between the north-east and Shetland. 'Hill of-', on the other hand, is represented by at least 109 names on the one-inch Ordnance Survey maps, such as Hill of Dale, Hill of Canisdale, Hill of Berry, Hill of Gunnista and so on. There are even more 'Loch of-' names, in fact a total of 137, on these maps: for instance, Loch of Spiggie, Loch of Grunnavoe, Loch of Lunnister, Loch of Kettlester, etc. Not infrequently, both 'hill' and 'loch' are combined with the same name in this way, such as Hill and Loch of Basta, and of Brindister, Burwick, Colvister, Garth, Girlsta, Grista, Houlland, Huxter, Kirkabister, etc. The types Point of Coppister, Head of Mula, Saddle of Swarister, Bight of Haggrister, Bay of Quendale, Isle of Noss and Mires of Linksetter reinforce the impression of basically Scots or English usage, and at the same time make it very likely that the 'A of B' pattern came to Shetland (and Orkney) as a ready-made name-type from Scotland with Scots-speaking incomers from the north-east mainland.

By the time this pattern reached Shetland there was no trace left of its Gaelic origins. It had become well established within the variety of Lowland Scots spoken by these incomers, and its usage seems to have become very popular in the developing Shetland dialect of Scots: so much so, that almost every Scandinavian geographical term which had been borrowed into that dialect could also appear as element A in the imported construction. There are countless examples of this, of which I can only mention a few: Wick of Collaster (O.N. *vík*), Ness of Wadbister (O.N. *nes*), Taing of Noustigarth (O.N. *tangi*), Geo of Henken (O.N. *gjá*), Ward of Clugan (O.N. *varða*), Keen of Hamar. (O.N. *kinn*), Holm of Skaw (O.N. *hólmr*), Lee of Saxavord (O.N. *hlíð*), Breck of Newgarth (O.N. *brekka*), Noup of Noss (O.N. *gnúpr*), Hamars of Houlland (O.N. *hamarr*), Cro of Ham (O.N. **kró*, a variety of *krá*), Stacks of Valsland [or Vataland?] (O.N. *stakkr*), and many others. The map of Shetland today tends to give the impression that this is perhaps the most common name-type at present, certainly with regard to the names of natural features. In colloquial usage the definite article is usually prefixed, and the 'f' of 'of' is elided (both under Scottish influence), so that we have de Bard o' Bressay (instead of Bard of Bressay), de Hevdin o' Waddersta (rather than Hevden of Wethersta), de Klepps o' Kollaster, de Kūl o' Fladabister, de Rogg o' Kirkabister, and so on.[14] Whether this pattern is still creative today is difficult to say, but its close proximity to ordinary appellative usage may still be keeping it alive, just as its popularity and impact are probably also due to its holding a position half-way between a proper name and a more syntactic unit used as a descriptive label. However that may be, it is undoubtedly the major contribution of Lowland Scots to the naming practices of Shetlanders, and to the map of Shetland, after 1469.

Nevertheless, it is not the most common type of adaptation of Norse names by incoming speakers of Scots and English, for out of the five different varieties mentioned, the fifth and last is also the most frequently employed, i.e. the phonological adaptation largely through the means of sound-substitution. The fact that Old Norse **leir-vík* has become Lerwick (and ['lɛrik] in Lerwick itself) and not remained *Leir-vík* as in Norway, that **þing-vǫllr* is Tingwall and not Norwegian *Tingvoll*, that **lyng-øy* is Linga today and not still *lyng-øy*, and that **hóland* has developed into Houlland and not into *Høy-land* are due to this adaptation. I am not saying that Shetland Norn would not have developed its own distinct forms anyhow – after all, Icelandic names sound quite different from their Norwegian counterparts today. But it is more than likely that these are not the forms which have been brought about, in spelling and in pronunciation, by five hundred years of Lowland Scots and English linguistic influence. It is improbable that there would have been any 'w' in the present-day Shetland pronunciation of names like Lerwick and Tingwall without such southern influence. The introduction of metathesis into such names as Brough (several instances), Gossabrough (Yell), and Snabrough (Fetlar), all containing the Old Norse *borg*, can also be ascribed to Scots influence (cf. the word *broch* itself), although spellings like Scousburgh, Sumburgh, and Cullinsburgh sometimes obscure this fact. The visitor by air now lands at Sumburgh and not at *Sumbrough. There is no genre of names in Shetland which has not been affected by this phonological process although it is perhaps more noticeable in the major names of the islands: settlement names, names of districts, the names of the islands themselves, and the names of all the major elevations, bays, headlands and so on. On the whole, this phonological adaptation has had the effect of making many of these names totally or partly meaningless for the present-day Shetlander who has no special training in the Scandinavian languages or in linguistics.

In general, this adaptation was easy because of the close relation which the two relevant languages then had, including their similar sound-system. There is a good research topic for a linguist in contrasting the stock of sounds which Shetland Norn is likely to have had in the fifteenth century with the phonological structure of Lowland Scots of the same period and during the two or three centuries which followed: for on that basis it might be possible to predict the kind of substitution to be expected. Our linguist could also offer a quantitative analysis of the influence which Lowland Scots (and latterly Scottish-English) have had on the Shetland Norn sound-system, and that with regard to more than place-names.

So much for adaptations which do not, after all, add anything substantially new to any nomenclature:[15] but are there any independently-created new names to be ascribed to the post-1469 period? We cannot distinguish any new Norse or Shetland Norn names from those coined before 1469 unless additional extra-linguistic information is available. In the case of Lowland Scots or English names, could we rule out the possibility of full translation from Norse or of an easy adaptation to a cognate phonological and lexical system? Jakobsen,[16] for instance, derives from Norse such names as Midhouse (Delting), Northus (Unst); Westhus (Dunrossness), Easter-, Mid- and Wester-tun (Unst), Langtun (Mainland) and Korstun (Dunrossness); but some at least of these may be of later origin since names ending in -hus and -tun are very common in Lowland Scots areas.

Sometimes it is possible to ferret out a replacement of an earlier name, such as Newhoos for an older *Skēva in Delting or West Yell for the earlier village called Strand;[17] but, on the whole, such replacements are just as difficult to determine as full translations. And even when we do know that a certain name mentioned in the sagas or in early documentary evidence has been lost,[18] we cannot know very easily whether it has been replaced by another name. This does not mean that there are no readily recognisable post-Norse names on the Shetland map today. Scots names like The Faulds in Yell and Aithsting, or The Links (in Unst and Dunrossness) belong to this category, as do modern English names like Belmont (Unst), Greenmeadow (Aithsting), Hillside (Delting), Roadside (Sandsting), Seafield (Mid Yell)[19] Fort Charlotte might be added here and Jarlshof too, as well as the street-names in Lerwick and Scalloway. Names of individual town-houses like Leagarth, Clairmont House, Rocklea, Gordon Cottage, Hillbank and Helenlea, which one notices in the capital of Shetland, would also have their place here; but although there are plenty of these, the additional place-name material which has come into the rural areas of Shetland appears to be rather small and limited when compared with the number of Scottish personal names which have been introduced into Shetland in the last five hundred years.

Of the 500 names included on the Ordnance Survey one-inch map for the parish of Dunrossness only a maximum of 40 (or 8 per cent) can be regarded as having independent post-Norse origins, and even this figure may hide a few full translations from Norse. The names in question apply almost without exception to such less important geographical features as stones or holes or small streams or to a few late settlements. And out of the 139 inhabited settlements in Shetland listed in the 1961 Census report, *Place-names and Population: Scotland*[20] only 9 look as though they have post-Norse names, viz. Bridgend, Freefield, Longfield, Lower Sound, Moors, Mossbank, Netherston, Northhouse and Whitefield; but, apart from Bridgend and perhaps Mossbank, the others could be adaptations. There are also five names of the 'A of B' type. It is by adaptation of existing names that Lowland Scots has made its impact since 1469.

Is there any possibility of dating this impact and of linking it to particular events? Only a diligent search of the existing documents could help us here and no one has yet made a comprehensive survey of the available sources relating to Shetland. But I have noted a number of points in my search for some kind of a chronology of naming. Perhaps it is not necessary to stress that there are very few names which can be dated as precisely as Fort Charlotte, named after the wife of George III in connection with the re-establishment of a garrison at Lerwick in 1782; or as Jarlshof, which makes its first appearance in Scott's *The Pirate* in 1821. But street-names should be readily datable from successions of street-plans and council minutes, while houses must also, in many cases, have datable names if it will not always be possible to discover why they were given the particular names they have – apart from reasons of euphony (the Victorian variety) and nostalgia. For the bulk of Shetland names, however, we must despair of absolute dating and can only hope to establish a relative chronology, for we must remember that the first reference to a place is normally not contemporary with the creation of the name by which it is called.

The first mention of something approaching a Scots place-name in Shetland seems to be a reference to the *Corss Kyrk* in Dunrossness in 1506.[21] *Newhous* and *Stansland* are mentioned in the Court Book of 1615[22] but we do not know, of course, whether these are Scottish or adapted Norse names. The pattern 'A of B' certainly existed at the beginning of the seventeenth century for the Court Book of 1615 has 'the mylne of Urafirthe', 'the...hill of Urafirth', 'the hous of Wasland' (or 'Vasland'), 'the hill of Quarfe', 'the ile of Moussay', 'the ile of Rue' and 'the hill of [Conn]sburch'; whereas one year earlier we find 'the loch of Coginsburch' and 'the ile of Wais', always with the definite article and still hovering on the brink between appellative and onomastic usage.[23] In the field of phonology we may note that, whereas in 1467 Tingwall is still spelt with a 'y' (Tyngvell),[24] in 1602 the Scots 'w' seems to have come to be there to stay (Tingwall).[25] The Scots metathesis of 'borg' to 'brough' is also in evidence at that time: not only for Brough in Gulberwick (which is spelt 'Bruche' and 'Burghe' in 1602) and for Sumburgh ('Soundbrughe'), but also for Hamburg as is shown by the mention of 'ane half Hambruch barrell of beiff' in 1615. The intrusive double 'l' in the spelling of Walls was still absent in 1510 ('Waas') and in 1614 ('Wais') and both spellings are very close to modern Shetland pronunciation of that place-name.

One difficulty in the dating of such linguistic changes lies in the fact that most of the relevant documents like the Court Books are in Scots, and they tend therefore to obscure rather than bring out the local pronunciation of the time. The records of Hanseatic towns are, therefore, a welcome non-Scots source for many of our names and may well be closer in many respects to local usage than are the contemporary official Scottish documents. An example of the value of non-British sources is to be found in the *Records of the Earldom of Orkney*[26] where there is a certification by the law-courts of Bergen of an agreement affecting lands in Shetland. Written in 1485, this document is in Norwegian and we get some lovely spellings – 'Liwngöy' for Linga, 'Hwalsöysund' for Whalsay Sound, 'Vlstadh' for Ulsta in Yell, and some others. That Norse place-nomenclature remained stable and unchanged even after the appearance of numerous Scottish surnames and their bearers in Shetland is clearly shown in such examples as this from the Court Book: at an assize on 21 August 1612, arranged for a 'dittay contra the egiptians for schlauchter', while the names of the persons involved are Schlaitter, Magnussone, Olasone, Kaid, Mowat, Coghill, another Mowat, Foster, Nicolsone, Olasone, another Magnussone, Bult, Smith and Wischart, all the place-names are Norse.[27] It is a situation which has, to all intents and purposes, continued until the present day when the discrepancy between surnames and place-names is still very notable.

In tackling such a seemingly unrewarding subject as the post-Norse place-names of Shetland, therefore, we meet a host of questions rather than answers: but we can come to certain general conclusions in spite of the comparative dearth of material and the little work which has been done so far. When Shetland was pledged to the Scottish crown in 1469 it contained such a wealth of named settlements and of named natural features that the necessity for fresh naming was not very great. The percentage of really new Scottish names given without reference to the existing Norse nomenclature was therefore very small, and it has been infinitesimal with regard to settlement names. The only major contribution made by the Scots incomers was the introduction of the pattern 'A of B' which became dominant in the secondary naming of natural features and thus quite typical of the Shetland onomastic dialect.[28] Otherwise, phonological adaptation as part of the general linguistic take-over has been the main process of change observed. This has meant that the place-nomenclature of Shetland today has remained close to the Shetland dialect in its ingredients but has retained a large Norse element because the meaningfulness which is essential to the retention of ordinary lexical items is not required in the retention of names. Perhaps one can say that the dialect is largely but not exclusively Scots in its phonology, morphology, and syntax but that it has a strong Norse admixture in its vocabulary, whereas the place-nomenclature is basically Norse with the addition of certain Scottish material. [29]

What *is* now necessary is the systematic collection, from oral tradition and from historical documents, of the place-names of Shetland; and I would therefore support Mr John Stewart's appeal for such a collection, made in the *New Shetlander* in 1951.[30] This collection should be made regardless of the linguistic origin of the names and should, if at all possible, consist not only of lists but also of map references and tape-recorded interviews with suitable informants. I am quite sure that the Scottish Place-Name Survey, with the Shetland Folk Society, could devise and implement such a scheme, calling if necessary on help from the schools. The immediate aim would be the preservation of material for future generations but it would not exclude analysis and interpretation. A Gaelic map of Scotland is being prepared for Gaelic speakers for use in school classrooms. A similar kind of map or series of maps which would show the place-names of Shetland in the Shetland dialect would be an interesting and very desirable parallel to the Ordnance Survey sheets produced by English-speaking publishers and intended for English-speaking users. What I envisage is not an etymological map or an antiquarian map going back to pre-1469 times but one which would reflect Shetland usage today. It would provide an immediate local stimulus for the collection of names and would thus repay the labours of those who were involved in its preparation.

Notes

1 See T.M.Y. Manson, 'The personal impact of Jakobsen in Shetland and Orkney' in *Fróðskaparrit*, xiii (1964), 9-13.

2 The late John Stewart.

3 For instance, the name Hawick in Southern Scotland is now meaningless although it is a Scottish-English name.

4 W.F.H. Nicolaisen, 'Norse settlement in the Northern and Western Isles: some place-name evidence' in *The Scottish Historical Review*, xlviii (Apr. 1969), 617.

5 There is an excellent analysis of these by John Stewart in Alan Small (ed.), *The Fourth Viking Congress* (Edinburgh, 1965), 247-260. The same author has a shorter account in A.T. Cluness (ed.), *The Shetland Book* (Lerwick, 167), 136-140.

6 For some general comments see W.F.H. Nicolaisen, 'The interpretation of name-changes' in *Scottish Studies*, v (1961), 85-96.

7 Like *Flókavágr* of the sagas and a number of others listed by A.B. Taylor in 'Shetland place-names in the sagas', in W. Douglas Simpson (ed.), *The Viking Congress, Lerwick: July 1950* (Edinburgh, 1954), 112-129. Losses are of no interest to us in the context of the present paper.

8 Jakob Jakobsen, *The Place-Names of Shetland* (London, 1936), 5.

9 *Ibid.*

10 'Dyke-end' may be much more recent than the phase of part-translation: many 'dyke-ends' seem to be nineteenth century in origin.

11 This type of name has been dealt with in a number of articles by the present writer in the series 'Notes on Scottish Place-Names' in *Scottish Studies*. See 'The Type "Burn of-" in Scottish Hydronymy', iii (1959), 92-102; 'Names containing the preposition "of"', iv (1960), 194-205; '"Hill of-" and "Loch of-"', ix (1965), 175-182.

12 Jakobsen, *Place-Names*, 6, where he suggests that de Hill o' de Waters (Yell) represents an older *Vatnahul* or *Vatnabrekk, and Hill o' Dale an older *Dalsfell*.

13 See *Scottish Studies*, iii (1959), 97-8.

14 Jakobsen, *Place-Names*, 9-10.

15 The type 'A of B', however, might well be regarded not only as an incorporating adaptation but as a kind of new formation which has added to the existing stock of name patterns and has in this way enriched the range of Shetland place-names, especially secondary and subsidiary names.

16 *Place-Names*, 129-130. (The names are here quoted in the forms given by Jakobsen).

17 *Ibid.*, 133.

18 See note 5 above.

19 Jakobsen, *Place-Names*, 7.

20 *Place-names and Population, Scotland: an alphabetical list of populated places derived from the Census of Scotland* (London, 1967).

21 Alfred W. and Amy Johnston (eds.), *Orkney and Shetland Records*, i: Old-Lore Series, vii (London, 1907-13), 249.

22 Robert S. Barclay (ed.), *The Court Books of Orkney and Shetland 1614-1615* (Scot. Hist. Soc., 1967).

23 *Ibid.*, 107-108. One of the finest references to this type of name is in a court case in connection with 'the thifteous steilling of twa sheip out of the nes of Kebusta, and ane other of nes of Gr[im]bista in Juni last on ane Sonday in the morneing, quhilk they pat in a boit and sauld to the Hollenderis at Brassay'.

24 Johnston, *Orkney and Shetland Records*, 51.

25 Gordon Donaldson (ed.), *The Court Book of Shetland 1602-1604* (Scot. Record Soc., 1954).

26 J. Storer Clouston (ed.), *Records of the Earldom of Orkney, 1299-1614* (Scot. Hist. Soc., 1914), 72-73.

27 Robert S. Barclay (ed.), *The Court Book of Orkney and Shetland, 1612-1613* (Kirkwall, 1962), 25-26.

28 The map forms do not, of course, always represent local usage faithfully. As we have seen (see p. 79 above), the preposition 'of ' is given locally rather as 'o' [ɔ]. The type as such, however, exists in oral tradition but is sometimes paralleled by the 'B-A' rather than 'A of B' construction.

29 See David Murison, 'Scots Speech in Shetland' in Simpson, *The Viking Congress, Lerwick: July 1950*, 255-260, and esp. 257.

30 John Stewart, 'The Shetland place-name collection' in *The New Shetlander*, no. 28 (May-June 1951), 7-8.

Names 32, 4 (Dec. 1984) 358-366

Maps of Space – Maps of Time*

THIS paper has from its very inception been intended to be a rather unusual one, from my point of view, insofar as it contains a great many questions without the concomitant balance of just as many answers. In addition, its basic attitude of critical interrogation is not directed at others, as is customary in scholarly enquiry, but rather at myself and at much of what I have tried to do with place-names, especially in Scotland, over the last thirty years or so. This is an uncomfortable, sometimes even painful, posture to take in public; but since persistent private questioning along the same lines has not been productive, because of an obvious lack of objectivity and distance, I feel that I have to take my disquiet to a forum such as the readership of this journal in the hope that the name scholars, cultural geographers, historians, archaeologists, and dialecticians among the readers of *Names*, as well as others well versed in the construction and interpretation of maps, will assist me in my plight. In particular, the person whom this special issue honours, Dr. Meredith Burrill, who has done so much to enlighten us on the geographical dimension of place-names, may well be able to bring his experience and wisdom to bear on the problem which worries me.

My discomfiture and plea have their origins in, have certainly been accelerated by, the ever-growing awareness – based on quotations, footnotes, offprints and personal communications – that other scholars are increasingly using some of the results of my research and are building their own strategies and conclusions on them. While this is naturally gratifying on the one hand, this realisation has also, on the other, created a new recognition of my responsibility toward others so that what I have been pleased and fortunate to find, or thought to have found, in my repeated encounters with Scotia Onomastica now appears to be no longer the intellectual property of an individual, curious and playful, but part of a larger body of knowledge to which others, with or without my consent, have easy access and which these others approach with, to me, an amazing trust in its validity and seemingly solidly grounded persuasiveness. I find this to be not only an amusing but also a quite frightening position. Call it an academic mid-life crisis, the need for a confessional, a longing for reassurance, or just the inevitable consequence of becoming an "authority" – whatever the reasons, I am prompted to re-examine and re-assess some of the tacit assumptions under which I have been working, and consequently some of the results based on these assumptions.

In the study of Scottish place-names my major preoccupation has been with that aspect of primary research which toponymic material everywhere serves so well, i.e., the importance of names as evidence for settlement history and linguistic stratification. It is only natural therefore, that I have found it necessary to translate, convert, and process their obvious spatial scatter into some kind of distribution in time. In fact, a large part of my book on Scottish place-names,[1] owes its organisation to this approach and derives its substance from the sequential exploration of linguistic strata as implied or suggested by place-name evidence. Many of the maps which give that evidence a visual dimension not only are included in the Medieval Atlas of Scotland[2] but also have been reprinted in several other publications. Are they reliable enough to warrant publication for my own immediate purposes, accompanied by relevant name lists, etymologies, and their detailed discussions, and also to merit re-publication in other contexts, often without much or any of the toponymic evidence itself?

There is no doubt in my mind that – human error apart – a name containing a certain generic element does indeed exist in the locality which is indicated by a dot or other symbol on my maps; that kind of reliability is expected of all good trait mapping. But I do have two main concerns. First, the general relationship between maps of space and maps of time; and second, the temporal conclusions that I have drawn, over the years, from spatial distributions. Let me briefly attend to the first and then discuss the second in more detail.

Place-names, and by that I mean names of any kind of geographical feature, whether natural or manmade, are onomastic items that have a definite locus and can be pinpointed on a map by coordinates. Place-names have a definite "there", answering the question "where?"; they identify a location. That location and the name attached to it, identifying it, are eminently mappable, whether this is done to record their very evidence or as part of a survey conducted with particular objectives in mind. Like all names, place-names exist not in isolation but should be considered in relation to other place-names, thus helping to hone their identifying function in a number of ways. Place-names, apart from their general identifying function, also share with other place-names certain characteristics, the same generics perhaps, or the same specific, or the same linguistic origin, or the same meaning, or the same kind of referent (mountain, bay, street, etc.), or some such quality. They exist in loosely arranged clusters or in more tightly structured onomastic fields. Such shared properties can be individually selected and comparatively easily plotted on two-dimensional maps. We can note and describe their geographical distribution in terms of other major named features – the field names of a farm, the street names of a city, the stream names of a certain catchment basin, names beginning with *Kil-* in the south of Scotland, Norse names in Lewis, names containing the Pictish element *Pit-* from the Firth of Forth to the Moray Firth, and so on. We can say where they are, and we can draw isonyms around the various mapped locations of certain selected name types or elements, and establish the existence and extent of onomastic dialects, especially toponymic dialects.[3] While we are doing these and many other things with place-names, we are in essence treating them as spatial phenomena, as items that have horizontal distribution in a two-dimensional framework; and a map of, let us say, place-names beginning with *Pit-*, while inclusive of, it is hoped, all of these in its symbolic representation, is at the same time exclusive of – the white spaces – all other names not sharing that particular, very specific feature. The names mapped in this selective fashion have been deprived of their primary function of turning a chaotic, potentially threatening wilderness into a structured, habitable landscape and have instead become manipulated raw material for scholarly investigation. There is nothing wrong with that, and I am simply noting it here, not condemning it.

Place-names do, however, also have a "then" answering to the question "when?", identifying a location in time: Old Aberdeen, medieval Glasgow, Sir Walter Scott's Edinburgh, or Shetland under Earl Patrick. The names themselves have a temporal dimension as well as a spatial one. They have continuity of existence, from 800 to the present day, let us say, or from the fifteenth century to the seventeenth century. They have changed as well as continued in time, pronunciation, morphology, and their semantic status. Many of them have undergone a development from easily accessible lexical meaning to complete semantic opacity; many of them have outlived the various languages that coined them. Their very capacity to be lexically meaningless while onomastically functional has given them a remarkable power of survival. Names are in time as well as in space, but it is much more difficult for us to pinpoint their temporal location when we lack, or can only approximate, the co-ordinates of time, and when we have to rely to a large extent on their spatial distributions to obtain a glimpse of their temporal ones.[4] And this is where the crux of the matter lies! How is the translation from one dimension into another achieved? How is temporal continuity made visible in spatially static representations? Do we have the means by which to apply the same, or at least similar, levels of rigor and reliability to an investigation of the former as to the latter? Or does time, which gets the better of us so often in our lives, thwart us here, too?

As I see it, the problem is twofold: One, we have to come to grips with the temporal dimension of the total extent of a particular linguistic stratum in contrast to all other strata, as indicated by the place-name evidence. Two, it is incumbent upon us to establish, if possible, sequential layers within each discrete linguistic stratum. In pursuit of the former, distribution maps of selected toponymic material serve primarily, although probably not exclusively, as visual illustrations, so that one can claim, for example, that a map of the distribution of all compound names beginning with *Pit*- shows the maximum extent of the area in which the historic Celtic-speaking Picts once settled, or that a map of the Scottish place-names containing the generic *baile*[5] says the same about Gaelic-speaking Scotland, or that the distribution of place-names containing Norse *bólstaðr*[6] provides us with a spatial image of the extent of Scotia Scandinavica in the north and west of the country. In all these instances, there is no other toponymic element referring to human habitation, in the three languages concerned, that has a wider distribution.[7] So far so good. We may even be able to say without much fear of contradiction that in all three instances names containing these elements were capable of being newly created throughout the whole period during which the languages in question are likely to have been spoken in Scotland, from the third to the tenth centuries for Pictish, let us say; from about 800 to the thirteenth century (or a little beyond) for Norse; and from the fifth century till the present for Gaelic. Naturally, that chronological framework is not derived from the toponymic material itself but from extra-onomastic sources. What we cannot say with ease, however, is when the place-names concerned reached their peak of productivity and whether that peak coincided with the most extensive use of the respective languages in Scotland. It is very probable that more names beginning with *Baile* (*Bal-*) were reated after Gaelic had already begun its retreat from English than before; similarly the majority of the surviving *Pit*- names appears to have been coined when Pictland had already become heavily Gaelicised. In contrast, it is possible that *bólstaðr*-names reached their productive peak long before Norse political, economic and linguistic power began to decline.

In addition, it is probably legitimate to claim that, as a rule of thumb, distribution maps like these tell us more about final stages, or even the end, of any given toponymic usage than about its beginning. After all, any place-name element or type known in the "homeland" at the time of colonisation might well have been employed from the very start to create new place-names in the territory to be colonised. For this purpose, it was not necessary for names or their morphological components to have accessible lexical meaning or to be of the latest and most fashionable type in the homeland. Anything in existence in the place-nomenclature of the country of origin at the time of the emigrants' departure might serve as a model for inexperienced namers. Our maps are almost completely silent on this question. Nevertheless, they are valuable and valid visual orientation aids in the determination of the ultimate extent of the settlement areas of certain linguistic people. One only has to look at statements concerning the location of Pictland made before Kenneth Jackson's illuminating place-name map of the mid-fifties (to the best of my knowledge, the first published toponymic distribution map of any kind in Scotland)[8] and compare these pronouncements with similar statements after its publication, in order to sense the way in which what was originally intended to be mere illustration of descriptive data began to generate new thinking and new perceptions and a much greater feeling of security. The map, as one end-product of rigorous research, thus became the stimulating beginning of further quests. Watson's very full name lists, with their excellent documentation and analyses, had been around for at least thirty years,[9] but it was not until after Jackson's map had appeared that the notion of Celtic-speaking Pictland took on some kind of recognisable shape. We are visual people living in an eye-oriented society and world.

Of the three maps referred to so far, the *baile-* and *bólstaðr-* ones are, apart from certain parts of the Hebrides, largely complementary and reinforce each other's chronological implications. If, as is likely, the Norsemen began to settle Caithness in the ninth century, then the Gaels cannot have reached that part of Scotland any earlier but probably rather simultaneously or a little later, because otherwise the strict division into a toponymically Scandinavian north-eastern section and a Gaelic south-western one, with only a narrow boundary zone, cannot be easily explained.[10] Thus these two maps define each other with regard to temporal qualities. Of course, the fact that one map represents a Celtic language and the other a Germanic one helps enormously.

We are on much less certain ground when it comes to an evaluation of names created by one *p*-Celtic language in contrast to those coined by another *p*-Celtic language. After all, not all toponymic generics of *p*-Celtic origin support the definitive and quite unequivocal pattern set by the *Pit*-names.[11] In fact, as it turns out, *pit-* is the only element which demonstrates such territorial exclusivity. Other generics, like *pert, lanerc, pevr* and *aber*, which in Scottish terms are mostly to be found in the area delineated by *pit-*, have exact counterparts in Wales; and *penn, pren, cair* and *tref* hardly occur in the *pit-* area, while being quite common in southern Scotland and, of course, also in Wales and Cornwall. For *tref* we have the peculiar situation that it predominates in southern Scotland as a first element but is also quite common in the northeast as a second component. Are we really doing this complex linguistic situation justice by calling all evidence north of the Forth-Clyde line "Pictish" and all evidence south of that line "Cumbric"? Are we perhaps over-exaggerating the separating force of elements like *pit-* in the face of so much shared material? Is the toponymic evidence sufficient to warrant the postulation of two different Celtic languages – Pictish and Cumbric – rather than of two closely related *p*-Celtic dialects with common affinities to Welsh and Cornish and perhaps Gaulish? Is there anything in these maps which might help us to understand the individuation of these early, pre-Gaelic Celtic languages in Scotland or must one simply be content with regarding the evidence we have for them as rather late and perhaps not fully representative of their most extensive distribution in both time and space? I view these maps at this stage as visual devices of description or depiction, the full implications of which are as yet not at all clear.

The problems just enumerated are, however, almost insignificant when compared with those which confront us when we make an attempt at breaking up the temporal continuity of a particular place nomenclature by establishing earlier and later phases of it through the use of spatial distribution maps. I indicated above that the distribution of names beginning with *baile* demonstrates the Gaelic-speaking settlement area at its most extensive. By definition, therefore, all other distribution maps of Gaelic toponymic elements should be less extensive than the *baile*-map, certainly not more extensive, if *baile* is indeed to be found wherever Gaelic has been or still is spoken in Scotland. Maps showing the scatter of other generics should therefore show either regional variations in the lexical or onomastic dialects, or chronological differences, or a mixture of both. I have, in the last twenty years, constructed a large number of such distribution maps and have found that only very few of these permit chronological conclusions. The others appear all to be regionally dialectal, and while this may be of interest to the lexicographer of Gaelic, it has little bearing on the question which we are discussing.

At one stage, for example, I made lists of all sorts of generics present in Gaelic mountain names and plotted them on maps; practically all of them turned out to have more or less limited distributions, sometimes mutually exclusive, sometimes overlapping, which allowed them to be read as spatial maps and nothing else.[12] Only one of them seemed to show some promise with regard to the potential identification of an early stratum of Gaelic names in Scotland, the element *sliabh*, or *slew*, in its Anglicised form. Its almost exclusive occurrence in the two parts nearest Ireland and known to have been settled earliest by the Scots, i.e. the Scottish *Dal Riata* and the Rinns of Galloway and adjacent parts, led me to conclude boldly that:

> The distribution of *sliabh* in Scottish place-names reflects the geographical extent to which Gaelic was spoken in Scotland a few centuries after the Dalriadic settlement, mainly in Galloway, Argyll (with special emphasis on Islay and Jura) and in the upper reaches of Tay and Spey. The exact point in time at which *sliabh* ceased to be productive toponymically is, of course, impossible to determine but it should be put well before the ninth century when Gaels and Norsemen confronted each other in the Hebrides and Caithness, and when Gaelic had already begun to infiltrate Pictland. *Sliabh* is conspicuously absent from all these areas, and the seventh century might well be considered (as) the end of the use of this element in place-names, at least in the northern parts of its geographical scatter.[13]

This confident statement requires some modification. While I still regard *sliabh* as one of our earliest Gaelic elements and quite vociferous as such, I was perhaps a little too hasty in trying to get my hand under the Norse "blanket" – toponymically speaking, that is – when I assigned the end of its productivity to the seventh century. It is, after all, well possible that *sliabh*, after its initial impact, continued to serve for several centuries as a creative *regional* place-name element in a limited area and that many of the *sliabh-* or *slew*-names were actually given much later than I had first envisaged. This does not invalidate them as evidence for early settlement, just as the many Picto-Gaelic hybrids do not invalidate *Pit-* as an important marker of the area of Pictish settlement, but caution is certainly the watchword for those trying to read relative chronological sequences out of spatial patterns, and one must keep one's eyes open for alternatives. More limited distribution is not always, as I once simplistically thought, an indicator of an earlier linguistic stratum, just as less density in distribution is not always a sign of a late phase. Such phenomena may occur at any time within the lifespan of a nomenclature.

I consider myself on much firmer ground, however, with regard to another important Gaelic place-name element – *cill* "church or churchyard". In its distribution, it is somewhere halfway between *sliabh* and *baile*.[14] Theoretically, it may therefore have been a feature either of a phase before the greatest extent of Gaelic-speaking settlement, or after it. I am, however, convinced that my conclusions derived from its scatter still stand:

> *Kil*-names had ceased to be created when Gaelic speakers moved into Pictish territory proper on any appreciable scale, and before Gaels and Norsemen stood facing each

other in Caithness…*Kil*-names in the northern part of Scotland … are in general not likely to be younger than 800.[15]

It seems unlikely that this does not apply to the rest of the country too, although *Kirk*-names and *Kil*-names may have alternated in the southwest a little longer. Why this confidence? The datable saints' names which occur as specifics with *Kil*- all commemorate saints of the sixth and seventh, and sometimes eighth, centuries, and there is no reason to believe that other, later, saints' names would not have been involved if *Kil*-names had been created at a later date.

It is rare for us to have such datable evidence when drawing chronological conclusions from spatial toponymic patterns but the saints commemorated in the *Kil*-names nevertheless point to a potential way out of our dilemma – the humble recognition of the limitations of place-name evidence and the use of appropriate and relevant extra-onomastic support material. This can come from a variety of sources: absolute historical dates like the conversion of the Angles of Northumbria to Christianity in 627 A.D. to date the earliest English names in Scotland; the first recorded instance of a name as a *datum ante quem*; geographical information as to the quality of a named site (soil analysis, shelter value, altitude above sea level, distance from other sites, etc.); geological data; social contexts; information about phonological and morphological changes; archaeological finds and other excavation results; legal and church history; and so on.[16] There seems to be much extra-onomastic evidence to facilitate the kind of relative and absolute dating which names themselves, even in their spatial distribution patterns, are so loath to reveal. Obviously, there remain sizable gaps in our avowed endeavour to turn maps of space into maps of time or, to be more precise, maps of spatial orientation and illustration into maps of temporal evidence, but perhaps the problem is not as perplexingly intractable as it seems, especially if close co-operation with experts in neighbouring disciplines, such as cultural geography, can be achieved.

Notes

*   This is a revised version of a paper first read under the title of' "Chronology and the Spatial Distribution of Names" at the Seventh International Congress of Celtic Studies in Oxford, England, July 1015, 1983. In its present form it is dedicated with heartfelt thanks to the great interpreter of the onomastic landscape, Meredith Burrill. With regard to the maps mentioned in the text, readers are encouraged to consult them in either of the two published sources referred to in notes 1 and 2. Although this may be somewhat inconvenient there seems to be no justification for reprinting: these maps yet another time.

1   W.F.H. Nicolaisen, *Scottish Place-Names: Their Study and Significance* (London: B.T. Batsford, 1976).

2   Peter McNeill and Ranald Nicholson (eds.), *An Historical Atlas of Scotland c400-cl600* (St. Andrews: Conference of Scottish Medievalists, 1975).

3   W.F.H. Nicolaisen, "Onomastic Dialects", *American Speech*, 55 (1980), 36-45.

4   See K.H. Jackson, "The Pictish Language". In: *The Problem of the Picts*. Ed. F.T. Wainwright (Edinburgh: Nelson, 1955), 147; Nicolaisen, *Scottish Place-Names*, 153; also William Kirk, "Prehistoric Scotland: The Regional Dimension." In: *Scotland: A New Study*. Ed. Chalmers M. Clapperton (Newton Abbot: David & Charles, 1983), 95.

5   Nicolaisen, *Scottish Place-Names*, 137.

6   *Ibid.*, 93.

7   Names in Old Norse *dalr* do, of course, have a wider distribution (Nicolaisen, *Scottish Place-Names*, 95) but most of them primarily applied to natural features and became settlement names only later. This makes them a very different kind of evidence, only tangentially related to the problem in hand.

8   Jackson, 147.

9   William J. Watson, *The History of the Celtic Place-Names of Scotland* (Edinburgh: Blackwood, 1926), 407-414.

10 W.F.H. Nicolaisen, "Scandinavians and Celts in Caithness: The Place-Name Evidence." In: *Caithness: A Cultural Crossroads*. Ed. John R. Baldwin (Edinburgh: Scottish Society for Northern Studies, 1982), 75-85.

11 Nicolaisen, *Scottish Place-Names*, 149-172.

12 W.F.H. Nicolaisen, "The Distribution of Certain Gaelic Mountain-Names." *Transactions of the Gaelic Society of Inverness*, 45 (1969), 113-128.

13 Nicolaisen, *Scottish Place-Names*, 122-123.

14 *Ibid.*, 142.

15 *Ibid.*, 143.

16 See, in this respect, the excellent work done by historical geographers, such as G. Whittington and J.A. Soulshy, "A Preliminary Report on an Investigation into *Pit* Place-Names," *Scottish Geographical Magazine*, 84 (1968), 117-125; and G. Whittington, "Place-names and the settlement pattern of dark age Scotland," *Proceedings of the Society of Antiquaries of Scotland*, 106 (1974-5), 99-110. Archaeologists are also very much aware of the problems and needs. See, for example, Ian Hodder and Clive Orton, *Spatial analysis in archaeology* (Cambridge: Cambridge University Press, 1976).

ICOS XV (1984): *Der Eigenname in Sprache und Gesellschaft*
Ernst Eichler et al. (eds.) Verhandlungen im Plenum
Leipzig (1985) 118-132

Socio-onomastics

To have been asked to deliver one of the plenary lectures at this congress is a matter for both gratitude and embarrassment on my part: gratitude because of the very special honour implied in this invitation, and embarrassment because carrying owls to Athens or coals to Newcastle are distinctly innovative acts compared with the attempt to say something new and perceptive about names in language and society in a place like Leipzig. One comes to Leipzig to learn about socio-onomastics, not to provide new insights or, even more redundantly, to offer definitions and clarifications. The title of this congress and the subject matter for which it stands are so clearly and legitimately the hallmark of *Onomastica Lipsiensis* that any outsider trying to make a contribution to a fuller understanding of its scope and limitations must humbly acknowledge that he finds himself on territory where all sensible angels with a bent toward name studies fear to tread. Since any endeavour to do full justice to the honour received is therefore doomed to failure from the outset, one can only hope to do the next best thing which is to rethink, to reargue, to rephrase, maybe even simply to renew and to reiterate some of the well-known concepts and issues already paraded by our current organisers and their friends as long ago as 1973.

I am referring, of course, to the anthology which appeared under the same title as our present meeting – Der Name in Sprache und Gesellschaft[1] – as part of the series of monographs devoted to name studies, published under the aegis of the Sächsische Akademie der Wissenschaften. What Ernst Eichler,[2] Hans Walther,[3] Wolfgang Fleischer[4] and others[5] have said there in a series of splendid articles anticipates just about any approach which one might try to devise or dream up for this presentation – as I have learned to my cost. In a sense, therefore, socio-onomastics already has its informative handbook and reliable guide, and anything one can say eleven years later can, one fears, only echo, bounce off or be honed by the views expressed in that volume. The excuse which I have manufactured for myself for not exclusively following that procedure is that this excellent work is still relatively unknown in the English-speaking world where access to scholarship published in German is often difficult and certainly time-consuming, sometimes impossible to gain. The study of *Names in Language and Society* is therefore by no means a well trodden scholarly path in the British Commonwealth and North America, let us say, and the exploration of this topic may still evoke a certain sense of intellectual adventure. Neither students of names nor linguists and sociologists have so far paid much attention to what, for better or worse, tends to be called socio-onomastics, and the absence of any systematic approach to the matter and the lack of a clearly developed and widely accepted terminology for its investigation and analysis are symptomatic for the pursuit of work in this field and the dearth of manageable and convincing concepts. It is, for example, not without significance that not one of the many study guides, monographs and anthologies devoted to the subject of socio-linguistics contains any reference to onomastic items.[6] Explanations why this should be so would be so speculative that they are not worth offering at this point but the fact that this state of affairs exists almost speaks for itself. Whatever the reasons for this neglect, there seems to be some urgency for this situation to be remedied. Bearing this background in mind, the diffuse comments and suggestions which I hope to offer in the following are therefore, perhaps, more intended for consumption by a particular corner of the world of onomastics rather than for the distinguished audience assembled here today. Please forgive me if I nevertheless shamelessly use you as catalysts.

At the outset, it is necessary to clarify one important point in which I tend to differ from one of the fundamental principles expressed several times very forcefully and persuasively in *Der Name in Sprache und Gesellschaft.* Please do not mis-understand me; this is not a retraction of my genuine praise for the volume, nor does it invalidate its most important findings. It simply signals a different viewpoint and one from which I have regarded the nature, function and study of names for several decades. Restating its premises and their implications is therefore not surprising, nor does it constitute any bizarre departure from my previous thinking. The basic issue in question is this.

Several contributors to the volume stress especially that behind their theoretical considerations lies the fundamental assumption that onomastics is a sub-discipline of linguistics or, more specifically, that names constitute a special sector of the lexicon.[7] It is probably correct to say that the writers in question express in these statements a view held widely not only in the socialist countries but wherever names are studied. In fact, it is probably no exaggeration to assume that this opinion is undoubtedly held by the majority of name scholars all over the world. Those, who make it their theoretical underpinning in the Leipzig volume are therefore in excellent company and, let me say this again, when consistently applied this position is a defensible, even productive stance to take although it leads, I believe, to a certain terminological fuzziness and consequently to conceptual dilemmas which are not easily resolved. This is particularly true of problems which arise from the difficulty to separate the meaning and function of names and of misunderstandings which occur in the handling of semantic phenomena. However frequently one emphasises that one has different kinds of meaning in mind and that lexical meaning differs from onomastic meaning or word meaning from name meaning, it is impossible to remove fully the ambiguities which are inherent in such parallel usage, and the one area in which names are acknowledged by everybody to be unlike words becomes an intellectual morass or a stretch of systemic quicksand in which one's footing is at best precarious.

Let us by all means admit, even highlight, the grammatical properties which names and some kinds of words, especially nouns, share; particularly their syntactic behaviour is practically identical with that of nouns in many languages. Their similarity in this respect is, in fact, so striking that these shared features – and these often include visual and audible representation, i.e. both spelling and pronunciation – give the initial impression that names are indeed words with peculiar additional or alternative properties. This is where the crux of the matter lies, for this extensive overlap in characteristics appears to suggest that what makes names specifically onomastic is a set of eccentric qualities which permit one to describe them, as has been done on occasion, as marginal lexical items on the periphery of the basic vocabulary.[8] Such a position which places or pushes names away from the central concerns of human communication has, as will be readily seen, far-reaching consequences for the theoretical occupation with matters of name competence, name acquisition, the role of names in language teaching and learning, and so on. It will also affect the perceived centrality or otherwise of the speech acts of identification and recognition in the conduct of human affairs, especially such notions as selfhood and landscape, for it prevents the essential realisation that, whereas words have meaning, names have content, and whereas the original shape and meaning of words can be discovered with the help of etymological strategies, such strategies are not always necessary, indeed often inappropriate, in the interpretation of names. The name scholar's major concern should be, to use a German punning contrast which is not possible in English, a persistent quest for *Deutung*, not a desperate search for *Bedeutung*.

The latter, the search for *Bedeutung* or meaning, is by definition almost exclusively diachronic, retrospective and historical. It is intensely concerned with origins and therefore with the act of naming. It attempts to discover, through a series of disclosing procedures, the linguistic affiliation, the lexical elements and their meaning which went into the making of a name. It tries to recapture the moment just before these elements enter a nomenclature. It has, however, little to say as to what happens once such words and morphemes have become names and have begun to function largely independent of their original lexical burden. The former, the quest for *Deutung*, is essentially interested in the interpretation and understanding of names in their full contexts at any time in their existence, quite apart from their linguistic embeddedness. It is, *mutatis mutandis*, synchronic in nature and focuses its attention chiefly on name usage rather than on name creation. While fully aware of the need for reliable etymologies and while utilising these for its own purposes whenever appropriate, it insists on viewing names, both those of persons and those of places, as integral parts of the building and maintenance of a structured society and of a life-sustaining habitat, and of the interaction between the two. It does not negate the linguistic aspects of names, it harnesses them. It sees names primarily as parts of an onomasticon rather than a lexicon although naturally acknowledging the original and sometimes continuing identity of the two. In a way, it recognises in daring reversal of the usually accepted terminology and diagrammatic representation that words and names are both appellatives[9] thus accounting for their shared features but also for their semantically and functionally very separate communicative lives.

It is therefore the quest for *Deutung* rather than the search for *Bedeutung* which colours my perspective of what a properly defined field of socio-onomastics is and what its legitimate pursuits should be. This does not call for a radically different perception of its subject matter from those already adopted by earlier scholars but it does ask us to consider socio-onomastics not entirely as a sector or branch of socio-linguistics but as a closely allied approach to the study of names in a social context, not tagging on a sociological set of values and procedures but merging them with the onomastic ones. If, as has been said, "Sociolinguistics ... is that part of linguistics which is concerned with language as a social and cultural phenomenon. It investigates the field of language and society",[10] then it is my contention that "Socio-onomastics is that part of onomastics which is concerned with names as social and cultural phenomena. It investigates the field of names and society". If you find it difficult to reconcile your own definition of socio-onomastics with mine, please be nevertheless patient with me while I try to enumerate, and comment briefly on, some of the several facets of socio-onomastic investigation in view of these introductory remarks. I hope that once exemplification has done its job we may not find ourselves so far apart, after all; for, as I see it, this is not an existential quarrel but rather a way of looking at the same material from a different point of view or with a different focus. Someone endowed with a sufficiently wide-angled vision may even be able to accommodate both views. If, on the other hand, they cannot be incorporated into one vision with even the best will in the world, they should still be able to enrich each other.

What, then, is the subject matter, scope and purpose of socio-onomastics, or, adapting a little frivolously the title of a famous German inaugural lecture written and offered not terribly far from here almost 200 years ago: "Was heißt und zu welchem Ende studiert man Sozio-onomastik?[11] When we attempt to answer this question, it becomes immediately obvious that what we have termed here socio-onomastics is narrower or more circumscribed than any definition which might be put forward by someone of a more generous inclination, for, in a sense, the whole field of onomastics is socio-onomastics since naming and using names are social phenomena, are unthinkable without society.[12] The individuation of persons and places through onomastic signs and the expression of the relationship to other persons and places individuated, by the same means create, maintain and structure society and the habitat in which it is located. When viewed this broadly, it is redundant to prefix the term *onomastics* with the qualifier *socio-*, as in some way every onomastic act is a social act and no name exists which is not part of the communicative system of a group, however large or small. If, despite this potential redundancy, we apply the term socio-onomastics more restrictively, we are following well-established practice, for socio-linguists have had to wrestle with exactly the same problem and, in defining this stance, have, in their turn, taken their cue from the dialectologists who are, after all, in many respects their precursors, and ours as well. Just as the central issue of socio-linguistics has become societally and culturally motivated and induced linguistic variability, so the study of societally and culturally engendered anthroponymic and toponymic variables is bound to be at the heart of all socio-onomastic endeavour. I am careful at this point not to rule out other lines of enquiry which might fruitfully explore the societal and cultural base of names but it seems to me that we have plenty on our plates as it is and have the consolation, if not the assurance, of being on fairly safe ground if primarily we concentrate on the issue of variety. I hope that I will also be forgiven if I avoid the, in an international forum like this, thorny question of the kinds of subdivisions and their underlying causes which make human society the multi-faceted phenomenon which it is perceived to be. For the sort of socio-onomastics I have in mind it is of secondary importance whether we speak of classes or strata or, more neutrally, of special groups within society,[13] since whatever terminology we choose will, for its own peculiar reasons and if argued consistently, adequately support the notion of *appropriateness* which is the ultimate arbiter in all onomastic usage.[14] To know and to use the right variable of a name under the right circumstances in the company of the right people is what makes for onomastic competence, and it is therefore my main argument that onomastic variables which are the legitimate subject matter of socio-onomastics are chiefly created by different societal and cultural *registers*. If I say "chiefly" and not "exclusively", this less than encompassing claim indicates awareness of the fact that there may also well be a historical dimension to socio-onomastics which accounts for diachronic change, the domain of a kind of "socio-historical onomastics" paralleling a proposed scholarly pursuit termed "socio-historical linguistics", with its own status and methodology.[15] Register is so much a feature of synchronic approaches that the juxtaposition of register and history or the impact of register on linguistic and onomastic change has so far received scant attention at a sufficiently abstract level although the concrete evidence is clearly available.[16] It is therefore at present difficult to gauge systematically the socio-historical factors which are accountable for, or at play in, contemporary onomastic variation.

As far as the contemporary scene is concerned, we cannot go far wrong in adapting for our purposes the principles of linguistic dialectology which for so many years have served so well the recognition and analysis of the spatial distribution of certain linguistic items, especially in the fields of pronunciation, word formation and lexis, as long as we bear in mind that geographical variants of names, too, are subject to appropriate usage in social and cultural registers, mostly with regard to their pronunciation and the existence and employment of alternative names.[17] There are no circumstances under which names are given and used in which social pressures of one kind or another can be discounted. If, however, we paint our picture with a fairly broad brush when plotting the geographical scatter of, let us say, certain place-name types or elements, as has been done many times over in many countries, we are well on our way toward establishing visual criteria for the isolation of onomastic dialects which may be closely related to linguistic dialects but are never identical with them. It has been shown quite convincingly that the distribution of certain place-name generics, though largely coinciding with that of the lexical items from the toponymic sector of the vocabulary from which they stem, is often either wider or more confined than that of its lexical counterparts.[18] The areas enclosed within most isonyms are not congruous with the areas bounded by the corresponding isoglosses, and it is therefore risky to use both words and names indiscriminately on the same map. Thus, even where close discernible links exist between the contemporary lexicon and the contemporary onomasticon, onomastic dialects and linguistic dialects are not the same.

This is even truer of the distribution of names which have no equivalent in the contemporary vocabulary, either because they are relics from an earlier phase of the language currently spoken or because they are survivals from a language now extinct. In Scotland, for example, the distribution of names ending in -*worth* or -*wick* or beginning with *Pit*- indicates onomastic dialect areas which, for these reasons, are nor matched in the contemporary lexicon. Even further removed, because completely unrelated, are onomastic dialects illustrated by names which have never been part of any language spoken in those parts of the country in which they occur and are therefore not accessible through etymological strategies. Prime examples of these are the so-called classical town names of North America, like Syracuse, Marathon, Homer, Vestal, Hannibal, Marcellus, and so on, which were transferred unanalysed, from the end of the eighteenth century onwards, from the Mediterranean to upstate New York and beyond.[19] In the New World, they have never been part of the lexicon but only of the onomasticon, specifically the toponymicon, and they have therefore never carried any lexical semantic freight but, at least initially, a great deal of onomastic contents; they are empty of *Bedeutung* but brimful of *Bedeutsamkeit*, to use Debus's helpful term[20] (they are empty of *meaning* but full of *meaningfulness*, as one might render this distinction in English). Their significance has always been social rather then linguistic, and while they deserve sustained onomastic attention, their interest to the socio-linguist is minimal. They undoubtedly identify real, recognisable places as successfully as any other name and are therefore perfectly adequate toponymic markers in the structuring of an actual landscape; in addition, however, they have created a landscape of the mind which has perhaps proved more durable than their toponymic constellations, insofar as their original political and cultural intentions bear no relationship to the places to which they apply. The "Military Tract" which inspired them is, after all, forgotten by all but historians, is a thing of the past, and the geographical distribution of these names, their onomastic dialect, no longer reflects the socio-psychological motivation which made them possible, indeed insisted on them, in the first place.

It could be argued that this last group of names – and there are hundreds of them – constitutes one kind of onomastic *field* rather than an onomastic *dialect*, and there would be some merit to that argument. It is always difficult to make a clear-cut distinction between these two modes of describing and defining clusters of names sharing identical or similar characteristics, for since toponymic items identify places, their relationship to each other never lacks a spatial element, and the idea of "field", though introduced into lexical and name studies metaphorically from physics, brings to the investigation of place-names an additional terminological poignancy, not inappropriate to the subject matter.[21] At any rate, the act of creating a landscape out of a wilderness through naming, thus introducing the potential for topographical as well as social orientation, not only identifies and individualises but makes other places and their names possible. Human beings live lives by spending time in and among locations, and any place-nomenclature is, for this reason, among other things also intensely, sometimes severely, social. The existence of one name anywhere is a contradiction in itself; identity hones itself on otherness and names shape each other. No name is without its field to which it belongs, and because we are not dealing with lexical semantics when determining such fields, the same name can be part of several of them. Within any one field, duplication is normally not possible, as onomastic contents cannot be shared by different names in the same register. Whereas in an onomastic dialect, in the strictest sense of that construct, geographical distribution is the only criterion, an onomastic field, while not without its spatial nuances, receives and maintains its variants usually from more then just a sense of person or space. Appropriate usage within the confines of a "field" demands, on the part of the competent user, sensitivities and delicateness beyond the skills immediately associated with the successful manipulation of names, both in their employment and in their interpretation. Through the felicitous constellation of place-names life and landscape approximate each other; similar anthroponymic constellations make personal inter-relationships communicable, on the level of both the signifier and the signified, as long as one prerequisite is fulfilled above all – a minimal amount of shared name contents on the part of speaker and listener, or writer and reader.

In this respect, it is important to note that in European and European-derived societies we have practically lost the immediate lexical-cum-onomastic access to the locus of the named person in the contemporary society in question. In Lowland Scotland, for example, the rule of thumb applies that until the fifteenth century most surnames were given and used with their full lexical force.[22] Somebody called *Baxter* was indeed a baker, somebody bearing the name *Cruickshank* would be bow-legged, somebody named Thomson would have a father named *Tom*, and somebody blessed with the name of *Buchan* would indeed somehow hail from or be connected with the region of *Buchan* in the Scottish northeast. The locus of identity of each person would be in the present, each name placing the named person in his or her proper position. When, mostly for administrative reasons, surnames became heritable, this locus of identity was shifted irrevocably to the past, at least in the formal register.[23] Lexical meaning and name contents became separated; after a while, congruity of name and occupation, or name and personal characteristics, or name and parentage, or name and locality was no longer expected, and in the rare instances when it occurred – a baker being called *Baxter*, let us say, or a man named *Thomson* having a father named *Tom* – would elicit a surprised lifting of an eyebrow or a knowing smile. The socio-onomastic implications of this revolutionary change are immense but have never been studied in full, partly, one feels, because a socio-onomastic "window" on this deeply significant and disquieting change was not available, despite a plethora of excellent limited studies which have provided valuable insights in many other respects.

Fortunately, however, register-specific variation has never been abandoned altogether, and neither the almost total lack of choice in the acquisition of one's surname nor the fairly circumscribed selection of first names from anthroponomica consisting either of names fit for the naming of girls or of names fit for the naming of boys, pared down further by other social constraints, has produced a person who bears only one name under all circumstances and at all times. Not only are there appropriate chronological changes which turn *Johnnie* first into *John* and then into *Mr John Macpherson* but both *Johnnie* and *John* are likely to persist in informal registers and perhaps *Johnnie the Post* is added or *Big John*, or both. As a by-product of her study of language death in Easter Sutherland, for example, Nancy Dorian has given us an illuminating account of by-names in the community in which she did her field-work and of the delicate rules which regulate their usage in the presence or absence of the person named.[24] All of us here are nostalgically familiar with teachers' nicknames from our own schooldays and their register-bound application. Under these and similar circumstances, translation of a name from one register to another, and perhaps to a third, is an essential part of name competence, and inappropriate usage may not only be impolite but may have disastrous results, as a consequence of breaking a societal code. Scottish place-name doublets like *Fraserburgh* and *The Broch*, or *Edinburgh* and *Auld Reekie* are still similarly restricted variables.

I have used the term "translation" deliberately in this context, knowing full well that it has frequently been argued to be a special characteristic of names that they are not translatable. My own observations have led me to the conclusion that this claim has little merit, not only when applied to the phenomenon of register-switching but also in the more accepted sense of translation from one language to another, as long as we recognise that the translation of names occurs mostly on an onomastic, and rarely on a lexical, level. French *Paris* [pa-'ri:] English *Paris* ['pa-rɪs], and German *Paris* [pa-'ri:s] all have the same name contents, despite their phonological differences. Italian *Milano*, English *Milan* and German *Mailand* belong to the same category; although their graphemic presentation is also different and the pronunciations are further apart. Pairs like German *München* – English *Munich*, German *Regensburg* – French *Ratisbone*, German *Wien* – English *Vienna*, German *Köln* – English *Cologne*, Danish *København* – and English *Copenhagen* (or German *Kopenhagen*), Italian *Firenze* and English *Florence* (or German *Florenz*) are additional examples with varying degrees of similarity. That phonological adaptations are not only the most common onomastic translations of place-names within the range of internationally known major names but also in bilingual and bicultural situations involving languages in contact in more regional or even local situations is demonstrated, for instance, by Gaelic and English names used by bilingual speakers for the same places in Scotland: Gaelic *Inbhir-nis* and English *Inverness*, Gaelic *Sleibhte* and English *Sleat*, Gaelic *Banbh* and English *Banff*, Gaelic *Raineach* and English *Rannoch*, and hundreds more. The next most common category consists of names which are completely unrelated to each other in the languages, from a lexically semantic point of view, like *Newton* and *Baile Mhic Phail*, and *Newtonferry* and *Port nan Long* in North Uist, or *Fort Augustus* and *Cill Chuimein*, *Ceannloch* and *Campbeltown*, and *Sutherland* and *Cataibh* on the mainland. Onomastic translations that are also lexical translations, like Gaelic *Cearamh Meadhonach* and English *Middlequarter*, or Gaelic *An t-Eilean Dubh* and English *Black Isle*, are much rarer, a fact which reinforces our contention that lexical meaning is of little or no consequence in such name usage.[25] Languages in contact therefore also create variants which are potential grist to the socio-onomastic mill, and one might even include such subtle variations as the local terms *Fawkirk*, *Glenleevet* and *Aynster* for the common Scottish English *Falkirk*, *Glenlivet* and *Anstruther*. Employment of the latter triad immediately stamps one as an outsider. The onomastic translation from one register to another, from one language to another, from standard to dialect or from general standard to local standard is not only possible but necessary and a ready-made area for socio-onomastic investigation.

Let me briefly draw your attention to one more intriguing phenomenon before attempting to draw these rather loosely woven threads together: In the secondary reinterpretation of names – I try to avoid the term "folk-etymology" because of its evaluative, usually pejorative, overtones – it happens quite frequently that the suggested lexical meaning is bolstered by, or is said to be the result of, an event which is narrated in connection with the reinterpretation.[26] Thus story becomes a name's new link with the lexicon; a name becomes narratable or a kind of shorthand for story. It is a fascinating thought that the speech acts of naming and narration, perhaps the most ubiquitous of all human intellectual traits, show themselves so closely allied in the process.[27] Not only *nominare* but also *narrare necesse est*! We survive because we can structure the world around us through identifying naming and also not less because we can create true chunks of the past through narration. My old friends *homo nominans* and *homo narrans*, turn out to be not just twins but one and the same.

What does it all add up to? As I said at the beginning, I would rather have carried owls to Athens than socio-onomastic thoughts to Leipzig, but perhaps a little re-thinking of well known matters has done no harm; each generation, each scholar has to plough furrows which others have ploughed before him; otherwise there would be no seed time and no new harvest. What is old in what I have said is painfully obvious; what has a certain degree of novelty is perhaps the insistence that name studies of all kinds must heed the realisation that names are part of an onomasticon rather than of a lexicon and that consequently the kinds of variables and variants we study from a socio-onomastic point of view must indeed be primarily onomastic ones. Above all, research into the social dimensions of onomastics must increasingly concentrate on name usage rather than on name giving and must become more strongly aware of the important role which register – and language – specific appropriateness plays in both name acquisition and name competence. Names as social and cultural phenomena, with special emphasis on onomastic variability, seem more central than one could perhaps have anticipated to all name study – *Quod erat demonstrandum*.

Notes

1   *Der Name in Sprache und Gesellschaft: Beiträge zur Theorie der Onomastik.* Deutsch-Slawische Forschungen zur Namenkunde und Siedlungsgeschichte Nr. 27 (Berlin: Akademie-Verlag, 1973).

2   Ernst Eichler, "Aufgaben und Perspektiven der Namenforschung in der Deutschen Demokratischen Republik" *Ibid.*, pp. 7-12.

3   Hans Walther, "Zu den gesellschaftswissenschaftlichen Grundpositionen der Namenforschung". *Ibid.* pp. 13-30.

4   Wolfgang Fleischer. "Variationen von Eigennamen". *Ibid.* pp. 52-63.

5   For example. Vincent Blanár, "Das spezifisch Onomastische". *Ibid.* pp. 31-51.

6   For instance. William Bright (editor). *Sociolinguistics: Proceedings of the UCLA Sociolinguistics Conference, 1964.* Janua Linguarum, Series Major XX (The Hague: Mouton & Co., 1966); Joshua A. Fishman, *Sociolinguistics: A Brief Introduction* (Rowley, Mass., Newbury House Publishers. 1970); Pier Paolo Giglioli (ed.), *Language and Social Context* (Harmondsworth, Middlesex: Penguin Books, 1972); John J. Gumpers and Dell Hymes (eds.), *Directions in*

Sociolinguistics: the ethnography of communication (New York: Holt, Rinehart and Winston, 1972); J .B. Pride and Janet Holmes (eds.), *Sociolinguistics: Selected Reading* (Harmondsworth, Middlesex: Penguin Books. 1972); Norbert Dittmar, *Soziolinguistik* (Frankfurt/Main: Athenäum, 1973); Roger T. Bell, *Sociolinguistics: goals, approaches and problems* (London: B.T. Batford Ltd., 1976); Robert N. St. Clair and Howard Giles (eds.). *The Social and Psychological Contexts of Language* (Hillsdale, N.J.: Laurence Erlbaum Associates, 1980); Suzanne Romaine, *Sociolinguistics: Variation in Speech Communities* (London: Edward Arnold, 1982); Peter Trudgill, *Sociolinguistics: An Introduction to Language and Society.* Revised Edition (Harmondsworth, Middlesex: Penguin Books, 1983); William Downes. *Language and Society* (London: Fontana Paperback, 1984). Several years ago, Victoria Belen'kaja drew attention to the need to study the social dimensions of names in her article "Die Toponomastik als soziolinguistisches Problem". In: *Sowjetische Namenforschung.* Eds. E. Eichler *et al.* (Berlin: Akademie-Verlag, 1975), p. 43.

7   Thus, for example, Hans Walther speaks of "Onomastik als Zweigbereich der Linguistik" (Walther, p. 13), but see also A.A. Reformatskij, "Zur Stellung der Onomastik innerhalb der Linguistik". *Sowjetische Namenforschung.* p. 11.

8   See J. Kuryłowich, *La position linguistique des noms propres. Onomastica* 2 (1956), p. 1.

9   See W.F.H. Nicolaisen, "The Semantics of Place-names and Their Elements". *Proceedings of the NORNA Conference.* Reykjavik, August, 1983; "Nomen, Noun and Name: The Lexical Horns of an Onomastic Dilemma". In: *Historical and Editorial studies in Medieval and Early Modern English,* forthcoming.

10   Trudgill, p. 32.

11   My parody is, of course, of Friedrich Schiller's famous "Was heißt und zu welchem Ende studiert man Universalgeschichte" the published version of his inaugural lecture at the University of Jena on May, 26, 1789.

12   For socio-linguistics this view is put forward by William Labov for whom there is no linguistics other than socio-linguistics which for him is therefore "an oddly redundant term" (William Labov, *Socio-linguistic Patterns*, Philadelphia: University of Pennsylvania Press, 1972, p. 183.

13   See, for example, Rainer Frank, *Zur Frage einer schichtenspezifischen Personennamengebung:* Kieler Beiträge zur deutschen Sprachgeschichte 1 (Neumünster: Karl Wachholtz Verlag, 1977).

14   From a socio-onomastic point of view, all onomastic usage is "situated" in Roger Bell's sense (Bell, p. 31).

15   See Suzanne Romaine, *Socio-Historical. Linguistics: its status and methodology* (Cambridge: Cambridge University Press. 1982).

16   In *Language Change: Progress or Decay?* (London: Fontana Paperbacks. 1982), Jean Aitchison discusses, among other things, some "socio-linguistic causes of linguistic change" (pp. 111-128).

17 See the seminal article by Friedhelm Debus, "Soziologische Namengeographie: Zur sprachgeographisch-soziologischen Betrachtung der Nomina propria". In: *Wortgeographie und Gesellschaft: Festgabe für Ludwig Erich Schmitt.* Ed. Walter Mitzka (Berlin: Erich Schmitt, 1968), pp. 28-48.

18 W.F.H. Nicolaisen, "Onomastic Dialects". *American Speech* 55 (1980), pp. 36-45.

19 Wilbur Zelinsky, "Classical Town Names in the United States: The Historical Geography of an American Idea". *Geographical Review* 57 (1967), pp. 463-495.

20 F.L. Debus, *Aspekte zum Verhältnis Name – Wort.* (Groningen: J.B. Wolters, 1966), p. 16.

21 See W.F.H. Nicolaisen, "Lexical and Onomastic Fields". *Proceedings of the Thirteenth International Conference of Onomastic Sciences*, Cracow 1978, Vol. II (Cracow 1982), pp. 209-216, and the literature mentioned there.

22 George F. Black, *The Surnames of Scotland: Their Origin, Meaning and History* (New York: The New York Public Library, 1946), pp. xix-xxxii.

23 See W.F.H. Nicolaisen, "Tension and Extension: Thoughts on Scottish surnames and Medieval Popular Culture". *Journal of Popular Culture* 14, 1 (Summer 1980), pp. 119-130.

24 Nancy C. Dorian, "East Sutherland By-Naming". *Scottish Studies* 14 (1970), pp. 59-65; "A substitute name system in the Scottish Highlands". *American Anthropologist* 72 (1970), pp. 303-319; *Language Death: The Life Cycle of a Scottish Gaelic Dialect* (Philadelphia: University of Pennsylvania Press, 1981), p. 57.

25 See also W.F.H. Nicolaisen, "Place-names in Bilingual Communities". *Names* 23 (1975), pp. 167-174; and *Scottish Place-Names: Their Study and Significance* (London: B.T. Batsford Ltd., 1976), pp. 53-56.

26 W.F.H. Nicolaisen, "Place-Name Legends: An Onomastic Mythology". *Folklore* 87 (1976), pp. 146-159; "Place-names and Their Stories". *Ortnamnssällskapets i Uppsala Årsskrift* 1977, pp. 23-29; "Some Humorous Folk-Etymological Narratives". *New York Folklore* 3 (1977), pp. 1-14.

27 W.F.H. Nicolaisen, "Names and Narratives". *Journal of American Folklore* 97 (1984), pp. 259-272.

Names 33, 1-2 (1985) 29-38

Burnside of Duntrune:
An Essay in Praise of Ordinariness

NAMES, and place-names in particular, have long been recognised as very special raw material for the study of linguistic stratification and settlement history. Their potential longevity, their often amazing power of survival, their ability to outlive the languages that coined them and the lexica from which they were coined provide them with an aura of fascination, and even the most hard-headed name scholar or linguist cannot help succumbing, on occasion, to what may almost be termed the romance of names. Exploring and exploiting this fascinating potential has therefore, in the course of the last two centuries, become the legitimate pursuit, if not the all-absorbing pre-occupation, of scholar and layman alike. As a result, our understanding of the nature of names has been greatly enhanced, our methods in handling them been greatly refined, and our strategies in laying bare their secrets become much more sophisticated.

It is probably no exaggeration to claim that much of this undoubted fascination of names and most of the very keen, and sometimes very passionate, interest taken in them by an ever-growing number of people[1] stem from a desire to make transparent what is opaque, to recover, or at least to establish, meaning for the meaningless, and to gain access to a seemingly inaccessible past. The investigation of names, demanding, as it does, the careful piecing together of scraps of evidence, from the earliest spelling to the modem pronunciation, pleases or arouses the detective that is in all of us, and the devices and successes of onomastic etymology become the appealing trappings of stealthy stalking and dramatic disclosure. Solving, to our own satisfaction if not necessarily to that of others, the "Case of the Mysterious River Name" creates a sense of achievement not easily rivalled by any other intellectual endeavour, and having "solved" it, we are not going to be stopped from taking on another case, and yet another, and another …, and we are not easily persuaded that sometimes our skills do not quite match our tasks.

Indeed, so strong is our concentration on the spectacular that we tend to ignore, or at least neglect, those names which do not challenge the onomastic Sherlock Holmes in us and which we therefore regard as blandly pedestrian or almost disconcertingly accessible without much work on our part and which, in our dismay at having been cheated, we dub "self-explanatory". What we presumably mean by this is that such names, which have an awful habit of being highly repetitive, from an etymological point of view wear their lexical meanings on their sleeves, so to speak, thus depriving us of satisfying our urge to unravel mysteries and to expose the hidden. It is to some of these Cinderellas of name studies that I wish to draw attention in this brief essay, taking as my starting-point the assumption that there is no such thing as a "self-explanatory" name, and that we are more likely to learn something of general significance about those characteristically human traits of names, naming and using names from the commonplace, ordinary and frequent than from the singular, extraordinary and rare, however attractive and revealing this latter group of names may be in other respects.

The evidence which I wish to discuss consists of names of populated places in Scotland as registered in the Census of April 23, 1961, the last census for which such detailed population figures are available.[2] All the names in question are, at least in a Scottish context, lexically transparent to speakers of English, and the places to which they apply are, more often than not, among the smaller settlements, having anything down to a dozen or two inhabitants. Because of their comparatively small size – quite often they are farms or little hamlets – and because all of them have been coined within the most recent stratum in Scottish linguistic history, English, there is little likelihood that these names have been given in imitation or commemoration of names of important places elsewhere; it therefore follows that, in their morphological structure as well as in their choice of elements, they resemble most closely a kind of English onomastic vernacular in Scotland, at least as far as the naming of inhabited places is concerned. Thus their significance as a corpus lies, on the whole, in their very insignificance as individual names. Blandness and humbleness are their virtues.

Naturally, it is impossible to survey, on this occasion, all the names which would fall into this category. I have therefore selected only those names which, in their choice of generics or specifics, or both, demonstrate an interlocking relationship with other names or an interdependence of the geographical features associated with the naming of the settlement. The purpose of this selection is to utilise this substantial so-called "self-explanatory" group of place-names for the furtherance of our understanding of how we create and view a landscape through the act of naming and of how confined, specific and almost predictable this process and its results really are. Our vision in creating a familiar habitat onomastically is fairly limited, it seems, but it is a vision which nevertheless deserves our best attention.

The prototype of the kind of name which will be at the heart of our discussion not only occurs most frequently in the census lists, it is also the name which, perhaps because of its frequency (16 occurrences), first made me aware of the peculiar properties of the group of names which it represents: *Burnside*. This name, on a Scottish map, in a Scottish landscape, offers absolutely no problems to the would-be onomastic etymologiser; its lexical meaning is as clear today as when it was first given, and the fact that its specific – *burn* – is the only word which anybody ever uses in Scotland in reference to a smallish water-course (larger water-courses are *rivers*) locates it without a doubt in a clearly definable and understood linguistic, cultural and even national context. *Burnside* is a *Scottish* place-name. At the same time, the same specific indicates one of the most favourite and most advantageous locations for any human settlement which is to have any real chance to prosper – near a stream, or at least near a source of water. As part of a compound name, *Burn-* speaks of the conscious and deliberate attention the namers (settlers?) gave to this choice of site and to the prominence of this relatively major geographical feature in the vicinity of the human habitation. The generic *-side* divulges the precise directory relationship which that habitation has to the geographical feature: It is located by the *side* of a *burn*, not anywhere else. It is where its name says it is. That a name like *Burnside* has taken on new toponymic content in addition to its lexical meaning or, in suburbia or in a cityscape where the original watercourse may have become all but invisible, to the exclusion of that lexical meaning, is another matter which cannot concern us as part of this discussion, although it points to some other very interesting aspects of the so-called "self-explanatory" name, as does the shift of the stress to the generic *-side* which clearly distinguishes the name *Burnsíde* from its lexical counterpart *búrnside*. *Burnsíde* can therefore not be anything but a name although its word origins are never in doubt.

Of course, the preceding commentary and analysis will not have created the kind of excitement which might have followed the rigorously argued and amply supported revelation that *Oxton* in Berwickshire (*Hulf-keliston, Ulfkeliston* 1206) was originally "Ulfkell's settlement", that *Leadburn* in Midlothian (*Legbernard* c. 1128) is a late re-interpretation by English speakers of a Gaelic name meaning "Bernard's stone", or that *Ancrum* in Roxburghshire (*Alnecrumba* c. 1124, *Alncromb* c. 1150) represents a development of an early Celtic name meaning "bend on the river *Ale* (*Alne* 1176)".[3] These three names are either misleading in their modern forms *(Oxton* and *Leadburn)* or completely opaque semantically (*Ancrum*). They masquerade in new guises, are not what they seem, whereas *Burnside* and the category of names for which it stands are exactly what they appear to be.[4] As individual etymological puzzles they have little or nothing to offer, but when taken out of their isolation they begin to speak of patterns, perceptions and polarities, and it is the very fact that their etymologies are not in doubt and do not have to be argued over that makes them such splendid evidence.

Burnside is given a much fuller sense when contrasted, on the one hand, with such names as *Birkenside, Bogside, Braeside, Damside, Denside, Dykeside, Gateside* (9 examples), *Glenside, Hillside, Kirkside, Knowside, Lochside* (4 examples), *Moss-side, Muirside, Myreside, Rigside, Roadside, Springside, Voeside, Waterside* and *Woodside* (5 examples), and, on the other hand, with *Burnfoot, Burnhead, Burnmouth* or even *Burnbrae, Burnbanks*. Not only does -*side* turn out to be an extremely popular toponymic generic (representing a popular location for a settlement in relation to a perceived geographical feature), but there are apparently other discernible locations along the course of a stream which by their very existence define -*side* as non-*foot*, non-*head*, non-*mouth*, non-*brae*, and non-*bank(s)*. *Burnside* as an isolated named feature is inconceivable without other named features (actual or potential) such as *Bogside, Glenside, Hillside* and *Woodside*, or *Burnfoot, Burnhead* and *Burnmouth*. Perhaps one might go even one step further and claim that a settlement name such as *Burnside* would be impossible without other settlements called *Bogside, Glenside, Hillside, Woodside, Burnfoot, Burnhead, Burnmouth* and so on; for it seems reasonable to adopt the premise that it is not necessary for a natural feature to have been named *Burnside, Woodside,* or *Burnmouth* before such a name could have been transferred to a settlement built in or near such a location.[5] *Burnside, Woodside,* and *Burnmouth,* may, in many instances, well have meant or have had the onomastic potential to mean from the very beginning "settlement on the side of a burn", "settlement on the side of a wood", or "settlement at the mouth of a burn", respectively. This is, however, a tangential consideration which does not affect the central thrust of the main argument advanced here which is rather an extension of the theory of "onomastic fields"[6] than an exposition of how words become names or what the relationship may be between lexical meaning and onomastic content.[7] Name transfer from a natural feature to a man-made one is, of course, always possible but only provable in the rarest of cases where the evidence permits such proof.

The two generics found compounded with *Burn-* which most emphatically indicate a locational relationship to a water-course, in addition to *-side*, i.e. *-head* and *-foot*, make quite frequent appearances in combination with other topographical specifics, often the same as those to which *-side* may be added. Thus we have: *Bankhead, Bayhead, Boghead, Braehead(s), Carsehead, Craighead, Crofthead, Damhead(s), Denhead* (5 examples), *Drumhead, Dykehead* and *Dykegatehead, Edgehead, Fauldhead, Gatehead, Glenhead, Greenhead, Haughhead, Heughhead, Hillhead* (5 examples), *Holmhead, Knowehead, Lawhead, Loanhead, Lochhead, Mosshead, Muirhead* and *Parkhead* (4 examples each), *Pathhead, Sandhead, Townhead* (7 examples), *Wellhead(s)* and *Woodhead(s)*; also *Bankfoot, Bridgefoot, Croftfoot, Glenfoot, Greenfoot, Lochfoot, Muirfoot, Townfoot* and *Waterfoot*. *Side, head,* and *foot* are paralleled by many names containing the element *end* which seemingly does not occur with *Burn-*, perhaps because of the semantically equivalent formation *Burnmouth*. Names with the generic *-end* are, for example: *Bankend, Bogend, Bridgend* (10 examples), *Broomend, Campend, Causewayend, Craigend(s), Denend, Greenend, Hillend* (4 examples), *Lochend, Moorend, Mossend, Muirend, Riggend,* and *Woodend* (8 examples). *Bank,* too, is found with specifics other than *Burn-*, such as: *Carsebank, Causewaybank, Chapelbank, Deanbank, Kirkbank, Kirkfieldbank, Mossbank, Springbank, Wellbank* and *Woodbank*.

These lists are, of course, not exhaustive but they are sufficiently representative to reveal that the geographical features which enter into these orientational names as specifics are not only small in number but convey the notion of landscape perceived in relatively simple terms – the hill, the wood, the burn, the bridge, the moor, the path or gate (road), the loch, the glen, etc. – and structured accordingly. On a taxonomical scale, these terms – and that applies to *bank, bog, dyke, dean, croft, dam, law, loan, knowe,* etc. as well – would be placed near the semantically least discriminatory end but this lack of semantic discrimination obviously does not disqualify them from providing an adequate or even satisfying, certainly a manageable, sense of landscape – quite the contrary. It is also worth noting that topographic terms adopted by Scottish English from Scottish Gaelic, such as *bog, brae, craig, drum, glen, loch* and others, feature prominently in these toponymic permutations, as expressions of the very Scottishness of the landscape perceived and named.[8] Vernacular landscapes are never culturally neutral, neither lexically nor onomastically.[9]

This becomes even more apparent when we widen the selective meshes of our investigatory net and also consider names in which the place of the lexical specific is taken by the name of a feature near the settlements in question. As far as the type *Burnside* is concerned, compounds containing names of water-courses are the most obvious examples, such as *Devonside, Earnside, Edenside, Leetside, Lochtayside, Lochyside, Ness-side*, or *Tarfside*. Similar names are found with the generics *bank* (*Almondbank, Blyth Bank, Clydebank, Cononbank, Deebank, Edenbank, Gala Bank, Gogar Bank, Luggiebank, Lunan Bank, Manor Bank, Noranbank,* and *Teviotbank*), *foot* (*Blackwaterfoot, Byreburnfoot, Caddonfoot, Elvanfoot* and *Lendalfoot*), *head* (*Kelvinhead, Lunanhead, Wanlockhead,* as well as *Lochdonhead, Lochearnhead,* and *Lochgilphead,* instead of the lexical *lochhead*), and *-mouth* (*Edenmouth, Eyemouth, Lossiemouth, Taymouth*). These toponymically oriented compounds for which there is, by their very nature, no equivalent or starting point in the lexicon make it clear that, as far as the creators of these settlement names were concerned, structured orientation in a landscape is achieved as much by relating to existing names as by discerning features picked out with the help of the topographic sector of the vocabulary. The inclusion of a river name like *Eden* or *Lunan* or *Teviot* gives the new settlement a specificity and locatory precision which words such as *burn* or *hill* or *loch* cannot provide. If the danger of creating an instant, easily misunderstood, hierarchy can be tolerated, one might be tempted to call *Devonside, Clydebank, Caddonfoot, Kelvinhead* and *Lossiemouth secondary* names which would not exist, or would certainly lose much of their structural function, without the *primary* names *Devon, Clyde, Caddon, Kelvin* and *Lossie* which they embrace. Such onomastic rather than lexical compounds also demonstrate that, despite their non-English or pre-English origins and their undoubted semantic opacity, *Devon, Clyde, Caddon, Kelvin,* and *Lossie* are toponymic (or hydronymic) ingredients of the English language and therefore on a par with *burn, hill,* or *loch,* and certainly with *Blackwater* and *Byreburn*.

That the equivalency of function is complete is shown by the onomastic contrasts *Edenside–Edenbank* and *Lunan Bank–Lunanhead* which parallel *Burnside–Burnbank* and *Burnbank–Burnhead*, respectively. *Clydebank–Clydeside* and *Deebank–Deeside* are other cases in point, although in these instances the *-side*-names represent districts or regions rather than well-defined settlements. When we look beyond the category of place-names derived from river names we discover that primary names can generate quite a few secondary names in this fashion, as, for example, *Ayton Castle, Cocklaw, Mains* and *-law*; *Caverton Hillhead, Mains* and *Mill*; *Fala Dam, Hill, Mains, Mill,* and *Cottages*; *Old Cambus East Mains, Townhead* and *West Mains*; or *Preston Grange, Links, Mains* and *-pans*. The primary names *Ayton, Caverton, Fala, Old Cambus,* and *Preston* are also extant.

This principle of onomastic contrast is even more apparent and more common in place-names in which a name, not a word, takes on the role of generic. In such names, distinctions and oppositions are achieved through appropriate lexical specifics, such as those referring to the points of the compass, so that we find *East* and *West Barns, Bennan, Blanerne, Brackly, Cairnbeg*, etc.; *Easter* and *Wester Balgedie, Broomhouse, Calcots, Cowden, Culmalundie, Friarton*, etc.; or *North* and *South Balfern, Belton, Boisdale, Braegar, Connel, Corston*, etc. Similar contrasts, usually supported by the lie of the land, are seen in such pairs as *Low* and *High Valleyfield; Lower* and *Upper Barvas, Bayble, Knockando, Largo* and *Milovaig; Nether* and *Upper Blainslie, Coullie, Dysart* and *Urquhart; or Nether* and *Over Hailes*. An original difference in size accounts for *Little* and *Meikle Clinterty, Pinkerton* and *Port of Spittal*; and earlier and later settlements are contrasted in *Old* and *New Belses, Deer, Downie, Pentland*, and *Scone*. The use of *Mid* and *Middle* implies a tripartite division perfectly represented by *East, Mid*, and *West Calder* but less so by *Mid* and *West Yell, Middle* and *Wester Norton*, and *Middle* and *Easter Softlaw*. In these last three instances, it is safe to assume that there used to be, or perhaps still are, an *East Yell*, an *Easter Norton*, and a *Wester Softlaw*, respectively, but is not necessary for the threesome to have been complete at one stage in all instances. *Little Ballinluig* is sufficiently distinguished from *Ballinluig, Little Brechin* from *Brechin, Little Haddo* from *Haddo*, and *Little Lour* from *Lour*, as not to call for the use of a contrasting epithet *Meikle;* the larger settlement is represented by the unmarked name in these cases. The same may well be true of *High Auldgirth* vs. *Auldgirth, High Blantyre* vs. *Blantyre, High Bonnybridge* vs. *Bonnybridge, High Burnside* (!) vs. *Burnside, Low Banton* vs. *Banton, Low Grange* vs. *Grange*, and perhaps even *Meikle Kilchattan* vs. *Urchany*, although for the use of *Meikle* the argument is not so easily supported. It is also well worthy of note that in the majority of examples the specific *New* is not paralleled by *Old*, just as the many *Newtons* or *Newtowns* do not have contrasting *Oldtons* or *Oldtowns*, and probably never had. *New Pitsligo* vs. *Pitsligo* expresses the relationship between these names and between the settlements to which they apply, quite adequately; the zero specific in *Pitsligo* has to be interpreted as "old".[10] In all these examples, however, flaws in the basic evidence created by incompleteness, the vagaries of survival and documentation, and historical change make it impossible to arrive at clear-cut pronouncements in each case. Historically, for example, *Northberwick* was contrasted with *Southberwick*; now the latter is always only *Berwick*, obscuring the meaning of *North-* in the former.

Some of the *Newtons* and *Newtowns* just mentioned may serve to build a bridge to our last category of names to be paraded, for both of them also occur quite frequently qualified by the name of the place which formed the "old town". Thus we find *Eccles Newton, Edrom Newton* and *Roxburgh Newtown*, But also

Newton Mearns and *Newtown St. Boswells*, as well as the name type *Newton of Airlie, Newton of Arbirlot, Newton of Balcanquhal, Newton of Balcormo, Newton of Ballunie, Newton of Darnaway, Newton of Falkland,* etc., and *Newtown of Ardtoe, Newtown of Beltrees* and *Newtown of Swiney.* In Scotland, this type is formed on a Gaelic phrase model like *Allt Bad nan Clach* "burn of the clump of the stones", *Allt Creag Chait* "burn of the rock of the cat" or *Allt Uamha na Muice* "burn of the cave of the pig".[11] In its simplest form it occurs in Scottish English names as *Burn of Corrhatnich, Burn of Badenhilt, Burn of Berryhill* or, with other generics, *Mains of Balmanno, Bridge of Orchy, Grange of Barry, Heights of Auchterneed, Banks of Strichen, Moss of Barmuckity, Barns of Claverhouse, Boat of Garten, Greens of Coxton, Hill of Gutcher, Point of Coppister,* etc. What distinguishes the formation *Newton of Ballunie* from, let us say, *Mains of Balmanno* is the observation that lexical compounds such as *Newton* and *Newtown* occur much more frequently as independent place-names than simple generics like *Mains.* In a way, therefore, *Newton of Ballunie* represents a kind of tertiary name because both components, generic and specific, are onomastic in nature. The Scottish map is full of illustrative examples in the appropriate regions, such as *Backmuir of New Gilston, Midtown of Barras, Bridgend of Lintrathen, Burnside (!) of Duntrune, Hilton of Cadboll, Eastertown of Auchleuchries, Kirkton of Glenisla, Milton of Balgonie, Muirton of Ardblair, Backhill of Clackriach, Bailiesland of Leuchars, Castletown of Blairfindy, Boreland of Southwick, Coaltown of Burnturk, Newlands of Clyth, Hatton of Eassie, Townhead of Greenlaw,* and many others. Among these there are several examples of binary oppositions, such as *Milton* and *Coaltown of Balgonie, Milton of Conon* and *West Grange of Conon, Milton of Finavon* and *West Mains of Finavon,* but usually the contrast is with names containing simple generics such as *Mains, Grange, Crofts,* and *Clachan* or, most frequently, with the unqualified primary name itself, like *Broomhill of Ord* vs. *Ord, Kirkton of Oyne* vs. *Oyne,* or *Burnside of Duntrune* vs. *Duntrune.*[11]

Such two-member clusters of related names may have been, or may still be, part of more diversified toponymic constellations involving several names; only a detailed examination of all the sources, contemporary and historical, would show this. There is ample evidence, however, that many primary names have spawned quite a variety of secondary and tertiary names which can only be fully understood as part of such self-contained "mini-fields". Such clusters or fields, in their turn, link up with, exist through contrast with other clusters and fields and individual names, mutually defining and legitimising each other. These are best identified and analysed through observation and description of their synchronic function and usage, and through the strategies of investigation which, for their own purposes, resist the lure of etymological detective work and historical interpretation. If approached in this manner they have a wealth of information and insight to offer to the scholar, and their lack of teasing obscurity turns out to be anything but pedestrian blandness. There is no name in the world that does not excite in some way or other; one only has to be sensitive and open-minded enough to notice its appeal.

Notes

1   For North America, this is demonstrated by the annual reports, ably edited by E.C. Ehrensperger for so many years, on published and projected work in the field of name studies.

2   General Register Office, Edinburgh. *Place-names and Population Scotland.* An alphabetical list of populated places derived from the Census of Scotland (Edinburgh: Her Majesty's Stationery Office, 1967).

3   For these names, see W.F.H. Nicolaisen, *Scottish Place-Names: Their Study and Significance* (London: B.T. Batsford, 1976), pp. 18, 172, and 186.

4   This does not mean that we can take these names at face value; their documentary record has to be thoroughly investigated. Otherwise *Primside* (Roxburghshire) which is *Prenwensete* in the Melrose Liber (i.e. Cumbric *pren wen* "white tree" plus Old English *sete* "seat"), or such Sutherland names as *Linside*, *Coulside* and *Fallside* which, as their Gaelic antecedents *Lìonasaid*, *Culasaid* and *Fealasaid* show, contain Old Norse *setr* or *sætr*, could easily be mistaken for our type of name. *Moorfoot* (Midlothian), too, has to be discarded because early spellings such as *Morthwait* 1140-53, *Morthwayt* pre-1153, *Morthweth* 1174, *Mortwait* and *Mortwath* 1361 and others persuasively argue for a derivation from Old Norse *morþveit* "moor place".

5   This is an argument which I put forward and developed in greater detail at a place-name symposium in Reykjavik (Iceland), August 11-13, 1983: "The Semantics of Place-names and Their Elements", *NORNA-rapporter*, 28 (1985), pp. 60-71.

6   See W.F.H. Nicolaisen, "Lexical and Onomastic Fields", *Proceedings of the Thirteenth International Congress of Onomastic Sciences*. Cracow 1978, Vol. II (Cracow, 1982), pp. 209-216.

7   'These, of course, are also very important considerations although not of direct relevance here. See, for example, W.F.H. Nicolaisen, "Words as Names", *Onoma*. 20 (1976), pp. 142-163.

8   For the definition and derivation of such terms and of words peculiar to Scottish English see William Grant and David Murison (eds.), *The Scottish National Dictionary* (Edinburgh: The Scottish National Dictionary Association, 1931-1976).

9   That this also applies to the onomastic structure of vernacular landscapes in literature is suggested by W.F.H. Nicolaisen, "An Onomastic Vernacular in Scottish Literature", in: J. Derrick McClure (ed.), *Scotland and the Lowland Tongue* (Aberdeen: Aberdeen University Press, 1983), pp. 209-218.

10 The opposite is true of *Old Aberdeen* vs. *Aberdeen*, *Old Montrose* vs. *Montrose*, *Old Meldrum* vs. *Meldrum*, and similar ones; in these names the unmarked partner in a pair is the more modern.

11 For a detailed account of the origins of this type of name in Scotland see W.F.H. Nicolaisen, "The Type *'Burn of-'* in Scottish Hydronymy", *Scottish Studies*, 3 (1959), pp. 92-102; "Names Containing the Preposition *o*'", *Scottish Studies*, 4 (1960), pp. 195-205; " *'Hill of-'* and *'Loch of'*", *Scottish Studies*, 9 (1965), pp. 175-182; also *Scottish Place-Names*, pp. 56-64.

Scottish Language **5** (1986) 140-146

Gaelic Place-Names in Scots

W HEN, well over a quarter of a century ago, I first read W.L. Lorimer's article on 'The Persistence of Gaelic in Galloway and Carrick',[1] it occurred to me that here was a field of research to which the study of names, particularly place-names, might one day make a major, maybe even a unique, elucidating contribution, for there seemed to be here, on the face of it, a classic case for the appropriate, even optimal, exploitation of onomastic evidence in the unravelling of regional linguistic history.

In his essay, Lorimer, on the basis of literary allusions, documented historical events, antiquarian comments, military reports, kirk session minutes, lexical borrowings, etc., came to the following conclusion: 'Scots was already in 1560 generally known throughout Galloway and Carrick, ... Gaelic wilted fast before Scots and English in the next hundred years, and perhaps by the middle, probably by the end, of the 17th century, it was extinct'.[2] Note that there is no mention here of place-names, which is probably not surprising in view of the observation that generally place-names do not contain any references to chronologically identifiable items or events which might facilitate absolute dating. What suggested itself to me, despite this well-known deficiency of all onomastic material, was that, as a result of a rigorous analysis both of the Scotticised Gaelic place-names as they are recorded in written sources and as they are spelt and pronounced today, and of their underlying Gaelic etyma, as conjectured from the Scotticised forms, it should nevertheless be possible through a process of careful matching to conclude, with a fair amount of precision, at what time the Gaelic names in question had passed into Scots. If this could be done, then the dates in question might further provide us with the chronological parameters of what might be termed the period of bi-lingualism and bi-culturalism in Galloway and Carrick during which Scots and Gaelic were contact languages in the area. Not only might we be able to give more substance to Lorimer's own conclusions, if necessary modifying them, but we might also be in a position to confirm or reject his idea of the century and a half between about 1550 and 1700 as the time when, he claims, one language, Scots, fairly rapidly replaced another, Gaelic.

There are, however, at least three reasons why in the 25 years or more that have gone past since I first read Lorimer's article I have never been able to realise that original vision. First, there is the paucity or absolute dearth of information regarding the pronunciation of Gaelic in the Scottish south-west, at any time of its currency there. When Sir Herbert Maxwell had, as an antiquarian rather than as a linguist, made a fairly comprehensive study of the place-names of Galloway,[3] he assumed that Gallovidian Gaelic was simply an offshoot of Irish Gaelic and had remained so as long as it was spoken in Wigtownshire and the Stewartry, and presumably also in Carrick. The conjectured etymologies which Maxwell provided for Gaelic place-names were therefore invariably Irish Gaelic, regardless of whether a name might have been amongst the earliest given or of much later coinage and application. In fact, internal stratification within the Gaelic place-nomenclature of the region appears to have been never envisaged by him. This oversimplified view of the linguistic situation clearly and blatantly falsifies reality, since it does not take into account either any significant continuing changes within the donor language that first coined, applied and used these names – Gaelic – or the characteristics of the recipient language through which the same names have been transmitted to us – Scots. For Maxwell, Gaelic never became Scottish Gaelic in the south-west; nor did he consider chronological layering a factor of moment. Unfortunately, while it is comparatively easy to level this kind of criticism at Maxwell and while we can say with conviction what should be done instead, this has to remain a statement of principle and intent for the present, for we simply do not have the evidence to proceed with its implementation, mainly because the history of Scottish Gaelic phonology still has to be written.

The second reason why the dream is still only a dream is the fact that at least 300 years have passed since native Gaelic – even at its most 'persistent', in Lorimer's terms – was last spoken in Galloway and Carrick. The closest I have ever come to hearing Ayrshire Gaelic pronounced was when, in the early sixties, I recorded the Gaelic pronunciation of such names as Kilwinning, Ayr and Kilmarnock from native speakers of Arran Gaelic,[4] just across the Firth of Clyde; but how are we to know what the relationship between Arran and Ayrshire Gaelic was and in what instances the insular pronunciation imitated the mainland one and in what cases it was distinct from it? Only a careful collection and evaluation of the written evidence, however unsatisfactory in certain respects, will supply at least some of the clues required.

Thirdly, my own field-work in the behaviour of place-names in bilingual situations (all of it conducted before 1969 when I went to North America) has been exclusively in parts of Scotland where Gaelic has been or is being superseded by Scottish English, not by Scots,[5] and although the principles will, to all intents and purposes, be the same, the details will, of course, be different. I therefore welcome the kind of work that Adam Watson and Elizabeth Allan did in Upper Deeside in the last ten years, resulting in that splendid volume which Aberdeen University Press published last year (1984),[6] and also the intensive investigation of Caithness place-names which Doreen Waugh has undertaken over the last several years.[7] All three of them have had the opportunity – on Deeside perhaps more than in Caithness – of observing and analysing situations in which Gaelic place-names have been adopted and adapted by speakers of Scots; and that, of course, parallels exactly, though three centuries later, the phenomena and the problems as we would have encountered them in sixteenth- and seventeenth-century Galloway and Carrick.

My purpose in this paper is to bring together some initial evidence and to examine it for potential underlying principles. From the work which I have done over the years on the fate of place-names in bilingual communities and, more generally, in the transmission of names from one linguistic embeddedness to another, it has become apparent that the most common way by which place-names pass from one language to another and ultimately even survive the death of the donor languages is through phonological adaptation in the receiver language. In practically all instances, this is accompanied by instant semantic opacity on the lexical level. This is, of course, a phenomenon that potentially applies to all names from the very moment when the lexical material from which they have been shaped takes on an onomastic function;[8] but it is especially prevalent, almost guaranteed, when a name changes its linguistic environment. As a consequence, the names in question become more than ever sequences of sound that have onomastic contents but lack semantic transparency on the lexical level. They are now truly part of an onomastic rather than a linguistic dialect.[9] This general observation naturally also applies to names which have passed from Gaelic into Scots, and I want to present and examine some of the consequences of that process, not as definitive answers but rather as hints and hunches of what seems to be happening. Of course, in the long run we cannot be satisfied with the presentation of the material alone but will have to be constantly aware of the question whether the same or similar changes would have taken place if the same names had been adapted by Scots from Gaelic elsewhere in Scotland, or at a different time, or both, and whether the same Gaelic name would have fared differently if the recipient language had been Scottish English, not Scots.

(1) One of the most common Gaelic suffixes to be found in Scottish place-names is *-ach*, primarily an adjectival ending meaning 'pertaining to', or the like, but in toponymic application often used nominally indicating a sense of a place abundant in or characterised by the base. In several well known place-names, mostly in the east of Scotland, this suffix has become *-o*, as in Balerno, Balmerino, Largo, Pitsligo, Aberlemno, Craigo, Stracathro, Balmanno, Cambo, Fetteresso, Haddo, and others. In all instances in which early recorded evidence is available,[10] the final voiceless fricative is preserved, as for Balerno MLO (*Balhernoch* 1280, *Balernaugh* 1283, *Balernaght* 1296, *Ballernache* 1375, *Balernoch* 1557, but *Ballerno* 1510, *Balerno* 1555), Balmerino FIF (*Balmorinac* 1227, *Balmurinach* 1235, *Balmerynacht* c. 1230, *Balmurynach* c. 1320, *Balmurinoc* 1421, *Balmorynoch* 1459, *Balmorinach* 1469, *Balmurinocht*, *Balmerinach* 1512, *Balmerynoch* as late as 1630, but *Balmerino* 1613), Pitsligo ABD (*Petslegach* 1408, 1426, but *Petsligo* 1505-6), Aberlemno ANG (*Aberlevinach* 1202, *Aberlimenach* 1242, *Abirlemenach* 1275, *Abrelemnach* 1359, *Abbyrlemnoch* 1488, *Abbirlennoch*, *Aberlennoch* 1504, but *Aberlemno* 1546), Stracathro, ANG (*Strukatherach* 1178-c. 1190, *Strukatharach* 1204-11, *Stracatherach* 1212, *Strucathrach* 1213, *Stracatherauch* 1226-31, but Stracathro 1525), Balmanno KCD (*Balmannov* 1448, *Balmannoch* 1459, *Balmannocht* 1520) and PER (*Balmanach* 1420, but *Balmanno* 1588), Fetteresso KCD (*Fodresach* Pict. Chron., *Fethiresach, Fetheressagh* 1287, *Fechiressoch, Federossow* 1419), Haddo ABD, several (*Haldouch* 1189, *Haldauach* 1414, *the twa Haddochis* 1487, *Haldauch* 1492, *Haddauch* 1538, *Haldocht* 1557, but *Haddow* 1528-9).[11] On the whole, the earliest forms of the thirteenth and fourteenth centuries preserve the original Gaelic *-ach* faithfully, but from the fifteenth century on forms in *-och, -auch* and *-augh* are the rule, indicating that rounding of the vowel from *-a-* to *-o-*, possibly under the influence of the following velar fricative, had already taken place; in fact, this tendency had obviously already existed for a while, as some of the thirteenth-century forms for Balerno MLO show, but spellings without the final fricative do not seem to be much recorded before the fifteenth century and only became plentiful from the sixteenth century onwards: *Ballerno* 1510, *Balmerino* 1613, *Pitslego* 1468, *Aberlemno* 1546, *Stracathro* 1525, *Gilberti de Balmanow* 1421, *Balmanno* 1588, *Cambow* 1316, *Federossow* 1419, *Haldow* 1527.

One might therefore say that when place-names ending in *-ach* were first adopted by Scots in the Scottish east and north-east (roughly the former Pictish territory) in the thirteenth century, they kept the unstressed suffix more or less intact but began changing it to -*och* almost immediately in isolated instances, and wholesale from the fifteenth century on; the loss of the final fricative, although recorded in the fourteenth century, becomes common in the sixteenth century. I know of no instance in which the loss of the fricative preceded the change from -*a*- to -*o*- in the vowel of the syllable. As Stracathro and Haddo demonstrate, these phonological developments are not confined to the adjectival or topographic suffix -*ach;* they are shared by genetive in *ach* and by words like *davach.*

Outside this area, a number of developments is possible: (a) the final fricative can be replaced by the homorganic voiceless stop as in the Dumfriesshire Dalgarnock which is *Dalgernoch* in 1273-79 and *Dalgarnach* in 1371, but also *Dalgernok* in 1200 *Dalegernoc* in 1209-11, and *Dalgarno* in 1473-4. Compare also Balerno near Edinburgh with Balernock near Garelochhead DNB. This is a phenomenon which can also occur in the -*ach* > -*och* > -*o* area, for the Fife Cambo is recorded as *Camboc* in 1171-74 (17c) and the Midlothian Cammo as *Cambok* in 1296. Not to be confused with this process are names like Greenock and Gourock in which -*ock* is the reflex of Gaelic –*ag.* (b) In areas which remained Gaelic-speaking much longer and in which Scottish English, rather than Scots, frequently replaced Gaelic, the change from -*ach* to -*och* occurs in the Scotticised names, as in Badenoch INV (*Badenach* 1224-33, *Badenoch* 1229, *Badenagh, Badenoughe* 1289, *Baydenach* 1361, *Baydenauch* 1371, *Badzenoch* 1517), Garioch ABD (*Garuiach* 1178-82, *Garwyach* 1189-90, *Garviach* 1190-95, *Garuiauch* 1350, *Garviauch* 1360), Balloch DNB (*Belach* 1225, *Ballach* 1238, *Belloch* 1508), Tulloch ROS (*Tulloch* 1507), Rannoch PER (*Ranath* 1449, *Rannach* 1505, *Ranoch* 1508; *Lochrannoch* 1506, *Kenlochrannocht* 1531), but the final fricative is retained. (c) Gaelic -*ach* remains unchanged not only in Gaelic map names but also in such names as The Cabrach BNF (*Cabrauch* 1397, *Cabrach* 1439, *the Cabbrach* 1463) or Coigach ROS (*Gogeach* 1502, *Coidgeach* 1538, *Cogeauch* 1572) although here, too, historical forms in -*auch* exist.

(2) Whenever the origin of -*o*, -*och*, or -*ock* is the adjectival toponymic suffix *ach*, the names in question reflect the nominative form or at least a regularised nominative. That names are not normally used in the nominative but rather in oblique cases, especially in the locative, is not difficult to demonstrate. Gaelic locatives in *aich*, earlier -*aigh*, have therefore provided many more Scots adaptations than -*ach*, as is shown by the many names in -*ie* or -*y* in the same area as our names in final -*o*, as for example Bognie, Cairnie, Cannie, Cluny, Coullie, Crathie, Footdee, Fyvie, Logie, Ordie, Petty, Pittulie, Tipperty, Towie, etc. The loss of the voiceless palatal fricative [ç] appears to have occurred more or less at the same time as that of its velar counterpart [x], perhaps even a little earlier since for many names ending in Scots *ie/y* no early spellings displaying

it are on record. In others there is confusion because sometimes nominative forms in *-ach* are recorded although the name later shows *-y* or the like, as in the Aberdeenshire Tillygreig, earlier *Tulachgrig*.[12] There seems to have operated a normalisation to *Tully-* or *Tilly-* when Gaelic *tulach*, *tuileach* 'a hillock' is the first element in compound names, except sometimes when the second element begins with a vowel, as in Tullichewan: Tillicoultry, Tillycorthy, Tillydrone, Tillyfour, Tillyhilt, Tulliallan, Tullibardine, Tullybod, Tulliebole, Tullybelton, Tullynessle, etc.[13]

(3) The phonological development of the Gaelic suffix *-ach* to *-och* is shared by the initial syllable of Gaelic *achadh* 'field' which is found in hundreds of place-names wherever Gaelic has been spoken in Scotland at one time or another.[14] Together with Gaelic *baile* it is the most prolific generic in all settlement names of Gaelic origin. Although names beginning with *Ach-* (like Achachork, Achadun, Acharacle, Acharn, Achininver, Achmore) do occur as Anglicised reflexes in the former counties of Argyllshire, Perthshire, Inverness-shire, Ross-shire, Sutherland and Caithness, i.e. in those areas in which Gaelic is still a force today or was until recently, most map spellings outside these counties begin with *Auch-*. Indeed, one could argue that most of them begin with *Auchen-* or *Auchin-*, for phonological processes have here created a new stereotyped element. While it is possible to claim that in all these instances – and there are hundreds of them – *Auchen-/Auchin-* in either spelling is a Scotticisation of the Gaelic diminutive *achadhan* 'little field', this would be an unacceptable generalisation in view of the frequency of this element and because the specifics qualifying *Auchen-/Auchin-* are by no means only personal names and adjectives. What has happened here is that, in the course of the phonological simplification which accompanied loss of lexical meaning, as well as depletion of morphological transparency, the two forms of the Gaelic definite article which are potential sources of *-en-/-in-* (the feminine singular genitive *na* and the genitive plural *nan*) became merged and indistinguishable. In addition, the same Scotticisations spread to compounds in which no such form would be appropriate in Gaelic, i.e. before masculine nouns, personal names and adjectives. It is difficult to judge whether this development took place during the end-phase of Gaelic before it succumbed completely to Scots and when inflexional features were breaking down, or whether it should be ascribed to the post-Scotticisation period, but there seems to be little doubt that it is the result of a bilingual situation. It certainly looks as if the Scotticised form *Auchen-/Auchin-* was regarded by non-Gaelic speakers as a fixed element, having become an indivisible morphological unit. My own view is that we are here faced with the creation of a new post-Gaelic generic as the result of phonological adaptation and simplification, and also secondary morphological

reinterpretation. Examples would be Auchenblae, Auchenbowie, Auchencairn, Auchencastle, Auchencrieve, Auchendinny, Auchendrane, Auchengray, Auchenshuggle, and, with *-in-*, Auchincruive, Auchindoir, Auchindown, Auchingoul, Auchinloch, Auchintore, and many others. *Auch*-names, of course, also exist, and there are those among them that use the definite article properly like Auchnacloich ARG and Auchnagatt ABD.

(4) Here are briefly some other features which throw light on the phonological processes which are symptomatic of what happens when Gaelic names pass into Scots:

(a) The Scots syllable *Auch-* not only represents Gaelic *Ach-*, as in *achadh* but also Gaelic *Uach-*, as in *Uachdar* 'an upland'. *Ua-* is, of course, a diphthong which is not part of the vowel system of Scots, and the numerous and sometimes quite amusing early spellings of this element in such names as Auchterarder PER (*Uchterardouer* 1201-3, *Huctherdardouer* c. 1221, *Vchterardouere* 1226, *Ouchyrardour* 1238, *Outerardouer* 1235, *Efferdardeuar* 1203, *hucterardouer* 1239-40, *Huchterardor* c. 1284, *Wterardore* c. 1290, *Hucterhardouer* 1251-69), Auchterderran FIF (*Ouchterdera* 1431-2, *Ouchtirdera* 1449, *Auchterderay* 1515), Auchterhouse ANG (*Huchtirhus* 1247, *Huterus*, *Hugterhus* 1287, *Uchterhouse* 1410, *Uchirhous* 1416, *Vchtirous* 1418), Auchtermuchty FIF (*Uchtermukethin* 1205-11, *Uctermukethi* 1209-10, *Hughtermukedy*, *Huctermukedy* 1207, *Ochtirmokadi* 1350), Auchtertool FIF (*Outhertule* 1122-3, *Ochtertuly* 1178-9, *Ochtirtule* c. 1229-36), Ochtertyre PER (*Wochtertiry* 1498, *Hochtertyre* 1653) bear witness to the difficulties scribes had when trying to represent unfamiliar phonemes in terms of Scottish orthography, before ultimately and very late settling for *Auchter-*, or, occasionally, *Ochter-*. A thorough study of the spelling conventions regarding the Scotticised form of this toponymic generic would certainly bear rich fruit and should be quite illuminating; such an undertaking should be helped by the fact that no orthographic norms had been developed during the period in question.

(b) Scotticised forms of Gaelic place-names tend to eliminate completely all grammatically or morphologically relevant binary oppositions in final consonants such as palatal vs. velar, or 'slender' vs. 'broad' *l*, *n*, or *r*. In each case these distinctive phonemes are simply replaced by allophones of the English sounds in question occurring in complementary distribution.

(c) Graphemically, Gaelic palatal *[ɲ]* is usually represented by *n* plus <3>, later by *n* plus <z> which either retains the pronunciation [j], as in (Castle) Menzies PER (*Menyheis* 1449, *Menzes* c. 1590), or leads to a spelling pronunciation as in Lenzie DNB (*Lanyn* 1238, *Leygneh* 1369, *Lenye* 1399, *Leinze* 1389, *Lanye* 1583).

(d) The Gaelic sequence *-oll-* often becomes *-ow*, sharing or following the well-known vocalisation of post-vocalic *l* in Scots, as in Cowie KCD (*Inuercollin* 1196-99, *Collyn* 1264-66, *Kollie* 1337, *Colly* 1400, *Cowy* 1430), from Gaelic *coll* 'hazel', Towie ABD (*de duabus Tollis* 1483, *Towiis* 1495, *Tolleys* 1504, *Tolly* 1511, *Tollie vel Towie* 1594) from Gaelic *Tollaigh* 'at hole-place', or Toward ARG (*Tollart* 1449, *Toward*, *Towart* 1498, *Tollard* 1513, *Tollort* 1526) from Gaelic *Tollard* 'hole-point'.

(e) The non-Gaelic consonant cluster [kw] plus vowel is usually substituted for Gaelic *Cua-* , as in Quaich, Queich, or Quoych for locatives of Gaelic *cuach* 'cup'. This substitution, including the shift of the stress to the second part of the diphthong, of course parallels a similar replacement in the lexical equivalents. The aspirated *Chu-* is often rendered [hw], as in Dalwhinnie INV (*Dallwhiny* 1746) from Gaelic *Dail-chuinnidh* 'champions' dale'.

These are only a few of the phonological, and sometimes morphological, consequences of the Scotticisation of Gaelic place-names. The list is not only incomplete but also unsystematic and in every case preliminary. It is full of fleeting glimpses of partially obliterated footprints. Nevertheless, it may perhaps be possible to reach a few tentative conclusions at this point:

(1) The time is more than overdue for a systematic investigation of the phonological adaptations and their graphemic representations of Gaelic place-names that have passed into or through Scots. Such an investigation would not only survey the end results but also the historical evidence, i.e. all spellings, their earliest and latest occurrences, their frequencies, and their regional distribution. One of its major aims would be the removal of the notion of arbitrariness and its replacement by perceived rules and regularities which cover the correspondences. It would do so selectively and gradually; there is much scope here for term papers and dissertations.

(2) Once such a systematic survey has been completed – region by region, or element by element, or sound change by sound change – it might serve as a major source for the identification of historical strata as well as of linguistic contact zones and periods; it might also enable us one day to complete the task to which I referred in my introduction.

(3) The call for such an investigation and such a survey, while taking it for granted that place-names are valuable source material for the elucidation of linguistic history, would also reaffirm that names are more than words and that the establishment of reliable etymologies is not the final but the initial step in all onomastic research. It would, if it is to succeed fully, have to be conceived as an onomastic, not only a linguistic undertaking.

Notes

1 W.L. Lorimer, 'The Persistence of Gaelic in Galloway and Carrick.' *Scottish Gaelic Studies* 6 (1949) pp. 113-36, and 7 (1951), pp. 26-46.

2 Ibid., p. 42.

3 Sir Herbert Maxwell, *Studies in the Topography* of *Galloway* (Edinburgh, 1887); later revised as *The Place-Names of Galloway* (Glasgow, 1930).

4 W.F.H. Nicolaisen, 'Notes on Scottish Place-Names: 21. Kilwinning'. *Scottish Studies* 7 (1963), pp. 199-200.

5 W.F.H. Nicolaisen, 'Place-Names in Bilingual Communities'. *Names* 23 (1975), pp. 167-74; *Scottish Place-Names: Their Study and Significance* (London, 1976), pp. 53-6.

6 Adam Watson and Elizabeth Allan, *The Place-names* of *Upper Deeside* (Aberdeen, 1984).

7 See Doreen Waugh's contribution to the volume, *Scottish Language* 5 (1986), pp. 147-155.

8 W.F.H. Nicolaisen, 'The Semantics of Place-names and Their Elements'. *NORNA-rapporter* 28 (1985), pp. 60-71, and earlier publications.

9 W.F.H. Nicolaisen, 'Onomastic Dialects'. *American Speech* 55 (1980), pp.36-45.

10 In the examples which follow, all early spellings have been culled from the as yet incomplete collections for my projected *Concise Dictionary of Scottish Place-names.*

11 This list includes two names of Pictish origin – Pitsligo and Aberlemno – but by the time these names passed into Scots they were, of course, Gaelic names; especially their second elements had been thoroughly Gaelicised.

12 According to William J. Watson, *The History* of *the Celtic Place-Names of Scotland* (Edinburgh, 1926), p. 324.

13 W.F.H. Nicolaisen, 'Scottish Place-names: 32. Gaelic *tulach* and *barr'*. *Scottish Studies* 13 (1969), pp. 159-66; also *Scottish Place-Names*, pp. 147-8.

14 W.F.H. Nicolaisen, 'Gaelic Place-names in Southern Scotland'. *Studia Celtica* 5 (1970), pp. 15-35; also *Scottish Place-Names*, pp. 125-8, 140-3.

Onomastica Canadiana: Journal of the Canadian Society for the Study of Names 68/2 (Dec. 1986) 58-66

Names as Intertextual Devices

AFTER having paid steady attention to names in literature for about a decade, I came to the conclusion a couple of years ago that I had probably exhausted the kinds of approach I was interested in and that there was nothing new left for me to say. A chapter in my scholarly activities seemed to be closed, and I even wrote what I regarded as my final overview of the subject, in which I pulled together from several previous articles various findings and statements, illustrating them from the range of literature I had covered.[1] I was not foolish enough to think that these findings and statements might in any way be regarded as definitive, but I certainly thought that they were my own last word on the subject; my future discipleship of literary onomastics would be largely confined to the role of recipient and connoisseur of what others would have to offer.

It was only when, almost two years later,[2] I began to think again about the function of names in literature and about the vogue that the study of literary onomastics currently enjoys among both students of names and students of literature, that I realised how limited my own attempts at investigating names in literary contexts had been, in scope as well as in depth. I became especially aware of the fact that my interrogations had been severely bounded by particular individual texts and that I had responded to the challenge of literary onomastics mainly by emphasising the function of names as texts within texts.[3] Practically all my studies had been based on the premise that names are, to all intents and purposes, intra-textual devices intended by their creative authors to provide locations, landscapes, social settings, identities, sources of recognition, characterisation, discernible structure within the covers of a book. In concert with other scholars in the field, I had viewed names almost exclusively as contributing factors to the textuality of a text, as tectonic features, and had derived from these perceived functions both their semantic status and their linguistic embeddedness, seeing names primarily as onomastic threads woven into the patterns of a text. Even names of actual persons and actual places incorporated by authors into fictional texts I had regarded essentially as intra-textual, once their transplantation had been completed, albeit with continuing, and sometimes disconcertingly strong and interfering, extra-textual links. That such names with a dual existence within and without the text are occasionally pressed into service beyond their frequent function of providing verisimilitude and a sort of verbal nudge in the direction of fictional veracity, seemed particularly apt.

Thus, Hardy's delineation of Wessex through the contrast of fictional names and non-fictional names,[4] or the creation of operational space within actual landscapes through the same kind of juxtaposition as in, let us say, the novels of such Scottish authors as John Galt, Lewis Grassic Gibbon or Compton Mackenzie,[5] or the establishment of onomastic links between the fictional and actual world for the purposes of travel, temporary removal of characters or the introduction of the outsider by, among others, Anthony Trollope, George Eliot, Elizabeth Gaskell and Emily Brontë[6] appeared to be almost too self-evident to merit mention or elaboration. After all, even those actual places or persons selected by authors for inclusion in their works of fiction have, with perhaps the slightest hint at metonymity, become part and parcel of a text, so that a journey from Barchester to Oxford[7] or a conversation between Edward Waverley and Bonnie Prince Charlie[8] does not violate textual integrity. This assertion might well find support in the observation that the Glasgow of William McIlvanney's Laidlaw and the Glasgow of George Blake's The Shipbuilders are different Glasgows,[9] or that Sir Walter Scott's Rob Roy Macgregor in Rob Roy and Nigel Tranter's Rob Roy Macgregor in The Patriot are not identical. All are verifiable only intra-textually, and the onomastic overlap in sound and spelling and certain other identifying characteristics is almost incidental. It is almost impossible to imagine that Scott's Bailie Nicol Jarvie could have spoken to Nigel Tranter's Captain Macgregor, or Tranter's Andrew Fletcher to Scott's Rob Roy. The purely intra-textual validity even of these extra-textually derived and documented names is thus never in doubt.

The only time at which I was at least dimly aware of the potential function of names as intertextual devices was when, in addition to sketching the essentially onomastic continuity of Hardy's Wessex and Trollope's Barsetshire, I drew attention to William Golding's playful use of the toponymy of the latter in The Pyramid[10] and to the extended employment of its toponymic features by Angela Thirkell in her re-creation of Trollope's fictional reality in her own series of novels, almost a hundred years later.[11] In both these instances, a case could be made for the introduction of onomastic, especially toponymic intertextuality[12] as a sort of legitimisation of a new fictive world. Angela Thirkell's Barsetshire became plausible because Anthony Trollope's Barsetshire had existed before it, and Golding's village of Stilbourne received its stamp of believability because it was said to be situated not far from Barchester (as well as being in the vicinity of Oxford). While these are undoubtedly important examples of the intertextual manipulation of onomastic items, they are, however, by no means the only onomastic resonances available as strategic devices to authors with intertextual intentions; there are other onomastic tactics that are perhaps subtler, more far-reaching and also more effective with regard to the weaving of a true web of intertextuality. That is why I have come out of my literary onomastic "retirement", in order to point out some of these possibilities as I see them now.

If I illustrate the points I wish to make from the works of Sir Walter Scott, this is, in the first place, a matter of convenience since during a five-year project of reading all of his Waverley Novels, I accumulated copious notes on onomastic usage on which I have drawn only sparingly so far. Scott's novels, however, also furnish much appropriate evidence for less personal reasons; for, next to Shakespeare and Milton, Scott is probably the most intertextually conscious writer in English, and reading the Waverley Novels from Waverley to Castle Dangerous has been largely responsible for my own awareness of the potent force of intertextuality. Much of Scott's evocative technique is, of course, not onomastic though decidedly verbal, the most prominent feature being his use of literary quotations, often verse, as mottoes at the beginning of each chapter. These usually provide an accumulation of thirty, forty or more intertextual items per novel, introducing chapters, summarising them in advance, commenting on them, highlighting their salient points, structuring each novel by their intervention between the end of one chapter and the beginning of the next, thus giving each chapter its identity as a separate though interlinked part of the story he tells. Nevertheless, these literary quotations are largely perceived as intrusive and therefore disregarded by readers without, in their opinion, serious damage to the integrity of the text. Their intertextual value is limited since they are so obviously extraneous additions, not truly capable of creating a vibrant intertext. It is probably more precise to describe them as one text enlightening another.

Next in importance are the many literary allusions within his texts, frequently in the form of quotations, not seldom identified and elaborated in Scott's own extensive Notes in his appendices. These allusions occur both as auctorial comments and embedded in the direct speech of his characters who are sometimes acting as the author's mouthpieces. Unlike the chapter headings and the Notes, they provide more than an obtrusive sense of deliberate, knowledgeable, and formative infiltration of textual matter which, at least on the surface, tempts the reader to ignore it or to treat it as an exposed but redundant display of authorial Belesenheit. As a result, Scott's texts are always intertexts, and the reader is not permitted to forget this fact.

This general intertextual climate, which makes him such an outstanding example for the student of literary onomastics, receives its most specific, most stringent, but also most elusive expression in the form of onomastic allusions, similes and metaphors incorporated in the text. Consequently, many of the Waverley Novels contain almost as many references to names of places and persons (especially the latter) outside the immediate topography and personnel of the work as to those within them and, because of this onomastically-based intertextual vibrancy, one can never be sure of the ultimate boundaries and potentialities of any given text. Names, in Scott's usage, seem to be like volcanoes forever on the brink of causing textual eruptions followed by an overflow of intertextual lava.

In the wake of such an extravagant claim, the question must inevitably be asked, what kinds of names are specifically involved and where their respective habitats are? Needless to say, a few illustrative instances must suffice to demonstrate the underlying principles.

In a self-conscious authorial aside intended to characterise, in essence, his own narrative craftsmanship and almost unlimited opportunities as a storyteller, Scott notes in Old Mortality:[13]

> It is fortunate for tale-tellers that they are not tied down like theatrical writers to the unities of time and place, but may conduct their personages to Athens and Thebes at their pleasure, and bring them back at their convenience.

If it is the storyteller's privilege and practice to create true chunks of the past by narrating them,[14] thus converting chronicle into story, then Athens and Thebes are, in the widest sense, toponymic metaphors for that storying ability. Granted they primarily designate locations, they also symbolise, as locatory devices, places prominent in classical culture and mythology conjuring up, on the one hand, persons and events specifically associated with them and, on the other, the whole world for which this culture and mythology stand – a time before our time, and yet, because of its pervasive influence, a time in our time, too. Taletellers may, indeed, "conduct their personages" to actual places called Athens and Thebes, and back again, but, whatever fabulating mediator may be the guide, these will undoubtedly be the Athens and Thebes of our occidental culture, strongholds in the classical landscape of the mind. Scott as the modern – i.e. "modern" in an early nineteenth-century sense – teller of tales identifies himself with the Homers and Virgils of old and, at least for the length of a dependent clause, panders to their ghostly acclaim. For the same length of time and, one suspects, for a considerable while after, the text of Old Mortality, in its particular sixteenth-century Scottish ambience, opens up to enfold over two thousand years of narrative creativity and to embrace the heroes and actions of classical adventure and cultural heritage – pervasive intertextuality is made possible through onomastic devices.

Scott's immediate practical purpose in this intertextual strategy is to make his readers aware, at the beginning of Chapter XXXVII of the novel, of the curious fact that more non-narrated time has passed since the end of the last chapter than the total of recounted time, both narrated and non-narrated, in the previous thirty-six. He therefore continues:

> Time, to use Rosalind's simile, has hitherto paced with the hero of our tale,[15] for, betwixt Morton's first appearance as a competitor for the popinjay, and his final departure for Holland, hardly two months elapsed. Years, however, glided away ere we find it possible to resume the thread of our narrative.

After the previous brief but somehow lasting intertextual excursion into classical textuality, this next evocation of another text, still employed for the same practical purposes, offers, for those in the know, a momentary glimpse of Shakespeare's As You Like It, not just in its express reference to a particular character's memorable saying within the dramatic framework of a scene, but to the whole of the intricate, bemusing and satisfying hilarity of that comedy. Shakespeare, in addition to Homer and Virgil, has entered the lists on behalf of the narrator, having been invoked just as obliquely, as well as unquestionably, as the other two. Scott's own manipulation of time has been sanctioned by the Swan of Avon if, that is, created characters can ever be said to speak on behalf of their creators. Would a Rosalind by any other name have been as effective an onomastic catalyst of dynamic intertextuality? The answer is obviously "NO"; neither interchangeability of name nor anonymity is possible under the circumstances.

Shakespeare is one of Scott's favourite sources for onomastically engendered intertextuality, frequently in the form of comparison or simile. Thus, in Guy Mannering we come across "a sort of female Rosencrantz and reverend Guildenstern, one in a tartan petticoats, the other in a cassock";[16] in The Monastery, Cristie tells his stories of the supernatural "while Dame Elspeth's curch bristled with horror, and Tibb Tacket, rejoiced to find herself once more in the company of a jack-man, listened to his tales, like Desdemona to Othello, with undisguised delight";[17] and in St. Ronan's Well, Lady Penelope exhorts the poet Tyrrell: "Confess that to a poet a seat unoccupied – the chair of Banquo – has more charms than if it were filled even as an alderman would fill it. What if 'the Dark Ladye' shall glide in to occupy it?"[18] Hamlet, Othello and what, for reasons of superstition, people within the theatre call "that Scottish play" all furnish onomastic nodes of intertextuality. In each instance, it is naturally first of all the exact scene referred to which, like Coleridge's "Dark Ladye",[19] glides into the text, to intermingle with it, to interfere with it, to occupy space and establish itself in it. Narrative borrows visuality and dynamics from the theatrical, whether as ironic reminder of a Shakespearean byplay, the domestication on a Scottish hearth of the sinister aspects of fateful jealousy, or the accusing consequences of murder done. The chair of Banquo in particular becomes a powerful symbol for "the seat unoccupied", but in all cases the intertextual evocation bursts wide open the covers of the novels in question, and it is hard to predict how timid or overwhelming the incoming tide will be.

In order to stem it or retain some control over it, Scott uses his Notes to direct the reader's attention to the exact significance of the onomastic allusion. There are at least three references to Sir Tristrem in his novels – in Ivanhoe, The Talisman, and The Betrothed. In the first, the phrase "the fabulous Sir Tristrem" is glossed: "...The origin of this science hunting was imputed to the celebrated Sir Tristrem, famous for his tragic intrigue with the beautiful Ysolte ... ".[20] In the second, King Richard commends the supposed Nubian mute: "'Thou canst well in woodcraft', said the King, after a pause, 'and has started thy game and brought him to bay as ably as if Tristrem himself had taught thee'."[21] This receives the gloss: "An universal tradition ascribed to Sir Tristrem, famous for his love of fair Queen Ysault ...".[22] And in the third, Damian, after having been termed earlier "the Timon of the woods", receives the accolade "a second Sir Tristrem", with regard to his superior woodcraft.[23] In all instances, Tristrem is used within the text as an onomastic metaphor for a great hunter and woodsman, but Scott is at pains to explain on two occasions that this is the same Tristrem whom the reader probably knows better as the tragic lover of Ysolte (Ysault) of the medieval romances. This is purposefully directed intertextuality which leaves the reader in no doubt as to the content and extent of the onomastic device employed, i.e. the name Tristrem. Some may regard this as crudely and unnecessarily manipulative on the part of the author but it may also be seen as a conscious attempt to ensure, as far as this can ever be achieved, congruity of authorially intended and reader-response perceived intertextuality, at least within Scott's own generation. After all, does not one of the great problems in reading Scott, or, even more markedly, Shakespeare or Milton, lie in the difficulty we have in recreating in our own minds onomastically engendered intertextuality because their onomastic allusions, references, hints or links are no longer easily understood and therefore either remain opaque or have to be made transparent with the aid of secondary sources? Most of us are no longer the targeted readership of the Waverley Novels, expected by the author to know our Classical Mythology, Shakespeare, Medieval and Arthurian Romances, Old Testament, Pilgrim's Progress, Chaucer, Cervantes, folktales, Burns, Taliessin, Thomas the Rhymer – some of Scott's most frequently quoted sources of allusion and simile, reference and commentary. Only very few of us would instantly understand the phrase "as Pugg says" in The Surgeon's Daughter as introducing a reference to Ben Jonson's The Devil is an Ass.[24] Not unexpectedly, our dimensions of onomastic literacy have changed: in certain respects they are shallower, in others narrower, in yet others just different. Mainly, they are hardly ever co-extensive with those of Scott (or Shakespeare or Milton), perhaps never have been, and that not just for historical reasons.

The result is a kind of intertextual no-man's-land, and a deplorable, though inevitable, loss of textuality as well. The great opportunities – one might almost say temptations – that names offer as intertextual devices here also expose their undoubted shortcomings. The very quality which recommends them, i.e. their severe focusing powers, can treacherously turn them into traps, leaving nothing but a vague blur. In a way, this risk, of course, reflects the general lack of lexical meaning which is inherent in their very nature as names. Intended onomastic intertextuality does not even have to be deliberately or carelessly obscure in order to demonstrate that the author's expectations have been misplaced; but the risk is nevertheless well worth taking on the part of both the author and the reader, because of that glorious condensation of content that makes names such attractive literary devices: a name, like a picture, can say more than a thousand words.

It follows that, in some sense, any name inserted into a text creates some kind of intertextuality or, perhaps more correctly, intercontextuality, since most names, textually embedded or infiltrated, do not relate to a different text in the strictest sense of that term but rather to a different, non-verbal context. In consequence of the unpredictable semantic freight they carry, this inter-contextuality can be various and cumulative: several other contexts may well be evoked by the same name. In true onomastically engendered intertextuality, this resulting network is likely to be more limited and the precise denotation of the other text to be more apparent, but even then much depends on the potential and, ultimately, on the realizable congruity of intertexts. Otherwise even a humouristically trivialising onomastic pun like Phoebe, as the name of Die Vernon's horse in Rob Roy,[25] loses its effectiveness.

Naturally, the onomastic chapter of the grammar of intertextuality will still have to be written, but perhaps the foregoing comments will help to start us thinking about it. Certainly the evocative power of names makes them ideal raw material for the mapping out of intertextual strategies. The conspicuous density of their semantic content and the intense single-mindedness of their denotative function provide them with concretising properties which far transcend mere verbal allusion, reference, quotation or incorporation. The simultaneity of their intra-textual and intertextual presence must surely rank them among the most tempting devices at hand to the creative author. It is up to the student of names to investigate and define what precisely the contribution of their very onomasticity is to the resonances they evoke in the precarious and precocious process of turning texts into intertexts.

Notes

1   W.F.H. Nicolaisen, "The Structure and Function of Names in English Literature", read at the Twelfth Triennial Conference of the International Association of University Professors of English, August 28-September 3, 1983, in Hamburg (West Germany); to be published in Studia Anglica Posnaniensia 18 (1985).

2   This is a much revised version of a paper first read at the annual meeting of the Canadian Society for the Study of Names in Montreal, June 3-4, 1985.

3   See, for example, W.F.H. Nicolaisen, "Literary Names as Texts: Personal Names in Sir Walter Scott's Waverley". Nomina 3 (1979) 29-39

4   W.F.H. Nicolaisen, "The Place-names of Wessex". Literary Onomastics Studies 2 (1975) 58-82.

5   W.F.H. Nicolaisen, "An Onomastic Vernacular in Scottish Literature". In: Scotland and the Lowland Tongue. Ed. J. Derrick McClure (Aberdeen: Aberdeen University Press, 1983) 209-218.

6   W.F.H. Nicolaisen, "The Toponymy of Literary Landscapes". Literary Onomastics Studies 6 (1979) 75-104.

7   Anthony Trollope, Barchester Towers, Chapter I.

8   Sir Walter Scott, Waverley, Chapter XL.

9   Nicolaisen, "An Onomastic Vernacular", 209.

10   W.F.H. Nicolaisen, "The Place-names of Barsetshire". Literary Onomastics Studies 3 (1976) 1-21.

11   Ibid.

12   The notion of intertextuality is used in so many different ways in contemporary literary criticism that it would be impossible to point to any one authoritative definition or application. Anyone employing this concept, however, cannot but be (intertextually!) aware of – or, better still, conversant with – the pronouncements of Jacques Derrida, Jonathan Culler and Roland Barthes in this area, even if their particular uses of this term have not been followed slavishly.

13 Sir Walter Scott, Old Mortality, Chapter XXXVII.

14 W.F.H. Nicolaisen, "Sir Walter Scott: The Folklorist as Novelist". In: Scott and His Influence. Eds. J.H. Alexander and David Hewitt (Aberdeen: Association for Scottish Literary Studies, 1983) 169-179, esp. 176.

15 Shakespeare, As You Like It, Act III, Scene 11: Rosalind in her little "Dissertation" on the subjectivity of time, ."Time travels in divers paces with divers persons". – Chapter XXXVII itself is also headed by another (slightly altered) quotation from the same scene; ."Whom does time gallop withal?" – Shakespeare's As You Like It had delighted Sir Walter when he was still a youngster (Edgar Johnson, Sir Walter Scott: The Great Unknown. Vol. I [London: Hamish Hamilton, 1970], 22).

16 Sir Walter Scott, Guy Mannering, Chapter XVIII; the reference is, of course, to Shakespeare's Hamlet.

17 Sir Walter Scott, The Monastery, Chapter XIV; Shakespeare's Othello, Act I, Scene III.

18 Sir Walter Scott, St. Ronan's Well, Chapter VI; Shakespeare's Macbeth, Act III, Scene IV.

19 In his own Note 4, Scott comments: "The Dark Ladye is one of the tantalising fragments in which Mr. Coleridge has shown us what exquisite powers of poetry he has suffered to remain uncultivated". The reference here is to Coleridge's The Ballad of the Dark Ladie. A Fragment. Like the "cypress and a myrtle bough" in the ballad, Scott here creates a little intertextual vignette himself, by intertwining two texts "around his harp".

20 Sir Walter Scott, Ivanhoe, Chapter V, and Note 5.

21 Sir Walter Scott, The Talisman, Chapter XXV.

22 Ibid., Note 10.

23 Sir Walter Scott, The Betrothed, Chapter XVII.

24 Sir Walter Scott, The Surgeon's Daughter, Chapter VI; Scott's literary memory is here, as so often, somewhat faulty, for the statement, "then there will be a pair of you", which he attributes to Pugg seems to be no more than a vague recollection of the amorous Pugg's "as who so ever is one, I will be another sure, I'll have my share" (Ben Jonson, The Devil is an Ass, Act II, Scene I). Perhaps it would be safer to speak in instances like this of intended intertextuality rather than of its verifiable counterpart although the question whether the verbal reference has to be verbatim is debatable. Onomastically, there is, of course, no problem.

25 Sir Walter Scott, Rob Roy, Chapter V.

perfectionist tendencies. Before we look at the actual, albeit limited, material and at several ways of interrogating it, let me make a few more points which have some bearing on the matter and which should help to eliminate some possible misconceptions and misunderstandings. When I look for signs of innovative onomastic acts on the part of Scandinavian settlers in Scotland, I am aware of a number of factors that may be of some significance in this respect, but which are very hard to prove or disprove when one can compare only the products of these acts and not the processes which ultimately resulted in them; the two most important of these have temporal and spatial connotations and implications, respectively. In the first instance, it is self-evident that the naming of places in Scotland by Scandinavians occurred over a considerable period of time, and was carried out by a number of generations from, let us say, about the beginning of the ninth century to at least the middle of the thirteenth. In instances in which local Norse dialects of the Northern Isles and Caithness (and under somewhat different circumstances in the Hebrides and on the Scottish west coast) adopted and used toponymic generics (and certain specifics) as part of the topographical sector of their lexica, these generics, and less importantly also the specifics, may well have continued to be fashionable and creative far beyond that time. As it is, and even without taking such extended usage into consideration, the relevant names which we can recover from modern maps or from historical documents, or both, form a kind of toponymic palimpsest – some may have survived for only a very short time, having been replaced by others or become irrelevant; these are now no longer traceable but leave important holes in our evidence. Others may be secondary names which may have obliterated completely the primary names of the same topographic features to which they refer. Others again may be secondary, but their primary predecessors may be still on record. Taking this potential sequencing even further, other names yet again may be tertiary, with the primary and secondary names also on record or not. Others, and one has more than a suspicion that most names belong to this category, can indeed be taken to be the only Scandinavian names which the features in question have ever had. Be all this as it may, it is more than reasonable to assume then, that, on the one hand, not all names were given at the same time, and that, on the other, we are likely to find much more information, and are therefore much more qualified to say something knowledgeable, about the later phases of name usage than about the earlier ones; i.e. it is easier to assess how long an element remained productive than when it first started becoming so. The implications of these two, somewhat connected, observations are obvious: earlier colonial settlers are presumably more inclined to be in touch with their homeland and therefore imitative rather than innovative, while later colonists may consider innovation or, when imitative, may have newly established 'colonial' models in mind rather than the toponymic baggage which their ancestors had brought with them. Such later imitation may, for example, apply to the naming of a later settlement after an earlier one elsewhere.

This brings me to the second major point, the spatial one. As there is no need to name every conceivable, discernible feature immediately, or even to discern it, the density of names increases as time goes on. In an insular environment, coastal features are likely, usually, to be named before inland ones, as are the best settlement sites on good soil before less desirable ones on poorer soil and in less favourable locations. In addition, colonists may encounter, even in comparatively small islands not all that far from home, topographical formations and sites with previously unencountered characteristics which may necessitate, or at least stimulate, innovative semantic shifts in existing toponymic elements, or even the coining of new elements from existing word stock or *ab novo*. New wildernesses offer new challenges; newly perceived referents ask for new kinds of references; consequently both lexical and onomastic fields re-arrange themselves.

Nevertheless, despite these qualifications and potential traps, it is, I think, legitimate, because capable of producing valid results, to take a restricted corpus of evidence and treat it as if it were undifferentiated in any of the temporal or spatial ways just mentioned, to think of it as two-dimensional, so to speak, reducing it from something ideal but unmanageable to something less perfect but manageable.

The restrictions which I have with great hesitation imposed upon this little survey are twofold: all the Scottish names on which it is based are only from the two northernmost Orcadian islands – North Ronaldsay and Sanday – and all of them are now, or once were, farm-names. Naturally, Hugh Marwick's *Orkney Farm-names*[1] is my convenient and reliable source of relevant material in this respect, whereas the multi-volume compilation of Rygh's *Norske Gaardnavne*[2] forms the compendium from which potential Norwegian equivalents have been culled. Since this is not a study in the regional origins of Scandinavian immigrants to Scotland in the manner of A.W. Brøgger,[3] no attempt has been made to establish this kind of relationship between Orkney and Norway. If a name or an element is found in both inventories, without regard to location or frequency, it has qualified as an identical equivalent. One occurrence in both, Marwick and Rygh, is sufficient, however disastrous this may sound to statisticians and others more easily convinced by numbers. Now that you know most of the confessed weaknesses of my presentation, let us see if it has any redeeming strengths.

The toponymic corpus which I have subjected to scrutiny consists of 136 names, 29 from North Ronaldsay and 107 from Sanday. Apart from a small minority, all of them are still in use today. Of these names, twelve are completely opaque, four are apparently pre-Norse Celtic, two are Scots, one is English, and one (Westove) is described by Marwick as 'erroneous', whatever that may be.[4] In the remaining 116 names, at least one element, usually the generic, is demonstrably Scandinavian; indeed, in a large percentage of them both elements of the compound – if they are compound names – are transparently of Scandinavian origin. Simple names obviously do not need this kind of double proof. The questions which interest us are how this residue of 116 names fares when compared with Norwegian farm-names, and what these names tell us about the forces of imitation and innovation to which the naming of farms in North Ronaldsay and Sanday by Scandinavians was subject, always bearing in mind that both imitation and innovation are creative acts, albeit triggered by different motivations and attitudes.

Let us begin by looking at the generics involved, as these are clearly of special, because basic, significance in the naming of places, whether from existing word-stock or derived from an inherited, familiar onomasticon. Scandinavian farm-names in the two islands contain the following 40 generics:

bólstaðr 'farm': Brabustir, Conglibist, Everbist, Hobbister, Kirbist, Neebister, Sellibister, Simbister, Skedgibist, Skelbister
borg 'fortress': Brough
brekka 'slope': Antabreck, Breck (2), Breckan, Hammerbrake
bústaðr 'farm': Busta (?)
bý/bœr 'farm': Erraby, Okamby, Suthirbie
bölkr 'wall': Garbo, Gerbo
dys 'mound': Disher
endi 'end': Airan
fjall 'hill': Fea
flata 'flat expanse of land': Lettan
garðr 'farm': Bressigar, Colligar, Finligar, Gardemeles, Garth, Hermisgarth, Housegarth, Isgarth, Leavsgarth, Neigarth, Northgarth, Scarrigar, Stretigar, Waldgarth
Norw. *gjorde* 'meadow field': Goir
gröf 'hollow': Gravity
haugr 'mound': Garso, Hellihowe, Hoosay, Howar (2), Hynegreenie
hlíð 'slope': Grindally
hóll 'hill': Gruthill, Hool
hólmr 'islet': Holm
hǫrgr 'stony hillock': Hargar

hús 'house': Appiehouse, Finyarhouse, Sugarhouse
klette 'rock': Cleat, Linklet, Whiteclett
kot 'cottage': Benziecot
kró 'nook': Houscrow
kvern 'mill': Hookin
kví 'enclosure': Boloquoy, Sholtisquoy
land 'land': Holland (2), Howland, Leyland, Noltland
ló 'low-lying flat': Whunderless
mýrar 'mires': Myres
nes 'headland': Burness, Elsness, Hacksness, Lamaness, Lopness, Ness, Rusness, Sennes, Tresness, Vaultness, Volunes
naustar 'boat landing place': Nouster
óss 'river mouth': Oyce
sandr 'sand': Sand (2)
setr 'dwelling': Curcasetter, Maizer, Seater, Stangasetter, Voxetter, Warsetter
skáli 'hall': Backaskail, Langskaill, Skaill (2)
stofa 'room': Stove
stæði 'foundation': Gairsty
topt 'house site': Howatoft, Kettletoft, Tafts
vágr 'bay': Southwall, Walls
vatn 'loch': (Over the Water)
vík 'bay': Braeswick
völlr 'field': Quivals, Savil

Every single one of these generics (with the possible exception of *bölkr* and *stæði*, for which I have yet to find Norwegian examples) also occurs in Norway. Whenever they appear in their uncompounded form, either in the singular or in the plural or in both, they also occur as Norwegian farm-names:

GENERIC	ORKNEY	NORWAY	RYGH
bólstað /bústaðr	Busta	Bolstad/Bustad	III, 389
borg	Brough	Borg(en)	I, 76
brekka	Breck(an)	Brekke(n)	many
dys	Disher	Dysjaa	VII, 302
fjall	Fea	Fjeld	many
flata	Lettan	Floter	I, 375
garðr	Garth	Gaard	many
haugr	Howar	Hauger	many
hóll	Hool	Hol	many
hólmr	Holm	Holm	many
hörgr	Hargar	Horge	XI, 250
klette	Cleat	Klet	XIV, 316

mýrar	Myres	Myrer	many
naustar	Nouster	Nøste, Nauste	several
nes	Ness	Nes	many
óss	Oyce	Os	many
sandr	Sand	Sand	many
setr	Seater	Sætre	III, 186
skáli	Skaill	Skaale	XI, 29
stofa	Stove	in compounds*	several
topt	Tafts	Tofte	several
vágr	Walls	Vaag(ene)	many; X, 348

*Eidstu (XIV, 367), Listo (XII, 393), Myklestad (XI, 168), Øfrestue (XI, 289), etc.

Marwick (p. 8) also conjectures that the Orkney name Goir is derived from, or cognate with, Norw. *gjorde* 'meadow field', for which Rygh does not seem to cite a toponymic example.

The kind of almost total congruity which the last table demonstrates should not come as a surprise, as the generics involved are, on the whole, semantically very general on any taxonomic scale. The man-made aspects of a farmstead are expressed in a few terms (*bólstaðr/bústaðr, bölkr, bý/bær, garðr, hús, kot, kvern, kví, setr, skáli, stæði, stofa, topt, völlr*), and *borgr* is the only artificial feature in the vicinity referred to. Obviously, an attempt was made by the namers to distinguish different types of homesteads, but these distinctions are not made on the basis of very fine nuances. The natural features of the surrounding landscape from which farm-names are derived in large measure include, on the coast, headlands (*nes*), bays (*vágr, vík*), river-mouths (*óss*), landing-places (*naustar*), islets (*hólmr*), sand (*sandr*), and, in the inland, eminences (*dýs, fjall, haugr, hóll, horgr, klettr*), slopes (*brekka, hlíð*), depressions (*gröf*), low (*ló*) and flat (*flata*) pieces of land, and features such as nooks (*kró*), ends (*endi*), mires (*mýrar*), lochs (*vatn*), or just land (*land*). Apart from some variation in the choice of terms for small hills, this is an unexciting landscape described in unexcited terms by unexcited, or even unexciting, people. Lack of refinement and detail is written all over it, as well as utilitarian rather than aesthetic purposes. What is discerned and toponymically structured here, one has seen at home before; it therefore asks for imitation, not innovation.

It is usually the task of specifics to provide some of the refinement that most generics cannot supply, and to a certain extent this is true in North Ronaldsay and Sanday, although quite a few elements that occur as generics are also used as specifics (*borg, garðr, haugr, hlíð, hús, kví, óss, skáli, vágr*). Other features in the landscape referred to are *velta* 'ploughed soil', *kirkja* 'church', *köngull* 'cluster of rocks', *vin* 'pasture', *á* 'water course', *hellir* 'cave', *grind* 'gate', *grjót* 'stones', *hóp* 'bay', *stöng* 'pole', *træ* 'tree', *varð* 'beacon hill', *eyrar* 'gravelly beach', *bakki* 'slope', *hamra* 'projecting rocks', *skarð* 'notch', and *skeið* 'track'. Flora and fauna have found their way into such names as Linklet (*lyng* 'heather'), Sennes (*selr* 'seal'), Whunderless (*hvönn* 'angelica'), Lamaness (*lamba* 'lamb'), Noltland (*naut* 'cattle'), Sellibister (*selja* 'willow'), Rusness (*hross* 'horse'), and Savil (*sáð* 'seed'). It is a landscape toponymically structured largely by relating features referred to in generics to other features referred to in specifics. Perhaps names containing directions also belong to this category, like *suð* 'south' in Sugarhouse, Suthirbie, Southwall and Simbister, *nord* 'north' in Northgarth, and *øfri* 'upper' in Appiehouse and Evirbist. Descriptive of the features themselves are *hó* 'high' (Holland), *vesall* 'poor, worthless' (Fisligar), *breiði* 'broad' (Brabustir, Skelbrae), *helgi* 'holy' (Hellihowe), *hlaupand* 'leaping' (Lopness), *ný* 'new' (Neebister, Neigarth), *langi* 'long' (Langskaill), *hvít* 'white' (Whiteclett), and, in some sense *streit* 'strife' (Stratigar). The largest group of names has a personal name as its specific: Bresigar, Boloquoy, Hermisgarth, Colligar, Kettletoft, Leavsgarth, Skedgibist. In the name Geiramont the original generic has been lost and only the anthroponymic specific remains.

There is again nothing particularly innovative or imaginative about these qualifying elements. What does interest us in our enquiry, however, is that, like the simple names, every one of them also occurs in Norwegian farm-names. Some of this congruency may be regarded as self-fulfilling prophecy or circular reasoning because some of the opaque names in the two Orcadian islands may contain specifics (or generics, for that matter) which have not been identified because they are not found in Norway or have not been recognised there, but if this is so, it would apply only to a very small number of elements and not change the overall picture.

SPECIFIC	ORKNEY	NORWAY
á	Hookin	Aarbakke, Aartun
bakki	Backaskail	Bakkeland, Bakkevik
borg	Burness	Baarhaug, Berhovde
breiði	Brabustir	Breiby, Breiset
garðr	Gairsty, Garbo, Garso, Gerbo, Sugarhouse	Garløs, Garvik
grind	Grindally	Grindaaker, Grindereng
grjót	Gruthill	Groterud, Grjotland
hamra	Hammerbrake	Hammeraas, Hammerberg
helgi	Hellihowe	Helgevold, Hægebostad
hellir	Elsness	Hellestveit, Hellesæter

hlaupand	Lopness	Laupstad
hóp	Hobbister	Hopland, Hopnese
hvít	Whiteclett	Hvitberg, Hvitstein
hvönn	Whunderless	Hvannes
kirkja	Kirbist	Kirkeby, Kirkegaard
kví	Quivals	Kviby, Kvistad
köngull	Conglibist	Kongelstad
langi	Langskaill	Langdalen, Langholt
lyng	Linklet	Lyngaas, Lyngnes
óss	Isgarth	Osbak, Osnes
sáð	Savil	Saadland, Saaset
selja	Sellibister	Seljord, Siljaas, Sølberg
skáli	Skelbister	Skaalevik, Skaaltveit
skarð	Scarrigar	Skar(d)berg, Skarderud
skeið	Skitho	Skeibrok, Skeidhaker
streit	Stretigar	Streituland
stöng	Stangasetter	Stangeby, Stangeland
træ	Tresness	Træsbakken, Træsdalen
vág	Voxetter, Waldgarth	Vaagen, Vagsvik
varð	Warsetter	Vardeberg, Vardeheien
velta	Vaultness	Veltbakken
vesall	Fisligar	Veslebraaten, (?) Veslengen
vin	Finyarhouse	Venneskaal, Vinjevold

PERSONAL NAMES

Bolli m.	Boloquoy	Bollerod, Bollgaarden
Brúsi m.	Bersigar	Bruserud. Brusevold
Geirmundr	Geiramunt	Gjermundsby, Gjermundstad
Hermundr	Hermisgarth	Hermundsal, Hermundstad
Ketil	Kettletoft	Ketilsaa, Ketilstad
Kolli m., *Kolla* f.	Colligar	Kollerud, Kolrøis
Leif	Leavsgarth	Lefsrod, Lefsaaker
Skeggi	Skedgibist	Skjeggeby, Skjeggenes

Not included in this list is *eyrar* 'gravelly beach', which in Orkney occurs in Airan and Erraby, but which I have so far been unable to trace in Norway.

Just as it is possible to find without much difficulty Orcadian specifics which in Norwegian farm-names are combined with generics other than the one(s) with which they have been employed to form farm-names in North Ronaldsay and Sanday, so it takes just a little patient search through the two compendia in question to discover generics which occur on both sides of the North Sea, though in combination with different specifics. Examples would be:

GENERIC	ORKNEY	NORWAY
brekka	Antabreck, Hammerbrake	Langebrekke, Sandbrekke, Solbrekke, Vandbrekke
endi	Airan	Sjuerød, Sjøren, Skogrem, Vassum
hús	Appiehouse, Finyarhouse	Bækhus, Enhus, Langhus, Nethus
klettr	Linklet, Whiteclett	Arekletten, Hovskletten, Lysklett, Duklett
kot	Benziecot	Kaapegot, Kallekot, Kalsgot
setr	Voxetter, Warsetter	Bruset, Furuset, Groset, Hellekindset
skáli	Backaskail, Langskaill	Eggeskal, Fjeldskaal, Reppeskaal, Venneskaal
völlr / vellir	Quivals, Savil	Brusvold, Havold, Hestevold, Jaavall, Myrvold

While it is of interest and significance in our quest to find both generics and specifics used in Orkney and Norway in unrelated formations, the most impressive and important category in our name corpus, of course, consists of the several Orkney compound names for which there are identical equivalents in Norway, for these are obviously witness to an attitude of imitation rather than innovation. These are:

NORSE NAME	ORKNEY	NORWAY	RYGH
Akrsnes (?)	Hacksness	Aksnes	XIII, 82, etc.
Haugagarðr	Housegarth	Hauggaard	I, 107; III, 183
Haugaland	Howland	Haugeland	many
Haugatopt	Howatoft	Haugetuft	VII, 23
Haugrinn grœni	Hynegreenie	cf. Grœnehaugen	X, 81
Haugskró	Houscrow	Huskroen	VII, 364
Hóland	Holland	Holand	many
Hrossanes	Rusness	Rossnes	XI, 390, 418
Húshaugr	Hoosay	Hushaug	XI, 79
Lambanes	Lamaness	Lambunes	XVIII, 300
Liða(r)land	Leyland	Liland	several
Nautland	Noltland	Nautland	IX, 214
Nordgaror	Northgarth	Nordgaard	I, 206, etc.
Nýgarðr	Neigarth	Nygaard	many
Sel(a)nes	Sennes	Selnes	several
Skjaldbreiðr	Shelbrae	Skjalbred	V, 245, etc.
Súðrbær/-by	Suthirbie	Subø	VII, 344

Súðrgarðr	Sugar (house)	Søgaard	I, 187, 331
Træsnes (?)	Tresness	Træsnes	VIII, 79
?	Volunes	Volnes	XVI, 109
Øfribólstaðr	Everbist	Øverbostad	XIII, 131

While this list of 21 names, even when augmented by the same number of simple names which occur on both sides of the North Sea, does not substantiate my impressionistic claim, made several years ago,[5] that it might be possible to find an identical equivalent in Norway for almost every Orkney farm-name, it nevertheless indicates that this is true of at least one third of the names in question, an indication even more noteworthy when one considers the rather scanty documentary evidence in Norway, as well as in the Northern Isles of Scotland.

It is not my intention on this occasion to re-open the debate as to whether these are mainly lexical or onomastic imitations, but there cannot be any doubt that the element of imitation is predominant, and that any innovative impulse is almost completely absent. There may be hints of innovation in the use of such terms as *bölkr*, *eyrar* and *stæði* in toponymic compounds, and of *stova* as an onomastic simplex in Orkney, when these elements do not seem to be used similarly in Norway; but, as always, it is dangerous to argue from the absence of evidence. There may also have been certain subtle semantic shifts which are not easily detected a thousand years later. In addition, *bólstaðr* was apparently employed more liberally in Orkney, perhaps as the result of a change in application. A name like Crotrive suggests that here a Scandinavian specific (ON *kró* 'enclosure, cattle fold') modifies a pre-Norse Gaelic generic (*trave* < *treabh*). While these may be glimpses of innovation, otherwise the cupboard is bare.

Colonists intent on making a living in a new environment (or at least in Orkney) are therefore, it seems, not very adventurous in their naming practices. They discern new landscapes in terms of the homeland and create a familiar habitat within the framework of these perceptions. It would be very surprising if a more comprehensive survey were to produce very different conclusions or alter the picture significantly. What we observe, if the Scandinavian farm-names of North Ronaldsay and Sanday are anything to go by, is not just a transferred nomenclature, but a transferred landscape.

Notes

This article is a revised version of a paper given on 29 March 1987 at the XIXth Annual Conference of the Council for Name Studies held at the University of Nottingham.

1   Hugh Marwick, *Orkney Farm-Names* (Kirkwall, 1952).

2   Olaf Rygh, *Norske Gaardnavne*, 19 vols (Christiania/Oslo, 1898-1936).

3   A.W. Brøgger, *Ancient Emigrants* (Oxford, 1929).

4. Marwick, 22.

5   W.F.H. Nicolaisen, 'Early Scandinavian naming in the Western and Northern Isles', *Northern Scotland* III, 2 (1979-80), 105-121, esp. 108.

NORNA – rapporter 34 (1987) 9–19

Semantic Causes of Structural
Changes in Place-names

THE subject which I have chosen for this presentation appeals to me for a number of reasons. In the first place, it gives me an opportunity to combine the two major topics listed separately, or at least independently, for this conference. This is not simply a personal preference because it is no secret that in all expressive culture form and meaning are closely linked. Although I have never quite believed those who claim that form is meaning and that the medium is the message, I am nevertheless convinced that form is more than a vehicle for meaning and has a much more complex relationship with the latter. As, over the years, I have come across many attempts by people fascinated with names to interpret them not in terms of their origins but within the framework of their own contemporary cultural notions, I think it would be fun to see whether there are examples of names on the Scottish map in which this kind of reanalysis has become permanent, so to speak; what I have in mind are names which, because they have been invested with new meaning by their users, have undergone morphological changes which are so reasonable and so plausible that they have become locked into the modern spelling and frequently also the modern pronunciation, although the two processes do not necessarily go hand in hand. This kind of development is naturally mostly, though not exclusively, to be expected at the seams of linguistic and cultural contact when a name passes from one language into another.

While this kind of investigation would have an objective quite appropriate for this conference and would be well worth undertaking just for that reason alone, it seems to offer not quite the right kind of scholarly satisfaction. Dealing with surfaces is one thing or with products of processes, but it is quite another to ferret out the motivations and conceptions, perhaps even the preconceptions, behind the processes that have produced the products or have supplied the surfaces. Underlying my choice of topic is therefore the more challenging realization that, in the course of my analysis and interpretation, I would have to come to grips with the contradictory claims made by the two tenets which have guided my onomastic endeavours over the last three decades or so: On the one hand, the firm conviction that names do not need lexical meaning in order to function adequately as names; and, on the other, the observation that name users often are not content with this semantic opacity of onomastic items and, through secondary re-interpretation, endow them with new lexical meaning, thus making the seemingly meaningless meaningful for themselves. The clash of these two principles is, for me at least, an intriguing one which cannot be resolved on a purely descriptive level. While it remains undoubtedly true that something happens to words when they are pressed into service for onomastic purposes, i.e. when names are "coined", as we say, from lexical material, this filling of words with onomastic contents and this establishment of new criteria and expectations which determine what happens to names in their various linguistic embeddednesses, are obviously not the whole story. As long as we are only concerned with the process of naming and concentrate on the moment of, what one might call, the onomasticisation of words and its consequences, one can speculate without any qualms about these theoretical matters and perhaps even successfully arrive at a theory of names or, a little more modestly, a theory about names. One can compare and contrast words and names with regard to their phonological, morphological, syntactic, or semantic properties, for instance; and this is something which I have been doing for many years.[1] One can even suggest a new hierarchical terminology which would allow one to regard, in defiance of long established tradition and well-ploughed furrows, both words and names as appellatives or appellations, thus conjuring up a convenient umbrella term and concept for them both.[2] And there is undoubtedly a great need for innovative thinking if we wish to convince ourselves, each other, and especially our colleagues in other disciplines that the study of names is not just the study of words with peculiar additional characteristics. In other words, it is absolutely essential that we must provide the theoretical underpinnings for what we do. It is not enough to assert that we know what we are doing. Indeed, research in this direction will enable us to get closer and closer to a fuller understanding of Man the Namer, of that elusive *homo nominans* who shares so many qualities with *homo ludens*, *homo faber* and *homo cogitans*. Well, you have heard me talk about all this before.

If, however, we were to lavish our attention exclusively on who names what, the processes by which names are given and the products of these processes, i.e. if we were to concentrate solely on namer, naming and name, we would probably ignore elements and components that, in my view, are perhaps even more important than the essential triad just mentioned, because no number of namers, no amount of naming and no corpus of names, however extensive, would have any impact on our lives, would turn a threatening wilderness into a familiar habitat or human chaos into an ordered society, without the name user, without the usage of names, without usage-oriented attitudes toward names. Our theories will never amount to much if we do not include in them a socio-onomastic dimension.[3] This may not be easy, it may frequently not be very comfortable, it may even sometimes demand intolerable adjustments in our thinking, but it is necessary if we want to be name scholars worth our salt. Ultimately, it is usage that matters and only through a thorough exploration and understanding of the onomastic registers and dialects involved and of the variations they produce can we hope to isolate, analyse and come to terms with this so obviously real but so difficult to conceptualise phenomenon which we call *name*.

The secondary semantic re-interpretation of names by their users is one important aspect to be examined by this socio-onomastic approach to names. We cannot be satisfied with the mere claim so often made by those whose fascination with names is not matched by equally well-developed interpretative skills, that a name has been "corrupted" by its users. In fact, the term "corruption" with its moral or moralistic overtones has no place in the vocabulary of our discipline. It may go against the grain when the well-established and well-cherished principles of etymology are ignored by those who, while using names, also redeploy their meaning; but instead of raving against the perpetrators of such unspeakable crimes that violate our precious academic sensibilities, we must endeavour to understand their motives and the results of their actions. Names are neither sacrosanct nor static, and the changes inherent in their dynamism can occur for many reasons, whether we, as scholars, approve of these reasons or not. We get upset when they do not fit the phonological patterns or the morphological systems which we have so painstakingly and with so much scholarly rigor, though without taking into account such "unreasonable" changes the history of many a name would be difficult to explain and we could not say how its original form of, let us say, a thousand years ago has become what it is now. That is the much more serious desideratum, then: a better understanding of name usage, the only method by which life-blood can be pumped into sterile structures. A non-applied name is no name or, putting it the other way round, names are there to be used. I have not been silent on this subject in the past either.

In some curious fashion, and much to my delight, this particular facet of name usage, the secondary re-interpretation of names in lexically valid semantic terms, also has strong links with that other basic and ubiquitous characteristic of all humankind – the telling of stories. Through stories we create believable chunks of the past.[4] The past does not exist unless it is narrated; otherwise it is only chronology. Only the past is narratable, and we use the present to create new pasts through narration. Occasionally we can also rehearse the future through story and thus make it less overwhelming, take the sting out of it.[5] The aetiological explanation of names does not escape this treatment for, to all intents and purposes, *homo nominans* and *homo narrans* are one and the same, mastering space through naming and conquering time through storying, thus locating us in space as well as in time. It is not surprising therefore that the secondary re-interpretation of names, their appropriation in contemporary lexical terms, is often accompanied by stories bolstering or confirming the linguistic act.[6] A past event is verbally re-enacted to give credence to the present name; the landscape is revealed as having historical structure as well as current existence. Life and landscape begin to approximate each other; names, in this sense, are plausible texts to be interrogated through story. As both purveyors and recipients of certain pasts in certain places, we are not only satisfied with stories, we demand them. The oral traditions to which we are exposed, mostly in the form of local or localized legends, may sometimes seem questionable in the light of our written documentation or should, at a minimum, raise a questioning eyebrow, but not only are we not put off by this dubiety, we are so endeared by it that we accept the bizarre and the exotic in our willingness to succumb to the reality of fiction as if it were the fiction of reality. Our disbelief does not have to be suspended because the truth of a story lies in its telling, and all narrated pasts, including those of the names on our maps, are true during the act of narration. Stories do not so much explain names, make excuses for them, they legitimize them beyond their obvious and pedestrian functionality. While perhaps not all names spell out for us an onomastic shorthand for story, many of them are eminently narratable because they encapsulate a past that has either been narrated before or is still to be told. The storying capacity of names is therefore enormous. Well, that, too, I have talked and written about before.

Where, then, do we go from here in view of this distinct lack of novelty, and what does the foregoing have to do with the purported topic in hand, the investigation of the potential impact of secondary semantic re-analysis on the structure of place-names? I hope to show in the remainder that all three aspects of onomasticity briefly alluded to – the lexical meaninglessness of names, the desire by name users to reinvent a lexical context for them, and the role which stories play in the creation of pasts for these names – have some bearing on our central subject. In fact, I would like to claim that we have secretly and without making much fuss about it – "auf Schleichwegen", as they would say in Germany – come quite close to our intended intellectual destination. All that remains for me to do is to provide the illustrations and to present these in some systematic fashion. My examples will all come from the place-nomenclature of Scotland; whenever possible, I have tried to include names that are ultimately of Scandinavian origin but, of necessity, there are also several other languages involved. Almost invariably the recipient language in question will be a form of English, and usually the semantic re-interpretations and the morphological re-structuring will therefore be within the linguistic embeddedness and features of that language. This is a matter of convenience rather than personal preference; naturally, the same phenomena and principles to be observed when Gaelic, Pictish, Cumbric, or Scandinavian names passed into English, must also have been observable when Scandinavian, Pictish or Cumbric names passed into Gaelic, but the all-important role of analogies and onomastic puns in these processes would be difficult to detect. Let us examine the process step by step:

(1) Fundamental to all our considerations remains the well-documented premise that names, if they have not already lost their lexical meaning in the donor language, will do so when they are transferred to a recipient language. Sometimes there remains some residual but very limited understanding of some of the most common generic elements but, on the whole, semantic opacity is inevitable and to be expected. English-speaking users of names like *Balloch, Cambusnethan, Freuch, Thwaite, Lerwick, Borgue* do not know that these names are derived from words meaning "pass", "bend on the (river) Nethan", "heather" in Gaelic, or "clearing", "mud-bay", or "fortification" in Norse, respectively. For them, all these names are meaningless sequences of sounds functioning as modern English place-names on the Scottish map.

(2) In this process of de-semanticisation, it happens not infrequently and accidentally – although one can never be sure what analogical forces have been at work, since analogy plays a much more important role in linguistic history than tidy textbooks can accommodate in their chapters and are therefore prepared to admit – that, as a result of the limited number of significant sound sequences which the phonological structure of a language will allow, an onomastically adopted and phonologically adapted name takes on the shape, both in spelling and pronunciation, of a meaningful word in English. Examples would be names like *Deer, Dollar, Inch, Petty, Rum*, and *Yell*. The fact that we can trace *Dollar* to Gaelic *dolair* "valley place", *Inch* to Gaelic *inis* "island", and *Petty* to Gaelic *peitigh*, the locative of *peiteach* "place of portions" (the first element is, of course, Pictish in origin), whereas we do not know the linguistic origins or meanings of *Deer*,

Rum or *Yell*, is of no consequence. It is their homonymity in English that matters, the punning potential of which has occasionally been exploited in jokes and riddles. What we have here is proto-story potential but, in general, no apparent deliberate or wrenching attempt at reshaping the name to fit English semantic patterns.

(3) Half understood, not understood or misunderstood names or their components are in some way rearranged, either audibly or visually, or both, to resemble English words, with various degrees of success, from near-plausibility to complete nonsensicality. The following examples represent only some of the possibilities:

(a) The river name *Adder*, which occurs twice as *Blackadder* and *Whiteadder* and which is identical in its Old European origins with the German river name *Oder*,[7] would not have been given its modern spelling and pronunciation without the existence and influence of the English word *adder* "a snake".

(b) The river name *Almond* (Perthshire: *Amun* 1162-64),[8] as **Ambona* of early Celtic or pre-Celtic provenance,[9] after adding the homorganic voiced stop [d] to the final [n], in a process quite common in Scots (West Lothian: *Aumond* 1420), sounded like the nut, the "almond", and therefore had an -*l*- added to its spelling (West Lothian: *Almond* 1593). Why anyone should think that this would be an appropriate name for a river, is another matter.

(c) The Pictish *Apercrossan* (*c.* 1088) "confluence by the cross" was partially re-interpreted as *Applecross* (*Appillcroce* 1510).

(d) The *Colbrandespade* of *c.* 1130 containing the Old Norse personal name *Kolbrandr* has, in a series of steps, become the modern *Cockburnspath* (*Cowbrandispeth* 1443, *Coburnspeth c.* 1485, *Cokbrandispeth* 1529, *Cok-burnispeth* 1664) in which a well-known Scottish surname has been substituted.

(e) The ecclesiastical place-name which appears in 1211 as *Eglesmagrill* and as *Eglesmagril* in 1211-14, "my-Grill's church", in some alarming secular turnabout now appears on the Scottish map as *Exmagirdle* (recorded as such as early as 1476, though still on record as *Eglismagirdill* in 1618), made possible by the common *r*-metathesis which initially produced -*girl* from *gril*.

(f) *Irongrey*, as in *Kirkpatrick Irongrey* (Kirkcudbrightshire), on record as *kyrkpatric cro* in 1287 and as *Kirkpatric-Garngray* in 1463 was originally a compound of Gaelic *earrann* "a portion" and the district name *Cro*.

(g) *King Edward* in Aberdeenshire is the most extreme and bizarre example of the very common hypercorrect substitution of *-ing* for *-in*. This name is on record in 1178 as *Kynedor* and in 1272 as *Kennedor*. However, as early as the thirteenth century the second element had begun to look like the personal name *Edward* in the spellings *Kenedward c.* 1250 and *Kyneduart* 1272. By 1531, the first component *Kin-* has been re-interpreted as *King-* so that we find *Kingedward*. Originally the name was composed of Gaelic *cinn* and *fothair*, meaning "(at the) end of the slope". The morpho-phonemic substitution of *-ing* for *-in* is very common; sometimes it has survived, as in *Stirling* (*Striuelin c.* 1123, *Striueling* 1147-53); sometimes it has been abandoned again, as in *Dunfermline* (*Dunfermelyn c.* 1125, *Dunfremling* 1490).

(h) The Gaelic *fid-nemed* "wood-sanctuary", after intermediate semantic opacity, has taken on a partial new meaning which seems to make sense in a topographic context. Though bearing witness to the scribes' struggle to represent unfamiliar sounds, its early spellings reflect its original meaning fairly well, such as *Fothneuyn* c. 1250, *Foþeneuyn* 1287, *Futhynevynt* 1370, *Fothnevyn*, *Fothenevin* 1374, and even *Fothneve* 1453, but only a few years later it is *Finevyn* in 1465 which thoroughly obscures the first element, and later it is recorded as *Finhevin* 1606, *Phinheavin* 1635, and *Phinhaven* 1672, all obvious forerunners of the modern *Finhaven*. Parallel evidence is provided by the name *Usan* whose fifteenth-century spellings partly foreshadow the modern form (*Owsawyn* 1485, *Owsane* 1487) or indicate re-interpretations similar to *Finhaven* (*Vllishavyn* 1492, *Houshavyn* 1493; also *Wolfishavyn* 1532). In this case, however, the re-interpreted forms have not prevailed.

(i) In Gaelic, *Legbernard c.* 1142, "Bernard's flagstone", and Cumbric *Pren ros* "tree of the moor", both components have been re-interpreted in terms of English, for the former is now *Leadburn* (*Letbernard* 1344, *Leadburn* 1773) and the latter *Primrose* (*Primros* 1154-59), while *Pren Wen* "white tree" with English *sete* "seat" added (*Prenwensete c.* 1200) is now *Primside* (*Promset* late 13th century, *Promside* 1430, *Primside* 1432).

(j) That re-analysis does not only take place when a name passes from one language into another, but can also happen within the historical development of the same language, especially if the underlying lexical items have themselves become obsolete or have undergone a semantic shift, is demonstrated by *Yetholm* (*Jetham* 1166-71) and *Twynholm* (*Tuinham* 1287), both originally *hām* names but now regarded as containing *holmr*, *Morebattle* (*Mereboda* c.1124, *Merbotil* 1174-99, *Morbottle* 1590, *Morbatle* 1675) and *Newbattle* (*Neubotle* 1124-40, *Newbattle* 1661) in which the no longer understood Old English *boþl* "a dwelling" has been replaced somewhat eccentrically by Modern English *battle*, and *Lillescliva c.* 1124, "Lillie's Cliff", which now appears as *Lilliesleaf* (*Lillessleyf* 1510).

In all these examples, and there are many more, secondary semantic re-interpretation has left the basic structure of the names affected intact. In compound names, for example, the boundary between first and second elements has not been violated although, because of the different word order, what used to be a sequence generic followed by specific in Gaelic, is now a sequence specific plus generic in English. Generally speaking, however, the reinterpretations have been purely semantic, with only minimal effect on the structure.

(4) The foregoing third group of names painlessly and almost imperceptibly leads us to the category which is the most central concern of this paper – names in which semantic re-analysis has caused structural reshapings of the names question. In each case a semantic cause has had morphological consequences.

(a) Perhaps the easiest type to begin with is represented by *Kinghorn* which derives from Gaelic *cinn-gronna* "bog-head" and which, for example, was *Kingorn c.* 1128. In the modern form of the name, the dental nasal [n] and the velar voiced stop [g] have been assimilated to the velar nasal [ŋ], perhaps somewhat assisted by the development of Gaelic *Cinn-* "head" to *King-* which I discussed earlier in connection with *King Edward*, and the second element, after loss of the initial *g-* to the previous syllable and *r*-metathesis, has been re-interpreted as English *horn* (*Kynhorn* 1419, *Kinghorn* 1595), a process also seen in *Dreghorn* (*Dreghorne* 1529) which was earlier *Dregerna* c.1240, and the like. The stress has been accommodated in initial position. The main point is that, as a result of the secondary semantic re-interpretation in terms of English, the boundary between the two elements has shifted from before the *g* to after it.

(b) In the Gaelic name which appears in 1200 as *Kyllosbern*, "Osbern's church", the last syllable has been reinterpreted as Scottish English *burn* "stream" and the generic *cill* "church", combined with the first syllable of the personal name, has been telescoped into and reinterpreted as *Close-*, so that the modern map name is now *Closeburn* (*Cloisborne* 1556), looking eminently English without being all that meaningful.

(c) *Dún Breatann*, the ancient "Fortress of the Britons" on the River Clyde, has undergone a morphological split in the second element which, as a result of *r*-metathesis and re-interpretation of the last syllable as *-ton* < earlier *-tūn*, now appears as *-barton*, and the whole name as *Dumbarton*, with the usual labialisation of *n* > *m* before *b* (*Dunbretane* 1238, *Dumbertan* 1271, *Dunbartane* 1508, *Dumpartane* 1525, *Dumbartoune* 1680).

(d) The final two examples of this kind, according to their modern spellings and pronunciations, both appear to contain the Scots word *-kirk* < Old Norse *kirkja* which would be quite appropriate in the part of Scotland in which they are found. They are *Westerkirk* and *Stoneykirk*; the two first elements seem to be straightforward, from an English point of view. It is only when we discover that *Westerkirk* was *Wathstirkir* "*Stýrkarr's* ford" in 1255 and *Wadsterkerin* in 1249, and that *Stoneykirk* was *Steinnaker* "the field of stones" as late as 1575 (*Stanacra* 1287, *Stennaker* 1534), that we realise how we have been fooled by the appearance of the modern names. In both instances, the last syllable has been separated and reinterpreted as Scots *-kirk*. In the first name, the meaningless bisyllabic jumble of *Wathstir-* was then reshaped as *Wester-* (*Westerker 1296*, *Westerkyrke* 1287), and in the second, *Stenna-*, i.e. the reflex of Norse *steinna* plus the initial *a-* of *akr*, have been sort of Anglicised as *Stoney-* (*Stainykirk* 1547, *Stonnykirk* 1615). Naturally, the unusual, though for the region appropriate, word order of *Vað-Stýrkarr* (inversion compound) has been obliterated and the stress has been shifted to its expected initial position.

(e) That morpheme boundaries can also be rearranged without the name passing into another language is shown by *Fortune*, a development and re-interpretation of *Forton* or *Fortoun* (*Fortona c.* 1150, *Fortoun* 1503, *Fortune* 1549-50). The really unusual feature about this name is that a compound name has been turned into a simple one which is the opposite of what one would have expected.

What is the upshot of all this? The material presented has, I hope, demonstrated that it would be dangerous for name scholars to leave the name user out of the picture. Whenever there is user interference, the expected results of phonological adaptation lose much of their predictability, and lexically meaningless onomastic functionality has all or part of its semantic transparency restored – or so it seems, for this process of restoration is largely dependent on re-interpretation within the framework of another language, in our case English, for which the rules of the game are somewhat different. Sometimes names simply begin to look like words familiar to speakers of that recipient language and invite punning in the way in which every homonym invites word play; sometimes a little cosmetic, often based on analogy, is needed to simulate full or partial meaning, but this removal of semantic opacity has no structural side-effects; sometimes again semantic re-interpretation is accompanied by the violation of morphological boundaries and the structural re-arrangement of morphemes.

To show that this last category exists and what some of its potential trends are, has been the point of this paper while, without being able to discuss this point in detail, I have also tried to highlight the possibility of such names as narratable texts (and sometimes also intertexts),[10] creating not just windows on the past but the past itself. My Sunday sermon therefore ends with a hallelujah for the existence of the name user who exasperates, thwarts and delights us, for without him or her we would be involved in a discipline bereft of the ever-changing patterns of the socio-onomastic kaleidoscope.

Notes

1   See, for example, W.F.H. Nicolaisen, "Onomastics – An Independent Discipline?". *Indiana Names* 3 (1972) 33-47; "Words as Names". *Onoma* 20 (1976) 142-163; "Are There Connotative Names?". *Names* 26 (1978) 40-47; "Onomastic Dialects". *American Speech* 55 (1980) 36-45; "Lexical and Onomastic Fields". *Proceedings of the Thirteenth International Congress of Onomastic Sciences*, Cracow 1978, Vol. 11 (Cracow 1982) 209-216.

2   W.F.H. Nicolaisen, "The Semantics of Place-names and Their Elements". *NORNA-rapporter* 28 (1985) 60-71; "Nomen, Noun and Name: The Lexical Horns of an Onomastic Dilemma", in: *Historical & Editorial Studies in Medieval and Early Modern English*. Eds. Mary-Jo Arn and Hanneke Wirtjes (Groningen: Wolters – Noordhoff, 1985) 63-72.

3   W.F.H. Nicolaisen, "Socio-onomastics". *Proceedings of the Fifteenth International Congress of Onomastic Sciences*, Leipzig 1984 (Leipzig: Karl-Marx-Universität, 1985) 118-132.

4   See W.F.H. Nicolaisen, "Legends as Narrative Response", in: *Perspectives on Contemporary Legend*. Ed. Paul Smith. CECTAL Conference Paper Series No 4 (Sheffield: University of Sheffield, 1984) 167-178.

5   W.F.H. Nicolaisen, "Rehearsing the Future in the Folktale". *New York Folklore* 11 (1985) 231-238. Pre-publication version available in: *Papers II – The 8th Congress for the International Society for Folk Narrative Research*. Eds. Reimund Kvideland and Torunn Selberg (Bergen 1984) 119-130.

6   W.F.H. Nicolaisen, "Place-Name Legends: An Onomastic Mythology". *Folklore* 87 (1976) 146-59: "Place-names and Their Stories". *Ortnamnssällskapets i Uppsala Ärsskrift* (1977) 23-29; "Some Humorous Folk-Etymological Narratives". *New York Folklore* 3 (1977) 1-14; "Names and Narratives". *Journal of American Folklore* 97 (1984) 259-272.

7   W.F.H. Nicolaisen, "Scottish Place-Names: 26. Blackadder and Whiteadder".
     Scottish Studies 10 (1966) 78-87; "Great Britain and Old Europe". *Namn och Bygd*
     59 (1971) 85-105; *Scottish Place-Names: Their Study and Significance* (London:
     B.T. Batsford, 1976) 184-186; "Thirty Years Later: Thoughts on a Viable Concept
     of Old European Hydronymy", in: *Festschrift für Johannes Hubschmid zum 65.
     Geburtstag.* Eds. Otto Winkelmann and Maria Braisch (Bern 1982) 139-148; "'Old
     European' Names in Britain". *Nomina* 6 (1982) 37-42.
8   All early spellings have been culled from the files of my as yet incomplete
     collections for a projected *Concise Dictionary of Scottish Place-names.*
9   Nicolaisen, *Scottish Place-Names*, p. 178.
10   W.F.H. Nicolaisen, "Names as Intertextual Devices". *Onomastica Canadiana* 68/2
     (1986).

Studia Onomastica: Festskrift till Thorsten Andersson
23 Feb. 1989 Lund (1989) 261-268

Place-Name Maps – How Reliable Are They?

IF it strikes the editors and readers of this festschrift as strange that the title of an essay written in honour of one of the foremost Scandinavian name scholars of our time, by someone who has been a devoted student of onomastics for almost forty years, is asking a question directed at the basics of name research, there is obvious justification for this initial reaction, for is it not rather late in the day for one sexagenarian to offer such a fundamental query as a birthday present to another sexagenarian, his friend? Such an interrogative pose seems to be particularly inappropriate for someone who, as recently as the XVIth International Congress of Onomastic Sciences in Quebec in August 1987 tried to make the case for a rigorously onomastic onomastics, i.e. a truly name-centred study of names,[1] after having earlier pleaded for a strict division of onomasticon and lexicon,[2] argued strongly for a separation of onomastic fields from lexical fields,[3] advocated the establishment of a sub-discipline of socio-onomastics to examine socially engendered variation in different onomastic registers,[4] proposed the concept of isonyms in the determination of regional onomastic dialects,[5] and, above all, drawn attention on several occasions to the semantically significant contrast between lexical meaning and onomastic content,[6] to mention only some of the theoretical underpinnings of his research into place-names as convenient and promising raw material for the investigation of linguistic history, into the function of names in literature, into the role of name aesthetics, into the implications of the transfer of unanalysed names and name models from one country or even continent to another, and into the necessity to name as an essential factor in human survival and mastery of the world.

Before any consternation or, at the very least, puzzlement at the title's disturbing indication of apparent uncertainty in the mind of somebody who should know better takes on unmanageable proportions, let me explain: In the first place, this questioner is not all of a sudden abandoning all his former convictions throwing doubt on his frequently stated commitment to the pursuit of research that takes the existence of a discrete phenomenon which we call "name" as a given and proceeds on that assumption. Nor does he, secondly, suddenly have qualms about the wisdom of his insistence on a loosening of the close ties which for so long had forced onomastics into a position of linguistic sub-discipline, or, thirdly, admit to a decrease in his strong belief that the extra-linguistic facets of names need increased emphasis in future onomastic research. In fact, the question posed by the title is much less universal and much more practical and circumscribed than might be imagined at first glance, and should not surprise those who are aware of the self-critical way in which the questioner has, in recent years, assessed some of the findings of his own toponymic research, or are acquainted with the friendly but probing criticism recently levelled at some of these findings by other scholars, not necessarily in the onomastic business themselves. This essay is, in part, a response to this outside criticism but the question which precedes it in its title should not be construed as an underhand attempt at turning a defensive position into an aggressive one by diverting attention from a matter of detail to a more general enquiry concerning the foundations of our discipline; for the truth is that the criticism in this case is by no means ill-founded because it exposes an overlooked flaw in the translation of the spatial distribution of place-names into chronological sequences – a kind of metaphorising of one pattern into another, so to speak – which lies at the heart of an argument regarding the naming of *Scotia Scandinavica* which I first put forward in 1969[8] and which has found its way into other publications since then.[9] More precisely, therefore, the questions to be explored are: "What kinds of convincing conclusions can we derive from the mapping of the distribution of place-names or their elements? What kind of evidence are names in that kind of context?"

The reason why an attempt at answering these questions is a suitable topic for a thoughtful contribution to this festschrift is that they have been prompted as the result of the interpretation of Scandinavian names in Scotland in answer to the where, when and why of their occurrence, a sort of extension to the study of names in the Scandinavian countries, especially Norway, themselves. That such names might make a profitable field of enquiry has been recognised on both sides of the North Sea for at least a century by such scholars as Jakobsen, Olsen, Marwick, Borgstrøm, Oftedal, Wainwright, Stewart, Fellows-Jensen, Fraser, Macaulay, Small, myself, and others, because they offer an opportunity to study onomastic problems of differing scope and varying degrees of elaboration, most of them with repercussions for scholarship in the "homeland", in a limited "colonial" setting. It is not necessary to enumerate them all; suffice it to say that one of them was, and still is, the perceived need to plot different categories of place-names or place-name elements on maps and to extract the largest amount of information possible from any distribution patterns which might emerge.

It was with this aim in mind that I set out in the sixties to map the occurrence of Scandinavian place-names in Scotland. The spatial scatters which this undertaking made visual suggested strongly three major concentrations which demanded separate evaluation and made nonsense of any kind of map that tried to depict an undifferentiated and unstratified Scandinavian nomenclature wherever names of Scandinavian origin happened to be encountered in Scotland.[10] The Scandinavian place-names in the Scottish south-west showed a close link with – in fact, proved themselves to be the extension of – an area of Scandinavian place-names in the English north-west,[11] – whereas in south-east Scotland the indirect Scandinavian contribution to the toponymic palimpsest demonstrably consisted mostly of personal names combined as specifics with English generics in compound names and consequently more indicative of the presence of English-speaking settlers with Scandinavian names than of any Scandinavians themselves.[12] Only in the Atlantic islands was a direct influence from the Scandinavian mainland, especially Norway, clearly discernible. As far as the "where" was concerned, the evidence of place-names had therefore served its purpose splendidly although the resulting maps, in their simple two-dimensional format, were still lacking in sophistication and cartographic detail.

Notably in recent years, however, some of the insights gained from these maps regarding the "when" of the names plotted have not gone unchallenged, and this not so much with regard to the scatter of individual names as with reference to the attempted sequencing of geographical distributions aimed at the disclosure and display of chronological layering within the Scandinavian stratum. In particular, some of the conclusions drawn from maps which I prepared in order to show the occurrence of certain Scandinavian name elements in the Northern and Western Isles have come under fire in this respect. Selecting from Marwick's and Wainwright's set of toponymic generics the four terms *staðr/staðir*, *setr/sætr*, *bólstaðr* and *dalr*, as significantly mappable, I had claimed that:

> the names in *staðir* provide us with a picture of what the Norse settlement area was like before and up to the middle of the ninth century, whereas *setr*-names speak of consolidation and expansion well into the second half of that century. The map of *bólstaðr* in its various disguises -*bister*, -*bster*, -*bost*, -*bus*, -*boll*, -*pol*, etc. supplies an overall visual impression of Scandinavian *settlement* in the north and west when

at its most extensive; and finally the distribution of *dalr* reminds us that settlement area and sphere of influence are not the same and that the Norsemen must have known the western coastal districts of the mainland from Cape Wrath to the Mull of Kintyre extremely well even if they never (or hardly ever) had any permanent farms or other settlements there.[13]

I later incorporated that claim in the chapter on "Scandinavian Names" in my book *Scottish Place-Names*[14] and in other related writings.

This perceived chronological sequence and its attribution to some approximate absolute dates have been questioned chiefly on the grounds that differences in the extent of a distribution do not necessarily imply differences in the length of time during which the names whose distribution is depicted were productive. As Gillian Fellows-Jensen says: "Nicolaisen has argued that the names in -*staðir* in the Isles belong to the earliest period because of their very restricted distribution [...], but the fact that *staðir*-names are common in Iceland shows that the generic must have remained productive until late in the ninth century at least."[15] Similarly, while agreeing that the pattern of distribution of names in -*bólstaðr* "formed the definitive map of Norse settlement in the area", she argues that "the mere fact that their distribution is much more widespread than that of place-names in -*setr* does not necessarily mean that *setr*-names ceased to be formed at an earlier period than did the *bólstaðr*-names. There may be other reasons for the absence of *setr*-names from Islay, Mull, Coll and Tiree than that these islands were not settled by Scandinavians until after the generic *setr* had ceased to be used to form place-names."[16] Another good friend, the historian Barbara E. Crawford, in her recent excellent book *Scandinavian Scotland*, after surveying the same map sequence and drawing into the discussion equivalent names not only in Iceland but also in the Isle of Man, comes to the conclusion that "the rigid chronological sequencing of these place-name elements does not seem necessary or realistic".[17] In addition, she advances the view, based on Margaret Gelling's investigation of early English names,[18] that "in one very important respect the place-name maps of the Norse settlement of Scotland are entirely defective, and that is because they do not include what are now recognised as being some of the earliest and most important farms of all: those with topographical names".[19]

Obviously it would not be enough for the originator of these maps to point out that, in his attempts to make distribution visible and to scan it for potential patterns he was breaking new ground in Scotland, although this was certainly the case in the sixties. Nor would it be sufficient to offer the reminder that to correlate distributions in space with distributions in time or, put somewhat differently, to equate certain spatial patterns with certain temporal patterns, was an equally innovative act in the context of the place-nomenclature of Scandinavian Scotland, that in the last two decades cartographic techniques have progressed significantly, accompanied by a concomitant rise in expectations, and that new evidence has come to light. Indeed, there is no need to be so defensive as to hide behind a beginner's or pioneer's inexperience or lack of analogies, for I believe that, in principle, the general methodology I employed in the sixties is still valid. What was at fault was not the notion of chronological sequencing of spatial patterns itself but the, admittedly far too simplistic, automatic equation of "less extensive" with "earlier" and of "more extensive" with "later".

In a way, I had foreseen these problems by ending my account in the original article with the statement: "If such a sequence of maps is acceptable, place-names have done their job without being pressed for information which they cannot give,"[20] and I reinforced this conditional rider by concluding the respective section in my book with the warning: "It would be risky to read any more out of or into these maps."[21] It is now clear that, having been seduced by the neatness of the equation, I had not listened to my own warning bells early enough and had omitted to take into account other interpretative possibilities. It is equally evident that, although it may sometimes or even frequently be the case, it is not permissible to assume that the peak of productivity of a place-name type or element (if such a peak can indeed be pinpointed) always coincides with the most extensive use of that type or element.[22] It is, for example, possible for a generic, let us say, to have been used early in a restricted area and to have remained fashionable within the limits of that area as long as the language in which the resulting names are embedded was spoken there. It is, however, also possible for a type or element to have been used early in a restricted area and to have become non-productive after a short time. Thirdly, one cannot ignore the possibility of an element being coined or becoming fashionable later in the history of the language to which it belongs and to have died out again soon thereafter, never spreading very far from its area of origin. There are, of course, still other variations on this theme of trying to interpret a limited distribution.

Indeed, the problem, as I see it, lies in the fact that it is very difficult if not impossible to trace the beginnings and early stages of any developing productivity or pattern, in the absence of contemporary evidence.[23] I therefore agree with Crawford when she says that "no map of these place-names, or of any group of them, is therefore a map of primary Norse settlement, but only of expansion in the following decades or centuries."[24] It is also self-evident, one would have thought, that most generic elements are likely to have been used concurrently for much of the time, a fact which may have been methodologically obscured by my earlier fervour to discover definite links between spatial distribution and chronological sequencing. This is, one would presume, especially true of generics referring to natural features like, for example, ON *dalr*. Although this and similar terms may well have been used, as Barbara Crawford says, to designate "some of the earliest and most important farms of all,"[25] it was apparently also still productive at the later stages when Scandinavians, from their main bases in the Hebrides, made forays into or maybe even settled, temporarily or permanently, on the adjacent west coast of the Scottish mainland. The fact that such toponymic generics and simple names may have been used early does not invalidate them as evidence for a relatively late development or, in fact, for anything in between. I cannot envisage a time in the Scandinavian period in Scotland when topographical names in -*dalr*, both as farm names and as names of valleys, were not given when appropriate, because of this generic's continuing productivity, but I also still stand by my conclusion of twenty years ago that the *dalr*-names outside the *bólstaðr*-area reflect, on the whole, less permanency in occupation, or at least a very different attitude towards the land, than farm names formed with this and other generics within that area. In general, however, it would probably be fair to say that the kinds of maps which I drew in the sixties are predominantly visual devices of description and depiction the full implications of which are as yet not at all clear.[26]

What is particularly missing from them, of course, is any real sense of tangible locality, and the call for greater attention to topographical details and for more field-work on the ground involving knowledgeable local historians is therefore not only valid but strongly to be endorsed,[27] as long as any preoccupation with isolated individual names in their very local settings does not obscure the wider vision which only cumulative and comparative evidence can provide as, for instance, in the detection of viable onomastic dialects; this is, in fact, exactly the kind of evidence for which maps can be both end product and starting point. Once, as the result of intense local field-work and sound abstraction from its findings, maps have been drawn, these can, if the circumstances and the angle of light are right, open up new possibilities for both more field-work and less myopic perspectives. There are many ways in which names and the places they name connect with each other and with other names and the places named by them. Apart from the establishment of "onomastic dialects", the concept of "onomastic fields"[28] comes to mind as one way of recognising and perhaps interpreting those various relationships. Far from resignedly abstaining from drawing place-name maps in future, we should endeavour to draw not only more of them but better ones based on more sophisticated evidence and taking particularly into account the several relevant extra-linguistic facets of names which my early maps almost completely ignored.

There is one other point worth making, however, and that is that toponymic maps do not only define each other, synchronically and diachronically, within the same linguistic matrix but also in juxtaposition to toponymic maps reflecting namings of other linguistic settlers, i.e. where two languages coincide or overlap at some point in history. With regard to Scottish names representing the coinages of Scandinavians this is especially relevant when one maps these alongside names and nomenclatures created by speakers of Scottish Gaelic within certain well defined areas of which Caithness would be a particularly instructive case in point.[29] Instead of simply plotting the occurrences of *staðir*, *bólstaðr*, and *setr*, and even *dalr* and linking them with Orkney, the drawing of similar maps of Gaelic *baile* and *achadh* – *the* most common and most widespread generics reflecting settlement – helps to define their almost complete mutual exclusivity, except for a narrow strip of overlap. When the respective isonyms are linked to Caithness topography, the confrontational patterns which emerge vividly illustrate not only where, but also why, and perhaps even when, Scandinavian and Gaelic settlers established the linguistic boundary which for many centuries divided the county. It might be instructive to conduct similar microtoponymic investigations in the Hebrides and on the western seaboard.

It may well be, then, that the maps which I drew in the sixties were no more than initial eye-openers, revealing distributions and suggesting patterns never made visible before. They may also have derived justification from the fact that, to the best of anyone's knowledge, each one of the hundreds of dots represented a name whose generic had been validated through the patient application of accepted etymological procedures. Their basic reliability is therefore perhaps their most important asset and legitimisation, in addition to their visual appeal. What they lack and what is gradually, competently and fortunately being supplied by linguists, geographers, historians, archaeologists and others are the local details and ancillary pieces of information which make their interpretation more rigorously persuasive. Those early maps – and it is difficult to believe that most of them are only about a quarter of a century old – have served their purpose as stimulants, and it is now up to those who have been stimulated by them to increase their reliability and to interrogate them in ways which were not even thought of at the time of their being drawn.

"Place-Name Maps How Reliable Are They?" The answer apparently is that they are as reliable as the scholarship that each new generation of researchers brings to them. What may be quite satisfactory for one generation may no longer be sufficient for the next. That is a healthy sign and worth celebrating. We should therefore keep on drawing and interpreting ever-better place-name maps, for while analogies from elsewhere – Norway, Iceland, England, the Isle of Man, let us say – may offer useful parallels, they may have been created under very different circumstances by very different people responding to a very different landscape. Fundamentally, the evidence has to come from within. Barbara Crawford has pointed out that any method which attempts to establish chronological sequencing on the basis of toponymic distribution maps, is "fraught with difficulties".[30] This may well be so but initial failure to overcome such difficulties should not stop us from trying again. Without place-name maps and without the potential they offer for time-oriented interpretations, we would be forced back into an era of lists and individual etymologies, and surely nobody would want that to happen.

Notes

1   W.F.H. Nicolaisen, "Onomastic Onomastics". Opening address, XVIth International Congress of Onomastic Sciences, August 23-29, 1987; to be published in the Congress Proceedings.

2   W.F.H. Nicolaisen, "Words as Names". *Onoma* 20 (1976) 142-163.

3   W.F.H. Nicolaisen, "Lexical and Onomastic Fields". *Proceedings of the Thirteenth International Congress of Onomastic Sciences, Cracow 1978*, Vol. II (Cracow, 1982) 209-216.

4   W.F.H. Nicolaisen, "Socio-onomastics". *Der Eigenname in Sprache und Gesellschaft*. 1. Verhandlungen im Plenum (XV. Internationaler Kongreß für Namenforschung, 13-17. August 1984). Eds. Ernst Eichler et al. (Leipzig: Karl-Marx-Universität, 1985) 118-132.

5   W.F.H. Nicolaisen, "Onomastic Dialects". *American Speech* 55 (1980) 36-45.

6   See, for example, W.F.H. Nicolaisen, "The Semantics of Place-names and Their Elements". *Merking staðfræðilegra samnafna i örnefnum*. Ed. Þórhallur Vilmundarson (*NORNA-rapporter* 28, Uppsala, 1985) 60-71.

7   W.F.H. Nicolaisen, "Maps of Space Maps of Time". *Names* 32 (1984) 358-366. In this essay the author discusses similar issues in a less restricted context.

8   W.F.H. Nicolaisen, "Norse Settlements in the Northern and Western Isles: Some Place-Name Evidence". *The Scottish Historical Review* 48,1 (1969) 6-17.

9   Particularly, W.F.H. Nicolaisen, *Scottish Place-Names: Their Study and Significance* (London: B.T. Batsford, 1976); and *An Historical Atlas of Scotland c.400-c.1600* (St. Andrews, 1975), but also several other publications of my own and by other scholars.

10 See, for example, "Fig. 16. Norse settlement in Scotland", as part of C.A.R. Redford's chapter "From Prehistory to History", in: Stuart Piggott (ed.), *The Prehistoric Peoples of Scotland* (London: Routledge and Kegan Paul, 1962).

11 W.F.H. Nicolaisen, "Norse Place-Names in South-West Scotland". *Scottish Studies* 4 (1960) 49-70.

12 W.F.H. Nicolaisen, "Scottish Place-Names: 29. Scandinavian Personal Names in the Place-Names of South-East Scotland". *Scottish Studies* 11 (1967) 223-236.

13 Nicolaisen, 1969, 17.

14 Nicolaisen, 1976, 96.

15 Gillian Fellows-Jensen, "Viking Settlement in the Northern and Western Isles – the Place-Name Evidence as seen from Denmark and the Danelaw". In: Alexander Fenton and Hermann Pálsson (eds.), *The Northern and Western Isles in the Viking World: Survival, Continuity and Change* (Edinburgh: John Donald, 1984) 158.

16 *Ibid.*, 160.

17 Barbara E. Crawford, *Scandinavian Scotland* (Leicester: Leicester University Press, 1987) 108.

18 Margaret Gelling, *Place-Names in the Landscape* (London: Dent, 1984).

19 Crawford, 1987, 111.

20 Nicolaisen, 1969, 17.

21 Nicolaisen, 1976, 96.

22 I made a similar point in Nicolaisen, 1984, 361.

23 Nicolaisen, 1984, 362.

24 Crawford, 1987, 114.

25 *Ibid.*, 111 (see above note 19).

26 Cf. Nicolaisen, 1984, 363.

27 Crawford, 1987, 110.

28 Cf. Nicolaisen, 1982.

29 See W.F.H. Nicolaisen, "Scandinavians and Celts in Caithness: The Place-Name Evidence". In: John R. Baldwin (ed.), *Caithness: A Cultural Crossroads* (Edinburgh: Scottish Society for Northern Studies and Edina Press, 1982) 75-85.

30 Crawford, 1987, 105.

Names 38, 3 (Sept. 1990) 193-207

Place-names and Politics

F ROM September 29 through October 3, 1985, I had the pleasure of being the official U.S. representative at an international conference in Bozen/ Bolzano (Italy), on the "Official Use of Geographic Names". This meeting, organised conjointly by the Südtiroler Kulturinstitut and the Landesverband für Heimatpflege in Südtirol, was attended by participants from eight different countries (Austria, Belgium, Canada, France, Italy, Netherlands, Switzerland, U.S.A.); the fifteen papers and reports presented were subsequently published, with German and Italian translations (if required), in a very full volume of *Proceedings* (Kühebacher).[1] Although these are therefore available in print, their accessibility is of necessity limited, since only the two North American papers were published in English. It can also be assumed that the *Proceedings* themselves are not easily obtainable in the English-speaking world. For these reasons, it is my intention to provide an overview of their contents, particularly as regards the insights they offer concerning the official treatment of place-names created and used by substantial cultural and linguistic minorities, within the countries represented at the conference.

The perspective from which I present this information is unavoidably scholarly and academic, as I am not normally involved in the political aspects of naming and name usage. In fact, this gathering of experts in Southern Tyrol was an eye-opener for me, because until then I had been almost exclusively concerned with such matters as the spelling, pronunciation, morphology, grammar, meaning, content, and usage of names in a descriptive, somewhat detached manner, deliberately setting aside emotive issues and anything that might smack of political controversy. After all, is it not the scholar's prerogative-indeed, his duty-to stand back and describe and interpret in neutral terms the evidence he interrogates?

The good folk at Bozen/Bolzano thought and felt, and presumably still think and feel, otherwise. To them, place-names, especially their officially sanctioned or decreed linguistic form(s), are a matter of intense interest, untouchable though threatened symbols of the region's cultural heritage. In such a context, the 1985 international symposium of experts was for them not so much an opportunity to gather objective evidence and carefully weighed scholarly opinion as a chance to discover what other countries with linguistic minorities might have to offer in the way of experience and advice to bolster the regional German-speaking population's struggle against what they perceive as the unwarranted "Italianisation" of their place-nomenclature. We had been invited, as it were, as consultants who might turn into secret allies in their just cause.

Having heard all the papers as they were originally delivered and having reread them in their printed form, I am not certain how much they actually contributed to the furtherance of that deeply felt cause and cultural commitment, but the published conference proceedings, as they reflect the information provided and echo the voices that provided it, are in themselves a valuable compendium of reports and comments on the political, social, and cultural circumstances under which names are coined and used, frequently imposed, in the countries represented. Obviously there are many other areas in the world faced with similar problems, but the eight countries[2] which had delegates at the symposium supply important pointers toward possible solutions.

In this essay I shall use the eight countries as focal points in the discussion of such a controversial topic as "Place-names and Politics". In order to avoid the temptation of writing a conference report, I shall present the overview of the internal situations as we find them in the countries in question in alphabetical order and not in the sequence in which the respective papers were originally delivered. The papers followed a brief account of the recommendations made by the relevant committee of the United Nations, whose primary interest lies, of course, in international standardisation but whose recommendations nevertheless require as an important basis consistent national policies regarding the written forms of names, as it is difficult to regiment pronunciation.

As this essay is not directly concerned with the knotty question of international standardisation, nor with the extent to which individual nations have implemented the recommendations of the several United Nations Conferences on the Standardisation of Geographical Names, the basic recommendations of 1967 are here included in an Appendix based on Dr. Josef Breu's paper "Die amtliche Schreibung geographischer Namen in der Sicht der Vereinten Nationen" (Kühebacher 40–41). They clearly contain agreed guidelines relevant not only to the U.S. Board on Geographic Names but also to the U.S. Place-name Commission and Place-name Survey of the Society which publishes this journal and should therefore be made known to all individuals and institutions involved in decisions concerning official name usage in this country.

It might be assumed that well thought-out, acceptable, or even accepted policies would ensure that politics are kept out of the processes of naming and using names, but experience shows that this is by no means always the case. In times of linguistic controversy and cultural friction, names are apt to generate emotional rather than rational responses, and their symbolic force should never be underestimated, especially in the realm of politics. Different political circumstances and attitudes also engender different solutions; what is plausible, indeed eminently feasible, in one country, is out of the question in another. What looks like sweet reasonableness in one set of conditions leads to strife and division in another. A basic attitude of tolerance produces different reactions from a fundamental stance of authoritarianism. Here are some illustrations.

Austria

An Austrian participant, Prof. Hermann M. Ölberg of the University of Innsbruck, after outlining some of the scholarly principles essential in the recovery of the pre-Bavarian Romance place-nomenclature in the Austrian North Tyrol and recognising that while it cannot be the academic's objective to undo secondary reinterpretations of names or historicising spellings, states that it is nevertheless the scholar's duty to describe the situation correctly (107). He also insists (110) that it cannot be the task of official place name commissions, as set up within the UN guidelines, to be prescriptive in their approach to the collection of regional place-nomenclatures, and that to make any name changes without the approval of the people affected by them goes against modern legal concepts. He also argues strongly for a clear-cut conceptual distinction between bilingualism (*Zweisprachigkeit*) and binominalism (*Zweinamigkeit*), the implication being that the former does not necessarily have to result in the latter on the current map or in current usage.

Another Austrian participant, Dr. Alfred Ogris of the University of Klagenfurt, who also argues against unwarranted interference in the historically developed place-nomenclature of a region, illustrates with the aid of examples from the bilingual German-Slovenian place-name signs of certain parts of Carinthia (Kärnten), how difficult it is to implement official acts and pronouncements even in a benign climate of opinion when emotive political factors come into play (157-90).

Federal Austrian law is not only tolerant of cultural and linguistic minorities in the country but actively supports them; the recent provision of bilingual place-name signs in designated areas is part of this policy. One of the major obstacles, however, in complying with the legal requirements is the transcription of names used in oral tradition into acceptable written forms, especially when regional usage differs from the linguistic standards developed in a neighboring country (Yugoslavia). Despite every effort on the part of well-trained and well-meaning scholars, politicisation of the issue becomes almost inevitable, preventing an objective handling of such highly sensitive questions, particularly in the face of extremists' vociferous and active, though uninformed, demands.

Belgium

Belgian authorities and scholars are faced with somewhat different issues. Having passed through a French (1795-1814) and a Dutch (1814-1830) phase, the country has, in the years since its foundation in 1830, experienced a series of changes in its administrative communities, especially their drastic reduction in 1977, which has necessitated a considerable amount of naming and renaming. After initially lacking the advice of knowledgeable name scholars, the Ministry of the Interior, in 1926, formed an advisory commission consisting of fifteen Flemish-speaking and fifteen French-speaking experts who scrutinise suggestions in their respective language areas and offer their opinions on them. One of the major problems on the Flemish side was the discrepancy between place-name spellings and the modernised spelling standards introduced for the Flemish and Dutch language in general in 1864, on the advice of de Vries and te Winkel. After a highly emotional campaign by the Flemish Movement and its supporters, the modernised spellings finally became official in 1937.

A new discrepancy was, however, created for some names when, in 1946 and 1947, Belgium and the Netherlands agreed on a moderate simplification of the de Vries-te Winkel system; two years later the spelling of the names affected by the reform was officially changed to comply with the new spelling rules. As Professor Jan Goossens of the University of Leuven points out (229-30), this apparently felicitous solution ignores the difference between lexical and onomastic characteristics and underestimates the importance of a name as an onomastic rather than as a linguistic sign. In its implementation it also has to overcome problems in the transformation of names with localised pronunciations and other dialect features to a standard, supra-regional orthography. This necessitated compromises but also occasionally led to faulty interpretations. The difficulties faced by any orthographic standardisation of French place-names in Belgium were even greater and standardisation has (therefore?) never been attempted. In the case of some officially bilingual communities, this has led to a curious juxtaposition of a modernised Flemish spelling and an old-fashioned one, as in *Schaarbek/Schaerbeek* or *Oudergem/Auderghem* (233).

The reduction of Belgian administrative communities through the combination of several smaller units into one larger one has also required the substitution of new street names for confusing homonyms and homophones. Although the responsibility for the naming of streets lies with the local authorities, the place-name commission also has an advisory role to play. In the Flemish part of the country which is now monolingually Flemish (Dutch), the commission advises on ways to eliminate the French influence to which street names had been subjected in the nineteenth and early twentieth centuries. As Professor de Smet points out, important criteria in the naming or renaming of streets are local history, art and culture, toponymy, and folklore (244).

Canada

The general trend toward greater decentralisation and more local or regional legislative authority and responsibility regarding place-names is also noticeable in Canada, where the provinces are in the process of acquiring effective control (267). Although Canada is officially bilingual, English and French, only in the province of New Brunswick are the two languages accorded official recognition and status at the provincial level, and even here only one geographical location (Grand Falls) has two official names, reinforcing the observation that official bilingualism does not have to result in official binominalism. The province of Quebec, of course, declared itself unilingually French in 1976, and the Northwest Territories where the country's aboriginal languages still hold their own has also been declared officially bilingual. Outside these areas, in Ontario for example, the position is that a locality should have no more than one approved official name in use at a given time so that, for instance, only *Lake of the Woods* is used to the exclusion of the Franco-Ontarian *Lac des Bois*, the all-important criterion being "current local usage". In Quebec, on the other hand, practically the whole of the English language geographical nomenclature has disappeared, having been "translated" into French as the result of political decisions which are intended to preserve and ensure the French character of the whole of Quebec's toponymic fabric (280). The agency responsible for these matters is the *Commission de toponymie*, whose work, in contrast to the rest of Canada on the provincial level, is chiefly prescriptive. The federal coordinating role is carried out by the Canadian Permanent Committee on Geographical Names in Ottawa.

France

From the highly political question of French names in Canada in general and in Quebec in particular, I turn to the treatment of non-French names in France. Here Alsace is the obvious focal point with its chequered history and, in recent centuries, its divided cultural and linguistic allegiances, for quite a while victim of the mistaken notion that national and linguistic boundaries are ideally identical ("*cujus regio, ejus lingua*"). After having been German for a thousand years, Alsace has changed hands five times since 1648; it has been part of France since 1945 and during this time the use of the regional Allemanic dialect has steadily regressed. Its field names, however, with very few exceptions go back to Middle High German or even Old High German, while its street names reflect more directly the changing political and linguistic fortunes, having been translated three times into French and twice into German.

In some of the more enlightened communities, including Strasbourg, some German dialect street-name signs have in recent years been added to the official French ones. Settlement names have largely kept their original, mostly Allemanic or Franconian names which were sometimes adapted to French pronunciation and in a few instances translated into French. In extreme cases, some places have three names: the original dialect one, the corresponding High German one, and the modern official French one, like *Nards/Nordhausen/Nordhouse* or *Kritt/Gereuth/Neubois* (215).

Italy

It is the current situation in the northernmost Italian province of Alto Adige (German Südtirol), which borders on Austria, that triggered the international conference the *Proceedings* of which form the basis of this paper. The problem is summarised by one of the main conference organisers, Egon Kühebacher, who also edited the published volume (11):

> It is the wish of the people of South Tyrol that in their part of the world (*Land*) only those place-names be retained and legally recognised which have grown historically. This would mean that the approximately 8,000 Italianised place designations which were introduced by Ettore Tolomei during the period of fascism be eliminated, except for two or three dozen Italian names which had existed when South Tyrol was almost completely German (and Ladino). The Italians in South Tyrol claim that for them who were born and have grown up here, the Italian place-names have also "grown" here. They admit that the Italian names were initially introduced without justification but feel that one cannot blame the current generation for an illegal act committed several decades ago. Many German-speaking South Tyrolians find this difficult to understand; but are the Italians wrong?[3]

Even without knowing the various complex details of the issues involved, it is easy for an outsider to see that this is a matter which virtually begs for emotive politicisation; a mediating middle ground is difficult to imagine in this divisive atmosphere. This is borne out by the several papers contributed to the conference on this subject, including those by Dr. Norbert Mumelter of

Bozen/Bolzano (43-61), Professors Giuseppe de Vergottini (63-70) and Luigi Heilmann (91-105) of the University of Bologna, Umberto Corsini (71-89) of the University of Venice, Giovanni Battista Pellegrini (115-31) of the University of Padua, and Ferian Ormeling (133-55) of the University of Utrecht. It would, of course, be impossible to do them all justice in this survey.

At the very heart of the problem lie the activities associated with Ettore Tolomei whose name was heard more often at the conference than any other because, in the wake of the occupation and subsequent annexation of this part of Austria by Italy after the First World War (and to considerable degree even before the Austrian defeat), he devised and had to a large extent made official a list of about 8,000 Italian names for mandatory use in South Tyrol. Practically all of these names – translations, Italianisations, innovations – had never been used before and were, in a process of deliberate denationalization, superimposed on the existing place-nomenclature, in addition to the few bilingual names that had "naturally" developed in boundary zones.

While this superimposition is seen by the German-speaking population of the province as an "unnatural", autocratic, even fascist act against the will of the majority of the population, it is pointed out by the Italian side that the special provision for bilingualism, including bilingual place-names, for the province was a measure devised to protect and support the German heritage which, on a national scale, is that of a minority. For the same reason, it is claimed, it would be illegal to deprive the Italian-speaking population in the province of their right to use Italian names with which they are now thoroughly familiar and identify, even if these names were introduced in an authoritarian fashion in 1923 (70). To the neutral observer it looks as if, despite more ameliorative decrees since World War II (88), laws which were originally conceived to guarantee the language rights of a national minority have the opposite effect in a part of the country in which this minority is in the majority, quite apart from the tacit, but by no means self-evident, assumption that bilingualism includes, implies, or directly leads to binominalism.

Switzerland

That place-names are an integral part of language is also a basic assumption of the language laws of Switzerland, which has four national languages: German, French, Italian, and Rhaeto-Romance. In 1983, the respective percentages were 73.6, 20.0, 4.5, and 0.9, and each of these languages is the only official means of communication in its own territory (191). This exclusivity includes education, and the rigorously enforced territorial principle demands assimilation of the individual in all public matters.

The same principle is echoed in the official place-nomenclature of the country, i.e. in all name categories except field names. This means that in German-speaking Switzerland only historically developed German names are acceptable, in French-speaking Switzerland equivalent French names, etc. Thus local usage determines official usage; the same is true in multilingual cantons. As a result, each place has only one official name, except for localities near linguistic boundaries; there many have two names if there is a linguistic minority of at least thirty per cent of the population. In such a rigorously enforced system political disputes about place-names are rare or nonexistent as they are inextricably linked to the languages which created them or in which they are embedded. A few individual exceptions do not break this rule, as even directional signs indicate the name form of the language area in which the destination lies (199).

United States

If this is the solution in a country which has four national languages, each strictly enforced in its own territory, then the situation in the United States is almost diametrically opposed, insofar as there is no official national language, although English has a special status because all the Federal laws are written in that language. From this follows that no language is "foreign" to the United States, and for that reason minority languages and the place-names they produce are probably best described as "non-English" (253). Many thousands of place-names have been transferred from other countries over the centuries and have been spread further throughout the country through internal migrations. Speakers of many languages have also coined new names in various parts of the country.

Any official effort on the standardisation or regularisation of place-name spellings has therefore to be usage oriented and cannot impose the traffic rules of one language upon another, especially since onomastic usage and linguistic provenance are frequently two very different matters, both historically and philosophically. The official editorial treatment of "non-English" geographical names can therefore only be part of the official treatment of *all* geographical names within the United States and its territories. This basic approach governs the U.S. Board on Geographic Names whose responsibility it is to "develop policies, principles, and procedures governing the use, spelling, and application of geographic names" (254) and naturally also applies to its Domestic Names Committee. The primary principle or philosophy of the board is its recognition of present-day local usage and preferences.

When it comes to the adaptation of names of non-English origin by English speakers and name users, what matters is the natural process of language, not an imposition by any naming authority. As far as Native American names are concerned, which in the early stages of European settlement were so often sadly mangled, misplaced, or ousted altogether, present attitudes are much more sympathetic; such names are, together with other ethnic names, generally acceptable. It may be said therefore that the absence of a single national language is advantageous to the official handling of geographic names in the United States, especially of those of non-English or minority provenance, as the possibility of political interference is highly circumscribed.

Summary

Naturally, the variety of ways in which place-names can become politicised is not limited to the instances presented here. One might think of the names along the German-Danish border at the end of the nineteenth and the beginning of the twentieth century, the treatment of names in the newly acquired parts of Western Poland after World War II, the treatment of Frisian names in the Netherlands, or of Gaelic or Welsh names in Britain, of Breton names in France, or of Hungarian names in Romania.[4] What nevertheless emerges from the illustrative examples offered here is the realisation that, contrary to their supposed "neutrality" in their primary task of designating individual geographical features, place-names when employed as evidence in the arena of politics become highly charged objects provoking emotive responses. Especially when identified with particular minority languages and cultures or with certain nationalistic movements, their treatment can become divisive and lead to strong political action.

Under those circumstances, it does matter in what form a name appears on a sign at the entrance to a village, and a missing accent can cause displeasure.

One of the major problems is caused by the confusion of linguistic and onomastic usage so that names, although fundamentally part of an onomasticon and not a lexicon, are made to conform to exclusively linguistic rules. This assumed but unjustified congruency is especially noticeable in bilingual regions which are by definition also considered binominal. This is, it seems, a misunderstanding that cannot be eradicated. Although two languages may indeed produce two names or name forms, this is not necessarily the case, and to argue otherwise is ill-informed, but this is where scholars and politicians, for the time being, can only accept a parting of the ways. Until a more enlightened attitude begins to prevail, one can only ask for as many detailed studies of local, regional, and national situations as possible in order to discuss patterns in the variety of official responses around the world in the fascinating realm of politics concerning place-names. One might also hope for greater tolerance.

Notes

1   All internal references in this paper are to the pagination in that volume.
2   Only seven of the eight countries represented will be referred to since the representative of the Netherlands chose to speak about names in the host province.

3   The English translation of the original German text is mine.

4   Just recently the London *Times* (March I, 1990), in an article on the "Saxons" (Germans) of Transylvania, reported a member of the German-speaking minority as complaining about post-revolutionary Romania: "They only speak about our rights but so far there has been no action. We cannot even erect a sign outside our German villages in German".

Works Cited

Breu, Josef. "The Official Spelling of Geographical Names in the Perspective of the United Nations" (German and Italian). In Kühebacher 23-41.

Corsini, Umberto. "Italian Placenames in Alto Adige" in the First Half of the Twentieth Century (Italian and German). In Kühebacher 71-89.

Glatthard, Peter. "On the Official Geographical Nomenclature of Switzerland" (German and Italian). In Kühebacher 191-208.

Goossens, Jan. "The Names of Belgian Communities and Their Spelling" (German and Italian). In Kühebacher 225-42.

Heilmann, Luigi. "Origin and Development of Place names in Alto Adige" (Italian and German). In Kühebacher 91-105.

Kühebacher, Egon, ed. *Amtlicher Gebrauch des geographischen Namengutes.* Bozen: Sudtiroler Kulturinstitut/Landesverband für Heimatpflege in Südtirol, 1986.

Meyer, Joseph. "Field, Street, and Placenames in Their Adaptability in Alsace" (German and Italian). In Kühebacher 209-23.

Mumelter, Norbert. "The Legal Position of Geographical Names in Südtirol since 1918" (German and Italian). In Kühebacher 43-61.

Nicolaisen, Wilhelm F. H. "The Official Treatment of Non-English Place-names in the United States" (English, German, and Italian). In Kühebacher 253-65.

Ölberg, Hermann. "Settlement Strata in a Tyrolian Community on the Basis of Names of Localities" (German and Italian). In Kühebacher 107-13.

Ogris, Alfred. "The Official Treatment of Bilingual Placenames in Kärnten from a Historical and Contemporary Perspective" (German and Italian). In Kühebacher 157-90.

Ormeling, Ferjan. "The Geographical Nomenclature of Südtirol from a Cartographical Perspective" (German and Italian). In Kühebacher 133-55.

Pellegrini, Giovanni Battista. "On the Bilingual Character of Placenames" (Italian and German). In Kühebacher 115-31.

Smart, Michael B. "Official Treatment of Geographical Names in Canada" (English, German, and Italian). In Kühebacher 267-313.

Smet, Gilbert de. "Street Names in Flanders" (German and Italian). In Kühebacher 243-52.

UN Department of Economic and Social Affairs. "Report of the Group of Experts on Geographical Names". *World* Cartography. New York: United Nations, 1962. 7: 7-18.

Vergottini, Giuseppe de. "Legal Guidelines for Place-nomenclatures" (Italian and German). In Kühebacher 63-70.

Northern Studies 27 (1990) 50–63

Aberdeen: A Toponymic Key to the Region

To have been asked to talk to you on the place-names of the region gives me particular pleasure because the occasion affords me the opportunity to try an experiment which I have been tempted to carry out for some considerable time: to take a single name and observe and interpret it from as many angles as possible and thus establish its locus not only in its relationship to other names in the onomasticon of which it is a part but also in its historical setting. So that you do not think that this is a rather long-winded way of saying that one wants to discover its etymology, let me immediately remove even the possibility of such a misunderstanding by stating at the outset that the place-name on which I want to focus this discussion – *Aberdeen* – is a compound consisting of a generic *aber* meaning "river mouth or confluence" and a specific which is undoubtedly the river name *Don*. Translated into Modern English, *Aberdeen* therefore means "Don-mouth". It is as simple as that, and if the etymology of the name *Aberdeen* were our only objective, the challenge would now be over because the mystery has been revealed.

I have, however, on several occasions stressed – and will stress it over and over again as long as anybody is willing to listen – that for a truly onomastic study of names, i.e. for one that regards them as names and not simply as linguistic items with some peculiar additional properties, their etymology is the necessary beginning and not the ultimate end of the exercise. It is the *conditio sine qua non* which makes all other onomastic research possible, for it is not enough, indeed misguided though tempting, to be satisfied with having reduced names to the words they once were. There is so much more to names than that. The starting point of our exploration is therefore the unchallenged and unchallengeable etymologisation of the place-name *Aberdeen* as "Don-mouth" (let me hasten to add in parenthesis that the name of the *Denburn* has been proposed as the specific in this name but I do not regard this suggestion as a serious challenge, and hope that the reasons for this rejection will become clear in the following).

Instead of chasing its etymology, then, or its lexical meaning I want to employ the name *Aberdeen* as a key, maybe as a whole door, to the nomenclature of the region in which this conference is being held. This seems to be appropriate not only because it is the name of our meeting place and the name of the major city in the Scottish north-east but also because it has been affected by at least three languages – Pictish, Gaelic and Scots – and can therefore be a lodestar in guiding us through the major linguistic and onomastic stratification of this part of the world. For these reasons, *Aberdeen* is a name worth conjuring with, and it has the additional advantage of being, as far as Scottish place-names go, fairly well documented; by that I mean that it has been frequently recorded since the first half of the twelfth century. Indeed, the major evidence at our disposal, apart from its modern pronunciation in both English and Gaelic, is hundreds of early spellings to be found in a variety of sources of the medieval and post-medieval periods. From a historical perspective, this is primarily a silent record that speaks to us visually, and it has to be further borne in mind that most of these visual representations are embedded in much of the record in the official Latin of the time, i.e. in alien, artificial surroundings, and that these spellings were often written (perhaps perpetrated would be a better term) by scribes not familiar with the name in its local setting, including its pronunciation, and were more often than not derived from earlier written sources establishing a kind of scribal onomastic convention. In such texts, frequently charters of one kind or another, place-names, and to a certain extent personal names, are usually the only vernacular intrusions and are sometimes, especially when used adjectivally, made to conform to their Latin textual environment. All this is possibly not as much of a handicap as it may sound but it is nevertheless worth remembering that much of our toponymic evidence is considerably removed or screened from any direct contact with the genuine, local pronunciation of its time, with the various intervening factors serving as effective buffers.

Another point worth making is that, even if we follow the golden rule of all onomastic research and give special status and credence to the earliest recorded spellings available, the earliest mention of the name in the third decade of the twelfth century is separated from the time at which the name is likely to have been coined and first used, by several hundred years. 1136 or 1137 may look pretty impressive in a general north-eastern Scottish context, and there are many names for which the earliest surviving record is much, much later, but such exceptionally early dates lie, after all, at the beginning of the interface between Gaelic and Scots in the area and anything we want to claim to be Pictish about

13th century

Aberden 1214-22
Abirden 1214-48
Abberden 1218-22
Abberden 1234
Habirden 1236
Haberden 1239
Abirden *c* 1260

Aberden 1266
Abeirden *c* 1272
Aberdene 1273
Aberdon 1287
Aberden 1287
Aberdene 1274-1307
Abberdene 1290

Haberdene 1290
Aberdene 1290
Aberden 1292
Abirdene 1296
Aberden 1296
Abbirden 1297

14th century

Aberdene 1306-29
Aberdene 1319
Abirden 1319
Abirdene 1323
Aberden 1326
Aberdeen 1330
Abryden 1331
Aberdene 1336
Abreden 1341
Abirdene 1341 *(bis)*

Abberden 1342
Aberdeine 1342
Abirdene 1342
Abredene 1342
Habirden 1345 *(bis)*
Abreden 1348
Abbirdene 1353
Abirreden 1354
Aberden 1357
Aberdene 1360

Abirdon 1362
Abirdone 1362
Aberdeen 1362
Abriden 1363
Abirden 1371
Abirden 1371-90
Abirdene 1373
Abbirden 1391
Abirden 1391

15th century

Abredene 1405
Abredon 1406
Abirden 1411
Abirdon 1417
Abbirdene 1426
Aberden 1433
Abirdeyn 1445
Abreden 1449
Abirdene 1451 *(bis)*

Aberdene 1453
Abyrdene 1457
Aberdene 1458
Abirdeyn 1461
Abbirden 1461
Abirden 1461
Abirdene 1461
Abbirdene 1461
Aberden 1465

Abbirden 1469
Abbirteyn 1470
Abyrdene 1482
Abberden 1492
Abyrdene 1492
Abyrdeyne 1492
Abirdene 1494

16th century

Abberdene 1500
Aberdeine 1500
Aberdone 1500-01
Abbyrdene 1510
Aburdyne 1524
Abirden 1525
Aberdon 1526

Abyrdon 1526
Abirdeyn 1527
Aberdene 1532
Abardyn 1535
Aberdyne 1537
Abyrdyne 1543
Aberdeine 1556

Obyrdin 1561
Abirdene 1589 *(bis)*
Aberdeyn 1591
Aberdone 1595
Abirdeyne 1596

17th century

Aberdein 1627-8
Aberdeine 1632
Aberdeene 1639

Aberdein 1641
Aberdone 1688
Abbertein 1696

Aberdein 1697
Aberdeen 1698

What can we read out of this evidence? Let us look to begin with at the first element, the generic aber: (FIG. 2). Of the spelling variations on the list, Aber- is by far the most common, with 60 examples; the only other spelling to rival it, Abir-. is found in 32 instances, while Abyr- occurs nine times. It is, I think, permissible to regard the –y- as a contemporary allograph of -i-, and no special significance should therefore be read into this variation; we might be quite justified in adding these two spelling variants together, giving us a total of 41. One of the major differences between the Aber- and Abir-/Abyr- spellings seems to be that while the former occurs from the beginning of the record till the end of the seventeenth century and beyond – from the twelfth century to the present day – the latter appear to peter out in the sixteenth century. It is improbable that these three spellings actually imply different pronunciations; they are more likely to be thought of as scribal conventions in particular documents or sets of documents,

FIG. 2 Aberdeen Chronological Typology of Early Spellings

ABER	(centuries)						-DEEN	(centuries)					
	12	13	14	15	16	17		12	13	14	15	16	17
Aber-	12	10	9	2	7	7	-don	10	1	2	2	2	
Abir-	4	4	10	8	5		-done	1		1			
Abyr-	2		2	3	1		-doen	2					
Abeir-		1					-deon	2					
Abur-					1		-den	7	12	14	6	1	
Abar-					1		-dene		8	10	9	4	
Abber-	1	3	1	1	1	1	-dein	1		1			3
Abbir-	3	1	2	4			-deyn				3	2	
Abbyr-					1		-deone			1		2	1
Abre-	1		6	3			-deyne				1	1	
Abri-		1					-dien			1			
Abirre-			1				-dyne					3	
Haber-		2					-din			1		1	
Habir-		1	1				-dyn					1	
Obyr-					1		-tein						1
Apar-		1					-djon		1				
							-den		1	1			

and the same is probably true of the hapax legomena Abeir-, Abur- and Abar-. That the initial vowel was always short in the centuries surveyed is indicated by the ten spellings with a double -bb-, and the strongly trilled and almost vocalic nature of the final -r is confirmed by the eleven spellings in Abre- and Abri-, practically all of which are confined to the fourteenth and fifteenth centuries. Metathesis of the -r- is , of course, a very common feature in Scottish English and by no means limited to place-names. It is certainly found. together with the other features already mentioned, in many other Aber- names, particularly Arbroath which is especially well documented (Abbrebrodoghe 1305, Abrebrothok 1306–7, Abrebroth 1320, Abrebrothot 1410, 1443, Abbribroth 1447). The singleton spelling Abirre- of 1354 seems to have it both ways, while the two Habers and the two Habirs of the thirteenth and early fourteenth centuries demonstrate French influence, not on the pronunciation but on the scribal habits. Obyr of 1561 is found in the Black Book of Taymouth which in many respects appears to have close connections with Gaelic, the modern pronunciation in that language being Obar Dheathan. The spelling Apardjon found in the thirteenth-century Orkneyinga Saga is also likely to reflect that pronunciation.

This brings us to the representation of the second element, the river name the mouth of which is indicated by *Aber-* (FIG 2). From the beginning of the record this is clearly divided into two parallel spelling traditions, one *Aberdon, Aberdone, Aberdoen*, and the other *Ab(b)erdeon, Aberden, Aberdene*. The former is preserved in the Latinised adjective *Aberdonensis;* the latter is, of course, the ancestor of the modern name *Aberdeen*. Watson derives the former (*Aberdon*, etc.) from a Pictish form of the river name corresponding to Old Welsh *Duion*, and the latter (*Aberdeon*, etc.) from a *Gaelic Deathan* for the same river.[1] This phonological interpretation is supported by the chronological evidence. Both spelling traditions are strong in the twelfth century but whereas *-don(e)* spellings occur only sporadically in later centuries, *-den(e)* – by far the largest proportion of all spellings encountered – continues in strength until the end of the sixteenth century. One is clearly a diminishing, the other an increasing tradition. Pictish, after all. must have been dead for at least two to three centuries when the first *-don* spelling is to be found in the surviving written record, while Gaelic must have been powerful at the time and must have continued to be spoken, side by side with the incoming English, for another five hundred years or so. The two *-doen/-deon* pairs of the twelfth century, at the very outset of our written corpus, most clearly mark the beginning of the dichotomy. Until the great vowel shift of the fifteenth century, *den* must have reflected a [de:n] pronunciation, and -dene, after the loss in pronunciation of the final -e, is likely to have become more and more attractive for the spelling of the same pronunciation, in contradistinction to [dEn]. Apart from a few early forerunners, *dein, deyn, deine, deyne, dien,* and certainly *dyne* spellings only occur after the great vowel shift when, in all varieties of standard English, [de:n] had become [di:n], a pronunciation most appropriately represented by *-deen* in modern English orthography. One cannot help wondering whether spellings that contain an *i* or a *y*, especially *-dyne*, reflect the north-east Scots development of [e:] to [ai] as in *quyne* referred to by Derrick McClure in another paper. The occasional *-din* (1330, 1561) and *-dyn* (1535) are difficult to assess, as to whether they really indicate short vowels and therefore a different pronunciation or are variants of *-dyne;* and *-tein* (1696) appears to display occasional Gaelic influence. One cannot discount either analogical changes in the pronunciation and spelling in the wake of the change from [de:] to [di:] in the nearby sister river to whose banks and mouth the city expanded and largely shifted in the post-medieval period.

The overall impression derived from the spelling history of the river name. then, is that the *-don(e)* set of spellings based on the Pictish form of the name is not very visible after the twelfth century, whereas the *-den(e)* group of spellings based on the Gaelic form gains in influence and finally dominates the scene, with the pronunciation changing from [de:n] to [di:n] under the influence of the great vowel shift; the *-dyne* type spellings are possibly a reflection of the Scots of the north-east. If one were to indulge in chronological speculation, which I am not tempted to do, of course, one might say that one might expect the name to occur as *Aberdon* or *Aberden* in the twelfth century, as *Aberden* or *-dene* in the thirteenth century, as *Aber-* or *Abir-den* or *-dene* in the fourteenth century, as *Abirden* or *-dene* in the fifteenth century, as *Aber-* and *Abir-* with a variety of river-name spellings in the sixteenth century, and culminating in *Aberdeen* at the end of the seventeenth century. Altogether, at least five languages – Pictish, Gaelic, English, Scots, and French – have left their mark at one time or another on the spelling of the name *Aberdeen*, and the *Apardjon* of the *Orkneyinga Saga* adds a Scandinavian touch which is otherwise completely lacking in native renderings in an area in which no Norse name can be reliably documented.

So much for the spelling of the river name *per se;* what does it stand for? How can, in fact, a single name like *Aberdeen* serve as a key to the whole region? Let us begin again with *Aber-* whose ultimate etymology is *ad-ber* from the root *bher-* "to bring".[2] It could therefore be somehow translated as "out-bring", a meaning which in the cases of our *Aber-* place-names is obviously applied to the "bringing out" of water at the mouth of a river or a confluence. The word *aber* is known as a common noun in Welsh and goes back to an Old Welsh *aper*. In Gaelic it is only found in place-names such as *Loch-abar* "Lochaber" and *a' Chomraich Abrach* "Applecross" but even in these instances one cannot be sure that they are not adaptations from pre-Gaelic Celtic. Anyhow, there can be no doubt about the large majority, if not all, of the Scottish place-names which have *Aber-* as an initial generic being not Gaelic but of *p*-Celtic origin. Since Pictish is the term applied to the variety of pre-Gaelic *p*-Celtic spoken in this part of the world between, let us say, 200 and 900 A.D., it is tempting to call the type of name of which *Aberdeen* is our prototype simply Pictish but, as two relevant distribution maps show,[3] it is not quite as simple as that.

Whereas place-names containing *pet* "a piece or share of land" (*Pitmedden, Pittodrie. Pitcaple, Pitfichie*, etc.) nicely conform in their distribution to what one might term our classical notion of Celtic-speaking Pictland – the north-east of Scotland bounded roughly by the Firth of Forth in the south and the Moray Firth in the north – *Aber-* names are also found in southern Scotland where the brand of *p*-Celtic spoken until the superimposition of Gaelic and Anglian is usually termed Cumbric, the major onomastic expression of which are the place-names containing the element *cair* "a fort", as in *Cramond, Carluke, Cathcart, Carfrae* and *Caerlanrig*, but also in the Cumberland names *Carlisle, Cardew* and *Cardurnock* which, according to Kenneth Jackson, were probably "given by British immigrants from Strathclyde who reoccupied Northern Cumberland in the tenth century".[4] Politically, this toponymic evidence is most likely associated with the kingdoms of Rheged and Strathclyde the latter of which had its capital at Dumbarton and its ecclesiastical centre in Glasgow. To the south of this area, names beginning with *cair* do not occur again until the Welsh borderland has been reached (there is a *Caradoc* in Herefordshire) and in Wales proper, as in *Cardiff, Carmarthen*, and the like. The distribution of *cair*-names is therefore clearly Cumbric and Welsh but, what is more important to our enquiry, decidedly *non-Pictish*.

What makes the late Frederick Wainwright's book title *The Problem* of *the Picts*[5] so applicable to the name *Aberdeen* and the other north-eastern Aber-names, such as *Aberdour, Arbroath, Aberfeldy, Abernethy, and Abertarff*, is the fact that some examples of this name type also occur in what is supposed to be Cumbric territory, as exemplified by our *cair-names*. Thus we have *Aberlady* in East Lothian, *Aberlosk* and the now obsolete *Abermilk* in Dumfriesshire, and *Abercarf* in Lanarkshire, and it is unlikely that such names were given by a few stray Pictish settlers in that part of the world. At best, we can therefore say that *aber* has a preponderantly north-easterly distribution, a scatter which implies that it was employed more productively – was more fashionable if you like – in the naming of places by the Picts than by the Cumbrians, as far as the *p*-Celts in Scotland were concerned. They also share with *cair*-names, of course, Welsh counterparts such as *Aberystwyth* and *Abergavenny*.

It is worth remembering, however, that *Aber*-names are not our only problem children in this respect, apparently contradicting the self-contained neatness of the distribution pattern of the *Pit*-names. The terms *pert* "a wood, a copse" which we know best from such place-names as *Perth* and *Larbert*, *lanerc* "a clearing" as in *Lanrick* and *Lendrick*, and *pevr* "radiant, beautiful" as in *Strathpeffer* and *Inverpeffray*, also occur occasionally in Cumbrian territory as, for example, *Pappert Law* in Selkirkshire, *Lanark* in Lanarkshire, and the two Peffers in East Lothian.[6] Whereas we can make the same claim for these three terms as for *aber* with regard to a predominantly "Pictish" distribution, the reverse seems to be true of the generics *penn* "end, head", *pren* "a tree" and *tref* "a settlement". These are strong in the south and rare in the north-east as, for instance, the older *Peanfanel* recorded by Bede for *Kinneil* or *Prinlaws* in Fife and *Kinpurnie* in Angus and are therefore primarily to be regarded as Cumbric.[7] Even more tantalising is the distribution of names containing *tref* which in Modern Welsh still means "town or home" and is prolific in place-names in Wales and Cornwall. The peculiar characteristic of *tref*-names in Scotland is that names in which this generic occurs as a first element (*Tranent*, *Traquair*, *Trabroun*) are found exclusively to the south of the Forth-Clyde line, while names in which it is the second element are also common north of that line, like *Cantra* (Inverness-shire) or *Menstrie* (Clackmannanshire), sometimes of identical derivation such as *Trostrie* (Kirkcudbrightshire) and *Troustrie* (Fife). Like the *Pit*-names, these north-eastern -*tref*-names often have Gaelic specifics, such as the common *Fintr(a)y* "white settlement" or *Clinterty* and the like, "sloping settlement", and also Moray, from an earlier Gaelic **Moirthreabh* = **mori-treb-* "sea settlement". As in the case of the many *Pit*-names in this area (*Pitmedden* comes to mind), part-translation is the most likely explanation for some of these names, while others may have been coined during a Pictish-Gaelic bilingual period in the ninth and tenth centuries.[8] The type *Fintr(a)y* would thus correspond exactly to the type *Pitmedden*. This is hinted at by an admittedly much later seventeenth-century entry in the *Register of the Great Seal* which says of the Aberdeenshire name *"Cantres* vulgo voc at. *Fintries* in parochia de Kingedward" (*Cantres* commonly called *Fintries* within the parish of Kingedward).

There is a hint regarding a similar process in at least one *Aber*-name: the Kincardineshire place-name *Inverbervie* on the Bervie Water near the sea, is recorded in 1290 as *Haberberui*, undoubtedly an *Aber*-name. It had already been on record as an *Inver*-name (Gaelic *inbhear* "confluence", from *in-ber-* "carry in") at least four times in the same century before that date (*Inuirberuyn* 1204–1214, *Inuerberuyn* 1232–1237, *Inirbervyn*

1266, and *Inuerberuy* 1287), and the single *Haberberui* is therefore clearly a relic from pre-Gaelic times, establishing a sequence *Aber-* to *Inver-*. One wonders how many of the *Inver*-names in the former Pictland had suffered a similar fate before the written record starts in the twelfth or thirteenth century but leaving no trace of an older *Aber-*. Hypothetically this might have been the case in all those names in which the river name which forms the specific cannot convincingly be said to be of Gaelic origin. For example, such Aberdeenshire names as *Inverernan* (not recorded till the sixteenth century), *Inverey* (on record only since the fifteenth century), and especially *Inverugie* (*Inuirugin* 1202–4) and *Inverurie* (*Enroury* 1172, and *Nrurin* in the Pictish Chronicle) may well fall into this category; and, as *Inverbervie* shows, although the river name *Bervie* is derivable from the Old Irish *berbaim* "I boil", this, too, may be a translation or an adaptation of an earlier *p*-Celtic name, as it is unlikely for *Aber-* to have been attached to a Gaelic name of the watercourse. At any rate, part-translation cannot be ruled out in a period of prolonged bilingualism, so that even names like *Inverallochy*, *Invermarkie* and *Invernochty* may have pre-Gaelic antecedents, and the number of *Aber*-names in this region be considerably higher than our late and accidental written record would lead us to believe.

Enough of speculation, however; our own current concern has to be with the status of confirmed *Aber*-names, such as the ones already mentioned as well as *Aberbothrie*, *Aberchirder*, *Abercrombie*, *Aberfoyle*, *Abergeldie*, *Aberlemno*, *Aberlour*, *Abernyte*, *Aberuchill*, *Aberuthven*, *Abriachan*, *Arbirlot*, and *Arbuthnott*. It must seem perhaps superfluous to be told that all these names designate places near streams, especially those close to their mouths or to their confluences with other watercourses. This apparently redundant observation does, however, point to the somewhat complementary nature of the two distribution patterns of *Pit*-names and *Aber*-names, respectively, within the Pictish settlement area. Just over twenty years ago, the geo-graphers Whittington and Soulsby published "A Preliminary Report on an Investigation into *Pit* Place-names", in which they offered the results of an examination which they, as geographers, had undertaken of the *Pit*-names of Fife and the adjacent parts of Angus, analysing each individual site so named, with a view to gathering information about "the preferred habitat of the Pictish people".[9] On the basis of the data collected, they came to the conclusion that the Picts generally did not favour the coastal zone and also avoided the floors of river valleys, and that because of the largely coastal area below and the adverse exposure conditions above, *Pit*-names are almost entirely restricted to a distribution between an altitude of 50 and 650 feet. Other factors such as distance to other sites with *Pit*-names, soil quality, shelter, good drainage, slope value, and a southerly component in the aspect of the chosen site also come into play. Altogether, the coiners of *Pit*-names emerge as inland people who would prefer to settle on loamy soils in well-sheltered and well-drained positions. Whittington largely confirms these conclusions in a later more extensive and more sophisticated study covering the whole of "Pictland".[10]

The distribution of *Aber*-names naturally does not follow this pattern, particularly with regard to altitude and the proximity to river beds or coastal areas, and probably one should add a rider to Whittington's (and Soulsby's) very valuable findings to the effect that there were also Picts who did not indulge in the kind of agricultural activities that many of the specifics in *Pit*-names imply and who preferred to live near water courses, especially near their mouths and confluences. An important consideration in this respect is the fact that all the *Aber*-names, or certainly a very high proportion of them, must be pre-Gaelic and therefore pre-850 or even centuries older (although I am not prepared to put this kind of compound formation too early in the period which we tend to assign to the historical Picts), while many, if not most of the *Pit*-names were coined by Gaels who had adopted *Pit*- as a place-name element or even as a lexical item, in the ninth and tenth centuries, or perhaps even later.[11]

Certainly there cannot be any doubt about the *Aber*-names within the rough boundaries of "Pictland" with justification being called Pictish, as long as one also recognises their wider distribution and affinity with Cumbric and Welsh, i.e. with the rest of the *p*-Celtic area of Britain. In contrast to the *Pit*-names which are only to be found in Pictland and a little beyond and which therefore can make certain claims for a separate Pictish toponymy and consequently for a separate Pictish language. *Aber*-names demonstrate that Pictish is likely to have shared many features with British Celtic as a whole, and is therefore not as isolated as the *Pit*-names appear to suggest. The non-Celtic component of Pictish is. of course, another thorny problem which does, however, not concern us in this context because there is no evidence that it affected Aberdeen and its hinterland.

This brings us to the last aspect of the name *Aberdeen* to which this discussion is intended to draw attention – the derivation and meaning of the river name which forms its specific and by which it is differentiated from all other *Aber*-names in Scotland (this does not mean that repetitions might not occur as the two *Aberdours* in Aberdeenshire and Fife show). It cannot come as a surprise that the river name which makes the uniqueness of the name *Aberdeen* possible, the *Don*. is, like the generic *aber*, also pre-Gaelic. W.J. Watson convincingly etymologised it as an early Celtic (which to us means Pictish) *Devona*, a river-goddess name derived from the word *devos* "a god", a cognate, for example, of

Latin *deus*.[12] The ending -*onā* is very common in Early Celtic names, both of rivers and of divinities, in Britain as well as on the Continent. For instance, in Gaulish, the major Continental form of Celtic known to us, the famous horse goddess *Eponā* would be a well-known example.

As far as Scottish river names are concerned, -*onā* is not confined to Pictland. and we find it in such names as the *Devon* in Perthshire and the *Black Devon* in Fife, both from **Dubona* "black one"; the *Lavern Burn* in Dumfriesshire, the *Levern Water* in Renfrewshire, the *Lowran Burn* in the Stewartry, all from **Labarona* "the talking one"; the three *Levens* in Argyllshire, Dumbartonshire and Fife, from **Lemona* "elm (river)"; the *Lyon* in Perthshire from **Limona* "the flooding one"; the *Burn* of *Brown* in Banffshire, from **Brutona* "the boiling one"; the *Ythan* in Aberdeenshire, from **Iektona* "the talking one"; the *Leithen Water* in Peeblesshire, from **Lektona* "the slow flowing one"; the *Nethan* in Lanarkshire, from **Nektona* "the washing one"; the *Conan* in Ross-shire, the "wolf river"; and several others including the *Almonds* in West Lothian and Perthshire, from **Ambona* "water", the *Calneburn* in East Lothian, the *Kale Water* in Roxburghshire, the *Caddon Water* in Selkirkshire, all from **Kalona* "hard water", and, best known of all, the several *Avons* from *Abona* which means simply "river". Our *Dēvonā* is therefore in excellent company as far as its morphological make-up as a complex name is concerned.[13]

Dēvonā also shares another characteristic with some of these names. For the *Avon*, for instance, there is an unextended parallel in the river and loch name *Awe* in Argyllshire (from **Abā*); for **Labarona* we have the parallel **Labarā* in the *Burn* of *Aberlour* in Banffshire; and for the **Limonā* (the Perthshire *Lyon*) we find, a little further afield, a **Limā* in the *Lymes* of Devon and Dorset. The unextended "twin" of the *Don* or **Devonā* is, of course, the *Dee* or **Dēvā* which also means simply "goddess" or, in its metaphorical sense, "divine river". What is special about the relationship between *Don* and *Dee*, however, is that they are rivers which flow in close proximity to each other and enter the North Sea only a very short distance apart.

That two such rivers should be designated by related but contrasting names – morphologically speaking – is also not unknown from other parts of Scotland. One only has to think of the *Black* and *White Cart* in Renfrewshire and the *Blackadder* and *Whiteadder* of Berwickshire in which the English colour adjectives *black* and *white* are used to make both the connection and the distinction. A Gaelic equivalent would be the *Findhorn* and the *Deveron* in which the Gaelic adjectives *fionn* "white" and *dubh* "black" have been added to otherwise identical river names. What is particularly fascinating about the *Blackadder* and the *Whiteadder* is that they seem to have also had connective names at a much earlier, perhaps even pre-Celtic, stage, insofar as one of them appears to have been the *Adara* and the other the *Adaria* (*Adara*, by the way, is also the origin of the river name *Oder* on the German-Polish border).[14] The similar morphological contrast *Dēvā* (*Dee*) – *Dēvonā* (*Don*) is, however, also documented in precisely the same way elsewhere in Scotland, in the river names *Dee* and *Doon* in the south-west of the country. In both these instances, as well as the others referred to, the namers and users of such river names were aware of, and continued this awareness, of close connections between the rivers concerned, whether they occurred in the same geographical neighbourhood or one was the tributary of the other. There is no *Don* without a *Dee*, and vice versa.

What singles out the *Don* (and the *Doon*) from the other names in *-onā* which usually refer to physical qualities of the watercourse concerned is the fact that it and its twin *Dee* unmistakably express the belief that the river has divine characteristics. I have tried to be very guarded and circumspect in my formulation because I am disinclined to assert or even suggest that the Picts indulged in river worship. Nevertheless, even if one is reluctant to do so, one cannot ignore the fact that two closely associated rivers are called "goddess" or "the holy one", i.e. *Dēvā* and *Dēvonā*, especially when they are not isolated instances. Mention has already been made of the *Dee* and the *Doon* in south-west Scotland, and there is, of course, also the *Dee* that for a long way forms the boundary between England and Wales and flows into the Irish Sea below Chester, and which is actually recorded as *Dēvā* by Ptolemy and others in the second, fifth and seventh centuries. In addition, we have at least two other names derived from *Dēvā* in Wales, a river *Dee* in Ireland and watercourses called *Deba* and *Dēvā* in Spain, all within ancient Celtic territory. Of the Welsh *Dee* at Chester, it is said that it was dedicated to or identified with the goddess of war,[15] and in general it has to be concluded that the Celtic people must have believed in the presence of a divinity in the water. I am, however, not aware of any account of any rituals associated with such a belief either among the Picts or the Celts in general. Anne Ross, in her study of the pagan Celts, has provided us with several examples of springs as significant places in the belief system of the Celts,[16] and most of us share the somewhat befuddled Tam o' Shanter's conviction that witches cannot cross running water. Further afield, the *Encyclopedia* of *Religion and Ethics* furnishes an abundance of examples of ways in which water and water goddesses play important roles in the magico-religious cults of primitive people as well as among the Babylonians, Egyptians, Greeks, Romans, Hebrews and Indians, whether in seasonal rites, as rain charms, in purification ceremonies, as a means of divination or as an ingredient in the overall response to the sacred and mysterious.[17] As part of this cosmogony, water gods play an important role.

The *Dee* the *Don* and other cognate rivers in Britain and on the Continent may well be indicative of any or all of these practices, rituals and beliefs, but apart from the names themselves, I have no specific evidence for such an assumption; in particular, this group of names does not allow us to pinpoint precisely any places along their banks where associated rites might have taken place or which were regarded as especially holy. It is not unlikely that the mouth of a river or a confluence might have been deemed special in this respect and that, if this is so, the original settlement called *Aberdeen* was not only founded near the mouth of the *Don* for economic and strategic, i.e. pragmatic, reasons but also because the "Don-mouth", the mouth of the goddess, was regarded as a sacred place. It would then have found its Christian successor in St. Machar's activities and foundation.

By the time the names of our two Pictish rivers, and particularly of the *Don*, were adopted and adapted by the Gaels, neither their original meaning nor any practices associated with it will have been remembered as the consequence of intensive Christianisation of the region. Among others, the crosses on some of the symbol stones testify to that. For the Gaels, as for us, *Deathan* and *Dé*, or *Don* and *Dee*, were simply lexically meaningless names of rivers, serving the usual identificatory functions of names very satisfactorily.

To sum up: in chronological sequence, the starting point for the name *Aberdeen* is a Celtic-Pictish river name *Dēvonā* meaning "goddess" and closely associated with the river name Dee (*Dēvā*). It must have been in existence in Roman times for the Roman camp at Kintore is referred to by Ptolomy in the second century A.D. as *Dēvanā*, a town of the Taexali, and by the Ravenna Geographer in the fourth century as *Devoni*.[18] Some time later during the Pictish period, most likely after the withdrawal of the Romans, a settlement was formed on the estuary of the river and called by the Picts *Aber-don "Don-mouth"*. In naming this place, the Picts used a term, *aber*, which they shared with other insular Celts, especially in southern Scotland and in Wales. Their language was therefore *p*-Celtic or British, and not *q*-Celtic or Goidelic. The spelling and pronunciation of the name have been affected by all the languages that have been spoken in this region since the Roman occupation: Pictish, Roman Latin, Gaelic, Scottish English and Scots, and we also encounter a Scandinavian form in the *Orkneyinga Saga* and traces of French-influenced scribal habits in some medieval spellings. The name Aberdeen, then, a splendid toponymic ruin in the modern linguistic landscape, can therefore serve well as a remarkable toponymic key to the history and prehistory of this region.

Notes

1   William J. Watson, *The History of the Celtic Place-Names of Scotland.* (Edinburgh 1926) 211-212.

2   *Ibid.*, 458.

3   W.F.H. Nicolaisen, *Scottish Place-Names: Their Study and Significance.* (London 1976) 153 and 163.

4   Kenneth H. Jackson, "Angles and Britons in Northumbria and Cumbria." In: Henry Lewis (ed.), *Angles and Britons* (Cardiff 1963) 81.

5   Frederick T. Wainwright, *The Problem of the Picts* (Edinburgh 1955).

6   A detailed discussion of these elements is to be found in Nicolaisen, 164-166.

7   *Loc. cit.*

8   Nicolaisen, 166-170.

9   G. Whittington and J.A. Soulsby, "A Preliminary Report on an Investigation into Pit Place-names". *Scottish Geographical Magazine* 84 (1968) 117-125.

10 G. Whittington, "Placenames and the settlement patterns of Dark-Age Scotland". *Proceedings of the Society of Antiquaries of Scotland* 106 (1977) 99-110.

11 See Nicolaisen, 156.

12 Watson, 211.

13 For a fuller discussion of this name type see Nicolaisen, 177-179.

14 See Nicolaisen, 184-186.

15 Eilert Ekwall, *English River-Names* (Oxford 1928) 118.

16 Anne Ross, *Pagan Celtic Britain* (London 1967) 20-33. For the potential veneration of rivers she mostly cites river names like the *Dee. Clyde. Severn, Boyne*, and *Shannon*. See also her *Everyday Life of the Pagan Celts* (London 1970) 164 and 166.

17 James Hastings (ed.), *Encyclopaedia* of *Religion and Ethics*. 12 vols. (Edinburgh 1908-1921). See particularly under "Picts" (X, 1918, 1-6) and "Water, Water-Gods" (XII, 1921, 704-719).

18 A.L.F. Rivet and Colin Smith, *The Place-Names* of *Roman Britain* (London 1979) 338.

Folklore 102 (1991) 3–15

The Past as Place: Names, Stories, and the Remembered Self

Katharine Briggs Memorial Lecture, November 6, 1990

> ONCE upon a time, and a long time ago, there was a young farmer whose farmlands bordered on the sea.[1]
>
> Once there was a time, and it was a long time ago, when two farmers called Hudden and Dudden lived in the west of Ireland.[2]
>
> In the great forests of the Atlas Mountains there once lived a widow and her young son, Khalid.[3]
>
> Beyond high mountains and beyond deep rivers, far in the east, almost at the Chinese borders, there was one big and splendid city.[4]

W HILE the treatment of time in, and the temporal structure of stories from the folk-cu ltural register have fascinated students of folk-narrative for a long time,[5] this fascination has reached a new peak in recent years.[6] There is now considerable agreement among scholars, and I subscribe to this view, that the folktale, and by that we mean essentially what in German is usually termed the *märchen*, is in its very nature ahistorical. For this reason, it narrates a past which cannot be accommodated in any identifiable historical, calendar, or clock-on-the-wall time-frame but rather is determined by the folktale's own narrative time. The formulaic introductory phrase 'Once upon a time' (*Es war einmal*) or one of its recognisable equivalents eases the listener/reader out of the historical time in which the story is being told (narration time) into this narrative time, providing an unmistakable linguistic signal that both the narrator's intentions and the listener's expectations will be markedly different from those involved in, let us say, a historian's chronicling of the past, an official report on a recent occurrence, or even a storyteller's rendering of a local legend. Once convincingly embedded in narrative time, any story's total recounted time is presented in narrated and non-narrated portions, of which the former – the narrated portions – which are roughly equivalent to the episodes of the narrative structure set out in Antti Aarne's and Stith Thompson's *Tale Type Index*[7] are normally proportionately less extensive than the latter – the non-narrated segments – thus giving folktales in their very telling a paradoxical lopsidedness towards silence, towards the redundance of the unsaid. The basic unit of this internal temporal structure is the day, and any further subdivision of its somewhat elastic diurnal frame of reference is dominated by the sundial, not the clock. Whether one agrees with this particular overview of this scheme of things or with the specific terminology through which it is expressed,. or not, there is no denying that the relationship between time and the folktale in the actualisation of which believable chunks of the past are created through narration, has been charted in great detail and that its description and analysis have been given noteworthy scholarly attention. Although, naturally, much work still remains to be done in the exploration of this particular facet of folktales, solid foundations have undoubtedly been laid on which a reliable intellectual edifice can be built. Even without further study, therefore, we can with some confidence already answer questions regarding the 'When' of the events which folktales depict.

In contrast, studies concerning the 'Where' of these self-same events have been much less frequent and also less intensive.[8] Apart from the ever-present, ever-new and often overwhelmingly debilitating human confrontation with the phenomenon of time, this may be partly due to the fact that, because of its dominant initial position in most opening sentences, the adverbial phrase 'once upon a time', or one of its several variants, attracts immediate attention, has almost become a seductive catch-phrase, thus effectively obscuring any reference to the spatial locus of folktale action; but this paucity of studies can probably also be accounted for by the predominantly, or even exclusively, temporal qualities with which we instinctively imbue the narrated past, as part of a general perception of pastness, not least because of the grammatical 'tense' employed in narrating it. As only the past, but not the present or the future, can be narrated,[9] and as the most appropriate linguistic medium through which this is commonly done is the past tense (or preterite), the illusion is quite easily formed that the past which is created through story – or chronicled through history, for that matter – is only a dimension of time but not of space, and that it is consequently only legitimate to ask *when* the world of the folktale was but not *where*. All this is quite understandable; in fact, it is almost natural that it should be so. In the unfortunate absence of an explicit opening phrase 'Once upon a place', it is therefore apparently necessary for the student of folktales to invent it in order to draw attention to the spatial facet of story, on the one hand, and to the perhaps surprising but undeniable realisation, on the other, that the past is as much located in space, whether as nameable place or not, as in time; in other words, the past is a place as well as a time.

Such a proposition finds easy and convincing support in the four introductory sentences which I quoted at the beginning. All of these have been culled at random from folktales which, in their published versions, have been adapted and retold for children. Their explicit references to 'farmlands bordered on the sea', 'the west of Ireland', 'the great forests of the Atlas Mountains', and, most tantalisingly specific of all, 'beyond high mountains and deep rivers, far in the east, almost at the Chinese borders' do not leave the reader/listener in any doubt about the topography, sometimes even the geography, of the stories in question. Responsible storytellers are obviously eager to convey to their audiences not just a sense of time but also a sense of place. That this is not just a feature of the genre when it is adapted for the entertainment of children is corroborated by the numerous excellent folktale collections from many different countries that derive more directly from oral tradition than the ones already cited. Here are just a few examples which can be said to be representative of hundreds, if not thousands, of similar openings:

On the edge of a large forest lived a woodcutter and his wife … [10]

Beyond the beyond. Beyond the seven seas, and beyond their farthest shores; there lived a poor Gypsy, who had three sons.[11]

Once upon a time, in a certain part of the wide world, there lived a poor man.[12]

Once upon a time, there was an old king, living beyond the beyond.[13]

A long time ago in a certain place …[14]

In a certain village there was a very rich family …[15]

In former times in a village in the Chü district …[16]

Very many years ago there lived a gentleman and a lady in a very beautiful part of the country.[17]

An old man and woman in the forest of Dean had twelve sons …[18]

An old woman and her son lived in a lonely wee house on the hillside.[19]

In Fifeshire there lived a farmer who had a lazy son…[20]

About the year 800, there lived a rich nobleman in a sequestered place in Scotland …[21]

There was once a wicked king who lived in a large castle which stood on a high hill in a lonely wood …[22]

There was once a farmer living in a wild part of the country where strangers seldom came …[23]

An old woman lived in a cottage on a hillside.[24]

Admittedly, there are many folktale openings in which no hint is given as to the locale in which the events take place or from which they are initiated but, then, as some of the examples just paraded indicate, this is, albeit to a lesser extent, also true of references to the temporal aspects of certain stories, perhaps mainly for stylistic reasons. Even a selective list of examples, like the fifteen just cited, surely demonstrates unequivocally the hidden, or often not so hidden, preoccupation of tellers of tales, in the folk-cultural register, with space as well as with time. If one is permitted to generalise on the basis of fifteen opening statements almost casually extracted from a handful of collections (in this case from Germany, Hungary, China and Britain), the a-historicity of *märchen* in matters temporal is dramatically matched, or at least paralleled, by a-cartographical characteristics in matters spatial. In the majority of the examples presented the location of the past is near the periphery of the map, just off the map or well beyond the map. One gets the impression that, to all intents and purposes, it is not really mappable: 'On the edge of a large forest', 'Beyond the beyond. Beyond the seven seas, and beyond their furthest shores', '… in a certain part of the wide world', 'beyond the beyond', 'in a certain place', 'in a certain village', 'in a very beautiful part of the country', 'in a lonely wee house on the hillside', 'in a sequestered part of Scotland', 'on a high hill in a lonely wood', 'in a wild part of the country where strangers seldom came', 'in a cottage on a hillside'. The language of such descriptions reminds us that any attempt to pinpoint any of these places by means of the conventional network of latitudes and longitudes, or by any other kind of accurate grid, is bound to end in failure. Even the more legend-like naming of places – 'in the Chü district', 'in the forest of Dean', 'in Fifeshire' – does not really hold out any greater promise in that respect, just as the phrase 'beyond high mountains and beyond deep rivers, far in the east, almost at the Chinese borders' is clearly only a named 'beyond the beyond', an expression which turns out to be a very popular because effective spatial equivalent of the temporal 'Once upon a time'. The past which is created through narration is therefore beyond the beyond of both time and place or, in a kind of inner removal from the reachable or knowable, in parts of the country that are 'sequestered', 'wild', or 'lonely', on hillsides and in forests. This past was 'once upon a time *and* place', and the world of the folktale exists in that doubly defined past.

Not unexpectedly, references to the spatial past are not confined to the first sentence of a story. Quite frequently, if the opening statement signals the temporal past as an introduction to narrative time, the second or third sentences elaborate on the question of narrative space, as in:

> In days of old when wishing still did some good, there lived a king whose daughters were all beautiful;… Near the royal manor was a big dark forest, and in that forest under an old linden was a well.[25]

There was once a man and his wife; for, a long time they had been longing for
a child. Finally the woman expected that God would fulfil her wish. At the
back of their house the couple had a little window overloooking a magnificent
garden...[26]

Once upon a time there was a king. He had a beautiful castle. In front of one window
there was a tree.[27]

There was once a rich knight whom the people called the Knight of the Glens and
Bens and Passes. Opposite this knight's castle was a pretty green knoll...[28]

The opening syntactic structure, then, of folktales, apart from informing
us about some of the most important personnel (the *who*) of a story (a king
whose daughters were all beautiful, a woodcutter and his wife, a man and his
wife, a poor Gypsy, a poor man, an old king, a very rich family, a poor youth, a
rich knight, a gentleman and a lady, and an old woman and her son, etc., etc.),
orients us in general as to its *when* and *where*, leaving what one might call the
actual landscaping of the story to the gradual unfolding of the plot. As detailed
description is not a characteristic of the *märchen* style, references to landscape
features are usually infrequent and sparse and tend to be at the general rather
than the specific end of any taxonomic hierarchy. They are only included in
the storying account if they have some direct bearing on the events narrated.
After all, narrative space, like narrative time, has mainly a distancing function,
removing characters and plots from the places in which we live and have our
being, to the 'beyond the beyond'.

As a consequence, and in keeping with the remarkably parallel treatment of
time and space in the folktale, the amount of actually narrated space is only a
very small proportion of the total recounted space of a tale.[29] It is probably true
to say, that even less space is narrated than time, although there is apparently a
close connection between the two. Time and space are, however, most closely
linked in the well-known episodic structure of folktales (to which I have
already referred) which is a result of the stories' single-strandedness and their
concomitant sequential arrangement of narrated events. The concept of episode
as one in a series of several 'thens' – and then and then and then … – convinces
with its no-nonsense commonsense and therefore easily grounds it in the realms
of temporality. One only has to leaf through the pages of the *Tale Type Index*[30]
to recognise that the kind of comparative folktale scholarship that has given us
this valuable descriptive and analytical tool understood episodes essentially as
chunks of time, as building blocks in a tale's selective realisation of temporal
processes, often in such manifestations as the journey, the quest, the rescue,
the destruction, the maturation, the deliverance, the (dis)enchantment, etc.,
etc. All these are action orientated, are human behaviour embedded in time.

Like the folk-narrative day, they are elastic in terms of how much or how little narrated substance they encompass, are in fact often contained within a day of narrative time, from sunrise to sunset, so to speak. It is, however, the episode as a significant portion of one of the most basic and therefore most commonly encountered movements in a folktale – the journey – which suggests that instead of being simplistically regarded as one of several 'thens', it should, in recognition of its equally important spatial dimension, be also seen as one of several 'then theres'. Even when, as often happens in a folktale, distances are measured in terms of time,[31] journeys are movements in time from place to place, requiring a multiplicity of localities in order to propel the protagonist from familiar habitat (home) to the incremental challenges of a threatening wilderness, and back home again.

Take, for example, this telescoped version of the Grimms' well-known multi-episodic tale of *The Town Musicians of Bremen* (Grimm 27, AT 130):[32]

> …a donkey…ran away, and set out for *Bremen* … After it had been going *for a while*, it met a hunting dog lying *on the roadway* … They went on. *A little later* they saw a cat sitting *on the roadway* … The cat went along. *Next* the three fugitives passed *a farmyard* where a cock was sitting *on the gate* … all four of them set forth together…they…*that evening got into a forest* … The donkey and the dog lay down *under a big tree* while the cat and the cock got up *into the branches*, the cock, in fact, flew up *to the very top* … *Then* … they started out *toward the light* … *until* they reached *a robbers' den* …The donkey…approached *the window* … *Then* they all plunged *through the window into the room* … *Now* the four companions sat down to *the table* … *When* the four minstrels were finished…the donkey lay down.*on the dungheap*, the dog *behind the door*, the cat by the warm ashes *on the hearth*, while the cock perched *on the rooftree* …, and so on.

In this skeletal outline which has stripped the story of everything not germane to the issue under discussion, the words and phrases I emphasised (the italics are mine) not only illustrate the very close connection between the 'thens' and the 'theres' in the sequential progression of events but also the carefully orchestrated locations and their relationships to each other when the action happens to be at a standstill, as in the forest or around the robbers' den.

Similarly, the adventures of the 'pretty and industrious' daughter at the bottom of the well in *Frau Holle* (Grimm 24, AT 480) are (sub-)episodic in their combined temporal/spatial sequencing:[33]

> …*when* she awoke…she was *in a beautiful meadow* … she walked *across the meadow* and came to *an oven* … *then* she stepped up…*then* she went on and came

to *a tree* ... *then* she shook the tree...*when* she'd gathered them the apples...she
went on. *Finally* she came to *a cottage* ... *after* she'd spent some time...*finally* she
realized...*at last* she said...*then* she took her by the hand and led her to *a big gate*
... *then* she went into her mother...

For what subsequently happens to the jealous sister who is 'ugly and lazy',
the same places (well – meadow – oven – apple tree – Frau Holle's cottage) serve
in the duplicated 'then there' sequence. It is therefore clearly not permissible,
even misleading, to think of folktale journeys in purely temporal terms, and
it is for the same reasons quite legitimate to enquire with some care into the
whereabouts of the folktale world.

While, as we have already seen, the world of the folktale may be unmappable
because it is essentially a-cartographical, and while its alleged locations are often
either peripheral or hard to find (lonely, sequestered, wild), it is by no means so
exotic in its eccentricity (in its non-centralness) as to be incomprehensible. Quite
the contrary! This landscape of otherness is largely a projection of the landscape
of home.[34] For example, to take a specific country, Ireland, the landscape of
Irish folktales, whether in this world or the other, is the landscape of Ireland.
In particular, since protagonists have to leave home in order to complete their
assigned tasks and ultimately to find themselves, it is the landscape of the roads
of Ireland.

It is also, as one would expect, a topography in which the sea plays an
important part. In many respects, the ocean is, in contrast to and in extension
of the internal road system, the main highway leading away from the landscape
of home into that big, wide world out there beyond the horizon. It gives almost
unimaginable scope and is therefore frequently imagined in connection with
the protagonists' need for travel, taking them to Greece or Rome, to *Lochlainn*
or New York, to the kingdom of the dark men and even to the otherworld. It
provides opportunity for adventure and a tearful path to exile. Where a harbour
juts into a strange island, the sailor moors his ship there for a precautionary 'year
and a day' even though he might be gone only for an hour: 'one rope landward
and two ropes towards the sea'[35] safeguarding his return.

In such a setting, the beach becomes the seam between land and sea and
a metaphor for the border between the known and familiar, the firm land, on
the one hand, and the threatening or at least unpredictable, the infirm sea, on
the other. It is a place of ambiguities. It is here that a routine evening stroll for
a pipeful of tobacco can turn into an unexpected sea voyage to New York and
Boston, as happened to one Seán Palmer who entered a fairy boat which took
him to the other side of the ocean and back again in very few hours.[36] It is here

on the strand that less peaceful encounters with the supernatural are a constant threat, as in the story of 'Young Conall of Howth':[37]

> ... it wasn't long before the daughter of the king of Ulster saw wading through the sea a huge warrior with a basket on his back. Whenever he spied a fish that he liked, he flicked it over his shoulder into the basket with his toes. She tried to hide herself from him as well as she could, but it was no use. He was so tall that even a bird on the ground couldn't escape his eye. He saw her easily and never stopped or stayed till he stood in front of her.

In spite of her entreaties and evasions, he makes her get into the basket and abducts her while her husband is asleep.

In a way, it is here on the shore that the concepts of time and space in these folktales mingle, for the beach is not only the tangible, observable boundary between the spaces of familiar habitat and an only-to-be-guessed-at topography of the unknown, it is also the limit of temporal existence, for there beyond the horizon, at the faraway edge of that vast expanse of water, lies Tir na nÓg, the island of eternal youth from which there is no return for ordinary mortals. Each voyage away from the strand, for whatever purpose, therefore only rehearses that future beyond all futures, and each quay, each jetty, each pier is only an extreme place of temporality occupying a little bit of space in the untempory ocean, just as each wave lapping the shore is a gentle intimation of eternity.

In other stories told in other countries, as we have seen, the land- and seascapes of otherness, in their specific features, portray a German, Hungarian, Chinese, Scottish or Moroccan 'beyond the beyond'; suffice it here to add that this homely familiarity, even in the thickest thicket of the forest or in the most remote and calamitous corner of earthly wilderness, is again not unlike the familiar units of time (day, morning, noon, evening, night) which give us access to the internal temporal structure of folktales. It is the landscaped world of the folktale not by *what* it is but by *where* it is. Narrative space may be unreachable now but it can be comprehended in tellers' and listeners' terms. It is its very lack of definition and seeming ubiquity that makes it possible for listeners/readers to recognise and interpret it in their own culture-specific (or even personal) way.

Where, then, is the past world of the folktale? It is beyond the beyond, in a wild part of the country where strangers seldom came, on a high hill in a lonely wood, or, more generally, in a certain place. Its location is remote and inaccessible and can yet be experienced in homely, familiar terms. It is other but not strange and is therefore recognisable; paradoxically, it can be on both sides of the high mountains and of the deep river and, contrary to what I once believed,[38] its role in stories told in the folk-cultural register is as significant as, and closely linked to, the function of time in these tales, especially in their shared distancing force and their mutually reinforcing episodic structuring. The world of the folktale is the unmappable, a-cartographic place where the a-historic past is created through narration.

In keeping with the nature of folktales, it is also a spatial past and world which is usually unnamed and therefore badly suited for any onomastic, particularly toponymic investigation. For a name-centred kind of interrogation of a spatially conceptualised past I therefore propose to explore in comparison another narrative genre, that of the personal experience story.

Before I do so, however, allow me to make a personal confession which, I hope, is appropriate in this context. During the many years in which my boyhood fascination with *märchen* turned into an academic pursuit and professional interest, there had been another part of me exploring systematically the kind of evidence place-names are in the investigation of linguistic history, in the establishment of relative chronological stratification, in the recapturing of the sense of place which had motivated the namers of geographical features and, perhaps most fundamentally, in the delineation of the changing contents of the various names in question, in addition to tracing their etymological origins. There had been these two *mes*, interrogating narratives and surveying nomenclatures for almost a scholar's lifetime as if these were two very separate and almost incompatible exercises, and realising only quite recently that *homo narrans* and *homo nominans* are, indeed, the same people responding to the same intellectual stimuli, essential and existential for the survival of *homo sapiens* – narrating and naming, telling stories and structuring the world around us through the imposition of names.[39] It is perhaps rather late in life for me to say that now I know better, but at least it gives me an opportunity to permit that newly reconstituted intellectual self to be in charge of the next part of this presentation.

To return to what I was saying before, while the geographical space of folktales has very little scope to offer to the name scholar, the places remembered and recorded in the autobiographical accounts of childhood are, in contrast, eminently namable and, therefore, frequently named or recalled as having had names, and are, as a result, ready grist to the onomatologist's mill, especially if that mill happens to be of the literary or textual kind. Presumably one can squabble over the degree of fictitiousness with which childhood reminiscences, even the seemingly most objective ones, are imbued; there can be little doubt, however, that such reflections, several decades and a bundle of experience later, reveal, filtered through the benign prism of hindsight, not only the personal deployment of subjective time but also the reconstructed localisations of subjective space

– space named to such an extent that, on the one hand, it persuades through its designated locatability and, on the other, condenses experience through toponymic encapsulations. There is, however, room for illusion here, for, while reminiscing writers are apparently making the spatial components of their early years known and accessible to the public, what really happens is that the private contents of named places remain essentially uncommunicated, particularly when readers have, in response, not much contents to bring themselves to the names displayed; that is, when they do not know them at all or know them only vaguely.

Let me illustrate what I mean by some examples from a volume, which triggered this train of thought, a fairly recent anthology entitled *A Scottish Childhood*,[40] to which about seventy well-known Scots contributed various kinds of childhood recollections. The oldest of the contributors, the novelist and travel and science fiction writer Naomi Mitchison (now in her nineties), after comparing the two houses of her childhood in urban Edinburgh, and in rural Cloan, Perthshire, describes in predominately spatial terms her grandfather's Edinburgh residence:[41]

> 10 Randolph Crescent towered five stories up in front, but, as it was built on the edge of a cliff above the Water of Leith, dropping down for countless storeys on the west side, past all of which one must climb to get to the gardens. This was a distinctly alarming process … All this was below the kitchens and the wine cellar, far below Grandpa's study where gentlemen were allowed to smoke, the dining-room, and above it the great double drawing-room and 'boudoir' where there was a singularly horrid picture on an easel of a boy looking good with long ringlets and a hockey stick…Above them again were the best bedrooms, and the narrower stairs to our room above. All has been remodelled inside into unrecognisability…

This is one half of a childhood remembered, indeed conceived in distinctly spatial terms. Even today still acknowledged as a 'good address' by the citizens of the Scottish capital, 10 Randolph Crescent is recollected here as an inside experience in unmistakable vertical relationships, spatial as well as social and more stratified than a mere upstairs-downstairs juxtaposition, each level from 'best bedrooms' to cellars, and ultimately to the gardens on the riverbank, assessed in their familial, aesthetic ascriptions: a childhood re-visualised as a traversing of their vertical layers with the help of stairs. This is 10 Randolph Crescent as it was about eighty-five years ago, cast in a kind of idealised reality, but its recognisability now obliterated, we are told, its reality now obscured and distorted by unthinking, falsifying remodelling, a past misplaced.

There is an almost ecstatic outward extension to Mrs. Mitchison's recollected inward space, a horizontal exterior to the vertical exterior, named in terms of some of Edinburgh's best known landmarks:[42]

> I was taken for walks, my hand held firmly, but I was allowed to run in Princes Street Gardens or in the Randolph Crescent gardens that sloped steeply to the Water of Leith and St. Bernard's Well, repaired by one of my forebears, but whose water I was wisely not allowed to drink.

In this private appropriation of named public places, she accommodates her nurturing childhood beliefs and traditions:[43]

> I often hoped I would see a would-be suicide floating down from the Dean Bridge, parachuted by a petticoat as the story had it. Edinburgh pavements were particularly appropriate for the lines and squares ritual with their huge granite sets. I avoided the lines as presumably, most right-thinking people do. Yet there must be some who actually step on the lines. It would be interesting to know with what other abnormality this is connected.

In contrast to Naomi Mitchison's upper-class reminiscences, Jack House's spatial focus of his Glasgow childhood, though eminently nameable and mappable for him and for certain knowledgeable Glaswegians, will elicit little recognition from those not familiar with the urban landscape of Scotland's Second City:[44]

> …the pavement, which we all preferred to the Field,…was in front of the four closes which made up the odd side of Kennyhill Square. A close, in case you don't know, is an entry to a tenement building. On each floor there were two facing flats, eight in all since it was a three-storey tenement. The numbers were 1, 3, 5 and 7 Kennyhill Square, looking straight at the entrance to the bowling green which separated the odd and even sides.

Like 10 Randolph Crescent, 7 Kennyhill Square is, to all intents and purposes, a postal address, the number distinguishing it from other addresses in Randolph Crescent or Kennyhill Square, the street name from other streets in Edinburgh or Glasgow. For Jack House and Naomi Mitchison, however, the numerical and onomastic precision with which they pinpoint their childhood space – who says anything of time here – is not for the convenience of some postman, now long gone, but is a fundamental act of named remembrance: 'Once upon a place I was a child'. Reminding us that these places were in Glasgow and Edinburgh, respectively, they toponymically assert their own non-interchangeability, their personal uniqueness, and embody an attempt at communicating their essentially private contents. Where Naomi Mitchison reports nostalgically on the gentility of her grandparents' residence, Jack House wistfully remembers the pavement of Kennyhill Square for his first love affair; what was Edinburgh's bourgeois Princes Street Gardens to the girl Naomi is epitomised in Glasgow's working-class Alexandra Park for the boy Jack, public ludic space away from the narrower confines of home – of 10 Randolph Crescent and 7 Kennyhill Square, that is – and yet somehow incorporated in a wider concept of homeliness in the place that once was childhood.

Several contributors to the anthology effectively use place-names to establish contrasts between city and country, working year and vacation, school and play, at home and abroad, war and peace, England and Scotland; to explore these contrasts in detail would require a paper in itself. Many of these accounts include journeys, mainly by train, not only initiated and terminated at named stations but often also punctuated by the names of intermediate stops. Walter Coutts, for instance, remembers:[45]

> At Easter, we used to go [to St. Fillans] by train, through the wonderful succession of now defunct stations – Gleneagles, Tullibardine, Highlandman, Muthil, Crieff, Comrie, Dalchonzie, and so to base.

Surely, these place-names, almost all of them of Gaelic origin and therefore lexically meaningless to the writer, both as a child and as an adult, and his family, are enumerated here not only to indicate the route taken and to shed a grown-up's tear over the loss of a railway line so important to childhood travel – even the stations have gone! – but also as a string of toponymic pearls, a succession of spellings and sounds associated with a loss of childhood itself and of its irrecoverable pleasures – place-names evocative of a loss of innocence, fossils not only linguistically but also generationally, reminders of a journey taken and completed.

The singer Moira Anderson also re-envisions her childhood holidays not just in terms of space occupied and explored but more particularly through the recollected reverberating toponymy of travel:[46]

> My parents, my two brothers, my sisters and I spent our holidays with my uncle Tom in Brora, Sutherland, and from there we explored Caithness to the north and Easter Ross to the south. We left Kirkintilloch in the early morning to travel to Glasgow's Buchanan Street Station where the north-bound train awaited us.

And then the inquisitive eyes of the travellers encountered a sequence of places mostly intimated through their named stations, a toponymic litany of the journeying child (and today's adult, for that matter): Stirling, Perth, Dunkeld, Pitlochry, Blair Atholl, Kingussie, Aviemore, Inverness, Lairg, Golspie, Dunrobin, and, the destination, Brora: '... when we finally tumbled out of our carriage we had been travelling for more than eight hours'. [47]

This is a list of names marking a desirable progression from south to north, from Lowland to Highland, from work and school to leisure and play – names which gradually increase in promise and hope and anticipation, the further afield the travellers journey and the closer they approach Brora, names that are stages in a journey of expectation and maturation, names that not only pace movement but also space the testimony of childish delight, names as symbols of the spatial accommodation of youthful adventure, in an unmistakably Scottish world.

Naturally, these are only a few telling examples of the toponymy of remembered childhood as offered in the anthology in question; there are dozens more like them in that collection. Instead of selecting several more of them to make my point even more emphatically, it seems to be preferable to turn, for my closing illustrations and comments, to autobiographies of three famous Scots of an earlier generation, as a kind of control to ensure that the pieces chosen for the anthology are not to any biasing extent coloured by the predilections of its editors. The eminent Scots I have in mind are R.H. Bruce Lockhart, the Rev. James L. Dow, and John Buchan. This is Lockhart writing in the mid-thirties:[48]

> I was born in Anstruther in the East Neuk of the Kingdom of Fife. The House in which I first raised my voice to the four winds was the Waid Academy, a small grammar school of which my father was then headmaster ... The East Neuk is that portion of the county of Fife which lies east of a perpendicular line drawn from St. Andrews to Largs. Anstruther itself bears the proud title of an ancient royal borough ... The town, which has a picturesque harbour, is lashed by the cold North Sea....

Book 1 of Lockhart's *My Scottish Youth* from which this passage has been extracted, is significantly called 'Son of the Soil'. Chapter 1 of James Dow's reminiscences, *No Better Than I Should Be*, bears the title 'A Paisley Lad':[49]

> Grandfather and Grandmother lived in a cottage at the foot of Taylor's Wynd in Dundee ... Ours was the last close in Greenlaw Avenue in Paisley and over the garden wall was a sizable piece of vacant ground which we called the Park, and where we played our games.

Both Lockhart and Dow are obviously place and name conscious, the former mostly in terms of the map and of his childhood's coordinates on it, the latitudes and longitudes of youth, so to speak, the latter predominately in the distancing separation of grandparental and parental home and of the contrast between walled-in domesticity ('the last close in Greenlaw Avenue') and playful exuberance and competition ('the Park').

I have deliberately left John Buchan's *Memory Hold-the-Door* till last, for in the opening statement of his first chapter whose place-oriented title is 'Wood, Water and Hill', this accomplished Scottish thinker, statesman and novelist says in felicitous prose what this interpreter could not even approach to express in similarly persuasive and sensitive language. Before I allow him the last word on my behalf, however, in the knowledge that the artist is always one step ahead of the scholar, permit me a brief onomastic summary of the second part of my presentation in my own much less adequate words: What this brief account has confirmed, I hope, is that the past, in the rearview mirror of autobiographical writing, is at least as much a place as a time but that, contrary to the treatment of past unmappable space in folktales, adult rememberers of childhood feel constrained to name the focussed, structured, private and public places in which they were children, or perhaps rather in which they re-envision, re-create, re-invent themselves as children. Thus the toponymy of remembered childhood, consisting of real names fictionalised in the imaginative process of remembering, is a valuable, externalising and, to us scholars, revealing, non-etymological landscape of symbols, a specialised onomastic field representing location, juxtaposition, journeying, shelter, generational interior and exterior space – playful, adventurous, dangerous, promising space, space of expectation and fulfilment – a constellation of named places whose major contents it is now to have once accommodated children.

And here is John Buchan:[50]

> As a child I must have differed in other things besides sanctity from the good Bernard of Clairvaux, who, we are told, could walk all day by the Lake of Geneva and never see the lake. My earliest recollections are not of myself, but of my environment. It is only reflection that fits my small presence into this picture. When a few months old I was brought by my parents to a little grey manse on the Fife coast. It was a square, stone house standing in a big garden, with a railway behind it, and in front, across a muddy by-road, a linoleum factory, a coal pit and a rope-walk, with a bleaching-works somewhere in the rear …

Where, then, is the toponymy, that named spatial past, of remembered childhood? Now we know – it is somewhere between the railway in front and the bleaching-works behind. No wonder, we sometimes have trouble finding it.

It may be in the very nature of the folktale to name sparsely or not at all, and it may be a chief characteristic of autobiographical writing, especially in the evocation of childhood, to name extensively and precisely, but whether a-historic and a-cartographic, or historical and eminently mappable, whether third-person fabulation unashamedly offering fictive events, or first-person reminiscence incorporating and fostering an illusion of identity and of a continuous self, the past does not exist until it has been narrated, has been created through story both as time and as space. Story, in this perspective, is understood as a contractual performance actualised in the space between the credibility of the teller and the credulity of the listener, in real and metaphorical narration space; is seen as the inevitable and necessary outcome of social interaction, of the need to narrate oneself and each other in never-ending fictions; is viewed as a true narration of a past that never was.[51] The past as place is the arena in which the past as time is allowed to create itself; past space makes past time possible.

'Beyond the beyond. Beyond the seven seas, and beyond the farthest shores, there lived a poor Gypsy, who had three sons' – 'Grandfather and Grandmother lived in a cottage at the foot of Taylor's Wynd in Dundee.' No matter how we narrate the past, we cannot help constructing it in spatial terms, as localised tectonic time. But construct it, create it, harness it we must, because without a narrated past we are incapable of dealing with the unnarratable present or of facing the otherwise overwhelming future. Story, it turns out, is an urgent matter of survival. We have to know where we once were in order to know where we are and where we are going, negotiating the challenges of crossroads and the ambiguities of our own shores on the way. *Tír na nÓg* is, after all, also just beyond our own horizons.

Acknowledgements

Substantial portions of three previously published papers of mine have been incorporated in this article, and I want to thank the editors of the publications in question for their kind permission to republish them, with some modifications. The papers are: 'Concepts of Time and Space in Irish Folktales', in: Patrick K. Ford (ed.), *Celtic Folklore and Christianity: Studies in Memory of William W. Heist* (Santa Barbara, CA, 1 083), 150-158; 'Once Upon a Place, or where is the World of the Folktale?', in: Albrecht Lehmann and Andreas Kuntz (eds.), *Sichtweisen der Volkskunde: Zur Geschichte und Forschungspraxis einer Disziplin* (Berlin-Hamburg, 1988) 359-366; 'The Toponymy of Remembered Childhood', *Names* 36 (1988), 133-141. A very brief summary was made available to students of the Department of English at the University of Aarhus (Denmark) in their *Dolphin Newsletter* 9 (May 1990), 25-26.

Notes

1   'The Seal Wife', in: Ruth Manning Sanders, *Scottish Folk Tales* (London: 1976), p. 44.

2   'Hudden and Dudden and Donald O'Neary', in: *Tales of the British Isles: As Told in Jackanory* (London 1977), p. 73.

3   'Khalid the Dreamer' in: *The Storyteller of Marrakesh Based on Traditional Tales from Morocco told by Ahmed Benchaga to Tony Barton* (London, 1980), p. 12.

4   *Aladdin and his Wonderful Lamp* (London 1876), p. 5.

5   See, for example, Edwin Sidney Hartland, *The Science of Fairy Tales* (London 1891), chapters 7-9.

6   Max Lüthi, *Once upon a Time: On the Nature of Fairy Tales* (Bloomington, IN, 1976), and other publications. Katharine M. Briggs, *The Vanishing People* (London 1978), pp. 11-26. W.F.H. Nicolaisen, 'Time in Folk-Narrative', in: Venetia J. Newall (ed.), *Folklore Studies in the Twentieth Century* (Woodbridge, Suffolk 1980), pp. 314-319; 'The Structure of Narrated Time in the Folktale', in: *Le conte, pourquoi? comment?* (Paris 1984), pp. 417-436; see also Acknowledgements above.

7   Antti Aarne and Stith Thompson, *The Types of the Folktale*, Folklore Fellows Communications 184 (Helsinki l961).

8   A recent attempt would be my own 'Space in Folk-Narrative', in: Nikolai Burlakoff and Carl Lindahl (eds.) *Folklore on Two Continents: Essays in Honor of Linda Dégh* (Bloomington, IN, 1980), pp. 14-18. There is also an unpublished Ph.D. thesis by Juliette Thomas on 'Geographical Themes in Medieval Celtic and Italian Folklore' (University of Pennsylvania, 1976).

9   See W.F.H. Nicolaisen, 'Rehearsing the Future in the Folktale', *New York Folklore* 11 (1985), pp. 231-238.

10 'A Child of Saint Mary' (Marienkind), in: *The Grimms' German Folk Tales*, translated by Francis P. Magoun Jr. and Alexander H. Krappe (Carbondale, IL, 1960), p. 8.

11 'Csucskari', in: Linda Dégh (ed.). *Folktales of Hungary* (London 1965), p. 15.

12 'Handsome András' *ibid.*, p. 28.

13 'The Tale of a King, a Prince and a Horse', *ibid.*, p. 57.

14 'Why Men are so Bad', in:Wolfgang Eberhard (ed.), *Folktales of China* (London 1965), p. 3.

15 'The Dissatisfied Benefactor', *ibid.*, p. 132.

16 'The Sacrifice of the Maiden' *ibid.*, p. 135.

17 'Ashpitel' in: Katharine M. Briggs, *A Dictionary of British Folk Tales*, Part A, Vol. I (London,1970), p. 138.

18 'Ashypelt' *ibid.*, p. 140.

19 'Billy Biter and the Parkin', *ibid.*, p.148.

20 'The Black Cat' *ibid.*, p.159.

21 'The Cruel Stepmother', *ibid.*, p.197. The precise time reference, 'about the year 800', more appropriate for the chronicle or the legend, shows that it can be dangerous to over-generalise in one's juxtaposition of genre characteristics.

22 'The Fairy and the Rings' *ibid.*, p. 226.

23 'The Flight of Birds', *ibid.*, p. 238.

24 'Food and Fire and Company', *ibid.*, p. 240.

25 'The Frog King, or Iron Henry' (Der Froschkönig oder der eiserne Heinrich), in: *The Grimms' German Folk Tales*, p. 3.

26 'Rampion' (Rapunzel), *ibid.*, p. 47.

27 'The Tree that Reached Up to the Sky', in: Dégh, p. 77.

28 'The Knight of the Glens and Bens and Passes', in: Ruth Ratcliff, *Scottish Folk, Tales* (London, 1976), p. 11.

29 I am deliberately using the same terminology as in my previous essay 'The Structure of Narrated Time in the Folktale' (see Note 6) in order to draw attention to the closely equivalent functions of time and space, in this context.

30 See Note 7.

31 Nicolaisen, 'Space in Folk Narrative', pp. 16-17.

32 *The Grimms' German Folk Tales*, pp. 105-108.

33 *Ibid.*, pp. 97-99.

34 Nicolaisen, 'Space in Folk Narrative', p. 17.

35 Seán Ó Súilleabháin, *Folktales of Ireland*, Folktales of the World 4 (Chicago, 1966), p. 87.

36 'Seán Palmer's Voyage to America with the Fairies', *ibid.*, pp. 210-220.

37 *Ibid.*, p. 85.

38 Nicolaisen, 'Space in Folk Narrative', p. 14.

39 W.F.H. Nicolaisen, 'Names and Narratives', *Journal of American Folklore* 97 (1984), pp. 259-272.

40 Antony Kamm and Anne Lean (eds.), *A Scottish Childhood: 70 Famous Scots Remember* (Glasgow, 1985).

41 *Ibid.*, p. 2.

42 *Ibid.*, p. 3.

43 *Loc. cit.*

44 *Ibid.*, p. 17.

45 *Ibid.*, p. 44.

46 *Ibid.*, p. 169.

47 *Ibid.*, p. 170.

48 R.H. Bruce Lockhart, *My Scottish Youth* (London, 1937), pp. 5-6.

49 James L. Dow, *No Better Than I Should Be* (London, 1975), pp. 14-15.

50 John Buchan, *Memory Hold-The-Door* (London, 1940), p. 13.

51 W.F.H. Nicolaisen, 'Why Tell Stories?', *Fabula* 31 (1990), pp. 5-10, esp. p. 10.

Nomina 15 (1991–92) 7–20

Pictish Place-Names as Scottish Surnames:
Origins, Dissemination and Current Status

T HE project on which this is an interim report[1] is a spin-off of two other undertakings, and the pilot study for a third. Of the first two, my *Concise Dictionary of Scottish Place-Names* has been in the making for eighteen years,[2] again and again posing the question of to what extent, and with what validity, spellings of place-names that have become surnames should be included in my inventory of early forms, especially after the fifteenth century when, in most parts of Scotland, surnames had become hereditary, and no longer reflected directly their lexical meaning – a man called *Smith* could now be a baker, someone with the name of *Wilson* could have a father named Peter, someone called *Cruikshanks* could have very straight legs, and someone answering to the name *Glasgow* could be, God forbid, from Edinburgh. It is, of course, the last of these four categories – surnames derived from place-names – which has caused problems in the selection of early spellings for my place-name dictionary and which will occupy our attention in this essay.

It is also this class of surnames which plays a similar role in my second project, which is tangentially related to, or derived from, the first: *A Comprehensive Dictionary of Pictish Place Names*, which, still in its infancy, is intended to bring together all the available evidence that has survived concerning Scottish place-names of Pictish or partially Pictish origin.[3] Here the question of the potential significance of surname spellings in the documentation and interpretation of place-names becomes even more acute, because of the comprehensive nature of the project. It is also this particular, more limited, but also more intensive enterprise that has suggested the special slant of this paper.

It is, however, the third project, as yet only in its early planning stages and somewhat vague in my mind, that has provided the most immediate impetus for this exploration. It has been an old dream of mine, hardly articulated and certainly not anywhere near realisation as yet, to investigate the ways in which place-names have become, and now function as, surnames, i.e. to find out what happens when an item in one onomastic category is transferred to another onomastic category, from a toponymicon to an anthroponymicon, so to speak, losing in the process the characteristics and contents of the former, the place-name, and taking on the qualities and the contents of the latter, the surname, and this so completely that, even if its toponymic origins, its previous status as place-name, are still transparent (as in the name *Glasgow*, for example), they are not allowed to interfere with or influence the new function. Instead of identifying a place and having an unequivocal locus in a structured landscape, the name helps to identify a person as an unmistakable individual in a complex society, especially, though not exclusively, his or her allegiance to a family unit within accepted and acceptable contemporary social organisation. As someone who has dabbled in the study of names for over forty years, I have felt for some time that name scholars, if they are aware of the problem at all, tend to treat this functional transfer, this dramatic transformation of onymic contents, too lightly, presumably because what was once a name continues to be a name. When a place-name becomes a surname, or when the opposite takes place (a development which can be illustrated extensively from North American maps), such a transfer does not differ essentially from the leap a word takes from its position in a lexicon to its new status in an onomasticon, instantly and immediately on the act of naming. Employing the place-name Glasgow – or Ross or Melrose or Stirling – as a surname is, in this respect, not any different from using the words *smith* (or *miller* or *wright* or *cruikshanks* or *brown* or *shakespeare*) as surnames, or a combination of name and common noun in patronymics such as Wilson or Macdonald. The degree of opacity associated with such a transfer can be such that, when attempting to discover the origins of a surname like Petty, we cannot normally be sure whether this is derived from a word like French *petit* or from a place-name like Petty in Inverness-shire or Aberdeenshire; similarly, a surname like Whitehill may originally have referred to someone living near a 'white hill' or to someone coming from one of several places called Whitehill. To some degree, the transformation of one kind of name into another, by waving the magic wand which we call naming, is an even more miraculous human intellectual act than a change of a lexical item, a word, into an onomastic one, a name.

While, therefore, I have been fascinated for a good many years by this multi-faceted relationship between names and names, not just within the same onomastic categories, but also in different ones, and particularly in the manner in which place-names and surnames inform each other, I have never regarded these questions as mere theoretical challenges. As an inveterate pattern-seeker, I have, in this context, found the prospect especially challenging that, as the result of a comprehensive survey of all Scottish surnames and of their systematic scrutiny according to certain discernible, though yet to be defined, criteria, it might one day be possible, not only to establish a system of classification, but also, more adventurously, to predict what sort of place-name has the greatest likelihood of being turned into a surname, and what groups of geographical names are least likely to cross the boundary from one kind of nomenclature to the other. If Scottish surnames are counted individually and not according to the number of their bearers, about half of them – approximately 2,500 in one major survey – are found to be derived from place-names.[4] The undertaking just described would, therefore, be a formidable task, requiring the co-operation of a team rather than the dedicated efforts of an individual.

For these reasons, a more circumscribed project is called for to test the potential viability of the ideal, larger exercise, and my current preoccupation with the Picts and the place-names they have left behind in the palimpsest of the Scottish map suggested that those Pictish place-names that have become Scottish surnames might form a more limited, and therefore also a more manageable inventory for such an investigation. In a sense, the selection of this particular class of Scottish surnames can, of course, be called arbitrary or whimsical, and not very different from choosing all names beginning with *S*- or ending in -*t*, or without an -*r*- in their spelling; for by the time certain Pictish place-names in Scotland became surnames, they had ceased to be Pictish place-names in a contemporary context, because Pictish, as a spoken language, had been dead for several hundred years. The names created by the Picts had, by this time, passed through Scottish Gaelic – adapted by it, modified by it, imitated by it – and were now used by speakers of Scottish English or Scots, with appropriate phonological and graphological adjustments, as designations of places in areas in which Pictish used to be spoken. Most of them had become either completely or partially meaningless as words, and this lexical opacity or near-opacity enabled them to be filled with toponymic contents only obliquely related to their word-meaning which their generics and specifics had possessed when they had offered themselves as reasonable, maybe even perfect, choices to the original Pictish namers. For these reasons, the epithet 'Pictish', when used in conjunction with these names, implies no more than a convenient sub-section of the Scottish place-nomenclature. On the other hand, even if 'Pictishness', is a criterion that is not any better or any worse than other properties one might have chosen, it does not invalidate the names in question as suitable, indeed appropriate, evidence in our quest.

There are, however, certain benefits outside these considerations. One is a mechanical one: since the great majority of Pictish place-names begin with the generics *aber* 'a confluence' or *pit* 'a piece of land', they tend to be clustered in certain parts of the alphabet and are therefore easily detected in, and extracted from, gazetteers and indices.[5] Also, with the exception of a very few ambiguous names, misunderstandings are rare and usually quickly resolved on the basis of medieval and early post-medieval spellings. The third benefit, however, though also largely practical, is even greater: the eponymous places of the surnames in question are to be found in a regionally well-defined distribution, i.e. in the original 'Pictland', a pre-Gaelic Celtic-speaking part of north-east Scotland, roughly from the Firth of Forth northwards to the Moray Firth and a little beyond into Easter Ross and Easter Sutherland, with the western boundary more or less identical with the northern part of the Great Glen and the Perthshire-Argyllshire border. It is not their special and undisputed linguistic origins (which, by the time some of them became surnames, had anyhow become largely irrelevant), but their remarkable regionality that highly recommends them as promising onomastic material for a pilot study. It may be argued that this severe regionality may make them unrepresentative of the whole of Scotland, that Pictish does, in fact, not equal Scottish, and may therefore introduce distortions; this may be so, but it is a small risk to take compared with the advantage of traceable origins, status and paths of dissemination.

Before the actual evidence is presented, attention should be drawn to a more general aspect of the topic under discussion: that association with a certain place, whether named or not, was one of the windows on a person's identity – the other three being parental descent (usually paternal), personal habits and qualities, and occupation – is a phenomenon which it would be thoughtless to take for granted. To establish who a person is by that person's residence or origin requires a sense of place more delicate than most of us are endowed with today. It also implies that one's current or former whereabouts may include the right to own a portion, however small, of the earth's surface. This is an assumption which is also inherent in the many place-names that contain personal names as specifics, like Johnston or Grimsetter. That this association of identifiable and recognisable personal individuality with a location is more significant than any other notable characteristics which a person may have is a further escalation of this mode of thinking, directly responsible for the large number of heritable surnames which have their origin somewhere in the landscape out there. This certainly holds true in the Lowlands, whereas the Highlands acquired a heritable system of surnames much later, one based almost exclusively on patronymics and clanship.[6] It is usually accepted that, in Scotland, toponymic surnames were first given to owners of large tracts of land with considerable standing in society,[7] and that this practice was later extended to the farming community and to people less settled, who had moved from one place to another and, in their new habitat, continued to be identified as incomers, strangers and outsiders; one might also say that they were branded as such, and that some of the resulting surnames therefore imply, not only awareness of outside origins, but also non-integration into, or even rejection by, the communities in which these incomers now lived, thus highlighting the very special role of the stranger in society. It is also worth remembering that, once place-names have been converted into surnames, they acquire a degree of mobility which had been almost completely denied to them before. They can go wherever a person can go; weighing their considerable anchors, so to speak, and casting their fast moorings, they become migratory.

Where does the use of Pictish place-names as Scottish surnames fit into this picture? As anticipated in a comment above, the central evidence for the propositions advanced in this paper will consist of names beginning with the generics *Aber-* and *Pit-*, as these are non-controversial, even if it has to be conceded that most of the *Pit*names, like Pitlochry, Pittentagart, Pittenweem, and so on, are Gaelic-Pictish hybrids.[8] By selecting these two major toponymic elements in the Pictish place-nomenclature to guide us, we are also in a position of perhaps catching two different groups of people within Pictland, from the point of view of both linguistic affinity and settlement preference. Whereas it can be said without much fear of contradiction that the element *pit* 'piece of land' occurs in place-names only within the boundaries of 'Pictland' proper, or very close to those boundaries, the element *aber* 'confluence' is, of course, also found in Wales. Whereas *pit*, therefore, gives the impression or illusion of a separate linguistic identity within the group of Celtic people, *aber* argues for close links, not only with Cumbric south of the Forth-Clyde line, but also with Welsh, despite the absence of *aber*-names in the English west between the Scottish and Welsh borders. The somewhat tenuous and by no means automatic connection between onomastic evidence and its linguistic underpinnings is thus again exposed.

Similarly, whereas Whittington and Soulsby have convincingly demonstrated that the people who gave *Pit*-names to their settlements avoided coastal areas and river valleys, preferring sites at a certain altitude, with favourable southern exposure, good soil and drainage and certain slope values, the Picts who coined Aber-names were obviously river-dwellers, with a special penchant for confluences, whether with another water-course or the sea.[9] These two types of Pictish settlers therefore complemented each other; how mutually exclusive they were is another question. Both types of names have become heritable Scottish surnames, although one cannot help feeling that the *Aber*-names had perhaps more status, both before and after their semantic conversion.

According to the best authorities, there are about seventy *Aber*-names in Scotland, and approximately 300 *Pit*-names. Of these, a remarkably small percentage seems to have been employed as surnames. George F. Black, in his *Surnames of Scotland*, lists only ten *Aber*-names and twenty-two *Pit*-names, including those documented only historically. What is even more astonishing, however, is the fact that only six *Aber*-names and seven *Pit*-names have survived to the present day. These are Abercorn, Abercrombie, Aberdeen, Aberdour, Abernethy and Arbuthnott, on the one hand, and Pitbladdo, Pitcairn, Pitcairns, Pitkaithly, Pitkeathly, Pittendreich, and Pittillo or Pattullo. Other promising candidates such as *Aberchirder*, *Aberdalgy*, *Aberlady*, *Abernyte* and *Arbroath*, as well as *Pitbauchly*, *Pitcarry*, *Pitcon*, *Pitlandy* and *Pitcruive*, have apparently fallen by the wayside. Since these now seemingly-obsolete surnames are all derived from place-names in the same area as those which have survived, the overall picture of geographical or regional origins would not have changed significantly, even if the evidence had been more substantial.

Here is a brief synopsis of the names in question:[10]

Abercorn (NT 0878) is in West Lothian, just south of the southern boundary of Pictland proper. It is mentioned as early as the eighth century by the Venerable Bede as *Æbbercurnig*, meaning 'horned confluence'.

Abercrombie (NO 5102) was a barony and is now a village in Fife.[11] There are medieval references to it in the twelfth century. While *aber* is Pictish, the specific element is a genitive *-crombaidh* of Gaelic *crombadh* 'bending'. The Gaelic adjective *crom* 'bent' from which it is derived may have replaced or 'translated' a Pictish word corresponding to Welsh *crwm* 'bent'.

Aberdeen (NJ 9306) is Scotland's third-largest city, at the mouths of Don and Dee on the Scottish north-east coast. The earliest spelling on record is *Aberdon* about 1124, a clear reference to the fact that the original Aberdeen was at the mouth of the Don.

Aberdour. There are two places called Aberdour, one in Aberdeenshire (NJ 8863) and the other in Fife (NT 1985). In both instances, the name of the river which forms the confluence is a simplex *dubron*, as in Welsh *dwfr*, *dwr*, and Gaelic *dobhar*, simply meaning 'water'. It is the Fife Aberdour which matters here, although the earliest references to Aberdour as a surname appear to be to the Aberdeenshire name.

Abernethy. Although there is another Abernethy further north (NH 9918), the surname must be derived from Abernethy in Perthshire (NO 1816), where there used to be a Culdee monastery. The first reference to the place goes back to about 1100 A.D., and the first person on record so named is Hugh, who died in the middle of the following century. *Nethy* is an Anglicisation of a Gaelic genitive of *Nethech* or *Neitheach*, which itself is an adaptation of the Pictish *Neithon*, earlier *Nectona* 'the pure one'.

Arbuthnott. *Aberbuthenoth* at the beginning of the thirteenth century, is in Kincardineshire (NO 7975). The unnamed burn on which it is situated must have been the *Buadhnat* (Gaelic) 'the little one of virtue', probably designating a stream with healing power.

Pitbladdo (NO 3617) is a thoroughly Pictish name in Fife which contains, as its second element, a genitive *blátha*, corresponding to Welsh *blawd* 'meal, flour', and was therefore probably the miller's portion of land.

Pitcairn which gave rise to the surname is in Fife (NO 1995); another Pitcairn is in Perthshire (NO 0627).[12] The specific in the name is clearly Gaelic *carn* 'a heap of stones, a cairn', and the name may have been given by speakers of Gaelic who had adopted the Pictish toponymic element *pit* to enrich their own vocabulary. The surname Pitcairns may be of the same origin. [13]

Pitcaithly (NO 1117) is in Perthshire near Perth. It is on record as *Pethkathilin* about 1230; its second element is probably the personal name *Cathalan*, a diminutive of *Cathal*, indicating proprietorship. Black claims that Pitkethly or Pitkeathley is of the same origin.[14]

Pittendreich. This is another place-name which occurs in a variety of forms as a surname, especially since it not only displays various spellings for the element *dreich*, but also has a telescoped first element in Pendreigh. A major problem is caused by the fact that there are at least ten places named Pittendreich, which are found not only in the Pictish heartland – Fife, Kinross, Perthshire, Angus, Kincardine and Aberdeen – but also in Banff and Elgin in the north, in Stirlingshire, actually now Penderich (NS 7997), and in Midlothian on the southern side of the Forth.[15] There is the distinct possibility of polygenesis for the surname, which may be derived from more than one location. The popularity of the place-name is undoubtedly linked with the meaning of the specific, Gaelic *dreach*, which signifies 'aspect, face, countenance', and refers to the favourable position of the places so named. Watson notes that 'the places of this name appear all to be situated on slopes, usually facing the sun'[16] – a kind of Pictish-Gaelic precursor of modem names like Morningside or Blinkbonny, and also toponymic proof of one major criterion isolated by Whittington and Soulsby in their investigation of the preferences which the coiners of *Pit*-names showed for certain favourite settlement sites.

Pittillock. Either Pittillock in Fife (NO 2705) or Pittilloch in Perthshire (NO 1310). This name, which has developed two quite different forms as a surname – Pittillo and Pattullo – has, as its second element, Gaelic *tulach* 'a hill'.

As is easily demonstrated, practically all the eponymous places involved are situated in a very compact area of Pictland, mostly in Fife and Perthshire, i.e. they are outside those parts of the formerly Pictish territory which, in the crucial centuries in which surnames became essentially heritable, were still thoroughly Gaelic, both linguistically and culturally, and therefore not given to coining fixed surnames, especially not from place-names. That is why not a single *Pit*-place-name now to be found in Easter Ross or Easter Sutherland, or in the westernmost parts of 'Pictland', has produced any surname. This attempt at an explanation unfortunately does not help us to deal satisfactorily with the other side of the coin, the absence of names in the corpus of surnames which one would have expected to be there, like Aberlemno, Abergeldie, Pittarow, Pitcaple, or Pittenweem, particularly the first two, since most *Pit*-names historically referred to small and medium-sized farms; many of them still do today.

So much for origins, but what about destinations? Or, where in Scotland are surnames of Pictish origin found in our time, and what are their respective strongholds (without considering names that appear in aristocratic titles)? In order to obtain a general overview of their local and regional presence and their frequency, I have consulted the relevant telephone directories in a process which I like to call telephonomastics.[17] Such an approach has obvious limitations, but it is nevertheless a convenient and useful beginning, as complete street directories are no longer available.

Again, let us first look at the *Aber*-names, beginning with Abercorn and Aberdour. About the former, Black conjectured half a century ago: 'The surname is now very uncommon if not extinct'.[18] Despite his gloomy prognosis, there are, almost fifty years later, still two individuals or households with the name of Abercorn at the end of a telephone. If one wanted to reach them, one would have to dial a Cumbernauld number. Although Cumbernauld is situated in what used to be a small enclave of Dumbartonshire, it is not very far from Abercorn in West Lothian, and one might therefore surmise that the surviving name has travelled a short distance only; but as Cumbernauld is one of the creations of the New Town movement in the sixties, the Abercorns may have reached it via Glasgow, which provided much of the overspill. Nevertheless, Abercorn is obviously a surname on the brink of extinction. We are not much better off with the surname Aberdour, which survives in only two Scottish locations – in Burntisland, just next door to the eponymous place on the southern Fife coast, and five times in Edinburgh across the Firth of Forth. If it ever migrated any further within Scotland, there is no trace of it in the contemporary record, and our already-small corpus of Pictish place-names that have become Scottish surnames may soon be reduced even further.

The surname Aberdeen is in a much healthier position, as there are currently thirty-seven subscribers of that name; but it, too, or its bearers do not seem to have had the itch to travel, for only one of them would answer the phone in Newtonmore (Inverness-shire), Stromness (Orkney), in Bonnyrigg, in Liston, in Auchterarder, in Fort William and in Smallholm, and two in Kirkcaldy. Of the remaining bearers of this name, eleven live in Dundee and sixteen in Aberdeen and environs. An additional curiosum is that only one of the citizens of Dundee and the one lone bearer of the name in Newtonmore spell their surnames the same way as the modern city, whereas all the others use a spelling Aberdein, which occurred occasionally in the twelfth, fourteenth and seventeenth centuries. What appears to have developed here is a spelling dichotomy between place-name and surname in the way in which we distinguish the word tailor from the surname Taylor. Although there are thirty-seven households of this name that have a telephone, the number of people involved is quite small, considering the size of the city.

In contrast, the migratory urge of the people who lived in Abercrombie in Fife and in Abernethy in Perthshire appears to have been quite strong, for of the 201 Abercrombies who have a telephone, at least 167 have left Pictland proper, and now have a strong representation in the Greater Glasgow area and around Edinburgh, but are also found as far as Berwick, Dunure in Ayrshire, and the Scottish Borders. Thirty-four of them still live in former Pictish territory. The impact of this surname is inverse to the size of the place from which it stems, and the social standing of the owner has obviously been a more important factor in the creation of such a large number of Abercrombie surnames, either spelt with a final -*ie* or a final -*y*. The name is found very early in the legal profession of the capital.

The presence of the name Abernethy is almost as numerous as that of Abercrombie, but with a different distribution. Thirty-five bearers of that name still live somewhere near Tayside and on Dee- and Don-side, and there is the expected contingent of sixty-eight in the Greater Glasgow area and of fifteen around Edinburgh, but twenty-four telephone subscribers of this name live in the Northern Isles, especially in Orkney as a result of movements of Scots into that part of the world. The name has been recorded in the island of Unst at least since 1822, and its presence there is most likely to be ascribed to the emigration of one particular family.[19] It would, of course, take some intensive local research to discover whether all the current Abernethys are offspring of the same prolific progenitor.

The Arbuthnotts, who originated in the Mearns, have perhaps the widest current distribution of all the names considered in this survey. Apart from the expected north-east home base and reasonable representations in Edinburgh and Glasgow, with nine and four respectively, the name occurs from Inverness to Stranraer and from Ardrossan to Tranent, although in these latter places, and in many others, only in single households.

Most of the Pit-names show a pattern of contemporary distribution that is similar to that of the Aber-names, i.e. strong continued regional presence in the area of origin and sizable numbers of bearers in the Glasgow and Edinburgh areas. This is, however, only partially true of the Fife name Pitbladdo, which seems to have stayed on the east coast – ten of them in Fife, six in Edinburgh, and one each in Aberdeen, Alloa, Dalkeith, Musselburgh and Queensferry.

Another Fife name, Pitcairn, occurs sixty-three times in the Scottish telephone directories, nineteen times in Fife and Kinross, twenty-five times in the Greater Glasgow area, fifteen times in Edinburgh, and four times in the Scottish south-west. The only subscriber with the name of Pitcairns one would have to ring in Dunfermline, also in Fife. It is curious that people bearing such a durable name appear to have been reluctant to move further north.

From small beginnings near Perth, the eighty-four Pitkaithleys, Pitkeathlys, Pitcaithlys, etc., have followed the usual dissemination pattern. Forty-five of them still live in Pictland, most of them in Perthshire or on Tayside, the others in Fife and Kinross; the remaining thirty nine have succumbed to the lures of the big cities and also moved further away. It is interesting to note that the spelling Pitcaithly predominates in Glasgow, while the spelling Pitkeathly is more common in Edinburgh.

In contrast to the Pitcairns and the Pitcaithly/Pitkeathlies, there are many Pittendreichs, forty-three of them in Aberdeenshire and the neighbouring north-east, this out of a total of fifty-nine. For them the pull of the big city lights seems to have been much less strong, for there are very few of them in Glasgow and Edinburgh. As already indicated, the picture is confused by the fact that several Pittendreichs in favourable locations vie for the honour of having spawned the current number of telephone subscribers named Pittendreich, though the more northerly examples are more likely to be the originators. The sub-set of Pendreichs are particularly numerous in the Edinburgh area, where forty-three out of a total of sixty-six live; the remaining distribution is very 'un-Pictish', and, unless a close connection with the Stirlingshire Pendreich can be established, suggests that this name-form may have developed later outside Pictland.

The Fife place-name Pittillock has produced two very different groups of onomastic offspring: the nine who spell their name Pittillo, with the exception of a Burntisland subscriber, have telephones in widely scattered locations in the Scottish south – Edinburgh, Kilbarchan, Paisley, Galashiels, Hawick and St Boswells. Those who spell their name Pattullo have largely stayed in Pictland, seventy-nine out of ninety-six, and for the rest of them, as for the Pittillos, the Glasgow area seems to have had little attraction. It might be better to put the argument the other way round, by saying that the spelling Pattullo developed mostly in the old Pictland and the spelling Pittillo elsewhere. It is nevertheless quite intriguing to observe how many of them stayed at or near home, mostly in Angus.

What, then, has happened to that comparatively small band of Scotsmen and Scotswomen who are bearers of surnames of Pictish origin and have telephones? Without being able to introduce into this discussion the hundreds of historical references, especially of the sixteenth, seventeenth and eighteenth centuries, which I have on file, I would claim that a remarkable number of them have not moved very far.[20] Most of these surnames are, therefore, still found in former Pictish territory.[21] This is particularly demonstrable with regard to the Pittillos/ Pattullos. Otherwise, Glasgow and Edinburgh and the areas surrounding them have been particularly attractive, mostly, one would think, because they have offered employment, largely of an industrial nature, over the last 150 years. The presence of the names in question further south, i.e. in the Lothians, the Borders, and the Scottish south-west, is sporadic, and follows no particular pattern. Much more spectacular, however, is the almost complete absence of such surnames in the Highlands and the Western Isles, and, with the exception of prolific Abernethys, also from the Northern Isles, westward and north-westward movement, involving the penetration of another culture area or the piercing of a formidable internal Scottish cultural frontier, appears not to have been on the list of priorities of people raised in the old Pictish territory; either that, or they immediately joined the system and became Macdonalds, Campbells or Frasers. This is the image with which we are left, apart from the observation that, if one comes across an Abercrombie, an Abernethy, an Arbuthnott, a Pitcairn, Pitcaithly or Pitkeathly, a Pitbladdo, Pittendreich or Pattullo somewhere between the north shores of the Firth of Forth and the southern shores of the Moray Firth, one is most likely in the presence of someone who, even 1000 years after the end of the Pictish kingdom and the death of the Pictish language, still has a drop of Pictish blood in his or her veins. For a Pictophile like myself, that is quite a fascinating thought.

Notes

1 Earlier versions of this report were read at the Annual Meeting of the Council for Name Studies in Great Britain and Ireland at the University of Leicester, April 5-8, 1991, and the International Conference of 'Frontiers of European culture' at the University of Aberdeen, July 1-4, 1991, respectively.

2 This was supported by a research grant from the National Endowment for the Humanities, 1983-1986.

3 Supported by a Fellowship from the National Endowment for the Humanities, January 1 to August 31, 1991.

4 This count is based on the list of names included in George F. Black, *The Surnames of Scotland* (New York, 1946).

5 See William J. Watson, *The History of the Celtic Place-Names of Scotland* (Edinburgh, 1926), pp. 407-11 and 458-67; K.H. Jackson, 'The Pictish language', in *The Problem of the Picts*, edited by F.T. Wainwright (Edinburgh, 1955), pp. 129-66; W.F.H. Nicolaisen, *Scottish Place-Names: their Study and Significance* (London, 1976), pp. 151-58 and 164-65.

6 See, for example, Alexander Macbain, 'Early Highland personal names', *Transactions of the Gaelic Society of Inverness*, 22 (1897-98), 152-68. A brief but very informative account of the subject is found in a pamphlet by William Matheson, *Highland Surnames* (Inverness and Glasgow, 1973).

7 See Black, *Surnames of Scotland*, p. xix.

8 See Watson, *Celtic Place-Names*, pp. 389-424; Nicolaisen, *Scottish Place-Names*, pp. 154-56.

9 G. Whittington and J.A. Soulsby, 'A preliminary report on an investigation into *Pit* place-names', *Scottish Geographical Magazine*, 84 (1968), 117-25; G. Whittington, 'Place-names and the settlement pattern of dark-age Scotland', *Proceedings of the Society of Antiquaries of Scotland*, 106 (1974-75), pp. 99-110.

10 The Scottish *Aber*-names have been comprehensively collected and published as part of Erskine Beveridge's *The 'Abers' and 'Invers' of Scotland* (Edinburgh, 1923). For the *Pit*-names there is no equivalent corpus; for an extensive but less than full listing see Watson, *Celtic Place-Names*, pp. 407-10.

11 It was also once the name of a parish which is now called St Monans: Beveridge, '*Abers' and 'Invers'*, p. 9, raises the possibility of a second Fife barony called Abercrombie.

12 The modern map shows only Pitcairngreen; a second Fife Pitcairn is at NO 2602.

13 There is, however, also a Pitcairns in Perthshire (NO 0214).

14 Black, *Surnames of Scotland*, p. 664.

15 William M. Alexander, *The Place-Names of Aberdeenshire* (Aberdeen, 1952), p. 352, lists a Pittendreich and a Pittendrigh, but etymologises them both differently.

16 Watson, *Celtic Place-Names*, p. 413.

17 W.F.H. Nicolaisen, 'Telephonomastics', *The Scots Magazine* (December, 1969), p. 243.

18 Black, *Surnames of Scotland*, p. 2.

19 Dr Doreen Waugh informs me that in Shetland the surname is pronounced with a stress on the first syllable.

20 The historical movements of a single surname within Scotland require diligent and detailed research; for a group of names like the ones under discussion, the task is even more formidable.

21 This limited mobility coincides with R.A. Mckinley's findings in England. See his *A History of British Surnames* (London, 1990), pp. 66-70, and also *Norfolk Surnames in the Sixteenth Century* (Leicester, 1969), pp. 21-23.

Names 41, 4 (Dec. 1993) 306–313

Scottish Place-Names as Evidence
for Language Change[1]

This paper traces several changes in the pronunciation of unaccented final syllables in Scottish place-names. It claims that place-names which are lexically opaque are more likely to reflect changes in pronunciation earlier than words the lexical meaning of which is well known. As a parallel, the loss of *-l* in words like *ball*, *wall* and *fall* is illustrated by the appearance of continuing usage of *Fal-* spellings in the name *Falkirk* in pronunciation; they nevertheless are invaluable evidence for change.

ALTHOUGH the illustrations for this brief enquiry will be culled from the place-nomenclature of Scotland (both Scottish Gaelic and Scottish English), it is my intention to re-emphasise in principle the special, indeed favourable, status of toponymic evidence in the investigation of language change. The basic assumption underlying such a claim is that, whereas lexical items cannot function properly, i.e. cannot be used competently, without transparent meaning, onomastic items, while of necessity embedded in language for the purposes of communication, function quite satisfactorily, i.e. can be used more or less competently, even when they are completely opaque semantically. Indeed, one might go one step further and say that all items which have crossed the threshold from lexicon to onomasticon function on the basis of their contents only, even if they continue to have fully or partially discernible lexical meaning. It is, however, the category of names which, in the act of naming and in the course of later usage, have become semantically opaque that deserves our special attention. Naturally, this process is particularly common, if not inevitable, when a subsequent language adopts and adapts names coined by speakers of a previous language but it is not confined to that kind of onomastic contact. I hope to offer a few examples of both situations – bilingual and monolingual.

Why should we have such high expectations of place-name evidence, especially when it has cast its lexical moorings and is semantically adrift? In answering this question it is arguable that a lexically meaningless sound sequence which (a) has no connections with the vocabulary of the language in which it is embedded, (b) additionally carries no or little semantic freight and is unencumbered etymologically, and (c) serves denotatively to identify a location as part of the process of creating a structured landscape through naming and the use of names, is much more likely to reflect the onset of impending linguistic changes than items that have easily understood connotations and meanings within a knowable and known lexicon in which they hone each other in various types of semantic fields. This is, of course, not to say that names are single, unconnected items that do not have reciprocal relationships or do not inform each other in onomastic fields; quite the contrary is the case, and it would therefore be ill-advised to rely solely on the evidence of individual names when searching for reflexes of language change, on whatever level.

The changes which I wish to examine are all phonological and mainly affect final consonants in unstressed syllables. The first of these is by no means confined to Scottish or even Northern English but is to be found in all varieties of English at one time or another under the appropriate triggering conditions – the change from a final velar nasal [ŋ] to an alveolar nasal [n], and vice versa (Nicolaisen 1989). Let us take as our starting point the well-known Scottish place-name *Stirling* for which no reliable linguistic ascription or acceptable etymology has ever been suggested and which is therefore prototypical as a "meaningless place-name". Its earliest recorded form is *Striuelin* in the early twelfth century, and *-n* endings, with and without a final *-e*, continue strongly until the middle of the sixteenth century in such spellings as *Struelin* and *Striulin*, as well as the most common *Striuelin(e)*, and the like, and, with metathesis, as *Stervlen* and *Styrvelyn*. Parallel to these forms, though much less frequently, we find early *Striueling* and *Strivling*, and later the metathesised *Steruelyng*, *Sterling* and *Stirling*. These *-ling* forms have, of course, become dominant and have been used exclusively since the middle of the seventeenth century. This brief list cannot convey more than a glimpse of the variety of spellings displayed in the historical record; nor is it an adequate indicator of the numerical occurrences of the various spellings, some of which are extremely numerous at certain times whereas others occur singly or only occasionally. For the purposes of this particular, very circumscribed investigation, the letters *i* and *y* can be legitimately treated as interchangeable allographs, but this is not to say that their presence and distribution may not yield important information in some other context. Broadly speaking, the picture which emerges is this: almost from the very beginning of the recorded history of the name *Stirling* in the first half of the twelfth century, *-lin* or *-lyn*, *-line* or *-lyne*, and *-ling* or *-lyng* spellings occur side by side although until the fifteenth century the *i*-spellings are much more common than the *y*-spellings. From the fifteenth century onwards, *-ling* or *-lyng* spellings predominate and take over completely from the second half of the sixteenth or the beginning of the seventeenth century on.

Another Scottish place-name whose relevant second element is lexically opaque is *Dunfermline*. For this name, *-lin* or *-lyn* spellings, like *Dunfermelyn* c. 1125 and *Dunfermelin* c. 1126, are by far the most common in the initial three centuries of its recorded history; apart from two puzzling earlier examples, *-ling* does not occur until the beginning of the fifteenth century but then predominates until the middle of the seventeenth century, with the original *-lin* ending petering out about a hundred years earlier. In contrast to *Stirling*, however, *-lin(e)* spellings begin to replace *-ling* spellings again in the middle of the seventeenth century, after a break in continuity of about a hundred years. This curious revival is, however, not relevant to the theme of this discussion.

The essential evidence provided by *Stirling* and *Dunfermline* is corroborated by several other Scottish place-names. For *Tealing* in Angus, for example, *-ing* spellings begin to appear in the fifteenth century and take over completely two centuries later. The name *Dupplin* in Perthshire has *-ing* intrusions in the sixteenth and seventeenth centuries; for the name *Roslin* in the Lothians *-ing* is found in the fifteenth and sixteenth centuries; for *Dunning* in Perthshire consistent *-ing* spellings begin in the sixteenth, for *Inverkeithing* in Fife and *Kilwinning* in Ayrshire by and large in the fifteenth century, and so on. The /-n/ > /-ŋ/ phenomenon is, however, not confined to final *-in* becoming *-ing*. For *Longmorn* in Moray, for instance, which contains Gaelic *lann* 'an enclosure', *Lang*-spellings begin to appear in the sixteenth century; similarly *Lhanbryde*, also in Moray, and *Longannet* in Stirlingshire display *Lang-* as a first element in the same century, in obvious analogy to Scots *lang* 'long', and there are numerous other illustrations.

What is to be made of this? Purely descriptively, we can say that while *-ing* is a possibility from the twelfth century, it becomes more frequent two hundred years later, reaching its peak in the sixteenth and, especially, the seventeenth century. The many coexistent spellings in *-n* and *-ng*, sometimes in the same document, often in the same source, argue against the possibility of *-n* and *-ng* reflecting different linguistic registers and for an explanation that postulates them as allographs, with one of them assuming the role of allographic norm. Nevertheless, the increasing appearance of *-ng* spellings in the fifteenth and sixteenth centuries, in names in which the original spelling and pronunciation had been clearly -*n*, does presuppose an underlying trend from -*n* to -*ng* in pronunciation at times when lexical material is either silent or, at least, not very eloquent on the subject.

Another historical change which is felicitously illustrated by place-names and hardly reflected at all in non-onomastic material concerns the loss of the final fricative [x] in what used to be the more easterly Gaelic-speaking parts of Scotland (Nicolaisen 1996). Although, as usual, the situation is quite complex, in its simplified form this development accounts for the changes of final Gaelic -*ach* (the old Celtic -*acum*) to *o*, via an intermediate step of -*och*, once the names in question had been adopted by speakers of Scottish English or of Scots. The Angus place-name *Aberlemno*, which is *Aberlimenach* in the thirteenth century and is recorded as *Abbyrlemnoch* in 1488, shows -o spellings from the fifteenth century onwards. The Fife name *Balmerino*, which is *Balmurinach* and the like from the end of the twelfth century on and shows -*auch* spellings from the following century onwards, is first recorded as *Balmurino* in 1423. Another Fife name, *Dunino*, shows -*ach* spellings from the thirteenth to the sixteenth centuries and -*och* spellings in the fifteenth and sixteenth centuries, but is recorded with a final -*o* from 1400 onwards. In these and dozens of other names, -*o* has become permanent whereas there are a few, mostly further west, in which -*o* is only temporary, and -*och* or -*ock* is the modern form (*Kirkintilloch, Cumnock*). In general, we can say that in the relevant corpus of names, -*ach* spellings usually belong to the twelfth, thirteenth and fourteenth centuries, -*och* spellings to the fifteenth through seventeenth centuries, and -*o* spellings to the fifteenth, sixteenth and later centuries. Since all these spellings are visual representations and, in many instances, are likely to have been copied from earlier written sources, it is difficult to gauge their actual relationship to contemporary pronunciation. Certainly, one has to take into account the delaying factor involved in scribal habits; it is therefore more than probable that changes in pronunciation had occurred already some time before they were reflected in these toponymic spellings; similarly, spellings may have been continued for a while after the pronunciations they represented had already undergone change. The considerable overlaps which are to be found in the written word in that respect are clear indications of this situation, for it is again important to stress that these spellings are not likely to stand for different simultaneous pronunciations being used side by side for a century or more, not even in different socio-onomastic registers.

What our evidence demonstrates very clearly is that change from -*ach* to -*och*, a precondition for the further change to [o:x] and finally to -*o*, is widespread from the fifteenth century onwards although there is some indication that it may have occurred as early as the twelfth and been latent for several hundred years. The difference between the second and third stages, i.e. between [ox] and [o:x] is not reflected in the spellings in any obvious way but when -*och* and -*o* spellings occur side by side for a period of time it would be legitimate to assume that both these spellings, at least initially, stand for [o:x]. Even if this problem cannot be resolved in purely visual terms, it is necessary to postulate the intermediate third stage [o:x] in order to reach the final destination [o:] because there is no evidence to suggest that the voiceless velar fricative [x] was ever lost in Scotland after short [o]. Parenthetically, it is worth pointing out that, on the other hand, certain Scottish place-names in a non-Gaelic English context show a loss of [x] after [o:] about the thirteenth century (*Fogo, Kelso, Minto* and *Stobo* in the Border country, all of which contain Old English *hoh* 'a projecting ridge of land'). It must be assumed that the language receiving Gaelic names in -*ach* did therefore at the time of their adoption not have the sequence [o:] + [x] in its phonological structure. This must also have applied to the more north-easterly region where the development [ɔ:x] > [o:x] > [o:] was mainly triggered in the sixteenth century, probably as the result of a bilingual Scottish Gaelic-Scottish English period or, perhaps more plausibly, of an early post-Gaelic one, periods about which we otherwise know practically nothing in that part of Scotland, regarding the linguistic contacts between Gaelic and Scots.

Let me add briefly that the development in the spelling of Scottish Gaelic locatives in -*aich* (earlier -*aigh*) to -*ie/-y* in Scottish English was along similar lines; that the loss of the final voiceless palatal fricative [ç] appears to have happened more or less at the same time as that of its velar counterpart [x], perhaps even a little earlier since for most eastern Scottish place-names now ending in -*ie/-y*, but most probably old dative-locatives in -*aich* (*Cluny, Downie, Logie*), no early spellings displaying a final consonant are on record. On the western seaboard, on the other hand, an ancient name like *Dunollie* in Argyll preserves an -*ich* ending at least until the end of the seventeenth century (*Dunollich* 1688).

A related linguistic development which is, however, usually associated with stressed syllables is the regular loss of post-vocalic -*l* in words such as *ball, hall, wall* which in Scotland become *ba', ha',* and *wa'* respectively. The resulting vowel has several dialectal allophonic variants from [ɔ:] to [a:]. The toponymic evidence for this phonological change has yet to be fully explored but one of the major place-names affected by it, *Falkirk*, has already had a certain amount of detailed treatment (Nicolaisen 1969; and 1976). As its early spellings (*Faukirk* 1298, *Fawkirk* 1391) and its modern local pronunciation show, the -*l* in the current official spelling and in the non-local pronunciation is not original to the name, the specific of which is Middle English *fawe, faze* 'variegated, of various colours'. The modern form *Falkirk*, first recorded in the middle of the fifteenth century, is undoubtedly a hyper-correct spelling which became possible or suggested itself after the -*l* had been dropped in Scots, i.e. before 1458, the date of the first known *Falkirk* spelling. It is always risky to base a general conclusion on the evidence of one name alone, particularly when the process observed and described works in reverse. In this case, we are, however, on safe ground because the *Faukirk/Falkirk* evidence is corroborated by many eastern Scottish place-names with the Gaelic element *baile* 'a homestead, etc.' which normally appears Scotticised as *Bal-* but occasionally produced spellings without the *l*, as in the Aberdeenshire names *Balbithan* (*Bawbethane* 1552), *Balcairn* (*Bawcarne* 1551), and *Balhaggardy* (*Bahagarty* 1551), the Angus names *Balgray* (*Bagra* 1527, *Bawgraw 1539*, *Bowgray* 1559), *Balhall* (*Bahawle* 1548), *Balmirmer* (*Bamirmour* 1387), and *Balwyllo* (*Bawillo* 1513; *Bawylo* 1549), and the Fife names *Balcarres* (*Baccarrus* 1589), *Balcaskie* (*Bawcasky* 1480, personal name), *Balcomie* (*Bawcomy* 1537), *Balgonie* (*Bawgouny* 1454), and *Balwearie* (*Bawery* 1497, 1524). Of these, the *Baw*-spellings are especially significant, since they occur in unstressed syllables. Most of the sporadic -*l*-less spellings are, of course, surrounded by many forms in which the -*l* is retained, pointing to a written record and, later, also a cartographic tradition. It is, however, noteworthy that the oral pronunciation asserts itself occasionally for we cannot regard all the -l-less spellings as scribal errors. Apart from some early murmurings in 1387 (*e.g.*, *Bamirmour*), such spellings occur between the end of the fifteenth century and the sixteenth century, having been made possible by a change in vernacular pronunciation during the preceding half century or so, as the earliest *Faukirk* spelling suggests. On the basis of the toponymic evidence, one would therefore be inclined to place the change from [fɔːl] to [fɔː], [faː] in that period, not forgetting the delaying factor already mentioned above. Much more material will, however, have to be examined before such a preliminary and tentative conclusion can be confirmed, and caution is still required in its acceptance.

There are, of course, other avenues still to be explored, some of them lexical, some of them morphological, but even the few phonological developments briefly examined here should have demonstrated. in defiance of a blinkered etymological approach to individual names, the significance of onomastic, in this case toponymic, evidence as signposting guidance to linguistic changes otherwise shrouded in the mists of history, because such changes are barely and certainly less immediately reflected in the lexical material. In view of this realisation, a more extensive, if not comprehensive, survey of other potential Scottish candidates for the exploration of early place-name spellings as evidence for otherwise completely hidden or sparsely documented linguistic change is

W.D.H. Sellar (ed.), *Moray: Province and People*
(Edinburgh: Scottish Society for Northern Studies. 1993)
253-262

Names in the Landscape of the Moray Firth

At the very outset, I would like to draw your attention to the exact wording of the title of this presentation – 'Names in the Landscape of the Moray Firth' – for it has been chosen with more than usual care. Titles anticipate and make promises; they summarise and raise expectations; they sometimes tease and woo us. Above all, however, they open gates to paths of intellectual exploration at the end of which the mind should be comfortably satisfied. It is for all these reasons, but especially the last, that titles should be as accurate and as directional as signposts, for the sake both of those who shape them and of those for whose guidance they are intended. Otherwise their paths and ours will diverge from the very beginning.

NOW that I have made you, the reader, disturbingly title conscious, you are entitled to know the reasons for this unusual preface. Why all this wordiness? Mainly to highlight the three major terms contained in the title – names, landscape, and Moray Firth – because these not only carry the greatest semantic freight but also represent the three key concepts of this discussion. They orient with regard to subject matter, setting and location or, put more simply, to the what, how and where. Let us briefly consider these points in reverse order.

It seems self-evident that, in a review of the place-names of Moray, somehow the notion of Moray has to be one of its major shaping components but the question is: which of the several possible Morays is it to be, since all of them are different in historical significance or spatial extent, or both? Is it to be the province, the diocese, the synod, the district? Is it to have largely historical, prehistoric, or ecclesiastical connotations, to express a nostalgic hankering after, or regret for, the passing of a comparatively recent administrative unit for which the name Moray had been revived earlier this century to replace the pair Elgin and Forres, or is it to acknowledge the current political status of the mauled district within the Grampian Region, i.e. what Donald Omand has called the 'new Moray'?[1] In order not to be bound by the implications of any of these several Morays, I have added the generic Firth to the name Moray, thus making most of that estuary's southern shore and the more or less immediate hinterland my bailiwick for the purposes of this essay. The northern delineation of the area to be surveyed is therefore unmistakable whereas its western, eastern and southern boundaries largely coincide with those of the former counties of Nairn, Moray and Banff.

The second semantically pregnant *term* – landscape – has also been chosen with deliberate care. After all, a title such as 'Place-names on the Moray Firth' or even 'Place-names in Moray' would have been quite an adequate successor to those used in past toponymic presentations to this Society by Ian Fraser, Gillian Fellows-Jensen and myself. The word 'landscape', however, is to serve as a reminder that place-names are not only embedded in language but also in the world out there. It would be misleading to regard names exclusively as the product of mental processes, and it is therefore understandable that some publications treat and present them, together with flora, fauna, rock formations, etc., almost like natural features, regarding the onomastic characteristics of a given area in more or less the same way as the botanical, zoological and geological ones, and not as past human footprints. There is, indeed, something almost 'natural' about the belongingness of names and their persuasive appropriateness. After all, it is through the process of naming, the speech act of identification, that we structure the actual world outside our minds as it offers itself to us, thus taming, mastering and domesticating a potentially threatening wilderness and turning it into a familiar habitat which we tend to call 'landscape'. There is no landscape without a network of names or, from the point of view of the creative act of naming, names make a landscape. It is therefore inevitable, because essential, that the word 'landscape' should appear in our title.

That the term 'names' is also part of it, is probably even more predictable as it points to the very subject matter to be explored, the 'what' of the triad. Naming is a ubiquitous activity; as far as we know, human beings everywhere and at all times have named and will go on doing so as long as man or woman draws breath. Names are so much more than lexical items with certain peculiar additional properties; they are a matter of survival, of orienting oneself in the world, and, for this reason, are as important as food, drink and shelter. Names never occur singly – this would be a *contradictio in adjecto* – but in their individuating function relate to other names through contrast, through juxtaposition, through stratification, thus forming onomastic fields which are ever-changing and ever-readjusting. To have a name is to be, but never in solitude. Without names we are lost.

A title like 'Names in the Landscape of the Moray Firth' therefore attempts to open a window on the toponymically structured, or perhaps rather the toponymically articulated, landscape of a region defined somewhat loosely and yet not without discernible boundaries. Harnessing this title for this essay is consequently an act of appropriation, a desirable closing in on the essence of 'Moray', whatever that may be these days. Only the people of Moray can decide that.

Naturally, there are several ways of going about this business. Over eighty years ago, Donald Matheson, in his *Place-names of Elginshire*,[2] now thoroughly out of date and even in its own days highly suspect, chose the acceptable, though deceptively disruptive, device of listing names in alphabetical order, his sole purpose being, consonant with the main tenor of name scholarship in his time, the ferreting out of the so-called 'meaning' of the names included in his alphabetical list. This approach assumes that it is possible, indeed incumbent upon us, to reduce names to the words they once were,[3] and that the restoration of such original meaning or etymology is the prime purpose of name studies. It completely ignores, or at least obscures, the fact that names – whether derived from words, other names, or from arbitrary sound sequences – at the very point of naming acquire a content independent of all lexical needs and considerations, and that it is this content and not their etymologies that allows names to function viably in our efforts at effective communication. Nevertheless, the recovery of lexical meaning and of linguistic affinities is, of course, when carried out with competence and circumspection and with due regard to all the available evidence including early spellings and modern pronunciation, an essential first step, a *sine qua non* in all onomastic research, a kind of linguistic archaeology. It is, however, not the be-all-and-end-all; nor should such a fundamentally lexical procedure be confused with a thoroughly onomastic approach which recognises and exploits the status and function of names as names.

More recently, in 1976, in his contribution to Donald Omand's *Moray Book*,[4] Donald Macaulay, bringing his considerable expertise as a Celtic scholar and his skills as a native speaker of Gaelic to bear on his investigation, chose to present the bulk of his material in several discrete categories, such as references to settlement, land division and fields, crops, domestic animals, 'activities', churches, and topographic elements, like water, raised ground, low ground, 'valleys', as well as non-domestic animals and birds, vegetation, shape and size, and colour. Such a classificatory approach takes it for granted that the etymology of each name thus classified has been satisfactorily established; it is therefore a kind of second step, the findings of which, when described in this fashion and systematically analysed, go a long way towards making good use of place-names as linguistic fossils and towards employing them in the reconstruction of past landscapes. If Donald Macaulay had not chosen to do this so recently, I might well have decided on such an approach for this investigation, but there is no need for this kind of duplication.

The third frequently practised and very fruitful method in the study of place-names also starts with the supposition that the first step in establishing reliable etymologies has already been successfully taken and that the names in question have been made lexically transparent, not just semantically but also with regard to, for example, their pronunciation and their morphology. Instead of focusing on the several distinctive categories of meaning involved, as in Donald Macaulay's treatment, it attempts to make constructive use, on the one hand, of the linguistic features of names and, on the other, of their onomastic properties. Taking into account the well-known fact that names, because of their virtual independence of lexical meaning, their desemanticisation, so to speak, often survive when words do not, this method tries to place-names and their elements in their relevant distribution patterns in time and space and, subsequently, to derive from these patterns information regarding the historical stratification of languages in a given area and the geographical scatter of settlers speaking the languages in question. This, mostly historical, orientation to name studies underlies, for instance, my own book on *Scottish Place-Names*[5] which, like Donald Macaulay's chapter, was also published in 1976. Again, it would be inappropriate to reiterate in detail its conclusions concerning Scotland as a whole and the Moray Firth area in particular but it may be helpful to sketch out, with a few strokes of a broad brush, the picture as it emerges from the place-name evidence. The discussion of principles and methods without the use of illustrative examples is a pointless enterprise.

Leaving aside for a moment the fascinating question of the possibility that the Celts may not have been the first Indo-Europeans to have reached these shores,[6] there cannot be any doubt that the region to the south of the Moray Firth was once settled by non-Gaelic speaking Celts whom we know as the Picts and whose linguistic connections were with southern Scotland and Wales and ultimately with the Celtic areas of the Continent, rather than with Ireland. According to that great Celticist, W.J. Watson, there are, or once were, fifteen names beginning with the generic *Pit-* in Banffshire, twelve in the county of Moray, and one in Nairnshire.[7] These names quite clearly form part of the larger area in the Scottish east and north-east in which compound names containing this generic can be found, from the Firth of Forth northwards. As has been demonstrated convincingly, *Pit-* is the modern reflex (practically all the earlier name spellings use a form *Pet-*) of a Pictish word for a portion of land derived from an early Celtic *petia* and therefore, in a roundabout way, via Latin, is cognate with our modern English word *piece*.[8] It is not found in the British Isles anywhere outside the area once settled by Pictish-speaking Celts, although it would be erroneous to assume that all the names in this group were actually given by Pictish speakers themselves. Many of the specifics in these names are, in fact, Gaelic.[9] Some of these may have been translated or adapted from Pictish but the majority of them must go back to speakers of Gaelic who had adopted *pit* or *pet* as an element suitable for the naming of places, especially of farm-like settlements. This is certainly true of Moray as Donald Macaulay has shown;[10] he cites *Pitchaish, Pitchroy, Pitcraigie, Pittendreich, Pittensier, Pitgaveny, Pitglassie*, and *Pittyvaich. Petty* also belongs here. It is unlikely that these names were given much before the tenth century from when on Gaelic-speaking settlers became well established in what had been Pictland. Such dating is supported by the dearth of ecclesiastical names beginning with *Kil-* (Gaelic *cill* 'church, churchyard') which seem to have become less fashionable or productive about. the time the Gaels entered Pictland.[11]

Other names which have survived from pre-Gaelic times are *Aberarder, Aberchirder* and *Aberlour* all of which contain river names as their specifics, and possibly *Fochabers*. Unlike *Pit-*, Pictish *aber* 'a river mouth or confluence' does, of course, occur in southern Scotland and also in Wales[12] but this wider distribution only emphasises the point that Pictish is not likely to have been as different from the Celtic languages south of the Firth of Forth which Professor Jackson calls Cumbric,[13] or from the Brittonic ancestor of Welsh, Cornish and Breton as the evidence of the *Pit*-names when viewed in isolation might lead one to conclude. *Pluscarden*, despite the shift of stress to the first syllable, also contains an element which places it alongside the *Aber*-names, a topographic term now represented by Welsh *cardden* 'thicket, brake'.[14] The area which has our attention was therefore once thoroughly Pictish, and we must assume that Pictish in this part of the world was a Celtic language, unlike the linguistic situation north of the Moray Firth.

As already indicated, these Pictish-speaking Celts on the south side of the firth were overrun and succeeded by Gaelic-speaking Celts from about the ninth century onwards. The incomers speaking this language not only utilised elements of the onomasticon, or name vocabulary, of their Pictish predecessors, like *Pit-*, but also brought with them and applied their own toponymic terminology. Chief among the generics used in settlement names and found wherever Gaelic speakers once settled in Scotland are the terms *baile* 'homestead' and *achadh* 'field'.[15] The landscape south of the Moray Firth yields many examples of both as, for instance for *baile, Balblair, Ballachurn, Ballanlish, Ballanloan, Ballenteem*,

Balgreen, Ballindalloch, Balnacree, Balnaferry, Balnageith, Balvenie, and many others, and, for *achadh, Achfad, Auchenhalrig, Auchindown, Auchingoul, Auchintoul, Achnahannet, Auchnarrow, Auchness,* and others. Just as this area was once solidly Pictish, so it participated fully in the Gaelic settlement which followed. In fact, it can easily be shown that the presence of Gaelic here for about a thousand years has left an indelible mark on the toponymic palimpsest of our maps. In view of this extended and extensive influence, it is not surprising that this stratum is distinctly stratified within itself, the last places in our area having been named possibly around the beginning of this century. There are hundreds, if not thousands, of names to vouch for such a claim. These incorporate a plethora of Gaelic generics and specifics including many of the most classical ones such as *blàr, ceann, torr, tom, allt, beinn, cnoc, dùn, druim, aodann, leitir, gleann, inis, inbhir, ràth, àrd, barr, clach, cùil, lann, loch, logach, màgh,* and the like. Most of these, like their Pictish counterparts, have in the course of time become semantically opaque to speakers of Scots or English who have gradually turned into the dominating linguistic force but the lexical opacity of these names has not in any way detracted from their staying fully functional as names. While meaning is no longer accessible, the all-important content still is, however much it may change from time to time and from person to person.

So much, or so little, for the Celts. As far as speakers of Germanic languages are concerned, there is, again in contrast to the region north of the Moray Firth,[16] no place-name evidence to indicate that any Scandinavians ever held sway over our area.[17] The Cromarty and Beauly Firths seem to have stopped even the boldest of them. Like the Romans before them, the Norsemen apparently never lived long enough in the Moray landscape to contribute to its articulation. As is to be expected, however, there is now a sizable crop of descriptive English names well anchored to the ground, such as *Berryhillock, Birkenbog, Cairnfield, Drybridge, Limehillock,* and so on. These are now all names of settlements and are lexically, on the whole, quite transparent. We know what they mean as words. They are, therefore, the kinds of names that name scholars in the past, and sometimes even in the present, have often regarded as pedestrian, boring and not worth bothering about, and have consequently been accorded left-handed comments such as 'meaning self-evident'. From a purely etymologically oriented approach to name studies, this may well be true but this lack of etymological challenge does not make them less valuable and functional or worthy of study than names whose meaning is now obscure and has to be recovered through complex and lengthy procedures, if it can be recovered at all. When Donald Macaulay comments on the name *Dyke*[18] that it probably means simply *dike*, there is that very kind of disappointment in his comment. I am myself not at all disillusioned by names like *Dyke* for I still want to know when and why they were first given. Because so many of them were coined so late and originally referred to rather minor features in the landscape, the recorded evidence for them is often almost non-existent, or at least scanty and hard to find. For example, in my extensive search for early spellings for my *Dictionary of Scottish Place-names* I have yet to find reliable documentary evidence for about half the names just listed, the 'self-evident' ones. They are thus among the most elusive toponymic material one comes across and are often traceable only in very local sources. In contrast, names which have come down to us from the Middle Ages or some other earlier period are usually so much better documented.

Another category of such comparatively recent names which, according to the language of the namers, can only be called English but which have local historical and genealogical, sometimes very personal, connections with this area, are those of the various ports and towns planned and developed from the seventeenth century onwards. Instances would be: *Dufftown*, founded in 1817 by James Duff, fourth Earl of Fife; *Gardenstown*, founded in 1720 by Alexander Garden of Troup; *Macduff* which was erected a burgh of barony for the Earl of Fiffe in 1783 and whose earlier name had been *Down* (1683); *Branderburgh* where Colonel Brander of Pitgaveny built a house for himself in 1830; *Castle Grant* which replaced *Freuchie* and *Ballochastell* when the Regality of Grant was erected in 1694; *Gordon Castle*, the old *Bog of Gight* (older *Geith*), named about 1685; and *Gordonstoun* which came into being when Sir Robert Gordon, from 1636 on, purchased such places as *Ogstoun*, *Plewlands*, *Ettles*, etc. to form the estate; Grantown-on-Spey, a town planned by Sir James Grant of Castle Grant in 1776; or *Cummingstown* whose proprietor, Sir William Cumming Gordon, planned it as a village in 1805. As a foreign intruder from south of the Border comes *Kingston* which, it is said, was created in 1784 by two Englishmen from Kingston-upon-Hull (even in Hull they don't call it Kingston any more).

A related group consists of names like *Portessie* which became a fishing station in 1727; *Portgordon*, founded in 1797 by the fourth Duke of Gordon; *Portknockie*, founded in 1677; *Portsoy* which became a burgh of barony for Ogilvy of Boyne in 1550; and even *Lossiemouth*, the harbour of which was constructed in 1698 and for which our earliest record is from 1702, and *Buckie* which grew out of several separate villages. Names like these, despite their obvious Gaelic antecedents, are largely post-Gaelic echoes of coming to terms with the riskful ambiguity of coastscapes, offering onomastic promises of shelter and haven and livelihood for those in peril on the sea.

These two groups of names are excellent examples of how the toponymic ingredient of our landscapes is forever changing and how the onomastic field changes with them. Landscape has historical structure as well as current existence.

That this process of change is not yet complete and will, to some extent, continue for ever, is demonstrated not only by the several distillery names made famous to thirsty imbibers of the water of life all over the world, but also by such seemingly mundane names as *Ballindalloch Station*, opened on July 1, 1863; and closed November 1968; *Alves Station*, opened on March 25,1858, and closed on November 7, 1966; *Dava Station*, opened on November 1, 1864, and closed on October 18, 1965; *Dunphail Station*, opened on August 3,1863, and closed on October 18, 1965; and *Fochabers Station*, opened October 23, 1893, and closed on March 28, 1966.[19] Although these stations do not exist any more, having mostly fallen prey to Dr Beeching's axe in the sixties, the small settlements so named still do, but their content has changed. In all these instances, the originally appropriate generic – *station* – obviously no longer applies but the name persists, fossilising toponymically a way of locomotion now no longer in need of stopping places in these locations. Who says that only the ancient has its fascination? We are still adding to the palimpsest that will one day be deciphered by our puzzled descendants.

It is also worth remembering that, in addition to or intermingled with, the official or standard place nomenclature there is the vernacular one that has never been recorded on any map and probably never will be. There are *Foggy* and the *Douce Burgh*, and further east there are the *Broch* and the *Blue Toon*, and I understand that no self-respecting native would ever call *Gardenstown* anything but *Gamrie*. This unofficial vernacular consists of alternative names, often nicknames, in non-standard or dialect forms, of additional names, of local pronunciations, but also of names in other languages like Gaelic. Mainly these operate in a different sociolinguistic register and are therefore appropriate under particular circumstances, in particular company, and as, largely informal, responses to particular stimuli. They have hardly been seriously studied at all because of their non-official popular associations but are a rich source of information for a differently articulated vernacular landscape that supplements, parallels or replaces the official one.

There is one more important point I would like to make. We have already seen that *Kingston* is an individual, possibly an intrusive, transferred name but sometimes, perhaps due to the motivation or the ability to innovate imaginatively or for other reasons, groups of names or nomenclatures are transferred, and with them whole landscapes. If W.J. Watson is right, such transference happened on a grand scale when Gaelic speakers first settled in this area.[20] The names which he groups together in support of such a claim are *Banff* which literally means 'sucking pig' but as *Banba* was also a name for Ireland; *Elgin* which as a Gaelic locative case *Eilginn* could be connected with a diminutive of *Elg*, another ancient name for Ireland; *Boyne* and *Boyndie* which have equivalents in Ireland; and especially *Findhorn* (*Fionn-Eire* 'white Ireland') which was *Invereren* in 1187–1203, the mouth of the *aqua de Eren*. Linking this with *Strathearn* (*Stratheren* 1236) and *Auldearn* (*Aldheren* 1238) = *Allt Eireann* 'Ireland's Burn', he postulates a district name *Eryn* 'Ireland', and if his interpretations are right this would indeed be a remarkable accumulation of names reinforcing each other in their direct links with the country from which the settlers or their ancestors had ultimately come. The problem I have with this cumulative evidence, despite my great admiration for Watson as a scholar, is that it is very difficult to reconcile such a wholesale transfer with the several river names in question. I have been studying river names for almost forty years now, and instinct tells me that they do not behave in this way. Animal names for rivers such as *Banff* are quite common in the Celtic world, and *Boyne* and *Boyndie* might well have been created independently. For the second part of *Findhorn* and *Auldearn*, as well as the related *Deveron*, an original river name is more likely and much points in this direction, i.e. of -*horn*, *earn* and -*eron* representing ancient river names meaning 'flowing water'. If this explanation is acceptable, one might further suggest that this older name belonged to a pre-Celtic Indo-European stratum to which the river name *Nairn* probably also goes back.[21] In addition, although an etymology is hard to establish, the name of the *Spey* may also belong here; a meaning 'hawthorn river' which Watson proposes for the most important river in the region is difficult to substantiate.

Whatever the explanation, it is highly probable that the Celtic people who settled in *Moray*, Gaelic *Moireabh*, the old *Murebe* or early Celtic *mori-treb* 'seaboard settlement',[22] may well have found other people already there whose language was very much akin to their own. *Moray* itself has an honourable, ancient history as a name but one would like to dig deeper. Unfortunately, the evidence that has come down to us does not allow much more than speculation, for even place-names, that wonderful inheritance from several linguistic pasts, are not inexhaustive in their provision of knowledge, and there comes a point in prehistory at which even names cease to speak and only things still have a voice.

No doubt there were topographic features asking to be named, no doubt there were namers equipped and willing to name them, no doubt as a result there were names, maybe not as many as today but still enough to create a landscape; but maps were only in people's minds, and the ears that heard them in oral tradition have long been unhearing. Names, those eloquent, informative witnesses for the last 3000 years or so, at that point offer nothing but silence.

Notes

1   Donald Omand (ed.), *The Moray Book* (Edinburgh: Paul Harris, 1976).

2   Donald Matheson, *The Place-names of Elginshire* (Stirling: Eneas Mackay, 1905).

3   See W.F.H. Nicolaisen 'Names Reduced to Words?: Purpose and Scope of a Dictionary of Scottish Place-names' in *Scottish Language and Literature, Mediaeval and Renaissance* eds. Dietrich Strauss and Horst W. Drescher (Frankfurt am Main: Peter Lang, 1986) 47-54.

4   Donald Macaulay 'Place-names' in Omand, *Moray Book* 248-263.

5   W.F.H. Nicolaisen, *Scottish Place-Names: Their Study and Significance* (London: B.T. Batsford, 1976).

6   Ibid., 173-191. Also: W.F.H. Nicolaisen 'Die alteuropäischen Gewässernamen der britischen Hauptinsel' in *Beiträge zur Namenforschung* 8 (1957) 211-268; 'Great Britain and Old Europe' in *Namn och Bygd* 59 (1971) 85-105, 'Thirty Years Later: Thoughts on a Viable Concept of Old European Hydronymy' in *Festschrift für Johannes Hubschmid zum 65 Geburtstag* eds,. Otto Winkelman and Maria Braisch (Bern; Switzerland 1982) 139-149; and 'Old European Names in Britain' in *Nomina* 6 (1982) 37-42.

7   William J. Watson, *The History of the Celtic Place-Names of Scotland* (Edinburgh: William Blackwood & Sons, 1926) 407.

8   Nicolaisen, *Scottish Place-names* 152.

9   Ibid., 154.

10   Macaulay 'Place-names' 249.

11   Nicolaisen, *Scottish Place-names* 143.

12   Ibid., 164-165.

13   See, for example, Kenneth Jackson 'Angles and Britons in Northumbria and Cumbria' in *Angles and Britons* ed. Henry Lewis (Cardiff: University of Wales Press, 1963) 60-84.

14   Nicolaisen, *Scottish Place-Names* 158-159.

15   Ibid., 136-143.

16.   See Ian A. Fraser 'Norse and Celtic Place-Names Around the Dornoch Firth' in *Firthlands of Ross and Sutherland* ed. John R. Baldwin (Edinburgh: Scottish Society for Northern Studies, 1986) 23-32, esp. 29-31.

17   A name like *Surradale* is a newcomer not recorded till the nineteenth century. I am grateful to Mr. Ian Keillar, Elgin for this information.

18   Macaulay 'Place-names' 260. *Dyke* is, on the other hand, a curiosum in so far as one would not expect an English name of such importance to have been recorded in the twelfth century in this part of the country. Is it possible that an English or Scandinavian loan-word in Gaelic was employed when this name was coined?

19   This information has been provided by the late Mr. Norris Forrest, Aberdeen.

20   Watson, *Celtic Place-Names* 228-232.

21   Nicolaisen, *Scottish Place-Names*, 187.

22   Watson, *Celtic Place-Names* 115-116.

Edith Marold and Christiane Zimmermann (eds.),
Nordwestgermanisch Berlin/New York: Walter de Gruyter
(1995) 106-114

Is There a Northwest Germanic Toponymy?

I

IT may seem inappropriate or even hazardous to have the question which is at
the heart of this brief essay raised by someone whose chief interest in onomastic
research has been the study of the place-names of Scotland where, for historical
reasons, English, i.e. Anglian, toponymic items are not found until the second
quarter of the seventh century at the earliest, and place-names of Scandinavian
origin do not occur until almost two hundred years later. On the other hand, a
Scottish perspective may have certain advantages over the points of view which
have dominated the debate, such as it is, so far: (1) Its northern peripheral vision
will help to distance any argumentation in which it might get involved from the
age-old and ever-present quest for a definition of the continental regions of origin
of the Angles, Saxons and Jutes (in Scotland they came from Northumbria!).
(2) Scotland's importation and continuing creation of Norse place-names,
especially in the Northern and Western Isles where Scandinavian settlement
predates the arrival of such settlers in England by about a hundred years, may
throw much needed light on the onomastic strategies and devices, particularly
under the impact of that ubiquitous and inescapable force, analogy, employed by
colonisers in a new land (almost every Norse place-name in Scotland ascribable
to the Viking Age has an identical counterpart in Norway!). (3) Scotland cannot
possibly claim to have been part of the Northwest Germanic sphere of influence,
however defined (it was too far away and Germanic languages reached it
too late). (4) As the historical and prehistoric location of at least three Celtic
languages (Cumbric, Pictish and Gaelic) it is more than a spectator in the lively
discussion of the origins, dissemination and evolution of Celtic, a discussion

which in many respects resembles that surrounding the concept of Northwest Germanic (What is the exact relationship of Pictish and Cumbric, for example? How did the Picts get to where we find them between 200 and 800 A.D.? What are the earliest Gaelic names in Scotland?). Nevertheless, the very detachment with which the Northwest Germanic question can be viewed from north of the Tweed and west of the North Sea, while advantageous in certain respects, may well imbue it with a sort of blandness and a concomitant lack of the kind of passion which is so often at the core of fruitful debates, but perhaps that is a risk worth taking even without an artificial injection of scholarly fervour.

Another, albeit minor, drawback faced by the writer of this essay is the fact that although this piece is intended to complement the other contributions on aspects of the toponymic evidence (Fellows-Jensen, Udolph, and also Andersson) in this volume, it may well overlap or compete with them in both subject matter and methodology since the other discussions are not available to the author at the time of writing and have therefore had to be mentally reconstructed in fragmentary form from memory of the performance of the papers at the symposium and on the basis of the presenters' handouts consisting mostly of illustrative examples.[1] For this shortcoming I apologise to both the authors and the readers. Aided by the titles, however, these imperfectly remembered presentations appear to indicate with some persuasion that the approach taken in the present paper will differ sufficiently to allow it space in the same volume. Even the same evidence when filtered through different minds and subjected to different interrogations can yield very different insights, a blending of which with what is already known may well illuminate the road ahead.

II

As the title of these musings makes clear, this essay is not meant to investigate whether toponymic evidence can be used either to prove or to disprove the existence of a phase in the development of the Germanic languages which might with justification be called Northwest Germanic. The questions asked are rather: Assuming that those who, though mindful of an extra-linguistic context, claim the reality of such a stage on linguistic grounds are right, i.e. assuming that Northwest Germanic as a discernible branch of Germanic once existed, (a) did it find expression as part of its creation of familiar landscapes in a distinctive Northwest Germanic toponymy, and (b) if it can be shown to have done so, how does this toponymy support or contradict or, more neutrally, interrelate with the conclusions reached mostly as the result of investigations of phonological and morphological material? That the concept of Northwest Germanic is more than a working hypothesis finds, in this writer's opinion, convincing substantiation in

H.F. Nielsen's two studies *Old English and the Continental Germanic Languages* (Nielsen 1981) and, most forcefully, *The Germanic Languages: Origins and Early Dialectal Interrelations* (Nielsen 1989) in which he demonstrates, mainly on the basis of thirteen changes shared by North and West Germanic not only that there must have been "a primary split of Germanic into Gothic and Northwest Germanic" (Nielsen 1989: 95) but also, more importantly, that these thirteen parallels which "carry much more weight than the one phonological agreement usually associated with North and East Germanic [...] must have arisen when North and West Germanic were *one* [italics mine] dialect" (Nielsen 1989: 96).

This is not the place to rehearse the factors, in particular the innovative isoglosses, which underpin Nielsen's findings; nor is it necessary to show in detail how these overlap with or subtly differ from the conclusions reached by other scholars, such as Adamus, Antonsen, Arndt, Bahnick, Haugen, Kuhn, Makaev, Lerchner, and others although, in view of the well-known lack of temporal specificity rightly attributed to place-name evidence, it may be worth reminding ourselves that Bahnick (1973: 193) suggests that the Northwest Germanic period was brought to an end "by the stabilization of the individual dialects: Old English, Old Saxon, Old High German and Common Nordic" (quoted in Nielsen 1989: 97), and also recalling that, according to Haugen (1970: 48), "the gradual transition from Northwest Germanic to Common Scandinavian takes place in the later runic inscriptions after 500" (also quoted in Nielsen 1989: 97). These statements clearly demand that we look to a contiguous toponymic dialect associated with, in the appropriate parts of the Germanic area from Friesland to Jutland and even Norway, Northwest Germanic before the middle of the fifth century.

III

In proposing such a search I am very conscious of Nielsen's own reservations about the usefulness of lexical items which he regards as "much more unstable than phonological, morphological or syntactic ones and therefore less suitable for determining prehistoric dialectal interrelations" (Nielsen 1989: 146). I do, however, take courage from his admission that "this is not to say that lexical parallels should be completely discarded" despite his view that they "do not carry the same weight" (Nielsen: loc.cit.). It cannot be part of the quest in hand to enquire what the criteria are that are applied, in such circumstances, in the "weighting" of comparable evidence. In fact, I would submit that it is arguable that even if it can be proved that lexical parallels are indeed more lightweight, onymic, in particular toponymic, parallels may form an exception to this rule insofar as they constitute parallels within the onomastica to be compared and not within the lexica with which they may have been associated or from which they may have been derived. Looking for evidence which may permit us to posit the former existence of a Northwest Germanic toponymy is more than, and different from, a search for lexical items in the topographical sector of the lexicon which have been incorporated into place-names both as generics and as specifics, especially the former. That is to say that our search would be less than successful and our conclusions less than persuasive if we were satisfied with the discovery of a network of words that these names had once been.

Admittedly, we have to try to gain access to the toponymicon through the lexicon and we may frequently have to manufacture toponymic conclusions on the basis of lexical evidence, but in the end there will have to be more than that, mainly because names are more than just words with additional peculiar properties. The promise which names offer with respect to turning the project which I wish to propose at the conclusion of this essay from what might potentially, almost predictably, be a burlesque wild-goose-chase into a solid and profitable scholarly enterprise stems from their very nature as names which allows them, indeed practically requires them, to shed their semantic transparency on the lexical level in order to absorb in its place a great variety of contents; in a nutshell: from their having become names instead of having remained words. It is for that reason that I am confident that onymic items, especially toponymic ones with their severely spatial contents and referents and their paradoxical ability to migrate while staying put simultaneously, may turn out to be more "suitable" and less "unstable" than lexical ones that have never crossed the threshold to an onomasticon, in our attempt to establish Northwest Germanic as what Nielsen (1981: 257) calls a "macro group", if we can trace them far enough back since written documentation in Friesland, in Lower Saxony, in Schleswig-Holstein, in Jutland, in Norway, in England, and presumably also in Scotland is, on the whole, centuries later than the purported Northwest Germanic period before 500 or 450 A.D.

IV

If we can trace them far enough back ...! This is the crux of the whole matter. Our attempt to find a method through which we can achieve this is, of course, not the first response to this challenge, and to a certain extent much of the groundwork has been laid, both on the continent and in Britain. In general, the objectives of these past exercises have been different or only tangentially related; several of them have tried to address the problem of the home areas from which the Anglian, Saxon and Jutish settlers emigrated to England. Such investigations regarded the study of the relevant place-names and their elements as a means towards an end, rather than as an end in itself. Here are just some of the more recent ones:

In 1965, Wolfgang Laur, the undisputed expert on the place-names of Schleswig-Holstein (Laur 1960, 1967 and 1992), examined this very problem in a paper entitled *Ortsnamen in England und in den festländischen Stammländern der Angelsachsen* in the course of which, following a number of earlier scholars, he tried to find answers to three questions which might almost be termed paradigmatic (Laur 1965: 300):

(1) Which place-names did the Anglo-Saxons transfer to Britain from their continental homes?

(2) Which name types did they bring with them and which of these types were used in the naming process in England?

(3) How does the English toponymy, i.e. the toponymy of Anglo-Saxon origin, differ from that of the Anglo-Saxon homeland on the continent?

Sensibly skirting the pitfalls associated with the first of these questions because the number of specific, unanalysed names consciously transferred is likely to have been very small (though usually exaggerated by non-scholarly enquirers who have the recent North-American scene in mind), he concentrates on the differences in the continental and insular place-nomenclatures while acknowledging Hans Kuhn's dictum that colonisation does not automatically imply an immediate complete disruption between the homeland and the colony (Kuhn 1955: 40; also 1966: 26). For Laur, location and distribution of relevant name types, by which he means categories of names formed with the same generic, are of prime importance. Examining names in *ing*, *-set* (*sætas*), *-ton* (*-tūn*), *-ham* (*-hām*), *-þrop*, *-bōðl/-bōtl*, *-hamm* and *stead*, he rehearses several different sets of circumstances, like innovative naming in England though grounded in continental naming habits (*-sǣtan*); presence in the Saxon homeland but full flowering in England (*-tūn*); transferred from the continent but becoming particularly productive in Britain, perhaps under the influence of the Frisian and Dutch coastal area (*-hām*); roots in the Germanic migration period (*stead*), and so on. Laur also (1965: 312) emphasises that place-name types can develop independent of each other, a possibilty which is easily and therefore frequently overlooked in any enthusiastic search for connections.

1979 saw the publication of Walter Piroth's earlier Frankfurt dissertation *Ortsnamenstudien zur angelsächsischen Wanderung: Ein Vergleich von -ingas, -ingaNamen in England mit ihren Entsprechungen auf dem Festland* (Piroth 1979). According to an English summary, it was the purpose of his thesis "to provide a list of parallels between the *-ingas* folk names found in the *-ingas/-*

inga-place-names in England and those found in the names of the Continental homelands" (Piroth 1977: 27). In contrast to the more cautious Laur who concentrated on discernible differences, Piroth concludes that

> the supposition of an accidental correspondence, based on the same linguistic background of the Anglo-Saxons in their Continental homeland and in Britain, becomes less and less likely. On the contrary, we may reasonably speculate that some name transfer may have taken place [...]. (Piroth: loc.cit.)

However, the fact that, for instance, *Aldringham* (*Alrincham* 1086) in Suffolk corresponds to *Ellringen* (in *Alaringi* 892) near Blackede, *Cocking* (*Cochinges* 1086) in Sussex to *Köchingen* in Braunschweig (*Cochigge* 12-13c), or *Hucking* (*Huggingas* 1195) in Kent to *Huckingen* (*Hukengen* 1218-31) near Duisburg (Piroth 1977: 28 and 29), does not necessarily imply the transfer of actual names but rather points to the emigrants' having taken with them across the Channel certain name models that could be activated whenever the circumstances provided the right triggering device. This view is supported by John Dodgson's extensively argued proposition that the names in *-ingas, -inga-* do not belong to the earliest stratum of names given by the new settlers (Dodgson 1966 and 1967). While the name formations investigated by Piroth are therefore not the most felicitous choices for the purpose for which he had selected them (see also Nielsen 1981: 262), his inventory of names might still be considered valid evidence for his hypothesis that the continental area in which they occur may "have been the starting point of a number of Anglo-Saxon tribal units during the migration period" (Piroth 1977: 28) if, that is, much of the cross-Channel migration was indeed tribal.

A third exploration of a similar kind though much more wide-ranging than Piroth's is contained in this volume (Udolph 1995). As the title of the essay indicates – *Die Landnahme Englands durch germanische Stämme im Lichte der Ortsnamen* – place-names are again pressed into service to illuminate the settlement history, i.e. point of departure and place of arrival, of a period for which there is very little other evidence. At the time of writing, Udolph's interpretation of the corpus of names listed in his handout and his presentation of the patterns which might potentially emerge from it are not available to me but a few comments are nevertheless in order; (a) Udolph's list contains both generics and specifics (the examples quoted under *skarn* are all specifics, except for one simple name) but it can hardly be claimed that specifics carry the same weight as generics. What they convey is that there are many dirty, mucky places and that *skarn, scearn, skern, etc.* was a word (maybe a fashionable word) available to all the namers in question who had been called upon to describe such places adequately without giving offence but distinguishing a *Sharnford*, let us say, from any other kind of *ford* in the vicinity. At most, *Sharnford*, *Harbach*, *Fenstad*, and the like may have been coined or transferred as whole names in imitation of toponymic models; otherwise what we have here is correspondence on the lexical, not the onomastic level. (b) As far as the linking of *büttel* and *botl/bold/boðl* is concerned, Laur's observation (1965: 308) is well worth bearing in mind that there is no connection between them, and that, as they do not belong to the oldest stratum, they entered the respective place-nomenclatures independently. They look seductively alike but are etymologically not identical. (c) The five English names containing *-ithi-* appear to be additional to the long list of such names previously published and discussed by Udolph (1991). They make a better claim for the inclusion of English names in the substantial *-ithi-*corpus than the mere reference to Old English appellatives like *gor*, *hēse*, *hosa* and *calwe/calwa* for continental names such as *Görde*, *Heisede*, *Höst* and *Kalbe* (Udolph 1991: 140). I am still not convinced, however, that *-ithi-* was once a productive element in the toponymy of Common Germanic, simply because of the employment of cognates of Gothic *hlainē* and *laus* in West Germanic names (Udolph: loc.cit.). It is more likely that *-ithi-* is a morphological element in Northwest Germanic that reaches right back to the time immediately after the separation of Gothic from the rest.

V

It is only natural and understandable that Laur, Piroth and Udolph, and others before them, look at the English evidence as keenly interested outsiders and utilise it for their own purposes which are largely concerned with the exploration of continental problems like dating and tribal homelands. Similarly, at the northern end of the island, A.W. Brøgger (1929: 77) attributed the presence of a Norse place-name generic like *setr* to emigration from a certain part of Norway. On the other hand, the recent chief concern of the insular insiders derives from an almost diametrically opposed perspective: the legitimate quest for the oldest English names in England. Until John Dodgson (1966 and 1967; see above) spoiled the party, place-names in *-ingas* and *ingahām* were regarded as among the earliest but their absence from areas of early Anglo-Saxon archaeological remains has made such an assumption highly doubtful. Instead, the prevailing view is now that topographical rather than habitative settlement names form the bottom layer chronologically and that, according to Margaret Gelling (1984: 6; see also 1978: 126), for three main reasons:

they predominate in areas where the earliest pagan Anglo-Saxon presence is attested by archaeology, they predominate as names of parishes, and they outnumber other types in the analysis of English place-names recorded by AD 730.

The last of these three references is to a survey of *The Place-Names of the Earliest English Records* conducted by Barrie Cox in which he found the following most frequent toponymic elements before 730 (Cox 1976: 66):

- Topographical: *burna, dūn, ēg, feld, ford, lēah;* possibly *hamm.*
- Habitative: *burh, ceaster, hām, hām-stede,* and *wīc.*
- District-name-forming: *gē.*
- Group-name-forming: *-ingas(-ingum* dat. pl.), *-inga.*

Soon after 730 topographical elements like *brōc, hyll, wella, worð* begin to appear in the written record in greater numbers.

What this list of name elements teaches us more than anything else, it seems, is, first, that it is probably a mistake to expect only one kind of name to have been given exclusively in the earliest settlement phase and, second, that it is not necessary for the name of a natural feature to be transferred secondarily to a settlement – for instance, a farm – but that a human habitation can directly be given the name of the topographical feature with which it is outwardly associated. This would explain the preponderance of topographical settlement names not only in the early stages of English settlement history but also in subsequent phases as Margaret Gelling's study of *Names in the Landscape* has demonstrated so vividly (Gelling 1984). This is also true of Scandinavian settlement in Scotland between the ninth and the thirteenth century where, apart from personal associations like ownership, the combination of two topographic terms to provide visual orientation was the most common way of creating names of human habitations (Nicolaisen 1994: 45).

VI

How does all this throw light on the question which this essay set out to answer: Is there a Northwest Germanic toponymy? What does all this cross-Channel or cross-North-Sea diffusion of place-names and *Landnahme* stuff have to do with the possibility of tracing at least remnants or echoes of a more or less unified, though not uniform, Northwest Germanic place-nomenclature, i.e. of a network of names which in many of its types and elements was shared by all Germanic people and their dialects except the Goths and Gothic and perhaps some other East Germanic linguistic tribes? Curiously, the key to meeting this challenge might again be found in England, and by extension in Scotland. In her chapter on the names of "Hills, Slopes and Ridges" (Gelling 1984: 124-187), Margaret Gelling discusses, among many others, the elements Old English (OE) *hlith* 'slope' (1984: 165-166), as in *Lyth Hall* (Shropshire), *Lenborough* (Buckinghamshire) and *Lytham* (Lancashire), and Old Norse (ON) *hlith* 'slope' (1984: 166-167), as in *Lythe* (Yorkshire), *Kelleth* (Westmorland) and *Litherland* (Lancashire). Since early spellings do not usually make a distinction between these two elements, scholars tend to distinguish them according to modern vowel quantity (sometimes), geographical location of the names in question and, when appropriate, the linguistic affinities of the other elements in compound names. Inevitably, there are overlaps and uncertainties in this sort of situation, and it is not surprising therefore that there are nine names in the West Riding of Yorkshire for which either element is considered possible (Smith 1962: 205; see also Smith 1956: 252-253); in five of these the ambiguous element is a generic in a compound name – *Gatecliff, Langcliffe, Risplith, Runley, Hanlith* – and one, *Lythe*, is a simplex. Only *Lythe* and *Hanlith*, as well as *Kirkleatham* and *Upleatham*, are included in Fellows-Jensen (1972: 78). Obviously, both these cognates have reached England through immigration, one from West Germanic, the other from North Germanic territory on the continent. The respective dates of their arrival lie less than five hundred years apart, and only a slightly longer time span separates the hypothetical break-up of Northwest Germanic into its constituents and the confusing application of these two toponymic elements in, let us say, the West Riding of Yorkshire but undoubtedly also elsewhere. It seems possible for that reason to turn the onomastic historian's dilemma into a positive asset. If it is fair to assume that two cognate terms with similar pronunciation and identical meaning, one of them Old English, i.e. West Germanic, and the other Old Norse, i.e. North Germanic, reached England as productive toponymic elements and not just as lexical items, then it is more than likely that they were also toponymically productive in their continental areas of origin at the time of their departure and, retrospectively, in earlier phases of an undifferentiated, or only minimally differentiated, Northwest Germanic toponymic dialect. This would be true regardless of whether such elements now overlap geographically in England as etymological alternatives or not. That ON *hlið* was productive in Scandinavia during the Viking Age is easily demonstrated by the many names in Oluf Rygh's multi-volume *Norske Gaardnavne* (see Rygh 1898: 65 for a listing). I am unfortunately not familiar with the situation in Anglian, Saxon, Jutish and Frisian territory on the continent.

A comparison of the indices of Gelling (1984: 256-326) and Rygh (1898: 41-88) shows that OE *hlið* and ON *hlið* are not the only cognate pair productive in the West and North Germanic toponymica, whether they occur together in

England (or Scotland) or not. Some others are: OE *ēa*, ON *á;* OE *æcer*, ON *akr;* OE *bæce, bece*, ON *bekkr;* OE *botm, bothm*, ON *botn;* OE *burh*, ON *borg;* OE *celde*, ON *kelda;* OE *clif;* ON *klif;* OE *dæl*, ON *dalr;* OE *ecg*, ON *egg;* OE *ēg*, ON *øy;* OE *flēot*, ON *fljót;* OE *hām*, ON *heimr;* OE *hēah*, ON *haugr;* OE *hæth, hāth*, ON *heiðr;* OE *hol*, ON *hol;* OE *holt*, ON *holt;* OE *heafod*, ON *hǫfuð;* OE *hūs*, ON *hús;* OE *lād*, ON *laða, hlaða;* OE *land*, ON *land;* OE *mōr*, ON *mor;* OE *moss*, ON *mósi;* OE *næss, ness*, ON *nes;* OE *rod, rodu, roð*, ON *ruð;* OE *hrycg*, ON *ryggr, hryggr;* OE *sand*, ON *sandr;* OE *set*, ON *setr;* OE *stede*, ON *staðr*, pl. *staðir;* OE *stig*, ON *stigr;* OE *sǣr*, ON *sǽr;* OE *þrop*, ON *þorp;* OE *þwit*, ON *þveit* (ablaut); OE *wǣd*, ON *vað;* OE *wæter*, ON *vatn;* OE *widu*, ON *viðr.* A diligent search would undoubtedly produce many more pairs of this kind.

It cannot be the purpose of this paper to fill in the gaps between the extreme northern and western branches of Northwest Germanic; it must suffice to add some which the place-nomenclature of Schleswig-Holstein provides: *au/aa, bek, burg, dorf, fleet, heim/hem, hus/haus, rade/rode, seet,* and *stedt* (Laur 1967: 219-222), from its German and North-Frisian stock. What is so significant about the toponymies which complement or collide with each other in England is that they presuppose a connecting centre, on the one hand, and a common ancestry, on the other. It would be absurd to regard all these terms purely as lexical items which could be employed in the naming process whenever required; they must have been part of a Northwest Germanic onomasticon, and not just of a lexicon.

VII

Let me try to weave these various strands together to see if any theoretical patterns emerge that can become blueprints for scholarly action: what the material and thoughts just paraded hint at is the existence of a Northwest Germanic toponymy from which the earliest strata, and not infrequently also later ones, are descended in the individual dialects. In order to establish its nature and structure, it appears desirable to shift the direction of previous research by looking from England to the continent instead of the other way round, thus combining the English quest for the earliest names in the island with the continental preoccupation with regions of origin in the period of the great migrations. Helpful in this respect would also be a change in emphasis from the intensive study of habitative names to a comprehensive survey of the kind of topographic names, whether also applied to habitations or not, which Margaret Gelling has so successfully studied (Gelling 1984) and which predominate not only in Cox's findings (Cox 1976) from which one could add to the ones already cited (see above) *beorg, brōc, celde, denu, ēa, flēot, hæð, heafod, hlid, holt, hyll, hyrst, (ge)lad, mersc, nos, ofer/ufer, ora, wald, widu* and *wudu*, but also in the

Old English/Old Norse pairs compiled from the English and Norwegian place-nomenclatures, sometimes involving the same words. There is a high degree of probability that the Northwest Germanic toponymy, like the earliest strata of the English and possibly also of the Norwegian place-name inventories, contained a high proportion of topographic names and it is therefore through the search for common ancestors of such names and name types that we will get closest to the goal of our quest.

Bibliography

Bahnick, Karen. 1973: *The Determination of Stages in the Historical Development of the Germanic Languages by Morphological Criteria*. The Hague.

Cox, Barrie. 1976: *The Place-Names of the Earliest English Records*. In: *The English Place-Name Society*, Journal 8 (1975-1976), pp. 12-66.

Dodgson, John M. 1966: *The Significance of the Distribution of the English Place-Names in -ingas, -inga in South-East England*. In: *Medieval Archaeology* 10, pp.1-29.

Dodgson, John M. 1967: *The -ing- in English Place-Names like Birmingham and Altrincham*. In: *Beiträge zur Namenforschung*. N.F. 2, 3, pp. 221-245.

Dodgson, John M. 1967: *Various Forms of Old English -ing- in English Place-Names*. In: *Beiträge zur Namenforschung*. N.F. 2, 4, pp. 325-396.

Dodgson, John M. 1968: *Various English Place-Name Formations Containing Old English -ing*. In: *Beiträge zur Namenforschung*. N.F. 3, 2, pp. 141-189.

Fellows-Jensen, Gillian. 1972: *Scandinavian Settlement Names in Yorkshire*. Copenhagen.

Gelling, Margaret. 1978: *Signposts to the Past: Place-names and the history of England*. London.

Gelling, Margaret. 1984: *Place-Names in the Landscape*. London.

Haugen, Einar. 1970: *The Language History of Scandinavia: A Profile of Problems*. In: Hreinn Benediktsson (ed.): *The Nordic Languages and Modern Linguistics*. Reykjavik.

Kuhn, Hans. 1955: *Zur Gliederung der germanischen Sprachen*. In: *Zeitschrift für deutsches Altertum und deutsche Literatur 86*, pp. 1-47.

Kuhn, Hans. 1966: *Die Ortsnamen der Kolonien und das Mutterland*. In: Blok, D.P. (ed.): *Proceedings of the Eighth International Congress of Onomastic Sciences*. The Hague, pp. 260-265.

Laur, Wolfgang. 1960: *Die Ortsnamen in Schleswig-Holstein*. Gottorfer Schriften VI. Schleswig.

Laur, Wolfgang. 1965: *Ortsnamen in England und in den festländischen Stammländern der Angelsachsen*. In: *Namenforschung: Festschrift zum 75. Geburtstag von Adolf Bach*. Heidelberg, pp. 300-312.

Laur, Wolfgang. 1967: *Historisches Ortsnamenlexikon von Schleswig-Holstein*. Gottorfer Schriften VIII. Schleswig.

Laur, Wolfgang. 1992: *Historisches Ortsnamenlexikon von Schleswig-Holstein*. 2. völlig veränderte und erweiterte Auflage. Neumünster.

Nicolaisen, W.F.H. 1994: *Viking Place-names in Scotland*. In: *NORNA-rapporter* 154, pp. 31-49.

Nielsen, Hans Frede. 1981: *Old English and the Continental Germanic Languages: A Survey of Morphological and Phonological Interrelations*. Innsbruck.

Nielsen, Hans Frede. 1989: *The Germanic Languages: Origins and Early Dialectal Interrelations*. Tuscaloosa, Alabama.

Piroth, Walter. 1977: *Studies on Place-Names and Anglo-Saxon Migration: A Comparison of -ingas, -inga-Names in England with their Parallels on the European Mainland*. In: *Nomina* 1, 2, pp. 27-31.

Piroth, Waiter. 1979: *Ortsnamenstudien zur angelsächsischen Wanderung: Ein Vergleich von -ingas, -inga- Namen in England mit ihren Entsprechungen auf dem europäischen Festland*. Wiesbaden.

Rygh, Oluf. 1898: *Norske Gaardnavne: Forord og Indledning*. Kristiania.

Smith, A.H. 1956: *English Place-Name Elements*. Part One. English Place-Name Society, Vol.25. Cambridge.

Smith, A.H. 1962: *The Place-Names of the West Riding of Yorkshire*. Vol.7. English Place-Name Society, Vol.36. Cambridge.

Udolph, Jürgen. 1991: *Die Ortsnamen auf -ithi*. In: Eichler, Ernst (Hg.): *Probleme der älteren Namenschichten*. Beiheft 32. Beiträge zur Namenforschung, N.F. Heidelberg.

Udolph, Jürgen. 1994: *Namenkundliche Studien zum Germanenproblem*. Berlin.

Udolph, Jürgen. 1995: *Die Landnahme Englands durch germanische Stämme im Lichte der Ortsnamen*. In: Marold, Edith und Zimmermann, Christiane (Hg.): *Nordwestgermanisch*. Berlin-New York, pp. 232-269.

Note

1   Both Dr Fellows-Jensen and Dr Udolph kindly made their papers available to me at a later date. After reading both of them, I am glad to say that this essay may still be legitimately regarded as complememtary rather than repetitive.

Ernst Eichler, et al. (eds.), *Name Studies:*
An International Handbook of Onomastics **1**
(Berlin/New York: Walter de Gruyter 1995) 384-392.

Name and Appellative

1. Introduction

As the copula "and" between the two key terms in the title of this article indicates, the discussion which follows will not be exclusively concerned with juxtaposing any concepts that may be claimed to lie behind them although that point of view will, of course, have to be prominently considered because it has dominated scholarly perception of their relationship for so long. Nor will this exploration of one of the most complex and vexing verbal expressions of two closely associated grammatical categories be capable of reaching conclusions which might be generally applicable to all language families. Even two cognate languages like English and German whose vocabulary feeds largely on the same sources show certain differences, particularly in their surface features, in the treatment of these two notions. Far from being intended to produce universally accepted or acceptable principles, this account will be chiefly devoted to the problems as they present themselves to users of English, since even translations from other languages involve the risk of misunderstanding and unwarranted assumptions. As this examination will demonstrate, a heading "Name and Word" might have been preferable from an English point of view because it would have pointed up the dilemma on the horns of which we find ourselves impaled (Nicolaisen 1985a), more accurately or, at least, more persuasively.

2. Terminology

2.1 Brief Terminological History

Before presenting in some detail the confusing current situation, a brief look at the history behind the present terminological disarray may help us to understand why, in English at least, the lexical field to which *noun*, *name*, and their associates belong is either overloaded or ill-defined in its constellations. In this connection it is worth remembering that the very word *name* has a genealogy which goes right back to the beginnings of the language family of which English is one of the descendants, and perhaps even beyond. Not only do Old English *nama* and *noma*, as well as Old Frisian *nama* and *noma*, Old Saxon *namo*, Old High German *namo*, Old Norse *nafn* and *namn*, and Gothic *namo*, presuppose a Germanic *namōn*, but Latin *nōmen* and Greek *ónoma* attest it for the classical world of the Mediterranean. In addition, there are cognates on record in Sanskrit, Avestic, Tokharian A and B, Old Slavonic, Old Prussian, Armenian, Albanian, Hittite, Old Irish, and Early Welsh, pointing to an Indo-European *en(o)mn-* and *(o)nomn-*, and *nōmn* as the common root and source for its variations (Pokorny 1949, 321; Onions 1966, 602; Kluge 1960, 501-502). There is therefore no doubt that the notion of name in the sense of "particular designation" is familiar to speakers of all Indo-European languages and must have been known to their common ancestor. Indeed, if Finno-Ugric *näm*, *nam*, *nem*, and *namma*, and Hungarian *név*, all meaning "name", are not very early loan-words – and the most competent etymologists seem to think that they are not – the idea of linguistically namable identity is likely to have even greater antiquity. It is not surprising therefore that the compilers of etymological dictionaries have treated this lexical family with reverence, terming it "an ancient and widespread word" or "one of the most archaic and honorable words still alive among us today" (Kluge 1960, 502). Naming and using names, identity and recognition, are consequently proven human traits: *homo nominans* shows himself or herself to be no recent interloper, and students of names therefore concern themselves with the very core of human existence and survival.

If English had solely inherited its genetic descendant of that lexical family, the word *name*, recorded from the eighth-century Beowulf "*is mīn nama*", the study of names and of their linguistic, especially grammatical, handling might well have been much simpler because terminologically less complex, perhaps also less exciting. However, cultural flotsam and jetsam washed onto the intellectual shores of Britain in the course of centuries have deprived onomastics of such dull simplicity, for at least three other Indo-European languages have deposited their versions of the same word, in varying contexts and at varying times, in the vocabulary of English, particularly in the language of grammar and the ways in which it classifies its words.

The most influential of these donated terms has obviously been Greek *ónoma*, not so much perhaps because it has become the basis for the internationally acknowledged designation of the discipline of onomastics "the study of names", but rather because of its indirect effectiveness as the ideological forebear, though genetic sister, of Latin *nomen* in those grammatical treatises which have shaped our thinking in the western world. I have particularly in mind the Latin grammar of Priscian (c 500 AD) which was largely modelled on the Greek system taken over from Dionysius Thrax (2nd cent. BC) by Apollonius Dyscolus (2nd cent. AD). *Ónoma* having started out in nontechnical usage exactly like English *name*, Plato (c 429-347 BC) had been the first to recognise it as one of the two major components of the sentence, contrasting it with *rhema*, or topic versus comment. Chrysippus (c 280-207 BC) who is quoted by Diogenes Laertius (3rd cent. AD) appears to have been the first to have divided *ónoma* into two classes, on the one hand *ónoma* itself which we might translate as *proper noun*, and on the other *prosēgoria*, our *common noun*. A similar distinction was made by the Stoics who established, in the Latin terminology of Priscian, five parts of speech: *nomen, appellatio, verbum, pronomen sive articulum, conjunctio*. In this set, *nomen* represents the 'proper noun' and *appellatio* the 'common noun'. In the final Greek system, *ónomata* and *prosēgoriai* were merged again into a single *ónoma* class, whereas for Dionysius Thrax "the Stoic *ónoma* or 'proper noun' and *proségoria* 'common noun' are regrouped as subclasses within the *ónoma* class". This, then is Priscian's *nomen* which is further subdivided into adjective and noun (Robins 1966; Michael 1970; Algeo 1973).

The word *noun* itself is not recorded in English until John of Trevisa uses it in 1398, and almost a hundred years later, in 1483, it is still glossed as *nomen* (Oxford English Dictionary (OED), s. v.). Having its origin in Old French *nun, num*, it is, of course, also an indirect descendant of Latin *nomen*. Since the end of the fourteenth century, then, English has had the possibility of distinguishing between *noun* and *name* as categories, but appears to have made only sporadic use of it, early English grammarians preferring instead to follow classical tradition and to preface either of the two terms with the epithets *common* and *proper*, thus making the same distinction between *noun* and *name* through the confusing and largely synonymous pairs of *common noun* and *proper noun*, on the one hand, and *common name* and *proper name*, on the other, or insisting on the contrasts *name–appellative*, as suggested by Priscian's word class system (Priscian 1961). The ways in which parts of speech are classified by the early English grammarians are full of uncertainties, diversities and inconsistencies (Michael 1970, 201); many of them define both nouns and substantives as names (for example, Lowe 1737: "The name of a thing is a Noun"). See also Herndon (1970, 55): "A noun is typically defined as the name of a person, place, or thing"; such a statement confirms the continuing survival of that heritage, as does the Oxford Dictionary of English Etymology in its glossing of noun: "(gram.) name of a person or thing" (Onions 1966: 616).

Quite apart from the philosophical implications of the notion of *name* which cannot be part of this discussion, the linguistic import of this usage is less than satisfying, not only from the point of view of modern theory but also in the context of modern dictionary making, as will be demonstrated below. What is, however, even more critical is that the situation, as established and perpetuated in the systems of classification most influential in their impact on the thinking of grammarians, has left the name scholar without a sound base from which to begin the construction of a "theory of names" or, less ambitiously, of a "theory about names" (Nicolaisen 1985b). If the linguistic dilemma is frustrating, its onomastic counterpart is crippling.

2.2 Alternative Model

It may not be idle hypothesising to speculate at this point whether there is still a possibility of getting out of the old grooves in an attempt to plough fresh furrows. Strangely, the potential "solution" may not lie so much in an imaginative leap forward as in a turning back of the wheel of history, for the system which would adequately take care of the major contingency has been known for over two millennia. Unfortunately, it has not had the influence on grammatical reasoning which it would have deserved and which would have greatly clarified our thinking many centuries ago. In this writer's view, we would do well to develop further a distinction which Marcus Terentius Varro (116-27 BC) made in his *De Lingua Latina* (Varro 1951) between *vocabula*, for which he cites Latin *scutum* "shield" and *gladium* "sword", and *nomina* which he illustrates by Romulus and Remus. These, as well as *provocabula* and *pronomina*, he calls the four *partes appellandi*, providing therefore the possibility of a term like *appellation* or *appellative* as the umbrella term for both *vocabula* which, with a little semantic license, can be translated as "word", and *nomen* "name". This would not only be helpful in recognising the existence of an onomasticon "a name vocabulary", as opposed to but also linked with a lexicon "a word vocabulary" but would also facilitate our awareness and analysis of onomastic dialects (Nicolaisen 1980) and socio-onomastic registers (Nicolaisen 1985d), in a variety of manifestations.

Even with these extended benefits, however, a subdivision of appellatives (or appellations) into words and names, without the employment of the epithets proper or common and without reference to the term *noun* (which would, or could, remain a lexical sub-category, though challenged in some quarters by *substantive*), would make much more economical use of the available English lexical resources and fresh thinking at least a possibility; it would also, in one of

nouns and names (Nicolaisen 1985: 64-67). Of the five dictionaries surveyed (American Heritage 1969; Webster 1973; Oxford 1975; Collins 1978; Chambers 1983), Webster's New Collegiate Dictionary most consistently includes names and persons only if they have also been transferred to lexical usage; as a corollary to this policy, it also has the largest number of lower case entries giving items of onomastic origin full noun status. In the other four dictionaries, small initials are rare; in those instances in which they are included, the American Heritage Dictionary almost invariably displays as its main entry for the items in question the name of the person or place with which it is linked, adding several names which do not occur in the other dictionaries and which have no apparent bearing on lexical usage. The remaining three dictionaries vary in selection and emphasis, with Collins least inclined to include names. In a way, the two extremes – Webster's and American Heritage – offer the fewest problems since lower-case nouns of whatever origin and capitalised names conform to the expected norm in modern English.

The inclusion of a large number of names in a dictionary is an important editorial decision, adding a limited onomasticon to an extensive lexicon, but once such a decision has been taken, the resulting toponymic and anthroponymic entries can be honestly distinguished both graphemically and semantically. More problematic are the entries which clearly indicate the onomastic provenance of a noun by retaining an initial capital, thus giving them dual or undecided status as both names and words. *Chablis* is an obvious example, since all five dictionaries list it only as the designation of "a very dry white Burgundy wine made at Chablis ..." (Chambers 1983, s. v.), but not as a place-name in its own right; similarly, most of the other "onomastic nouns" refer to some kind of product associated with a place or person, like *Chantilly* (lace) and *Chippendale* (furniture). Their onomastic rather than lexical derivation – and this applies also when they are presented with lower-case initials – is made obvious when they are explained by reference to places where this particular wine grows or lace was first made, or to the maker and designer of a special kind of furniture at a certain time, whereas words (nouns, appellatives) are followed by their lexical etymologies. There is, of course, no point in etymologising the eponymous places or persons involved, just as the entries presented as names differ in their definitions from those presented as words. The "meaning" of these names (or, as we will see, rather their "content") lives in their denotative, singularising function, not in their connotative inclusiveness. Although they depend for their communicative potential on a nucleus of stable, public content, their socio-onomastic meaning may differ considerably in extent and emphasis depending on the user. Any additional private content cannot be sufficiently abstracted or generalised for inclusion in a dictionary. In neither their public nor their private function do etymologies have any role to play.

4. Of Meaning and Function

The divergent treatment applied by dictionary makers to words and names (or to appellatives and names, in the jargon of the accepted terminology) is a practical reflection of the realisation that names, whether one accords them primarily linguistic status or not, have properties which are not shared by words. The problem is how to discern and articulate them. As one attractive way out of this dilemma, John Algeo in his excellent monograph entitled On Defining the Proper Name, very sensibly suggests that much depends on the level on which the seemingly conflicting terminology is used, and he therefore makes the following distinctions: "... on the orthographic level, there are ORTHOGRAPHIC NAMES or CAPITALISED WORDS versus UNCAPITALISED WORDS; on the morphosyntactic level, there are PROPER NOUNS versus COMMON NOUNS; on the referential level, there are SINGULAR TERMS versus GENERAL TERMS; on the semantic level, there are PROPER NAMES or simply NAMES versus COMMON NAMES or APPELLATIVES" (Algeo 1973: 13). What is worrying about his pluralistic terminology, however, is the observation that the term *name* (or *proper name*) only comes into its own on the semantic level, even here finding itself set up in contradistinction to appellatives (or common names)! Are we to infer from this that any one onomastic item we study – *Scotland*, let us say, both as a place-name and as a surname – is orthographically a capitalised word, morphosyntactically a proper noun, referentially a singular term, and semantically a proper name. Does not this nagging confusion and profusion arise from a perceived inability to maintain conceptually the discrete integrity of an onomastic item on all these levels by refusing to call it a name under all these circumstances? Instead of running "the risk of hypostatizing a linguistic fiction" (Algeo 1973: 13), why not assume that there is a "linguistic fact", called *name*, which looks like a capitalized word in English orthography (but not in German, for example, where all nouns are capitalised, too), is often formed and behaves in many respects syntactically like a noun, is usually definite, particular, or singular in its reference (though not unique), and has onomastic meaning (or content) rather than lexical meaning. On all these levels, and normally on several or even all of them simultaneously, the name functions in the speech act of identification which is the prerequisite for the speech act of recognition.

In the end, however, it all boils down to socio-onomastic usage (Nicolaisen 1984) and therefore to meaning and function, two aspects of the act of naming, its product the name, and the employment of that product, processes which are frequently confused. Everything else is language specific, especially if one adds notable distinctions in pronunciation (*búrnside* vs. *Burnside*) and spelling (*tailor* vs. *Taylor*) to Algeo's list.

4.1 The Question of Meaning

The question whether names mean in the way that words mean has been central to most discussions of the relationship between names and words (appellatives) for hundreds, if not thousands, of years. It found its extreme answer in Sir Alan Gardiner's dictum: "The purest of proper names are wholly arbitrary and totally without significance", although he admits that "the fact that ... names [like Smith and Brown] have some significance does detract a little, but only a little, from their purity" (Gardiner 1954, 19). Presumably what is at issue here when Gardiner speaks of "significance" is the lexical meaning of a name or the meaning it may have had as a word before it was pressed into onomastic service. If this is so, then the reaction provoked by his statement has to be that lexical meaninglessness (or lack of descriptive potential) is not a condition sine qua non of onomastic "purity"; it is, on the other hand, frequently an outstanding characteristic of names so that semantic transparency is more often than not only established after a number of devious manoeuvres requiring special knowledge and methodological approaches. Whether the search for meaningfulness on the lexical level is always desirable or helpful, is an open question; such a quest is, however, always bound to reduce a name to the word it once was. Thus the attempt to answer the question "What does such and such a name mean (or what is its significance)?", i.e. the etymologising of a name, is the process by which lexical meaning is added to, or takes the place of the onomastically meaningful. It is a purely linguistic process which the name scholar may use as the beginning but certainly not as the sole end of his or her researches and enquiries (Nicolaisen 1976, 145). Semantic opacity does not detract from the onomastic essence of a name, nor does it in any way prevent it from functioning effectively as a name when it performs what Searle has called "the speech act of identifying reference" (Searle 1969, 174). Indeed, semantic transparency is not expected of a name in our western cultures, and when we become aware of it, it can be quite baffling and unsettling. One might argue that, in order to function well in their onomastic capacity as identifiers, names cannot be completely without what Gardiner calls "significance", and it would be difficult as well as unnecessary to refute such an argument, as long as names do not have to be (although they sometimes are) "significant" on the lexical level. Instead this required "significance" might be termed "onomastic meaning", or, in order to avoid confusion, "name content", translating the useful German term *Nameninhalt* (Solmsen 1922, 5; Pulgram

1954, 23). In its most severe form, one might express this contrast in the formula: Words (= appellatives) must have meaning in order to function, names must have content. In this respect, lexical meaning if transparent or lexical etymology if ascertainable may contradict or be completely unrelated to the content of an onomastic item – somebody called *Smith* may be a baker, *Fiona* (from Gaelic *fionn* "white") may be a girl with a dark complexion, *Cambridge* may be on the Charles River, and *Perth* may be a city (rather than a thicket). In extension of the underlying principle at work here, this process may also apply to intra-onomastic shifts so that one kind of name may become another kind of name – a person may bear the place-name *Washington*, a ship may be called *Queen Mary* or *Arundel Castle*, a horse may be given the name *Pinocchio*, and one may live in *Dallas* (a Scottish place-name that after becoming a surname turned into a place-name again).

4.1.1 Longevity of Names

One important consequence of the fact that names can and do function without lexical meaning is their potential longevity. Whereas words (appellatives) must be semantically transparent in order to be used appropriately and competently, names can be, and often are, completely opaque semantically, can be empty shells waiting to be filled with onomastic content. They are therefore not only capable of surviving the death of the words that went into their making initially, but also the demise of the very language that coined them. After certain acoustic and visual adjustments, they can become embedded in another language and sometimes in more than one. For this reason, they tend to be important raw material for the study of linguistic stratification and of the earlier stages of individual languages. They speak at times when words (appellatives) are silent. In parenthesis, it should be noted that names can also complete the circle by becoming words again – a *balaclava* is a helmet or headgear, a *mosel* a wine, an *ohm* a unit of electrical resistance.

4.2 Onomastic Fields

It has sometimes been claimed that all names are "isolates" the analysis of which cannot produce any patterns. This is a mistaken conclusion, for names, despite their individuating function, do not exist in isolation; quite the contrary, they are part of textured structures in which they hone each other in mutual interdependence. They belong to a variety of discrete onomastic "fields" (Moser 1957 and 1958; Fleischer 1962; Nicolaisen 1982). The suggestion of, and successful search for, the concept of an "onomastic field" presupposes the acceptance of the notion that, in addition to a workable lexicon or repertoire of words, all speakers of any language have and use a discrete onomasticon or repertoire of names (Nicolaisen 1978) that is separate from, but by no means completely without links with, the vocabulary, past and present. It further requires recognition of the fact that, apart from potential dialects (Nicolaisen 1980) and idiolects, the user of such onomastica will display different levels of competence in their onomastic range, their precision of usage, and in the act of naming. Onomastica, in general, and personal name repertoires in particular, tend to be culture bound. Their actual articulation – their phonological realisation, for example, or their syntactic rules – is often language-specific. But perhaps the most important point to remember is that, since the major difference between words and names lies in their semantic characteristics and in their function, it is not likely that a concept of "field", which has been found helpful in the investigation of the interdependence of connotative words displaying lexical meaning, can automatically, and without considerable modification, be extended to an examination of the patterning of denotative names displacing onomastic meaning (or having content). There is, however, also no reason why the "field" concept cannot be applied to onomastic circumstances and requirements a priori. The concept of "onomastic field" was first pioneered by the German scholar Wilhelm Will who introduced it to the onomastic sciences because he saw "the place-names as a whole as a large 'linguistic' field on which, in continuous reciprocal action between names and appellatives, new conceptual and morphological materials are employed" (Will 1943: 237). As is to be expected, Will's original definition has over the years undergone a number of changes, not all of which, however, have led to an acceptable articulation of what an "onomastic" field actually is, mainly because of their preoccupation with lexically meaningful items and because they have neglected an essential ingredient in the determination of such a concept, particularly in toponymy, i.e. their spatial dimension, especially in its circumscribed realisation as "region" (Nicolaisen 1982: 214).

Place-names structure our immediate landscape, as personal names structure our immediate society, but both fields are open beyond these immediate boundaries. Since we know so little about the extent and nature of such fields, the compilation of a large number of name repertoires, both of individual name users and of speech communities in which they live, is a very strong desideratum. This leads to the even more important consideration that it is impossible to lay bare – to discover – onomastic fields without close attention to the geographical features or persons who bear the names in question. Rudolf Šrámek has said that in the act of naming the relationship between the name giver and the reality to be named comes consciously into play (Šrámek 1972/73: 63). This statement is probably even truer when applied to the act of using a name, and therefore to the competent employment of a name as part of an onomasticon. George R. Stewart's penetrating question "What is named?" (Stewart 1943) has consequently to be followed by an enquiry into "What names are used?", by individuals or by speech communities (or should these be called "onomastic communities"?). Obviously, there is bound to be a considerable difference between active name usage and a more extensive passive name knowledge. There will also be limited or more expansive repertoires, but whatever the scope, Šrámek's dictum still stands that "Ein Name ist ... immer systemtragend" (Šrámek 1972/73: 74). Indeed, that landscape out there is structured for us through the place-names we know; that society round us is systematised for us through the personal names we have acquired. Anonymity may be permissible but namelessness is not.

Jost Trier claimed that behind each "lexical field" there is a "conceptual field" (Trier 1931: 1). Analogously, we may suggest that behind or parallel to each "onomastic field", each field of *nomina*, there is a "field of named items", of *nominata*, whose constellation locates each *nomen* in its field. It follows from this that the characteristics of these named items, of these *nominata*, not just inform but form the contents of the names, are their meaning. There is no *nomen* without a *nominatum*, and when we engage in the "speech act of identifying reference" (Searle 1969: 174), i.e. when we use names, we do not perform an isolated deictic act but select from a patterned, structured nomenclature, and whatever denotative name we use is delineated and shaped in its content by the contents of other names which we know but do not use on that occasion. The more content a name has for us, the better we know it, the richer its associations and relations in a "field" are likely to be. This is not to say that we must have a working knowledge of the whole nomenclature; a much spottier competence is fortunately quite enough. In order to use a name or a set of names precisely, or rather felicitously (for precision is only one aspect of felicity), we must, however, have a thorough knowledge of its content. Through "onomastic fields" (constituted by names almost regardless of their linguistic affinities, lexical meaning, or morphological makeup), then, we structure the world around us, overwhelm it, harness it – one is almost tempted to say "create" it – in the thought processes of the human mind. *Homo nominans* turns the threatening wilderness into a beneficent habitat which makes survival of body and mind possible.

5. Analogical Naming

In a sense, the binary opposition of lexical meaning and onomastic content and, by implication, of word (appellative) and name, is too simplistic if it is taken to exclude ambiguities that straddle the boundary between the two categories. This becomes clear when we look closely at colonial naming or naming in new territory ingeneral, whether it be in the parts of Scotland settled by Scandinavians or in the New World.

5.1 American Name Transfers

In the latter part of the world, semantically unanalysed name transfers from the eastern side of the Atlantic abound, usually for commemorative or nostalgic reasons. Such names, however, are later also transplanted within the country in the course of the westward movement of exploration and settlement. A special case in this respect are the cultural transfers in the "classical belt" (Stewart 1945, 185), like *Marathon, Homer, Rome, Ithaca,* or *Troy,* which Zelinsky has studied extensively and which, to borrow a phrase from the introductory sentence of his article, meant in their time "that the United States is the latter-day embodiment of the virtues and ideals of ancient Greece and Rome" (Zelinsky 1967, 463), or in Stewart's words, spoke "of ancient glory renewed" (Stewart 1945, 18), in the spirit of the post- and anti-British Classical Revival. Such names exist only as names and are nothing but names. That they may have been words once, in Greek or in some other Mediterranean language, is of no consequence in this context. They may be significant ingredients of the cultural, social, political, local history of a region, but are hardly ever part of its linguistic history, and it is in this realm of transfers that the methodological distance between etymological research and onomastic enquiry is particularly noticeable.

5.2 Scandinavian Names in Scotland

Undoubtedly, such unanalysed name transfers also occurred from Norway to Scotland during the period of Scandinavian settlement in the Northern and Western Isles and on the adjacent mainland, between the ninth and thirteenth centuries. As an alternative mode of naming in unfamiliar territory, the creation of new names from a suitable, in many instances traditional, word stock must also have been widespread, thus continuously transferring items from a lexicon to an onomasticon, i.e. from a vocabulary of words to a vocabulary of names. As most of those new names were compounds morphologically, both their generics and their specifics were selected from available appellatives practically all of which would have been used before and continued to be used in the homeland, although sometimes semantic shifts might have been needed to satisfy the requirements of the new habitat (Nicolaisen 1985c). Analogy is the dominating force in such situations (Nicolaisen 1991), and there can be little doubt that most of the names contributed by Scandinavians to the Scottish place-nomenclature were coined in this fashion, i.e. by lexically meaningful appellatives becoming onomastically contentful names. In addition to the commemorative or nostalgic transfer of actual names from the homeland and the creation of names from familiar items in the topographical sector of the lexicon, there was, however, a third way of naming places through the analogical application of name models or "names off-the-peg", so to speak. This recreative process would consist of the giving of types of ready-made names, without any specific reference to or connection with any actual, locatable names in Norway, like *Sandvík* (not lexically *sand* + *vík*) for a sandy bay, or *Ørfirisey* (not lexically *ørfir(is)* + *ey* for an island cut off at high tide but connected to another island or the mainland at low tide (Nicolaisen 1978: 43–47; see also Dalberg 1985). Such name models which would have formed part of the mental baggage of the emigrants and would have appealed to their conservative and imitative tendencies (Nicolaisen 1987) are obviously onomastic in origin but nevertheless contain certain appellative features, including almost always semantic transparency. It has to be assumed that they form a much richer source for the naming process than has so far been thought.

6. The Question of Function

As the discussion of the "meaning" of names and words has shown, there is a close connection between onomastic content and function (Nicolaisen 1978: 42); yet these two major aspects of name usage (and also, of course, of word usage) must not be confused. While semantically words have meaning and names have content, functionally words connote and names denote; put somewhat differently, words include, comprehend, embrace, whereas names exclude, isolate, individualise (Nicolaisen 1978). More than any other quality, the functional aspects of names remind us that it is not necessary to understand a name in order to use it competently, but that it is essential to know it. Acquiring a name, i.e. adding it to one's onomastic idiolect, one's personal name-inventory, is therefore the process by which one gets to know it, and that newly acquired knowledge includes its function as well as its content (see also *Koß* 1990: 67-73). The basic isolatory, individuating nature of names has sometimes led to the claim that names must be unique in order to function effectively, but this is obviously an impossible demand which can only be met, and then only with difficulty, in a small circle of persons or a circumscribed area. Otherwise identical names can have different content; the same first name might be used in different families or even in different generations of the same family, and the same place-name may be found in adjacent valleys separated by a watershed, or the same field name on adjacent farms. It is also worth remembering that names of the type *Sandvík* and *Ørfirisey* often straddle the boundary between connotative words and denotative names and may therefore be termed "connotative names". Such names, as well as their elements, are largely responsible for the shaping of onomastic dialects (Nicolaisen 1980). When words cross the threshold from a lexicon to an onomasticon they become instantly denotative names; the opposite happens when names are admitted to the lexicon. With reference to the discussion under 3.1., one might add that, if *proper* and *common* are considered roughly to be alternatives for *denotative* and *connotative* and are, for that reason, found useful in English descriptive grammar, they should nevertheless be used in contrasting fashion; only the designations *common nouns* and *proper names* would be permissible but definitely not *common names* and *proper nouns*. As already argued, the use of these epithets is, however, unnecessary and accordingly restricted to employment as stylistic devices.

7. Conclusion

Complementary to perspectives which see names as integral to the lexicon (Algeo 1973 and 1985; Wimmer 1973; Pamp 1985; Werner 1987; Christoph 1991, etc.), it has been argued in this exposition that, while names share certain characteristics with words (appellatives), they are more than just words with peculiar additional qualities. Ideally, both words and names should be subsumed under the umbrella term *appellative* but this would necessitate radical changes – a revolution might be the right term – in the current terminology and the concepts it represents. In contrasting members of a lexicon with members of an onomasticon, it becomes clear that lexical items (words) have meaning and connote, whereas onomastic items (names) have content and denote. On the surface level, this may be expressed in English both visually (spelling) and orally/aurally (pronunciation). While it may be inappropriate to call onomastics a discipline separate from linguistics (Nicolaisen 1972), it is highly desirable that the special nature of names should lead to a more onomastic orientation of onomastics (Nicolaisen 1990) and to the recognition of the powerful force of analogy in the naming process (Albøge et al. 1991).

8. Selected Bibliography

Albøge, Gordon et al. (1991): Analogi i Navngivning. *NORNA-rapporter* 45. Uppsala.
Algeo, John (1973): On Defining the Proper Name (University of Florida Humanities Monograph 41). Gainesville, FL.
Algeo, John (1985): Is a Theory of Names Possible? In: Nicolaisen 1985b, 136-144.
American Heritage (1969) = The American Heritage Dictionary of the English Language. Boston.

Chambers (1983) = Chambers 20th Century Dictionary, new edition. Edinburgh.

Christoph, Ernst-Michael (1991): Eigennamen als Bestandteil des Lexikons? Ein Diskussionsbeitrag zur Semantikforschung in der Onomastik. In: Zeitschrift für Phonetik, Sprachwissenschaft und Kommunikationsforschung 44, 357-371.

Collins (1978) = Collins Concise Dictionary of the English Language. London and Glasgow.

Dalberg, Vibeke (1985): On Homonymy between Proper Name and Appellative. In: Nicolaisen 1985b, 127-135.

Fleischer, Wolfgang (1962): Zur Frage der Namenfelder. In: Wissenschaftliche Zeitschrift der Karl Marx Universität Leipzig 11, 319-326.

Gardiner, Sir Alan H. (1954): The Theory of Proper Names. 2nd edition. London.

Herndon, Jeanne H. (1970): A Survey of Modern Grammars. New York.

Jespersen, Otto (1924): The Philosophy of Grammar. London.

Kluge, Friedrich (1960). Etymologisches Wörterbuch der deutschen Sprache. 18th edition, ed. by Walther Mitzka. Berlin.

Koß, Gerhard (1990): Namenforschung: Eine Einführung in die Onomastik (Germanistische Arbeitshefte 34). Tübingen.

Langendon, D. Terence (1970): Essentials of English Grammar. New York.

Lowe, Solomon (1737): English Grammar Reformed into a small compass and easy method for the readier learning and better understanding of the English tongue by way of introduction to other languages. London.

Michael, Ian (1970): English Grammatical Categories and the Tradition to 1800. Cambridge.

Moser, Hugo (1957): Namenfelder. In: Der Deutschunterricht 9, 5, 51-72.

Moser, Hugo (1958): Zum Problem der Namenfelder. In: Actes et mémoires du cinquième congrès international de toponymie et d'anthroponymie, Salamanca 1955. Vol. I, Salamanca, 161-164.

Nicolaisen, Wilhelm F.H. (1972): Onomastics – An Independent Discipline? In: Indiana Names 3, 33-47.

Nicolaisen, Wilhelm F.H. (1976): Words as Names. In: Onoma 20, 142-163.

Nicolaisen, Wilhelm F.H. (1978): Are there Connotative Names? In: Names 26, 40-47.

Nicolaisen, Wilhelm F.H. (1980): Onomastic Dialects. In: American Speech 55, 36-45.

Nicolaisen, Wilhelm F.H. (1982): Lexical and Onomastic Fields. In: Proceedings of the Thirteenth International Congress of Onomastic Sciences, Cracow 1978, Vol. II. Cracow, 209-216.

Nicolaisen, Wilhelm F.H. (1985a): Nomen, Noun, and Name: The Lexical Horns of an Onomastic Dilemma. In: Historical and Editorial Studies in Medieval and Early Modern English. Groningen, 63-72.

Nicolaisen, Wilhelm F.H. (1985b). Ed.: Special Issue on Theory about Names (Names 33/3).

Nicolaisen, Wilhelm F.H. (1985c): The Semantics of Place-Names and Their Elements. In: *NORNArapporter* 28, 60-71.

Nicolaisen, Wilhelm F.H. (1985d): Socio-onomastics. In: Der Eigenname in Sprache und Gesellschaft, I. Verhandlungen im Plenum. Leipzig, 118-132.

Nicolaisen, Wilhelm F. H. (1987): Imitation and Innovation in the Scandinavian Place-Names of the Northern Isles of Scotland. In: Nomina 11, 75-85.

Nicolaisen, Wilhelm F.H. (1990): Onomastic Onomastics. In: Proceedings of the XVIth International Congress of Onomastic Sciences, Quebec 1987. Quebec, 3-14.

Nicolaisen, Wilhelm F.H. (1991): Scottish Analogues of Scandinavian Place-names. In: Albøge et al. 1991, 147-155.

Onions, C.T. (1966): The Oxford Dictionary of English Etymology. Oxford.

Oxford (1975) = The Oxford Illustrated Dictionary. Oxford.

Pamp, Bengt (1985): Ten Theses on Proper Names. In: Nicolaisen 1985b, 111-118.

Pei, Mario, Gaynor, Frank (1965): A Dictionary of Linguistics. London.

Pokorny, Julius (1949): Indogermanisches etymologisches Wörterbuch. Bern.

Priscian (1961): Grammatici Latini ex recensione Henrici Keilii. II. Prisciani Institutionum Grammaticarum Libri i–xii ex recensione Martini Hertzii [reprinted]. Hildesheim.

Pulgram, Ernst (1954): Theory of Names. Berkeley, CA.

Quirk, Randolph, Greenbaum, Sidney (1973): A University Grammar of English. London.

Robins, R.H. (1966): The Development of the Word Class System of the European Grammatical Tradition. In: Foundations of Language 2, 3-19.

Scott, F.S. et al. (1968): English Grammar: A Linguistic Study of its Classes and Structures. London.

Searle, John R. (1969): Speech Acts: An Essay in the Philosophy of Language. Cambridge.

Solmsen, F. (1922): Indogermanische Eigennamen als Spiegel der Kulturgeschichte, ed. E. Fraenkel, Heidelberg.

Šrámek, Rudolf (1972/73): 'Modell' and 'System' in the Toponomastik. In: Onoma 17, 55-75.

Stewart, G.R. (1943): What is Named? – Towns, Islands, Mountains, Rivers, Capes. In: California University Publications in English 14, 223-232.

Stewart, G.R. (1945): Names on the Land. New York.

Strang, Barbara M.H. (1968): Modern English Structure (second edition).

Sweet, Henry (1892): A New English Grammar. Oxford.

Trier, Jost (1931): Der deutsche Wortschatz im Sinnbezirk des Verstandes. Vol. I Heidelberg.

Varro (1951): Varro on the Latin Language, with an English translation by Roland G. Kent, H. Cambridge, MA, 406-407.

Webster (1973) = Webster's New Collegiate Dictionary. Springfield, MA.

Will, Wilhelm (1943): Ortsnamen. In: Maurer, F., Stroh, F. (eds.): Deutsche Wortgeschichte. Berlin.

Werner, Otmar (1974): Appellativa – Nomina Propria. In: Proceedings of the Eleventh International Congress of Linguistics, Bologna – Florence 1972, II. Bologna, 171-187.

Wimmer, Rainer (1973): Der Eigenname im Deutschen: Ein Beitrag zu seiner linguistischen Beschreibung. Tübingen.

Zelinsky, Wilbur (1967): Classical Town Names in the United States: The Historical Geography of an American Idea. In: The Geographical Review 57, 463-495.

You name it: Perspectives on onomastic research.
Eds. Ritva Liisa Pitkänen and Kaija Mallat. Helsinki (1996)
57-62

One name but many systems

W HEN one thinks of Eero Kiviniemi's major contributions to the study
of names, key concepts like typology, system, theory, etc., immediately come
to mind. As much as anybody he has, over the last quarter of a century or
so, attempted to distil, from a vast number of individual names that make a
nomenclature, general principles and basic rules, thus moving far beyond
the search for the meaning of single names that is so often taken to be the be
all and end all of onomastic research. For those of us who were privileged
to participate in the XVIIth International Congress of Onomastic Sciences in
Helsinki in 1990, of which he was one of the presidents and prime movers, it did
not therefore come as a surprise when one of its main themes was announced
to be "Name Systems"; the many intriguing variations on that theme offered
in response by scholars from such countries as Czechoslovakia (both Czech
and Slovak), Estonia, France, Germany, Israel, Italy, the Netherlands, Poland,
Portugal, Romania, Russia, Scotland, Sweden, and the U.S.A., persuasively
corroborated or at least paralleled the Finnish experience. Most of these
contributions[1] provided convincing proof that the intellectual endeavour which
we call Onomastics even six years ago was well on the way towards establishing
itself as a discipline intent on exploring the environment in which names hone,
depend on and interact with each other systematically, and capable of subjecting
this interconnected evidence to rigorous and fruitful investigation.[2]

My own contribution was concerned with the growth of name systems,[3]
emphasising that it would be misleading, indeed sterile, to look upon them in
purely synchronic or static terms. I used some Scottish place-names to make my
point, coming to the conclusion that certain devices like subdivision, contrast,

addition, "allow a toponymic system to reflect on itself ... and to increase the number of items in the system without having to coin an unlimited number of new, independent names. This trick permits the paradox of a name system which is to all intents and purposes closed to grow substantially, nevertheless having nothing but itself to feed on".[4] There cannot be any doubt, therefore, that my thinking on these matters moves in the same direction as Kiviniemi's and tries to promote methods and approaches which will argue over and over again the case for intra- and inter-systemic investigations in all fields of name research.

Having said all this, it may seem strange or even contradictory for me to have chosen for my contribution to a Festschrift honouring one of our great systemic thinkers in the discipline a close look at an individual name, but it will, I hope, become clear in the course of this brief discussion that this is an attempt to enhance rather than abandon systemic thinking in onomastics, particularly toponymics, using an individual name as a key to open a door into a larger room, maybe even several of them.

The name which I have selected for my purposes is *Hatton of Fintray*, which designates a small hamlet north-west of Aberdeen (Scotland). To the best of my knowledge it admirably fulfils the individualising requirements of a name insofar as it is unique (unless somebody has nostalgically transferred it as a house name or the like). It applies to this one small settlement on the B977 from Balmedie to Kintore, and none other. In a contemporary setting it distinguishes, within the neighbouring nomenclature of the region, this one place from other named places nearby such as *Kinmuck, Newmachar, Blackburn, Kemnay, Port Elphinstone, Potterton, Belhelvie*, and so on. As part of a wider inventory of place-names in north-east Scotland, it indicates that *Hatton of Fintray* is not *Inverurie, Aberdeen, Peterhead, Fraserburgh, Elgin*, or any one of hundreds of other settled places, large and small. Casting our net even wider it makes it unmistakably clear that anyone living in *Hatton of Fintray* does not live in *Edinburgh, Glasgow, Birmingham, London, Paris, Helsinki*, or even *Capetown, Bombay, Tokyo, Montreal*, or *Melbourne*. Thus it functions effectively as one name in the worldwide network of named locations. This is the first system to which it belongs, and yet it does not accomplish its expected onymic task by itself but through a set of manoeuvres and strategies as part of a number of discrete systems or fields.[5] It manages to do so because it has absorbed the ingredients of several linguistic strata and their toponymic manifestations which, though also discernible in other place-names of the Scottish north-east, have, over the centuries, created its uniqueness in a complex, cumulative fashion, with some of the elements involved being lexically transparent to current speakers of Scottish English and its regional dialect, and others being totally opaque.

As far as the first part of the name, *Hatton*, is concerned, only its generic, *-ton*, is accessible to the naive user, as it is a reflex of the most common term employed in settlement names of English origin on the Scottish map. Identical with English *town* but often applied to farms and farm-like habitations, it has been around ever since speakers of English (Anglian) first set foot on what is now Scottish soil at the beginning of the seventh century AD and has accompanied them wherever they have moved or settled down. As *-toun* [tu:n], it is the toponymic element par excellence of a Scottish English presence and, in its role of a generic has, because of its ubiquity, had a wide variety of specifics attached to it, as in *Bridgeton*, *Milton*, *Middleton*, *Thornton*, *Newton*, *Scotston*, *Westerton*, *Yonderton*, *Potterton*, *Muirton*, *Kirkton*, *Bishopston*, *Chapelton*, *Upperton*, and a large assortment of others.[6] *Hatton*, despite the opacity of its specific *Hat-*, therefore takes its place typologically in one respect in this group of settlement names and is easily recognisable as such. It is at the same time excluded from name types having other habitative terms as their generics, such as *croft*, *house*, *seat*, *mains*, *castle*, or *grange*. A place called *Hatton* is not a *Bridgeton*, *Thornton*, *Middleton*, etc. In its most localised usage it is not *Milton of Fintray* as it is not *Mill of Fintray* or *Wester Fintray*.

As the earliest documented spelling of our name – *Haltoun de Fintray* 1582 – shows, it contains the word *hall* and therefore represents a superior dwelling such as a farmer's house in contrast to a cottar's house, or something even more socially respectable (cf. *Hatton Castle* near Turriff). There are many other *Hattons* not only in Aberdeenshire but also elsewhere in Scotland, many of which occur in the construction "Hatton of X" as, for example, *Hatton of Ardoyne* (*Haltoun de Ardune* 1512-13, *Haltoun* 1550), *Hatton of Auchterless* (*Haltoun* 1546, *Halton de Ochterles* 1570), *Hatton of Lumphanan* (*Haltoun de Lumfannane* 1546-47), or, historically, *Haltoun of Belhelveis* 1607 (= *Hatton of Belhelvie*) and *Hattown of Forest* 1769 (in Strichen). Beyond Aberdeenshire, "Hatton of X" constructions are found in good numbers in Banffshire, Kincardineshire, Angus, Fife, Perthshire, quite apart from several other unspecified *Hattons*.

As we have already seen, *Hatton of Fintray* achieves partial identity through its contrast with *Milton of Fintray* (and perhaps also with a nearby Newton). In order to give it further specificity on its path towards onymic uniqueness, it hones its individuality in its contrast to such other names as *Hatton of Ardoyne*, *Hatton of Auchterless*, *Hatton of Lumphanan* or, at one time, *Hatton of Belhelvie*, citing just Aberdeenshire names. The morphological structure of this device – "X of Y" – is now thoroughly English but has its origin in earlier underlying Gaelic patterns, like *Allt Uamha na Muice* 'burn of the stream of the pig' or *Drochaid Chonoglas* 'bridge of (the river) Conglass'.[7] In a series of steps, this model was adopted by English-speaking namers of geographical features so that we find constructions like *Burn of Y, Water of Y, Mill of Y, Mains of Y, Hill of Y*, and so on. Of these, *Mains of Y* is perhaps most closely related to the formula *Hatton of Y*. In achieving a further degree of individuality and non-interchangeability, our name has therefore incorporated a pre-English Gaelic pattern into its make-up. As a result, it has become part of yet another system which, on the one hand, links and, on the other, contrasts it with similarly constructed names in the vicinity, like *Netherton of Balquhain, Hillhead of Pitbee, Chapel of Garioch, West Mains of Harlaw, Burnside of Pitcaple*, and many others, including its own descendant *Boat of Hatton* (in reference to a former ferry boat). For a while, this model "X of Y" was regarded as a nineteenth-century map-makers' invention perhaps derived from earlier estate maps and the like but, as the examples already quoted have demonstrated, it has been around for quite a few centuries, and Gaelic origin is the preferred explanation.

The last, and probably the most important, element in the complex nature of *Hatton of Fintray* as an effective onymic device is, of course, the name *Fintray*[8] which preceded both the transitional Gaelic pattern just discussed and, by many centuries, the Scottish English emergence of *toun*-names in the north-east, including *Hatton*. *Fintray* (*Fintrach* 1175; *Fintreth* 1180, 1490; *Fintray* 1654)[9] is itself a linguistic hybrid presenting quite a challenge to the would-be interpreter. Its second element, the generic, is cognate with Welsh *tref* 'town, home' commonly found in place-names in Wales, such as *Trecwn, Trecynon, Tregarth, Tremain, Tredegar* but also occurring in Cumbric p-Celtic south of the Forth-Clyde line in names like *Tranent, Traquair, Traprain, Terregles*, etc.[10] When it is found as the first part of a compound name its geographical distribution is clear-cut, emphasising the close relationship between Cumbric and Welsh (and also Cornish). The situation is, however, quite different when it comes to the spatial scatter, in Scotland, of place-names in which it occurs as the second element. As is to be expected, it is found in Cumbric territory: *Niddry* (several), *Ochiltree, Soutra*, and the like. It does, however, also occur in "Pictland", from Fife to the Moray Firth: *Capledrae, Clentry, Fortree*, and especially in the district name *Moray* (*Murebe* 1032, *Moreb* 1130), a reflex of Celtic **mori-treb-* 'sea settlement'.[11] The major difference between the Cumbric and Pictish evidence is that in the former group of names the first element, the specific, is also p-Celtic, whereas in the latter in tends to be Gaelic although in some instances in which the same name is found both south and north of the Forth-Clyde line, like *Rattra, Rattray, Rattrey* and *Trostrie, Troustrie*,[12] it is difficult to ascribe with certainty the linguistic affiliation of the first element. Presumably, the normal division also applies.

Our *Fintray* undoubtedly belongs to the "northern" subcategory in which the specific is Gaelic, in this case Gaelic *fionn* 'white'. It is, however, by no means unique for there is another example in Aberdeenshire, *Fintry* (*Meikle Fyntra* 1375)[13] and the same name also occurs in Stirlingshire (*Fyntrif* 1225, *Fyntryf* 1225-70)[14] and Angus. It is tempting to regard these four names as part-translations of a p-Celtic forerunner, and this is apparently proved by the entry, for the other Aberdeenshire *Fintry*, in the Register of the Great Seal "terras et baroniam de Cantries vulgo vocat. Fintries in parochia de Kingeduard" (1634, similar in 1625), which suggests that the original name was something like **can-dref-* < **cantro-treb-* 'white settlement'. Alternatively, the p-Celtic original could have been something like **gwendref*, with the same meaning.[15] It is perhaps also not to be ignored that Gaelic *fionn* can mean 'holy'; a cultic connection might explain the frequency of the name.

That part-translation is, however, not as common as is often assumed: as shown by the well-known group of place-names in our area, compounded with Pictish *pett* 'a portion of land' and a Gaelic specific; there are several of these not far from *Hatton of Fintray*, such as *Pitcaple*, *Pitbee*, *Pitmedden*, *Petmathen*, and *Pittodrie*. These have been shown[16] to have been created in the bilingual Pictish-Gaelic and immediate post-Pictish periods, mainly in the ninth and tenth centuries. As it cannot be proved, however, that *–tref* was adopted like Pictish *pett* as a productive Gaelic topographic term, part-translation of the specific is perhaps the most probable explanation. It is also worth noting that, whereas *pett* never occurs as a second element, *tref* is never found as the first element of a compound name in Pictish territory. While their morphological usage is therefore mutually exclusive, they may yet be semantically closely related, almost complementary. The Aberdeenshire *Pitcaple* and the name *Capledrae* in Fife, for instance, both contain references to horses (Gaelic *capull* 'horse'), and *Pit*-names and *Tref*-names may also not be dissimilar in status. Thus the name *Fintray* provides a link with the Pictish past of the region, especially as adapted by the Gaelic-speaking successors to the Picts.

Diachronically, *Hatton of Fintray* has therefore shared in practically all the known linguistic and toponymic phases which have affected the Scottish north-east in post-Roman times: Pictish, Gaelic-Pictish, Gaelic, Gaelic-English, and Scottish-English. In each of these strata, it has been part of a prevailing system from a synchronic point of view, being successively defined by such oppositions as *Fintray-Trostrie*, *Fintray-Pitcaple*, *Hatton of Fintray-Hatton of Auchterless*, *Hatton of Fintray-Milton of Fintray*, and *Hatton-Newton*. As an individual, individualising name in current usage, it receives its unique effectiveness from a combination of all of these. Even today it therefore participates in, and benefits from, a multiplicity of systems, both by what it is and by what it is not. Consequently, there can be no doubt that it is *Hatton of Fintray* and not, let us say, *Tuusula*!

Notes

1   Available in Eeva Maria Närhi (ed.), *Proceedings of the XVIIth International Congress of Onomastic Sciences*. Two volumes. Helsinki: The University of Helsinki and the Finnish Research Centre for Domestic Languages, 1990.

2   Kiviniemi himself contributed a plenary lecture to the congress on "Die lexikalischen Grundzüge des toponymischen Systems in Finnland", *ibid.*, I, 69-83.

3   *Ibid.*, II, 203-210.

4   *Ibid.*, II. 209.

5   All these names are found not far from *Hatton of Fintray*.

6   See, for example, W.F.H. Nicolaisen, "Lexical and Onomastic Fields", *Proceedings of the Thirteenth International Congress of Onomastic Sciences*, Cracow 1978. Two volumes. Cracow: 1982, II, 209-216.

7   See W.F.H. Nicolaisen, *Scottish Place-Names: Their Study and Significance*. London: B.T. Batsford, 1976, 57-64.

8   *Ibid.*, 169-170.

9   For a discussion of these spellings see, William M. Alexander, *The Place-Names of Aberdeenshire*. Aberdeen: The Third Spalding Club, 1952, 57.

10 William J. Watson, *The History of the Celtic Place-Names of Scotland*. Edinburgh: William Blackwood, 1926, 357-365; and Nicolaisen, *Scottish Place-Names*, 166-168.

11 Watson, 115–116. For the wider issue see Nicolaisen, *Scottish Place-Names*, 168-170.

12 Nicolaisen, *ibid.*, 169.

13 Alexander, 9.

14 Watson, 364.

15 *Ibid.*

16 See Watson, 407-414; Nicolaisen *Scottish Place-Names*, 151-158; also Nicolaisen, *The Picts and their Place-names*. Rosemarkie: Groam House Museum, 1996.

Onomata 16 (2000-2001) 327-336

Landscape as Plot: Place-Names in R.L. Stevenson's Fiction

T HE title of this paper[1] is to be understood as a promise to myself as well as to any potential reader; its first half is the rather audacious and perhaps not fully justified condensation of memories of earlier, much earlier, readings of Stevenson's fiction. Instead of being a considered, though provocative, statement based on solid evidence, it therefore turned into a challenging question when I recently interrogated the same texts with the specific purpose of this brief essay in mind, and this presentation will probably not only reveal its questioning but also its questionable nature. The second half of the title should certainly be augmented, and through augmentation be restricted by the addition of the adjective "Scottish" before the word "Fiction", mainly because of the general framework of this enquiry but also because my familiarity with literary onomastics, i.e. with the ways in which names function in literature, does not extend much beyond the British Isles and has for the last twenty years or so been chiefly focused on Scotland, with special emphasis on Sir Walter Scott.[2]

The phrase "R.L. Stevenson's Fiction", in turn, refers essentially to the three major novels finished by Stevenson himself – *Kidnapped* (1886), *Catriona* (1893), and *The Master of Ballantrae* (1889) – since it is difficult to assess the role of names in a literary work if that work is either unfinished or has been completed, however felicitously, by somebody else. The same applies, of course, to the unfolding of plots. A name-ful and plot-ful novel thrives on completeness, from the first page to the last, from opening paragraph to the last sentence, just as anything one might usefully say about these matters must essentially be confined to what one discovers between the two covers of the book. But more about that later.

This is, as I have already implied, not my first tussle with the intricacies and very special qualities of the onomastics of Scottish literature[3] but it is the first time that I am attempting to apply my ideas to Stevenson, mainly, I presume, to get away from Sir Walter for a while but also because it is something I have been wanting to do for a long time. In our Edinburgh days in the fifties and sixties we could see his "cottage" at Swanston, just below the T-Wood, from our bedroom window and often strolled past it on our Sunday afternoon walks, and the urge to "do something with Stevenson one of these days" has never left me since. After all, we were spatial neighbours for a while though temporal strangers.

As, over the years, I have investigated quite a number of Scottish fictive texts from a variety of perspectives, I would consider it redundant, if not boring, to examine Stevenson's fiction from one or other, or even all, of the same angles, even though such parallel examination might well be useful for comparative purposes. In order to draw readers' attention to certain approaches, however, and to demonstrate how my thinking on the subject has developed over the last two decades and where I think I now stand in matters literary and onomastic it is necessary to devote at least a little space to some of the more general issues which confront us when we try to come to grips with the ways in which names mean and function in a particular work of fiction, in an author's complete literary output, or in a set of onomastically related fictions. As is to be expected, the title of this essay demands that, in this brief preamble, I concentrate almost exclusively on the names of places.

At the beginning of the newly found and rapidly developing interest in the study of names in literature, about a quarter of a century ago, both students of names and critics of fiction were pre-occupied with the analysis of names in specific works by specific authors, more often than not searching for or at least speculating about the etymologies and lexical resonances of individual names. The most frequently asked question was: Why did this author choose this particular name or this particular character or place? This question and approach dominated the field of literary onomastics far beyond its initial stages and is even today probably the most popular strategy in that kind of research. While acknowledging the need for such investigations and the validity of such approaches, I have over the years found them too limiting, especially when pursued as ends in themselves, and have therefore advocated for some time to regard the nomenclature of a single literary work – the toponymic inventory of a novel, let us say – as a text within a text[4] and to read that embedded text not only in its entirety but also in its relationship to the larger text in which it is enclosed. This intra-textual perspective is in itself, of course, also only a step, although an essential one, in the direction of the examination of names as extremely effective and economical intertextual devices that have a special niche in the production of parodies and of sequels,[5] such as Anna L'Estrange's *Return to Wuthering Heights* (1977), Alexander Ripley's *Scarlett* (1991), and nearer to home, John Goldsmith's *Return to Treasure Island* (1985). There are also Jeffrey Caine's *Heathcliff* (1978) which attempts to fill a famous gap in Emily Bronte's novel, and Jean Rhys's *Wide Sargasso Sea* (1966) which narrates events preceding Jane Eyre's encounter with Mr. Rochester. What such creative and re-creative tactics recognise and build on is the basic lexical meaninglessness of names which makes them available as empty shells to be filled with whatever contents an imaginative author chooses. The risks involved in this kind of onomastic enterprise are, however, at least twofold: Either, as Sir Walter Scott discovered after his invention of the name *Waverley*,[6] a name can take on a seductive power of its own to which even its inventor gradually and irresistibly succumbs; or, and this is, of course, a dilemma not limited to onomastic inventiveness, elusive readers bring to names in fiction their own unpredictable biases, prejudices, and experiences in general which may only partially coincide with the author's intentions or even differ from them altogether.

This is particularly true if, from a toponymic point of view, the authors in question have included, for whatever reason, in their works of fiction real names of real places suggesting, perhaps for the sake of verisimilitude, that such names lend credibility to the plot and setting, or at least to the fictitious names which the author has inserted into the interstices, the as yet open spaces among them. The interaction of these two kinds of names is in itself a fascinating field of study, as it apparently creates an intertextuality, or perhaps better an inter-contextuality, between the landscapes of fiction and those in the actual world out there. When closely examining this phenomenon, however,[7] one becomes aware of the fact that the inclusion of what I have just called "real names" fictionalises them to such an extent that they become indistinguishable from those created by the author, or that, even if one does know that Edinburgh, Colinton, and Cramond are real names and Essendean and the House of Shaws are not, in each other's company the first three become fictionalised by a kind of authorial act of contamination, whereas the second two are well on the road to factualisation so that David Balfour on his way from Essendean to the House of Shaws can get a glimpse of Edinburgh, pass to the west of Colinton, and enter the parish of Cramond. For that reason, it is difficult, if not impossible, to make a clear-cut and convincing distinction between fictional and non-fictional names, an observation which obviously equally applies to names of places and of people. In the end, the creative levelling process makes them equally factual and fictitious.

Stevenson himself was well aware of this, as the very first sentence of his dedication of *Kidnapped* to Charles Baxter demonstrates:

"If you ever read this tale" he begins, "you will likely ask yourself more questions than I should care to answer: as for instance how the Appin murder has come to fall in the year 1751, how the Torran rocks have crept so near to Earraid, or why the printed trial is silent as to all that touches David Balfour. These are nuts beyond my ability to crack."[8]

Authors are always so much ahead of their critics and therefore in a position to tease them mercilessly! Stevenson's legitimate right to introduce his own chronology (the Appin murder was actually committed one year later, in 1752), his own topography (by shifting the location of two topographical features with "real" names), and his own human constellations (through the association of the fictitious David Balfour with the historical Alan Breck) cannot be challenged, and he knows it. What concerns us most in this triad is naturally the question of "how the Torran rocks have crept so near to Earraid" although you will not find me attempting a definite answer because we are confronted by Stevenson's Torran rocks and Stevenson's Earraid or, if you like, David Balfour's Torran rocks and David Balfour's Earraid, and not by places with which we may be familiar or can visit, and, if I may return to an earlier comment, it is also utterly irrelevant what the etymology of these names is or what Stevenson thought it was. Certainly David Balfour did not care!

What we are here invited to respond to are landscapes of the mind,[9] our minds as well as the author's who sometimes feels constrained to help us in our quest for them by providing visual cartographical aids, maps which may or may not have a pivotal function in the narrative plot itself. Although there is no need to remind readers of the central role which Captain Flint's map plays in *Treasure Island*, there is no harm in taking another look at it since it is germane to the topic of this essay.

This is how the discovery of the map is described by Stevenson in the persona of Jim Hawkins:[10]

The paper had been sealed in several places with a thimble by way of seal ... . The doctor opened the seals with great care, and there fell out the map of an island, with latitude and longitude, soundings, names of hills, and bays and inlets, and every particular that would be needed to bring a ship to a safe anchorage upon its shores. It was about nine miles long and five across, shaped, you might say, like a fat dragon standing up, and had two fine landlocked harbours, and a hill in the centre part marked 'The Spyglass'. There were several additions of a later date; but, above all, three crosses of red ink – two on the north part of the island, one in the south-west, and beside this last, in the same red ink, and in a small, neat hand, very different from the captain's tottery characters, these words: 'Bulk of treasure here'.

Over on the back the same hand had written this further information:

'Tall tree, Spy glass shoulder, bearing a point to the N. of NNE'.

'Skeleton Island ESE and by E'.

'Ten feet'.

'The bar silver is in the north cache: you can find it by the trend of the east hummock, ten fathoms south of the black crag with the face on it'.

'The arms are easy found, in the sand hill, N. point of north inlet cape, bearing E. and a quarter N'

'J.F.'

The discovery of the map initiates the hazardous trip to the island to which it refers and which gives the novel its title. Without this central, focal, plot-generating map or chart there would be no story, or only a very feeble one.

It is, of course, comparatively easy to persuade, perhaps even convince, readers that the kind of landscape created with the help of fictitious place-names on a fictitious map is purely imaginary and therefore exclusively lodged in the mind. The visit to *Treasure Island* narrated by Stevenson cannot be repeated physically (you and I cannot hire a ship to go there); Treasure Island is off the map. We are, however, confronted with a very different situation when it comes to landscapes that are largely narrated in terms of real names and therefore in the shadow of their mappability; landscapes, that is, which permit, indeed invite, us to locate them and, if we wish, to travel to and through them.

That we succumb to this temptation or, if you like, accept this invitation is proved by an article by Rennie McOwan in *The Scots Magazine*[11] in which he suggests that the area around Bridge of Allan and Stirling, including Dumyat and the Ochils, inspired Stevenson in the creation of many of his landscapes, among them those of *Treasure Island* and *Kidnapped*. In the course of his argument, the writer also mentions having walked (and sailed) with friends "the 270-mile route undertaken by the fictitious David Balfour and partly-fictitious Alan Breck".[12] Only a little later, BBC Television showed a special *Omnibus* double on "Stevenson's Travels", including both his own and those of his fictional characters. Both the article and the television programme were welcome responses to the centenary year of R.L.S.'s death, and I hope that it will not seem churlish if I nevertheless voice some reservations.

These are based on the realisation that, however fascinating repeat journeys in the footsteps of some famous personage may be and however much they may bring to life the detective and explorer in us, they are ultimately confined to anachronistic, superficial, perhaps even futile imitation. This is disturbing enough when one observes the several pilgrims who have followed the routes of Johnson and Boswell on their *Tour* to and of the *Hebrides*, for we cannot make their landscapes our landscapes just as these are not likely to have been the landscapes perceived by their contemporaries or, to return to our author, as Stevenson's *Cevennes* never have been the *Cevennes* of their inhabitants, nor of other travellers through the region.[13] All this becomes, of course, even more problematic when the original traveller is a fictitious character whose journey happened only within the covers of an adventure story and whose traceable named places have become as fictionalised as the invented ones, or as Stevenson's portrait of Alan Breck.

Please, do not misunderstand me: I am not denying that some knowledge of the actual places mentioned in *Kidnapped* does shape our perception of their fictionalised counterparts. I am only too aware of this myself, since my response to David Balfour's trials and tribulations on Mull was greatly enriched by my having done extensive field-work on the island, including the Ross and the area around Torosay. And yet, along with this enrichment also came distortion because the experience of my own cycling trips round the island brought to Stevenson's narrative images and interpretations which interfered with those intended and conjured up by the author, and I am not sure whether my initial naive, maybe even poverty-stricken, reaction to my first reading, many years ago, of *Kidnapped* was not preferable at a time when my acquaintance with the landscapes traversed by David and Alan was almost completely derived from the novel and I was unable to distinguish between so-called real names and invented ones, a distinction which to make never occurred to me at the time, and did not spoil or enhance my enjoyment of the narrative. There must have been many readers like me in the last century or so for whom their mental map of *Mull* has been, let us say, in the same category as *Treasure Island*. Germans, for example who might well have grouped *Die Entführung* together with *Die Schatzinsel*.[14]

Or, put somewhat differently, how many readers, unless very familiar with *Glencoe* and *Loch Leven*, would know whether the *Haugh of Corrynakiegh* where David and Alan hide and *Koalisnacoan* where Alan places a cross in John Breck Maccoll's window[15] are real names or imaginary ones. As it happens, *Caolinacoan* is still marked on the Ordnance Survey map on the south side of *Loch Leven* while, in the absence of the name *Coire na Ciche*, the map shows the nearby *Sgór na Ciche* (or *Pap of Glencoe*) on the slopes of which the corrie must have been situated. Stevenson's Lowland term *heugh*, by the way, looks surprisingly out of place linguistically in what was in the middle of the eighteenth century a solidly Gaelic-speaking area but, then, if the Selkirkshire narrator/protagonist says that this is what it was called, that must have been what it was called, and we cannot quarrel with it; after all, we did not look with him down "upon a part of Mamore, and on the sea-loch that divides that country from Appin", from this "cleft in the head of a great mountain" and did not hide from the red-coats there.[16]

It is surely also significant that Stevenson, in the persona of his narrator David Balfour, is not concerned with the lexical meaning of any of the place-names mentioned and does not offer any translations into English, as Scott might have done in keeping with the device of sending a stranger on our behalf into the Highlands in order to convey to his non-Highland readers the nature of the countryside and the characteristics of its inhabitants.[17] A name is a name, and in the case of *Kidnapped* the semantic opacity of names like *Torran, Earraid, Kinlochaline, Appin, Aucharn, Caolisnacoan, Benalder, Balquhidder,* etc. imbues them with an aura of romantic exoticism, both attractive and threatening, which they would not have had if they had been linguistically accessible to speakers of Scots or of English in general. Because of this opacity and semantic emptiness, the author is able to fill them with contents of his own making, relevant to the story he is telling.

There is only one point in his narrative at which he comes close to toying with the meaning of a name, and that is when David Balfour describes the place called *Lettermore* "(or Lettervore, for I have heard it both ways)" as "a wood of birches growing on a steep, craggy side of a mountain that overhung the loch"[18] and it is probably worth noting at least in parenthesis that this is the only instance in which he provides alternative forms of a name, in this case depending on the grammatical gender of the Gaelic noun *leitir* "a steep slope".

But to our tale. When assessing the function of place-names in *Kidnapped* it is necessary to realise that this novel is essentially the narrative of a journey. My former colleague in the U.S., the late John Gardner, author, for instance, of *Grendel* and *The King's Indian*, claimed that there are only two basic plots in the world: Either someone goes on a journey, or a stranger comes into town.[19] I have a feeling that the plot of *Kidnapped*, like that of many other novels, is perhaps a mixture of both of these. Very much in the tradition of folktales, the journey in *Kidnapped* operates on two levels: On the surface it takes the protagonist. one David Balfour, through actual landscapes in which trees are trees, burns are burns, rocks are rocks, and heather is heather. On a metaphorical level, on the other hand, his journey is a projection of David's maturation, of a boy turning into a young man, of someone becoming who he is supposed to be, and since he cannot achieve this by himself – again a common folktale trait – he has a helper by his side, admittedly a somewhat tricky helper and by no means an unselfish and always reliable one, but a helper nevertheless. On this journey, which, like all journeys, is movement through space in time, place-names, whether real or fictitious, but mostly the former, assist in the creation of a spatial framework, of mapping out the protagonist's travels, of foregrounding as adventures the hazards and pleasures of growing up, of becoming oneself. In particular, they pace and space the journey undertaken, however unwillingly, most frequently as destinations which become new points of departure: From Queensferry past Dysart north to the Northern Isles and then south again past Hebridean islands and west coast promontories to the Torran Rocks and Earraid, the Ross of Mull and Torosay, back to the mainland at Kinlochaline and through Appin and Glencoe and over Ben Alder, across Loch Errocht, past Loch Rannoch by Kippen to Balquhidder, and in the end to Queensferry again.

This is by no means a complete list of all the places the names of which punctuate the journey's outward progress but they are amongst the major ones. Despite the hunted fugitive's exertions and despite the time spent in moving from one named place to the next, these names are, at first glance, a static element in the narrative, designating locations with definite intersecting degrees of latitude and of longitude, or eastings and northings in the national grid. They are fixed points, and it is up to the traveller to strain for them or to avoid them, or to leave them behind. In their fixity, they create a constant measurable space, an identifiable and recognisable topography that is an important background ingredient in what is often termed "setting". There is nothing new about this observation, and if that were all I had to say, I would be wasting my readers' time.

I do, however, want to throw caution to the wind and somewhat boldly and injudiciously take us one step further by suggesting that most of the place-names incorporated in *Kidnapped* also have a dynamic dimension which not only moves the plot forward but also becomes a significant active part of the plot itself. Just as there are friendly and unfriendly, kind and cruel, helpful and unhelpful named characters in the story, it also contains friendly and unfriendly, kind and cruel, helpful and unhelpful named places and landscapes, and of course also seascapes:[20]

> "We'll have to play at being hares", said Alan.·
> "Do you see yon mountain?" pointing to one on the north-eastern sky.
> "Ay", said I.
> "Well, then, Says he, "let us strike for that. The name is Ben Alder. It is a wild, desert mountain full of hills and hollows, and if we can win to it before morn…".

Or, a little earlier, at the Heugh of Corrynaskiegh:[21]

"There was a low concealed place, in turning of the glen, where we were so bold as to make fire; so that we could warm ourselves when the clouds set in, and cook porridge, and grill the little trouts that we caught with our hands under the stones and overhanging banks of the burn."

On the other hand, at the Torran Rocks:[22]

"The reef on which we had struck was close in under the south-west end of Mull, off a little isle they called Earraid, which lay low and black upon the larboard ... and then "For God's sake, hold on". We knew by his tone that it was something more than ordinary; and sure enough, there followed a sea so huge that it lifted the brig right up and canted her over on her beam."

Thus, *Ben Alder* and *Corrynaskiegh* stand for shelter and relative safety but the *Torran Rocks* mean danger and shipwreck.

The point I am trying to make is particularly well demonstrated in Chapter 14 "The Islet" which tells the episode of David Balfour's terrifying stay on the inhospitable island of Earraid which imprisons him in the loneliness of its own sea-encircled bounds and in his own despair, in contrast to the safety and shelter of the island of Iona so clearly visible not far away:

"... my way was stopped by a creek or inlet of the sea, which seemed to run pretty deep into the land; and as I had no means to get across I must needs change my direction to go about the end of it. It was still the roughest kind of walking; indeed, the whole, not only of Earraid, but of the neighbouring part of Mull (which they call the Ross) is nothing but a jumble of granite rocks with heather in among. At first the creek kept narrowing as I had looked to see; but presently to my surprise it began to widen out again. At this I scratched my head but had still no notion of the truth; until at last I came to a rising ground, and it burst upon me all in a moment that I was cast upon a little, barren isle, and cut off on every side by the salt seas."

It is only when it is pointed out to him by passing fishermen that the island is tidal that he realises that escape to the Ross of Mull is possible. *Earraid* at this point ceases to be part of a threatening coastscape and takes on, indeed, the role of a place which offers the possibility of survival. The content of the name *Earraid* changes from black despair to justifiable hope, but whether one or the other, *Earraid*, as well as *Ben Alder, Coire na Ciche, Torran*, and most of the other named places are within the covers of this book, condensations of key elements in a landscape that is actively involved in the journey upon which our protagonist and his helper have embarked. This landscape is never neutral and, in contrast to our own lives, there are no place-names to spare that do not touch upon the life of the journeying David Balfour. The semantics of this toponymic text within the larger narrative one exists independently of its lexical meaning and it is largely irrelevant that the names Queensferry and Limekilns are English, Torosay and Eriskay Norse, and Coire na Ciche and Glencoe Gaelic. For the life of David Balfour they take on meaning unconnected with etymological considerations, historical significance, or linguistic ascription, and thus become the toponymic iconographic topography of a journey in search of self, severely focused symbols of the paraphernalia of living, of fear, promise, companionship, pain, obstacles to be overcome, hopes dashed and realised, and ultimate rejoicing – all, of course, within the literary creation called *Kidnapped* and nowhere else.

It was at this point in writing this paper that I realised that I would not be able to do equal justice to *Catriona* and The *Master of Ballantrae* but this imbalance is not as unfortunate as it may seem, for neither of these two novels has the toponymic richness of *Kidnapped*. This was particularly disappointing for me with regard to *Catriona* since I had hoped, indeed expected to find there, too, some of the onomastic devices which I had come across in other sequels as mentioned earlier. *Catriona* is, however, much more a novel of people than of places, and the main links with *Kidnapped* are made through shared personnel, or at least through characters bearing the same names. Of course, Essendean, Appin, Balquhidder, Ardshiel, the House of Shaws and such like are mentioned but largely incidentally as ingredients of actions of the past, the consequences of which are still to be resolved. There are very few private places apart from the Bass Rock, and even the names of the places by which it is reached in the narrative[23] – Stockbridge, Silverwells, Broughton, Picardy, Lochend, Musselburgh, Prestonpans, Gladsmuir, Cockenzie, Linton, Gullane, North Berwick, Dirleton, and so on – smack more of a geography well-remembered from afar of the environs to the east of the Scottish capital than of personal icons. Even David's, sometimes quite detailed movements within Edinburgh have a touch of locations remembered from abroad, of street names as reminiscences rather than of a cityscape vitally involved in the plot. One does not have to consult the relevant nostalgic passage in the dedication to come to that conclusion; the text itself is transparent enough. Admittedly, these names fulfil their primary function of creating believable geographic space but somehow the spark is missing that converts them into lively metaphors. One gets the impression that they are pressed into service rather than creatively employed.

In *The Master of Ballantrae* my disappointment was of a different kind. I had been looking forward to toponymic reflections of Stevenson's personal knowledge of the Hudson Valley, especially of its upper reaches, as the result of his stay at Saranac Lake, and was quite willing to pit my own acquaintance with upstate New York against his. Unfortunately, apart from the names of the river and of the state capital, Albany, that particular landscape is practically nameless. A brief perusal of the accounts of the other wanderings, absences and journeys of the *Master* elsewhere seems to indicate that they are not very different in that respect.

My conclusion has therefore to be more in the nature of a warning than a summary: Beware of generalisations even with regard to one and the same author. Whereas my memory was correct concerning the use of place-names in *Kidnapped*, it had played me false in that regard in what I had remembered about *Catriona* and *The Master of Ballantrae*. There is consequently no such phenomenon as *the* use of place-names in Stevenson's fiction. The plot of *Kidnapped*, presumably because of its underlying structure of a journey of adventure, fully confirms my hunch that named places can, indeed, become active forces in a plot, both on the actual and on the metaphorical level. The other two novels, on the other hand, do not support this concept, or support it only minimally. Perhaps, it is a consolation that my own experience in my interrogation of these stories may save others from similar disappointments. At any rate, I would enthusiastically encourage you, the readers, to re-read *Kidnapped* and, if you like somebody else's maps, also *Treasure Island*, with the same onomastic concerns in mind which I have tried to touch on in this brief essay. The notion of landscapes as plots is not as far-fetched as it may seem.

Notes

1   This is a much revised version of a paper read by the author at the one-day conference on "Stevenson and the Scots Tongue", held in the University of Glasgow on 26 November 1994.

2   See, for instance, W.F.H. Nicolaisen, "Literary Names as Text: Personal Names in Sir Walter Scott's *Waverley*", *Nomina* 3 (1979) 29-39; "Inverlochy: Place-names as Ruins", *Literary Onomastics Studies* 8 (1981) 27-38; "What is your name?: The Question of Identity in some of the *Waverley Novels*", *Names* 28 (1980) 255-266.

3   In addition to my papers on Scott, see "An Onomastic Vernacular in Scottish Literature". In: *Scotland and the Lowland Tongue*. Ed. J. Derrick McClure (Aberdeen: Aberdeen University Press, 1983) 209-218.

4   W.F.H. Nicolaisen, "Literary Names as Text" (see Note 2 above).

5   W.F.H. Nicolaisen, "Names in Derivative Literature and Parodies", *Literary Onomastics Studies* 14 (1987) 49-67.

6   Sir Walter Scott, *Waverley*, Chapter 1.

7   W.F.H. Nicolaisen, "Names as Intertextual Devices", *Onomastica Canadiana* 68/2 (December 1986) 58-66.

8   Preceding Chapter 1 in all editions of the novel.

9   Cf. W.F.H. Nicolaisen, "Maps of Fiction: The Cartography of the Landscape of the Mind", *Onomastica Canadiana* 72 (1990) 57-68.

10 *Treasure Island*, Chapter 6. Because of the large number of editions of Stevenson's works, references are here given by chapter rather than by precise pagination, in order to avoid confusion.

11 Rennie McOwan, "The Cradle of *Kidnapped*", *The Scots Magazine* 141/6 (December 1994) 602-609.

12 *Ibid.*, 603.

13 Robert Louis Stevenson, *Travels with a Donkey in the Cevennes* (1879).

14 These are titles of the German Translations of *Kidnapped* and *Treasure Island*, respectively.

15 *Kidnapped*, Chapter 21.

16 *Ibid.*

17 As in Scott's novel *Waverley*.

18 *Kidnapped*, Chapter 17.

19 John Gardner, Verbal communication to the author, State University of New York at Binghamton, N.Y., U.S.A.

20 *Kidnapped*, Chapter 22.

21 *Ibid.*, Chapter 21.

22 *Ibid.*, Chapter 13.

23 See Note 5 above.

Nomina 24 (2001) 5-14

'A Change of Place is a Change of Fortune': Place-Names as Structuring Devices in Chaim Bermant's Novels

CHAIM Bermant (1929-1998), the Jewish novelist and journalist, has been one of my favourite writers since the last third of the last century of the last millennium. Anybody who claims to have spoken 'The Queen's Yiddish' is likely to attract my attention for the wit and humour which this phrase epitomises, and his pre-occupation, in several of his eighteen novels, with the lives and fortunes of middle-class Glasgow Jewry has acted as a further incentive for keeping my interest alive throughout his publishing career as a writer of narrative fiction. Although that fundamental humour which, like all good wit, is capable of perceptive observation and profound comment, is also to be found in Bermant's non-Scottish novels, it seems to have entered a particularly effective symbiosis when it has drawn on both Jewish and Scottish, especially Glaswegian, tributaries which, once channelled into a common bed, produce a delightful blend of crackling spiritedness and sensitive insights. For these reasons, though not for them alone, it appeared to be appropriate to explore Bermant's employment of names as stylistic devices in some of his novels,[1] in order to ascertain how much and in what way they contribute to the special tone, characterisation, and storying qualities which mark the author's narratives as distinctively and recognisably his.

As is often the case, when such an inventory has been finally assembled, any analysis beyond a mere listing tends to suggest directions which were not originally envisaged and to deflect the intended investigation from its laid-out paths; in other words, as the third section of this brief essay will demonstrate, there are always surprises. Readers are therefore encouraged to regard the opening two sections as preliminary to the purposes and strategies of the third.

In the first place, in the process of sorting and labelling the evidence, it became clear very quickly that it would be difficult, if not impossible, to divorce any examination of, and comment on, the use of personal names from the skilful and obviously competent and comfortable insertion of Yiddish or Hebrew words and phrases into the English texts. This is all the more significant since the first-person narrators of all the novels scrutinised for this study are Jewish in either the religious or secular sense and are, in one way or another, in their fictional autobiographies, concerned with a variety of aspects of their Jewish identity, from full acceptance via puzzled confrontation to severe questioning. It is therefore only to be expected and right that the narrating personae should, according to their position within the Jewish community and their linguistic ability, intersperse their English vocabulary with Yiddish/Hebrew expressions. How else could narrators like Jericho 'Jerry' Broch (JSA), Berl Brisker (BMT), Ben Bindle (BPU), Joshua 'Josh' Daniel Whitberg (SMW), Samuel 'Sam' Zucker (RBP), Sidney Newman (NNO), Henrietta 'Ducks' Courlander (THW) or Harry Newman (DB) be made to speak authentically? And Bermant's narratives are full of direct speech. Any writer who uses a mixed idiom like this – generally English but with occasional Yiddish/Hebrew encroachments – and relying on context for its intelligibility, does of course run the risk of satisfying neither of his main two audiences, but Bermant's interpolations adroitly avoid any problems that might have arisen. As is to be expected, most of his non-English lexicon refers to facets of Jewish religious practices or culinary items, although it is not limited to these.

On the whole, the items encountered might be placed in several categories of technical, homespun or apparently untranslatable terminology. Among them we find, without any attempt at classification, *sheigetz, ganef, shiksekricher, tzores, naches, lantsleit, Bar Mitzvah, Torah, shul, Mincha, Maariv, Bachad, kibbutz(im), Shabbat, cholent, lockshen, kreplech, tzimmes, meshuga, schmock, schwantz, wursht, uf-ruf, maazeltov, tachles, kosher, goy(im), kadish-seggers, chazan, Rosh Hashona, Yom Kippur, Succoth, Yeshiva, chupah, seder, kurve, kishkes, putzcha, mamzer, heimisch, yohr-tzeit, mentsch, shikse, klapping* vs *knipping, alter bock, schmaltz, shtum, cacker, bris, youngatz, schwartzer, schnorrer*, etc. When listed like this, they look quite overwhelming, but sprinkled judiciously over many pages of text in helpful contexts they lose their threat for the general reader. Together with certain syntactic constructions,[2] they serve Bermant's purposes well and helpfully underpin and accompany usage of personal names, effectively intertwining lexical and onomastic elements of his fictions.

In the world depicted by the Brochs, Briskers, Bindles, Whitbergs, Zuckers, Newmans and Courlanders, the Jewish communities to which they belong or of which they have knowledge are therefore peopled, in different capacities and with varying social and occupational status, by individuals like Luis Baranovitz, Philip Cohen, Ray Cranman, Ninna Boaz, Harry Levy, Inis Klein, Benny Black, a Mr Scholemazel, Katrina Kamenetz-Podolsk, Mr Epstein, Simcha Smeltzer, Mrs Nussbaum, a Board of Management of a synagogue consisting of Messrs Schrayer, Bills, Balls, Arkard, Balchack, Basil Plotz (cantor), and Asher Ochsher (beadle), Mrs Glober, Mrs Schmaltzhalter, gentlemen called Liftchick, Krapotkin, Greenfield, Slutzki, Shutef, Sheineretzke, Korncob, Abraham Pickholtz, Mr and Mrs Bosun, Monty Koch, Kluvnick (another cantor), Pushkin, Levine, Fish, Klapholtz, Drapkin, Grisewold, Grosschalk, Kravis, Kriskol, Flecker, Edwin T. Telfer, Otto Shoenberg, Katanchick, Eissemachar, Ignatz Wolf, Jacob and Avner Markovitch, Rhiner and so on. Like the above word list, this remarkable and often ludically selected anthroponymic palette suggests ironic exaggeration bordering on parody when presented in such density, but one has to recall that the occurrence of these names, alone or in clusters, is spread over a number of novels and thus never loses its effectiveness or detracts from the credibility of the characters so named; it is also worth remembering that in much of his novelistic output Chaim Bermant writes Human Comedy against a background of frequently unspeakable Tragedy.

This becomes especially poignant when he wryly refers to the onomastic means by which a certain amount of outward acculturation is achieved, as when recognisably Jewish surnames are altered by their bearers into what sound or look like Gentile equivalents, thus not only obliterating the original ethnic environment of the names but also suggesting a false onomastic heritage. Thus he comments on (fictive) name changes such as Schwartzenheimer to Blackholm, Cohen to Colquhoun or Connelly, Laski to MacLuskie, Malchaski to MacDonald, Kropotkin to Carmichael, Abraham to Ballantyne, Tiffenbron to Tiffen, Courlander to Lander or Lancer, Moshe Markovitch to Maurice Marshall, and (Nahum) Robinowitz to Raeburn. In particular, he plays, in *The Second Mrs Whitby*, with the varied forms of their name which members and descendants of the enormously rich Schwartzwald clan have adopted, such as Schwartz, Wald, Walden, de Walden, Black, Blackwood, Blaikie, and even Du Bois. Bermant, in general, manages to see the funny side of such name changes without losing sight of their more serious implications, especially in terms of his covert or overt quest for the nature or essence of Jewishness, or what some of his characters call 'Jewish Jewishness', a theme which is also central to his extensive journalistic and other non-fiction writings.[3] It goes without saying that, apart from scenarios set in Israel, the bearers of the names in question usually inhabit minority enclaves – social, cultural, religious, linguistic, customary – embedded in non-Jewish societies, mostly in cities like Glasgow or London, although these can shift within the cityscapes.

As indicated earlier, these brief surveys of the incorporation of Jewish lexical and onomastic items into some sample narratives of Bermant's are only intended to provide a surface impression of the presence of such devices in his novels. The temptation is, of course, considerable to flesh out these skeletal lists further but this would, in its over-simplification, not do a writer of Bermant's stylistic accomplishments any justice. It suffices to have drawn attention to his abilities as a name-conscious and linguistically sensitive writer, qualities that permeate all his novels, not just the ones investigated in this essay.

Instead of pursuing this undeniable strain in his fictions any further, we will therefore turn to an onomastic strategy in his novels which, after initially appearing to be mere accidence, on closer reading reveals itself as having considerable significance particularly in the toponymic marking of locational continuity or movement in the narrative structure; this device is better known from the temporal-spatial sequencing of events in the episodic arrangement of traditional folk-narratives, the single-stranded storying patterns of which are not dissimilar from those of first-person reminiscences or accounts, like those of Bermant's favourite protagonists – young people about to enter mature adulthood and old persons faced with or experiencing the challenges of retirement or the loneliness of widowerhood.

Let us look at two prominent examples of such human beings on thresholds in their lives; at the very beginning of the very first chapter of *Ben Preserve Us*, the young Ben Bindle, who has already spent three years in Cambridge and two in Jerusalem during named phases of his education, is about to leave London to become a Rabbi to a Jewish congregation in a Scottish town. That is a very prosaic summary of Chaim Bermant's inimitable version of a dialogue between a Jewish mother and her son (*Ben Preserve Us*, pp. 5-6):

> Mother jumped into the taxi as it was beginning to move.
> "Where are you going to?" I said.
> "I'm seeing you off to the station."
> "But I don't like being seen off. You know I don't. I've told you I don't."
> "All right, I'm not seeing you off. I'm taking a ride in the taxi. I like taxi rides. Do you mind? It's not as if it's going to cost you any more, and if it does, I'll pay for it."
> We travelled on in silence for a time. Then she said.
> "Do you still want to go?"

I sighed but did not answer.

"All right," she went on, "all right. You want to be a Rabbi? Be a Rabbi. Be anything you like. Be a dustman, a-a-scavanger, a strip-tease dancer. It's your life. You want to throw it away? Throw it away. But if you must be a Rabbi, why not in London? What's wrong with London, tell me? Ten million people live in London, but it's not good enough for my prince. Tell me what's wrong with it? I live in London, all my family live in London, the Queen, all the best people. Do you have to run away five hundred miles to what-do-you-call-that-place?"

"Auchenbother."

"Auchen who?"

"Auchenbother, I've told you a hundred times."

"If you would tell me a thousand times I still wouldn't be able to pronounce it. All I know about the place is that Aunt Hilda lives there, which believe me is a good enough reason for not going there. Did I ever tell you about Aunt – "

"A hundred times."

Thus, personal development – from student to Rabbi – is mapped by two named places, one London (fictionalised reality), the other Auchenbother (factualised fiction). What cannot be achieved in London, in spite of his mother's insistent protestations, appears to be possible in Auchenbother, several hundred miles away; therefore, relocation is required. The train journey from one location to the other is a rite of passage which allows Ben to become what he is destined, or at least wants, to be, with London as the named place of departure and the somewhat parodic Auchenbother as the named place of destination.

At the other end of the spectrum – again at the beginning of the first chapter – Sidney Newman recently retired, titular protagonist of *Now Newman Was Old*, reluctantly, on the verge of leaving London for Crocus Hill by the seaside near Brighton, rehearses again with his wife Dora the arguments for and against their imminent departure (*Now Newman Was Old*, p. 3):

"That's it then." I said when the removal van pulled up.

"You got regrets?" asked Dora

"Sure I've got regrets."

"Habit's everything with you," she said. "You'd have regrets leaving hell."

"Sure I'd have regrets. You got no regrets at all?"

"No I haven't. The stairs is killing me. I can't wait to have everything on one floor."

"We could have let the top floor."

"*Let* the top floor? I should keep lodgers at my age?"

"What's age got to do with it? And besides they wouldn't be lodgers, they'd be tenants."

"They'd have been coming through our hallway and up the stairs there, right?"
"Right."
"They'd be lodgers."·
We had been through all that before, if not a hundred times then a thousand times, and of course she was right. The house was big, it was difficult to get help (and expensive when you could get it), and the stairs were awkward.

Or, as Sidney puts it a little later (p. 7): "It was taken for granted, at least by Dora, that once I retired we would move house."
As in Ben Bindle's case, London remains the place to which one returns, for various reasons, from time to time, but Auchenbother and Crocus Hill are, after the initial leap in the dark, the places where their respective lives are now moored and, it must be said, flourish. Both Ben Bindle and Sidney Newman continue to make smaller journeys or sorties from time to time; the latter even travels to California (one of the most humorous episodes in the novel) before ending up in a nameless mental hospital, but the main change in their lives is flanked by the name London, on the one hand, and Auchenbother or Crocus Hill, on the other. It is probably not without significance that the latter two are acartographic.
Other novels, too, link named places with phases in Bermant's protagonists' lives, utilising them as stations on a journey, so to speak, mainly to be stopped at for a while for a particular purpose but always with the possibility of being revisited. Change of location as an outward sign of innovative action and new experiences is, of course, employed quite frequently as one of a storyteller's tricks of the trade, but what is remarkable about Chaim Bermant's stories is that many of these significant locations are named. Heinz/Heinschein, puzzled and sometimes confused identity seeker in *Dancing Bear*, for instance, has to go to Frankfurt to lose his virginity, and 'Ducks' Courlander in *The House of Women* loses hers in Leeds, both places having been primarily the destinations of journeys for other purposes. Heinschein is perhaps more than any other of Bermant's first-person narrators associated with a series of named places in his two-pronged quest for professional advancement and discovery of self. Resznitz on the Latvian-Polish border (boyhood), Cairo (further education), Oxford (study), Frankfurt (see above), London (bank), Gulf States (tour), South Kensington (love-making), Firwood Hall (falls in love), Moscow (professional posting), Yalta (holiday, breakdown of his marriage), London (meets former girl-friend again), Cairo, Riga and Resznitz (revisits), house in Brondesbury Park (circumcision of his son Jacob), Chicago (checking on his parentage, especially his mother), New York (professional assignment), London (return for professional reasons). No wonder the narrator, in an outburst of frustration, comments at one

point (p. 91): "I had been a Latvian, a German, and an Egyptian, and I was finally becoming an Englishman, and did not want the added complication of being a Jew." Heinschein's expression of vexation is a negative mirror image of the Prologue with which Bermant prefaces his largely autobiographical account *Coming Home* (p. 11):[4]

> I was born in a part of Lithuania which was then Poland and is now Russia. When I was three my family moved to Latvia; when five I was sent to a school in Poland; at eight we all moved to Scotland; at twenty I first went to Israel. In Latvia I was known as a Polack, in Poland as a Lett, and in Scotland as a foreigner. In Israel, however, I was known as a Scot. In a sense I had come home.

It is perhaps not too far-fetched to seek a source for the novelist's practice of naming places as geographical as well as structural markers in the voluntary or involuntary mobility which underlies such personal experience, as well as the behaviour of many of the community to which he belongs.[5] As Josh Whitberg, the narrator of *The Second Mrs Whitberg*, silently exclaims in exasperated commentary (p. 146):

> My fellow Jews. Bless 'em, are caught up in a leap-frog game all their life. No sooner are they established in one place, than whoop! They're off to another, a third, a fourth. They're the answer to an estate agent's dream (which is perhaps why so many of them are estate agents). You would think they were living in tents. Earlier generations – in Russia at least – had to keep moving because they weren't allowed to stay and I suppose if you're used to doing things one way for two thousand years, you can't change to another overnight, but somebody had to make a start

Characteristically, though, Josh Whitberg's vision of greater permanency in a more settled life style is also named as a Glasgow street called Tulloch Terrace, and specifically number twenty-two, a domicile which he refuses to leave even after most of the Jews who had lived there (Walden, Carmichael, Kropotkin, Klapholtz, Ballantyne, Abrahmski, Kluvnick, Pushkin, Levine, Fish etc.) "had fled to Gimmock, to Whitecraigs, to Newton Mearns" (p. 55) and had been replaced mostly by Pakistanis. His daughter, when he visits her in America, accuses him of regarding "Tulloch Terrace, Glasgow" as "paradise" (p. 82), and he chides her in return: "You've only been married four years and you've already moved twice", now living, as she admits, "sort of nowhere".

While it is dangerous to allow an author's fictional creations to speak for him, it seems nevertheless permissible to interpret frequently expressed opinions and attitudes, and especially the repeated use of particular devices, as echoing some of the writer's own predilections and basic instincts. The assumption is therefore not misleading that even more fundamental to Bermant's naming practices in the depiction of locations as holding areas in temporal developments in somebody's life is the author's innate, ingrained sense of space, for even when movement is absent or not yet contemplated, spatial relationships are prominently displayed, as in young Jericho Broch's description of Glasgow as seen from the university, a view familiar to numerous students (*Jericho Sleep Alone*, p. 47):

> As we stood by the University flagstaff on Gilmore hill we could see much of Glasgow stretched out below us: the Gingerbread pile of the art gallery, the children's hospital, like an Oldham mill; the river Kelvin, white with foam, gushing its noxious way, and in the distance the scaffolding and cranes of the ship-yards like a black, leafless forest, and beyond them the hills of the Clyde, grey-green.

If one adds to this nostalgic vision names (all with different functions in the plot) like Langside, The Victoria Infirmary, Queens Park, the Cosmo (cinema), Bath Street, the Langside, Gorbals, and Mitchell libraries, the Campsie Hills, Gorbals Cross, Ayr, the Maryhill Barracks, Pollockshields, the Trossachs, Kelvin Avenue, Loch Lomond, Woodland Road, St Andrew's Hall, Camphill, the image of the city of Glasgow, and of the delightful places to which Glaswegians can escape so easily, becomes irresistible. 'Jerry' Broch, of course, also travels as he grows up – to Thackford in Essex, to London, to Tel-Aviv, Haifa, Jerusalem and a kibbutz in Israel, but Glasgow remains both origin and satisfying destination of his life: "All was well with the world and the world was well with me" (*Jericho Sleep Alone*, p. 218).

It is not surprising that Bermant's novels do not contain many references to named places which are of little relevance or none at all to the plot for, in practically all instances, places that are given names by the author have some bearing on the lives of his protagonists, like a holiday trip from Crumpshall to Frinton's Queen Anne hotel and Clapton, or a day visit to Dorset in *The Companion*, the education of the girls in *The House of Women* at a boarding school called Hellenslea, Berl Brisker's offer of a job on a farm near Bletchley and his ultimate return to Eastleigh in *Berl Make Tea*, Bournemouth as a holiday destination in *Ben Preserve Us*, Sunday trips to the Strath-Eden hotel in Helensburgh for kosher suppers in *The Second Mrs Whitberg*, or an unexpected invitation to provide musical entertainment in Pontefract in *Roses are Blooming in Picardy*. While some of these may be of little significance, most of them represent important stepping stones, for in the terms of Uncle Yehudah's favourite Talmudic saying in *Jericho Sleep Alone*, *Meshane Hamokom, Meshane Hamazel* "a change of place is a change of fortune" (p. 32, also p. 300).

As is appropriate, in a corpus of novels like Chaim Bermant's, Israel is a frequent destination of those who travel to or settle in named places. It is therefore somewhat presumptuous of a student of literary onomastics to highlight only those aspects of Bermant's works which illuminate the use of names as structuring devices because, in the end, many of these novels, as well as his non-fiction writings, are about something even more fundamental than names, as this exchange between Mrs Kamanetz-Podolsk and Berl Brisker in *Berl Make Tea* demonstrates (p. 56):

> Mrs K.-P.: "... for ordinary people like you and me, Berl, if we're not Jewish we're nothing."
>
> B.B.: "Mrs K.-P., I'm as Jewish today as I was the day I was circumcised, and heaven forbid that I shall ever try to be anything else – because I should never get away with it. It's built into me."

This is a heart-felt, profound sense of identity which even the strong individuating power of names can foreground only with difficulty, but perhaps even the limited examination of the presence and function of names in some of the humorous novels of an accomplished Jewish writer like Chaim Bermant has made some kind of acceptable contribution to that fascinating and ever-growing field of intellectual endeavour – literary onomastics.

Notes

1 The novels in question are: BMT, *Berl Make Tea* (London, 1965); BPU, *Ben Preserve Us* (London, 1965); DB, *Dancing Bear* (London, 1984), JSA, *Jericho Sleep Alone* (London, 1964); NNO, *Now Newman Was Old* (London, 1978); RBP, *Roses Are Blooming in Picardy* (London, 1972); SMW, *The Second Mrs Whitberg* (London, 1976); TC, *The Companion* (London, 1987); THW, *The House of Women* (London, 1983).

2 Also in that most deprecating of Jewish verbal shoulder-shrugs: "Blows up, schmoz up", "Your Ninnas and Schminnas", "sermon schmermon".

3 Bermant was on the staff of the (London) *Jewish Chronicle* from 1961-1966. Many of his journalistic writings are collected in *Murmurings of a Licensed Heretic* (1990). Relevant non-fiction books are *Israel* (1967), *Troubled Eden* (1967), *The Cousinhood* (1971), *The Walled Garden* (1974), *Point of Arrival* (1975), *The Jews* (1978).

4 *Coming Home* (London, 1976). Parts of this book had previously appeared in the *Jewish Chronicle*, *The Observer* and *Present Tense*.

5 This is reflected both in the first volume of his autobiography, *Genesis*, published posthumously a few months after his death, and in his fictional "Jewish family saga" *The Patriarch* (London, 1981).

Lucie A. Möller and J.K. Jacobs (eds.), 2 vols.,
Nomina Africana 15, 1 & 2 (2000, pub. 2003) 80-86

On English and Gaelic Place-Names
in Medieval North-East Scotland

OVER the last few years, one of my main research projects has been an investigation of the earliest English place-names in North-East Scotland (Nicolaisen 1999), i.e. roughly in an area from the Mearns to Moray, and adjacently to Angus in the south and Nairn in the north-west. This research has inevitably led to a close examination of the linguistic, onomastic, and cultural contacts between English in its several varieties, as the most recent addition to the toponymic palimpsest that is the map of the region, and the preceding stratum, Gaelic. In my conceptualisation of the nature of these contacts, I have deliberately avoided notions like substratum and superstratum as far too rigid in their chronological sequencing. Although adstratum might have been a term more appropriately describing the actual contact situations, even it seemed inadequate when applied to the various observable complexities and nuances, even from a synchronic point of view. After all, in some parts of the north-east English and Gaelic have been, until fairly recently, spoken side by side for about 800 years, whereas in others native Gaelic must have ceased to be the daily means of communication several centuries ago; if we consider the extremes of the presence of Gaelic in the region from the arrival of the Scots in what used to be Celtic Pictland in the ninth century to the survival of a single speaker – so I am told – in a nursing home on Deeside in our own time, we can reckon with a span of almost a dozen centuries. Gaelic has therefore been more, much more, than an interim linguistic layer between Pictish and English, even though the former appears to have influenced it during the first few generations of Gaelic-speaking settlement, and the latter began to make its presence felt after a comparatively short period – perhaps only two or three hundred years –

during which Gaelic held sway as the dominant, or even exclusive language of the north-east, a thought which strikes some modern north-easterners, so firmly rooted in the Scots ('Doric') culture of the region as surprising, not to say bizarre or even unwelcome.

The political impetus and demographic movement which effectively opened the doors to English in the north-east was the feudalisation of Scotland under the royal brothers Edgar, Alexander I, and especially David I (between 1097 and 1153), at whose invitation the first Anglo-Norman nobles made their appearance in Scotland, a process intensified north of the Forth and Clyde in the reigns of David's grandsons Malcolm IV (1154-65) and William the Lion (1165-1214). Initially, this affected mostly the urban areas, particularly as a result of the creation of royal and other burghs, such as Aberdeen, Forres, Elgin, and Inverness (Pryde 1965), in the second half of the twelfth century, but then also spread to the rural hinterland of the burghs and to more remote areas. The documented use of English in the region as a whole did, however, not follow immediately, for two reasons, one general and the other specific: there is generally a noticeable time lag between the arrival of a language in an area and the appearance of its toponymic effects in the written record, and more specifically, the process in the north-east, as in other parts of Scotland, was in its early stages more one of upper-class Normanisation than of pervasive Anglicisation (Simpson 1943: 132, and 1949: 10).

Documentation for the coining of English place-names in the north-east begins at the turn of the twelfth to the thirteenth century, the first recorded instance being the spelling *Le harlav* for *Harlaw* (Aberdeenshire) 'grey hill' or 'hill with stony ground', near Inverurie, in a charter of Earl David of Huntingdon's some time between 1185 and 1219 (Stinger 1985: 223). To this solitary potential example of a late twelfth-century coinage we can add in the first half of the thirteenth century, as Geoffrey Barrow has shown (Barrow 1980: 201-202), about another eighteen names without any discernible overall pattern, although two small clusters of them are to be found in the Ellon/Logie-Buchan area of Aberdeenshire and in Strathisla in Banffshire, respectively. These clusters are both recorded in charters by William Comyn, Earl of Buchan, and may therefore be indicative of a greater density of speakers of English at that time on the Earl's possessions, one of the centres of which was Ellon. Practically all the names in this small inventory designate minor habitative or natural features in the landscape, although there are one or two exceptions, to one of which, Scotston (Scottistun), we will return later. Even in the first half of the thirteenth century the sources in which these place-names occur are, however, quite exceptional, insofar as the hundreds of other contemporary charters relevant to the north-east do not give the slightest hint of any localisation of English at all.

One might have been justified to expect a gradual increase in the recorded number of place-names of English origin in our region during the second half of the thirteenth century but, for some reason, this is not the case. Only about a dozen names have been identified so far (Nicolaisen 1999: 75). The reason for this decrease cannot solely be ascribed to incomplete documentation and, if place-name evidence is of any value at all in this kind of investigation, must mainly be looked for in a temporary slow-down of the localisation of English and of .its speakers in the Scottish north-east. This does not mean that the situation remained completely static, for several new types began to appear towards the end of this period which, it seems, reflect the beginnings of a new relationship between the incomers and both the land and the population they encountered. Representative of this new type of name are habitation names like Estertully (1287) in Culter and Estirgedeys (1295) in Nairn in which an English term is added to the existing Gaelic names Tully and Geddes (Gedeys) which also continue as designations of settlements near which, or as subdivisions of which, new habitations, presumably by speakers of English, were inserted into the landscape. These names and others like them are symptomatic of the kind of process, both in local settlement patterns and in their toponymic reflexes, which typify an important strand in the ever-increasing number of English contributions to the place-nomenclature of the Scottish north-east from the fourteenth century onwards, a process which has continued in the rural parts of the region almost to this very day – continuity and change encapsulated in a preponderant place-name type. Though nothing is ever self-evident in place-name research, it is surely not too adventurous to assert that such names were given by speakers of English who settled among their Gaelic-speaking neighbours whose place-names they had adopted and indeed made their own through phonological adaptation (cf. Taylor 1994).

If the real impact of English on the north-east of Scotland in terms of place-name creation can confidently be dated from the fourteenth century onwards (Nicolaisen 1999: 76-77), it follows that Gaelic must have remained the dominant language in the region until that time, and it is therefore not surprising that, as a consequence, the landscape of the region is saturated with names of Gaelic origin, names which designate every imaginable kind of geographic feature. Four and a half centuries are obviously quite a sufficient stretch of time for a blanket Gaelic place-nomenclature to have been created, even if one takes into account the strong possibility of a period of Pictish-Gaelic bilingualism straddling the year 900 and the sporadic English intrusions from about 1200 of which we have already spoken. In terms of linguistic and onomastic stratification it would therefore, as I have already stressed, be quite misleading to think of the Gaelic layer in the north-east merely as a transitional stage between Pictish and English. Quite the contrary is true, and its substantial one-time presence, including the pre-Gaelic components it had absorbed from Pictish and other less well-defined earlier strata, is apparent everywhere in the cartographic palimpsest that is the map of the north-east of Scotland.

It would be a worthwhile undertaking to describe and analyse the nature, structure, contents and vocabulary of this Gaelic toponymy but such a project would not likely make any practical contribution to a quest to which I have begun to give some thought in extension of my search for the earliest English names, both as a general matter of available evidence and research strategies and its specific application to the north-east. In a sense, what I have in mind may be regarded as the flipside of the same coin which I have already scrutinised, if such a colloquial numismatic metaphor is appropriate under these circumstances.

If, as I have already attempted to demonstrate, it is possible to search for and find examples of the earliest English place-names and their immediate successors from about 1200 onwards and to utilise them as evidence for the initial phases of the location of English in the region, it may also not be starting a wild-goose chase to look for toponymic material which might be useful not only in delineating the seam between Gaelic and English but also in tracing the gradual regression of Gaelic concomitant, if not always precisely concurrent, with the unstoppable progress of English. Or, put somewhat differently, to try and detect signposts which might somehow point to an answer to the question: For how long did Gaelic remain productive in the creation of geographical names in the north-east, in the face of the ever-increasing impact of English? What makes such a double quest so difficult is the fact that one is primarily looking for absences rather than presences, seeking out negative evidence, so to speak.

Strange as it may seem at first glance, such a search has apparently more chances of success at the early stages of the development which it is trying to track than at the later ones. In 1230, for instance, in reference to the name Wardlaw near Beauly, an entry in the *Register of the Bishopric of Moray* reads "locus qui dicitur Wardelau Scotice Balabrach", or, as a later charter has it, *Balcabrach*, i.e. "the place which is called *Wardelau* or in Gaelic Bal(c)abrach" (Barrow 1980: 201). This entry not only implies a name change from Gaelic to English in the making but also confirms the reality of a period of bilingualism at the charter date. Both names are obviously used side by side for a while, presumably *Wardelau* by speakers of English and *Balcabrach* by speakers of Gaelic, but it does not come as a surprise that not much later Gaelic *Balcabrach* "township of the tree trunks or rafters" is completely replaced by English *Wardlaw* "watching hill" which is still the designation of the place today.[1] Without these fortuitous entries we would never have been aware of a pre-existing Gaelic name for *Wardlaw*, and one cannot help wondering how many other Gaelic place-names have been obliterated by English replacements, in this case by one which has no semantic connection with its Gaelic forerunner and clearly looks at the same site from a very different perspective. Not unrelated is the question as to when native speakers of Gaelic, after learning the language of the incomers, began to use *Wardlaw* themselves when speaking English or, in a further step away from true bilingualism, started to coin geographic names in English.

Another entry of interest in this connection is found in a somewhat later thirteenth-century taxation register of about 1275, in reference to the name Codylstane in Cromar (Alexander 1952: 223; Barrow 1992: 225; Nicolaisen 1999: 75-6). This stands out as a single and singular exception in a fairly long list of Gaelic place-names, testifying very likely to a minimal presence of English speakers in Cromar (Aberdeenshire). Further light on its somewhat unexpected occurrence in this listing is thrown by a gloss in the margin of a 1268 document which comments that a place which was once called *Hachadgouan* "is now called Cuthilstone"; we find, too, that in 1228-39 it had been simply *Hachagouane* and continued as such for another twenty years. The substitution can therefore be placed around 1270.

The two spellings of the Gaelic name represent attempts by – presumably French-speaking – scribes to render Gaelic *Achadh Ghobhann* "the Smith's field", and its English equivalent, the modern form of which is *Coldstone*, pronounced ['kol-stən], possibly means "trysting stone", therefore again introducing a completely unrelated meaning. The morphology of *Cuthilstone* is, however, more complex as the first element may be Gaelic *comhdail* "assembly, meeting, conference, tryst" (Barrow 1992: 219-28). The significant difference between the pairs *Wardlau/Balcabrach* and *Hachadgouan/Cuthilstone* is that the former appears to indicate the onset of bilingualism whereas the latter implies that the substitution of English for Gaelic has reached a further stage.

Straying a little to the south into Angus, we come across a reference in 1256, in a perambulation of the marches of Kingoldrum, to a place called "Hachethm<i>ethoner quod anglice dicitur midefeld", *i.e. Achadh Meadhonach* which in English is called *Midfield* (Barrow 1980: 201). It is worth noting that in this instance the Gaelic name of the location is given first, with the English name added as a translation. This is of special interest since in a later description of the marches of the same lands in the first half of the fifteenth century only the English name *Mydfield* is used, an indication that all memory of the Gaelic name seems to. have been lost by that time. Perhaps one is allowed to conclude, even on the basis of so little evidence, that the demise of Gaelic in this western part of Angus took place between the middle of the thirteenth and some time in the fifteenth century.

These isolated recorded examples may not be much to go by but their survival permits us at least glimpses into the process of de-Gaelicisation, and especially in the north-east. They appear to be our best bet in the furthering of our exploration.

This does not mean that all other doors are completely closed although the criteria and strategies for opening them will still have to be much better honed. It might be possible, for instance, to tap into chronological sequences of the written record of names and explore their implications for phonological change. Major candidates for this kind of approach might well be a large group of place-names in which the Gaelic suffix *-ach* has become *-o*, the distribution of which is predominantly eastern and north-eastern although it also extends into Perthshire. As I tried to show in the festschrift for Derick Thompson (Nicolaisen 1996), the recorded forms allow us to reconstruct a sequence *-ach> -och> -oh> -o*, as, for example in Durno (Aberdeenshire) which is recorded as *Durnach* from about 1180 to 1380, as *Durnoch* in the sixteenth and seventeenth centuries, and as *Durno* from the end of the fifteenth century to the present day; or *Fetteresso* in the Mearns which has an *-ach*-ending in the thirteenth and fourteenth centuries, an *-och*-spelling in the fifteenth century, and an *-o*-ending from the fifteenth century to the present day (with a forerunner in *-eau* in 1204-11); or *Inchmarlo*, also in the Mearns, which is recorded as *Inchmerlach* in 1494, as *Inchmarloch* and the like from the second half of the fifteenth century to the middle of the seventeenth century, and as *Inchmarlo* from the sixteenth century onwards. Other north-east examples would be *Aberlemno*, *Ardo*, *Ardoe*, *Balbegno*, *Balwyllo*, *Braco*, *Craigo*, *Knockando*, *Pitsligo*, and *Stracathro*, and there are several instances to be found in Fife and Perthshire. Depending on whether one considers the change from *-ach* to *-och* as intra-Gaelic or as post-Gaelic, one can utilise either the *–ach > -och* or the *-och > -oh* change as a benchmark for an intended representation of the pronunciation by Gaelic or Scots speakers. As a rule of thumb, one might then conclude either that the domination of Gaelic ceased in the fifteenth century in the more easterly locations and in the sixteenth century in Perthshire, or roughly a hundred years later in both areas, if *-ō* is considered to be the post-Gaelic spelling. Naturally, the written record is not seamless nor is it free from overlaps; one also has again to be aware of the usual time-lag between language change and the recorded toponymic reflexes of that change which I mentioned earlier. Nevertheless, phonological evidence is, with all its flaws, likely to be an important source for our detective story.

Other possibilities might be the search for new Gaelic name types or elements as they may appear in the record, or an investigation of the qualities of the sites to which the names are attached. A late onset of the record of a name, though not necessarily relevant, may in some cases serve as a pointer in the right direction. The various places called *Scotston* may also have potential in this respect, if they turn out to be names given by English-speaking neighbours to habitations in which speakers of Gaelic lived. This name type does, however, often admit of alternative etymologies and has to be handled with care.

There may well be other criteria and potential strategies which we have not yet recognised, and extra-onomastic evidence may also come into play, sometimes providing critical supportive or contradictory arguments. Ideally, one would look, of course, for several criteria to support each other. We are, however, still in the initial phases of this explorative survey and much remains still to be done. In spite of the paucity of relevant evidence, the quest is by no means a hopeless one, and one day we may indeed be able to establish one of the most elusive phenomena in place-name research – the stratum within the stratum – while moving a step nearer redefining part of what Geoffrey Barrow has called "The Lost Gaidhealtachd" (Barrow 1992: 105).

Note

Since writing this article I have learned that the name *Cabrich* (NH 5343) still exists. It is in the modern parish of Kirkhill (NH 5545) which is incorporated in the parish of Wardlaw. – W.F.H.N.

References

Alexander, W.M. 1952. *The Place-Names of Aberdeenshire*. Aberdeen: Third Spalding Club.

Barrow, G.W.S. 1980. *The Anglo-Norman Era in Scottish History*. Oxford: Clarendon Press.

Barrow, G.W.S. 1992. *Scotland and its Neighbours in the Middle Ages*. London/Rio Grande: The Hambledon Press.

Nicolaisen, W.F.H. 1996. Gaelic *-ach* to Scots *-o* in Scottish Place-names. *Scottish Gaelic Studies* 17: 278-291.

Nicolaisen, W.F.H. 1999. The Earliest English Place-names in North East Scotland. *Northern Scotland* 18: 67-82.

Pryde, G.S. 1965. *The Burghs of Scotland*. Oxford: University Press.

Simpson, W.D. 1943. *The Province of Mar*. Aberdeen University Studies 121. Aberdeen: University Press.

Simpson, W.D. 1949. *The Earldom of Mar*. Aberdeen University Studies 126. Aberdeen: University Press

Stringer, K.J. 1985. *Earl David of Huntington* 1152-1219. Edinburgh: University Press.

Taylor, S. 1994. Babbet and Bridin Pudding and Polyglot Fife in the Middle Ages. *Nomina* 17:99-118.

Sea Change: Orkney and Northern Europe
in the later Iron Age AD 300-800.
Eds. Jane Downes and Anna Ritchie.
Balgavies, Angus (2003) 139-144

Perspectives on the Pre-Norse language(s) of Orkney

There [is no] way of knowing who these pre-Scandinavian people were
(Fellows-Jensen 1984, 151)

NOBODY but a fool – especially the proverbial old fool! – would have allowed himself to be persuaded to stand up in the capital of Orkney in front of a knowledgeable audience, to find words which will with even a smidgen of conviction convey some sensible information on what can only be regarded as a non-subject: the linguistic situation in Orkney before the arrival of the Scandinavians. As the programme indicates, and as several lectures have already confirmed, this conference is centrally concerned with 'The Later Iron Age', a title which unmistakably points to its focus on prehistoric material culture, indeed to the metal itself which, though by no means innovative any more and, as one might say, already well worked, sustained many tangible aspects of the culture of that Age. Presumably it was thought by the conference organisers, with considerable justification, that people who make things, not only with iron, also use language to communicate with each other which prompted the idea of an enquiry into the nature of that language; but whereas the corpus of material finds allows the perspicacious archaeologist to piece together a recognisable composite picture of life in these islands, both within the space of this archipelago and in a wider context, any equivalent discoveries in the linguistic sphere have simply not occurred and are not likely to happen in the foreseeable future. The chief reason for this current and unfortunately also anticipatory lack of relevant evidence is the realisation that, as far as Orkney itself, the Northern Isles in general, and, even more widely, the whole of the north of Scotland are concerned, we are, between AD 300 and 800, moving very close to the edge of the earliest known, even knowable, stratum of linguistic prehistory in this part of the world. Even the study of place-names, both habitative and topographical, which, with the help of a toponymic palimpsest, are usually the most ancient and persuasive evidence available in the reconstruction of a historical stratification, tends to fail us when we expectantly turn to it almost exclusively for this unpromising, highly speculative exploration. Let us therefore, with trepidation, enter this uninviting terrain.

Because of the extreme sparseness of the evidence, and in pursuit of fairly well proven pedagogical principles, our first step will have to be to widen our horizons by asking not only what our problem is but also whether Orkney faces a unique dilemma or can look for helpful analogues in similar situations elsewhere.

First of all, then, what is our problem? In contrast to the continuity, although perhaps not wealth, of archaeological evidence for the presence of people in pre-Scandinavian Orkney (Ritchie 1973, 1976-7) toponymic evidence for the centuries leading up to AD 800, let us say, is practically non-existent, apart from the name Orkney itself which, as *Orcades*, has been known at least since the middle of the first century AD when the Roman geographer Mela refers to this group of 30 islands by this designation. (Watson 1926, 6). Whether the name should be linked to actual pigs (boars), or whales or to the tribal totem animal of its inhabitants, the *Orcs* or 'boar people', is uncertain but the last of these meanings is the most convincing. *Inse Orc* is in early Irish literature paralleled by *Inse Catt* for Shetland (Watson 1926, 30) the latter, *Catt*, also being the totem name of the neighbouring mainland tribe, the 'Cat people' which has survived in the Gaelic name for Sutherland, *Cataibh* 'among the Cats' (Watson 1906, 235-6; 1926, 30), just as the Gaelic name for Orkney is *Arcaibh*, from *Orcaibh*. There is little doubt about the name's Celtic origin, and it is instructive to note that the Norsemen who must have known the name for some considerable time treated it similarly to the tribe of the Cats, i.e. adding their term for islands to the former, *Orkneyjar* (although reinterpreting it as 'seal islands'), and for a promontory to the latter, *Katanes*, the modern *Caithness*. As names are not usually given by the inhabitants of a territory or feature themselves but by their neighbours, all we can definitely say is that the neighbouring coiners and users of the name *Orcades* were Celts although this does not rule out the possibility of the Orcadians at that time, the beginning of the first millennium AD, being Celts themselves.

I am making this statement so cautiously because there is no place-name evidence at our disposal that allows us to be more positive. I am fully aware of attempts by reputable scholars (Hugh Marwick amongst them) to trace Celtic toponymic elements in the Orcadian place-nomenclature but ultimately with very limited success. The difficulty in this understandable, even necessary enterprise lies in the ability, or perhaps rather the inability, to prove that the potential toponymic candidates are indeed pre-Norse, i.e. belong at least to the period with which this conference is concerned. Almost forty years ago, F.T. Wainwright, reviewing the whole inventory of Marwick's candidates in great detail, was able to demonstrate that the terms in question, whether originally p-Celtic or Gaelic, have to be ascribed to Scandinavian contact with Gaelic speakers outside Orkney and are therefore to be understood in a Norse-Gaelic context elsewhere (Wainwright 1964). They are consequently not eligible as markers of survivals from pre-Norse times in Orkney (Wainwright 1964, 100-6). I have refrained from rehearsing the evidence and the arguments again since these have been part and parcel of the various discussions that have gone on on this subject ever since Marwick published his paper (Marwick 1923). It is only fair to add, that Marwick himself, however, whose article on the 'Celtic Place-Names in Orkney' had originally been prompted by a similar study of Jakob Jakobsen's in Shetland (Jakobsen 1901, 211-51), later in his magnum opus, *Orkney Farm-Names*, published in 1952, came to the conclusion that probably about 99 per cent of Orkney farm-names are of Norse origin and that the farms bearing names to which in the earlier paper he had ascribed 'pre-Norse provenance' 'cannot be regarded as having been in existence or so named in pre-Norse times'. His explanation was that the names of such farms 'merely denote words which had been borrowed from the earlier race and applied to the countryside which later [i.e. in Norse times] became farms' (Marwick 1952, 227). Without going over the details again, it must be said that the epithet 'earlier', if it is intended to refer to pre-Norse times in Orkney, is not applicable to practically any of the terms considered either.

The most promising toponymic candidates as witnesses for a potential pre-Norse Celtic presence are several place-names which appear to contain the genitive plural *Petta* of the Norse term *Pettr* referring to a 'Pict'. In Orkney, examples would be Pittaquoy, Pickiequoy, and Quoypettie which Marwick regards as compounds of *Petta* and ON *kví* 'cattle enclosure' (Marwick 1923, 262-3). As these were offered by Marwick again as complements to Jakobsen's Shetland names such as Pettadale, Pettawater, Petester, Pettafell, Pettigarthsfell and Pettyfirth, i.e. the valley, water, homestead, cattle enclosure and firth of the Picts (Jakobsen 1901, 169), it might be useful to deal with the evidence for the whole of the Northern Isles as one. Nobody would, of course, claim that these are Celtic place-names; as the generic elements ON *kví, dalr, vatn, setr, fjall, garðr, and fjörðr* show, they are thoroughly Norse containing, after all, the Norse form of the name *Picts*. It could, however, be argued that they do refer to the continual presence of some pre-Norse Picts among the Scandinavian incomers, perhaps living in small clusters or groups, identifiable and therefore nameable among the rest of the population. While this would be a reasonable interpretation of these place-names, if it were possible to show that the names in question are early enough to be at least near-contemporary with the arrival of Norse settlers in the Northern Isles, it becomes less plausible if one considers that the names are first recorded well into the Viking period (800-1100) or even later. It is therefore useful to consider seriously Barbara Crawford's observation that 'by the twelfth century ... the former native population of Orkney had been invested with supernatural qualities who in the *Historia Norvegiae* were described as dwarves who lived in underground houses' (Crawford 1987, 211). In fact, the context of *Petta*-names suggests that the previous inhabitants very soon became regarded more or less as trolls who inhabited certain lowly places' (*ibid*). As a folklorist, I find this information appealing, especially when it is supplemented by the belief expressed in the *Historia Norvegiae* using a well-known folklore motif that the Picts lost all their strength in the middle of the day. While one or two of the *petta*-place-names may preserve for us references to real Picts living in isolated or at least separate locations among the Norse, it is much more likely that these toponymic encapsulations have their origins. in oral tradition derived from the super-naturalisation of the Picts, and for that reason, play only an indirect, second-hand role in our quest for pre-Norse toponymic evidence.

Since it is the *Historia Norvegiae* which brings together the Peti (i.e. the *Pettar* or Picts) and the *Papae* (i.e. the *papar*, the 'Celtic priests'), a brief look at the placenames in which a reference to them is incorporated, seems to be in order at this point. What are of chief interest to us here are again the toponymic reflexes consisting mostly of Norse island names in which ON *ey* is the generic, like *Papa, Papa Stour, Papa Little* (in Shetland), and *Papa Stronsay, Papa Westray* (in Orkney) but also of other compounds such as *Papa Geo, Papa Skerry, Papdale*, as well as the Shetland *Papal* and Orkney *Papley* which contain ON *boeli* or *byli* 'a house or homestead' (see for instance Lamb 1995). Without wishing to go into detail regarding the anchoritic or monastic activities of these *papar* (perhaps one of them inscribed the ogham on the spindle whorl of Buckquoy or in the knife of Gurness?), neither they nor the geographical names traditionally attached to them, can tell us anything definite about the language of the pre-Norse inhabitants of Orkney and Shetland, except that there were amongst them Irish-speaking churchmen and their followers. It is also significant that Aidan MacDonald, with his life-long interest in the *papar* (MacDonald 1979), in a revised version of a paper he presented to a conference completely devoted to this topic in February 2001 (MacDonald 2002), suggests strongly that, instead of belonging mainly to the earliest phase of direct contact, they were coined and applied retrospectively, in a fashion not dissimilar from Crawford's views on the reshaping, in oral tradition, of the *Petta*-names. According to MacDonald, the *papar*-place-names themselves, once established, then contributed to the learned rationalisation of the traditions that had grown up around them (MacDonald 2002). Again I must confess that, as a folklorist, I find this argument attractive, and I am grateful to Aidan MacDonald for having made a preprint typescript of his paper available to me. My summary of his position is, of course, an oversimplification. Whether others find it acceptable or not, it does not affect the fundamental recognition that the *papar*-place-names, too, fail to serve as key witnesses for the general linguistic situation in pre-Norse Orkney.

There is one more facet of the Orcadian place-nomenclature which has sometimes been thrown into the discussion as being relevant to our quest and that is the type 'X of Y', like the three stream names *The Burn of Turnitail*, *Tne Burn of Gue*, and *The Burn of Vacquoy* (Nicolaisen 1976, 63; 2001, 83). In the early twentieth century, this type was sometimes regarded as being an adaptation of a Norse pattern, especially since occasionally both elements were of Norse origin, as in the Shetland names *Wick of Collaster*, *Holm of Skaw* and *Breck of Newgarth*. A detailed search has, however, revealed that there is no Scandinavian model for this pattern which is recorded from the very end of the fifteenth century (1492) onwards: *Nethertown of Grenyng*, *Bull of Rapness*, *Bull of Kerston*. The Shetland record for this type begins even later, for in 1615 we find the *Hill of Quarfe*, the *Isle of Moussay*, the *Hous of Wasland*. These examples, even if one takes patchy documentation and a certain delay between the creation of a productive type and its first documented occurrence into account, places the arrival of the 'X of Y' pattern in Orkney centuries beyond the Viking period. This morphological structure is, in fact, an import from the Scottish mainland, chiefly from the north-east, where the type is quite common, as in *Burn of Glendies* ABD, *Burn of Melmannoch* KCD, *Water of Buchat* ABD, *Mains of Keithfield* ABD, *Bridge of Don* ABD, and so on (Nicolaisen 1976, 63-4; 2001, 83-4). This Scottish import into the Northern Isles is itself the product of linguistic, or more precisely toponymic, contact, having started out in Gaelic as *Allt an t-Sluic Leith* 'burn of the green hollow' (1976, 59; 2001, 79). What we have here is therefore a Gaelic grammatical pattern which was taken over by speakers of Scots and subsequently exported to the Northern Isles, and there was for that reason no direct contact between Norse and Gaelic involved in its creation. The suggestion that 'the underlying pattern seems to be French' (Sandnes 1997, 128) is intriguing but not persuasive.

After this brief survey of the qualifications of some of the claimants or rather of their disqualifications, what is the toponymic residue? We have already singled out the name *Orcades*. It has also occasionally been proposed that the first elements in the island names *Shapinsay* and *Stronsay* may be derived from pre-Norse antecedents as there is no obvious Norse etymological connection (Thomson 2001, 42) but this does not help us much further. It is, however, worth our while to look at names of islands, especially the larger ones, for inspiration for, if we start casting around for potential analogues elsewhere, we note that Shetland has what looks like promising help to offer in the shape of the island names *Unst*, *Yell* and *Fetlar* (Crawford 1987, 104) which are semantically opaque and which have so far eluded ascription to any known language. They are certainly neither Norse nor Celtic, though they are likely to have been known to the Norsemen for some considerable time before they set out to settle in the Northern Isles. These names introduce an element which opens up a different linguistic perspective, that of a non-Germanic, non-Celtic, indeed a non-Indo-European presence in the Northern Isles, perhaps preceding them all, and therefore also not Pictish. I mention this possibility for during the last few years Katharine Forsyth, who has done so much for the deciphering of ogham inscriptions and whose scholarship I admire greatly, has led a vigorous and well-argued campaign against non-Indo-European Pictish (Forsyth 1995; 1997), mainly in the form of a repudiation of Kenneth Jackson's proposal of a second Pictish language of non-Indo-European provenance, in addition or parallel to p-Celtic Pictish which has emerged as the preferred ambience of the language of the Picts (Jackson 1955).

However, the epithet non-Indo-European, attached to these island names finds some justification and support not terribly far from Shetland in another group of islands which to a considerable extent shares the linguistic predicament of the Northern Isles: their western counterpart, the *Hebrides*. One of the puzzles of the toponymic stratification of these islands is that the large number of Norse place-names dating back from the beginning of the ninth to the middle of the thirteenth century do not contain any Gaelic element, as one would have expected, whereas the presumably later Gaelic place-names are replete with terms of Norse origin. This is such a curious state of affairs that Magne Oftedal observed in frustration: 'A logical consequence of this would be to infer that the areas in question were completely Norse, linguistically speaking, during a considerable period, or very nearly so, and that Gaelic was introduced, or reintroduced, afterward' (Oftedal 1955, 112). As in the situation in the Northern

Isles, there is, in the Western Isles, an almost complete absence of place-name evidence for the presence of the Celtic language which should have preceded the arrival of the Norsemen – Gaelic in the Hebrides and Pictish in Orkney and Shetland. As Pictish was nearing its demise everywhere soon after the beginning of the Viking Age, whereas Gaelic was on the ascendancy, the post-Norse linguistic development took, of course, very different courses in these two island groups.

Otherwise, the resemblance of the situations in the Northern and Western Isles does not end here, though, for the Hebrides have their *Unst, Yell*, and *Fetlar*, too, only there these are called *Lewis, Uist, Skye, Mull, Islay, Arran*, and possibly some others like *Bute, St Kilda* and *Tiree*. Most of these have become Scandinavianised in Norse usage, like *Ívist* for Uist, *Skíð* for Skye, *Myl* for Mull, *Bot* for Bute, *Íl* for Islay, and particularly *Ljóðhús* for Lewis which attempts to make sense of an otherwise opaque name by secondary re-interpretation in Norse or, as has been suggested, by renaming it after a market-town near Gothenburg (Pálsson 1996, 122-3). The details may differ but, on the whole, the Northern and Western Isles have much in common toponymically for the Norse period, not least the presence of a large number of *Pabay*-names, presumably reflecting very similar religious circumstances and activities in pre-Norse or early Norse times.

It would be as difficult to find Celtic or Indo-European etymologies for *Lewis, Uist*, and *Skye*, as for *Unst, Yell*, and *Fetlar*. A similar prospect would undoubtedly be encountered by any attempt to etymologise names like *Tuesis, Kailios*, and *Loxa* which are recorded by Ptolemy as belonging to rivers flowing into the Moray Firth in the middle of the second century AD, or even earlier (Watson 1926, 48-9). However helpless we may feel in facing their challenge, our ignorance regarding their linguistic provenance cannot seriously contradict their validity as evidence for a non- or preCeltic, non-Indo-European presence in the Northern and Western Isles, and presumably also on the Scottish mainland, in what is acknowledged p-Celtic Pictish territory, for which the strongest support comes from place-names such as those beginning with Pictish *pet(t)* (Pitlurg, Pittodrie, Pitmedden, Pitlochry, etc) (Nicolaisen 1996, 6-15). Names like *Unst, Skye* and *Kailios* do not weaken Katharine Forsyth's argument against non-Indo-European Picts but, when interrogated as linguistic evidence and taken to their logical conclusion, testify to the presence of people who were neither Picts nor Celts. Whether they were, at least in Orkney, the *Orcs*, 'the boar people', against whom expeditions by Pictish kings are recorded in Irish sources 'in 682 when "the Orkneys were utterly destroyed by Brude" and in 709' (Watson 1926, 62, note 2), is a different question, but these annals show that as late as the century preceding the arrival of the Norsemen, the Orcs were regarded in Ireland as different from the Picts. Such a view would coincide with the perception of the Pentland Firth (ON *Péttlands fjörðr*; Latin *Petlandicum mare*) as the northern boundary of 'Pictland' in the Norse sagas; it would, however, not rule out Pictish political overlordship over Orkney.

If, on the other hand, as the archaeological record is believed to indicate (Ritchie 1973; 1977; 1993, 25-8) and certain inscriptions appear to support (Forsyth 1996; 1997, 31-6), there were Picts in Orkney immediately before the Scandinavians, in spite of the absence of any reliable toponymic evidence, it is difficult to imagine that they shared with the contemporary mainland Picts of the Scottish north-east, the cultural richness which their place names and material and artistic remains display. For a proper evaluation of this combined evidence it is, of course necessary to remember that there is nothing static about a people and that, therefore, the tribal cluster whom the Romans called Picts was, probably, in many aspects quite different from the Picts with whom the Scotti merged in the ninth century. As far as the toponymic heritage is concerned, the element *pett* itself refers in the later stages in many instances not just to pieces of land but to 'estates' and even 'manor houses', as part of agricultural management and landscape maintenance, a fact which is still confirmed by the attachment of such names to modem castles and 'big houses' (Pitcaple, Pitfichie, Pittodrie, Pitmedden, etc) (Barrow 1973, 59-60; Taylor 1997). *Pit-*names, at least in the late Pictish dialect of the eighth and ninth centuries encountered by Gaelic speakers, also reveal, among other characteristics, individual ownership, including churches and Christian clerics but also preferred sites for agricultural and pastoral activities (*Pittendreich*). *Aber-* names (Aberdeen, Arbuthnott, Abernethy) point not only to important topographical locations at river-mouths, but also, in several instances to activities connected with river-worship in those locations (Nicholaisen 1996, 15-23; 1997*a*, 113-8; 1997*b*, 247-53). Even if Picts with close links to their mainland counterparts were the inhabitants of Orkney when, or before, the Scandinavian settlers came, the complete disappearance of such a varied and sophisticated toponymic tapestry and of the culture which it reflects would be astonishing.

No wonder that the complete absence of toponymic evidence for the presence of linguistic Picts (or *Orcs*, for that matter, apart from the name of the archipelago) in pre-Norse Orkney has aroused so much scholarly controversy which has split the experts into two major camps: those who believe in peaceful settlement by the Norse incomers and those who imagine a violent take-over (most recently Smith 2001 and Backlund 2001); for a balanced, dispassionate overview of the 'War' and 'Peace' theories see Chapter 3 of Thomson's new *History of Orkney*

(2001, 43-7)[1]. From a toponymic point of view, it is difficult to see how the obvious lack of relevant evidence can make any major contribution in support of either stance. As we have already seen, little consolation or assistance can be gained from those who have investigated the equivalent situation in the Hebrides, although, as Gillian Fellows-Jensen points out, 'in the Western Isles ... Gaelic-speaking people would seem to have survived' (Fellows-Jensen 1984, 151); she also admits, however, that 'it is impossible to be sure ... whether or not all or even most of the Gaelic speakers were descended from the pre-Norse population of the Hebrides' (*ibid*). In the terminology assessing the toponymic situation in the Northern Isles, words like 'overwhelmed' 'obliteration', 'submerged' etc frequently occur, smacking of replacements enforced by superior numbers of settlers, faced with a relatively thin population. If we were to transfer Hermann Pálsson's statement concerning Lewis and Harris to Orkney, we might get a little closer to discerning what may have happened: 'Having rejected the nomenclature used by previous occupants, the Norwegian settlers ... undertook the daunting task of finding appropriate names, not only for their own homesteads but also for numerous natural features of the insular landscape' (Pálsson 1996, 314). The term 'rejection', however, implies a conscious choice between a knowable, existing place-nomenclature and one's own imports. Perhaps a somewhat different nuance of Pálsson's explanation may at least partially account for the exclusive use of Norse place-name materials, without siding with either the 'Peace' or the 'War' factions among scholars.

It appears to be increasingly believed that the colonising expansion from Norway to what became *Scotia Scandinavica* had already begun within Norway as a westward movement which then spilled over across the sea. As I have pointed out elsewhere (Nicolaisen 1987; 1991), the colonists brought with them in their mental baggage not just a lexicon of words, as part of their linguistic expertise, but also an onomasticon of names, including a toponymicon of place-names, which they applied to the features of the islands on which they settled. Being inexperienced namers, they were imitative rather than innovative in their naming practices, thus re-creating to a considerable extent the landscapes of the homeland. Whether they had sufficient contact with an existing population or not, it never occurred to them that it might be possible to apply somebody else's nomenclature to their 'New Norway'. It is also worth remembering in this respect that they had available to them the whole range of contemporary name types and elements with which they had been familiar at home, regardless of their historical status or etymologies, and did therefore not selectively apply them in some kind of chronological sequence (Thomson 1995, 48). It is for this reason not surprising that the proportion of names which had no equivalent in

Norway, either identically or as morphological models, was comparatively small. It seems that this conscious or subconscious desire to transfer the landscape of home to the strange land with the aid of place-names, both topographic and habitative, may well have been an essential factor in accounting for the neglect (not rejection!) of what were, after all, structuring devices of somebody else's habitat. The colonisers' apparent ignorance of any language pre-existing their arrival probably encouraged such a process, anyhow.

While perhaps making a small. contribution to the puzzling question concerning the lack of pre-Norse toponymic survivals in Orkney, this theory does not, indeed cannot, aid a quest for the nature and identity of the pre-Norse language(s) of Orkney but that has, after all, been an impossible task from the beginning.[2]

Notes

1   I am most grateful to Willie Thomson for all his help and good advice, and especially for making a draft copy of the typescript of Chapter 3 ('Place-Names and the Pictish-Norse Transition') of his *New History of Orkney* (Thomson 2001, 40-55) available to me in which everything is set out so much more clearly and in a more balanced fashion than anything I could have attempted. Without his positive support my task would have been more daunting. That it has remained a Fool's Errand is my fault, not his.

2   Since completing this paper, the author has had the benefit of a lecture on 'Genetics and Genealogy' at the 2002 meeting of The Scottish Medievalists, by the eminent geneticist Professor Bryan Sykes of Wolfson College, Oxford. Analysing DNA samples, Professor Sykes has studied, among others, relevant genetic features of Orcadians, and his, as yet unpublished, results have shown the Norse vs. non-Norse (possibly Celtic) genetic evidence for Orcadians to be 60-40 in favour of the latter (the non-Norse). Even if only a small proportion of the non-Norse evidence can be linked with a pre-Norse population, these findings make the absence of pre-Norse place-names in Orkney all the more enigmatic and would, it seems, contradict any notion of a complete or partial rout of the pre-Norse inhabitants.

References

Bäcklund, J. 2001 'War or Peace? The relations between the Picts and the Norse in Orkney', *Northern Studies*, 36 (2001), 33-47.

Barrow, G.W.S. 1973 *The Kingdom of the Scots*. London: E. Arnold.

Crawford, B.E. 1987 *Scandinavian Scotland: Scotland in the Early Middle Ages*. Leicester: Leicester University Press.

Fellows-Jensen, G. 1984 'Viking Settlement in the Northern and Western Isles – the Place-Name Evidence as seen from Denmark and the Danelaw'. In Fenton, A & Pálsson, H. (eds) *The Northern and Western Isles in the Viking World: Survival, Continuity and Change*, 148-68. Edinburgh: John Donald.

Forsyth, K. 1995 'Language in Pictland: Spoken and Written'. In Nicoll, E.H. (ed) *A Pictish Panorama*, 7-10. Balgavies, Angus: The Pinkfoot Press.

Forsyth, K.S. 1996 *The Ogham Inscriptions of Scotland: An Edited Corpus*. Harvard University Thesis (April 1996). Ann Arbor, MI: UMI Dissertation Services 1998.

Forsyth, K. 1997 *Language in Pictland: the case against 'non-Indo-European' Pictish*. Studia Hameliana 2. Utrecht: de Keltische Draak.

Jackson, K.H. 1955 'The Pictish Language'. In Wainwright, F.T. (ed) *The Problem of the Picts*, 129-66. Edinburgh: Nelson.

Jakobsen, J. 1901 *Shetlandsøernes stednavne*. Aarbøger for nordisk Oldkyndighed og Historie 16, 55-258 (English translation: *The Place-Names of Shetland* London – Copenhagen: D. Nutt & V. The Orcadian Limited 1993.)

Lamb, R. 1995 'Papil, Picts and Papar', *in* Crawford, B.E. (ed) *Northern Isles Connections, essays from Orkney and Shetland presented to Per Sveaas Andersen*, 9-27. Kirkwall: The Orkney Press.

MacDonald, A. 1977 'Old Norse Papar Names in N. and W. Scotland: A Summary'. In Laing, L. (ed) *Studies in Celtic Survival*, 107-11. Oxford: BAR Brit Ser 37.

MacDonald, A. 2002 'The Papar and Some Problems: A Brief Review', *in* Crawford B.E. (ed) *The Papar in the North Atlantic: Environment and History*, 13-30. St Andrews: St John's House Papers 10.

Marwick, H. 1923 'Celtic Place-Names in Orkney', *Proc. Soc. Antiq. Scot.*, 57 (1922-3), 251-65.

Marwick, H. 1952 *Orkney Farm Names*. Kirkwall: W.R. Mackintosh.

Nicolaisen, W.F.H. 1976 *Scottish Place-Names: Their Study and Significance*. London: B.T. Batsford.

Nicolaisen, W.F.H. 1987 'Imitation and Innovation in the Scandinavian Place-Names of the Northern Isles', *Nomina* 11 (1987), 75-85.

Nicolaisen, W.F.H. 1991 'Scottish analogues of Scandinavian place names', *NORNA-rapporter*. 45 (1991), 147-55.

Nicolaisen, W.F.H. 1996 *The Picts and Their Place Names*. Rosemarkie: Groam House.

Nicolaisen, W.F.H. 1997a 'On Pictish Rivers and Their Confluences' In Henry, D. (ed) *The worm, the germ, and the thorn: Pictish and related studies presented to Isabel Henderson*, 113-18. Balgavies, Angus: The Pinkfoot Press.

Nicolaisen, W.F.H. 1997b 'The Dee at Chester and Aberdeen'. In Rumble, A.R. & Mills, A.D. (eds) *Names, Places and People, An Onomastic Miscellany in Memory of John McNeal Dodgson*, 247-53. Stanford: Paul Watkins.

Nicolaisen, W.F.H. 2001 *Scottish Place-Names: Their Study and Significance*. New Edition. Edinburgh: John Donald. (Originally published in 1976.)

Oftedal, M. 1955 'Norse Place-Names in the Hebrides' In Falck, D. (ed) 1955 *Annen Viking Kongress Bergen* 1953, 107-12. Universitetet: Bergen Årbok. Bergen: Grieg.

Pálsson, H. 1996 'Aspects of Norse Place Names in the Western Isles', *Northern Studies*, 31 (1996), 7-24.

Ritchie, A. 1973 'Empty Islands or Integration? An Archaeological Estimate of the Norse Impact in the Northern Isles', *Northern Studies*, 1 (1973), 23-5.

Ritchie, A. 1977 'Excavation of Pictish and Viking-age farmsteads at Buckquoy, Orkney', *Proc. Soc. Antiq. Scot.*, 108 (1976-7), 174-227.

Ritchie, A. 1985 'Orkney in the Pictish Kingdom' *in* Renfrew, C. (ed) *The Prehistory of Orkney B.C. 400-1000 A.D.*, 183–204. Edinburgh: University Press (reprinted in 1990). Ritchie, A. 1993 *Viking Scotland* London: B.T. Batsford.

Sandnes, B. 1997 'The Bu of Orphir, Burn of Gueth – a Gaelic Pattern in Orkney Place-Names', *Northern Studies*, 32 (1997), 125-8

Smith, R. 2001 'The Picts and the Martyrs or Did Vikings Kill the Native Population of Orkney and Shetland?', *Northern Studies*, 36 (2001), 7-32.

Taylor, S. 1997 'Generic Element Variation, with Special Reference to Eastern,Scotland', *Nomina*, 20 (1997), 1-22.

Thomson, W.P.L. 1995 'Orkney farm-names: a re-assessment of their chronology'. In Crawford, B.E. (ed) *Scandinavian Settlement in Northern Britain*, 42-62. Leicester: Leicester University Press. Thomson, W.P.L. 2001 *New History of Orkney*. Edinburgh: Mercat Press.

Wainwright, F.T. (ed) 1964 *The Northern Isles*. Edinburgh: Nelson; particularly 'Picts and Scots', 91-116.

Watson, W.J. 1906 'Some Sutherland Names of Places', *The Celtic Review*, 2 (1905-6), 232-42 and 360-8.

Watson, W.J. 1926 *The History of the Celtic Place-Names of Scotland*. Edinburgh: Blackwood.

Revised version of material which first appeared as part
of an entry 'Seenamen' (Lake Names) in the *Reallexikon
der Germanischen Altertumskunde* **28** (2005) 49-51

'Scottish Loch Names'

IN contrast to the cognate Welsh *llwch* but conforming to Irish *lough*, Scottish
Gaelic *loch* is the dominant, indeed the almost exclusive designation for an
expanse of standing water surrounded by firm ground. When *lake* occurs, it is,
with the exception of the *Lake of Menteith*, in reference to an artificial water
feature or, regionally, to a very small course of running water. The presence
of the hydronymic element water in the Northern Isles is discussed below (2).
Since *loch* is also the exclusively used lexical item referring to a natural expanse
of water of any size, in all varieties of Scottish English, *lake* being regarded
as peculiarly English, it will be used as the appropriate term in this discussion
of names of such features in Scotland; calling a *loch* a *lake*, even generically,
would seem unnatural.

Although Northumbrian *lūh* is found in the Lindisfarne Gospel (1) and
also occurs sporadically in geographical names in the north of England (4), this
is itself a loan from British. If this reached the south-east corner of Scotland
with the arrival of Angles from Northumbria in the seventh century A.D.,
it is nevertheless not likely to have been the sole source of *loch* in Anglian
Scotland; if it did make an appearance, it must have been soon reinforced or
supplanted by Gaelic *loch* which had arrived from Ireland from the 5th century
onwards. A more likely explanation is, however, that, both in the lexicon and in
the onomasticon, Scottish *loch* derives from its Irish counterpart; this applies
not only to names of Gaelic origin, whether in their Gaelic or their Anglicised/
Scotticised form, but also to those names in which it forms a compound with an
English generic, such as *Lochburn*, *Lochend*, *Lochfauld*, *Lochfield*, *Lochgate*,
Lochgreen, *Lochhead*, *Lochhill Lochpark*, *Lochrig*, *Lochside*, *Lochton*,

Lochtower, *Lochview*, *Lochwood*. Some of these names may well be translations from Gaelic, especially when they occur in former or present Gaelic-speaking areas, as, for instance, Lochend or Lochhead from Kinloch (Gaelic *Ceann Locha*), or Lochton from Balloch (Gaelic *Baile an Locha*), but this is not a precondition since *loch* (like *glen* 'valley' and *bog*) has been fully integrated into the Scottish English vocabulary. This is also shown by other loch-names in which *loch* occurs as the second element as, for example, with an attributive adjective: *Blackloch* (Gaelic *Loch Dubh*), *The Holy Loch* (*An Loch Sianta*), *Long Loch*, *Mikle Loch*, *North Loch*, *White Loch*, or with the name of a neighbourhood feature as a specific (*Carlingwark* Loch, *Carsford* Loch, *Clatteringshaw* Loch, *Houlaw* Loch, *Kilbirnie* Loch, *Kilconquhar* Loch, *Lindores* Loch, *Milton* Loch, *Portmore* Loch, *Rescobie* Loch, *Yetholm* Loch; and even the curious *Lochend* Loch). A subgroup of the latter category consists of names of the '*x* of *y*' pattern, which has its origins in Gaelic *Loch a' Bhealaich Bheithe*, *Loch a' Chaoruinn*) but has developed a separate existence in non-Gaelic-speaking environments in Scotland (2), (*Loch of Broadhouse*, *Loch of Brough*, *Loch of Clunie*, *Durness*, *Forfar*, *Fyvie*, *Kirbister*, *Lintrathen*, *Mortlach*, *Skene*, *Spiggie*, *Tingwall*).

One of the most notable categories of Scottish loch names derives from the name of the river which flows out of or through it. This group includes some of the major water-courses, among them pre-Gaelic Pictish and Old European names. Important examples are: Loch and River *Awe* (Gaelic *Abhainn Obha*), Loch and River *Brora*, Loch and River *Carron* (Gaelic *Carrann*), Loch and River *Doon*, Loch and River *Earn* (*Eireann*), Loch and River *Garry* (*Garadh*), Lochy (*Lòchaidh*), Lomond (*Laomainn*, the modern form of the river name is *Leven*), *Lyon* (*Líomhann*), *Naver* (*Nabhair*), *Ness* (*Nis*), *Nevis* (*Nibheis*), *Shiel* (*Seile*), *Shin* (*Sin*), *Tay* (*Tatha*), *Tummel* (*Teimhil*).

Naturally, the great majority of names in which *loch* occurs in its original linguistic habitat, Gaelic, is found in the Highlands and Western Isles, with its semantic connotations covering the full expected range, from the colour (*Loch Buidhe* 'yellow'; *Loch Dubh* 'black') or shape (*Loch Fada* 'long'; *Loch Mór* 'large', *Geárrloch* 'short') of the loch itself to, most commonly, references to features of the landscape in the vicinity (*Loch a' Bhealaich Beithe* 'a birch pass'; *Loch na Cille* 'church, churchyard'; *Loch a' Chàirn Bhàin* 'white cairn'; *Loch a' Choire* 'corrie'; *Loch a' Ghlinne* 'valley'; *Loch nan Eilean* 'islands') as well as to animal life (*Loch an Daimh* 'stag'; *Loch nam Breac* 'trout, salmon'; *Loch nan Eun* 'birds').

On the Scottish west coast and in the Western Isles (Hebrides), the term *loch* refers specifically also to coastal features, so-called 'sea-lochs', like *Loch Alsh*, *Loch Broom*, *Loch Etive*, *Loch Fyne*, *Loch Gilp*, *Loch Goil*, *Loch Hourn*, *Loch*

Indaal, *Loch Linnhe*, *Loch Long*, *Loch Morar*, *Loch Scridain*, *Loch Scriven*, *Loch Tarbert* and *Loch Torridon*. When these inlets from the sea were fairly narrow and tapered off, they often had previous Scandinavian names containing the element *fjörðr* 'fjord'; these have been incorporated in the Gaelic names, sometimes with hardly recognisable results (3): *Loch Ailort* (Gaelic *Loch Ailleart*), *Loch Ainort* (Gaelic *Loch Aineort*), *Loch Dionard* (Gaelic *Dionard*), *Loch Eishort* (*Eiseort*), *Loch Eport* (*Euphort*), *Loch Erisort* (*Eireasort*), (*Loch Eynort* (*Aineort*), *Loch Gruinart* (*Gruinneard*), *Loch Laxford* (*Luiseard*), *Loch Melfort* (*Meileart*), *Loch Moidart* (*Mhuideart*), *Loch Seaforth* (*Shiophort*), *Loch Skiport* (*Sgioport*), *Loch Snizort* (*Sniothasort*), *Loch Sunart* (*Suaineart*), and others. It is obvious that the final reinterpretation of the meaningless *-ort*, *-ard*, *-art* as *-port* *-fort* *–ford* *–forth* took place mostly in the post-Gaelic Anglicisation phase, although *–phort* > *port* may have been the result of an erroneous, intermediate perception of the Scandinavian initial *f* as a Gaelic aspirated *ph*.

Other names of sea-lochs in the same area contain Scandinavian *vágr* 'bay', (*Loch Carloway*, *Loch Scadaway*, *Loch Stornoway*) and *vík* 'bay' (*Loch Varkasaig*), and inland lochs incorporate Scandinavian loch names in *-vatn* 'water' (*Loch Caravat*, *Loch Grunavat*, *Loch Langavat* or *Langabhat*, *Loch Laxavat*, *Loch Scaravat*, *Loch Shanndabhat* and *Loch Strandavat*). *Loch Watten* in the north of Scotland (Caithness) also belongs to this group. In the Northern Isles, on the other hand, where the '*x* of *y*' formation (*Loch of Setter*, *Loch of Swartmill*) has become dominant as the result of the replacement of Norn by Scots, there are several examples of loch names in which Norse *vatn* has been substituted by English *water* (*Gossa Water*, *Housa Water*, *Lunga Water*, *Maa Water*, *Roer Water*, *Scarf Water*, *Simna Water*, etc.), as well as the completely Scots *Muckle Water* and *Peerie Water*.

Although the term *loch* can be applied to inland expanses of water of any size, its diminutive *lochan* is frequently used in the Gaelic designation of the smaller lochs, displaying a wide range of shades of meaning expressed in the specifics, as in *Lochan a' Chairn* 'small loch of the cairn', *Lochan Dubh* 'small black loch', *Lochan Fada* 'small long loch', *Lochan Gaineamhach* 'small sandy loch', *Lochan na h-Earba* 'small loch of the roe', *Lochan na Lairige* 'small loch of the mountain pass'.

Notes

(1) Sir W.A. Craigie, A.J. Aitken (Eds.), A Dictionary of the Older Scottish Tongue 3, 1963.

(2) W.F.H. Nicolaisen, Scottish Place-Names: Their Study and Significance, 1976, rev. ed. 2001.

(3) Idem, Fjord- and Bay-Names in Scotia Scandinavica, in: B. Sandnes et al. (eds.),
     NORNA-rapporter 70B, 2000, 161-168.
(4) A.H. Smith, English Place-Name Elements 2, 1956.
(5) W.J. Watson, The History of the Celtic Place-Names of Scotland, 1926.

Onoma 39 (2004, publ. 2007) 19-28

Teaching names: a personal account

1. In over fifty years ...

IN over fifty years of academic teaching and research, I have had the good fortune to be able to offer a number of courses, partial courses, contributions to courses and individual lectures to a variety of audiences, many of them academic but also others outside academe. While conditions, expectations and methods have varied from occasion to occasion, the basic substance and message have never changed: to make listeners aware of the significance and function of names, especially as part of an onomasticon, in contrast to a lexicon of words. It so happened that from the beginning of the initial collection of material for my PhD thesis from 1951 onwards, the chief focus has been on place-names though not to the exclusion of personal names and names of objects like boats, cars, pets, etc. The arrangement of my comments will be both chronological and according to the nature of the educational event, since there has been no clear cut systematic progression in my teaching from individual presentations to more complex courses. Opportunities had to be taken as they offered themselves.

Looking back over an endless-seeming string of 'talks', as I used to call them, the pattern was set in 1957 at a pre-historic conference in St Andrews on the Scottish east coast when I was asked to discuss the use of place-names as evidence for Scottish settlement history and linguistic stratification. I remember very clearly, but also with dismay, the fact that I enthusiastically went over my allotted time in an attempt to tell my kindly audience everything I knew on the subject. From then on, the format of my talks has changed very little: slides of distribution maps of certain name types or elements derived from material gathered by the Scottish Place-Name Survey, integrated into the verbal presentation, thus revealing the various linguistic strata, of which there are at least half a dozen in Scotland. What did change, however, was the choice of examples tailored to the location of the organisation into the programme of which my presentation had been slotted – extra-mural study groups of the Universities of Edinburgh and Glasgow, local historical societies, professional associations of all kinds, school classes, church discussion groups, etc. On these occasions, and there might be more than half a dozen during a winter season, I was always conscious of the fact that I was expected to teach my audiences something in an entertaining manner and in response to their background and perceived interests, but also of my own inadequacy regarding my lack of the specific local knowledge which many members of my audiences possessed and were able to contribute to what often turned into a dialogue, rather than a straightforward one-sided lecture. I also soon learned to engage audiences more personally by using a discussion of the names of some of the people present as an introduction even for talks on place-names, thus personalizing the general characteristics of names.

2. Diversified courses

While I have continued this mode of teaching names through single lectures embedded in thematic frameworks, on both sides of the Atlantic, to the present day and still find it an attractive way of reaching, mostly adult, audiences in unrepeatable contacts, a more intensive and extensive didactic medium has been for me the contribution of larger portions to appropriate, more structured courses, usually within an academic environment. The first of these arose when I was asked by the Geography Department of the University of Edinburgh to conduct several classes on Scottish place-names within their 'Cultural Geography' option. It goes without saying that geography can be a very suitable and welcoming discipline to take an interest in toponymic matters especially when the teacher is allowed to engage the students cooperatively in the construction of distribution maps, on the basis of material never mapped before and therefore quite uncertain in the outcome of the exercise. This innovative contribution to knowledge on the part of students is a creative device which results in active participation in the teaching process which, in my experience, has produced a better understanding of the role of place-names on maps and of the part these play in the making of landscapes.

Whereas a survey of the geography of names permits special emphasis on the extra-linguistic, spatial aspects of onymic evidence, an embedding of sections on name studies in courses on the History of English (or any other language) allows greater stress on the chronological facets of that evidence, particularly in their relationship to and relevance for linguistic development in the subject. Many experts in onomastics have come to this subject from the study of language history and are thus given an opportunity to instruct students in the semantic and functional differences between words and names as, for instance in the contrast between lexical meaning and onymic contents, lexical and onymic dialects, or their contrastive behaviour in linguistic contact situations; etymological concerns find this a hospitable environment, too. Other more encompassing subjects like 'Cultural History', 'Cultural Studies' or 'Tradition and Culture' have also been attractive hosts for the injection of onomastic sections, the latter especially offering opportunities for the display of the characteristics of names in oral usage and transmission, in informal, unofficial socio-onomastic registers.

3. The advantage of long term teaching

It goes without saying that the most promising environment for the teaching of names is in self-contained courses extending over a whole semester, trimester, term module, or whatever the time-table of the respective curricular structure might be. Above all, such courses provide an opportunity to concentrate on names as names and to draw attention to the several onomastic properties of names rather treating these aspects separately within the intellectual frameworks of other disciplines – linguistic, cultural, geographical, historical, and so on.

The first time I had a chance to avail myself of such an approach was in 1966-67 when, as a Visiting Professor at Ohio State University, I was requested by its Department of English to teach a graduate course in name studies. The task was both challenging and satisfying, and the experience stimulating enough to wish for its repetition. During my 23 years at the State University of New York in Binghamton, three more opportunities came along, a graduate course in 1972, and undergraduate courses in 1982 and 1986. These gave me a chance to hone both the format and the presentation; in each case the student response was very gratifying.

Paradoxically, it has been since my 'retirement' from SUNY-Binghamton and my return to Scotland, that courses in name studies have been most in demand, exclusively under the aegis of Aberdeen University's Centre for Continuing Education or, as it is called now, Centre for Lifelong Learning. As its title indicates, the Centre caters mainly for 'mature students', frequently people who have retired from earlier jobs, are completing previously interrupted degree studies, are attempting to improve their education or are aiming at intellectual stimulation. For these reasons, courses are run in the evening or at weekends. While some of them take place on the King's College campus of the University of Aberdeen, other venues are in smaller communities in northern and north-eastern Scotland, the university's natural hinterland. Weekend courses normally meet in situ for about six hours a month during the semester; evening classes are taught weekly or fortnightly from a studio on the university campus, with audio links by telephone to a large number of potential contact points in the region (recently I have also taught classes by video-link for the University of the Highlands and Islands, reaching out to an even more widespread clientele). Students are usually expected to sit a final examination on subject matter covered in the course, and to complete a substantial project in some aspect of names in their own area. The latter has been one of the most successful aspects of these courses, especially if students have previously taken a course in regional or even local history. The finished project is usually expected to contain maps, photographs, drawings, tape recordings, etc., beyond the essential verbal presentation; fieldwork and library work are normally also involved.

4. Workbooks

In order to give participating students information and direction in between actual class sessions, workbooks are provided to guide them through the course, including bibliographical aids and photocopies of important articles. The courses are usually entitled 'Names in ...', with specific reference to the area studied ('Names in Northern Scotland', 'Names in Orkney', 'Names in North-East Scotland', 'Names in Ross and Cromarty'). Please see the Appendix for sample pages from a workbook on 'Names in North-East Scotland', as an integral component of a larger group of courses in 'North-East Studies'.

In my personal experience, the 'Teaching of Names' has taken many forms, with different degrees of efficiency and intensity. For the study of place-names it is beneficial to get beyond the classroom walls. Personal visits by the tutor to classes in the region are perhaps most beneficial while reaching out into the community with the help of audio- and video-links harnesses modern technology in the course of modern name studies. Whatever teaching mode or method is chosen, it is important to involve students actively and to avoid situations in which the words of the teacher simply become the words of the students. Names of any kind are intrinsically fascinating to people and anybody wishing to teach their study and significance will therefore start with a great advantage over the teachers of many other subjects.

Appendix

Names in North-East Scotland
Course Themes

Theme 1:   Words and Names
Theme 2:   Personal Names
           (a) Family and Community
           (b) Unofficial Names
Theme 3:   Place-Names
           (a) Names on Maps
           (b) Street Names
           (c) House Names
Theme 4:   Linguistic Stratification
           (a) Gaelic
           (b) Pictish
           (c) Scottish/English
Theme 5:   Features Named
           (a) Natural
           (b) Manmade
Theme 6:   Names and History

Description

The course will examine the wide spectrum of names which occur in North-East Scotland: its methodology and aims will be based on the assumption that, as names are more than just words, they can be utilised as valuable raw materials in the study of a region like the North-East where we find a nomenclature that contains ample traces of languages no longer spoken in these parts and of the people who spoke them. The major languages involved are Pictish, Gaelic and Scottish/English, and this course will explore their presence or survival in personal names and place-names, in both official and unofficial usage. Special emphasis will be placed on name systems of all kinds, including street names, field names, farm, house and boat names. Each student will undertake a direct research project on his or her special topic of interest.

Suggestions for projects

Make sure that the project you choose is appropriate in its subject matter, precise in its formulation and manageable in extent. Projects which are vaguely formulated and too large in size tend to produce very unsatisfactory results. A length of about 5–6000 words is recommended but does not have to be slavishly adhered to.

Potential topics (randomly selected)

- A study of the street names in your community.
- A study of the house names in your community
- A study of the fishing boat names in your port.
- A study of the first names of pupils in a school.
- A study of the most common surnames in your community.
- A study of the nicknames in any group.
- A study of the field names in your community.
- A study of the names of particular types of topographic features in your area in the North-East in general, i.e. names of streams, hills, coastal features, etc. Concentrate on one type of feature. An account of name changes in your area.
- A study of the lingering presence of Gaelic in your area.
- A study of surnames derived from place-names and their role in the establishment of mobility patterns.
- A study of the influence of the Doric on the place-names of the region.

Course themes – here only Theme 1: *Words as names* is given in full

If you consult a dictionary that contains both words and names, you will discover that their treatment differs considerably. Here is an example.

In the Second College Edition of Webster's New World Dictionary of the American Language, the word *cord* is listed as a noun and transitive verb with its pronunciation, etymology and definitions, such as "thick string or thin rope, any force acting as a tie or bond; to fasten, to connect, or provide with a rod or cords", and so on, but *Cordoba* (with a capital C) is, after a transcript of its English and Spanish pronunciations, described as "1. City in NC Argentina; pop.589,000 and 2. City in Spain, on the Guadalquivir River; pop. 215,000." In between these two entries lies *Cordelia* (also a capital C) which, after an indication of its pronunciation, is followed by the comment "prob. ult. < Celt. *Creiryddlydd*, lit., daughter of the sea" and then defined as "1. A feminine name and 2. In Shakespeare's *King Lear*, the youngest of Lear's three daughters, and the only one faithful to him." The relevant items of information with regard to the place-name *Cordoba* are therefore: (a) *city* (i.e. kind of topographic feature), (b) NC Argentina or S. Spain, or perhaps both (i.e. location), and (c) the population figures (i.e. size); and the feminine personal name *Cordelia* is isolated by its denotative reference to a female character in a Shakespeare tragedy who has a certain genealogical and moral relationship with the central character of that play, and by its purported etymology.

Although not directly relevant to the Scottish North-East, these three entries – *cord, Cordoba* and *Cordelia* – illustrate persuasively the basic difference between word (*cord*) and name (*Cordoba* and *Cordelia*). In current usage – and that is what matters here – the word *cord* has to have *meaning* in order to function, and the names *Cordoba* and

Cordelia need *contents* (the etymology provided by the dictionary maker for the latter is redundant, insofar as it is not a necessary prerequisite for any competent use of the name). Translated into North-Eastern Scottish terms, this same distinction could be illustrated by the contrast between words like *hill, football, quine* or *loon,* and names like *Aberdeen* and *Banff, Dod* or *Bunty.* If we do not know the *meaning* of the four words listed, we cannot use them correctly; on the other hand, there is no need for us to know the word meaning of the four names, as long as we can identify the places and persons concerned by their location, size, population, or any other characteristic that *Aberdeen* or *Banff* may have, or by knowing the surname, address, occupation, age, etc. of *Dod* and *Bunty,* i.e. the *contents* of these names. It can probably be claimed without much fear of contradiction that most people familiar with *Aberdeen* and *Banff* or with some *Dod* or *Bunty* will have used these names competently without knowing their word meaning.

It also becomes clear that, whereas the words listed, and any other words we can think of, may refer to any of a large number of hills, footballs, quines and loons, the names quoted individualise, single out certain places and persons even though they are not unique in their reference. Words connote or include, but names denote or exclude. Although *names* are embedded in language for purposes of communication, they are not simply linguistic items. Many of them may have been *words* once, i.e. may have belonged to a *lexicon,* but as *names* they now belong to an *onomasticon,* and any connection which they may still show with the words they once were is now practically irrelevant to their function, even if those words are still recognisable, as in *Boghead, Newton* or *Nethermuir.*

All this may sound very theoretical and far removed from the announced, very practical aims of this course but this fundamental distinction between words and names gives the latter a very special status and makes them excellent raw material for the study of settlement history, social relations, and the like. Names can survive when the languages that evolved them have died out altogether and this process can be repeated several times over, as happened in the North-East with regard to Pictish, Gaelic and English.

When all is said and done, however, what matters most is usage, and much of this course and many of the projects to be undertaken will therefore be concerned with the use of names, either singly or in clusters. Quite clearly, names do not exist in isolation but in relationship to other names, forming what have been called "onomastic fields", "networks", or "systems". Special attention will therefore be given to such groups of names, applying a variety of criteria. Investigations may range from the "system" of street names in a small town to the motivations for given first names in certain families or the choice of names for fishing-boats in a certain port (in comparison with another port, perhaps).

Terminology

In order to be able to make precise statements about issues such as the relationship between words and names or particular categories of names, the following terms will be used frequently in this course:

lexical: pertaining to words
lexicon: a vocabulary of words
onomastic: pertaining to names
onomasticon: a vocabulary of names
toponymy: the study of place-names
anthroponymy: the study of personal names

Matters to think about

1   Try to verify the basic contention of this introduction by thinking of, and perhaps making lists of, some of the place-names in your area, contrasting those, the word (*lexical*) meaning of which you easily recognise with those whose meaning is opaque. Does it matter, from the point of view of competent usage, whether these names are in the first or the second category?

2   Do you know the meaning of any of the first names in your family? Have any of them been chosen because of their meaning?

3   Make a list of about a dozen place-names in your vicinity, together with what you would regard as their contents.

4   Make a similar list of the names of about a dozen people you know. What is the minimum amount of shared contents required to have an intelligent conversation about any one person.

5   Make a list of names that have become words (*balaclava, volt*) thus losing their special onomastic status. In which sectors of the lexicon do they particularly occur?

Background reading

Nicolaisen, W.F.H. 1976. Words as names. *Onoma* 20, 142-163.

Nicolaisen, W.F.H. 1982. Lexical and onomastic fields. In: Rymut Kazimierz (ed.), *Proceedings of the Thirteenth International Congress of Onomastic Sciences*. Cracow, August 21-25, 1978. Vol. II, 209-216. Wrocław–Warszawa–Kraków–Gdańsk–Łódź:Ossolineum.

Nicolaisen, W.F.H. 1990. The growth of name systems. In: Eeva Maria Närhi (ed.), *Proceedings of the XVIIth International Congress of Onomastic Sciences*. Vol. 2, 203-210. Helsinki: The University of Helsinki and The Finnish Research Centre for Domestic Languages.

List of Publications

This list does not include any references to about 230 reviews, a similar number of mostly one-page articles in *The Scots Magazine* (August 1960-January 1971 and December 1975-April 1976) and *Leopard* (April 1993-December 2004).

Books

With Margaret Gelling and Melville Richards, *The Names of Towns and Cities in Britain* (London: B.T. Batsford 1970.

Scottish Place-Names: Their Study and Significance (London: B.T. Batsford, 1976).

The Picts and Their Place Names (Groam House Museum Trust, 1996).

Scottish Place-Names: Their Study and Significance. New edition (Edinburgh: John Donald, 2001).

Editions and other editorial works

Associate Editor: *Scottish Studies* 1-9 (1957-1965).

Editor: *Transactions of the Third International Congress of Celtic Studies, Edinburgh 1967* (Edinburgh 1968).

Editor: Hugh Marwick, *The Place-Names of Birsay* (Aberdeen: Aberdeen University Press, 1970).

Assistant Editor: *Educational Opportunity Programs: Another Look.* Proceedings of the Institute on Innovative Teaching and Counseling IV (Binghamton NY, 1974).

Guest Editor: Special issue: "Type 425 'The Search for the Lost Husband'" *Midwestern Folklore* 15 (1989).

Editor: Special Issue on Theory about Names. *Names* 33, 3 (September 1985).

Editor: *Oral Tradition in the Middle Ages* (Binghamton NY: Medieval and Renaissance Texts and Studies, 1995).

Editor: 'The Year's Work in Scottish Literary and Linguistic Study 1993-1994'. (Glasgow: Association of Scottish Literary Studies, 1997).

Editor: *Proceedings of the XIXth International Congress of Onomastic Sciences, Aberdeen 1996.* 3 volumes (Aberdeen: Department of English, University of Aberdeen, 1998).

Editor: 'The Year's Work 1995-1996'. *Scottish Literary Journal* (Association of Scottish Literary Studies, 2001).

Co-editor: *Onomastik.* Acta of the XVIIIth International Congress of Onomastic Sciences, Trier 1993. Vol. VI. *Patronymica Romania* 19 (Tübingen: Niemeyer, 2002).

Articles and Reports

1957

"Die alteuropäischen Gewässernamen der britischen Hauptinsel". *Beiträge zur Namenforschung* 8 (1957) 211-268.

"The Semantic Structure of Scottish Hydronymy". *Scottish Studies* 1 (1957) 211-240.

1958

"Notes on Scottish Place-Names: 1. Armaidh; 2. Caddon Water; 3. Livet; 4. Forth". *Scottish Studies* 2 (1958) 109-112.

"Notes on Scottish Place-Names: 5. Shin; 6. Tain; 7. Gaelic *lón* in Stream-Names", *Scottish Studies* 2 (1958) 189-205.

1959

"Notes on Scottish Place-Names: 9. Dryfesdale. 10. The Type 'Burn of–' in Scottish Hydronymy". *Scottish Studies* 3 (1959) 88-102.

"Notes on Scottish Place-Names: 12. Nevis". *Scottish Studies* 3 (1959) 214-218.

1960

"Norse Place-Names in South-West Scotland". *Scottish Studies* 4 (1960) 49-70.

"The Fascination of Scottish Place Names". *The Scots Magazine* 73 (July 1960) 261-267.

"Notes on Scottish Place-Names: 13. Some Early Name-Forms of the Stirlingshire *Carron*". *Scottish Studies* 4 (1960) 96-104

"Notes on Scottish Place Names: 14. Avon; 15. Names Containing the Preposition *of*". *Scottish Studies* 4 (1960) 187-205.

1961

"Field-Work in Place-Name Research". *Studia Hibernica* 1 (1961) 74-88.

"The Historical Stratification of Scottish Hydronymy". *Sixth International Congress of Onomastic Sciences (Munich 1958) Reports. Vol. 3* (Munich 1961) 561-571.

"Notes on Scottish Place-Names: 16. The Interpretation of Name-changes". *Scottish Studies* 5 (1961) 85-96.

"Some Minor Manuscripts Sources of Scottish Place-Names". *Scottish Studies* 5 (1961) 209-211.

1962

"Notes on Scottish Place-Names: 18. *Lane* in Galloway". *Scottish Studies* 6 (1962) 85-87.

"Notes on Scottish Place-Names: 19. Further Minor Elements in Scottish River-Names". *Scottish Studies* 6 (1962) 210-217.

"Council for Name Studies: Great Britain and Ireland". *Scottish Studies* 6 (1962) 93-94.

1963

"The Collection and Transcription of Scottish Place-Names" *Atti e Memorie del VII Congresso Internazionale di Scienze Onomastiche* (Firenze 1963), Vol. 4 (Florence 1963) 104-114.

"A Short Comparative List of Celtic Bird Names of the British Isles". In: *Birds of the British Isles*, Vol. 12 (Edinburgh 1963) 405-423.

"Notes on Scottish Place-Names: 20. Path". *Scottish Studies* 7 (1963) 83-85.

"Notes on Scottish Place-Names: 21. Kilwinning". *Scottish Studies* 7 (1963) 199-200.

"Some Gaelic Place-Rhymes". *Scottish Studies* 7 (1963) 100-102.

1964

"Anglo-Saxons and Celts in the Scottish Border Counties". *Scottish Studies* 8 (1964) 141-171.

"Notes on Scottish Place-Names: 23. Old Norse *þveit*, etc." *Scottish Studies* 8 (1964) 96-103.

"Notes on Scottish Place-Names: 23. The Distribution of Old Norse *býr* and *fjall*". *Scottish Studies* 8 (1964) 208-213.

"A Gaelic Map of Scotland". *The Cartographic Journal* 1, No. 1 (June 1964) 44.

"Name-Spelling on Scottish Maps". *The Scotsman,* August 29, 1964.

1965

"Regional Ethnology in European Universities" (Summary). *Volkskunde* 66 (1965) 103-105.

"Scottish Studies in 1964: An Annual Bibliography." *Scottish Studies* 9 (1965) 225-235.

With O.K. Schram *et al.*: "Place Names", in *The Reader's Digest Complete Atlas of the British Isles* (1965) 124-125.

"Scottish Place-Names: 24. *Slew-* and *sliabh*". *Scottish Studies* 9 (1965) 91-106.

"Scottish Place-Names: 'Hill of -', and 'Loch of -'."*Scottish Studies* 9 (1965) 175-182.

1966

"Scottish Water-Courses as Boundaries". *Proceedings of the Eighth International Congress of Onomastic Sciences* (Amsterdam 1963) 327-333. The Hague 1966.

"Scottish Studies in 1965: An Annual Bibliography". *Scottish Studies* 10 (1966) 214-224.

"Index *Scottish Studies* Vols. 1 (1957)–10 (1966)". *Scottish Studies* 10 (1966) 225-268.

"Scottish Place-Names: 26. Blackadder and Whiteadder". *Scottish Studies* 10 (1966) 78-87.

"Scottish Place-Names: 27. Thurso". *Scottish Studies* 10 (1966) 171-176.

1967

"Scottish Studies in 1966: An Annual Bibliography". *Scottish Studies* 11 (1967) 252-264.

"Scottish Place-Names: 28. Old English *wic* in Scottish Place-Names", *Scottish Studies* 11 (1967) 75-84

"Scottish Place-Names: 29. Scandinavian Personal Names in the Place-Names of South-East Scotland". *Scottish Studies* 11 (1967) 223-236.

"Internationaler Kongress fur Namenforschung". *Beiträge zur Namenforschung* (Neue Folge) 2 (1967) 121-123.

1968

"The Prodigious Jump: A Contribution to the Study of the Relationship between Folklore and Place-names". *Volksüberlieferung*, Festschrift für Kurt Ranke (Göttingen 1968) 431-442.

"Place-Names of the Dundee Region". In: S.J. Jones (ed.), *Dundee and District*. British Association for the Advancement of Science (Dundee 1966) 144-152

"Scottish Studies in 1967: An Annual Bibliography". *Scottish Studies* 12 (1968) 207-218.

"Scottish Place-Names: 30. Fintry". *Scottish Studies* 12 (1968) 179-182.

1969

"Norse Settlement in the Northern and Western Isles". *Scottish Historical Review* 48 (1969) 6-17, + 4 maps.

"Some Problems of Chronology in Southern Scotland". *Proceedings of the Ninth International Congress of Onomastic Sciences* (London 1966) 340-347. Louvain 1969.

"The Distribution of Certain Gaelic Mountain-Names". *Transactions of the Gaelic Society of Inverness* 45 (1969) 113-128, + 7 maps.

"Aspects of Scottish Mountain-Names". *Disputationes ad Montium Vocabula alierumque nominum significationes pertinentes* (Tenth International Congress of Onomastic Sciences, Vienna 1969), Vol. 1, 109-115. Vienna 1969.

"Scottish Studies in 1968: An Annual Bibliography". *Scottish Studies* 13 (1969) 189-202.

Scottish section in *Place-Names on Maps of Scotland and Wales*. Ordnance Survey, Southampton 1969.

"Scottish Place-Names: 31. Falkirk". *Scottish Studies* 13 (1969) 47-59.

"Scottish Place-Names: 32. Gaelic *tulach* and *barr"*. *Scottish Studies* 13 (1969) 159-166.

1970

"Gaelic Place-Names in Southern Scotland". *Studia Celtica* 5 (1970) 15-35.

"Council for Name Studies in Great Britain and Ireland". *Onoma* 15, No. 1 (1970) 151-153.

1971

"National and International Folklore". *The Bulletin of the Pennsylvania State Modern Language Association* 49, Nos. 1-2 (Fall 1970–Spring 1971) 17-24.

"Early Spellings and Scottish Place-Names". *Edinburgh Studies in English and Scots* (London 1971) 210-233.

1972

"The Mapping of Folk Culture as Applied Folklore". *Folklore Forum*, Bibliographic and Special Studies No. 8 (1971) 26-30

"Great Britain and Old Europe". *Namn och Bygd* 59 (1971) 85-105.

"Onomastics – An Independent Discipline?". *Indiana Names* 3 (1972) 33-47.

"P-Celtic Place-Names in Scotland: A Reappraisal." *Studia Celtica* 7 (1972) 1-11.

1973

"Folklore and Geography: Towards an Atlas of American Folk Culture". *New York Folklore Quarterly* 29 (1973) 3-20.

"Place-Names in Traditional Ballads". *Folklore* 84 (1973) 299-312.

1974

"Place-Names in Traditional Ballads". *Literary Onomastics Studies* 1 (1974) 84-102 (revised version of paper published in *Folklore* 84).

"Names as Verbal Icons". *Names* 22 (1974) 104-110.

1975

"The Place-Names of Wessex". *Literary Onomastics Studies* 2 (1975) 58-82.

"Place-Name Evidence" (16 maps and accompanying text). In: *An Historical Atlas of Scotland c. 400-c. 1600* (St. Andrews 1975) 2-7 and 106-113.

"Surveying and Mapping North American Culture". *Mid-South Folklore* 3, No. 2 (Summer 1975) 35-40.

"Place-Names in Bilingual Communities". *Names* 23 (1975) 167-174.

1976

"Folk and Habitat". *Studia Fennica* 20 (1976) 324-330.

"The Place-Names of Barsetshire". *Literary Onomastics Studies* 3 (1976) 1-21.

"Scandinavian Place Names in Scotland as a Source of Knowledge". *Northern Studies* 7/8 (1976) 14-24.

"Place-Name Legends: An Onomastic Mythology". *Folklore* 87 (1976) 146-159.

"Onomastic Activities in the United States: A Personal postscript". *Onoma* 19 (1975; published 1976) 555-573.

"Words as Names". *Onoma* 20 (1976) 142-163.

"Name Aesthetics". *Midwestern Journal of Language and Folklore* 2 (1976) 56-63.

1977

"Line and Sentence in Dunbar's Poetry". In: *Bards and Makars,* eds. A.J. Aitken *et al.,* Glasgow 1977, 61-71.

"Place-Names and their Stories". *Ortnamnssällskapets i Uppsala Årsskrift* 1977: 23-29.

"Celtic Toponymics in Scotland". *Word* 28 (1976; pub. 1977) 117-139

"Folk Literature". In: "The Year's Work in Scottish Literary Studies". *Scottish Literary Journal*, Supplement No.4 (Autumn 1977) 9-14.

1978

"The Folk and the Region". *New York Folklore* 2, Nos. 3 & 4 (Winter 1976; publ. 1978) 143-149.

"Are There Connotative Names?". *Names* 26 (1978) 40-47.

"Desert Island Onomastics". *Literary Onomastics Studies* 5 (1978) 110-151.

"Between Berne and Cracow – Some Reflections". *Onoma* 21 (1977; publ. 1978) 549-556.

"English Jack and American Jack". *Midwestern Journal of Language and Folklore* 4, No. 1 (Spring 1978) 27-36.

"Recognition and Identity: Place Names as Keys and Disguises in the Regional Novel". *Onomastica* 53 (June 1978) 1-9.

"Ordering the Chaos: Name Strategies in Robert Kroetsch's Novels". *Essays on Canadian Writing* 11 (Summer 1978) 55-65.

"How Incremental is Incremental Repetition?". *Ballads and Ballad Research.* Ed. Patricia Conroy. Seattle, Washington, 1978, 122-133.

1979

"Celtic Place Names in America B.C.". *Vermont History* 47, No. 2 (Spring 1979) 148-160.

"Some Humorous Folk-Etymological Narratives". *New York Folklore* 3 (1997; publ. 1979) 1-14.

"The Toponymy of Literary Landscapes". *Literary Onomastics Studies* 6 (1979) 75-104.

"Field Collecting in Onomastics". *Names* 27 (1979) 162-178.

"Distorted Function in the Material Aspects of Culture". *Folklore Forum* 12, Nos. 2 & 3 (1979) 223-235.

"Literary Names as Text: Personal Names in Sir Walter Scott's *Waverley*". *Nomina* 3 (1979) 29-39.

1980

"Onomastic Dialects", *American Speech* 55 (1980) 36-45.

"Place Names as Evidence for Linguistic Stratification in Scotland". Sprogvidenskabelig Udnyttelse af Stednavnematerialet, eds. Vibeke Da1berg *et al., NORNA–rapporter* 18 (Uppsala 1980) 211-231.

"Tension and Extension: Thoughts on Scottish Surnames and Medieval Popular Culture". *Journal of Popular Culture* 14, 1 (Summer 1980) 119-130.

"'When I First Remember Talcottville …': Place Names in a Recollected Landscape". *Names Northeast* 1 (1979; publ. 1980) 17-27.

"Early Scandinavian Naming in the Northern and Western Isles". *Northern Scotland* 3, 2 (1979-80) 105-121.

"Masks and Illusions: 'The Function of Names of Robertson Davies. Deptford Trilogy'". *Onomastica* 58 (December 1980) 1-12.

"Space in Folk Narrative". In: *Folklore on Two Continents* – Essays in Honor of Linda Dégh. (Bloomington, Indiana: Trickster Press, 1980) 14-18.

"Scottish Folk Literature 1977 and 1978". *Scottish Literary Journal*, Supplement 13 (Winter 1980) 21-29.

"Time in Folk-Narrative". In: Venetia J. Newall (ed.), *Folklore Studies in the Twentieth Century.* (Woodridge, Suffolk: D.S. Brewer, 1980) 314-319.

"Über Namen in der Literatur". *Namenkundliche Informationen* 38 (1980) 13-25.

1981

"Personal Names in Traditional Ballads: A Proposal for a Ballad Onomasticon". Journal of American Folklore 94 (1981) 229-232.

"*Bagimond's Roll* as a toponymic text". In: Michael Benskin and M.L. Samuels (eds*.), So Many People Longages and Tonges,* philological essays in Scots and mediaeval English presented to Angus McIntosh (Edinburgh 1981) 173-185.

"Inverlochy: Place Names as Ruins". *Literary Onomastics Studies* 8 (1981) 27-38.

"Zur Namenforschung in den USA." *Namenkundliche Mitteilungen* 39 (1981) 37-45.

"'A colony for New England': New York Places and Their Names in Timothy Dwight's *Travels in New England and New York.*" *Names Northeast* 2 (1980; publ. 1981) 100-111.

"Robinsons as Namers". In: Fred Tarpley (ed.), *The Scope of Names,* South Central Names Institute Publication 7 (Commerce, Texas, 1981) 1-9.

1982

"Variant, Dialect and Region: An Exploration in the Geography of Tradition". *New York Folklore* 6, 3-4 (Winter 1980; publ. 1982) 137-149.

"What is your name? The Question of Identity in some of the *Waverley Novels.*" *Names* 28, 4 (December 1980; publ. 1982) 255-266.

"Why Study Names in Literature?". *Literary Onomastics Studies* 9 (1982) 1-20

"Lexical and Onomastic Fields". *Proceedings of the Thirteenth International Congress of Onomastic Sciences,* Cracow 1978, Vol. 2 (Cracow 1982) 209-216.

"P.W. Joyce and Scotland". *Topothesia:* Essays in Honour of T.S. O'Maille (Galway Ireland, 1982) 72-89.

"Scandinavians and Celts in Caithness: The Place-Name Evidence". In: John R. Baldwin (ed.), *Caithness: A Cultural Crossroads.* (Edinburgh 1982) 75-85.

"Salterton and Deptford: A Comparison of Onomastic Structures". *Onomastica Canadiana* 62 (1982) 14-22.

"Thirty Years Later: Thoughts on a Viable Concept of Old European Hydronymy". In: Otto Winkelmann and Maria Braisch (eds.), *Festschrift für Johannes Hubschmid zum 65. Geburtstag* (Bern, Switzerland, 1982) 139-148.

"The Viking Settlement of Scotland: Evidence of Place Names". In: R.T. Farrell (ed.), *The Vikings* (Chichester: Phillimore, 1982) 95-115.

"'The Lord is not at Home': A Brief Diversion". Proceedings of the 12th International Folk Ballad Conference. *CVV-Studies* 1 (1982) 206-213.

"AT 1535 in Beech Mountain, North Carolina". *ARV = Scandinavian Yearbook of Folklore* 36 (1980; publ. 1982) 99-106.

1983

"'Old European' Names in Britain". *Nomina* 6 (1982; publ. 1983) 37-42.

"Scott and the Folk Tradition". In: Alan Bold (ed.), *Sir Walter Scott: The LongForgotten Melody* (London: Vision Press, 1983) 127-142.

"'What a Name. Stephen Halifax.' Onomastic Modes in Three Novels by Margaret Drabble". *Literary Onomastics Studies* 10 (1983) 269-283.

"'Concepts of Time and Space in Irish Folktales". In: *Celtic Folklore and Christianity: Studies in Memory of William W. Heist.* Ed. Patrick K. Ford (Santa Barbara: McNally and Lofton, 1983) 150-158.

"The Post-Norse Place-Names of Shetland". In: *Shetland and the Outside World 1469-1969.* Ed. Donald R. Withrington. Aberdeen University Studies 157 (Oxford: Oxford University Press, 1983) 69-85.

"An Onomastic Vernacular in Scottish Literature". In: *Scotland and the Lowland Tongue.* Ed. J. Derrick McClure (Aberdeen: Aberdeen University Press, 1983) 209-218.

"Theodor Fontane's 'Sir Patrick Spens'". In: *The Ballad Image: Essays Presented to Bertrand Harris Bronson.* Ed. James Porter (Los Angeles: Center for the Study of Comparative Folklore and Mythology, University of California, 1983) 3-19

"The Folk in Literature: Some Comments on Sir Walter Scott's Scottish Novels". *Kentucky Folklore Record* 28, 1-4 (1982; publ. 1983) 48-60.

"Scandinavian Shore Names in Shetland: The Onomastic Subdialect of a Coastscape". *Språk och tradition.* Festskrift till Sven Benson (Uppsala: Almqvist & Wiksell, 1983) 144-152 [= *Svenska Landsmål och Svenskt Folkliv* 106 (1983)].

"Folklore and … What?" *New York Folklore* 9, 1-2 (Summer 1983) 89-98.

"Opening Address to the XIVth International Congress of Onomastic Sciences at Ann Arbor (1981)". *Onoma* 26 (1982; publ. 1983) 28-31 .

"Sir Walter Scott: The Folklorist as Novelist", in: *Scott and His Influence.* Eds. J.H. Alexander and David Hewitt (Aberdeen: Association for Scottish Literary 1983) 169-179.

Report: "Journées d'Etudes en Litterature Orale: 'Analyse des contes – problémes de methode', Paris, March 23-26, 1982." *Fabula* 24 (1983) 277-278.

1984

"What Crisis in Onomastics?" *Names* 32 (1984) 14-25.

"Folklore and Names". *Names Northeast* 3 (1984) 14-21.

"Place Names in Early New England Literature". *Names Northeast* 4 (1984) 67-76.

"The Structure of Narrated Time in the Folktale". *Le conte pourquoi? comment?* Paris: Editions du Centre National de la Recherche Scientifique, 1984) 417-436.

"Names and Narratives". *Journal of American Folklore* 97 (1984) 259-272.

"Legends as Narrative Response". In: *Perspectives on Contemporary Legend.* Ed. Paul Smith. CECTAL Conference Paper Series No. 4 (Sheffield: University of Sheffield, 1984) 167-178.

"Maps of Space – Maps of Time". *Names* 32 (1984) 358-366.

Report: "Perspectives on Contemporary Legend: A Second International Seminar". Centre for English Cultural Tradition and Language. University of Sheffield, August 1-7, 1983". *Fabula* 25 (1984) 113-114.

1985

"The Semantics of Place Names and Their Elements". *NORNA–rapporter* 28 (1985) 60-71.

"Nomen, Noun and Name: The Lexical Horns of an Onomastic Dilemma". In: *Historical & Editorial Studies in Medieval & Early Modern English.* Eds. Mary Jo Arn and Hanneke Wirtjes (Groningen: Wolters – Noordhoff, 1985) 63-72.

"Tartan and Kilt, Whisky and Bagpipe: Living Scottish Traditions in America". *New Jersey Folklore* 10 (1985) 17-21.

"Burnside of Duntrune: An Essay in Praise of Ordinariness". *Names* 33 (1985) 29-38.

"'There was a Lord in Ambertown': Fictitious Place Names in the Ballad Landscape." In: *Narrative Folksong – New Directions: Essays in Appreciation of W. Edson Richmond.* Eds. Carol L. Edwards and Kathleen E.B. Manley (Boulder, Colorado: Westview Press, 1985) 73-81.

''Recent Publications in German Onomastics". *Names* 33 (1985) 158-168.

"Introduction", Special Issue on Theory About Names. *Names* 33, 3 (September 1985) 109-110.

"Rehearsing the Future in the Folktale". *New York Folklore* 11 (1985) 231-238 .

"Reminiscences". *New York Folklore* 11 (1985) 18-20

"Socio-onomastics". In: *Der Eigenname in Sprache und Gesellschaft.* I. Verhandlungen im Plenum (XV. Internationaler Kongress für Namenforschung, 1317 August 1984). Eds. Ernst Eichler *et al.* (Leipzig: Karl-Marx-Universität, 1985) 118-132 .

1986

"Response to James Porter's 'Ballad Explanations, Ballad Reality, and the Singer's Epistemics'". *Western Folklore* 45, No. 2 (April 1986) 125-127.

"Perspectives on Contemporary Legend". *Fabula* 26, Nos. 34 (1985; publ. 1986) 213-218.

"Names Reduced to Words?: Purpose and Scope of a Dictionary of Scottish Place Names". In: *Scottish Language and Literature. Medieval and Renaissance.* Eds. Dietrich Strauss and Horst W. Drescher (Frankfurt am Main: Peter Lang, 1986) 47-54.

"Gaelic Place Names in Scots". *Scottish Language* 5 (Autumn 1986) 140-146

"Names of Strangers in Traditional Ballads: A Response to Sheila Douglas". In: *Ballad Research: The Stranger in Ballad Narrative and Other Topics.* Ed. Hugh Shields. Dublin: Folk Music Society of Ireland, 1986) 111-113.

"Fun and Names". *Grazer Linguistische Studien* 25 (1986) 215-220

"Personal Names as Place Names". In: *Personnamni Stadnamn,* Ed. Ola Stemshaug. *NORNA–rapporter* 33 (1986) 207-216.

"The Structure and Function of Names in English Literature". *Studia Anglica posnaniensia* 18 (1986) 139-152.

"Naming and Abstraction". In: *From Oz to Onion Patch.* Ed. Edward Callary. Publications of the North Central Name Society 1 (1986) 11-26

"Names as Intertextual Devices". *Onomastica Canadiana* 68/2 (December 1986) 58-66.
"The Official Treatment of Non-English Placenames in the United States". In:
Amtlicher Gebrauch des Geographischen Namengutes (Bozen 1986) 253-265.

1987

"Is There Room for Name Studies in Geolinguistics?" In: *Geolinguistic Perspectives.*
Eds. Jesse Levitt, *et al.* (Lanham: University Press of America, 1987) 129-137.
"Names in Derivative Literature and Parodies". *Literary Onomastics Studies* 14 (1987)
49-67.
"The Linguistic Structure of Legends". In: *Perspectives on Contemporary Legend.* Vol.
II. Eds. Gillian Bennett, *et al.* CECTAL Conference Paper Series No. 5 (Sheffield:
Sheffield Academic Press, 1987) 61-76.
"Semantic Causes of Structural Changes in Place Names". *NORNA–rapporter* 34
(Uppsala, 1987) 9-19.
"Imitation and Innovation in the Scandinavian Place-Names of the Northern Isles of
Scotland". *Nomina* 11 (1987; publ. 1988) 75-85.

1988

"Introduction: Folk-Narrative Research in the U.S.A". *Fabula* 29, 3-4 (1988) 286-289.
"Once Upon a Place, or where is the World of Folktale?" In: *Sichtweisen der Volks-
kunde: Zur Geschichte und Forschungspraxis einer Disziplin.* Eds. Albrecht
Lehmann and Andreas Kuntz. *Lebensformen* 3 Berlin – Hamburg: Dietrich Reimer,
1988) 358-366.
"German *Sage* and English *Legend*: Terminology and Conceptual Problems". In:
Monsters with Iron Teeth. Eds. Gillian Bennett and Paul Smith. Perspectives on
Contemporary legend III (Sheffield: Sheffield Academic Press, 1988) 79-87.
"Place Names in Badenoch". *Moray Field Club Bulletin* 16 (December 1988) 21.

1989

"Name Spelling and Identity". *Journal of the North Central Name Society* (Winter
1988-89) 13-21.
"Place-Name Maps: How Reliable Are They?" *Studia Onomastica:* Festskrift Till
Thorsten Anderson 13 Februari 1989 (Lund: Bloms, 1989) 261-268.
"Kurt Ranke and Einfache Formen". *Folklore* 100 (1989) 113-119.
"The Spelling of Scottish Place Names as a Linguistic Resource: Stirling vs.
Dunfermline". In: *In Other Words.* Eds. J. Lachlan Mackenzie and Richard Todd
(Dordrecht, Holland: Foris, 1989, 301-314.
"The Toponymy of Remembered Childhood". *Names* 36 (1988; publ. 1989) 133-142.
"What Have Our Histories Taught Us". *The Folklore Historian* 6, 1 (Spring 1989)
12-15.
"Hartland, Edwin Sidney". *Enzyklopädie des Märchens* 6, 2–3 (1989) 528-530.
"Henderson, Hamish". *Enzyklopädie des Märchens* 6, 2–3 (1989) 812-813.
"Definitional Problems in Oral Narrative". In: Gillian Bennett and Paul Smith (eds.),
The Questing Beast. Perspectives on Contemporary Legend IV (Sheffield:
Sheffield Academic Press, 1989) 77-89.

"Guest Editor's Foreword". Special Issue: Type 425, 'The Search for the Lost Husband'. *Midwestern Folklore* 15 (1989) 69-70.

"Stories and Storytelling in Barbour's *Brus.*" In: J. Derick McClure and Michael Spiller (eds.) *Bryght Lanterns: Essays on the Language and Literature of Medieval and Renaissance Scotland* (Aberdeen: Aberdeen University Press, 1989) 55-66.

1990

"Variability and Creativity in the Folktale". In: *D'Un Conte ... a l'Autre: La variabilite dans la litterature orale* (Paris: Editions du C.N.R.S., 1990) 39-46

"The Past as Place". *Dolphin Newsletter* 9 (May 1990) 25-26.

"Why Tell Stories?". *Fabula* 31, 1–2 (1990) 5-10

"Gaelic and Scots 1300–1600: Some Place-Name Evidence". In: Derick S. Thomson (ed.), *Gaelic and Scots in Harmony* (Glasgow: Department of Celtic, University of Glasgow, 1990) 20-35

"Dons Meet to Study Tall Tales Told by Our Friends". Preface to Gillian Bennett and Paul Smith (eds.), *Contemporary Legend: The First Five Years* (Sheffield: Sheffield Academic Press, 1990) 7-15.

"Placenames and Politics". *Names* 38 (1990) 193-207.

"Onomastic Onomastics". In: Jean-Claude Boulanger (ed.), *Proceedings of the XVIth International Congress of Onomastic Sciences, Quebec 1987* (Quebec: Les Presses de l' Université Laval, 1990) 3-14.

"Linguistic Aspects of the *Vanishing Hitchhiker*". In: Leander Petzoldt and Stefaan Top (eds.), *Dona Folcloristica: Festschrift für Lutz Röhrich ...* (Frankfurt /Bern/New York: P. Lang, 1990) 187-199 .

"Maps of Fiction: The Cartography of the Landscape of the Mind". *Onomastica Canadiana* 72 (1990) 57-68.

"The Growth of Name Systems". *Proceedings of the XVIIth International Congress of Onomastic Sciences.* Ed. Eeva Maria Närhi (Helsinki 1990) II, 203-210.

"Aberdeen: A Toponymic Key to the Region". *Northern Studies* 27 (1990) 50-63.

1991

"The Past as Place: Names, Stories and the Remembered Self". *Folklore* 102 (1991) 3-15.

"Scottish Analogues of Scandinavian Place Names". In: Gordon Albøge, *et al.* (eds.), *Analogi i Navngivning. NORNA–rapporter* 45 (Uppsala 1991) 147-155.

"Celtic and Pre-Celtic Place-Name Elements in Scotland". In Benjamin T. Hudson and Vickie Ziegler (eds.), *Crossed Paths: Methodological Approaches to the Celtic Aspects of the European Middle Ages.* Lanham, CT/New York/London: University Press of America. (1991) 1-10.

"Name that Past: Place Names in Autobiographical Writings". *Names* 39 (1991) 239-248.

"Die ältesten Namenschichten auf den Britischen Inseln". In: Ernst Eichler (ed.), *Probleme der ältesten Namenschichten.* Beiträge zur Namenforschung, N.F., Beiheft 32 (Heidelberg: Carl Winter, 1991) 67-74.

"A Folklorist Looks at (S)NACS". *North American Culture* 6 (1990) 1-11.

1992

"Humour in Traditional Ballads (Mainly Scottish)". *Folklore* 103 (1992) 27-39.

"Pictish Place-Names as Scottish Surnames: Origins, Dissemination and Current Status". *Nomina* 15 (1991-92) 7-20.

"Arran Place Names: A Fresh Look". *Northern Studies* 28 (1992) 1-13.

"Contemporary Legends: Narrative Texts vs. Summaries". *Contemporary Legend* 2 (1992) 71-91.

"Onomastic Aspects of Clerk Colville". *Arv* 48 (1992) 31-41.

1993

"Why Tell Stories about Innocent, Persecuted Heroines?". *Western Folklore* 52. 1 (1993) 61-71.

"Wortloses Erzählen". In: Leander Petzoldt, *et al.* (eds.), *Bild und Text.* Beiträge zur Europäischen Ethnologie und Folklore, Reihe B: Tagungsberichte und Materialien (Bratislava, Slovakia: Slovak Academic Press, 1993) 154-162.

"Names in the Landscape of the Moray Firth". In: W.D.H. Sellar (ed.), *Moray Province and People* (Edinburgh: Scottish Society for Northern Studies, 1993) 253-262.

"Scottish Place-Names as Evidence for Language Change". *Names* 41 (1993) 306-313.

"Onomastic Interaction in the Waverley Novels". In: J.H. Alexander and David Hewitt (eds.), *Scott in Carnival* (Aberdeen: Association for Scottish Literary Studies, 1993) 133-144.

"Kaiser und Abt". *Enzyklopädie des Märchens* 7, 2–3 (Berlin/New York, 1991). 845-852.

"A Response to William Harmon". *Connotations* 3 (1993) 44-47.

1994

"More Fun and Names". *Grazer Linguistische Monographien* 11 (1994) 157-162.

"Viking place names in Scotland". *NORNA–rapporter* 54 (1994) 31-49.

"The Teller and the Tale: Storytelling on Beech Mountain". In: William B. McCarthy (ed.), *Jack in Two Worlds* (Chapel Hill, NC: University of North Carolina Press 1994) 123-149.

"The genealogy of 'Lord Randal': onomastic evidence and dissemination". *Lore and Language* 12 (1994) 150-172.

"The Proverbial Scot". *Proverbium* 11 (1994) 197-206.

1995

"Narrare Necesse Est: Gedanken über das Jenseits in den Raum- und Zeitvorstellungen von Volkserzählungen". In: Carola Lipp (ed.), *Medien popularer Kultur* (Frankfurt/ New York: Campus Verlag, 1995) 172-181.

"König und kluger Knabe". *Enzyklopädie des Märchens* 8, 1. (Berlin/New York, 1995) 156-159.

"The Onomastic Legacy of Gaelic in Scotland". In Barbara Hillers and Jerry Hunter (eds.), *Proceedings of the Harvard Celtic Colloquium* (May 1-3, 1992) 12 (1992; publ. 1995) 1-15.

"Name and Appellative". In: *Name Studies: An International Handbook of Onomastics,* Vol. I (Berlin/New York: Walter de Gruyter, 1995) 384-393.

"Names in English Literature". *Ibid.,* 560-568.

"A Gleaner's Vision". *Folklore* 106 (1995) 71-76.

"Pictish Place Names". In: Eric H. Nicoll (ed.), *A Pictish Panorama* (Balgavies, Angus: The Pinkfoot Press, 1995) 11-13.

"Is There a Northwest Germanic Toponymy? Some Thoughts and a Proposal". In: Edith Marold and Christiane Zimmerman (eds.), *Nordwestgermanisch* (Berlin: de Gruyter, 1995) 103-114.

"Something Old, Something New from the Land of the Picts". In: Michaela Ofitsch and Christian Zinko (eds.), *Studia Onomastica et Indogermanica:* Festschrift für Fritz Lochner von Hütttenbach zum 65. Geburtstag. Arbeiten aus der Abteilung 'Vergleichende Sprachwissenschaft' Graz 10 (1995) 137-142.

"In Praise of William J. Watson (1865-1948): Celtic Place-Name Scholar". *Scottish Language* 14/15 (1995-96) 15-30.

"The Year's Work in Language". *The Year's Work 1991-1992. Scottish Literary Journal.* Association for Scottish Literary Studies (1995) 117-150.

1996

"Scottish Place-Names". In: *Name Studies: An International Handbook of Onomastics.* Vol. II (Berlin/New York: Walter de Gruyter, 1996) 1409-1413.

"Language Contact and Onomastics". In: *Contact Linguistics: An International Handbook of Contemporary Research* Vol. I (Berlin – New York: Walter de Gruyter, 1996) 549-554.

"Pictish and British Place Names" (50-51), "Gaelic Place Names" (58-60), "Anglian Place Names" (61), "Scandinavian Place Names and Settlements" (64-70). In: Peter G.B. McNeill and Hector L. MacQueen (eds.), *Atlas of Scottish History to 1707* (Edinburgh: The Scottish Medievalists and Department of Geography, University of Edinburgh, 1996).

"Gaelic *-ach* to Scots *-o* in Scottish Place Names". *Scottish Gaelic-Studies* 17 (1996) 278-291.

"Legends as Narrative Response". Reprinted in Gillian Bennett and Paul Smith (eds.), *Contemporary Legend: A Reader* (New York – London: Garland Publishing, 1996) 91-101 (First published in 1984).

"Thirty Years Later: Thoughts on a Viable Concept of an Old European Hydronymy". Reprinted in: Friedelm Debus and Wilfried Seibicke (eds.), *Reader zur Namenkunde* III, 2. *Toponymie* (Hildesheim, etc.: Georg Olms; 1996) 705-710 (First published in 1982).

1997

"One name but many systems". In: Ritva-Liisa Pitkänen and Kaija Mallat (eds.), *You name it – Perspectives on Onomastic Research.* Studia Fennica Linguistica 7 (Helsinki: Finnish Literature Society, 1997) 57-62.

"Names and Words – Yet Again". In: Marianne Blomqvist (ed.), *Ord och Några Visor.* Meddelanden från Institutionen för nordiska språk och nordisk litteratur vid Helsingfors universitet, B.18 (1997) 199-203.

"The *Dee* at Chester and Aberdeen: Thoughts on Rivers and Divinities". In: Alexander R. Rumble and A.D. Mills (eds.), *Names Places and People: An Onomastic Miscellany in Memory of John McNeal Dodgson* (Stamford: Paul Watkins, 1997) 247-253.

"On Pictish Rivers and their Confluences". In: David Henry (ed.), *The worm the germ and the thorn: Pictish. and related studies presented to Isabel Henderson* (Balgavies, Angus: The Pinkfoot Press, 1997) 113-118.

"Von der 'Namenablehnung' bis zum 'Namenzusatz'". In: Karlheinz Hengst, *et al.* (eds.), *Wort und Name im deutsch-slavischen Sprachkontakt* (Köln: Böhlau, 1997) 59-77 .

"Patterns in the Specifics of Scandinavian Place Names in Scotland". In: Kristoffer Kruken (ed.), *Den ellevte nordiske navneforskerkongressen* (Sundvollen 19-23. juni 1994). *NORNA–rapporter* 60 (Uppsala 1996, publ. 1997) 373-381.

"The Ballad and the Folklorist". *Folk Music Journal* 7, 3 (1997) 351-356.

"The *Cante Fable* in Occidental Folk Narrative". In: Joseph Harris and Karl Reichl (eds.), *Prosimetrum; Cross-Cultural Perspectives on Narrative in Prose and Verse* (Woodbridge, Suffolk: D.S. Brewer, 1997) 183-211.

"Periodization in the History of English". *General Linguistics* 75 (1997) 157-176.

1998

"Afterword". In: Simon Taylor (ed.), *The Uses of Place-Names*. St. John's House Papers No 7, St. Andrews (Edinburgh: Scottish Cultural Press, 1998) 180-181.

Entries in Thomas A. Green (ed.), *Folklore: An Encyclopedia of Beliefs, Customs, Music and Art.* 2 vols. (Santa Barbara, CA: ABC–CLIO, 1997: 'Academic Programs in Folklore, International' (3-5); 'Anecdote' (17-19), 'Style' (776-777).

"Von der Verharmlosung der Namen". In: Kurt Franz and Albrecht Greule (eds.), *Namenforschung und Namen didaktik* (Hohengehren: Schneider, 1998) 226-30.

"The Ballad and the Folklorist: David Buchan 1939-1994". *Aberdeen University Review* 57, no. 200 (Autumn 1998) 327-333 earlier version published in 1997).

Entries in Mary Ellen Brown and Bruce A. Rosenberg (eds.), *Encyclopedia of Folklore and Literature* (Santa Barbara, CA: ABC–CLIO 1998): "Folk Etymology" (213-215), "Formula Tale" (225-226), "Johann Gottfried Herder" (298-300), "Kenneth Hurlstone Jackson" (327-328), "Names" (435-437), "Kurt Ranke" (538-539), "Sir Walter Scott" (593-594).

"Die Welt der Namen*". Namenkundliche Informationen* 74 (1998) 9-28.

1999

"The Earliest English Place Names in North East Scotland". *Northern Scotland* 18 (1999) 67-82.

"The World of Names". *Ainm* 7 (1996-7; publ. 1999) 28-43.

"An Onomastic Autobiography, or, In the beginning was the Name". *Onomastik: Akten des 18. Internationalen Kongresses für Namenforschung.* Trier, 12-17. April 1999. Vol. III: Namensoziologie (Tübingen: Max Niemeyer, 1999) 24-29; also an illustrated version in *Names* 47, 3 (1999) 179-190.

"Einbruch und Einbrecher in der modernen Sage". In: Christoph Schmitt (ed.), *Homo narrans* (Münster: Waxmann, 1999) 181-190.

Entry on "Name". *Enzyklopädie des Märchens* 9, 3 (1999) 1157-1163.

"How Celtic Are Celtic Narratives?". In: Ingo Schneider (ed.), *Europäische Ethnologie und Folklore im internationalen Kontext* (Frankfurt am Main: Peter Lang, 1999) 203-211.

"Place-Names in the Shadow of Cairngorm". Appendix X in the reprint of William Forsyth, *In the Shadow of Cairngorm* (Lynwilg Press, 1999) 375-377.

2000

"Fjord- and Bay-Names in Scotia Scandinavica". In Berit Sandnes, *et al*, Oluf Rygh: Rapport fra Symposium pa Stiklestad 13–15 mai 1999. *NORNA–rapporter* 70B Uppsala 2000) 161-168.

"Place Names in the Landscapes of Fifteenth-Century Scotland". In: Gunther Hirschfelder *et al* (eds.), *Kulturen – Sprachen – Übergänge: Festschrift für H.L. Cox zum 65. Geburtstag* (Köln: Böhlau, 2000) 95-102.

"Place Names". In: Carl Lindahl *et al.* (eds.) *Medieval Folklore: An Encyclopedia of Myths Legends, Tales, Beliefs and Customs.* 2 vols. (Santa Barbara, CA: ABC–CLIO, 2000) II, 201-203.

"The Past in the Present". *Onomastické Práce, Svazek* 4 (Praha: Ustav pro Jazyk Ceský ov, CR 2000) 333-339.

"Personennamen und Ortsnamen: Intra-onomastische Beziehungen". In: H. Tiefenbach and H. Löffler (eds.), *Personenname und Ortsname* (Heidelberg: C. Winter, 2000) 11-20.

"Marking Time – Marking Space". *Names* 48 (2000) 275-282.

"Fifty Years *Onoma* (1950-2000)". *Onoma* 35 (2000) 5-16.

"Landscape as Plot: Place Names in Robert Louis Stevenson's Fiction". *Onomata* 16 (2000-2001) 327-337.

2001

"International Name Studies in the Nineties: A Report on ICOS XIX". In: Gunella Harling Kranck (ed.), *Namn i en föränderlig värld.* Studier i Nordisk Filologi 78 (2001) 210-218.

"Thomas Percy". *Enzyklopädie des Märchens* 10, 2 (2001) 727-730.

"Burglars and Burglaries in Contemporary Legends". *Folklore* 112, 2 (October 2001) 137-146.

"Language". In: *The Year's Work 1995-1996.* Scottish Literary Journal. Association for Scottish Literary Studies (2001) 168-192.

"Onomastics". In: N.J. Smelser and P.B. Baltes (eds.), 2001 *International Encyclopedia of the Social & Behavioral Sciences* (Oxford: Pergamon, 2001) Vol. 11, 10859-10867.

"A Change of Place is a Change of Fortune: Place Names as Structuring Devices in Chaim Bermant's Novels". *Nomina* 24 (2001) 5-15.

2002

"Narrating Names". *Folklore* 11 (2002) 1-9.

"Uses of Names in Fiction". *il Nome mel testo* 4 (2002) 157-168.

"From *Aucassin et Nicolette* to the 'Humorous Grace'" *Lore and Language* 15 (1997; publ. 2002) 23-47. (Shortened and somewhat revised version of "The Cante Fable in Occidental Folklore" (publ. in 1997, see above).

"Place-Name Index". In Patrick Shuldham-Shaw *et al.* (eds.), *The Greig-Duncan Folk Song Collection*, Vol. 8 (Edinburgh: Mercat Press, 2002), 603-623.

Contribution to Panel Discussion "Name Studies and Literature". In: Ana Isabel Bullén Aguelo (ed.), *Acta* ICOS XX (1994). Santiago de Composbela. Vol. I pp. 43-46. Publ. 2002.

2003

"Orts- und Hofnamen: Scotland". In Heinrich Beck *et al.* (eds.), *Reallexikon der Germanischen Altertumskunde* 22. (Berlin: Walter de Gruyter, 2003), 300-302.

"Orkneyinseln: Onomastics". *Ibid.*, 214-215.

"Uses of Names in Fictional Narratives". In Wayne H. Finke and Leonard R.N. Ashley (eds.), (New York: Cummings & Hathaway, 2003). 1-14. [Revised version of "Uses of Names in Fiction", 2002.]

"Presidential Preferences", *Folklore* 114, 1 (April 2003), 1-12.

"Perspectives on the Pre-Norse Language(s) of Orkney". In J. Downes and A. Ritchie (eds., *Sea-Change: Orkney and Northern Europe in the later Iron Age AD 300-800*. (Balgavies: The Pinkfoot Press, 2003) 139-144.

"On English and Gaelic Place Names in Medieval N.E. Scotland". In *A World of Names*, Lucie A. Möller and J.V. Jacobs (eds.), 2 vols. Special Issue, *Nomina Africana* 15, 1 & 2 [2001, publ. 2003] I, 80-86.

2004

"A Gallimaufry of Languages". In Astrid van Nahl *et al.* (eds.), *Namenwelten*: Ergänzungsband zum *Reallexikon der Germanischen Altertumskunde* 44 (Berlin/New York: Walter de Gruyter, 2004) 233-240.

"Methoden der literarischen Onomastik". In Andrea and Silvio Brendler (eds.), *Ein Lehrbuch für das Studium der Onomastik* (Hamburg: Baar, 2004) 247-257.

"Erzählen als kulturelle Legitimierung". In Sabine Wienker-Piepho and Klaus Roth (eds.), *Erzählen zwischen den Kulturen*. (Münster: Waxmain, 2004) 143-155.

"The functions of suffixes in early Scottish hydronymy". In Thorsten Andersson and Eva Nyman (eds.), *Suffixbildungen in alten Ortsnamen*. Acta Academiae Regiac Custavi Adolphi 88, (Uppsala 2004) 109-117.

"A Cluster of Dictionaries". *Names* 52, 2 (June 2004) 29-139.

2005

"Scoten: Onomastics". In *Reallexikon der Germanischen Altertumskunde* 27 (Berlin: Walter de Gruyter, 2005) 632-633.

"Gerhard Koss zum 70. Geburtstag". *Namenkundliche Informationen* 85/86 (2004; publ. 2005) 399-401.

"Place Names as evidence in the history of Scots". In Christian J. Kay and Margaret A. Mackay (eds.), *Perspectives on the Older Scottish Tongue* (Edinburgh: University Press, 2005) 112-118.

"Seenamen 3, C: Scotland". *Reallexikon der Germanischen Altertumskunde* 44 (Berlin: Walter de Gruyter, 2005) 49-51.

Section of Doctoral Oral Examination, Berit Sandnes (May 3, 2003) *namn og nemne* 20-21 (2003/04; publ. 2005) 37-40.

"Foreword" to Ian Keillar, *Romans in Moray* (Elgin: Moray New Horizons, 2005) 7-8.

"Manly Characters in Contemporary Legends: A Preliminary Survey". In: Simon J. Bonner (ed.), *Manly Traditions: The Folk Roots of American Masculinities* (Bloomington, IN: Indiana University Press, 2005) 247-260.

"Introduction". *Cultural Contacts in the North Atlantic Region: The Evidence of Names* (eds. Peder Gammeltoft, *et al.*) (Lerwick, 2005) 3-4.

2006

"Suðreyar", *Reallexikon der Germanischen Altertumskunde* 30 Berlin: Walter de Gruyter, 2006) 103-107.

"Pictish". *Encyclopedia of Language and Linguistics* 2nd Ed. Edited by Keith Brown (Oxford: Elsevier 2006) vol. 9, 539-591.

"In praise of collegial friendship". In: Peder Gammeltoft and Bent Jorgensen, *Names through the Looking-Glass*. (Copenhagen: G.A. Reitzells, 2006) 146-150.

Articles on "Atlas" (I, 57-58); "Cultural Register" (I. 295-296); "Dialect" (I. 304-307), with Simon J. Bonner; "Names" (III, 850-858) with Ronald L. Baker and Simon J. Bonner; "Region" (III. 1076-1038), with Simon J. Bonner. In *Encyclopaedia of American Folklife*, ed. Simon J. Bonner (Armonk, N.Y.: M.E. Sharpe, 2006).

"They Come and They Go. Random Thoughts on the Precarious Life of a Folk-Narrative Genre". Paul Catteeuw *et al.* (eds.) *Topline: Stories and Songs, Basis 3* (Trier: Wissenschaftlicher Verlag, 2006) 137-144.

2007

"Teaching Names: A Personal Account". *Onoma* 39 (2004, publ. 2007) 19-28

"Gaelic *sliabh* Revisited". In: Sharon Arbuthnott and Karina Hullo (eds.) *Fil súil nglais: A Grey Eye Looks Back;* a Festschrift in honour of Colm Ó Baoill (Ceann Dorchaid, Perthshire: Clann Tuiru, 2007) 175-186 plus bibliography 325-334.

"Place-Name Studies in Scotland: A Brief History". *Scottish Place-Name News* 23 (Autumn 2007) 2-6.

"The change from Pictish to Gaelic in Scotland". In: Paul Cavill and George Roderick (eds.) *Language Content in the Place Names of Britain and Ireland*. The English Place Name Series – Extra Series 3 (Nottingham: English Place-Name Society, 2007) 111-122.

"'As I cam' in by Ythanside': On the function of Place Names in the Greig-Duncan Folk Song Collection". In Frances J. Fischer and Sigrid Rieuwerts (eds.), *Emily Lyle: The Persistent Scholar. Basis 5* (Trier: Wissenschaftlicher Verlag, 2007) 231-240.

"From Florence 1951 to Pisa 2005: An Onomastic Journey". In: Maria Giovanna Arcamone *et al.*, (eds.), Atti del XXII Congresso Internazionale di Scienze Onomastiche, Pisa, 28 agosto-4 settembre 2005, Vol. 1 (Piza Editione ETS, 2007) 93-101.

2008

"Time and Place". In: Donald Haase (ed.), *The Greenwood Encyclopedia of Folktales and Fairy Tales* (Westport, Conn.: Greenwood Press, 2008) III, 973-976.

"Die Minderheit über die Mehrheit: Der Traveller Stanley Robertson". In: Susanne Hose (ed.), *Minderheiten und Mehrheiten in der Erzählkultur. Schriften des sorbischen Instituts* 46 (Bautzen: Domowina-Verlag, 2008) 90-95.

"Schliesslich... Beschäftigung mit Namen in der Literatur" (Finally … investigating names in literature). *Onoma* 40 (2005; publ. 2008) 29-41.

"Contemporary Legends in der englischsprachigen Presse: Moderne Sagen als Zeitungsnachricht". In: Christoph Schmitt (ed.), *Erzählkulturen im Medienwandel* (Münster: Waxmann, 2008) 215-224.

"On Names in Literature". *Nomina* 31 (2008) 89-98.